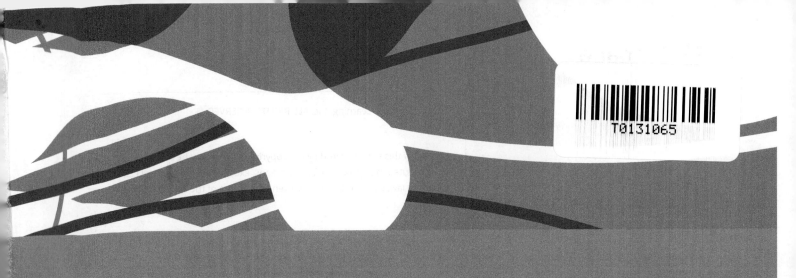

Programming with

C++

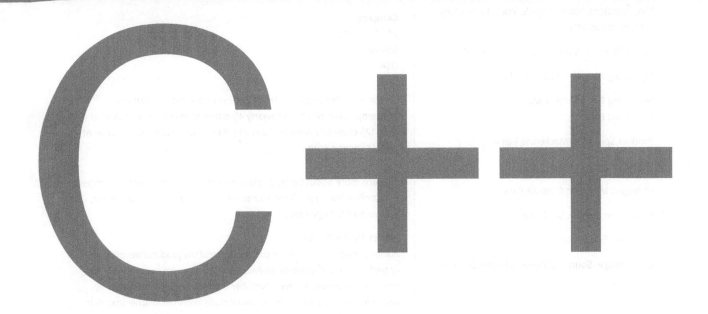

KYLA McMULLEN
ELIZABETH MATTHEWS
JUNE JAMRICH PARSONS

✷ Cengage

Australia • Brazil • Canada • Mexico • Singapore • United Kingdom • United States

Cengage

Readings from Programming with C++
**Kyla McMullen, Elizabeth Matthews,
June Jamrich Parsons**

SVP, Higher Education Product Management:
Erin Joyner

VP, Product Management: Thais Alencar

Product Team Manager: Kristin McNary

Associate Product Manager: Tran Pham

Product Assistant: Tom Benedetto

Learning Designer: Mary Convertino

Senior Content Manager: Maria Garguilo

Digital Delivery Lead: David O'Connor

Technical Editor: John Freitas

Developmental Editor: Lisa Ruffolo

Vice President, Marketing – Science, Technology,
& Math: Jason Sakos

Senior Director, Marketing: Michele McTighe

Marketing Manager: Cassie L. Cloutier

Marketing Development Manager:
Samantha Best

Product Specialist: Mackenzie Paine

IP Analyst: Ashley Maynard

IP Project Manager: Cassidie Parker

Production Service: SPi Global

Designer: Erin Griffin

Cover Image Source: echo3005/ShutterStock.com

For product information and technology assistance, contact us at
**Cengage Customer & Sales Support, 1-800-354-9706
or support.cengage.com.**

For permission to use material from this text or product, submit all
requests online at **www.copyright.com.**

Library of Congress Control Number: 2020922802

ISBN: 978-0-357-63775-3

Cengage
200 Pier 4 Boulevard
Boston, MA 02210
USA

Cengage is a leading provider of customized learning solutions
with employees residing in nearly 40 different countries and sales in more
than 125 countries around the world. Find your local representative at:
www.cengage.com.

To learn more about Cengage platforms and services, register or access
your online learning solution, or purchase materials for your course,
visit **www.cengage.com.**

Notice to the Reader

Printed at CLDPC, USA, 04-24

BRIEF CONTENTS

PREFACE   **XIII**

MODULE 1
Computational Thinking   1

MODULE 2
Programming Tools   15

MODULE 3
Literals, Variables, and Constants   35

MODULE 4
Numeric Data Types and Expressions   49

MODULE 5
Character and String Data Types   63

MODULE 6
Decision Control Structures   83

MODULE 7
Repetition Control Structures   103

MODULE 8
Arrays   125

MODULE 9
Functions   145

MODULE 10
Recursion   165

MODULE 11
Exceptions   185

MODULE 12
File Operations   205

MODULE 13
Classes and Objects   231

MODULE 14
Methods   245

MODULE 15
Encapsulation   271

MODULE 16
Inheritance   291

MODULE 17
Polymorphism   309

MODULE 18
Templates   319

MODULE 19
Linked List Data Structures   333

MODULE 20
Stacks and Queues   353

MODULE 21
Trees and Graphs   371

MODULE 22
Algorithm Complexity and Big-O Notation   395

MODULE 23
Search Algorithms   411

MODULE 24
Sorting Algorithms   427

MODULE 25
Processor Architecture   455

MODULE 26
Data Representation   469

MODULE 27
Programming Paradigms   491

MODULE 28
User Interfaces   507

MODULE 29
Software Development Methodologies   525

MODULE 30
Pseudocode, Flowcharts, and Decision Tables   541

MODULE 31
Unified Modeling Language   557

GLOSSARY   **569**
INDEX   **583**

TABLE OF CONTENTS

PREFACE   XIII

MODULE 1
COMPUTATIONAL THINKING   1

Algorithms   2
  Algorithm Basics   2
  Programming Algorithms   2
  "Good" Algorithms   3
  Selecting and Creating Algorithms   4
Decomposition   4
  Decomposition Basics   4
  Structural Decomposition   5
  Functional Decomposition   6
  Object-Oriented Decomposition   7
  Dependencies and Cohesion   7
Pattern Identification   8
  Pattern Identification Basics   8
  Repetitive Patterns   8
  Classification Patterns   9
Abstraction   9
  Abstraction Basics   9
  Classes and Objects   10
  Black Boxes   11
  Levels of Abstraction   12
SUMMARY   12
KEY TERMS   13

MODULE 2
PROGRAMMING TOOLS   15

Programming Languages   16
  Hello World!   16
  Programming Language Basics   16
  Syntax and Semantics   17
  Core Elements   19
  Your Toolbox   19
Coding Tools   20
  Program Editors   20
  Basic Structure   21

Build Tools   22
  The Toolset   22
  Compilers   23
  Preprocessors and Linkers   24
  Virtual Machines   25
  Interpreters   26
Debugging Tools   27
  Programming Errors   27
  Syntax Errors   28
  Runtime Errors   29
  Semantic Errors   29
  Debugging Utilities   30
IDEs and SDKs   32
  Integrated Development Environments   32
  Software Development Kits   32
SUMMARY   33
KEY TERMS   34

MODULE 3
LITERALS, VARIABLES, AND
CONSTANTS   35

Literals   36
  Numeric Literals   36
  Character and String Literals   37
  Tricky Literals   38
Variables and Constants   38
  Variables   38
  Constants   40
  The Memory Connection   41
Assignment Statements   41
  Declaring Variables   41
  Initializing Variables   42
  Assigning Variables   43
Input and Output   44
  Input to a Variable   44
  Output from a Variable   46
SUMMARY   46
KEY TERMS   47

MODULE 4

NUMERIC DATA TYPES AND EXPRESSIONS   49

Primitive Data Types	50
Data Types	50
Primitive Data Types	50
Composite Data Types	51
Numeric Data Types	52
Integer Data Types	52
Floating-Point Data Types	53
Mathematical Expressions	54
Arithmetic Operators	54
Order of Operations	56
Compound Operators	56
Numeric Data Type Conversion	58
Convert Integers and Floating-Point Numbers	58
Rounding Quirks	59
Formatting Output	60
Formatted Output	60
Formatting Parameters	60
SUMMARY	**62**
KEY TERMS	**62**

MODULE 5

CHARACTER AND STRING DATA TYPES   63

Character Data Types	64
Working with Character Data	64
Character Memory Allocation	65
Digits	66
Character Output Format	67
Character Manipulation	68
String Data Types	69
Working with String Data	69
Escape Characters	70
String Indexes	71
String Functions	72
String Manipulation	72
String Length	72
Change Case	73
Find the Location of a Character	74
Retrieve a Substring	75
Concatenation and Typecasting	76
Concatenated Output	76
Concatenated Variables	77
Coercion and Typecasting	78
SUMMARY	**80**
KEY TERMS	**81**

MODULE 6

DECISION CONTROL STRUCTURES   83

If-Then Control Structures	84
Control Structures	84
Decision Logic	85
If-Then Structures	85
Relational Operators	87
The Equal Operator	87
Using Relational Operators	88
Boolean Expressions and Data Types	89
Multiple Conditions	91
If-Then-Else Structures	91
Nested-If Structures	93
Else If Structures	96
Fall Through	97
Conditional Logical Operators	100
The AND Operator	100
The OR Operator	101
SUMMARY	**102**
KEY TERMS	**102**

MODULE 7

REPETITION CONTROL STRUCTURES   103

Count-Controlled Loops	104
Loop Basics	104
Control Statements	105
For-Loops	105
User-Controlled Loops	108
Counters and Accumulators	109
Loops That Count	109
Loops That Accumulate	111
Nested Loops	112
Loops Within Loops	112
Inner and Outer Loops	113
Pre-Test Loops	116
While-Loops	116
Infinite Loops	117
Breaking Out of Loops	118
Post-Test Loops	120
Do-Loops	120
Test Conditions and Terminating Conditions	123
SUMMARY	**124**
KEY TERMS	**124**

MODULE 8
ARRAYS   125

Array Basics   126
Magic Rectangles   126
Array Characteristics   127
Array Use Cases   128

One-Dimensional Arrays   128
Initialize Numeric Arrays   128
Initialize String Arrays   130

Array Input and Output   130
Output an Array Element   130
Index Errors   131
Traverse an Array   132
Input Array Elements   133

Array Operations   135
Change an Array Element   135
Find an Array Element   135
Sum Array Elements   137

Two-Dimensional Arrays   137
Two-Dimensional Array Basics   137
Initialize a Two-Dimensional Array   138
Output a Two-Dimensional Array   139
Sum Array Columns and Rows   141

SUMMARY   **143**

KEY TERMS   **144**

MODULE 9
FUNCTIONS   145

Function Basics   146
Function Classifications   146
Programmer-Defined Functions   146
Flow of Execution   147
Function Advantages   147

Void Functions   148
Void Function Basics   148
Function Pseudocode   149

Functions with Parameters   150
Function Parameters   150
Function Arguments   150
The Handoff   152

Return Values   153
Return Values   153
Return Type   156
Function Signature   157

Scope   157
Scope Basics   157
Pass by Value   160

Pass by Reference   161
Namespaces   162

SUMMARY   **163**

KEY TERMS   **163**

MODULE 10
RECURSION   165

Key Components of Recursion   165
The Recursive Mindset   165
Recursion Basics   167
When to Use Recursion   171

Using Recursion to Solve Complex
Problems   171
Designing Recursive Structures   171
Linear Recursion   174
Branching Recursion   175

Managing Memory during Recursion   179
Memory Management   179
Stable Recursion   182

SUMMARY   **183**

KEY TERMS   **183**

MODULE 11
EXCEPTIONS   185

Defining Exceptions   185
Errors in Code   185
Exception Types   187

Dealing with Exceptions   189
Handling Others' Exceptions   189
Try and Catch Blocks   189

Using Exceptions   198
Throwing Exceptions   198
When to Bail   202

SUMMARY   **203**

KEY TERMS   **203**

MODULE 12
FILE OPERATIONS   205

File Input and Output   206
The Purpose of Files   206
Anatomy of a File   210
File Usage   212

Processing a File   214
Accessing Files   214
Streaming and Buffering   214

Reading from a File   216
  Opening a File for Reading   216
  Reading from a File   218
Closing a File   222
  Closing Files after Use   222
  Trying to Close a File   222
Creating and Writing New Files   222
  Creating a File   222
  Opening a File for Writing   223
  Writing to and Appending a File   224
  Anticipating Exceptions   228
SUMMARY   229
KEY TERMS   230

MODULE 13
CLASSES AND OBJECTS   231

Classes in Object-Oriented Programming   232
  Representing the Real World with Code   232
  Using Classes   232
  Class Components   233
Using Objects   236
  Creating Objects   236
  Objects as Variables   238
  Object-Oriented Features and Principles   238
Using Static Elements in a Class   239
  Static Member Variables   239
  Static Methods   240
  Static Classes   241
Characteristics of Objects
  in Object-Oriented Programs   242
  Object Identity   242
  Object State   242
  Object Behavior   243
SUMMARY   244
KEY TERMS   244

MODULE 14
METHODS   245

Using Methods   245
  Why Use Methods?   245
  Anatomy of a Method   251
  Using Methods   251
Changing the Default Behavior
  of an Object   255
  Using Objects as Regular Variables   255
  Overloading Methods   258
  Setting One Object to Equal Another   262

Method Cascading and Method Chaining   263
  Calling Multiple Methods on the Same Object 263
Using Constructors   266
  Specifying How to Construct an Object   266
  Constructing an Object from Another Object 268
SUMMARY   269
KEY TERMS   269

MODULE 15
ENCAPSULATION   271

Components of Class Structure   271
  Data Hiding   271
  Designing Objects   273
  Self-Reference Scope   276
Accessor and Mutator Context   277
  Viewing Data from an Object   277
  Changing Data in an Object   278
Using Constructors   280
  Parameters and Arguments   280
  Default Parameters and Constructor
    Overloading   281
Encapsulation Enforcement
  with Access Modifiers   283
  Access Modifiers   283
  Public Variables and Methods   283
  Private Variables and Methods   284
Interfaces and Headers   286
  Interfaces   286
  Programming an Interface   287
SUMMARY   290
KEY TERMS   290

MODULE 16
INHERITANCE   291

Using Inheritance   291
  Creating Classes from Other Classes   291
  Family Trees in OOP   292
  Levels of Access   295
Necessary Components for Inheritance   296
  Defining a Parent Class   296
  Defining a Child Class   297
Creating a Child Class That Inherits
  from a Parent Class   298
  Inheritance Syntax   298
  Customizing Behavior   301
SUMMARY   307
KEY TERMS   307

MODULE 17
POLYMORPHISM   309

The Purpose of Polymorphism   309
  Flexibility While Coding   309
  Dynamic Binding Under the Hood   314
Polymorphism Basics   314
  Classes Within Classes   314
  Objects as Other Objects   315
Virtual Functions   316
  Anticipating Customization   316
  Abstract Classes   317
SUMMARY   **318**
KEY TERMS   **318**

MODULE 18
TEMPLATES   319

Template Basics   319
  Data Abstraction   319
  Template Structure and Use   322
Tricky Templating   328
  Advanced Templating   328
  Templated Objects as Arguments   330
Templates as a Problem-Solving
Approach   331
  Designing a Template   331
  When to Use Templates   331
SUMMARY   **331**
KEY TERMS   **332**

MODULE 19
LINKED LIST DATA
STRUCTURES   333

Linked List Structures   334
  Data Structure Selection   334
  Data Structure Implementation   335
  Linked List Basics   336
Types of Linked Lists   337
  Singly Linked Lists   337
  Doubly Linked Lists   338
  Circular Linked Lists   339
  Linked List Characteristics   339
Code a Linked List   342
  The `Node` Class   342
  The `LinkedList` Class   343
  The `Append` Method   343
  Linked List Traversal   345

The Find Method   346
The Insert Method   347
SUMMARY   **350**
KEY TERMS   **351**

MODULE 20
STACKS AND QUEUES   353

Stacks   353
  Stack Basics   353
  Stack Use Cases   355
  Built-in Stacks   356
  Code a Stack   357
Queues   362
  Queue Basics   362
  Queue Use Cases   363
  Code a Queue   364
SUMMARY   **369**
KEY TERMS   **369**

MODULE 21
TREES AND GRAPHS   371

Nonlinear Data Structures   371
  Linear versus Nonlinear Structures   371
  Nonlinear Building Blocks   373
Tree Structures   373
  Tree Basics   373
  Tree Properties   376
  Trees as Recursive Structures   376
Solving Problems Using Trees   379
  Tree Applications   379
  Data Storage in Trees   380
Graph Structures   387
  Graph Basics   387
  Directed and Undirected Graphs   388
Solving Problems with Graphs   388
  Graph Applications   388
  Computing Paths   389
SUMMARY   **394**
KEY TERMS   **394**

MODULE 22
ALGORITHM COMPLEXITY
AND BIG-O NOTATION   395

Big-O Notation   396
  Algorithm Complexity   396

Asymptotic Analysis   397
Asymptotic Notation   398
Time Complexity   398
  Big-O Metrics   398
  Constant Time   399
  Linear Time   399
  Quadratic Time   400
  Logarithmic Time   401
Space Complexity   403
  Memory Space   403
  Constant Space Complexity   404
  Linear Space Complexity   404
Complexity Calculations   405
  Line-by-Line Time Complexity   405
  Combine and Simplify   406
  A Mystery Algorithm   407
SUMMARY   409
KEY TERMS   409

MODULE 23
SEARCH ALGORITHMS   411
Using Search Algorithms   412
  Search Basics   412
Performing a Linear Search   413
  Looking for a Needle in a Haystack   413
  Evaluating Search Time   416
Performing a Binary Search   416
  Shrinking the Search Space   416
  Implementing Binary Search   418
Using Regular Expressions
  in Search Algorithms   423
  Specifying a Search Pattern   423
  Regular Expression Search Operators   423
SUMMARY   426
KEY TERMS   426

MODULE 24
SORTING ALGORITHMS   427
Qualities of Sorting Algorithms   428
  Ordering Items   428
  Time Complexity in Sorting Algorithms   428
  Sorting Properties   430
Bubble Sort   431
  Defining the Bubble Sort Algorithm   431
  Bubble Sort Properties   437

Quicksort   438
  Defining the Quicksort Algorithm   438
  Quicksort Properties   446
Merge Sort   447
  Defining the Merge Sort Algorithm   447
  Merge Sort Properties   453
SUMMARY   454
KEY TERMS   454

MODULE 25
PROCESSOR ARCHITECTURE   455
Processor Organization   456
  Integrated Circuits   456
  Moore's Law   458
  CPUs   458
Low-Level Instruction Sets   459
  Microprocessor Instruction Sets   459
  RISC and CISC   460
  Machine Language   460
  Assembly Language   461
Microprocessor Operations   462
  Processing an Instruction   462
  The Instruction Cycle   462
High-Level Programming Languages   464
  Evolution   464
  Teaching Languages   465
  The C Family   465
  Web Programming Languages   466
  Characteristics   466
  Advantages and Disadvantages   467
SUMMARY   467
KEY TERMS   468

MODULE 26
DATA REPRESENTATION   469
Bits and Bytes   470
  Digital Data   470
  Bits   471
  Bytes   472
Binary   474
  Binary Numbers   474
  Binary to Decimal   475
  Decimal to Binary   476
  Binary Addition   477
  Negative Numbers   478
Hexadecimal   480
  Colors   480
  Hexadecimal Numbers   481

Binary-Hex-Binary Conversions   481
Hex-Decimal Conversion   482
Information Density   483
ASCII and Unicode   483
    ASCII   483
    Extended ASCII   484
    Unicode   485
Memory Allocation   486
    Memory and Storage   486
    Storage Devices   487
    Memory   487
SUMMARY   489
KEY TERMS   489

MODULE 27
PROGRAMMING PARADIGMS   491

Imperative and Declarative Paradigms   492
    Think Outside the Box   492
The Procedural Paradigm   493
    Procedural Basics   493
    Characteristics of Procedural Programs   494
    Procedural Paradigm Applications   496
The Object-Oriented Paradigm   497
    Objects, Classes, and Methods   497
    Characteristics of Object-Oriented Programs 499
    Object-Oriented Applications   501
Declarative Paradigms   501
    Declarative Basics   501
    Characteristics of the Declarative
        Paradigm   504
    Applications for Declarative Paradigms   504
SUMMARY   505
KEY TERMS   505

MODULE 28
USER INTERFACES   507

User Interface Basics   508
    UI and UX   508
    UI Components   508
    Selecting a UI   510
Command-Line User Interfaces   510
    Command-Line Basics   510
    Command-Line Program Design   510
Graphical User Interfaces   512
    GUI Basics   512
    GUI Program Design   514
Voice User Interfaces   515
    Voice Interface Basics   515
    Speech Recognition   515

Speech Synthesis   516
Designing Programs for Voice User Interfaces   517
Virtual Environment Interfaces   517
    Virtual Environments   517
    Virtual Environment Interface Components   518
    Programming the Virtual Interface   519
Accessibility and Inclusion   520
    Accessibility Guidelines   520
    Inclusive Design   521
SUMMARY   524
KEY TERMS   524

MODULE 29
SOFTWARE DEVELOPMENT
METHODOLOGIES   525

Software Development   526
    The Software Development Life Cycle   526
    Efficiency, Quality, and Security   527
The Waterfall Model   528
    Structured Analysis and Design   528
    Waterfall Advantages and Disadvantages   529
The Agile Model   530
    Incremental Development   530
    Agile Methodologies   530
    Agile Advantages and Disadvantages   531
Coding Principles   532
    Efficient Coding   532
    Modularized Code   533
    Clean Coding   534
    Secure Coding   534
    Success Factors   536
Testing   536
    Levels of Testing   536
    Unit Testing   537
    Integration Testing   538
    System Testing   539
    Acceptance Testing   539
    Regression Testing   539
SUMMARY   540
KEY TERMS   540

MODULE 30
PSEUDOCODE, FLOWCHARTS,
AND DECISION TABLES   541

Pseudocode   542
    From Algorithms to Pseudocode   542
    Pseudocode Basics   544
    Pseudocode Guidelines   545
    Writing Pseudocode   547

Flowcharts   548
    Flowchart Basics   548
    Drawing Flowcharts   548
    Flowchart Tools   549
Decision Tables   551
    Decision Table Basics   551
    List the Conditions   551
    List All Possible Alternatives   552
    Specify Results and Rules   552
    Interpret Rules   553
    Optimize the Rules   554
    Check for Completeness and Accuracy   555
SUMMARY   **555**
KEY TERMS   **556**

MODULE 31
UNIFIED MODELING LANGUAGE   557

Purpose of Unified Modeling
  Language (UML)   557
    Communicating Ideas to Other Programmers   557

UML Diagram Parts   558
    Class Diagram Basics   558
    Use Case Diagram Basics   559
    Sequence Diagrams   561
Using UML to Structure Programs   562
    UML Associations   562
    Translating UML to Code   564
SUMMARY   **568**
KEY TERMS   **568**

GLOSSARY   **569**
INDEX   **583**

Welcome to *Readings from Programming with C++*. This text includes the stand-alone lessons and readings from MindTap for *Programming with C++* and is intended to be used in conjunction with the MindTap Reader for a complete learning experience.

MindTap Overview

Programming with C++ presents conceptual, language-agnostic narrative with language-specific assets, ungraded C++ coding Snippets, language-agnostic test banks, and additional instructor resources. The goal of this digital product is to develop content around the concepts that are essential for understanding Computer Science from a language-agnostic perspective. Learners will gain a foundational understanding of procedural programming, computer science concepts, and object-oriented programming. Instructors have identified the need for language-agnostic, conceptual content that can be paired with hands-on practice in a specific language. This 31-module text is designed to provide that conceptual content paired with language-specific examples and hands-on learning activities in C++.

Course Objectives:

- Develop a foundational knowledge of coding principles, vocabulary, and core concepts.
- Use new foundational knowledge to learn C++ programming skills.
- Practice emerging coding skills in a low-risk environment.
- Apply learned concepts and skills to assignments/activities that mimic real-world experiences and environments.

C++ Version

We recommend downloading the latest version of C++ before beginning this text. C++14 was used to test all C++ code presented in the module figures.

MindTap Features

In addition to the readings included within this text, the MindTap includes the following:

Course Orientation: Custom videos and readings prepare students for the material and coding experiences they will encounter in their course.

Videos: Animated videos demonstrate new programming terms and concepts in an easy-to-understand format, increasing student confidence and learning.

Coding Snippets: These short, ungraded coding activities are embedded within the MindTap Reader and provide students an opportunity to practice new programming concepts "in-the-moment." Additional language-specific "bridge content" helps transition the student from conceptual understanding to application of C++ code.

Language-specific Examples: Figures within the narrative illustrate the application of general concepts in C++ code.

Instructor & Student Resources

Additional instructor and student resources for this product are available online. Instructor assets include an Instructor's Manual, Teaching Online Guide, PowerPoint® slides, and a test bank powered by Cognero®. Student assets include source code files and coding Snippets ReadMe. Sign up or sign in at **www.cengage.com** to search for and access this product and its online resources.

ABOUT THE AUTHORS

Dr. Kyla McMullen is a tenure-track faculty member in the University of Florida's Computer & Information Sciences & Engineering Department, specializing in Human-Centered Computing. Her research interests are in the perception, applications, and development of 3D audio technologies. Dr. McMullen has authored over 30 manuscripts in this line of research and is the primary investigator for over 2 million dollars' worth of sponsored research projects.

Dr. Elizabeth A. Matthews is an Assistant Professor of Computer Science at Washington and Lee University. She has taught computer science since 2013 and has been an active researcher in human–computer interaction and human-centered computing. Matthews has published research in the areas of procedural generation, video game enjoyment factors, and freshwater algae identification with HCI.

June Jamrich Parsons is an educator, digital book pioneer, and co-author of Texty and McGuffey Award-winning textbooks. She co-developed the first commercially successful multimedia, interactive digital textbook; one that set the bar for platforms now being developed by educational publishers. Her career includes extensive classroom teaching, product design for eCourseware, textbook authoring for Course Technology and Cengage, Creative Strategist for MediaTechnics Corporation, and Director of Content for Veative Virtual Reality Labs.

ACKNOWLEDGMENTS

The unique approach for this book required a seasoned team. Our thanks to Maria Garguilo who ushered the manuscripts through every iteration and kept tight rein on the schedule; to Mary E. Convertino who supplied her expertise in learning design; to Lisa Ruffolo for her excellent developmental edit; to Courtney Cozzy who coordinated the project; to Kristin McNary for her leadership in Cengage's computing materials; to Rajiv Malkan (Lone Star College) for his instructional input; to Wade Schofield (Liberty University) for his reviewing expertise; and to John Freitas for his meticulous code review. It was a pleasure to be part of this professional and talented team. We hope that instructors and students will appreciate our efforts to provide this unique approach to computer science and programming.

Kyla McMullen: Above all things, I would like to thank God for giving me the gifts and talents that were utilized to write this book. I would like to thank my amazing husband Ade Kumuyi for always being my rock, sounding board, and biggest cheerleader. I thank my parents, Rita and James McMullen for all of their sacrifices to raise me. Last but not least, I thank my spirited friends who help me to remain sane, remind me of who I am, and never let me forget whose I am.

Elizabeth Matthews: I want to thank my parents, Drs. Geoff and Robin Matthews, for their support and understanding in my journey. I would also like to thank my advisor, Dr. Juan Gilbert, for seeing my dream to the end. Finally, I would like to thank my cats, Oreo and Laptop, who made sure that writing this book was interrupted as often as possible.

June Jamrich Parsons: Computer programming can be a truly satisfying experience. The reward when a program runs flawlessly has to bring a smile even to the most seasoned programmers. Working with three programming languages for this project at the same time was certainly challenging but provided insights that can help students understand computational thinking. I've thoroughly enjoyed working with the team to create these versatile learning resources and would like to dedicate my efforts to my mom, who has been a steadfast cheerleader for me throughout my career. To the instructors and students who use this book, my hope is that you enjoy programming as much as I do.

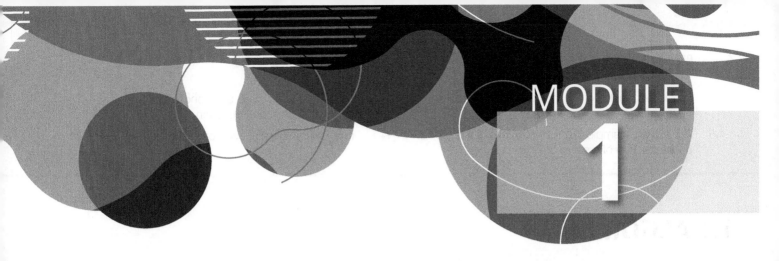

MODULE 1

COMPUTATIONAL THINKING

LEARNING OBJECTIVES:

1.1 ALGORITHMS

1.1.1 Define the term "algorithm" as a series of steps for solving a problem or carrying out a task.

1.1.2 State that algorithms are the underlying logic for computer programs.

1.1.3 Define the term "computer program."

1.1.4 Provide examples of algorithms used in everyday technology applications.

1.1.5 Confirm that there can be more than one algorithm for a task or problem and that some algorithms may be more efficient than others.

1.1.6 Explain why computer scientists are interested in algorithm efficiency.

1.1.7 List the characteristics of an effective algorithm.

1.1.8 Write an algorithm for accomplishing a simple, everyday technology application.

1.1.9 Write an alternate algorithm for an everyday technology task.

1.1.10 Select the more efficient of the two algorithms you have written.

1.2 DECOMPOSITION

1.2.1 Define the term "decomposition" as a technique for dividing a complex problem or solution into smaller parts.

1.2.2 Explain why decomposition is an important tool for computer scientists.

1.2.3 Differentiate the concepts of algorithms and decomposition.

1.2.4 Identify examples of structural decomposition.

1.2.5 Identify examples of functional decomposition.

1.2.6 Identify examples of object-oriented decomposition.

1.2.7 Provide examples of decomposition in technology applications.

1.2.8 Explain how dependencies and cohesion relate to decomposition.

1.3 PATTERN IDENTIFICATION

1.3.1 Define the term "pattern identification" as a technique for recognizing similarities or characteristics among the elements of a task or problem.

1.3.2 Identify examples of fill-in-the-blank patterns.

1.3.3 Identify examples of repetitive patterns.

1.3.4 Identify examples of classification patterns.

1.3.5 Provide examples of pattern identification in the real world and in technology applications.

1.4 ABSTRACTION

1.4.1 Define the term "abstraction" as a technique for generalization and for simplifying levels of complexity.

1.4.2 Explain why abstraction is an important computer science concept.

1.4.3 Provide an example illustrating how abstraction can help identify variables.

1.4.4   Provide examples of technology applications that have abstracted or hidden details.

1.4.5   Provide an example illustrating the use of a class as an abstraction of a set of objects.

1.4.6   Explain how the black box concept is an implementation of abstraction.

1.4.7   Identify appropriate levels of abstraction.

1.1 ALGORITHMS

Algorithm Basics (1.1.1, 1.1.4)

A password might not be enough to protect your online accounts. Two-factor authentication adds an extra layer of protection. A common form of two-factor authentication sends a personal identification number (PIN) to your cell phone. To log in, you perform the series of steps shown in **Figure 1-1**.

Connect to the site's login page.
Enter your user ID.
Enter your password.
Wait for a text message containing a PIN
    to arrive on your smartphone.
On the site's the login page, enter the PIN.

Figure 1-1   Steps for two-factor authentication

The procedure for two-factor authentication is an example of an algorithm. In a general sense, an **algorithm** is a series of steps for solving a problem or carrying out a task.

Algorithms exist for everyday tasks and tasks that involve technology. Here are some examples:

- A recipe for baking brownies
- The steps for changing a tire
- The instructions for pairing a smart watch with your phone
- The payment process at an online store
- The procedure for posting a tweet

Programming Algorithms (1.1.2, 1.1.3, 1.1.5)

Algorithms are also an important tool for programmers. A **programming algorithm** is a set of steps that specifies the underlying logic and structure for the statements in a computer program. You can think of programming algorithms as the blueprints for computer programs.

A **computer program** is a set of instructions, written in a programming language such as C++, Python, or Java, that performs a specific task when executed by a digital device. A computer program is an implementation of an algorithm.

Q Programming algorithms tell the computer what to do. Can you tell which of these algorithms is a programming algorithm?

Algorithm 1:

Connect to the website's login page.

Enter your user ID.

Enter your password.

Wait for a text message containing a PIN to arrive on your smartphone.

On the website's login page, enter the PIN.

Algorithm 2:

Prompt the user to enter a user ID.

Prompt the user to enter a password.

Make sure that the user ID and password match.

If the user ID and password match:

Generate a random PIN.

Send the PIN to user's phone.

Prompt the user to enter the PIN.

If the PIN is correct:

Allow access.

A Algorithm 1 is not a programming algorithm because it outlines instructions for the user. Algorithm 2 is a programming algorithm because it specifies what the computer is supposed to do. When you formulate a programming algorithm, the instructions should be for the computer, not the user.

There can be more than one programming algorithm for solving a problem or performing a task, but some algorithms are more efficient than others.

Q Here are two algorithms for summing the numbers from 1 to 10. Which algorithm is more efficient?

Algorithm 1:

Add 1 + 2 to get a total.

Repeat these steps nine times:

Get the next number.

Add this number to the total.

Algorithm 2:

Get the last number in the series (10).

Divide 10 by 2 to get a result.

Add 10 + 1 to get a sum.

Multiply the result by the sum.

A Both algorithms contain four instructions, but Algorithm 2 is more efficient. You can use it to amaze your friends by quickly calculating the total in only four steps. Algorithm 1 is also four lines long, but two of the instructions are repeated nine times. Counting the first step, that's 19 steps to complete this task!

"Good" Algorithms (1.1.6, 1.1.7)

Computer scientists are interested in designing what they call "good" algorithms. A good algorithm tends to produce a computer program that operates efficiently, quickly, and reliably. Good algorithms have these characteristics:

Input: The algorithm applies to a set of specified inputs.

Output: The algorithm produces one or more outputs.

Finite: The algorithm terminates after a finite number of steps.

Precise: Each step of the algorithm is clear and unambiguous.

Effective: The algorithm successfully produces the correct output.

When formulating an algorithm, you can easily check to make sure it satisfies all the criteria for a good algorithm. You can see how these criteria apply to an algorithm in **Figure 1-2**.

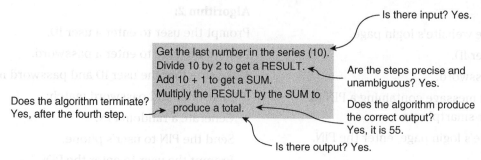

Figure 1-2   Is this a good algorithm?

Selecting and Creating Algorithms (1.1.8, 1.1.9, 1.1.10)

Before coding, programmers consider various algorithms that might apply to a problem. You can come up with an algorithm in three ways:

Use a standard algorithm. Programmers have created effective algorithms for many computing tasks, such as sorting, searching, manipulating text, encrypting data, and finding the shortest path. When you are familiar with these standard algorithms, you can easily incorporate them in programs.

Perform the task manually. When you can't find a standard algorithm, you can formulate an algorithm by stepping through a process manually, recording those steps, and then analyzing their effectiveness.

Apply computational thinking techniques. Computational thinking is a set of techniques designed to formulate problems and their solutions. You can use computational thinking techniques such as decomposition, pattern identification, and abstraction to devise efficient algorithms. Let's take a look at these techniques in more detail.

1.2 DECOMPOSITION

Decomposition Basics (1.2.1)

A mobile banking app contains many components. It has to provide a secure login procedure, allow users to manage preferences, display account balances, push out alerts, read checks for deposit, and perform other tasks shown in **Figure 1-3**.

The algorithm for such an extensive app would be difficult to formulate without dividing it into smaller parts, a process called decomposition. When devising an algorithm for a complex problem or task, decomposition can help you deal with smaller, more manageable pieces of the puzzle.

Figure 1-3 A mobile banking app handles many interacting tasks

Structural Decomposition (1.2.2, 1.2.3, 1.2.4, 1.2.7)

The first step in decomposition is to identify structural units that perform distinct tasks. **Figure 1-4** illustrates how you might divide a mobile banking app into structural units, called modules.

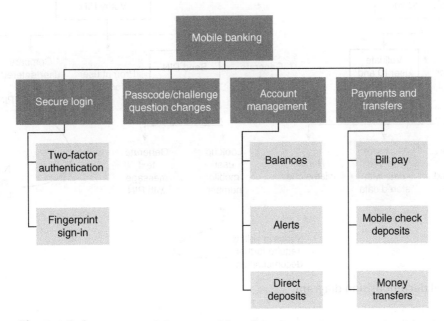

Figure 1-4 Structural decomposition diagram

Structural decomposition is a process that identifies a hierarchy of structural units. At the lowest levels of the hierarchy are modules, indicated in yellow in Figure 1-4, that have a manageable scope for creating algorithms.

Q Which module of the hierarchy chart is not fully decomposed?

A The module for modifying passwords and challenge questions could be further decomposed into two modules: one module that allows users to change their passwords and one for changing their challenge questions.

Here are some tips for creating a structural decomposition diagram:

- Use a top-down approach. The nodes at the top break down into component parts in the nodes below them.
- Label nodes with nouns and adjectives, rather than verbs. For example, "Account management" is the correct noun phrase, rather than a verb phrase, such as "Manage accounts."
- Don't worry about sequencing. Except for the actual login process, the components in a mobile banking system could be accessed in any order. This is a key difference between an algorithm and decomposition. An algorithm specifies an order of activities, whereas decomposition specifies the parts of a task.

Functional Decomposition (1.2.5)

Functional decomposition breaks down modules into smaller actions, processes, or steps. **Figure 1-5** illustrates a functional decomposition of the two-factor authentication module.

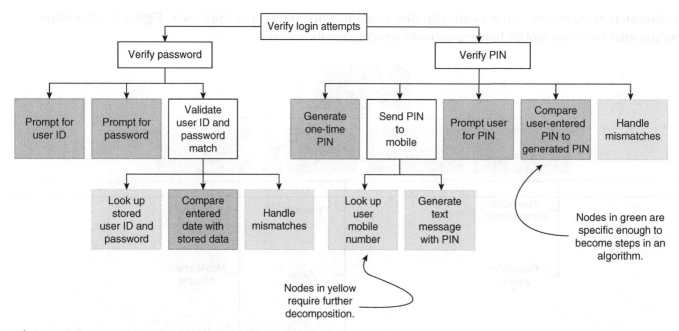

Figure 1-5   Functional decomposition diagram

Notice how the levels of the functional decomposition diagram get more specific until the nodes in the lowest levels begin to reveal instructions that should be incorporated in an algorithm.

Here are some tips for constructing functional decomposition diagrams and deriving algorithms from them:

- Label nodes with verb phrases. In contrast to the nodes of a structural decomposition diagram, the nodes of a functional decomposition are labeled with verb phrases that indicate "what" is to be done.
- Sequence from left to right. Reading left to right on the diagram should correspond to the sequence in which steps in the algorithm are performed.

Object-Oriented Decomposition (1.2.6)

Another way to apply decomposition to a module is to look for logical and physical objects that a computer program will manipulate. **Figure 1-6** illustrates an object-oriented decomposition of the two-factor authentication module.

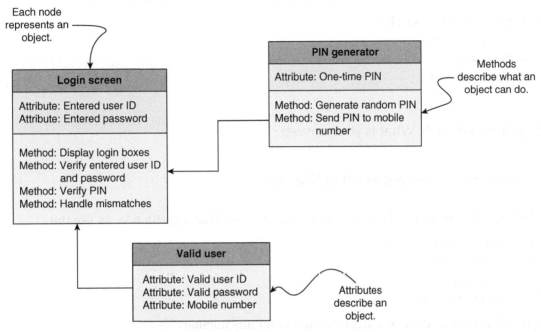

Figure 1-6   Object-oriented decomposition diagram

An object-oriented decomposition does not produce a hierarchy. Instead it produces a collection of objects that can represent people, places, or things.

Tips for object-oriented decomposition:

- Node titles are nouns. Each node in the object-oriented decomposition diagram is labeled with a noun.
- Attributes are nouns. A node can contain a list of attributes, which relate to the characteristics of an object.
- Methods are verb phrases. An object can also contain methods, which are actions that an object can perform. You may need to devise an algorithm for each method.
- Sketch in connection arrows. Connection arrows help you visualize how objects share data.

Dependencies and Cohesion (1.2.8)

You might wonder if there is a correct way to decompose a problem or task. In practice, there may be several viable ways to apply decomposition, but an effective breakdown minimizes dependencies and maximizes cohesion among the various parts.

The principles of decomposition are:

- Minimize dependencies. Although input and output may flow between nodes, changing the instructions in one module or object should not require changes to others.
- Maximize cohesion. Each object or module contains attributes, methods, or instructions that perform a single logical task or represent a single entity.

1.3 PATTERN IDENTIFICATION

Pattern Identification Basics (1.3.1, 1.3.2)

The Amaze-Your-Friends math trick for quickly adding numbers from 1 to 10 is very simple:

Get the last number in the series (10).
Divide 10 by 2 to get a result.
Add 10 + 1 to get a sum.
Multiply the result by the sum.

Q Try the algorithm yourself. What is your answer?

A If your math is correct, your answer should be 55.

Now, what if the challenge is to add the numbers from 1 to 200? That algorithm looks like this:

Get the last number in the series (200).
Divide 200 by 2 to get a result.
Add 200 + 1 to get a sum.
Multiply the result by the sum.

Notice a pattern? This fill-in-the-blank algorithm works for any number:

Get the last number in the series (_____).
Divide _____ by 2 to get a result.
Add _____ + 1 to get a sum.
Multiply the result by the sum.

The process of finding similarities in procedures and tasks is called **pattern identification**. It is a useful computational thinking technique for creating algorithms that can be used and reused on different data sets. By recognizing the pattern in the Amaze-Your-Friends math trick, you can use the algorithm to find the total of any series of numbers.

Repetitive Patterns (1.3.3)

In addition to fill-in-the-blank patterns, you might also find repetitive patterns as you analyze tasks and problems. Think about this algorithm, which handles logins to a social media site:

Get a user ID.
Get a password.
If the password is correct, allow access.
If the password is not correct, get the password again.
If the password is correct, allow access.
If the password is not correct, get the password again.
If the password is correct, allow access.
If the password is not correct, get the password again.
If the password is correct, allow access.
If the password is not correct, lock the account.

Q How many repetition patterns do you recognize?

A Two lines are repeated three times:
If the password is not correct, get the password again.
If the password is correct, allow access.

Recognizing this repetition, you can streamline the algorithm like this:
Get a password.
Repeat three times:
    If the password is correct, allow access.
    If the password is not correct, get the password again.
If the password is correct, allow access.
If the password is not correct, lock the account.

Classification Patterns (1.3.4, 1.3.5)

Everyone who subscribes to a social media site has a set of login credentials. Here are Lee's and Priya's:

Lee's login credentials:

Lee's user ID: LeezyBranson@gmail.com

Lee's password: MyCat411

Lee's mobile number: 415-999-1234

Priya's login credentials:

Priya's user ID: PriyaMontell@gmail.com

Priya's password: ouY52311v

Priya's mobile number: 906-222-0987

The series of attributes that define each user's login credentials have a pattern of similarities. Each user has three attributes: a user ID, a password, and a mobile number. By recognizing this pattern, you can create a template for any user's login credentials like this:

User ID: _____
Password: _____
Mobile number: _____

You can often discover **classification patterns** in the attributes that describe any person or object. Identifying classification patterns can help you design programs that involve databases because the template identifies fields, such as User ID, that contain data.

Classification patterns also come in handy if you want to design programs based on the interactions among a variety of objects, rather than a step-by-step algorithm. In some programming circles, templates are called **classes** because they specify the attributes for a classification of objects. For example, people classified as social media subscribers have attributes for login credentials. Vehicles classified as cars have attributes such as color, make, model, and VIN number. Businesses classified as restaurants have a name, hours of operation, and a menu.

1.4 ABSTRACTION

Abstraction Basics (1.4.1, 1.4.2, 1.4.3)

Think back to the Amaze-Your-Friends math trick. By identifying a pattern, you formulated a general algorithm that works for a sequence of any length, whether it is a sequence of 1 to 10 or 1 to 200.

Get the last number in the series (_____).
Divide _____ by 2 to get a result.

Add _____ + 1 to get a sum.
Multiply the result by the sum.

In this algorithm, the blank line is an abstraction that represents the last number in the sequence. An **abstraction** hides details, simplifies complexity, substitutes a generalization for something specific, and allows an algorithm to work for multiple inputs.

Abstraction is a key element of computational thinking and helps programmers in a multitude of ways.

If you've programmed before, you'll recognize that in the Amaze-Your-Friends algorithm, the blanks could become a variable with a name such as last_number. Result and sum are also variables because they represent values that change depending on the numbers in the sequence

Get the `last_number`
Divide `last_number` by 2 to get a `result`.
Add `last_number` + 1 to get a `sum`.
Multiply the `result` by the `sum`.

A variable is an abstraction because rather than representing a specific number, it can be used to represent many different numbers.

Classes and Objects (1.4.4, 1.4.5)

Abstraction has uses other than identifying variables. It is important for understanding how to represent real-world and conceptual objects. Remember the pattern you discovered for social media login credentials? With a little modification, it becomes a template that can be applied to any subscriber:

Class: LoginCredentials
Attribute: user_ID
Attribute: user_password
Attribute: mobile_number

The LoginCredentials class is an abstraction that contains a set of attributes. The class was formed by abstracting away, or removing, details for any specific subscriber.

Abstractions are handy for any programs that deal with real-world objects in addition to technology objects, such as login credentials.

Q Can you envision a class that's an abstraction of the collection of objects shown in **Figure 1-7**?

12 oz water glass   5 oz martini glass   8 oz wine glass   10 oz water goblet

Budnyi/Shutterstock.com

Figure 1-7   Abstract the details from this collection of glassware

A The glassware class could have these attributes:
Class: Glassware
Attribute: Color
Attribute: Capacity
Attribute: Style

Black Boxes (1.4.6)

To drive a car, you don't have to know exactly what goes on under the hood. The engine is essentially a "black box" that you control using a few simple inputs such as the gas pedal, brake, and steering wheel. The details of the engine are hidden. In computer science terminology, these details have been "abstracted away." See **Figure 1-8**.

You can drive a car without knowing the details of what's under the hood.

Figure 1-8   The controls for a car are an abstraction of its detailed mechanics

In concept, a black box is anything that accepts some type of input and performs a specific process to produce output without requiring an understanding of its internal workings. See **Figure 1-9**.

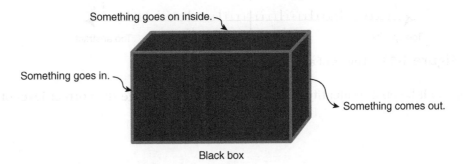

Something goes on inside.

Something goes in.

Something comes out.

Black box

Figure 1-9   Black box abstraction

The black-box concept of abstraction is a fundamental aspect of computer science. Think about it. Computer programs are abstractions. For example, you can use a social media app without knowing anything about the programming that makes it work. The icons that you touch on the screen abstract away the details of the underlying programming.

Programmers make extensive use of abstraction within programs by creating a set of instructions that functions like a black box. For example, you could bundle the instructions that handle login attempts into a black box like the one in **Figure 1-10**.

Programming languages also have built-in abstractions that perform standard tasks. For example, the built-in random function generates a random number when given a range, such as 1–100. You can incorporate the random function in a program without knowing how it works internally.

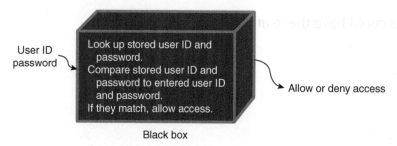

Figure 1-10   A login abstraction

Levels of Abstraction (1.4.7)

After you get the hang of abstraction, you'll see examples of this computational thinking concept everywhere. Applying the correct level of abstraction to your programs may take a little practice.

A **level of abstraction** relates to the amount of detail that is hidden. Abstracting out too much detail can make a program too generalized. Neglecting abstraction can produce programs that are too specific to work with a wide variety of data. See **Figure 1-11**.

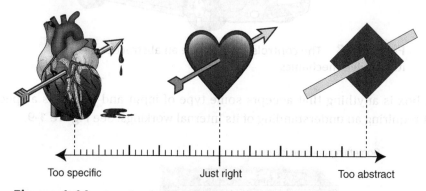

Figure 1-11   Levels of abstraction

With experience, you'll be able to identify useful abstractions and gauge the correct level of abstraction to use.

SUMMARY

- Computational thinking techniques help programmers define problems, find solutions, delineate tasks, and devise algorithms.
- An algorithm is a series of steps for solving a problem or carrying out a task. Programming algorithms are the blueprints for computer programs.
- Standard algorithms exist for many computing tasks. When an algorithm does not exist, you can step through a process manually and record the steps, or apply computational thinking techniques, such as decomposition, pattern identification, and abstraction.
- Decomposition divides a complex problem or task into manageable units.
- Pattern identification reveals sequences and repetitive tasks that can lead to algorithm efficiencies.
- Abstraction is a key computer science concept that suppresses details, substitutes a generalization for something specific, and allows an algorithm to work for multiple inputs.

Key Terms

abstraction

algorithm

attributes

classes

classification patterns

Computational thinking

computer program

decomposition

Functional decomposition

level of abstraction

methods

modules

objects

object-oriented decomposition

pattern identification

programming algorithm

Structural decomposition

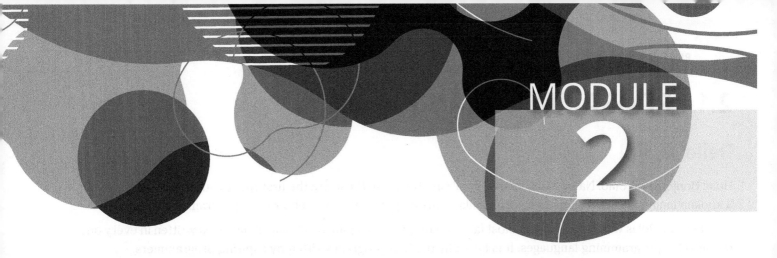

MODULE 2

PROGRAMMING TOOLS

LEARNING OBJECTIVES:

2.1 PROGRAMMING LANGUAGES

2.1.1 Explain the significance of the Hello World! program.

2.1.2 Reiterate that programming languages are used to create software.

2.1.3 Name some popular programming languages.

2.1.4 Distinguish between syntax and semantics in the context of programming languages.

2.1.5 Identify the key characteristics common to programming languages.

2.1.6 Explain options for accessing programming language implementations.

2.1.7 Identify programming tools.

2.2 CODING TOOLS

2.2.1 Define a program editor as the tool used to enter program code.

2.2.2 List the types of editors that can be used for coding.

2.2.3 List some handy features of code editors and explain how they help programmers create clean code.

2.2.4 Identify the basic structure and syntactical elements for a program written in the programming language you use.

2.3 BUILD TOOLS

2.3.1 Explain the purpose of build tools.

2.3.2 Explain the difference between source code and object code.

2.3.3 Describe how a compiler works.

2.3.4 Explain the purpose of a preprocessor.

2.3.5 Explain the purpose of a linker.

2.3.6 Associate virtual machines with Java and bytecode.

2.3.7 Explain how an interpreter works.

2.3.8 Differentiate between source code, bytecode, object code, and executable code.

2.4 DEBUGGING TOOLS

2.4.1 Explain the purpose of debugging.

2.4.2 List common syntax errors.

2.4.3 List common runtime errors.

2.4.4 List common logic errors.

2.4.5 Classify program errors as syntax errors, logic errors, or runtime errors.

2.4.6 Classify a debugger as utility software that allows programmers to walk through the code of a target program to find errors.

2.4.7 List handy features provided by a debugger.

2.5 IDEs AND SDKs

2.5.1 List the purpose and typical features of an integrated development environment (IDE).

2.5.2 Explain how IDEs support visual programming.

2.5.3 Confirm that some IDEs are installed locally, while other IDEs are accessed online.

2.5.4 Identify popular IDEs.

2.5.5 List the purpose and typical features of a software development kit (SDK).

2.5.6 Provide examples of SDK functionality.

2.5.7 Identify popular SDKs.

2.1 PROGRAMMING LANGUAGES

Hello World! (2.1.1)

Hola! Bonjour! Hi! Ciao! Namaste! Salaam! Nihau! Greetings like these are the first thing you learn when studying a spoken language. Programmers have a similar starting point. It is the Hello World! program.

Hello World! is without doubt the most famous computer program of all time. It has been written in every one of the 700+ programming languages. It is typically the first program written by aspiring programmers.

Q Take a look at the Hello World! programs in **Figure 2-1**. They are written in three popular programming languages, C++, Java, and Python. What differences can you identify?

Hello World! in C++	Hello World! in Java	Hello World! in Python

```
#include <iostream>
using namespace std;
int main()
{
  cout <<"Hello World!";
  return 0;
}
```

```
class HelloWorld {
  public static void main(String[] args) {
    System.out.println("Hello World!");
  }
}
```

```
print("Hello World!")
```

Figure 2-1   Hello World in C++, Java, and Python

A You probably noticed the following differences:
Length: Some Hello World! programs required more instructions than others.
Punctuation: Some programs used lots of curly brackets and semicolons.
Wording: One program used the word **cout** where the other programs used **System.out. println** and **print**.
Complexity: Some programs seemed easier to interpret than others.

A lot of backstory is bundled into the Hello World! program that can be applied to learning a programming language. Let's unbundle this famous program to discover the basics about your programming language.

Programming Language Basics (2.1.2, 2.1.3)

A programming language is a notation for specifying the steps in an algorithm that are supposed to be performed by a digital device. Programming languages such as C++, Java, and Python are classified as high-level programming languages because they provide a way for you as a programmer to compose human-readable instructions that direct the operations performed by a computing device.

How does your programming language stack up to other popular languages and where does it shine? Check out the list in **Figure 2-2**.

Using a high-level programming language, you can specify a set of instructions that correspond to the steps in an algorithm. Each instruction is referred to as a statement. The set of statements you generate using a programming language is called program code, or simply code. Your code can become a computer program, which can be distributed as computer software, desktop applications, web apps, and mobile apps.

Logo	Programming Language	Where It Shines
JS	JavaScript	Consumer-facing web development, server-side web development
	Python	Server-side web development, scripting, machine learning, data science, desktop applications, robotics
Java	Java	Server-side web development, desktop applications, mobile development, Internet of Things
C	C	Systems programming, embedded applications, Internet of Things
C++	C++	Systems programming, game development, desktop applications embedded applications, robotics
php	PHP	Server-side web development
	Swift	Desktop and mobile applications for Apple devices
C#	C#	Desktop applications, game development, virtual reality, mobile development
	Ruby	Server-side web development
	Go	Server-side web development, systems programming, Internet of Things

Figure 2-2   Popular programming languages

Syntax and Semantics (2.1.4)

When learning a programming language, where do you start? Programming languages have two key elements: semantics and syntax.

Semantics refers to the meaning and validity of program statements. In a natural language, such as English, it is perfectly fine to say, "Let's start the game" or "Let's start the car," but "Let's start the pen" doesn't make any sense. It is not semantically valid.

Programming languages include keywords, such as `print` and `cout`. These words are a subset of a programming language's reserved words, which are reserved for special purposes. You cannot use reserved words when you create names for variables, functions, or classes in your programs.

One aspect of learning a programming language is to become familiar with its keywords and their use. When learning C++, for example, you'll need to remember that `cout` sends output to a display device. But if you're learning Java, the keyword is `System.out.println`. In Python the keyword is `print`. **Figure 2-3** lists keywords that are common to many programming languages.

Keyword	Purpose
int	Define a value as an integer.
float	Define a value as a floating-point number.
char	Define something as a letter, numeral, punctuation mark, or symbol.
class	Define the characteristics of a person, place, or thing.
new	Create an object based on the characteristics of a class.
if then else	Execute program statements when a condition is true.
case switch	Specify several alternative conditions or decisions.
for while do	Begin a section of code that repeats one or more times.
return	Bring a value back from a function.
import	Incorporate a prewritten code module in a program.
try	Catch errors and handle them gracefully.

Figure 2-3 Keywords common to programming languages

Q Suppose you want to code a program to output "Hello World!" 10 times. What keyword could you use?

A Figure 2-3 lists the **for**, **while**, and **do** keywords for specifying code that repeats one or more times.

You'll acquire a vocabulary of keywords for your programming language gradually. Language references provide a list of keywords and examples of their use. You can find language references online. In fact, it is often helpful to create or find a "cheat sheet" of keywords to keep beside your computer as you learn a new language.

The syntax of a programming language is equivalent to the grammar rules of a written language, such as English or Cyrillic. Syntax defines the order of words and the punctuation you are required to use when composing statements.

Various programming languages use different punctuation syntax. One of the early steps in learning a programming language is to get a handle on its syntax.

Remember the different use of punctuation in the C++, Java, and Python Hello World! programs? Take a closer look in **Figure 2-4** and notice how punctuation helps to separate and structure the statements in a C++ program.

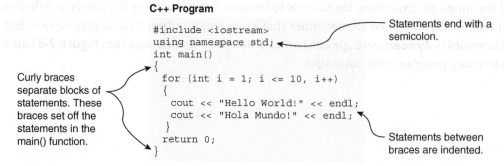

C++ Program

```
#include <iostream>
using namespace std;
int main()
{
    for (int i = 1; i <= 10, i++)
    {
      cout << "Hello World!" << endl;
      cout << "Hola Mundo!" << endl;
    }
    return 0;
}
```

Statements end with a semicolon.

Curly braces separate blocks of statements. These braces set off the statements in the main() function.

Statements between braces are indented.

Figure 2-4 C++ syntax style

Like C++, Java also uses lots of punctuation. **Figure 2-5** points out how the commonly used style for placing curly braces in Java is slightly different from C++. However, either style works equally well as long as the braces are paired. The key is consistency in the project you are working on.

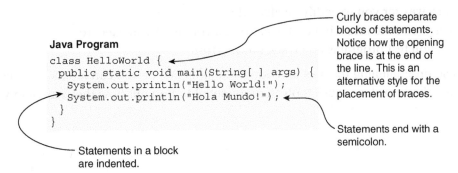

Figure 2-5   Java syntax style

Python uses quite a different approach to punctuation. See if you can spot the differences in **Figure 2-6**.

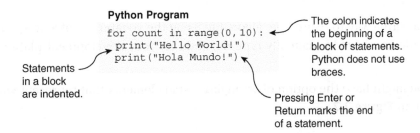

Figure 2-6   Python syntax style

In C++ and Java, statements are enclosed in a structure of curly braces and each statement ends with a semicolon. In contrast, Python uses indents to structure statements, and the linefeed that is generated when you press the Enter key marks the end of a statement. Remember the punctuation style for the language that you are using.

Core Elements (2.1.5)

Although programming languages have differing syntax and semantics, they have common elements. If you look for the ways that your programming language implements the elements in the following list, you will be well on your way through the initial learning curve.

Variables that can be assigned values and structures
Arithmetic operators that can be used to perform calculations
Keywords that perform operations such as print or append
Data types that define values and text
Branching controls that change the sequence in which statements are executed
Repetition controls that repeat a series of statements
Syntax rules for constructing valid statements
Terminology for describing the components of a language and their functions

Your Toolbox (2.1.6, 2.1.7)

Before you can write your Hello World! program, you need access to tools for coding instructions and executing them on a digital device. These tools are sometimes referred to as software development platforms, programming platforms, or development environments.

Programming tools are available as system utility software that can be installed on your computer. Another option is to use an online programming app.

Your programming toolbox includes the following essentials:

Coding tools provide a way for you to codify an algorithm.

Build tools transform your code into a binary format that a computer can execute.

Debugging tools help you test programs and track down errors.

You can acquire these programming tools as individual components, or you can look for a comprehensive development environment. Let's explore these tools in more detail to find out how they can help you develop brilliant programs.

2.2 CODING TOOLS

Program Editors (2.2.1, 2.2.2, 2.2.3)

Coding tools provide you with a way to express an algorithm using the vocabulary of a programming language. Just how much of the code you have to manually type depends on your development platform. Here are the options:

Visual platform: You might have the option of arranging visual elements that represent various statements, as shown in **Figure 2-7**.

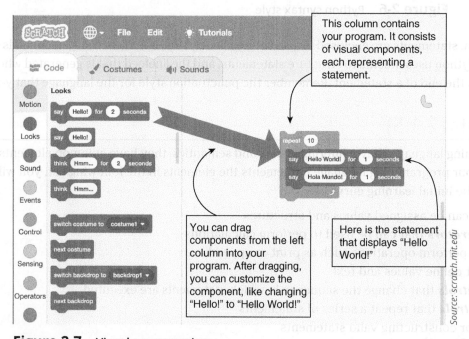

Figure 2-7   Visual programming

Word processor: Despite the attraction of visual programming tools, you will likely end up typing some if not all of the statements for your programs. For that task, you could use a word processor, but it embeds all kinds of codes for formatting and font effects which can't be included in your high-level code.

Text editor: A text editor such as Windows Notepad can produce plain ASCII text, but offers no features designed to help programmers. Using a generic text editor is a bare-bones approach. There are much better coding tools.

Code editor: A code editor is a type of text editor specially designed for entering high-level programming code. It can help you correctly use punctuation and indents, as well as remember variable names and ensure that you use valid keywords. Some handy features of code editors are highlighted in **Figure 2-8**.

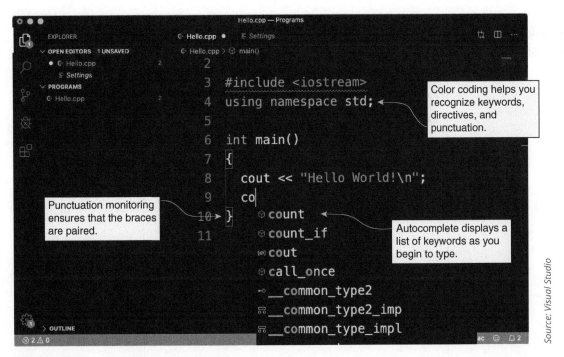

Figure 2-8   Visual Studio code editor

When using a code editor, you can simply type your commands. As you type, pay attention to color coding, autocomplete, and other helpful cues that the editor offers.

Basic Structure (2.2.4)

A programming language has structural and syntax conventions for writing code. When you become familiar with these conventions, they will be the underlying foundation for most of the programs you create. Browse through the following list before you try to identify the conventions in the next figure.

Comments: A comment provides an explanation of your code. At the beginning of a program, you can routinely include a comment with the program title and your name. Comments can be included anywhere in your code to annotate aspects of the program that might not be clear to other programmers who test or modify your code. Computers ignore comments as they are intended for documentation only.

Directives: A directive tells the computer how to handle the program rather than how to perform an algorithm. For example, a directive might specify the name of an external file that is supposed to be incorporated with the rest of your program code. Directives may begin with keywords such as **#include**, **import,** or **using.**

main() function: Many programming languages use **main()** to denote the entry point for program execution. The line of code following **main()** corresponds to the first step in the algorithm you designed for a problem or task.

Statements: Just as human-readable text is divided into sentences and paragraphs, your code should be divided into statements and blocks. A program statement is similar to a sentence; it contains one instruction. In languages such as C++ and Java, statements end with a semicolon. In Python, you end a statement by pressing the Enter or Return key.

Code blocks: A code block is similar to a paragraph; it contains multiple statements that have a specific purpose. In C++ and Java, you use braces (also known as curly brackets) to enclose code blocks. In Python, code blocks are indented.

Q Take a look at **Figure 2-9** and see if you can identify comments, directives, the `main()` function, statements, and code blocks.

```cpp
//Hello World! in English and Spanish
#include <iostream>
using namespace std;
int main()
{
    for (int i = 1; i <= 10, i++)
    {
        cout << "Hello World!" << endl;
        cout << "Hola Mundo!" << endl;
    }
    return 0;
}
```

Figure 2-9   Find the structural and syntax conventions in this code

A The comment is `//Hello World! in English and Spanish`.

There are two directives: `#include <iostream>` and `using namespace std`.

The main() function is labeled `int main()`.

Every line of the program is a statement.

The `for..return` statement is one block. The two `cout` statements form a block within the `for..return` block.

2.3 BUILD TOOLS

The Toolset (2.3.1)

The high-level code that you produce using an editor cannot be directly executed by a computer's microprocessor. Microprocessors have a machine language instruction set based on binary codes. There is no `print` instruction in the microprocessor's instruction set, for example.

Before a program can run, your code has to be converted into machine code consisting of machine language instructions. This executable code is stored in an executable file that can be run, processed, and executed by the microprocessor. Build tools convert your code into a program that a computer can execute.

As a programmer, you'll eventually want to package your programs and distribute them so that they can be installed on a digital device and run with a click, just like the Hola Mundo! program in **Figure 2-10**.

Figure 2-10   Hola Mundo! installed on a Windows computer

A little background about build tools can help you understand some of the weird statements, such as `#include<iostream>`, that you have to include in programs. Also, a passing knowledge of build tools such as compilers, preprocessors, linkers, virtual machines, and interpreters will help you hold your own at late-night parties in Silicon Valley.

Compilers (2.3.2, 2.3.3)

A compiler translates code written in one programming language into another language. The original code is called source code, and the code a compiler produces is called object code. Object code is stored in a standalone file that is separate from the file that holds your source code. See **Figure 2-11**.

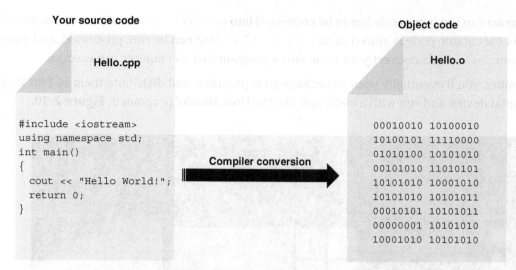

Figure 2-11 When the compiler creates machine code, the resulting file is executable

Q If a compiler is converting C++ code into machine code, what is the source code and what is the object code?

A The C++ code is the source code. The machine code is the object code.

Preprocessors and Linkers (2.3.4, 2.3.5)

The journey from source code to an executable program doesn't usually happen in one magical step. Your source code may be analyzed by a preprocessor and combined with other code by a linker.

A **preprocessor** is a software utility that performs housekeeping tasks before the compiler gets to work. Experienced programmers can creatively use preprocessors to make source programs easy to compile for various software platforms.

For languages such as C++, even basic programs require preprocessing and **preprocessor directives** such as `#include<iostream>` to be routinely included in the program code. After these directives are carried out by the preprocessor, they can be ignored by the compiler.

A **linker** is a software utility that converts one or more object files into a binary executable file. Linking takes place *after* compiling. Your source code is the main object file for linking, but you can specify additional object files that you've created or that are available from third parties. When you see the keyword `import`, it is a clue that an external file needs to be linked in.

Figure 2-12 can help you visualize the build process when a preprocessor and linker are involved.

Preprocessing and linking are not consistent for all programming languages. Your takeaways are:

- Several steps are required to convert your code into a file containing an executable program.
- You may have to include preprocessor directives in your code.

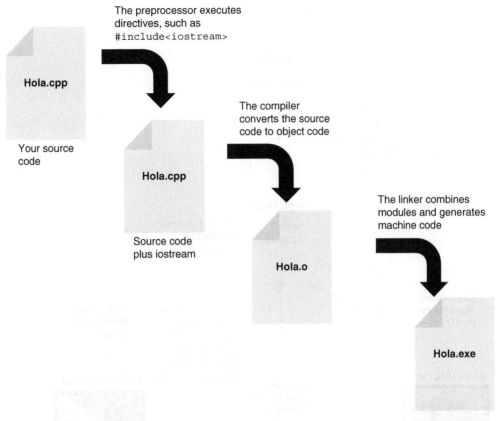

The preprocessor executes directives, such as #include<iostream>

Hola.cpp

Your source code

The compiler converts the source code to object code

Hola.cpp

Source code plus iostream

The linker combines modules and generates machine code

Hola.o

Hola.exe

Figure 2-12   Preprocessing, compiling, and linking the Hola Mundo! program

Virtual Machines (2.3.6)

The product of a compiler is not necessarily machine code. Some compilers convert source code into semi-compiled code called bytecode. Software called a virtual machine converts the bytecode into machine code as the program executes.

What's the point of a virtual machine? The Java Virtual Machine (JVM) offers some insight. The backstory is that an executable file designed to run on a computer with the Microsoft Windows operating system won't work on a computer running macOS. You could develop one version of a program for Microsoft Windows and one for macOS. Or, you can use the Java programming language to create one version of the program and compile it to bytecode.

You can distribute the same bytecode to Windows and Mac users. Windows users have the Windows version of the JVM. Mac users have another version. The virtual machine software converts the bytecode into code that works on the host platform. **Figure 2-13** can help you understand how the JVM works and the value of bytecode.

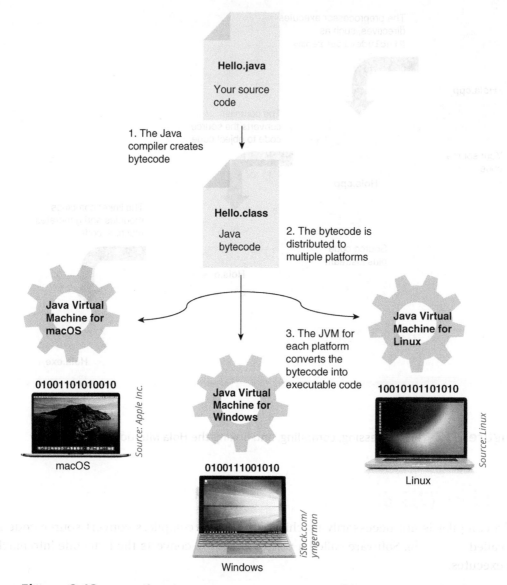

Figure 2-13   The Java Virtual Machine

Interpreters (2.3.7, 2.3.8)

There is one other tool for executing software. An **interpreter** is a software utility that begins with the first statement in your program, preprocesses it into a binary instruction, and then executes it. One by one, each statement in your program is interpreted and run, as illustrated in **Figure 2-14**.

The way an interpreter works is a huge contrast to the activity of a compiler, which preprocesses and converts all of the statements in a program into a binary file before handing it over for execution.

Using an interpreter is convenient for coding and testing your programs because the code executes one line at a time. Execution stops if there is an error, and you can easily see where that error occurred. Modern programming development environments may come bundled with tools for interpreting code, compiling it, or doing both.

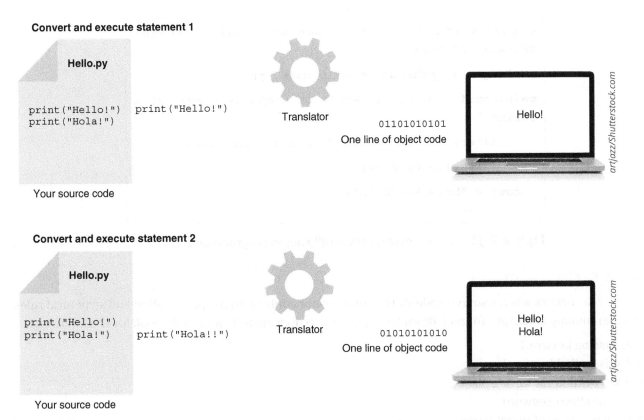

Figure 2-14 An interpreter converts source code into object code one statement at a time

Q For programs that you plan to distribute to other users, why would you want to compile them?

A For distributing software, you should compile your code to produce bytecode or an executable file. Distributing source code that has to be interpreted is awkward for users and exposes your code to unauthorized copying and hacking.

2.4 DEBUGGING TOOLS

Programming Errors (2.4.1)

Yikes! You've written a Spanish version of the Hello World! program, but when you try to run it, all you see is an error message like the one in **Figure 2-15**.

Every programmer makes programming errors, but don't worry. You can quickly track down and fix errors using a variety of programming and debugging tools.

Debugging is programming jargon for finding and correcting errors—or "bugs"—that prevent software from performing correctly. A popular meme dates the origin of the term "debug" to an event in 1947 when a programmer named Grace Hopper fixed a malfunctioning computer by removing a moth. That fact may come in handy when you play Trivia.

Programming errors can be classified into three categories: syntax errors, runtime errors, and logic errors. Knowing the common errors in each of these categories can help you quickly spot bugs in your programs and fix them.

```
clang   version   7.0.0-3~ubuntu0.18.04.1   (tags/
RELEASE_700/final)
> clang++-7 -pthread -o main main.cpp
main.cpp:4:8 warning: result of comparison against a
string
        literal is unspecified (use strcmp instead)
        [-Wstring-compare]
    cout < "Hola Mundo!\n";
         ^~~~~~~~~~~~~~~~~
```

Figure 2-15   Error messages reveal glitches in program code

Syntax Errors (2.4.2)

A **syntax error** occurs when a source code statement does not conform to the punctuation and structural rules of the programming language. To track down the cause of a syntax error in your code, look for the following:

- A missing keyword
- A misspelled keyword
- A keyword in the wrong place
- A capitalized keyword
- Incorrect type of punctuation
- Unpaired quotes or brackets
- Incorrect indentation
- An empty block
- Embedded characters
- Incorrect method parameters
- Missing return type

Q Syntax errors are typically caught by the compiler, which generates an error message. In **Figure 2-16**, can you use the error message to figure out what is wrong with the program?

```
main.cpp    ▤    ⟳ saved
1    #include <iostream>
2
3    using namespace std;
4    int main()
5    {
6        cout << "Hello World!";
7        cout << "Hola Mundo!;
8    }
```

```
clang version 7.0.0-3~ubuntu0.18.04.1 (tags/RELE
ASE_700/final)
> clang++-7 -pthread -o main main.cpp
main.cpp:7:11: warning: missing terminating
      '"' character [-Winvalid-pp-token]
   cout << "Hola Mundo!;
         ^
main.cpp:7:11: error: expected expression
1 warning and 1 error generated.
compiler exit status 1
>
```

Program   Output

Figure 2-16   Where is the error?

A A quotation mark is missing at the end of "Hola Mundo!" After the word "warning," the error message says, "missing terminating ' " ' character." The green ^ symbol indicates the general location of the error.

Runtime Errors (2.4.3)

Whoa! Your program just crashed. It cleared the compiler without any syntax errors, so what caused your program to come to an unexpected halt? A **runtime error** occurs when something in your program code goes wrong during runtime while it is executed by the microprocessor.

If you encounter a runtime error, look for these common problems:

- Division by zero
- Expressions that use incompatible data types
- Forgetting to declare a variable before using it
- Accessing a file that does not exist
- Running out of memory

In **Figure 2-17**, notice that the computer executed the first two lines of the program, but then it crashed when attempting to execute the last line containing a statement to divide by zero, which is not possible.

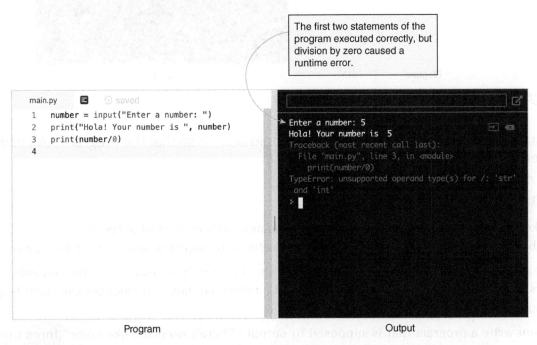

The first two statements of the program executed correctly, but division by zero caused a runtime error.

Program   Output

Figure 2-17   Runtime errors might not be discovered until your program is running

When a program partially executes, then unexpectedly halts, you can be fairly certain of a runtime error. Some compilers can spot common runtime errors and will not allow your program to run until you've corrected them. Even though these common errors might be caught by the compiler, be aware that they are still classified as runtime errors not syntax errors.

Semantic Errors (2.4.4, 2.4.5)

Recall that the semantics of a program statement relate to its meaning. A **semantic error** occurs when your program runs without crashing but produces an incorrect result. Semantic errors are also called logic errors because the algorithm might be based on flawed logic.

More commonly, semantic errors are caused by careless mistakes such as these:

- Using the wrong expression for a decision
- Using the wrong name for a variable

- Forgetting the order of operations
- Setting the wrong loop counter
- Indenting a block to the wrong level or incorrect placement of braces

Q In **Figure 2-18**, can you spot the logical error?

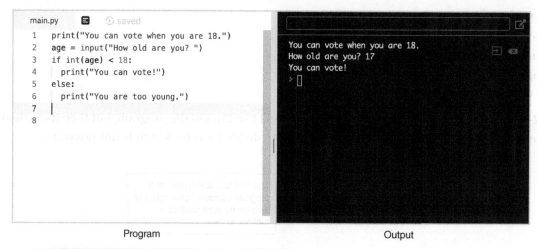

Figure 2-18   What is wrong with this program?

A The `if` statement is incorrect. The < symbol should be > = so that the program says you can vote when your age is greater than or equal to 18.

Debugging Utilities (2.4.6, 2.4.7)

Compilers, linkers, and interpreters can catch some programming errors. Special purpose debugging utilities are also available for your use. These tools offer two nifty features: breakpoints and program animation.

A breakpoint specifies a line of code where execution should pause to let you look at the contents of variables, registers, and other execution elements. If you find unexpected data, a breakpoint can often help you identify the source of an error.

Suppose you write a program that is supposed to output "There's no place like home" three times. In **Figure 2-19**, you can see the program and its output, which is not what you expected. There are only two lines of output, not three.

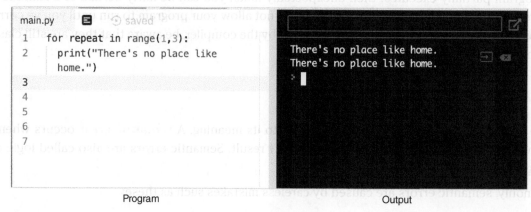

Figure 2-19   Logic errors produce the wrong result

By setting a breakpoint after the line containing "There's no place like home," you could examine the content of the variable called **repeat**. The variable **repeat** controls the number of times "There's no place like home" is output. In **Figure 2-20**, notice how the breakpoint pauses execution so that you can see the value of **repeat** as the program progresses.

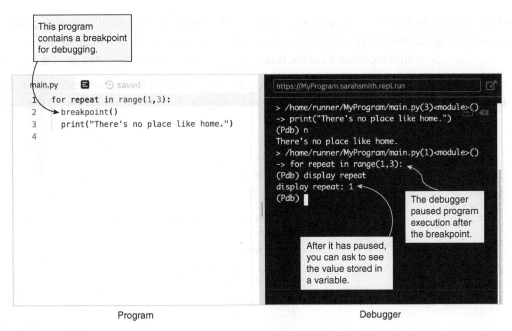

Figure 2-20   A debugger can be used to set breakpoints

By looking at the value of **repeat** when the program is complete, you'd find that it contains 2, which means "There's no place like home" was only output twice, not three times. That discrepancy would direct your attention to the **range(1,3)** statement that controls the number of times the print statement is repeated. It should be **range(0,3)** or **range(1,4)** because the first number in the range is where it starts, but the repetition stops *before* getting to the other number.

Debugging utilities also have a **program animation** feature that lets you watch the status of variables and other program elements as each line of your program is executed. This feature is useful when you run into an error that has you confounded. The program in **Figure 2-21** produced an error. The debugger helps you discover the source of that error.

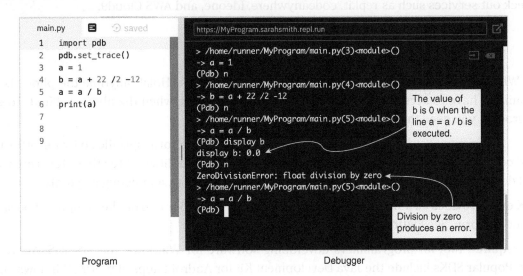

Figure 2-21   A step-by-step search for errors using a debugger's program animation

2.5 IDEs AND SDKs

Integrated Development Environments (2.5.1, 2.5.2, 2.5.3, 2.5.4)

Some experienced programmers like to create a customized development environment containing their favorite editing, compiling, and debugging tools. For your initial foray into programming, it is easier to use an **integrated development environment (IDE)** that includes all of the tools you need to code, compile, link, and debug your work.

Many IDEs support some level of visual programming so that you can define program elements using menus while dragging and dropping variables into program statements. **Figure 2-22** highlights some of the key features of an IDE.

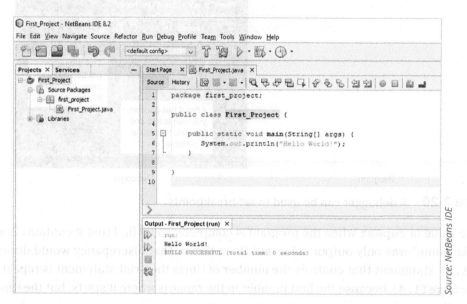

Source: NetBeans IDE

Figure 2-22   IDEs provide an integrated set of editing, debugging, and build tools

Popular IDEs include Visual Studio, Xcode, Eclipse, Netbeans, and PyCharm. To use these IDEs, you have to download and install them on a computer. If you prefer to work with an **online IDE** (or web IDE) that requires no installation, check out services such as repl.it, codeanywhere, Ideone, and AWS Cloud9.

Software Development Kits (2.5.5, 2.5.6, 2.5.7)

Here's an idea: What about creating a program for iPhones that displays "Hola!" anytime the phone is picked up? Your program will have to access the phone's accelerometer to sense when the phone is lifted. To get this project off the ground, you need the iOS SDK.

A **software development kit (SDK)** is a set of tools for developing platform-specific software. SDKs include preprogrammed code libraries, code samples, documentation, and other utilities. Often these tools are wrapped in an integrated development environment that provides coding, compiling, and debugging tools.

The iOS SDK even provides an iPhone simulator so that you can test your app on the computer you are using as a development platform. See **Figure 2-23**.

SDKs are a required tool for programmers developing software for Windows, macOS, iOS, Android, and other platforms. Popular SDKs include the Java Development Kit for Android apps, iOS SDK, Windows SDK, and Facebook SDK.

Figure 2-23   iOS SDK with iPhone simulator

SUMMARY

- Programming languages such as C++, Java, and Python are classified as high-level programming languages because they provide a way for you as a programmer to compose human-readable instructions that direct the operations performed by a computing device.
- Semantics refers to the meaning and validity of program statements. Keywords have specific semantic purposes and programmers have to learn how to use them correctly.
- Syntax defines the order of words and the punctuation you are required to use when composing statements. Each programming language has a unique syntax.
- Programming requires code editors, compilers, and debugging utilities.
- Code editors help you enter statements correctly, using standard conventions for comments, directives, functions, statements, and code blocks.
- Before a program can run, your code has to be converted into machine code, which is stored in an executable file. Compilers, preprocessors, linkers, and interpreters convert your code into a program that a computer can execute.
- A compiler translates source code written in one programming language into a file containing object code in another language.
- A preprocessor is a software utility that performs housekeeping tasks before the compiler gets to work. A linker is a software utility that converts one or more object files into a binary executable file. Linking takes place *after* compiling.
- Some compilers convert source code into semi-compiled code called bytecode. Software called a virtual machine translates bytecode into machine code just prior to its execution.
- An interpreter is a software utility that begins with the first statement in your program, preprocesses it into a binary instruction, and then executes it.
- Debugging is programming jargon for finding and correcting errors—or "bugs"—that prevent software from performing correctly. Debugging can reveal syntax, runtime, and semantic errors in a program.
- An IDE is an integrated development environment that typically includes a code editor, debugger, compiler, and linker. It might offer a visual environment to simplify coding.
- In addition to an IDE, a software development kit (SDK) provides platform-specific development tools.

Key Terms

breakpoint	integrated development	programming language
build tools	environment (IDE)	reserved words
bytecode	interpreter	runtime error
code block	Java Virtual Machine (JVM)	semantic error
code editor	keywords	semantics
comment	linker	software development
compiler	machine code	kit (SDK)
computer program	object code	source code
debugging	online IDE	statement
debugging utilities	preprocessor	syntax
directive	preprocessor directives	syntax error
executable file	program animation	text editor
high-level programming languages	program code	virtual machine

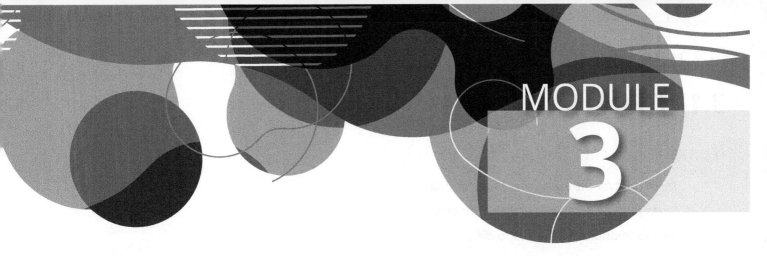

MODULE 3

LITERALS, VARIABLES, AND CONSTANTS

LEARNING OBJECTIVES:

3.1 LITERALS

3.1.1 Define the term "literal" in the context of programming.

3.1.2 Identify numeric literals.

3.1.3 Provide examples of integer literals and floating-point literals.

3.1.4 Identify character and string literals.

3.1.5 Provide use cases for string literals that look like numbers.

3.1.6 Identify Boolean literals.

3.2 VARIABLES AND CONSTANTS

3.2.1 List the characteristics of a program variable.

3.2.2 Create descriptive variable names using appropriate style conventions.

3.2.3 Describe the purpose of a constant.

3.2.4 Use standard naming conventions for constants.

3.2.5 Explain the difference between a variable, a constant, and a literal.

3.2.6 Explain the relationship between variables and memory.

3.3 ASSIGNMENT STATEMENTS

3.3.1 Differentiate between undefined and defined variables.

3.3.2 Identify statements that declare variables.

3.3.3 Identify statements that initialize variables.

3.3.4 Explain how dynamic typing and static typing can affect the way variables are initialized.

3.3.5 Explain the meaning of type inference.

3.3.6 Explain the concept of a null variable.

3.3.7 Identify assignment statements that change the value of a variable.

3.3.8 Differentiate declaring, initializing, and assigning variables.

3.4 INPUT AND OUTPUT

3.4.1 State the algorithm for collecting input from a user and placing it in a variable.

3.4.2 Transform the user input algorithm into pseudocode.

3.4.3 Trace the pseudocode that outputs the value of a variable that is input by a user.

3.1 LITERALS

Numeric Literals (3.1.1, 3.1.2, 3.1.3)

Three rings for the elven-kings under that sky,

Seven for the dwarf-lords in their halls of stone,

Nine for mortal men doomed to die. . .

In J.R.R. Tolkien's classic fantasy book, *The Hobbit*, nineteen rings are endowed with magic powers and distributed to elves, dwarves, and humans in Middle Earth. The rings, which might look like those in **Figure 3-1**, can help explain the concept of literals, which are a basic element in programming.

Elnur/Shutterstock.com   *Shmer/Shutterstock.com*   *Milos Stojiljkovic/ Shutterstock.com*

Figure 3-1   Three rings for the elven kings under the sky. . .

When you get down to basics, programming is a simple activity. You put data into the memory of a computer, then you tell the computer how to manipulate the data according to an algorithm.

Any element of data that you specify for a program is referred to as a **literal**. In Middle Earth, the elven kings had three rings. You can express this idea as:

```
elven_rings = 3
```

In this statement, 3 is a literal. It is a value that you specify as representing a quantity. The literal 3 always means three things, never four things. In that sense, 3 is a fixed value. But this is important: **elven_rings** is not fixed. If one ring is lost, then **elven_rings** can become 2.

Literals 3 and 2 are classified as numeric literals. A **numeric literal** is composed of one or more digits that can represent integers or floating-point numbers containing a decimal point.

Q What are the numeric literals in the following list?

```
dwarf_rings = 7

One

1

ring_thickness = 2.7

dark_lord = "Sauron"
```

A The numeric literals are 7, 1, and 2.7. Literals 7 and 1 are integers, while 2.7 is a floating-point number.

Okay, so numeric literals can be divided into integers and floating points. **Figure 3-2** illustrates the variety of numeric literals you can use in your programs.

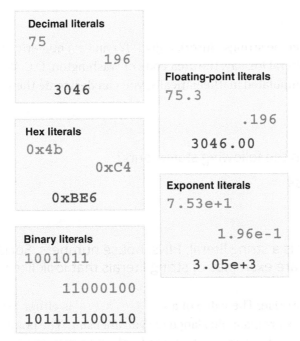

Figure 3-2   Common numeric literals

Q What is the literal in the following statement?

```
elven_rings = 0b00000011
```

A The literal is 0b00000011, which is the binary integer 3.

Character and String Literals (3.1.4)

In addition to numeric data, you'll want your programs to work with data such as letters, symbols, words, and sentences. These non-numeric literals come in two categories: character and string.

A **character literal** is a single letter or symbol. Programmers usually enclose character literals in single quotes, like these examples:

```
'a'
```

```
'@'
```

A **string literal** contains one or more characters and is typically denoted with double quotes, like these examples:

```
"Mordor"
```

```
"Three rings for the elven kings..."
```

```
"bilbo@theshire.com"
```

Q How would you classify `"J.R.R. Tolkien"`?

A It is a string literal because it contains more than one character.

Tricky Literals (3.1.5, 3.1.6)

Literals that look like numbers could be strings. Surprisingly, 202 can be a numeric literal for the value two hundred and two or it can be a string literal for, say, the area code of Washington, D.C. When working with numerals in a context where they are not manipulated mathematically, you can designate them as string literals by enclosing them in double quotes.

Q Where is the string literal in the following statements?

```
distance_to_mordor = 156
unlock_code = "156"
```

A Yes, the unlock code "156" is a string literal. PINs, house numbers, Social Security numbers, area codes, and zip codes are examples of string literals that look like numbers.

Boolean literals are another surprise. The value of a **Boolean literal** is either True or False. Whether those words are capitalized depends on the programming language you are using. The point, however, is that the words True and False look like string literals, but because they are Boolean literals, they are not enclosed in single or double quotes.

Booleans have lots of uses in programming, such as setting a fact as true:

```
bilbo_has_ring = True
```

This statement means that Bilbo has a ring. In contrast, the statement `bilbo_has_ring = "True"` might mean that the ring in Bilbo's possession is named "True" rather than "The One Ring."

3.2 VARIABLES AND CONSTANTS

Variables (3.2.1, 3.2.2)

One for the Dark Lord on his dark throne

In the land of Mordor where the shadows lie.

The evil sorcerer, Sauron, forges a powerful ring in the fires of Mount Doom. He wears the ring until he is defeated in battle. The ring then passes to a warrior named Isildur, who loses it while swimming across the Anduin River. For a very long time, the location of the ring is unknown.

Unlike Sauron's ring, you don't want your data to end up in some unknown location in the computer's memory. To use literals, you have to put them in a known location so that they can be accessed by the statements in your programs. Variables and constants provide these locations.

In the context of programming, a **variable** is a named memory location that temporarily holds text or a numeric value. See **Figure 3-3**.

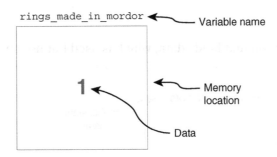

Figure 3-3   A variable is a named memory location that temporarily holds data

Variables have three important characteristics:

- A variable has a name.
- A variable corresponds to a memory location where data can be stored.
- The data in a variable can be changed.

You have lots of flexibility when naming variables, with the exception that you cannot use any of your programming language's reserved words. A reserved word, such as `print`, is used by a programming language for a specific purpose. You can find a list of reserved words in the reference for your programming language.

The names you use for variables should be descriptive. Can you guess what the programmer had in mind by calling a variable **er** and putting 3 into it?

`er = 3`

The variable name er might refer to an emergency room, explicit rate, or the small country of Eritrea. If 3 is the number of elven rings, however, a variable name such as **elven_rings** is much more descriptive.

`elven_rings = 3`

The style for variable names differs based on programming language syntax and project team standards. Some programming languages require variable names to begin with a lowercase letter, while other languages require an uppercase letter.

Variable names cannot contain any spaces, but a single word may not provide a very descriptive variable name. The two most prevalent conventions for combining words for variable names are camel case and snake case.

Camel case begins with a lowercase letter, but each subsequent word is capitalized. Snake case uses all lowercase and separates words with an underscore. **Figure 3-4** provides examples.

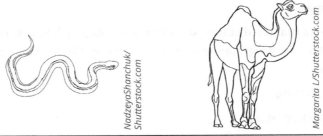

Snake case	Camel case
elven_rings	elvenRings
made_in_mordor	madeInMordor
hobbit	hobbit
multiples_of_2	multiplesOf2

Figure 3-4   Snake case and camel case for formatting variable names

Constants (3.2.3, 3.2.4, 3.2.5)

A **constant** is a named memory location that holds data, which is used but not changed by the statements in a program. See **Figure 3-5**.

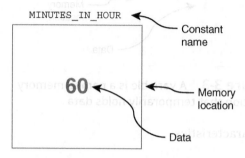

Figure 3-5   A constant is a named memory location that holds data that does not change

The three important characteristics of constants are:

- A constant has a name.
- A constant corresponds to a memory location where data can be stored.
- The data in a constant is not meant to be changed.

Constants are sometimes confused with literals because both may be described as "fixed." Your takeaway is that a literal is a data element, but a constant is a *place* in memory that holds a value that does not change.

As with variables, the name you use for a constant should be descriptive. To differentiate constants from variables, the convention in C++, Java, and Python is to name constants in all uppercase with an underscore separating words. Here are some examples:

```
MINUTES_IN_HOUR = 60

MAXIMUM_USERS = 1024

OHIO_ABBREVIATION = "OH"
```

You might wonder why programmers use named constants instead of simply using the actual value in calculations or processes. Well, suppose a NASA programmer uses 238,900 miles as the distance from the Earth to the Moon in a series of 20 or more formulas, beginning with these:

```
round_trip = 238900 * 2

travel_time = 238900/speed
```

Later the programmer discovers that the distance should be expressed in kilometers, not miles, or the lunar probe will miss its landing site. A smart programmer would have set up the formulas with a constant such as **DISTANCE_EARTH_MOON** like this:

```
DISTANCE_EARTH_MOON = 238900

round_trip = DISTANCE_EARTH_MOON * 2

travel_time = DISTANCE_EARTH_MOON /speed
```

Changing the distance to kilometers then requires a change in only one line, instead of all of the formulas.

```
DISTANCE_EARTH_MOON = 384400

round_trip = DISTANCE_EARTH_MOON * 2

travel_time = DISTANCE_EARTH_MOON /speed
```

The Memory Connection (3.2.6)

Variables and constants correspond to memory locations where data can be stored. Each memory location has a unique address that is expressed as a long binary number or an intimidating hex number such as 0xE2452440. Thankfully, you can put data into a memory location without dealing with those addresses.

Figure 3-6 shows that when you specify the name for a variable or constant, your programming language ties it to a memory location where you can put data.

Figure 3-6   Variable names correspond to memory locations

3.3 ASSIGNMENT STATEMENTS

Declaring Variables (3.3.1, 3.3.2)

The One Ring forged by Sauron bears an inscription that is only visible when the ring is placed in a fire:

> *One ring to rule them all,*
>
> *One ring to find them,*
>
> *One ring to bring them all,*
>
> *And in the darkness bind them.*

Just as the One Ring was designed to create a binding that controlled the other nineteen rings, programmers can define a variable by binding its name to a memory location. Using an undefined variable produces a runtime error, so it is essential to define the variables that you use in programs.

Variables can be declared, initialized, and assigned. Depending on your programming language and your algorithm, each of these operations might require a separate step or they can be combined.

To declare a variable means specifying a name that is assigned, or bound, to a memory location. Most programming languages require you to specify whether the variable will hold an integer, floating-point number, Boolean, character, or string.

Figure 3-7 shows how to declare a variable in pseudocode and in a programming language.

Declaration statements	
Pseudocode	`declare total_rings as integer` `declare first_letter as character`
Programming language	`int total_rings;` `char first_letter;`

Figure 3-7   Declaring a variable

Q Why would you declare a variable if you don't have any data to put in it?

A There are several reasons.

- You might not know the value of a variable until a user enters one.
- You might need a variable that will hold the value of a calculation after it is performed.
- You could be specifying the instance variables that describe an object's attributes, such as **ring_size**, that have an unknown value until you create a specific ring.

Initializing Variables (3.3.3, 3.3.4, 3.3.5, 3.3.6)

To **initialize a variable** means specifying a name and a value. In pseudocode, you can specify an initialization statement like this:

```
initialize total_rings = 20
```

This initialization statement creates a variable called **total_rings** and sets its value to 20. In pseudocode, it is handy to use the word **initialize**, but that word is not required when you code an initialization statement in a programming language such as C++, Java, or Python.

As with declaring variables, some languages require initialization statements to specify the type of data that will be placed in the variable. **Figure 3-8** shows the simple syntax for initializing a variable in pseudocode and three popular programming languages.

Initialization statements	
Pseudocode	`initialize total_rings = 20 as integer` `initialize first_letter = 'A' as character`
C++	`int total_rings = 20;` `char first_letter = 'A';`
Java	`int total_rings = 20;` `char first_letter = 'A';`
Python	`total_rings = 20` `first_letter = 'A'`

Figure 3-8   Initializing a variable

Q What do you notice is different about the Python syntax for initializing a variable?

A Python does not specify the type of data. The initialization statements don't include **int** or **char**.

Python is a dynamically typed programming language that allows a variable to take on any type of data during program execution. The language deduces the data type based on the presence or absence of a decimal point and quote marks. This process is referred to as type inference. For example, in a dynamically typed language, the following code is perfectly acceptable.

```
total_rings = 19

total_rings = 20

total_rings = "unknown"
```

With dynamic typing you can initialize `total_rings` as 19, which is a number. You can then change the value to 20, and then change it to a text string.

Languages such as C++ and Java are statically typed. After you specify a variable's data type, it cannot hold any other type of data. In the following code, it is acceptable to initialize `total_rings` as an integer with a value of 19. You can then change that value to another integer, such as 20. But you cannot place the word "unknown" into `total_rings` because that variable was initialized to hold an integer.

```
int total_rings = 19

total_rings = 20

total_rings = "unknown"
```

As you begin learning a programming language, be sure to find out if it uses dynamic typing or static typing, so you know how to properly declare, initialize, and change the values in variables.

What role does initialization play in your programming? Let's look at some examples.

Starting values. You can initialize a variable with a literal if you know its starting value when the program begins. Using pseudocode, you can specify that there are three elven rings as:

```
initialize elven_rings = 3
```

Initial value of counter. The integer variables that you plan to use to count repetitions can be initialized with 0 or 1, depending on the control structure that operates the loop. Here is an example:

```
initialize counter = 0
```

Null variables. A null variable is one that has no value. A null variable is not the same as a variable that has been initialized with 0. Zero is a value; null means no value. Programming languages handle null values in different ways. Initialization with null such as the following is best avoided when possible.

```
initialize ring_location = null
```

Q Instead of using null, how would you initialize the ring location if you don't know where the ring can be found at the beginning of the program?

A You could use this initialization statement:

```
initialize ring_location = "Unknown"
```

Assigning Variables (3.3.7, 3.3.8)

Assigning variables refers to any process that sets or changes the value of a variable. An assignment statement sets or changes the value that is stored in a variable. **Figure 3-9** explains the syntax of an assignment statement.

```
variable_name  =  expression
dwarf_rings     =  7 - 1
dwarf_rings     =  dwarf_rings - 1
total_rings     =  3 + 7 + 9 + 1
ring_location   =  "Anduin River"
ring_location   =  "Bilbo's pocket"
```

Figure 3-9   General syntax for assignment statements

Assignment statements and initializations look the same. An initialization is a type of assignment. Initialization is the term used for the first time you set the value of a variable. Later in your program, you can use an assignment statement to change the value of a variable.

In the following pseudocode, the variable **total_rings** is initialized as 0, then an assignment statement changes that value to the total number of rings. In pseudocode, **compute** is the keyword used for assignment statements that deal with numeric values.

```
initialize total_rings = 0

compute total_rings = 3 + 7 + 9 + 1
```

As you can see, assignment statements are a handy way to perform calculations and place the result into a variable. You can then use that variable for further calculation or as the source of output you display to users.

You can also use assignment statements to change the value of a string literal that is stored in a variable. Here is an example:

```
initialize who_has_the_ring = "Sauron"

assign who_has_the_ring = "Isildur"
```

Variables play several essential roles in your programs:

- Variables provide the perfect place to put the literals that your programs use as input, manipulations, and output.
- Variables can hold intermediate data while multistep calculations are performed.
- Variables can act as counters to control the number of repetitions a program performs.
- The value in a variable can be used as the basis for sections of an algorithm that hinge on decisions.

3.4 INPUT AND OUTPUT

Input to a Variable (3.4.1, 3.4.2)

A creature named Gollum lives in the dreary caves and tunnels below the Misty Mountains. His prize possession is a magical gold Ring. One day, the Ring somehow ends up on the ground in a lonely tunnel. Before Gollum knows the ring is gone, a hobbit called Bilbo Baggins, who is crawling through the dark tunnel, stretches out his hand, finds the Ring, and promptly tucks it in his pocket.

Think of the Ring as a data object from the outside world. As a programmer, you can collect data from an outside source and tuck it into a variable. It is a handy way to obtain some or all of the data your program is designed to process. The algorithm for collecting data from a user goes like this:

Initialize a variable to hold the user's input.

Prompt the user to enter data.

Collect the data in the initialized variable.

To get data from a user, you typically supply a prompt that explains what you want the user to enter. For example, if your program is collecting answers for a trivia game, one prompt might be, "In Middle Earth, how many rings were given to the dwarf lords?"

Using this prompt, here is the pseudocode to initialize a variable, display a prompt, and then collect an answer from the user:

```
initialize dwarf_rings = 0

display "In Middle Earth, how many rings were given to the dwarf lords? "

input dwarf_rings
```

When you code and run this program, the trivia player would see something like **Figure 3-10**.

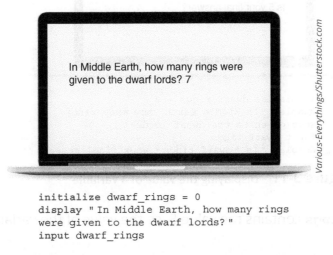

```
initialize dwarf_rings = 0
display " In Middle Earth, how many rings
were given to the dwarf lords? "
input dwarf_rings
```

Figure 3-10   Loading a variable with data entered by a user

Q In Figure 3-10, which line of code initializes the variable `dwarf_rings` and which line places the user's input in that variable?

A The line `initialize dwarf_rings = 0` initializes the variable. The line `input dwarf_rings` places the user's input into the variable.

Output from a Variable (3.4.3)

Suppose the trivia player responds to the question about dwarf rings by entering 5. That is not the correct answer. You can then ask if 5 is the final answer. Here's the pseudocode.

```
initialize dwarf_rings = 0

display "In Middle Earth, how many rings were given to the dwarf lords? "

input dwarf_rings

display "Is " dwarf_rings " your final answer?"
```

Q Look at the program in **Figure 3-11**. Where does the 5 come from in the last line?

Various-Everythings/Shutterstock.com

```
initialize dwarf_rings = 0
display "In Middle Earth, how many rings
were given to the dwarf lords? "
input dwarf_rings
display "Is "dwarf_rings" your final answer? "
```

Figure 3-11   Displaying the value of a variable

A The variable **dwarf_rings** contains the value 5, so the *value* of the variable appeared in the displayed line.

When variables are output to a display or printer, the output is the *value* of the variable, not the variable name.

SUMMARY

- Any element of data that you specify for a program is referred to as a literal. There are several types of literals, such as integer, floating point, character, string, and Boolean.
- Literals that look like numbers are sometimes treated as strings when they are not intended to be used in calculations. Telephone numbers, PINs, house numbers, Social Security numbers, area codes, and zip codes are examples of string literals that look like numbers.
- A variable is a named memory location that temporarily holds text or a numeric value.
- Variable names should be descriptive but cannot be reserved words used for special purposes by the programming language. Variable names are usually formatted in camel case or snake case.

- A constant is a named memory location that holds data that is not changed by the statements in a program.
- Variables and constants correspond to memory locations where data can be stored. When you specify the name for a variable or constant, your programming language ties it to a memory location where you can place data.
- Using undefined variables can produce runtime or compile-time errors. To define a variable, you can declare it or initialize it. When a language is statically typed, the first appearance of a variable in code must include a specification for the type of data it will hold. Dynamically typed languages do not require you to specify a data type. Type is inferred by the assignment and may be changed with a new assignment.
- Assignment statements can be used to initialize a variable or change its value. In statically typed languages, variables can only be assigned values that are the same type of data specified when the variable was declared or initialized.
- Programmers can assign values to variables or they can collect values from external sources, such as user input. The values of variables can be output to a printer, display, or other device.

Key Terms

assignment statement	initialize a variable	statically typed
Boolean literal	literal	string literal
Camel case	null variable	type inference
character literal	numeric literal	undefined variable
constant	prompt	variable
declare a variable	reserved word	
dynamically typed	Snake case	

NUMERIC DATA TYPES AND EXPRESSIONS

LEARNING OBJECTIVES:

4.1 PRIMITIVE DATA TYPES

4.1.1 Define the term "data type."

4.1.2 List four common primitive data types.

4.1.3 Explain the purpose of primitive data types.

4.1.4 Distinguish between primitive data types and composite data types.

4.2 NUMERIC DATA TYPES

4.2.1 List the characteristics of integer data.

4.2.2 Provide examples of integer data that might be incorporated in a computer program.

4.2.3 Explain the difference between a signed and an unsigned integer.

4.2.4 State the memory requirements for signed and unsigned integers.

4.2.5 List the characteristics of floating-point data.

4.2.6 Provide examples of floating-point data that might be incorporated in a computer program.

4.2.7 Recall that floating-point data is not stored in conventional binary format.

4.2.8 Compare and contrast the use of integer data with floating-point data.

4.3 MATHEMATICAL EXPRESSIONS

4.3.1 List the symbols used for the following mathematical operations: addition, subtraction, multiplication, division, exponentiation, and modulo division.

4.3.2 Provide examples of program statements in which the result of a mathematical operation is stored in a variable.

4.3.3 Describe the mathematical order of operations.

4.3.4 Provide examples illustrating the use of parentheses to change the order of operations.

4.3.5 Explain the use of compound operators such as += −+ *= /= and %=.

4.4 NUMERIC DATA TYPE CONVERSION

4.4.1 Provide examples of when a programmer might convert integer or floating-point data to a different data type.

4.4.2 Explain the disadvantage of converting floating-point data to integer data.

4.4.3 Explain the significance of rounding for floating-point calculations.

4.5 FORMATTING OUTPUT

4.5.1 Explain the advantage of formatting output.

4.5.2 List the elements that can be specified when formatting numeric output.

4.5.3 Use formatting parameters to specify the output format of numeric data.

4.1 PRIMITIVE DATA TYPES

Data Types (4.1.1)

iTunes provides detailed information about each of the albums in its collection. In **Figure 4-1**, you can easily identify the album price, release date, the number of reviewers, song list, song times, popularity, and song prices.

Figure 4-1   The data displayed for a music album is stored in variables

This data can be stored in variables. But wait. If you are writing a program and want to assign the value of 3:56 to a variable called **song_time**, your programming language is likely to generate an error. The problem with values such as 3:56 is related to data types, so let's dive into the topic.

The term **data type** refers to a way of categorizing data. For example, the number 21 could be categorized as an integer data type because it is a whole number without decimal places. As a programmer, you need a good understanding of data types because they are a key element of the variables that are the foundation for your programs.

Programmers work with two main classifications of data types: primitive data types and composite data types.

Primitive Data Types (4.1.2, 4.1.3)

Primitive data types are built into your programming language. **Figure 4-2** provides a list of them.

Primitive data types are important time savers because your programming language knows how to allocate memory for storing these data types. For example, suppose you want to store the number of songs—23—for the first act of the *Hamilton* soundtrack in a variable called **act1_song_count**. Because

Primitive Data Type	Keyword	Description	Examples
Character	`char`	A single letter, symbol, or numeral	'a' '@'
Integer	`int`	A whole number without any decimal places	1 128 3056 –2
Floating point	`float`	A number that includes decimal places	12.99 0.26 –3.56
Double floating point	`double`	A very large number that includes decimal places	3.84147098480789672
Boolean	`bool`	A logical value of True or False	True False
Valueless	`void`	No value	
Wide character	`wchar_t`	A Unicode character that requires more than 8 bits	€ ® ¥

Figure 4-2   Primitive data types

the integer 23 is classified as a primitive data type, your programming language knows how much memory space to allocate for it.

Your programming language also knows how to manipulate primitive data types. For numbers such as 23, your language can perform addition, subtraction, and other mathematical operations.

Programming languages provide functions to manipulate data. A **function** is a named procedure that performs a specific task. The **abs()** function, for example, returns the absolute, unsigned value of an integer.

Q What are the two key characteristics of primitive data types?

A The key characteristics are as follows:
1. The programming language knows how much memory to allocate.
2. The programming language knows how to manipulate that type of data.

The takeaway for primitive data types is that you can tell the programming language what to do with them, but you don't have to explain how to do it. You don't have to specify the mechanics of storing or adding two numbers; you just have to specify the variables or values that you want to add.

Composite Data Types (4.1.4)

Composite data types are not built into your programming language but can be constructed from primitive data types. Composite data types are programmer defined or available in add-on libraries of program code. In most programming languages, data that represents time would be handled as a composite data type.

The first song on the *Hamilton* soundtrack is 3:56 minutes long. This value is not an integer, floating-point number, or other primitive data type. To use this value in a program, you would need to create a composite data type and code routines for manipulating it.

You will discover more about composite data types as you continue to learn about functions and data structures. For now, let's focus on primitive data types that involve integers and floating-point numbers.

4.2 NUMERIC DATA TYPES

Integer Data Types (4.2.1, 4.2.2, 4.2.3, 4.2.4)

Whole numbers are classified as integer data types. Integer data types have the following characteristics:

- Must be whole numbers without decimal places or fractions.
- Can be positive or negative. An integer without a plus or minus symbol is called an unsigned integer and assumed to be a positive number. An integer that begins with a plus or minus symbol is a signed integer.
- Can be a decimal, binary, or hexadecimal number.

Figure 4-3 contains examples of signed and unsigned integer data that you might incorporate into computer programs.

Integer Data	Signedness	Description
23	Unsigned	Number of songs
+363	Signed	Number of reviewers
1460000	Unsigned	Number of *Hamilton* albums sold
7722333444	Unsigned	World population
−40	Signed	Coldest temperature recorded in Kansas
0b00000101	Unsigned	Binary 5
0x6C	Unsigned	Hexadecimal 108

Figure 4-3   Integer data types

In statically typed languages, such as C++ or Java, integers are designated with the keyword `int` when a variable is declared or initialized, like this:

```
int number_of_songs = 23
```

In dynamically typed languages, such as Python, the data type for a variable is inferred, so programmers do not need to declare a data type.

Integers, such as 23, are stored as binary numbers in memory locations. Each memory location holds 1 byte of data composed of eight digits. The binary number 11111111, which is 255, is the largest number that fits in 1 byte. One byte can hold unsigned integers ranging from 0 to 255.

A signed integer requires one digit as the sign, so only seven digits remain for the number. One byte provides enough storage space for signed integers ranging from −127 to +127. **Figure 4-4** further explains this important idea.

Because integers are a primitive data type, your programming language sets aside an appropriate amount of memory to store them. Your programs generally deal with integers that are larger than 255, so languages such as C++ and Java set aside 4 bytes of memory for each integer. Python sets aside even more.

Four bytes can hold integers ranging from −2,147,483,648 to +2,147,483,647. As long as you are working with numbers in these ranges, the basic integer data type is all you'll need.

| 00000000 (0) | 11111111 (255) |

One byte of memory holds eight binary digits. Unsigned integers range from 00000000 to 11111111, which is 0 to 255.

| 01111111 (−127) | 11111111 (+127) |

Signed integers use the leftmost bit to indicate a + or − sign. The range for signed integers is −1111111 to +1111111, which is −127 to +127.

Figure 4-4   Integer storage allocation

Floating-Point Data Types (4.2.5, 4.2.6, 4.2.7, 4.2.8)

Numbers with decimal places are classified as **floating-point data types**. These numbers include a decimal point and values to the right of the decimal point. **Figure 4-5** contains examples of signed and unsigned floating-point data that you might incorporate into computer programs.

Floating-Point Number	Signedness	Description
19.99	Unsigned	Price of the *Hamilton* album
4.8	Unsigned	Customer rating
.08	Unsigned	Tax rate
2.998E8	Unsigned	Speed of light (meters/second)
−4.5967E2	Signed	Absolute zero

Figure 4-5   Floating-point data types

Floating-point numbers can be positive or negative and they can be expressed in decimal notation or E notation. **E notation** is similar to scientific notation, which formats numbers as powers of 10. For example, 459.67 in E notation is 4.5967E2. Notice the 2 to the right of E. It means the decimal point was moved two places to the left, with each place representing a power of 10.

Q What is the E notation for .4996?

A It is 4.996E−1. E notation always displays one number to the left of the decimal, so the decimal point moved to the right. When the decimal point moves to the right, the exponent is negative.

Whether you initialize a variable as .4996 or 4.996E−1, your floating-point numbers are stored in E notation. In **Figure 4-6**, you can see the space used for each component when a floating-point number is stored in 4 bytes.

Byte 1	Byte 2	Byte 3	Byte 4
11111111	**11111111**	**11111111**	**11111111**

1 Sign bit   8 Exponent bits   23 Data bits

Figure 4-6   Floating-point storage allocation

Because of the space used to store the sign and exponent, 4 bytes can store floating-point numbers in the range of ±3.4E−38 to ±3.4E38. These 4-byte numbers are referred to as single precision numbers.

In statically typed languages, such as C++ and Java, single precision floating-point numbers are designated with the keyword **float** when a variable is declared or initialized, like this:

```
float albums_sold = 42335500000
```

When floating-point data is stored in 8 bytes, it is referred to as double precision. Double precision numbers can range from ±1.7E−308 to ±1.7E308. Double precision numbers are typically declared with the keyword **double**.

4.3 MATHEMATICAL EXPRESSIONS

Arithmetic Operators (4.3.1, 4.3.2)

Integers and floating-point numbers are used for calculations. The result of a calculation is generally stored in a variable. Here is an example:

```
discount_price = album_price - 2.99
```

Discount_price is the variable that will hold the result of the calculation. On the right side of the = symbol, **album_price - 2.99** is an expression. An expression is a programming statement that has a value and usually includes one or more arithmetic operators, such as + or −, and one or more operands, such as **album_price** or **2.99**.

To construct expressions, you can use the arithmetic operators listed in **Figure 4-7**.

Operator	Operation	Example
+	Addition	`song_count = 23 + 22`
−	Subtraction	`discount_price = album_price - 2.99`
*	Multiplication	`tax = discount_price * tax_rate`
/	Division	`average_rating = total / number_of_reviewers`
%	Modulo division	`remainder = 23 % 6`

Figure 4-7   Arithmetic operators

Q From the examples in Figure 4-7, can you conclude that arithmetic operators work only for literals?

A No. You can see that arithmetic operations can manipulate variables, such as **tax_rate**, as well as literals, such as **2.99**.

Arithmetic operators generally work as you'd expect, but note these important takeaways:

Integer division. When integer division produces a fractional part, it may not be included in the result. For example, **7 / 2 = 3.5**, but the result might be **3** depending on the programming language you are using.
Modulo division. The % operator produces the *remainder* of a division operation. The result of dividing 11 by 3 is 3 with 2 as the remainder. So, **11 % 3** produces **2** as the result.

Q What is the result of **6 % 2**?

A The result is 0 because 6 divided by 2 is 3 with no remainder. The remainder is 0. So, **6 % 2 = 0**.

You can use the modulo operator in an algorithm to determine if a number is odd or even. Here is the pseudocode.

```
initialize my_number = 6
if my_number % 2 is 0 then
    output "The number is even."
    else output "The number is odd."
```

This algorithm works because even numbers can be divided by 2 with no remainder. When **my_number % 2 = 0**, **my_number** is even. In **Figure 4-8** you can see how this algorithm works in actual code.

```
#include <iostream>
using namespace std;
int main()
{
    int my_number = 6;
    if (my_number % 2 == 0)
        cout << "The number is even.";
    else
        cout << "The number is odd.";
}
OUTPUT:
The number is even.
```

Figure 4-8 Checking if a number is even or odd

Order of Operations (4.3.3, 4.3.4)

What is the solution to the expression 2 + 3 * (5 + 1)? If you answered 20, you're on point with the order of operations, which specifies the sequence in which to perform arithmetic operations. Here's the sequence:

1. Do the math in parentheses first.
2. Carry out exponentiation and roots.
3. Perform multiplication, division, and modulo division as they appear from left to right.
4. Execute addition and subtraction as they appear from left to right.

To solve 2 + 3 * (5 + 1), first add 5 + 1 because it is in parentheses. Now you have 2 + 3 * 6. Next do the multiplication, so the expression becomes 2 + 18. Finally, add those numbers and the result is 20.

Q Got it? Let's see. What is the result of 2 + 3 % 2 * (4 + 1)?

A The result is 7. First add 4 + 1 because it is in parentheses. The modulo division 3 % 2 is next to yield a remainder of 1. Then multiply 1 * 5 and add the result to 2.

Parentheses are the key for changing the order of operations. Here is a simple example. 3 + 2 * 5 = 13 because the order of operations specifies that the multiplication comes before the addition.

But suppose you want to add 3 + 2 before multiplying it by 5. Simply add parentheses around the operation you want to go first: (3 + 2) * 5. Now the result is 25! **Figure 4-9** shows both expressions in code and the results.

```
#include <iostream>

using namespace std;

int main()

{

    int without_parenths = 3 + 2 * 5;

    int with_parenths = (3 + 2) * 5;

    cout << "Without parentheses: " << without_parenths << endl;

    cout << "With parentheses: " << with_parenths << endl;

}
OUTPUT:

Without parentheses: 13

With parentheses: 25
```

Figure 4-9   Changing the order of operations

Compound Operators (4.3.5)

Most programming languages offer a set of compound operators that provide handy shortcuts for some common arithmetic operations. Programmers frequently want to keep track of repetitions by incrementing a counter by 1. The usual code for incrementing a counter is shown in **Figure 4-10**.

```
#include <iostream>
using namespace std;
int main()
{
   int counter = 1;
   counter = counter + 1;
   cout << counter;
}
OUTPUT:
2
```

Figure 4-10 Incrementing a counter

The variable **counter** begins with the value 1. The computation adds 1 to the **counter** so its value becomes 2.

The compound += operator does the same thing with the code shown in **Figure 4-11**.

```
#include <iostream>
using namespace std;
int main()
{
   int counter = 1;
   counter += 1;
   cout << counter;
}
OUTPUT:
2
```

Figure 4-11 Using a compound operator

Figure 4-12 provides examples of the most commonly used compound operators.

Compound Operator	Example	Result
+=	`initialize counter = 1` `compute counter += 1`	2
-=	`initialize counter = 1` `compute counter -= 1`	0
*=	`initialize counter = 10` `compute counter *= 2`	20
/=	`initialize counter = 12` `compute counter /= 2`	6
%=	`initialize counter = 7` `compute counter %= 2`	1

Figure 4-12 Compound operators

4.4 NUMERIC DATA TYPE CONVERSION

Convert Integers and Floating-Point Numbers (4.4.1, 4.4.2)

Sometimes mathematical expressions contain different data types, such as an integer and a floating-point number. Here is a simple example designed to calculate the price of purchasing two albums:

```
initialize number_of_albums = 2

compute total_price = 19.99
```

The 19.99 price of one album is a floating-point number. The number of albums—2—is an integer. Some programming languages handle this expression gracefully using a process called coercion. Coercion automatically decides which data type to use for a calculation. For the expression 19.99 * 2, your programming language might use coercion to handle the integer 2 as a floating-point 2.0 when carrying out the calculation.

Coercion doesn't change the data type of the variable. The variable `number_of_albums` continues to hold the integer 2. Its value is coerced into a floating-point number only for the calculation. You can think of the calculation as happening on a scratch pad. This is the only place that the integer 2 becomes 2.0.

Depending on coercion is not necessarily a best practice, especially if you don't carefully track its effects through a series of calculations. You can manually convert a value to a different data type through a process that is sometimes called type casting, or simply "casting."

Suppose that you have collected ratings for the *Hamilton* soundtrack from thousands of music fans. The combined rating for 2,360 customers is 10,456. To find the average rating, you can use a statement like this:

```
compute average_rating = 10456.2 / 2361
```

The result stored in `average_rating` is 4.42872, but if you want to convert that number to an integer, you can use the `int()` function. Look for the `int()` function in **Figure 4-13** to see how it converts the floating point `average_rating` into an integer stored in `rounded_average`.

```cpp
#include <iostream>
using namespace std;

int main()
{
    int customers = 2361;
    float sum_of_ratings = 10456.2;
    float average_rating = sum_of_ratings / customers;
    int rounded_average = int(average_rating);
    cout << "Average: " << average_rating << endl;
    cout << "Rounded average: " << rounded_average << endl;
}
OUTPUT:
Average: 4.42872
Rounded average: 4
```

Figure 4-13   Converting a floating-point number to an integer

The use of the `int()` function converts the value in **average_rating** to an integer and stores 4 in **rounded_average**. Be aware, however, that the conversion has lost information. The fractional part to the right of the decimal is not stored in **rounded_average**.

Rounding Quirks (4.4.3)

Programming languages have some quirks when it comes to numeric data. Here's a puzzler:

What is the correct result for the expression **1 / 2**? You would be astonished if the computer produced 0 as the result. **Figure 4-14** explains how your programming language handles this situation.

C++ produces 0 as the result of 1 / 2, even if the result is assigned to a **float** data type. The reason is that 1 and 2 appear to be integers; they contain no decimal point.

```
#include <iostream>

using namespace std;

int main()

{

    float solution = 1 / 2;

    cout << solution;

}
```
OUTPUT:

0

To get the expected result, you can enter one or more of the numbers with a decimal place, which forces C++ to produce a floating-point result.

```
#include <iostream>

using namespace std;

int main()

{

    float solution = 1.0 / 2.0;

    cout << solution;

}
```
OUTPUT:

0.5

Figure 4-14   Floating-point quirks

Here is another oddity. What do you expect as the result of the expression **.1 + .2**? Would it surprise you if the computer produced 0.3000000119 or 0.30000000000000004? **Figure 4-15** reveals this strange result.

The result of .1 + .2 should be .3, so where do the other fractional numbers come from?

These odd results stem from a rounding quirk related to the computer's reliance on binary numbers. The binary representation of a floating-point number is an approximation because binary numbers don't yield the same fractions as decimal numbers.

The use of `#include <iomanip>` and the `setprecision()` function shows the contents of the variable with 10 decimal places.

```
#include <iostream>
#include <iomanip>
using namespace std;
int main()
{
  float solution = .1 + .2;
  cout << "What's displayed: " << solution << endl;
  cout << "What's in the variable: " << setprecision(10) << solution << endl;
}
OUTPUT:
What's displayed: 0.3
What's in the variable: 0.3000000119
```

Figure 4-15   Floating-point decimal quirks

When working with numbers that have many significant decimal places, you may have to use math functions to truncate or round the numbers. Modern high-level languages such as C++, Java, and Python have math libraries with a wealth of functionality, including rounding of numbers.

4.5 FORMATTING OUTPUT

Formatted Output (4.5.1)

The danger of converting floating-point data to integers is that significant data can be lost. When you want to eliminate trailing zeros or decimal places from displayed data, you can specify an output format without changing the actual data in a variable.

When you format output, variables retain their values, but you specify how much or how little of that information is displayed. The variable **average** contains 4.43050. You can use formatting to output any of the following:

4.43050
4
4.4
4.43050E0
004.43100

Formatting Parameters (4.5.2, 4.5.3)

Each programming language has a unique syntax for formatting output. Regardless of the syntax, you can control the following elements, called **formatting parameters**:

Width. The number of spaces allocated to the output. This element is especially useful when outputting columns of numbers.
Fill. Pad with spaces or zeros.

Alignment. Align left or right within the specified width.

Decimal point display. The presence or absence of a decimal point.

Precision. The number of places displayed after the decimal point.

Type. Integer, floating point, decimal, binary, hexadecimal, character, or E notation.

Sign. The inclusion of a + or − sign.

Figure 4-16 illustrates the use of these formatting parameters to change the appearance of 4.43050 when it is output.

Original value	Formatting parameters
4.43050	
4.431	Precision = 3. Displays three decimal places.
_ _ _ _4.431	Width = 9. Fixes the width at 9 leaving four blank spaces in front of the number.
>>>>4.431	Fill = >. Fill spaces with the specified character.

Figure 4-16   Using formatting parameters

The program in **Figure 4-17** illustrates how you can use formatting parameters to change the appearance of numeric output.

Handy math functions for formatting output are available in the iomanip and cmath libraries. Including these libraries as headers allows you to use their functions in a program.

```
#include <iostream>

#include <iomanip>

#include <cmath>

using namespace std;

int main()

{

  float average = 4.43050;

  cout << "Original: " << average << endl;

  cout << "Three decimal places: " << setprecision(4) << average << endl;

  cout << "Width of 9: " << setw(9) << average << endl;

  cout << "Pad with a character: " << setw(9) << setfill('>') << average << endl;

}
```

OUTPUT:

```
Original: 4.4305

Three decimal places: 4.431

Width of 9: 4.431

Pad with a character: >>>>4.431
```

Figure 4-17   Formatting numeric output

One note of practical caution here: If your program outputs a formatted value but continues to use the more precise value in subsequent calculations, the user may see apparent discrepancies in the data.

SUMMARY

- The term data type refers to a way of categorizing data. Primitive data types are built into your programming language. Composite data types are programmer defined, available in functions, or provided by methods.
- Whole numbers are classified as integer data types. They can be signed or unsigned, decimal, binary, or hexadecimal.
- Integers are typically stored in 4 bytes of data, but long integers are stored in 8 bytes and can take on larger values.
- Numbers with decimal places are classified as floating-point data types. Floating-point numbers can be positive or negative and expressed in decimal notation or E notation, which is similar to scientific notation.
- Single precision floating-point numbers can be stored in 4 bytes of memory. Double precision numbers are typically stored in 8 bytes of memory.
- Integer and floating-point numbers can be used in expressions, along with arithmetic operators, such as + − * / and %. These operators are processed in a sequence called the order of operations.
- Programmers need to be aware of data types because mixing them in a single expression sometimes produces unexpected results. Also, rounding errors may produce quirks that can affect the results of calculations.
- Programming languages may use coercion to automatically change the data type of a value as a calculation proceeds. Programmers can manually change the data type of a value by type casting. The int() and float() functions allow programmers to specify or change a numeric data type.
- Programming languages provide extensive formatting parameters that can be used to change the appearance a number without changing the data stored in the corresponding variable.

Key Terms

arithmetic operators	E notation	order of operations
coercion	expression	primitive data types
composite data types	floating-point data types	signed integer
compound operators	formatting parameters	single precision
data type	function	type casting
double precision	integer data types	unsigned integer

MODULE 5

CHARACTER AND STRING DATA TYPES

LEARNING OBJECTIVES:

5.1 CHARACTER DATA TYPES

5.1.1 List the variety of data that is characterized by the character data type.

5.1.2 Initialize data as a character data type.

5.1.3 Describe the punctuation conventions used for character data.

5.1.4 State the storage required for ASCII character data.

5.1.5 Explain the difference between numbers and digits.

5.1.6 Format character output separated by spaces or on separate lines.

5.1.7 List some common functions or methods available for manipulating character data.

5.2 STRING DATA TYPES

5.2.1 Explain that characters combine to form strings.

5.2.2 State that strings are classified as a composite data type in some languages.

5.2.3 Describe the punctuation conventions used for string literals.

5.2.4 Specify when an escape sequence is necessary.

5.2.5 Describe the memory allocation for strings.

5.2.6 Identify the index values for characters in a string.

5.3 STRING FUNCTIONS

5.3.1 List commonly used functions and methods that programming languages provide to manipulate strings.

5.3.2 Identify code that produces the length of a string.

5.3.3 Identify code that changes the case of a string.

5.3.4 Explain the significance of case sensitivity.

5.3.5 Provide use cases for finding a character in a string.

5.3.6 Explain the general approach to retrieving substrings.

5.4 CONCATENATION AND TYPECASTING

5.4.1 Explain the meaning of concatenation and identify the concatenation operator.

5.4.2 Provide an example of when a programmer would concatenate a string.

5.4.3 Concatenate a string during output.

5.4.4 Concatenate the contents of multiple variables.

5.4.5 State which data types can be successfully concatenated.

5.4.6 Explain the meanings of coercion and typecasting in the context of data types.

5.1 CHARACTER DATA TYPES

Working with Character Data (5.1.1, 5.1.2, 5.1.3)

"Alphabet soup." The term can refer to letter-shaped pasta floating in a salty broth (**Figure 5-1**) or to the slew of acronyms, such as the WPA, CCC, CWA, SEC, FHA, and PWA, that stand for government agencies created by President Franklin Roosevelt in the 1930s. Let's see how programmers work with an alphabet soup of data: letters, words, sentences, and documents.

Figure 5-1   Character data is like the letters in alphabet soup

The **character data type** is the classification that programmers use for variables that hold a single letter of the alphabet, a symbol, or a numeral from 0 to 9. It is a primitive data type that you can assign to any variable that should hold a single character. You might use the character data type in a program that asks for a person's middle initial or when designing an alphabet program for a preschooler.

When you initialize or assign a character literal to a variable, the convention is to surround the literal with single quotes.

```
initialize first_letter = 'a'
```

The quotes are stripped off when the literal is stored and are not included when the character is output. In **Figure 5-2**, the program outputs the contents of **first_letter** without quotes.

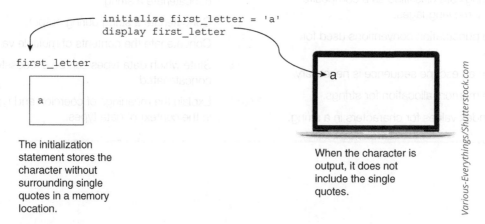

The initialization statement stores the character without surrounding single quotes in a memory location.

When the character is output, it does not include the single quotes.

Figure 5-2   Character data initialization and storage

A standard initialization statement creates a variable containing character data, as shown in **Figure 5-3**.

Syntax:

```
char variable_name = 'x'  where x is a single character.
```

Example:

```
char first_letter = 'a';
```

Character data can be output using `cout`. Including `endl` in the output stream completes the output and moves the cursor to the next line. Because the variable does not store the single quotes, they are not displayed in the output stream.

```
#include <iostream>

using namespace std;

int main()
{
    char first_letter = 'a';
    cout << first_letter << endl;
}
```

OUTPUT:

```
a
```

Figure 5-3   Character initialization and sample code

Character Memory Allocation (5.1.4)

Character data is stored in ASCII format. **ASCII (American Standard Code for Information Interchange)** is an encoding method that assigns a unique sequence of 8 bits to each character. For example, the letter 'a' is represented by the 8-bit ASCII code 01100001, which happens to be decimal 97. Remember this for later!

All of the uppercase letters, lowercase letters, numerals, and symbols on your computer keyboard have a unique ASCII value. These commonly used characters can be stored in 1 byte of memory. See **Figure 5-4**.

Every uppercase letter, lowercase letter, digit, and symbol on the keyboard has an 8-bit ASCII representation.

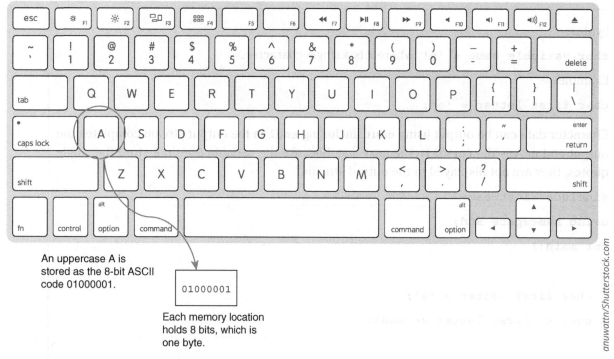

An uppercase A is stored as the 8-bit ASCII code 01000001.

01000001

Each memory location holds 8 bits, which is one byte.

Figure 5-4   Basic character data requires one byte of storage

Digits (5.1.5)

The single quotes surrounding character literals are important, especially when you are working with digits 0 to 9. Without surrounding punctuation, 2 is an integer that you can use in calculations. With surrounding punctuation, however, '2' is simply a squiggly digit that does not have the value of "two."

Q What would you expect as output from the code for the following Digits program?

```
initialize first_digit = '2'
initialize second_digit = '5'
display first_digit + second_digit
```

A Did you answer 25? **Figure 5-5** illustrates the difference between digits used as characters and numbers used as integers.

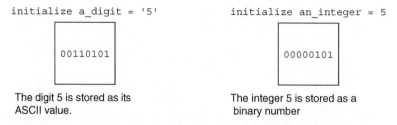

initialize a_digit = '5'

00110101

The digit 5 is stored as its ASCII value.

initialize an_integer = 5

00000101

The integer 5 is stored as a binary number

Figure 5-5   Digits are stored as ASCII codes, but integer numbers are stored as binary numbers

anuwattn/Shutterstock.com

Attempting to add digits that are character data types can produce surprising results, depending on your programming language. Just remember that the data for calculations should be assigned numeric data types, not character data types.

Character Output Format (5.1.6)

In the Digits program, the output looked like the value 25, but the output was actually the digit 2 and the digit 5. To make that clear, you can insert a space between the digits by including a blank character in the output statement, as shown in the last line of the program in **Figure 5-6**.

```
#include <iostream>

using namespace std;

int main()

{

  char first_digit = '2';

  char second_digit = '5';

  cout << first_digit << ' ' << second_digit << endl;

}

OUTPUT:

2 5
```

Figure 5-6   Insert a space in the output stream

Another option would be to output each digit on a separate line as shown in **Figure 5-7**.

```
Including endl in the output stream between the variables places the second digit on a new line.

#include <iostream>

using namespace std;

int main()

{

char first_digit = '2';

char second_digit = '5';

cout << first_digit << endl << second_digit << endl;

}

OUTPUT:

2

5
```

Figure 5-7   Output to separate lines

Character Manipulation (5.1.7)

Programming languages provide built-in tools for manipulating character data. These tools are called functions or methods, depending on your programming language.

One commonly used function changes a character from uppercase to lowercase. A similar function changes lowercase to uppercase. You might use the uppercase function to make sure that a person's middle initial is stored as an uppercase letter. See **Figure 5-8**.

The `toupper()` function produces the uppercase version of a character. If there is no uppercase version, such as for the # sign, then the character remains unchanged. The syntax for this function is:

```
variable_name = toupper(variable_name);
```

In the following program, `cin >>` is used to collect input from the keyboard and place it in the variable called `initial`. Notice that the uppercase character replaces the lowercase character in the variable called `initial`.

```
#include <iostream>

using namespace std;

int main()
{
  char initial;

  cout << "Enter initial: ";

  cin >> initial;

  initial = toupper(initial);

  cout << initial;
}
```

OUTPUT:

```
Enter initial: b [Enter]

B
```

Figure 5-8   Change the case of a character

Do you remember that the ASCII value for 'a' is 97? There is a function that displays the ASCII value of any character. You'll find the syntax for that and other handy functions in **Figure 5-9**.

Character Function/Method	Example	Data	Result
Check if the character is a letter of the alphabet	`isalpha(initial)` `isalpha(choice)`	`initial = 'a'` `char choice = '2'`	`True` `False`
Check if the character is a digit	`isdigit(initial)` `isdigit(choice)`	`char initial = 'a'` `char choice = '2'`	`False` `True`
Change to uppercase	`toupper(initial)`	`char initial = 'a'`	`A`
Change to lowercase	`tolower(initial)`	`char initial = 'A'`	`a`
Display the character for the specified ASCII value	`char(num)`	`int num = 97`	`a`
Display the ASCII value for the character	`int(initial)`	`char initial = 'a'`	`97`

Figure 5-9   Character functions

5.2 STRING DATA TYPES

Working with String Data (5.2.1, 5.2.2, 5.2.3)

A sequence of alphanumeric characters is classified as a **string**. You can use the **string data type** for working with variables that contain words, phrases, sentences, and other text.

In some programming languages, strings are a primitive data type, but in other languages, they are a composite data type. In either case, your programming language provides a variety of tools for working with strings.

String literals are typically enclosed in quotation marks for initialization statements, assignment statements, and prompts. The Alphabet Soup pseudocode in **Figure 5-10** uses strings in several ways.

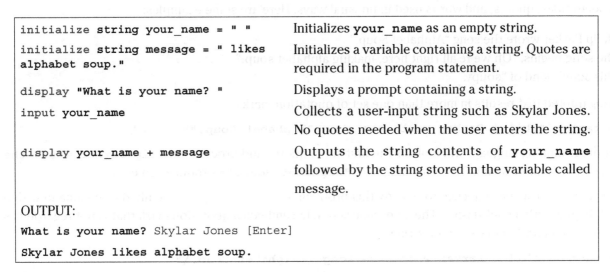

`initialize string your_name = " "`	Initializes **your_name** as an empty string.
`initialize string message = " likes alphabet soup."`	Initializes a variable containing a string. Quotes are required in the program statement.
`display "What is your name? "`	Displays a prompt containing a string.
`input your_name`	Collects a user-input string such as Skylar Jones. No quotes needed when the user enters the string.
`display your_name + message`	Outputs the string contents of **your_name** followed by the string stored in the variable called message.

OUTPUT:
What is your name? Skylar Jones [Enter]
Skylar Jones likes alphabet soup.

Figure 5-10   Strings can be initialized, input, and displayed

When initializing string variables, be sure to enclose the string in quotation marks. The quotation marks are not stored in the variable and will not appear in the output. Let's turn the Alphabet Soup pseudocode into program code. See **Figure 5-11**.

To work with strings, use the **#include <string>** header at the beginning of your program. You can also use the **getline()** function to collect input until the Enter key is pressed. The function **getline (cin, your_name);** collects input from the keyboard, designated **cin**, and stores it in the variable **your_name**.

```
#include <iostream>
#include <string>
using namespace std;
int main()
{
   string your_name;
   string message = " likes alphabet soup.";
   cout << "What's your name? ";
   getline (cin, your_name);
   cout << your_name << message << endl;
}
OUTPUT:
What is your name? Skylar Jones [Enter]
Skylar Jones likes alphabet soup.
```

Figure 5-11   Code for the Alphabet Soup program

Escape Characters (5.2.4)

The trouble with enclosing strings in quotation marks is that they are also used as punctuation in real world data, such as poem titles, quotes, and words used in unusual ways. Here are some examples:

- Philip Parker wrote the song "Alphabet Soup."
- The song begins, "Oh we're all right here, making alphabet soup."
- This song's kind of "soupy."

Storing quoted text results in more than one set of quotation marks:

fun_fact = "Philip Parker wrote the song "Alphabet Soup.""

Your programming language will look for the first set of quotes and process **"Philip Parker wrote the song "** as the complete string. The remaining text, **"Alphabet Soup.""** produces an error.

You can use an escape sequence to remedy this problem. An escape sequence embeds a command within a string. It begins with a backslash \. The **\"** escape sequence embeds a quotation mark that is not regarded as the start or end quotation mark for the string.

fun_fact = "Philip Parker wrote the song \"Alphabet Soup.\""

When using escape sequences, do not include a space after the backslash. **Figure 5-12** lists common escape sequences.

Escape Sequence	Name	Use
\"	Quotation mark	For strings that include quotation marks
\'	Apostrophe	For strings that include apostrophes
\\	Backslash	For strings that include a backslash
\n	Newline	To insert a line break in a string
\t	Tab	To insert a tab in a string

Figure 5-12   Escape sequences

Q Based on the escape sequences in Figure 5-12, what do you expect as the output from this code?

```
review = "This song\'s kind of \n \"SOUPY!\""
output review
```

A Did you catch that SOUPY! is output on a separate line?

```
This song's kind of
"SOUPY!"
```

String Indexes (5.2.5, 5.2.6)

Strings are stored in a succession of memory locations. Each character in the string has an **index**, which is a number that indicates its position in the string. The first character in the string is referenced by index 0, the next character is index 1. Index numbers are enclosed in square brackets, as in **Figure 5-13**.

Memory Location	0x0075	0x0076	0x0077	0x0078	0x0079	0x007A	0x007B	0x007C	0x007D	0x007E
Data	C	a	m	p	b	e	l	l	'	s
Index	[0]	[1]	[2]	[3]	[4]	[5]	[6]	[7]	[8]	[9]

Figure 5-13   Each character in a string is stored in a memory location referenced by an index

You can find the character at any position in a string based on its index number. For example, suppose you want to make sure that the first letter of a person's name is an uppercase letter. Trace through the following pseudocode to see how indexing works to produce the first letter of a word.

```
initialize string company_name = "Campbell's"
initialize letter as character
letter = company_name[0]
output letter
OUTPUT:
C
```

Q What would you change in the following line of code to find the third letter of the company name?

```
letter = company_name[0]
```

A You would change the index for company_name to [2]. Remember that the index begins with 0, so the third letter's index is 2. **Figure 5-14** shows the code and output.

```
#include <iostream>
#include <string>
using namespace std;
int main()
{
  string company_name = "Campbell's";
  char letter = company_name[2];
  cout << letter << endl;
}
OUTPUT:
m
```

Figure 5-14   Using the index to retrieve a specific element in a string

5.3 STRING FUNCTIONS

String Manipulation (5.3.1)

In addition to using indexes, you may want to manipulate strings in other ways. Here are some examples:

- Find the length of a string
- Change the case of a string
- Check if a string contains a specific character
- Retrieve a substring from a longer string

Let's take a look at some examples to assess their usefulness.

String Length (5.3.2)

Knowing the length of a string can come in handy to ensure that the string is complete. It might also be a step in an algorithm for reversing a string or checking that a string is not too long for a data entry box. **Figure 5-15** details the syntax for the **length()** function and illustrates its use to determine if a string containing the alphabet contains all 26 letters.

The output of the `length()` function is stored in an integer variable. The syntax for the `length()` function is:

```
int the_length = variable_name.length();
```

Here's the code that checks the length of a string containing the alphabet.

```
#include <iostream>
using namespace std;
int main()
{
   string alphabet = "ABCDEFGHIJKLMOPQRSTUVWXYZ";
   int the_length = alphabet.length();
   cout << the_length << endl;
}
OUTPUT:
25
```

Figure 5-15   Finding the length of a string

Q The alphabet has 26 letters, but the length of the string in the **alphabet** variable is only 25. Assuming no duplicates, that means one letter must be missing from the string in the initialization statement. Can you see which letter is missing?

A The missing letter is N.

Change Case (5.3.3, 5.3.4)

As with character data, you can change a string to uppercase or lowercase, and some programming languages provide a function to uppercase the first character in a string.

Case can be significant when searching and sorting data. The string **"Soup"** is not the same as **"SOUP"** or **"soup"**. Why? Because uppercase characters have different ASCII codes than lowercase characters. An uppercase S has an ASCII code of 01010011, whereas a lowercase s has an ASCII code of 01110011.

The ASCII codes for S and s are not the same, so Soup does not match soup. The concept that uppercase letters are different from lowercase letters is called **case sensitivity**. Passwords and variable names are common examples of case-sensitive data.

String comparisons used for searching and sorting are case sensitive. When creating a program to search through an inventory of groceries, be aware that a search for "alphabet soup" will not match "Alphabet Soup" unless you include code to handle variations of upper and lowercase.

One solution to case variations is to use the lowercase function. Here is a program that checks if two strings are the same regardless of case.

```
initialize first_item = "Soup"

initialize second_item = "soup"

if lowercase(first_item) = lowercase(second_item) then

    display "The words are the same."
```

To code this algorithm, you need a function to turn the entire string to lowercase. **Figure 5-16** explains how to do that.

C++ does not have a built-in function that elegantly converts an entire string to uppercase or lowercase. The **transform()** function does the job but requires headers **#include <cctype>** and **#include <algorithm>**.

Also, because strings are fundamentally an array of characters, the **transform()** function requires begin and end parameters. This code changes Campbell's to all lowercase:

```cpp
#include <algorithm>

#include <cctype>

#include <iostream>

#include <string>

using namespace std;

int main()
{
    string company_name="Campbell's";
    transform(company_name.begin(), company_name.end(),
    company_name.begin(), ::tolower);;
    cout << company_name ;
}
```
OUTPUT:

```
campbell's
```

Figure 5-16   Converting a string to lowercase

Find the Location of a Character (5.3.5)

You can determine if a string contains a specific character. When a string contains a space, you can assume that the string holds more than one word. A comma might indicate that a string holds a list of words. You might then write code to break the string into separate words.

The function for finding the position of a character produces the index position of the specified character. Remember that the first character in the string is index position [0].

Q In the following pseudocode, what does the `find()` function produce?

```
initialize string product_name = "Campbell's Alphabet Soup"
where = find(" ") in product_name
```

A It produces 10. Make sure you understand why.

To find the location of a character, you can use a built-in function. **Figure 5-17** provides the syntax and an example.

The `find()` function looks for a string specified in the parentheses. The code `find(" ")` looks for a blank character. The code `find("Soup")` would find the position of the string "Soup". To specify which variable you want to search, place it in front of the `find()` function separated by a dot.

```
int integer_variable = variable_name.find("string");
```

If the string is found, C++ returns its starting index location. If the string is not found, C++ returns -1. The following code looks for a blank space in the **product_name** string.

```
#include <iostream>
#include <string>
using namespace std;
int main()
{
   string product_name = "Campbell's Alphabet Soup";
   int where = product_name.find(" ");
   cout << where << endl;
}
OUTPUT:
10
```

Figure 5-17   Finding a character's location in a string

Retrieve a Substring (5.3.6)

Sometimes you might want to deal with a substring rather than the entire string. Working with substrings is a component of search engines and several text-processing algorithms. **Figure 5-18** explains how to find a substring and store it in a variable.

You can retrieve a substring by indicating where it should begin and how many characters you want to collect. Remember that the elements of a string are indexed beginning with [0].

The syntax for retrieving a substring is:

```
string new_string = variable_name.substr(start,length);
```

Trace through the code and see if you can determine what the variable **sub_string** will contain.

```
#include <iostream>
#include <string>
using namespace std;
int main()
{
    string alphabet = "ABCDEFGHIJKLMNOPQRSTUVWXYZ";
    string sub_string = alphabet.substr(3,5);
    cout << sub_string << endl;
}
```

OUTPUT:

```
DEFGH
```

The variable **sub_string** contains DEFGH as specified by the parameter (3, 5). The substring begins at D because A is index 0, B is index 1, C is index 2, so D is index 3. Starting with D, **sub_string** contains 5 letters.

Figure 5-18   Collecting a substring

5.4 CONCATENATION AND TYPECASTING

Concatenated Output (5.4.1, 5.4.2, 5.4.3)

Asking for a person's first and last name in one statement might not be the best practice. Sometimes, you might want to output Philip Parker as Parker, Philip. It would be best to store the first name in one variable and the last name in another variable.

To output the strings in two or more variables, you can use a process called concatenation. Concatenation means chaining two or more elements in sequence. The + sign is the concatenation operator. Trace through the following pseudocode to see how the **first_name** and **last_name** variables can be concatenated in output statements.

```
initialize string first_name = " "
initialize string last_name = " "


display "What is your first name? "
input first_name
```

```
display "What is your last name? "
input last_name
output "Hello, " + first_name
output "You are filed under " + last_name + ", " + first_name
```

OUTPUT:

What is your first name? Philip [Enter]

What is your last name? Parker [Enter]

Hello, Philip

You are filed as Parker, Philip

Let's see how this algorithm works. Check out the last line of code in **Figure 5-19** to see how to concatenate output.

C++ does not require a concatenation operator in the cout statement. The << operator allows you to combine strings and variables in the output stream.

```cpp
#include <iostream>
#include <string>
using namespace std;
int main()
{
  string first_name = "Philip";
  string last_name = "Parker";
  cout << "Hello, " << first_name << endl ;
  cout << "You are filed as " << last_name << ", " << first_name;
}
```

OUTPUT:

Hello, Philip

You are filed as Parker, Philip

Figure 5-19   Concatenated output

Concatenated Variables (5.4.4)

Concatenation is not just for output. You can also concatenate one or more variables and store the combined string in a new variable.

```
initialize string company_name = "Campbell's"
initialize string soup_name = "Alphabet Soup"
initialize string product_name = " "
assign product_name = company_name + " " + soup_name
output product_name
```

Q What ends up in the variable `product_name`?

A The variable `product_name` contains the string `Campbell's Alphabet Soup`.

Coding a concatenation is easy. Just make sure to declare the variables as strings. In **Figure 5-20**, look carefully at the variable declarations.

```cpp
#include <iostream>
#include <string>
using namespace std;
int main()
{
  string company_name = "Campbell's";
  string soup_name = "Alphabet Soup";
  string product_name = company_name + " " + soup_name;
  cout << product_name << endl;
}
OUTPUT:
Campbell's Alphabet Soup
```

Figure 5-20   Concatenating variables

The key takeaway here is that the variable `product_name` contains `Campbell's Alphabet Soup`, which is a result of concatenating the contents of the `company_name` and `soup_name` variables with the addition of a space in between.

The best practice for concatenating variables is to use a new variable for the concatenated string. It would be possible, but confusing, to put `company_name + soup_name` into the `company_name` variable. So, using a third variable called `product_name` is a better option.

Coercion and Typecasting (5.4.5, 5.4.6)

With most programming languages, strings can be concatenated with other strings and character data, but not with integer or floating-point data. Concatenating or appending mixed data types often leads to trouble. Here's an example of an attempt to concatenate a house number stored as an integer with a street name stored as a string.

```
initialize int house_number = 101
initialize string space = " "
initialize string street_name = "Main Street"
initialize string full_address = " "
```

```
output house_number
output street_name
full_address = house_number + space + street_name
output full_address
```

OUTPUT

```
Type mismatch error!!!
```

An attempt to concatenate an integer with a string can produce an error. Some programming languages try to adjust the data types through coercion. For example, your language's compiler or interpreter might attempt to coerce an integer into a string so that the concatenation can take place.

To manually fix an integer-string type mismatch, you can use typecasting to convert the integer to a string. **Figure 5-21** explains how to do it.

The **to_string()** function converts an integer or floating-point number into a string. The syntax is:

```
string converted_string = to_string(variable_name);
```

This code converts the integer 101 to a string so it can be concatenated with the string "Main Street".

```
#include <iostream>
#include <string>
using namespace std;
int main()
{
    int house_number = 101;
    string street_name = "Main Street";
    string space = " ";
    string full_address = to_string(house_number) + space + street_name;
    cout << full_address;
}
```

OUTPUT:

```
101 Main Street
```

Figure 5-21   Typecasting: Integer to string

How about converting a string to an integer? Of course! You might want to do that when you've got a string that contains digits you'd like to use for a calculation. The program in **Figure 5-22** gets the first two elements of a string, converts them to an integer, and then adds 1.

The **stoi()** function converts a string to an integer. Make sure the variable in parentheses has an integer value. Here is the syntax:

```
int integer_variable = stoi(string_variable);
```

In this program, the first two characters of the date are collected using the **substr()** function, then converted into an integer. Adding 1 to the day number produces the next day's date.

```
#include <iostream>
#include <string>
using namespace std;
int main()
{
    string today = "15 February";
    string today_substring = today.substr(0, 2);
    int day_number = stoi(today_substring);
    int tomorrow = day_number + 1;
    cout << tomorrow << endl;
}
OUTPUT:
16
```

Figure 5-22   Typecasting: String to integer

SUMMARY

- The character data type is a classification that programmers use for variables that hold a single letter of the alphabet, a symbol, or a numeral from 0 to 9.
- When you initialize or assign a character literal to a variable, the convention is to surround the literal with single quotes.
- Commonly used character data is stored in ASCII format, encoded as 8 binary digits.
- Programming languages supply built-in functions for manipulating character data.
- Variables that hold a sequence of characters are assigned the string data type.
- In some programming languages, strings are a primitive data type, but in other languages they are a composite data type.
- Strings are stored in a succession of memory locations, each referenced by an index value. The first character in a string has an index value of [0].
- When you initialize or assign a string to a variable, the convention is to surround the string with quotation marks.
- An escape sequence beginning with a backslash \ embeds a command within a string. Use the \" escape sequence for strings that already include quotation marks.
- Programming languages provide built-in string functions, such as finding the location of a character in a string or collecting a substring.
- Strings can be combined in a process called concatenation. It is also possible to change the data type using typecasting functions provided by your programming language.

Key Terms

ASCII (American Standard Code for
  Information Interchange)
case sensitivity

character data type
concatenation
escape sequence

index
string
string data type

MODULE 6

DECISION CONTROL STRUCTURES

LEARNING OBJECTIVES:

6.1 IF-THEN CONTROL STRUCTURES

6.1.1 Describe the purpose of control structures.

6.1.2 Identify parts of algorithms that require decision control structures.

6.1.3 Provide examples of algorithms that incorporate conditions or decisions.

6.1.4 Illustrate an if-then structure using a flowchart.

6.1.5 Write an if-then structure in pseudocode.

6.1.6 Identify the conditional statement in an if-then structure.

6.1.7 Use programming language syntax to code an if-then structure.

6.2 RELATIONAL OPERATORS

6.2.1 Differentiate between the = operator and the == operator.

6.2.2 List and define relational operators.

6.2.3 Identify the relational operators in example expressions.

6.2.4 Provide examples of Boolean expressions.

6.2.5 Initialize a Boolean variable using an assignment statement.

6.2.6 Differentiate a Boolean expression from a Boolean data type.

6.3 MULTIPLE CONDITIONS

6.3.1 Write an if-then-else structure in pseudocode.

6.3.2 Illustrate an if-then-else structure using a flowchart.

6.3.3 Code an if-then-else structure.

6.3.4 Trace the flow of an algorithm that contains a nested-if structure.

6.3.5 Trace the flow of an algorithm that contains an else-if structure.

6.3.6 Explain the concept of fall through in the context of decision control structures.

6.3.7 Explain the use of break statements in the context of fall through.

6.4 CONDITIONAL LOGICAL OPERATORS

6.4.1 Identify logical operators in expressions.

6.4.2 Identify the outcomes for AND operations as illustrated in a truth table.

6.4.3 Identify the outcomes for OR operations as illustrated in a truth table.

6.4.4 Create expressions using logical operators.

6.1 IF-THEN CONTROL STRUCTURES

Control Structures (6.1.1, 6.1.2)

Got a problem with your cable or Internet service? Customers who call their service providers typically interact with an automated voice response system. You know how it goes: "Press 1 if you need account information; press 2 if you need to troubleshoot your cable service..." See **Figure 6-1**.

Figure 6-1   Voice response systems require programming logic

Computer programs for these automated systems contain control structures that branch off to different paths based on options selected by the user. A control structure alters the sequential execution of statements in a computer program. A decision control structure alters the sequential flow by branching to specific statements based on a condition or decision.

Here is an algorithm for a sequential program that begins with a menu of choices. The program proceeds in sequence by asking for the customer's details, connecting to an agent, connecting to the cable troubleshooter, then to the Internet troubleshooter, and finally ending the call.

Output "Say or press 1 to connect to an account agent."
Output "Say or press 2 to troubleshoot your cable service."
Output "Say or press 3 to troubleshoot your Internet service."
Output "Say or press 0 to quit."

Ask for customer's name.
Ask for customer's account number.
Provide current account status.
Connect to next available agent.

Connect user to automated cable troubleshooter.

Connect user to automated Internet troubleshooter.
Make sure the user really wants to quit.
Output goodbye message.

Clearly, this algorithm should not be sequential. It needs to branch to a specific action depending on the customer's menu selection. If the customer has an intermittent Internet connection, for example, selecting 3 should branch directly to the Internet troubleshooter.

Q How many distinct branches should this algorithm have?

A The algorithm should have four branches, one for each of the menu options to select 1, 2, 3, or 0.

Decision Logic (6.1.3)

Decision control structures play a key role in just about every computer program. These structures help programs seem intelligent because they can make responses that correspond to user input.

Decision control structures also allow programs to handle data based on differing values. Here are just a few examples.

- Deciding who is eligible to vote based on age and citizenship
- Determining if a polynomial has zero, one, or two real roots
- Assigning a letter grade based on a quiz score
- Figuring out whether to apply a bank service charge based on the account balance
- Operating a furnace or air conditioner based on room temperature
- Checking if a number is odd or even based on modulo division
- Offering free shipping based on the amount purchased or VIP status

Let's break down decision control structures to see how they work and how to incorporate them in your programs.

If-Then Structures (6.1.4, 6.1.5, 6.1.6, 6.1.7)

A basic voice response system might simply tell customers to find their account number, then press 1 when they are ready to connect to an agent. You can diagram this logic as a flowchart using a diamond shape for the decision. See **Figure 6-2**.

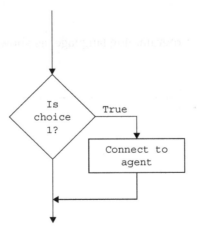

Figure 6-2   A flowchart for an if-then structure

The diamond symbol in a flowchart indicates a decision point and contains a question that specifies a condition. When the answer to the question is True, an arrow directs the flow to one or more statements in the conditional block. When the answer is not True, the flow bypasses the conditional block. This logic is referred to as an if-then structure and can be presented in pseudocode using keywords `if` and `then`.

In pseudocode, any statements that are executed on the True branch should be indented.

```
if choice == 1 then
   connect user to an agent
output "Bye"
```

The if-then structure is based on a conditional statement that directs the program flow to the correct set of statements when the condition is True. So, when the input is 1, the program directs the customer to an agent. When the conditional statement is not True—if the customer presses 9, for example—the program continues on a sequential path to the next statement, which in this case terminates the program with a message that says "Bye."

Figure 6-3 illustrates the general syntax and usage rules for an if-then structure.

Syntax:

```
if (condition)
    single statement;

if (condition)
{
statement;

statement;

}
```

Rules and best practices:

- Place the condition in parenthesis.
- No punctuation is necessary after the closing parenthesis.
- Indent any statements included in the if-then structure.
- End indented statements with a semicolon as usual.
- Use curly braces when the conditional statement is followed by more than one additional statement.

Figure 6-3   Syntax for an if-then structure

You can code if-then structures in your programming language, as shown in **Figure 6-4**.

```
#include <iostream>
using namespace std;


int main()
{
   int choice;
   cout << "Press or say 1 when you are ready to" << endl;
   cout << "connect to an account agent: ";
```

Figure 6-4   A program with a simple if-then structure (*Continued*)

```
    cin >> choice;

    if (choice == 1)

    {

        cout << "You chose option " << choice << endl;

        cout << "Connecting you now" << endl;

    }

    cout << "Bye";

}


OUTPUT:

Press or say 1 when you are ready to

connect to an account agent: 1[Enter]

You chose option 1

Connecting you now

Bye
```

Figure 6-4   A program with a simple if-then structure

Q Trace through the program code in the previous figure. What happens if the user presses a number other than 1?

A The program outputs **Bye** and the program ends.

6.2 RELATIONAL OPERATORS

The Equal Operator (6.2.1)

The conditional statement in the simple voice response system is peculiar. It contains double equal symbols:

`if choice == 1 then`

The == is the **equal operator**, which checks to see if two operands, such as **choice** and **1**, are equal to each other. The == equal operator is quite different from the = assignment operator that you use to initialize variables. Using the assignment operator in a conditional statement is likely to produce an error. **Figure 6-5** points out the difference between the assignment operator and the equal operator.

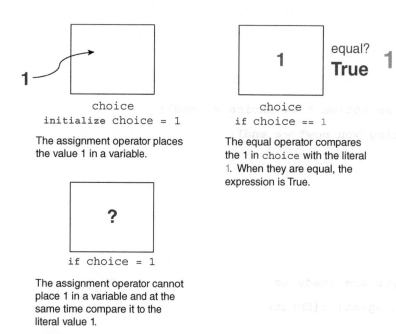

Figure 6-5   Using the assignment operator in a conditional statement is likely to produce an error

Using Relational Operators (6.2.2, 6.2.3)

The equal operator is one of several relational operators that you can use when constructing conditional expressions. A **relational operator** specifies a comparison between two operands. The operands could be:

- Two literals, such as **7** and **9**
- Two variables, such as **airtime** and **limit**
- One variable and one literal such as **airtime** and **1000**

Figure 6-6 provides a list of relational operators and examples of their use.

Operator	Description	Examples Where airtime = 1056	Result
==	Equal to	(airtime == 1056) (airtime == 566)	True False
!=	Not equal to	(airtime != 1056) (airtime != 566)	False True
<	Less than	(airtime < 2000) (2000 < airtime)	True False
>	Greater than	(airtime > 56) (56 > airtime)	True False
<=	Less than or equal to	(airtime <= 1056) (airtime <= 29)	True False
>=	Greater than or equal to	(airtime >= airtime) (airtime >= 2000)	True False

Figure 6-6   Relational operators

Relational operators provide lots of flexibility for crafting conditional expressions. For example, you can use the != operator to validate input for the voice response system in the following pseudocode:

```
output "Press or say 1 when you are ready to"
output "connect to an account agent: "
input choice
if choice != 1 then
    output "You chose option " + choice
    output "Invalid input"
```

Figure 6-7 illustrates this algorithm in code.

```cpp
#include <iostream>
using namespace std;


int main()
{
    int choice;
    cout << "Press or say 1 when you are ready to" << endl;
    cout << "connect to an account agent: ";
    cin >> choice;
    if (choice != 1)
    {
        cout << "You chose option " << choice << endl;
        cout << "Invalid input" << endl;
    }
}


OUTPUT:
Press or say 1 when you are ready to
connect to an account agent: 9 [Enter]
You chose option 9
Invalid input
```

Figure 6-7   Using a decision structure to validate input

Boolean Expressions and Data Types (6.2.4, 6.2.5, 6.2.6)

Relational operators and operands form **Boolean expressions** that evaluate to True or False. For example, choice != 1 is a Boolean expression that is True when the customer does not select 1. The Boolean expression is False when the customer selects 1.

Boolean expressions have similarities to Boolean data types. Both carry a value of True or False. In practice, however, you use a Boolean expression as part of a conditional statement, whereas you use a Boolean data type when making declaration or assignment statements.

For example, you might want a variable called **vip** to hold True or False, depending on whether the customer has VIP status. In pseudocode you can initialize a Boolean variable like this:

```
initialize bool vip = True
```

In memory, Boolean variables hold 0 representing False, or 1 representing True. Theoretically, a Boolean requires only 1 bit of storage, but the actual storage requirements vary by language.

Some programming languages, such as Python, require that True and False are capitalized. In other languages, such as C++ and Java, true and false have to be lowercase. In pseudocode, True and False are capitalized. Now take a look at the following pseudocode:

```
declare bool vip

assign vip = True

if vip then

    output "Transferring you to the VIP agent."
```

Q What is the Boolean variable in the pseudocode above? What is the conditional statement? What is the Boolean expression?

A The Boolean variable is **vip**, which appears in the declaration and assignment statements. The conditional statement is **if vip then**. The Boolean expression is simply **vip** in the conditional statement.

When a Boolean variable is used in a conditional statement, it does not need a relational operator. The Boolean is already either True or False, so it does not need a redundant expression, such as **if vip == True**. **Figure 6-8** illustrates how this works in code.

```
#include <iostream>
using namespace std;

int main()
{
    bool vip = true;

    if (vip)

        cout << "You get the VIP discount!" << endl;
}

OUTPUT:

You get the VIP discount!
```

Boolean variable initialization with "true" in lowercase for C++ syntax.

Boolean variable used in a conditional statement.

Figure 6-8   Using a Boolean variable in a conditional statement

6.3 MULTIPLE CONDITIONS

If-Then-Else Structures (6.3.1, 6.3.2, 6.3.3)

Suppose a voice response system gives customers two options:

Press or say 1 when you are ready to connect to an account agent.
Press or say 0 to quit.

Figure 6-9 illustrates a flowchart for this algorithm. Notice that both the True and False branches contain statements. The program follows one of these branches based on the outcome of the Boolean expression.

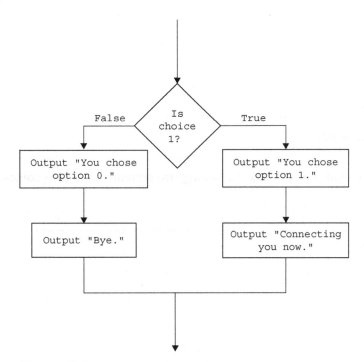

Figure 6-9   The if-then-else structure

A decision coded as two possible paths is called an **if-then-else structure**. The pseudocode for the voice response algorithm uses the keyword **else** to designate the alternative execution path.

```
output "Press or say 1 when you are ready to"

output "connect to an account agent."

output "Press or say 0 to quit."

input choice

if choice = 1 then

    output "You chose option 1."

    output "Connecting you now."

else

    output "You chose option 0."

    output "Bye."
```

Figure 6-10 illustrates the syntax, rules, and best practices for if-then-else structures.

Syntax:	Rules and best practices:

```if (condition)```
 ```{```
    ```statement;```
    ```statement;```
 ```}```
 ```else```
 ```{```
    ```statement;```
    ```statement;```
 ```}```
	• Place the **else** keyword on a separate line and at the same indent level as the **if** statement.
	 • Use curly braces when the else-block contains more than one statement.
	 • No semicolon is necessary after the keyword **else**.

Figure 6-10   The if-then-else syntax

The code in **Figure 6-11** includes an if-block containing two statements. It also contains an else-block with two statements.

```
#include <iostream>
using namespace std;


int main()
{
   int choice;
   cout << "Press or say 1 when you are ready to" << endl;
   cout << "connect to an account agent." << endl;
   cout << "Press or say 0 to quit." << endl;
   cin >> choice;
   if (choice == 1)
   {
     cout << "You chose option 1." << endl;
     cout << "Connecting you now." << endl;
   }
   else
   {
     cout << "You chose option 0." << endl;
```

Figure 6-11   Sample code for the if-then-else structure (*Continued*)

```
        cout << "Bye." << endl;
    }
}


OUTPUT:
Press or say 1 when you are ready to
connect to an account agent.
Press or say 0 to quit.
0 [Enter]


You chose option 0.
Bye.
```

Figure 6-11   Sample code for the if-then-else structure

Nested-If Structures (6.3.4)

Sometimes programs need to make decisions within decisions. As an example, suppose that after a customer selects the Quit option, you want to check if the customer really wants to quit. The Quit option involves one decision, but within that decision is the second decision to quit or send the customer to the help desk.

Decisions within decisions are often referred to as **nested-if structures**. **Figure 6-12** illustrates the nested-if flowchart for customers who want to quit.

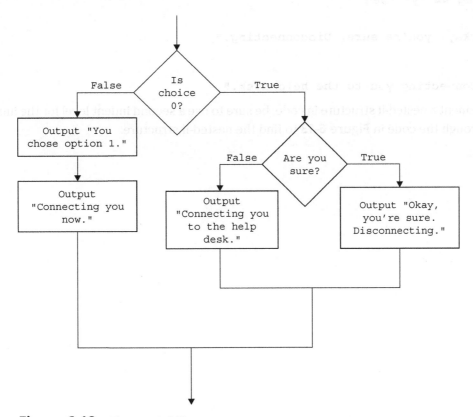

Figure 6-12   The nested-if structure

The following pseudocode contains a nested-if structure that confirms if the customer wants to quit. Based on the input, the customer is either disconnected or connected to the help desk.

```
output "Press or say 1 when you are ready to"
output "connect to an account agent."
output "Press or say 0 to quit."
input choice
if choice == 0 then
    output "Are you sure you want to quit? "
    input sure_thing
        if sure_thing == 'y' then
            output "Okay, you're sure. Disconnecting."
        else
            output "Connecting you to the help desk."
else
    output "You chose option 1."
    output "Connecting you now."
```

Q Which lines of the pseudocode above are the inner level of the nested-if structure?

A
```
if sure_thing == 'y' then

        output "Okay, you're sure. Disconnecting."
    else
        output "Connecting you to the help desk."
```

When you implement a nested-if structure in code, be sure to use a second indent level for the inner decision structure. Trace through the code in **Figure 6-13** to find the nested-if structure.

```cpp
#include <iostream>
using namespace std;


int main()
{
    int choice;
    char sure_thing;
    cout << "Press or say 1 when you are ready to" << endl;
    cout << "connect to an account agent." << endl;
    cout << "Press or say 0 to quit." << endl;
    cin >> choice;
    if (choice == 0)
    {
        cout << "Are you sure you want to quit?" << endl;
        cin >> sure_thing;
        if (sure_thing == 'y')
            cout << "Okay, you're sure. Disconnecting." << endl;
        else
            cout << "Connecting you to the help desk." << endl;
    }
    else
    {
        cout << "You chose option 1." << endl;
        cout << "Connecting you now." << endl;
    }
}
OUTPUT:


Press or say 1 when you are ready to
connect to an account agent.
Press or say 0 to quit.
0 [Enter]
Are you sure you want to quit?
y [Enter]
Okay, you're sure. Disconnecting.
```

Figure 6-13   Sample code for the nested-if structure

Else If Structures (6.3.5)

Programming languages provide syntax for structures that involve multiple conditions. Suppose you want to offer customers a menu of the following options:

Press or say 1 to connect to an account agent.
Press or say 2 to troubleshoot your cable service.
Press or say 3 to troubleshoot your Internet connection.
Press or say 0 to quit.

To handle algorithms that require multiple conditions, you can use an **else-if structure**. **Figure 6-14** provides the syntax, rules, and best practices.

Syntax:

```
if (condition)

    statement;

else if (condition)

    statement;

else if (condition)

    {

    statement;

    statement;

    }

else

    statement;
```

Rules and best practices:

- Begin with an **if** statement.
- Use the keyword **else if** for subsequent conditional statements.
- When else-if blocks contain more than one statement, use curly braces.
- Use the keyword **else** for the final condition.
- No semicolon is necessary after the parentheses or **else** keyword.

Figure 6-14   Syntax for an else-if structure

Figure 6-15 contains code for a program that uses an else-if structure to handle menu selections.

```cpp
#include <iostream>
using namespace std;


int main()
{
    int choice;
    cout << "Press or say 1 to connect to an account agent." << endl;
    cout << "Press or say 2 to troubleshoot your cable service." << endl;
    cout << "Press or say 3 to troubleshoot your Internet service." << endl;
    cout << "Press or say 0 to quit." << endl;
    cin >> choice;
    if (choice == 0)
        cout << "Bye.";
    else if (choice == 1)
        cout << "Transferring you to an account agent." << endl;
    else if (choice == 2)
        cout << "Connecting you to a cable technician." << endl;
    else if (choice == 3)
        cout << "Connecting you to an Internet specialist." << endl;
    else
        cout << "Invalid input." << endl;
}
```

Figure 6-15   Code for an else-if structure

Q When you trace through the program, what is the output if a customer enters 2? What is the output if the customer enters 7?

A When the customer enters 2, the output is `Connecting you to a cable technician.` When the customer enters 7 the output is `Invalid input.`

Fall Through (6.3.6, 6.3.7)

You might ask, why use an else-if structure instead of a series of `if` statements? What is the advantage of an else-if structure? The answer is that in a series of plain `if` statements, every one of the statements is evaluated and executed if true. In an else-if structure, however, the computer evaluates statements only until one of the conditions is true. The remaining else-if statements are not evaluated or executed.

To illustrate this concept, suppose you have the following pseudocode:

```
if choice == 1
    output "One"
```

```
else if choice == 2

   output "Two"

else if choice == 2

   output "Daisy"

else

   output "Stop"
```

Q What is the output when a user enters 2?

A The output will be **Two**. The output will not include **Daisy** even though the condition **choice == 2** is true because execution of the else-if structure terminated after the first true condition.

In programmer lingo, the else-if structure has no *fall through*. **Fall through** refers to program execution that continues to the next conditional statement within a structure. If the above pseudocode used a fall-through structure, the output would be **Two Daisy**.

Fall through can be implemented in a **switch-case structure** that contains a series of case statements. The pseudocode for a switch-case structure looks like this:

```
switch (choice)

case 1: output "Monday"

case 2: output "Tuesday"

case 3: output "Wednesday"

case 4: output "Thursday"

case 5: output "Friday"

case 6: output "Saturday"

case 7: output "Sunday"

default: output "Invalid input"
```

A fall-through structure can be useful when you'd like a decision to produce a sequence of outputs. Suppose the variable **choice** contains the value 5 when the switch-case structure begins. Because the switch-case structure falls through, the output will be:

```
Friday

Saturday

Sunday

Invalid input
```

To prevent fall through, you can add a **break** keyword to each case:

```
case 1: output "Monday"; break;

case 2: output "Tuesday"; break;
```

Figure 6-16 offers implementation notes for the switch-case structure.

Fall-through Syntax:

```
switch (variable)
{
case literal: statement;
case literal: statement;
default: statement;
}
```

No Fall-through Syntax:

```
switch (variable)
{
case literal: statement;
break;
case literal: statement;
break;
default: statement;
}
```

```
#include <iostream>
using namespace std;

int main()
{
   int choice;
   cout << "Enter a number from 1 to 7: ";
   cin >> choice;
   switch (choice)
   {
     case 1: cout << "Monday" << endl;
     case 2: cout << "Tuesday" << endl;
     case 3: cout << "Wednesday" << endl;
     case 4: cout << "Thursday" << endl;
     case 5: cout << "Friday" << endl;
     case 6: cout << "Saturday" << endl;
     case 7: cout << "Sunday" << endl;
     default: cout << "End" << endl;
   }
}
```

OUTPUT:

```
Enter a number from 1 to 7: 5 [Enter]


Friday
Saturday
Sunday
End
```

Figure 6-16   Switch-case structures

6.4 CONDITIONAL LOGICAL OPERATORS

The AND Operator (6.4.1, 6.4.2)

A simple conditional statement such as `choice == 1` contains a Boolean expression with one relational operator. You can specify more complex logic by adding conditional logical operators for AND and OR conditions. A conditional logical operator combines the outcomes of two or more Boolean expressions.

Suppose that you have a menu such as the following:

```
Press or say 1 to connect to an account agent.

Press or say 2 to troubleshoot your cable service.

Press or say 3 to troubleshoot your Internet service.

Press or say 9 to get help.

Press or say 0 to quit.
```

Valid input is 0, 1, 2, 3, and 9. You can filter out invalid input such as 4, 5, 6, 7, and 8 with the following:

```
input choice

if choice > 3 AND choice != 9 then

    output "Invalid input."
```

In the conditional expression, when `choice` is greater than 3 and `choice` is not 9, then the input is not valid.

To determine if the program takes the True or the False path out of the `if` statement, each of the relational expressions is evaluated and then the results are combined. Suppose the variable `choice` contains 7. Here's what the program does:

1. Evaluates `choice > 3`, which is True because 7 > 3.
2. Evaluates `choice != 9`, which is True because 7 != 9.
3. Evaluates True AND True from steps 1 and 2, which is True.
4. The result is True and the output is `"Invalid input"`.

Q What happens if choice contains 9?

A The `if` statement evaluates to True AND False, which is False. The invalid output message is not produced.

The AND operator requires that both conditions are true. A table summarizing the possible outcomes for logical operations is called a truth table. The truth table in **Figure 6-17** summarizes all the possible combinations for the AND operator and provides a code snippet to show it in action.

The && (AND) Operator

choice > 3	choice != 9	choice > 3 && choice != 9
true	true	true
true	false	false
false	true	false
false	false	false

```
if (choice > 3 && choice != 9)
{
    cout << "Invalid input." << endl;
}
```

Figure 6-17   Truth table for the AND operator

The OR Operator (6.4.3, 6.4.4)

The OR operator requires that only one of the conditions is true. Suppose an online store offers free shipping to customers who purchase more than $100.00 of merchandise or are VIP club members. As you can see from the table and the code snippet in **Figure 6-18**, only one of the conditions has to be true for free shipping.

The || (OR) Operator

purchase > 100.00	vip	purchase > 100.00 || vip
true	true	true
true	false	true
false	true	true
false	false	false

```
#include <iostream>
using namespace std;

int main()
{
    float purchase = 80.00;
    bool vip = true;
    if (purchase > 100.00 || vip)
        cout <<"Free shipping!";

}
```

OUTPUT:

```
Free shipping!
```

Figure 6-18   Truth table for the OR operator

You might find it necessary to use more than one logical operator in a conditional statement. When converting a pseudocode statement, such as if ((vip == False AND purchase < 100) || free_shipping_ coupon == True)), to code, use parentheses to ensure that the logic is carried out in the correct sequence.

SUMMARY

- A control structure alters the sequential execution of statements in a computer program. A decision control structure alters the sequential flow by branching to specific statements based on a condition or decision. Decision control structures help programs seem intelligent because they can make responses that correspond to user input.
- Decision control structures can be classified as if-then, if-then-else, nested-if, else-if, and switch-case.
- Decision control structures begin with a conditional statement such as `if choice == 1`.
- Conditional statements include relational operators, such as == != > < >= and <=.
- The == equal operator, not the = assignment operator, is used in conditional statements.
- Relational operators and operands form Boolean expressions, such as `choice == 1`, that evaluate to True or False.
- Boolean expressions have similarities to Boolean data types. Both carry a value of True or False. In practice, however, you use a Boolean expression as part of a conditional statement, whereas you use a Boolean data type when making declaration or assignment statements.
- Fall through refers to program execution that continues to the next conditional statement within a structure. Switch-case structures typically have fall through unless break keywords are added.
- The conditional logical operators AND and OR can be used to specify more complex logic for conditional statements. The results of AND and OR operations are summarized in truth tables.

Key Terms

Boolean expressions	decision control structure	if-then-else structure
conditional logical operator	else-if structure	nested-if structures
conditional statement	equal operator	relational operator
control structure	fall through	switch-case structure
	if-then structure	truth table

REPETITION CONTROL STRUCTURES

LEARNING OBJECTIVES:

7.1 COUNT-CONTROLLED LOOPS

7.1.1 Identify parts of algorithms that require repetition controls.

7.1.2 Specify the counting sequence produced by loop control statements.

7.1.3 Specify the use case for count-controlled loops.

7.1.4 Select the correct format for writing count-controlled loops in pseudocode.

7.1.5 Identify loop control statements, loop counters, and test conditions.

7.1.6 Use language-specific syntax to code a count-controlled loop.

7.1.7 Provide an example of an algorithm that requires a user-controlled loop.

7.1.8 Collect user input to control a loop.

7.2 COUNTERS AND ACCUMULATORS

7.2.1 Provide an example of a loop that requires a counter.

7.2.2 Explain the advantages and disadvantages of using the loop counter variable as an output source.

7.2.3 Provide examples of loops that require an accumulator.

7.2.4 Describe the general syntax for expressions that serve as accumulators.

7.3 NESTED LOOPS

7.3.1 Draw a flowchart that illustrates a nested loop.

7.3.2 Identify nested loops in pseudocode.

7.3.3 Describe common naming conventions for the variables used as counters in nested loops.

7.3.4 Use language-specific syntax to code a nested loop.

7.3.5 Analyze a nested loop to understand the results it produces.

7.4 PRE-TEST LOOPS

7.4.1 Draw a flowchart that illustrates a pre-test loop.

7.4.2 Identify algorithms that require a pre-test loop.

7.4.3 Identify pre-test loops in pseudocode.

7.4.4 Use language-specific syntax to code a pre-test loop.

7.4.5 Identify infinite loops.

7.4.6 State how to terminate an infinite loop.

7.4.7 Explain the advantages and disadvantages of using the break statement to exit a loop.

7.5 POST-TEST LOOPS

7.5.1 Draw a flowchart that illustrates a post-test loop.

7.5.2 Identify algorithms that require a post-test loop.

7.5.3 Identify post-test loops in pseudocode.

7.5.4 Use language-specific syntax to code a post-test loop.

7.5.5 Differentiate between a test condition and a terminating condition in the context of loops.

7.5.6 Select appropriate test conditions and terminating conditions for loops.

7.1 COUNT-CONTROLLED LOOPS

Loop Basics (7.1.1)

Pumping iron. Every lift requires repetitions using barbells, kettlebells, or free weights similar to those in **Figure 7-1**.

Jan Kvita/Shutterstock.com

Figure 7-1   Barbells, kettlebells, and free weights

Like weight-lifting exercises, computer programs can perform reps using **repetition control structures**, or "loops" as they are called in programming jargon. You can visualize a **loop** as a block of code with an entry point, a number of statements that repeat, and an exit point. See **Figure 7-2**.

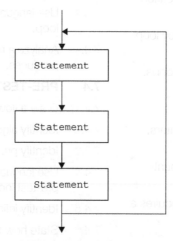

Figure 7-2   Repetition control structures repeat blocks of code

Loops are handy for many tasks within an algorithm, such as the following:

- Processing a series of records in a database or the items in a list
- Keeping a running count
- Accumulating totals
- Solving recursive math problems

There are three basic types of repetition control structures:

- Count-controlled loops
- Pre-test loops
- Post-test loops

In this module, you'll learn how to apply each of these control structures. Are you ready to strengthen your programming skills by discovering loops? Let's get started.

Control Statements (7.1.2)

The simplest repetition control structure is the count-controlled loop, which repeats a specified number of times. This type of loop begins with a control statement that contains one or more of the following parameters for controlling the loop.

- A variable for the loop counter that tracks the number of times a loop has repeated
- A starting value for the loop counter
- A test condition containing logic that continues or ends the loop
- An incrementation value that increases or decreases the loop counter
- The number of repetitions to perform

Figure 7-3 provides some examples of loop parameters. Pay attention to the counting sequence that each example produces.

Control Statement Parameters	Counting Sequence
(start = 1, test = 10, increment = 1)	1 2 3 4 5 6 7 8 9
(start = 1, test <= 10, increment = 1)	1 2 3 4 5 6 7 8 9 10
(start = 0, test = 20, increment = 2)	0 2 4 6 8 10 12 14 16 18
(repetitions = 5)	1 2 3 4 5

Figure 7-3   Loop counters

Q When the loop counter's test condition is set as = 10, what is the last number in the count?

A The last number is 9. When the test condition specifies a value with an = sign, it means "up to, but not including" the ending value.

When working with count-controlled loops, just remember that when your program runs, the test condition is evaluated *before* each iteration of the loop. If the test condition is false, program execution bypasses the loop and jumps to the statement after the end of the loop.

For-Loops (7.1.3, 7.1.4, 7.1.5, 7.1.6)

The for-loop is a count-controlled loop that works well when you know how many times you want a loop to repeat. For-loops are also called for-next loops. A for-loop can be depicted by the flowchart in **Figure 7-4**.

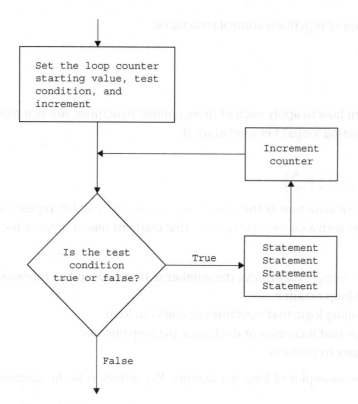

Figure 7-4   For-loop flowchart

You can write language-agnostic pseudocode for a for-loop using the **for** keyword at the beginning of the loop and the **next** keyword at the end. Here is the pseudocode for a program that outputs verbal guidance for two repetitions of the bench press lift.

```
for i (start: i = 1, test: i <= 2, increment = 1)

    output "Lift"

    output "Pause"

    output "Lower"
next
```

OUTPUT:

Lift

Pause

Lower

Lift

Pause

Lower

Q Can you identify the loop control statement, the loop counter, and the test condition in the preceding pseudocode?

A The loop control statement is **for i (start: i = 1, test: i <= 2, increment = 1)**. The loop counter is **i**. The test condition is **i <= 2**. The loop counter increments by 1 after each repetition.

When writing pseudocode for for-loops, you must specify the start and test conditions. Specifying the increment is optional. If you don't specify the incrementation value, it is assumed to be 1.

Programmers typically use the letter i for the loop counter's variable name. The i probably stands for *iteration*, which is a synonym for repetition. **Figure 7-5** provides the general syntax for a basic for-loop.

```
Syntax:
for (int i = initial value; i <= terminating value; i++)
{

    statement 1;

    statement 2;

}
```

Rules and best practices:

- The loop counter variable should always be defined as an integer.
- The test expression can be set as < or as < =. If you use < =, the terminating value will be included in the count.
- i+ + specifies that the count increments by 1 for each iteration.
- i+ =2 specifies that the count increments by 2 for each iteration.
- i− − specifies that the count decrements by 1 for each iteration.
- Avoid modifying the loop counter variable within the loop. For example, do not use i in an arithmetic operation inside the loop.

Figure 7-5   For-loop syntax, rules, and best practices

By applying the for-loop syntax, you can code the following program that guides a bench press exercise by outputting "Lift pause lower" for three repetitions. Take a close look at the syntax for the test condition, punctuation, and indentation in **Figure 7-6**.

```cpp
#include <iostream>
using namespace std;


int main()
{
    for (int i = 1; i <= 3; i++)

    {
    cout << "Lift"<< endl;

    cout << "Pause"<< endl;

    cout << "Lower"<< endl << endl;

    }

}
```

Figure 7-6   Code for three repetitions of bench press guidance (*Continued*)

OUTPUT:
```
Lift
Pause
Lower


Lift
Pause
Lower


Lift
Pause
Lower
```

Figure 7-6   Code for three repetitions of bench press guidance

User-Controlled Loops (7.1.7, 7.1.8)

You can allow users to determine the number of times a loop repeats. A **user-controlled loop** specifies the value for the loop counter during runtime by obtaining user input for its value. Users can control for-loops as well as pre-test and post-test loops.

Suppose that a weightlifter wants to do five reps of the bench press exercise. The following pseudocode collects the input for reps and uses it to control the loop.

```
initialize reps = 0
output "How many reps? "
input reps
for i (start: i = 1, test: i <= reps)
    output "Lift, pause, lower"
next
```

OUTPUT:
```
How many reps? 5 [Enter]
Lift, pause, lower
Lift, pause, lower
Lift, pause, lower
Lift, pause, lower
Lift, pause, lower
```

Coding this algorithm produces the program in **Figure 7-7**. Look for the use of the variable `reps` in the input statement and in the for-loop test condition.

```cpp
#include <iostream>
using namespace std;


int main()
{
  int reps;
  cout << "How many reps? ";
  cin >> reps;
  for (int i = 1; i <= reps; i++)
    cout << "Lift, pause, lower" << endl;
}
OUTPUT:
How many reps? 5 [Enter]
Lift, pause, lower
Lift, pause, lower
Lift, pause, lower
Lift, pause, lower
Lift, pause, lower
```

Figure 7-7   User-controlled for-loop

7.2 COUNTERS AND ACCUMULATORS

Loops That Count (7.2.1, 7.2.2)

Count-controlled loops have a built-in counter that you can use for algorithms that need to count or accumulate totals. The values in the loop counter follow a sequence of numbers similar to counting 1 2 3, or 2 4 6.

You can set the loop's increment to count by ones, by twos, by tens, or by other whole numbers using incrementation expressions such as `i++`, `i+=2`, and `i+=10`. This feature is useful when you create programs that include some counting component, such as a math program to count by twos or to output multiplication tables.

After setting the loop counter parameters for a counting sequence, you can simply output the value for i during each iteration. **Figure 7-8** contains the code for a program that outputs even numbers from 2 to 10. Be sure to study the parameters for the variable i.

```
#include <iostream>
using namespace std;


int main()
{
  for (int i = 2; i <= 10; i+=2)
   cout << i << endl;
}
OUTPUT:
2
4
6
8
10
```

Figure 7-8   A loop that counts by twos

It is good programming practice to avoid using the loop counter variable in other statements within the loop. The previous program used i in the output statement. To avoid reuse, and the possibility that the counter variable might be inadvertently changed, you can set up a separate variable for the output and increment it within the loop, as shown in **Figure 7-9**.

```
#include <iostream>
using namespace std;


int main()
{
  int count_out = 0;
  for (int i = 2; i <= 10; i+=2)
  {
    count_out +=2;
    cout << count_out << endl;
  }
}
```

Figure 7-9   A loop that uses a variable called count_out as a separate counter (*Continued*)

```
OUTPUT:
2
4
6
8
10
```

Figure 7-9   A loop that uses a variable called `count_out` as a separate counter

Q Instead of outputting i in the preceding program, which variable is used as a counter and for output?

A The variable `count_out` is used as a counter and for output.

Loops That Accumulate (7.2.3, 7.2.4)

Another application of loops is to accumulate a total by repeatedly adding values. Suppose you are bench pressing 15-pound weights in each hand and want to know the total weight that you've lifted after three repetitions.

You can set up a variable called `total_weight` that accumulates the sum of weight lifted during the bench press session. As a bonus, the cumulative totals can be output for each repetition. The pseudocode looks like this:

```
output "How many reps?"
input reps
output "What size weights are you using?"
input weight
for i (start: i = 1, test: i <= reps)
    total_weight = total_weight + (weight * 2)
    output "Rep " + i + " " + total_weight + "lbs."
next
```

Notice the statement that creates the accumulator: `total_weight = total_weight + (weight * 2)`. In general, the syntax for an accumulator looks like this:

```
accumulator_variable = accumulator_variable + some_other_variable
```

The code and output for the total-weight algorithm are in **Figure 7-10**.

```cpp
#include <iostream>
using namespace std;


int main()
{
  int reps;
  int weight;
  int total_weight = 0;
  cout << "How many reps? ";
  cin >> reps;
  cout << "What size weights are you using? ";
  cin >> weight;
  for (int i = 1; i <= reps; i ++)
  {
    total_weight = total_weight + (weight * 2);
    cout << "Rep " << i << " " << total_weight << " lbs so far." << endl;
  }
  cout << "Your total lift is: " << total_weight << " lbs." << endl;
}
```

OUTPUT:

How many reps? 3 [Enter]

What size weights are you using? 15 [Enter]

Rep 1 30 lbs so far.

Rep 2 60 lbs so far.

Rep 3 90 lbs so far.

Your total lift is: 90 lbs.

Figure 7-10   A loop that includes an accumulator for `total_weight`

Q Why is the weight multiplied by 2 before adding it to the accumulator?

A Because each hand is holding a weight. If each hand holds a 15 lb. weight, then each lift is 30 lbs.

7.3 NESTED LOOPS

Loops Within Loops (7.3.1, 7.3.2)

A **nested-loop** is a loop within a loop. These loops contain multiple control statements and loop counters. Weight lifting provides an insight into how these nested loops work.

Weight training exercises usually involve sets of repetitions. For example, set 1 for a bench press might involve four repetitions. Set 2 might involve another four repetitions and a third set might involve four more repetitions. The sets repeat three times, and each set has four reps. The sets are the outer loop. The reps are the inner loop.

A flowchart for a nested loop is illustrated in **Figure 7-11**. Trace the True paths through the loop to reinforce the idea that the computer does one outer loop, then repeats the inner loops before doing the next outer loop.

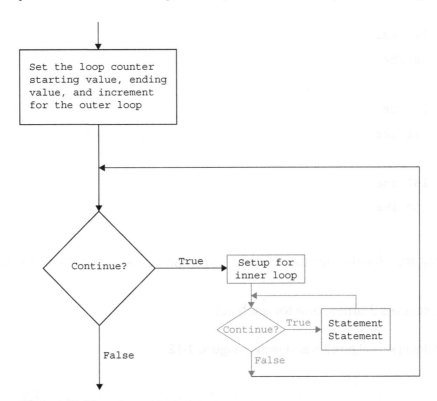

Figure 7-11   Nested-loop flowchart

Inner and Outer Loops (7.3.3, 7.3.4, 7.3.5)

When writing nested loops in pseudocode, the inner loop is indented from the outer loop and ends with its own **next** keyword. Each loop control variable must be unique. Programmers typically use j for the inner loop variable.

```
output "What size weights are you using?"

input weight

output "How many sets?"

input sets

display "How many reps per set?"

input reps

for i (start: i = 1, test: i <= sets)

    output "Set: " + i

    for j (start: j = 1, test: j <= reps)

        total_weight = total_weight + (weight * 2)

        output " Rep: " + j + " Progress: " + total_weight + " lbs. "

    next

next
```

OUTPUT:

```
What size weights are you using? 15 [Enter]
How many sets? 3 [Enter]
How many reps per set? 2 [Enter]
Set: 1
 Rep: 1 Progress: 30 lbs.
 Rep: 2 Progress: 60 lbs.
Set: 2
 Rep: 1 Progress: 90 lbs.
 Rep: 2 Progress: 120 lbs.
Set: 3
 Rep: 1 Progress: 150 lbs.
 Rep: 2 Progress: 180 lbs.
```

Q When the user enters 3 for the number of sets, how many times does the outer loop iterate?

A The outer loop executes 3 times, one for each set.

The code for the training-sets algorithm is shown in **Figure 7-12**.

```cpp
#include <iostream>
using namespace std;


int main()
{
    int weight, sets, reps;
    int total_weight = 0;
    cout << "What size weights are you using? ";
    cin >> weight;
    cout << "How many sets? ";
    cin >> sets;
    cout << "How many reps per set? ";
    cin >> reps;
    for (int i = 1; i <= sets; i++)
```

Figure 7-12   Code for a nested for-loop (*Continued*)

```
   {
     cout << "Set: " << i << endl;
     for(int j = 1; j <= reps; j++)
     {
       total_weight = total_weight + (weight * 2);
       cout << " Rep: " << j << " Progress: ";
       cout << total_weight << " lbs." << endl;
     }
   }
   cout << "Your total lift is: " << total_weight << " lbs." << endl;
}
```

OUTPUT:

```
What size weights are you using? 15 [Enter]
How many sets? 3 [Enter]
How many reps per set? 2 [Enter]
Set: 1
 Rep: 1 Progress: 30 lbs.
 Rep: 2 Progress: 60 lbs.
Set: 2
 Rep: 1 Progress: 90 lbs.
 Rep: 2 Progress: 120 lbs.
Set: 3
 Rep: 1 Progress: 150 lbs.
 Rep: 2 Progress: 180 lbs.
Your total lift is: 180 lbs.
```

Figure 7-12   Code for a nested for-loop

Q In the preceding program, why isn't "Set: 1" printed on the line for each repetition in the set as follows?

Set: 1 Rep: 1 Progress: 30 lbs.
Set: 1 Rep: 2 Progress: 60 lbs.

A The statement that outputs the set number is before the beginning of the inner loop. If you want tasks performed only by the outer loop, do not place them within the code for the inner loop.

7.4 PRE-TEST LOOPS

While-Loops (7.4.1, 7.4.2, 7.4.3, 7.4.4)

Loops are not always controlled by a counter. A condition-controlled loop is regulated by conditional statements containing Boolean expressions similar to those that control decision structures, such as if-then and else-if.

A pre-test loop begins with a condition. A condition-controlled pre-test loop executes only if the test condition is true and continues executing until the condition is no longer true or until the loop encounters a **break** statement.

A flowchart for a pre-test loop is illustrated in **Figure 7-13**.

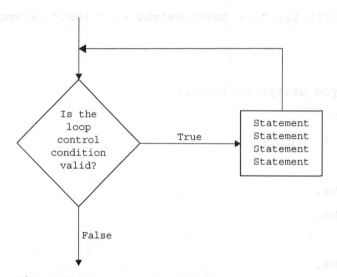

Figure 7-13   Pre-test loop flowchart

Pre-test loops are handy for validating input. You can set up a loop that implements the following algorithm:

Ask user for input.
If the input is not valid, output a message that asks for a valid entry.
Check the entry again and repeat until the entry is valid.

The pseudocode for a pre-test loop typically uses the keywords **while** and **do**. Here is the pseudocode that validates input in the range 1 to 25. This pre-test loop repeats as many times as necessary until the user enters a value in the range 1 to 25.

```
output "Enter the number of reps for this lifting exercise: "
input reps
while (reps < 1 OR reps > 25) do
    output "Try again. Reps have to be in the range 1 to 25."
    input reps
output "Okay, you want to do " + reps + " reps."
```

A while-loop provides the syntax for implementing a pre-test loop. In **Figure 7-14**, pay attention to the syntax and then see how it is applied in the example code.

```
Syntax:

while (condition)

{

   statement;

   statement;

}
```

```cpp
#include <iostream>

using namespace std;

int main()

{

   int reps;

   cout << ("Enter the number of reps for this lifting exercise: ");

   cin >> reps;

   while (reps <1 || reps > 25)

   {

      cout << "Try again. Reps have to be in the range 1 to 25:" << endl;

      cin >> reps;

   }

   cout << "Okay, you want to do " << reps << " reps.";

}
```

OUTPUT:

```
Enter the number of reps for this lifting exercise: 38 [Enter]

Try again. Reps have to be in the range 1 to 25: 20 [Enter]

Okay, you want to do 20 reps.
```

Figure 7-14   While-loop syntax and example

Infinite Loops (7.4.5)

When validating input, what happens if the weightlifter continues to enter 0? The validation loop could continue forever, a condition known as an **infinite loop**. Infinite loops can be caused by several factors, including the following:

- Invalid input that does not end an input loop.
- Input that changes the value of the loop counter.
- A programmer error in specifying the loop conditional statement.
- Using the loop counter variable in a mathematical operation inside the loop.
- Using the same loop counter variable for the inner and outer loops of a nested loop.

Trace through the following pseudocode and see if you can discover the error that creates an infinite loop.

```
output "Enter the number of reps: "
input reps
while reps < 1 OR reps > 25 do
    output "Try again. Enter a number in the range 1 to 25: "
output "Okay, you want to do " + reps + " reps."
```

OUTPUT:

```
Enter the number of reps: 0 [Enter]
Try again. Enter a number in the range 1 to 25:
Try again. Enter a number in the range 1 to 25:
Try again. Enter a number in the range 1 to 25:
Try again. Enter a number in the range 1 to 25:
. . .
```

Q Did you find the error?

A The error is that there is no input statement within the loop. The user never has a chance to enter a value other than the 0 entered at the first prompt.

If your program inadvertently goes into an infinite loop, you may be able to terminate it by pressing Ctrl+C a few times. Online compilers usually have a Stop button for use in such a situation.

Breaking Out of Loops (7.4.6, 7.4.7)

Using Ctrl+C to terminate a loop is not something you can expect users to do. Your program always should provide a clean exit path from a loop, preferably from within the logic of the loop control statement.

To prevent an endless loop when validating input, you can provide an exit strategy in the body of the loop. Look for the exit strategy in the following pseudocode.

```
output "Enter the number of reps: "
input reps
while (reps < 1 OR reps > 25) AND (reps != 999) do
    output "Try again. Enter a number in the range 1 to 25,
    output "or enter 999 to exit: "
    input reps
if reps == 999 then
    output "Bye."
else
    output "Okay, you want to do " + reps + " reps."
```

OUTPUT:

```
Enter the number of reps: 0 [Enter]
Try again. Enter a number in the range 1 to 25,
or enter 999 to exit: 999 [Enter]
Bye.
```

The user is given the option of entering 999 to exit the loop. This logic is handled by the parameters for the **while** statement (**reps < 1 OR reps > 25 AND (reps != 999)**). The if-else statements later in the loop provide additional logic necessary to either quit or output the number of reps.

It is also possible to use a **break** statement to exit a loop as in the following pseudocode, but the result might have unintended consequences.

```
output "Enter the number of reps: "
input reps
while (reps < 1 OR reps > 25) do
    output "Try again. Enter a number in the range 1 to 25,
    output "or enter 999 to exit: "
    input reps
    if reps == 999 then
        output "Bye."
        break
output "Okay, you want to do " + reps + " reps."
```

OUTPUT:

```
Enter the number of reps: 0 [Enter]
Try again. Enter a number in the range 1 to 25,
or enter 999 to exit: 999 [Enter]
Bye. Okay, you want to do 999 reps.
```

Q What is wrong with the logic in the preceding pseudocode?

A The loop exits with 999 in the variable **reps** and the last statement outputs the "Okay . . ." message, even though the loop terminated.

Because **break** statements can have unexpected effects, it is best to avoid their use within the body of a loop. The better practice is to design the control parameters to provide a graceful way to exit loops. Loops containing **break** statements are widely used by professional developers, however, so as a programmer you should have the flexibility to use them or avoid them as required by the specifications for each project.

7.5 POST-TEST LOOPS

Do-Loops (7.5.1, 7.5.2, 7.5.3, 7.5.4)

A **post-test loop** is structured with the conditional statement at the end of the loop. The first pass through the loop is executed unconditionally. Subsequent passes are controlled by the conditional statement. A flowchart for a post-test loop is illustrated in **Figure 7-15**.

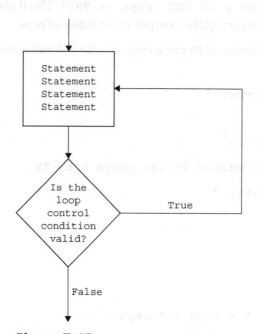

Figure 7-15   Post-test loop flowchart

Post-test loops are useful for any part of an algorithm that should be performed at least once but may need to be repeated in a loop. These loops are especially handy when you want to display a menu, collect input, perform the selected task, and display the menu again when the task is complete.

For post-test loop pseudocode, use the keywords `do..while`. Pseudocode such as the following could handle a menu of weight training choices.

```
do
    display "1. Bench press"
    display "2. Shoulder press"
    display "3. Hammer curl"
    display "4. Step ups"
    display "0. Quit"
    input "Your choice: "
    if choice != 0 then:
        display "Let's get started with lift #" + choice
        display "Press any key when you are done: "
        input any_key
while choice != 0
```

OUTPUT:

```
1. Bench press

2. Shoulder press

3. Hammer curl

4. Step ups

0. Quit

Your choice: 2 [Enter]

Let's get started with lift #2

Press any key when you are done: z [Enter]


1. Bench press

2. Shoulder press

3. Hammer curl

4. Step ups

0. Quit

Your choice:
```

Q Can you explain why there is an if-then structure within the do-while loop shown above?

A The if-then structure prevents the program from displaying `Let's get started with lift #0` if the user selects the Quit item from the menu.

Most programming languages have a post-test loop structure. **Figure 7-16** provides details for post-test loops in your programming language.

The do-while structure provides a post-test loop that begins with a **do** statement.

The body of the loop is contained in curly braces. The loop terminates with a **while** statement that specifies the condition for the loop to repeat. The **while** statement is outside of the curly braces that define the body of the loop.

Syntax:
```
do
{
    statement;
    statement;
    statement;
}
while (conditional expression);
```

Figure 7-16   Code for a post-test loop that displays a menu (*Continued*)

Trace through the following code to locate the statements that begin and end the loop.

```cpp
#include <iostream>
using namespace std;

int main()
{
  int choice;
  char any_key;
  do
  {
    cout << "1. Bench press"<< endl;
    cout << "2. Shoulder press" << endl;
    cout << "3. Hammer curl" << endl;
    cout << "4. Step ups" << endl;
    cout << "0. Quit" << endl;
    cout << "Your choice: ";
    cin >> choice;
    if (choice != 0)
    {
      cout << "Let's get started with lift #" << choice << endl;
      cout << "Press any key when you are done: ";
      cin >> any_key;
    }
  }
  while (choice != 0);
}
```

Figure 7-16   Code for a post-test loop that displays a menu

Test Conditions and Terminating Conditions (7.5.5, 7.5.6)

The ability of a loop to iterate depends on a test condition and its corresponding terminating condition. A loop's test condition is the expression that allows the loop to execute. A loop's **terminating condition** is the expression that stops the loop. Take another look at the following pseudocode.

```
do
    display "1. Bench press"
    display "2. Shoulder press"
    display "3. Hammer curl"
    display "4. Step ups"
    display "0. Quit"
    input "Your choice: "
    if choice != 0 then:
        display "Let's get started with lift #" + choice
        display "Press any key when you are done: "
        input any_key
while choice != 0
```

The test condition is **choice != 0**. That means the loop continues when the value of choice is not 0. The implied terminating condition is **choice == 0**. The terminating condition is not explicitly stated in code, but whenever you set a test condition, it is a good idea to make sure the terminating condition will stop the loop in all necessary cases.

The following algorithm is supposed to count by twos up to 10.

```
count = 1
do
  display count
  count = count + 2
while count != 10
```

The output of this program is an infinite loop beginning 1 3 5 7 9 11 13. What's wrong? The terminating condition is **count == 10**, but that number is never a value of **count** because **count** contains only odd numbers.

Q How would you change the test condition so that the terminating condition does not allow the loop to go past 10?

A You can change the test condition to **while count <= 10**. That logic makes the terminating condition broader and stops the loop when the value in **count** is any number greater than 10.

SUMMARY

- A repetition control structure creates a loop that has an entry point, a number of statements that repeat, and an exit point.
- A count-controlled loop repeats a specified number of times. This type of loop begins with a control statement that establishes a loop counter. A loop counter sets up a variable that tracks the number of times the loop repeats.
- The for-loop is a count-controlled loop that works well when you know how many times you want a loop to repeat.
- Users can specify the value for a loop counter during runtime by providing input for the value of the loop counter. Users can control for-loops as well as pre-test and post-test loops.
- Loops can be used to output counting sequences and to sum values in an accumulator.
- Nested loops are loops within loops. The outer loop and inner loop are controlled by different variables.
- A pre-test loop begins with a condition. The loop executes only if that condition is true and continues executing until the condition is no longer true or until it encounters a **break** statement. Pre-test loops are handy for validating input.
- An infinite loop has no means of termination other than user intervention and is generally considered an error condition. To manually terminate an infinite loop, press Ctrl+C or the Run/Stop button provided by a development environment. Although it is possible to include **break** statements to exit a loop, a better practice is to provide a clean exit path from within the logic of the loop's control statement.
- A post-test loop is structured with the conditional statement at the end of the loop. The first pass through the loop is executed unconditionally. Subsequent passes are controlled by the conditional statement. These loops are especially useful for displaying a menu, collecting input, performing a selected task, and displaying the menu again when the task is complete.
- A loop's test condition is the expression that allows the loop to execute. A loop's terminating condition is the expression that stops the loop. The terminating condition is not explicitly stated in code, but whenever you set a test condition, it is a good idea to make sure the terminating condition will stop the loop in all necessary cases.

Key Terms

condition-controlled loop

control statement

count-controlled loop

for-loop

infinite loop

iteration

loop

loop counter

nested-loop

post-test loop

pre-test loop

repetition control structures

terminating condition

test condition

user-controlled loop

while-loop

MODULE 8

ARRAYS

LEARNING OBJECTIVES:

8.1 ARRAY BASICS

8.1.1 Categorize an array as a data structure and a composite data type.

8.1.2 Distinguish one-dimensional arrays from two-dimensional arrays.

8.1.3 List the three characteristics of an array.

8.1.4 List the types of data that an array can hold.

8.1.5 Explain the use of array indexes.

8.1.6 Illustrate the layout of a one-dimensional array in memory.

8.1.7 Identify use cases for one-dimensional and two-dimensional arrays.

8.2 ONE-DIMENSIONAL ARRAYS

8.2.1 Identify variables that represent a one-dimensional array.

8.2.2 Declare and initialize one-dimensional numeric and string arrays.

8.3 ARRAY INPUT AND OUTPUT

8.3.1 Output a single array element.

8.3.2 Explain the cause of an index error in the context of arrays.

8.3.3 Use a loop to traverse an array.

8.3.4 Input array elements at runtime.

8.4 ARRAY OPERATIONS

8.4.1 Change the value of an array element.

8.4.2 Find an element in an array.

8.4.3 Find the sum of elements in a one-dimensional array.

8.5 TWO-DIMENSIONAL ARRAYS

8.5.1 Identify variables that represent two-dimensional arrays.

8.5.2 Associate two-dimensional arrays with tables, grids, and matrices.

8.5.3 Illustrate the way a two-dimensional array is stored in memory.

8.5.4 Initialize a two-dimensional array.

8.5.5 Explain the need for nested loops to traverse a two-dimensional array.

8.5.6 Output the elements of a two-dimensional array.

8.5.7 Sum the rows and columns in a two-dimensional array.

8.1 ARRAY BASICS

Magic Rectangles (8.1.1, 8.1.2)

A magic rectangle is a matrix filled with numbers. Look at the magic rectangle in **Figure 8-1**. Two numbers are missing. Can you figure out how to correctly fill in the missing square?

6	7	8	9	10
13	3	1	11	12
	14	15	4	

Figure 8-1 An incomplete magic rectangle

To complete the puzzle, you have to understand the following properties of a magic rectangle:

- Each cell contains a unique number.
- With 15 cells, the numbers are 1 through 15.
- The numbers in each row produce equal sums. In this rectangle, the sum for each row should be 40.
- The numbers in each column produce equal sums, but that sum does not need to be the same as the row sum. In this magic rectangle, each column should sum to 24.

Q What numbers would complete the magic rectangle?

A The lower-left cell should contain 5. The lower-right cell has to contain 2.

A magic rectangle is an example of an array. In the context of programming, an **array** is a data structure that stores a collection of elements that all have the same data type. The magic rectangle is an array that contains a collection of integers.

Arrays are also classified as composite data types because they are constructed from primitive data types, such as integers or characters.

Programmers typically work with one-dimensional and two-dimensional arrays.

- A **one-dimensional array** is linear. The first row of the magic rectangle with its five elements is a one-dimensional array.
- A **two-dimensional array** has rows and columns that form a matrix. The entire magic rectangle is a two-dimensional array.

Array Characteristics (8.1.3, 8.1.4, 8.1.5, 8.1.6)

Arrays are homogeneous, ordered, and finite.

Homogeneous. Arrays can be filled with character, Boolean, integer, floating-point, or string data. Remember, however, that all the elements of an array have to be the same data type, a characteristic referred to as homogeneous. An array can be filled with integer data, but you cannot have an array containing some integers and some strings.

Ordered. Arrays are stored in consecutive memory addresses and each element is identified by a sequential array index enclosed in square brackets. Array indexes are sometimes referred to as subscripts.

The first element in an array has an index of [0]. The remaining array elements in a one-dimensional array are indexed in sequence as shown in **Figure 8-2**.

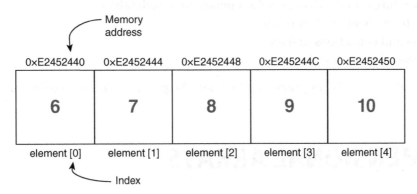

Figure 8-2   Memory allocation for a one-dimensional array

Finite. Because an array is stored in a set of consecutive memory locations, an array cannot have an infinite number of elements. In most programming languages, you have to define the number of elements in an array when you create it.

Technically, an array is fixed to the size you specify. You can change the elements in the array, but you cannot add more elements. To expand an array, you must create a new, larger array, move the original elements to the new array, and then add the new elements. Some programming languages provide work-arounds to this limitation. For example, C++ provides ATL vectors and Python provides lists that allow for dynamic sizing.

Here's a little gotcha. The first row of the magic rectangle is an array of five elements, but the index for the final element is [4], not [5] as shown in **Figure 8-3**. Keep this in mind as you work with arrays!

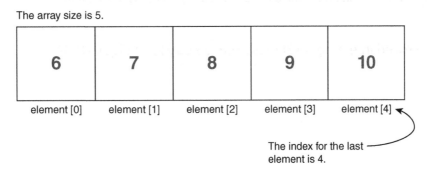

Figure 8-3   The index value for the last element in an array is one less than the number of elements in the array

Array Use Cases (8.1.7)

Arrays are an indispensable part of your programming toolbox. Suppose you want to a find the average of 100 rainfall measurements. Initializing 100 variables would be tedious. Instead, you can create a single named array, such as `rainfall[100]`, to hold all of the data.

Arrays are a great way to:

- Store lists of data.
- Represent a collection of integer or floating-point data that you want to process using the same algorithm.
- Sort a collection of numeric or string data.
- Manipulate the characters in a word or phrase by reversing them or encrypting them.
- Process images that are stored as a matrix of pixels.
- Store menus for program control.
- Implement data structures such as lists, stacks, queues, and hash tables.
- Store and manipulate mathematical matrices.
- Search through lists and collections of data.
- Process lists or tables of statistical data.

To discover more about this handy programming tool, let's begin by exploring one-dimensional arrays.

8.2 ONE-DIMENSIONAL ARRAYS

Initialize Numeric Arrays (8.2.1)

A one-dimensional array has a name and uses a single index to identify array elements. When naming an array, use the same conventions as naming a variable. The first row of the magic rectangle can be coded as an array called `magic_array[]`. The array contains five integers indexed [0] through [4] as shown in **Figure 8-4**.

| magic_array [0] | magic_array [1] | magic_array [2] | magic_array [3] | magic_array [4] |

Figure 8-4   An array called `magic_array[]` contains five elements

Q What is the value stored in element [2] of `magic_array[]` in Figure 8-4?

A It is 8.

To create an array, you can use a declaration statement to give the array a name and specify its length. This process is sometimes called *dimensioning an array*.

In pseudocode, an array declaration should include three parameters:

- The name of the array
- The type of data in the array
- The number of elements you intend to place in the array

To declare an array of five integers called magic_array, use the following pseudocode:

```
declare int magic_array[5]
```

You can also declare and initialize an array with its data elements in a single statement. The elements of the array are either enclosed in curly braces or square brackets, depending on your programming language. For pseudocode, curly braces are a common notation.

```
initialize int magic_array[5] = {6, 7, 8, 9, 10}
```

Figure 8-5 provides details on how to set up one-dimensional arrays in your programming language.

Syntax to declare an array:

```
data_type array_name[number_of_array_elements];
```

Example:

```
int magic_array[5];
```

Syntax to declare and initialize an array:

```
data_type array_name[number_of_array_elements] = {element, element, element};
```

Example:

```
int magic_array[5] = {6, 7, 8, 9, 10};
```

Figure 8-5 Declare and initialize one-dimensional arrays

Initialize String Arrays (8.2.2)

Building an array containing text is similar to creating an array of numbers. Use the string data type and enclose each string in quotes. In pseudocode, you can specify a string array like this:

```
initialize string sizes[3] = {"small", "medium", "large"}
```

Figure 8-6 provides code for initializing a string array called `sizes[]`.

```
#include <iostream>
#include <string>
using namespace std;

int main()
{
  string sizes[3] = {"small", "medium", "large"};
}
```

Rules and best practices:

- Designate the data type as string.
- When working with strings, don't forget to include the `<string>` library.
- Enclose string elements in quotes.

Figure 8-6 Initialize a string array

8.3 ARRAY INPUT AND OUTPUT

Output an Array Element (8.3.1)

You'll find it easy to output a single element of an array using its index value. In pseudocode, the following statement outputs the value for the array element referenced by index [3].

```
initialize int magic_array[5] = {6, 7, 8, 9, 10}
```

```
output magic_array[3]
```

OUTPUT:

9

The code for this operation is in **Figure 8-7**.

```cpp
#include <iostream>

using namespace std;


int main()
{
    int magic_array[5] = {6, 7, 8, 9, 10};
    cout << magic_array[3] << endl;
}


OUTPUT:
9
```

Figure 8-7   Output an array element

Index Errors (8.3.2)

Using an index for an element that is not within the array produces an index error or a compiler warning. For example, if you have **magic_array[]** dimensioned to hold five elements, and you attempt to access or output **magic_array[6]**, your programming environment might produce a message similar to the one in **Figure 8-8**.

```cpp
#include <iostream>
using namespace std;


int main()
{
    int magic_array[5] = {6, 7, 8, 9, 10};
    cout << magic_array[6];
}


OUTPUT:
main.cpp:7:11: warning: array index 6 is
        past the end of the array (which
        contains 5 elements) [-Warray-bounds]
    cout << magic_array[6];
```

Figure 8-8   An index error message

Index errors are sometimes referred to as boundary errors, out-of-bounds exceptions, or subscript errors. These errors are easy to make, but they are also easy to correct by paying attention to the index values in loops, calculations, and output statements.

Traverse an Array (8.3.3)

Arrays have multiple elements. To output all the elements in **magic_array**, you could use a brute-force algorithm like this:

output **magic_array[0]**

output **magic_array[1]**

output **magic_array[2]**

output **magic_array[3]**

output **magic_array[4]**

Obviously that algorithm is not very efficient. Attempting to simply execute a statement such as output **magic_array**, however, can lead to unexpected consequences. Depending on your programming language, such an output statement might produce a hexadecimal number such as 0x7ffc01070b60. That number is the memory address of the first element in the array, rather than a list of elements in the array.

You can use a loop to output the elements in an array. Accessing each array element in sequence is called *traversing an array*. You can traverse an array to output every element, count the total number of elements, search for an element, or sum the elements.

The pseudocode for traversing **magic_array[]** to output each element goes like this:

initialize **int magic_array[5] = {6, 7, 8, 9, 10}**

for i (start: i = 0, test: i < 5)

    output **magic_array[i]**

Look back at the pseudocode and notice the following:

- The loop counter begins at 0.
- The test condition ends the loop when the counter is < 5 because the counter begins at 0.
- In the output statement, the index for **magic_array[]** contains the variable i that counts the loops.

Figure 8-9 contains the code for traversing an array to output its elements.

```
#include <iostream>
#include <iomanip>
using namespace std;

int main()
{
    int i;
    int magic_array[5] = {6, 7, 8, 9, 10};
    for (i = 0; i < 5; i++)
```

Figure 8-9   Traverse an array with a count-controlled loop (*Continued*)

```
   {
      cout << setw(3) << magic_array[i];
   }
cout << endl;
}
```

OUTPUT:

```
   6   7   8   9  10
```

Rules and best practices:

- Use a count-controlled loop with the test value set at < the array size.
- To format the output with even spacing, use the `setw()` function to set the field width and right-justify the numbers.
- Include the `<iomanip>` library to access the `setw()` function.

Figure 8-9   Traverse an array with a count-controlled loop

Input Array Elements (8.3.4)

Your programs can collect elements for an array at runtime. The trick is remembering that in most programming languages, you need to declare the array and its size before you can add elements. If you know the size of the array, the algorithm goes like this:

```
declare int magic_array[5]
output "Enter five numbers for the array: "
for i (start: i = 0, test: i < 5)
    input magic_array[i]
```

You can see that with a known number of array elements, such as five, the loop counter can be set so that the loop makes five repetitions and collects five values for the array.

But what if you don't know how many elements will be entered at runtime? You can handle this situation by asking for the number of elements and storing that number in a variable, such as **max**. That variable will control the test condition in the loop.

```
output "How many numbers in the array? "
input max
declare int magic_array[max]
output "Enter " + max + " numbers for the array: "
for i (start: i = 0, test: i < max)
    input magic_array[i]
for i (start: i = 0, test: i < max)
    output magic_array[i]
```

The code in **Figure 8-10** contains the code for this algorithm, traces the input, and shows the output.

```cpp
#include <iostream>
#include <iomanip>
using namespace std;


int main()
{
  int i;
  int max = 0;


  cout << ("How many numbers in the array? ");
  cin >> max;
  int magic_array[max];
  cout << "Enter " << max << " numbers for the array:" << endl;
    for (i = 0; i < max; i++)
      cin >> magic_array[i];


  cout << endl << "Here are your numbers: ";
  for (i = 0; i < max; i++)
    cout << setw(3) << magic_array[i];
cout << endl;
}
```

OUTPUT:

How many numbers in the array? 3 [Enter]

Enter 3 numbers for the array:

55 [Enter]

22 [Enter]

9 [Enter]

Here are your numbers: 55 22   9

Figure 8-10   Runtime input to an array

Q In Figure 8-10, the variable **max** is the test condition for both the input and the output loops. Where does the value for **max** originate?

A The value for **max** is obtained by the **cin >> max** statement when the user responds to the prompt **"How many numbers in the array?"**

8.4 ARRAY OPERATIONS

Change an Array Element (8.4.1)

You can change the value of any array element using an assignment statement. Just remember to include the index value for the element you want to change. Take a look at the code in **Figure 8-11**. Which element is changed?

```
#include <iostream>
#include <iomanip>
using namespace std;

int main()
{
  int i;
  int magic_array[5] = {6, 7, 8, 9, 10};
  magic_array[3] = 22;
   for (i = 0; i < 5; i++)
      cout << setw(3) << magic_array[i];
}

OUTPUT:
  6   7   8 22 10
```

Figure 8-11   Change an array element

A statement such as **magic_array[3] = 22** changes the value of the fourth element in the array because the first element's index is [0]. The program changed the array value 9 to 22.

Find an Array Element (8.4.2)

Suppose you have a big array and want to know if it contains the value 22. You can loop through the array and compare each array item to the target value. You can also include an accumulator that records the number of times the target element appears in the array.

Trace through the following pseudocode to make sure you can identify the loop, the comparison operation, and the accumulator.

```
initialize int count = 0
initialize int magic_array[10] = {6, 22, 8, 22, 12, 6, 99, 20, 2, 4};
for i (start: i = 0, test i < 10)
   if magic_array[i] == 22 then
      count = count + 1
output "The array contains " + count + " instances of 22."
```

Q In the above pseudocode, which statement is the accumulator?

A The accumulator is **count = count + 1**.

The code for the search algorithm is in **Figure 8-12**.

```
#include <iostream>
using namespace std;


int main()
{
   int i;
   int count = 0;
   int magic_array[10] = {6, 22, 8, 22, 12, 6, 99, 20, 2, 4};
   for (i = 0; i < 10; i++)
   {
      if (magic_array[i] == 22)
         count = count + 1;
   }
   cout << "The array contains " << count << " instances of 22." << endl;
}

OUTPUT:
The array contains 2 instances of 22.
```

Figure 8-12   Find elements in an array

Sum Array Elements (8.4.3)

In the magic rectangle, the sum of each row is supposed to be the same. Let's use an accumulator named `total` to find the sum of the elements in the first row of the magic rectangle.

```cpp
#include <iostream>
using namespace std;


int main()
{
  int i;
  int total = 0;
  int magic_array[5] = {6, 7, 8, 9, 10};
  for (i = 0; i < 5; i++)
  {
    total =                      ;
  }
  cout << "The sum of the array: " << total << endl;
}


OUTPUT:
The sum of the array: 40
```

Figure 8-13 Sum array elements

Q The shaded box in **Figure 8-13** indicates that a part of the statement for the accumulator is missing. What is the missing expression?

A The missing expression is `total + magic_array[i]`.

8.5 TWO-DIMENSIONAL ARRAYS

Two-Dimensional Array Basics (8.5.1, 8.5.2, 8.5.3)

A magic rectangle is a two-dimensional array that has multiple rows and columns. Conceptually, two-dimensional arrays appear to be tables, grids, or matrices. Each cell in a two-dimensional array is referenced by two index values: one to indicate the row and one to indicate the column as shown in **Figure 8-14**.

	Column [0]	Column [1]	Column [2]	Column [3]	Column [4]
Row [0]	6 [0][0]	7 [0][1]	8 [0][2]	9 [0][3]	10 [0][4]
Row [1]	13 [1][0]	3 [1][1]	1 [1][2]	11 [1][3]	12 [1][4]
Row [2]	5 [2][0]	14 [2][1]	15 [2][2]	4 [2][3]	2 [2][4]

Figure 8-14   Two-dimensional array indexes

Q If the magic rectangle in Figure 8-14 is represented by an array called **magic_array[][]**, how would you refer to the cell that contains 11?

A The value 11 is in row 1, column 3. Using two indexes, the cell that holds 11 is **magic_array[1][3]**.

Although a two-dimensional array appears to be a grid of rows and columns, in memory these arrays are stored in a single row of memory locations. **Figure 8-15** can help you visualize the layout.

Address	0x40	0x44	0x48	0x4C	0x50	0x54	0x58	0x5C	0x60	0x64	0x68	0x6C	0x70	0x74	0x78
Elements	6	7	8	9	10	13	3	1	11	12	5	14	15	4	2

Row 0 of the array   Row 1 of the array   Row 2 of the array

Figure 8-15   Two-dimensional array memory allocation

Initialize a Two-Dimensional Array (8.5.4)

In pseudocode, you can declare a two-dimensional array using two indexes. The following pseudocode declares the magic rectangle with three rows and five columns.

```
declare int magic_array[3][5]
```

The pseudocode for initializing the magic rectangle requires each row of values to be enclosed in curly braces. Programmers like to align the data so it resembles a matrix.

```
initialize int magic_array[3][5] = {{6, 7, 8, 9, 10},
                                    {13, 3, 1, 11, 12},
                                    {5, 14, 15, 4, 2}}
```

Figure 8-16 provides details for coding two-dimensional arrays in your programming language.

Syntax to declare a two-dimensional array:

```
data_type array_name[rows][columns];
```

Example:

```
int magic_array[3][5];
```

Syntax to declare and initialize a two-dimensional array:

```
data_type array_name[rows][columns] = {{element, element, element}, {element,
element, element}};
```

Example:

```
int magic_array[3][5] = {{6, 7, 8, 9, 10},
                         {13, 3, 1, 11, 12},
                         {5, 14, 15, 4, 2}};
```

Figure 8-16 Declare and initialize a two-dimensional array

Output a Two-Dimensional Array (8.5.5, 8.5.6)

Traversing a two-dimensional array typically requires a nested loop. The outer loop controls the iteration through each row, while the inner loop controls the iterations through the columns. For `magic_array[][]`, the loop begins in row 0 to output the values in cells with these indexes:

[0][0] [0][1] [0][2] [0][3] [0][4]

Next, the loop outputs the values in row 1. The cells have these indexes:

[1][0] [1][1] [1][2] [1][3] [1][4]

And finally, in the last row:

[2][0] [2][1] [2][2] [2][3] [2][4]

Q In the following pseudocode, what is the test value for the outer loop i? For the inner loop j?

```
initialize int magic_array[3][5] = {{6, 7, 8, 9, 10},
                                     {13, 3, 1, 11, 12},
                                     {5, 14, 15, 4, 2}};
```

```
for i (start: i = 0, test: i < 3)

   for j (start: j = 0, test: j < 5)

      output magic_array[i][j]
```

A The outer loop's test value is `i < 3`. The test value for the inner loop is `j < 5`.

When coding array output, you might want to add some formatting parameters to align the output values. **Figure 8-17** provides some tips.

The `setw()` function from `<iomanip>` helps to arrange numbers in columns. The parameter `setw(4)` provides spacing for two-digit numbers.

```cpp
#include <iostream>

#include <iomanip>

using namespace std;


int main()
{
  int i = 0;

  int j = 0;

  int magic_array[3][5] = {{6, 7, 8, 9, 10},

                           {13, 3, 1, 11, 12},

                           {5, 14, 15, 4, 2}};

  for (i = 0; i < 3; i++)

  {

     for (j = 0; j < 5; j++)

     {

      cout << setw(4) << (magic_array[i][j]);

     }

      cout << endl;

  }
}
```

OUTPUT:
```
   6   7   8   9  10
  13   3   1  11  12
   5  14  15   4   2
```

Figure 8-17   Traverse a two-dimensional array

Sum Array Columns and Rows (8.5.7)

Each row in the magic rectangle is supposed to produce 40 as the sum of its elements. To confirm that is the case, you can write a program to sum each row. The algorithm requires a nested loop and an accumulator that is reset to zero for each row.

Q In the following pseudocode, can you identify the accumulator and the statement that resets it to zero for each row?

```
initialize int magic_array[3][5] = {{6, 7, 8, 9, 10},
                                     {13, 3, 1, 11, 12},
                                     {5, 14, 15, 4, 2}};
for i (start: i = 0, test: i < 3)
   row_sum = 0
   for j (start: j = 0, test: j < 5)
      row_sum = row_sum + magic_array[i][j]
      output magic_array[i][j]
   output "    " + row_sum
```

A The accumulator is **row_sum**. It is reset to 0 after the outer loop begins, but before the inner loop begins.

Now, what about printing the sum for each column? You can add a loop for that operation. The trick to getting the column sums is to reverse the indexes to [j][i] instead of [i][j]. Pay attention to the second nested loop in the following pseudocode:

```
initialize int magic_array[3][5] = {{6, 7, 8, 9, 10},
                                     {13, 3, 1, 11, 12},
                                     {5, 14, 15, 4, 2}};


for i (start: i = 0, test: i < 5)
   column_sum = 0
   for j (start: j = 0, test: j < 3)
      column_sum = column_sum + magic_array[j][i]


   output column_sum
```

After you understand the looping operations, the code for this algorithm is easy to grasp. In **Figure 8-18**, can you locate the loop that sums the row and the loop that sums the column?

```cpp
#include <iostream>
#include <iomanip>
using namespace std;


int main()
{
  int i = 0;
  int j = 0;
  int row_sum, column_sum;
  int magic_array[3][5] = {{6, 7, 8, 9, 10},
                           {13, 3, 1, 11, 12},
                           {5, 14, 15, 4, 2}};
  for (i = 0; i <3; i++)
  {
    row_sum = 0;
    for (j = 0; j < 5; j++)
    {
      row_sum = row_sum + magic_array[i][j];
      cout << setw(4) << (magic_array[i][j]);
    }
    cout<< "     " << row_sum;
    cout << endl;
  }
  cout << endl;

  for (i = 0; i < 5; i++)
  {
    column_sum = 0;
    for(j = 0; j < 3; j++)
```

Figure 8-18 Sum the rows and columns in a two-dimensional array (*Continued*)

```
      {
          column_sum = column_sum + magic_array[j][i];
      }
          cout << setw(4) << column_sum;
  }
  cout << endl;
}
```

OUTPUT:

```
  6   7   8   9  10      40
 13   3   1  11  12      40
  5  14  15   4   2      40

 24  24  24  24  24
```

Figure 8-18   Sum the rows and columns in a two-dimensional array

In addition to summing rows and columns, you can traverse two-dimensional arrays to find elements, change elements, and perform other operations. When you design programs that handle two-dimensional arrays, use decomposition techniques to break down the algorithm into manageable chunks. For example, you can work out the algorithm for a one-dimensional array first, and then adapt it for a two-dimensional array.

SUMMARY

- An array is a data structure that stores a collection of elements that all have the same data type. Arrays are also classified as composite data types because they are constructed from primitive data types, such as integers or characters.
- Arrays are homogeneous, ordered, and finite. They have a variety of use cases for working with collections of data.
- Programmers typically work with one-dimensional and two-dimensional arrays. A one-dimensional array is linear. A two-dimensional array has rows and columns that form a matrix.
- Both one-dimensional and two-dimensional arrays are stored in consecutive memory addresses. In program code, each element of an array is identified by an index value enclosed in brackets.
- One-dimensional array elements have one index. Two-dimensional array elements have a row index and a column index. Index errors in program code are common but are easy to identify and correct.

- Accessing each array element in sequence is called traversing an array. Loops are typically used to traverse arrays. A single loop can traverse a one-dimensional array. A nested loop is required to traverse a two-dimensional array.
- Common array operations include outputting elements, changing elements, searching for elements, inputting elements at runtime, and summing elements.

Key Terms

array	index error	two-dimensional array
array index	one-dimensional array	
homogeneous	traversing an array	

MODULE 9

FUNCTIONS

LEARNING OBJECTIVES:

9.1 FUNCTION BASICS

9.1.1 Differentiate between built-in functions, imported functions, and programmer-defined functions.

9.1.2 Associate functions with modular programming.

9.1.3 State the purpose of a function call.

9.1.4 Trace the flow of a program that includes programmer-defined functions.

9.1.5 State the advantages of programmer-defined functions.

9.1.6 Provide an example of a programmer-defined function.

9.2 VOID FUNCTIONS

9.2.1 Describe the key characteristics of a void function.

9.2.2 Compare the naming conventions for functions with those of variables.

9.2.3 Identify components in the declaration and body of a void function.

9.2.4 Identify functions and function calls in source code.

9.2.5 Identify functions and function calls in pseudocode.

9.3 FUNCTIONS WITH PARAMETERS

9.3.1 Explain the purpose of function parameters in a function declaration.

9.3.2 Explain the use of typed parameters.

9.3.3 Identify the arguments in a function call.

9.3.4 Differentiate arguments from parameters.

9.3.5 Identify the correspondence between the arguments in a function call and the parameters declared in a function declaration.

9.3.6 Trace data as it is handed off from a function call to a function.

9.4 RETURN VALUES

9.4.1 State the purpose of a function's return value.

9.4.2 Compose an assignment statement that collects a return value in a variable.

9.4.3 Trace the logic of a program that passes values to a function and returns a value to the main program.

9.4.4 Explain the purpose of declaring a function's return type.

9.4.5 Define the term "function signature" and identify examples.

9.5 SCOPE

9.5.1 Explain the concept of scope as it relates to variables in functions.

9.5.2 Explain the difference between global and local variables.

9.5.3 Declare global and local variables.

9.5.4 Identify global and local variables in code and state best practices for their use.

9.5.5 Explain the meaning of "pass by value" in the context of functions.

9.5.6 Explain the meaning of "pass by reference" in the context of functions.

9.5.7 Explain the purpose of namespaces.

9.1 FUNCTION BASICS

Function Classifications (9.1.1)

Trivia night is a popular event at pizzerias (**Figure 9-1**), and players can brush up ahead of time with online games. Trivia's question-and-answer format provides a great use case for incorporating functions into your programs.

Jog.cz/Shutterstock.com

Figure 9-1   Pizza-night trivia

A function is a named block of program code that performs a specific task. Functions can be classified into three categories:

- ***Built-in functions*** are provided by a programming language, without the need to import modules, libraries, packages, or other components. Most programming languages include basic math functions, such as **abs()** for finding the absolute value of a number.
- ***Imported functions*** are packaged in libraries and modules. They are distributed with a programming environment but need to be explicitly added to a program using a statement, such as **include** or **import**. A random number generator is an example of an imported function that you can include in your programs.
- ***Programmer-defined functions*** are created by you, the programmer, to perform customized operations within a program. You can create these functions to modularize your programs and perform repetitive tasks.

Programmer-Defined Functions (9.1.2)

In this module, the focus is on programmer-defined functions that you can create to perform a specific task, routine, operation, or process accessed by your main program. Suppose you're creating a Trivia program. For each question, there is the user's answer and the correct answer. You could use a linear algorithm and check the answer after each question, like this:

```
output "Lake Chapala is the largest freshwater lake in which country? "

input answer

if answer == "Mexico" then

    output "Correct!"

    output "You earn 1 point."

    score = score + 1
```

```
else

    output "That is not correct."


output "Mac Gargan is the alter ego of what Spider-Man villain? "
input answer
if answer == "Scorpion" then

    output "Correct!"

    output "You earn 1 point."

    score = score + 1
else

    output "That is not correct."
```

Notice that with the exception of the actual answers, "Mexico" and "Scorpion," the if-else logic to check the answers is similar for each question. Eliminating that repetition is exactly where programmer-defined functions shine.

Flow of Execution (9.1.3, 9.1.4)

You can create a single function that is activated for every question to check the answer. The function can be triggered by a **function call** from multiple locations in a program. The flow of execution jumps to the function, performs the statements it contains, and then returns to the previous execution path. **Figure 9-2** helps you visualize how functions affect the flow of program execution.

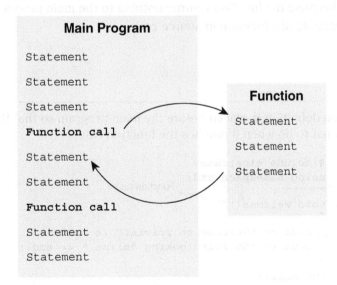

Figure 9-2   Function calls transfer execution to the specified function; flow returns to the previous execution path when the function is completed

Function Advantages (9.1.5, 9.1.6)

The Trivia program is one use case for programmer-defined functions. Functions help you do the following:

- Modularize your code by grouping statements that perform each task.
- Simplify modifications because they are more likely to affect only the code in a function rather than statements scattered throughout the program.

- Reduce the amount of coding by creating blocks of code that can be reused multiple times in a program.
- Encapsulate code to simplify debugging.

Let's take a closer look at functions, starting with a simple example before working up to a more robust version that checks answers and scores Trivia questions.

9.2 VOID FUNCTIONS

Void Function Basics (9.2.1, 9.2.2, 9.2.3, 9.2.4)

A **void function** is probably the simplest type of function because it performs a task, such as displaying a message or sum, without returning any values to the main program. For example, you could create a void function for a Trivia program that outputs a Welcome! message and rules at the start of the game.

```
function void welcome()

    display "Welcome to Trivia!"

    display "No fair looking online."
```

This function, like all functions, begins with a one-line **function declaration** (or *function header*) that specifies its name and other essential descriptors. The **function name** ends with () parentheses and uses the same naming conventions as a variable. The **function body** is a block of statements that defines what the function does.

The two statements in the body of the **welcome()** function directly output messages. The messages are not returned to the main program. Because the function returns nothing to the main program, the function is void. **Figure 9-3** illustrates the components of a function in source code.

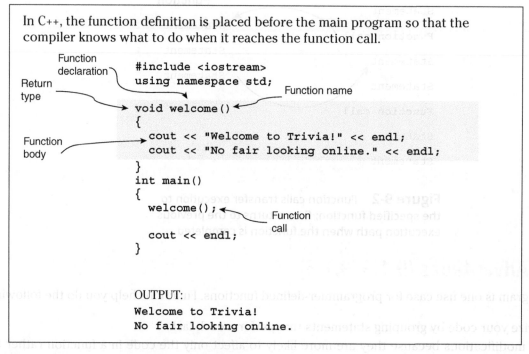

In C++, the function definition is placed before the main program so that the compiler knows what to do when it reaches the function call.

```
                        #include <iostream>
Function                using namespace std;
declaration
Return                                              Function name
type                    void welcome()
                        {
Function                    cout << "Welcome to Trivia!" << endl;
body                        cout << "No fair looking online." << endl;
                        }
                        int main()
                        {
                            welcome();
                                              Function
                                              call
                            cout << endl;
                        }


                        OUTPUT:
                        Welcome to Trivia!
                        No fair looking online.
```

Figure 9-3   Components of a function

Function Pseudocode (9.2.5)

When reading pseudocode for functions, you may see the following conventions:

- The keyword `function` begins the function declaration.
- The body of the function is indented.
- The keyword `call` indicates a function call.
- The function definition is placed before the main program, regardless of its position required by the programming language compiler or interpreter.

Here's the pseudocode that calls the `correct()` function for each correct answer in a Trivia game. Make sure that you can identify the three lines of function code and the two function calls.

```
function correct()

    display "Correct!"

    display "You earn 1 point."


output "Lake Chapala is the largest freshwater lake in which country? "

input answer

if answer == "Mexico" then

    call correct()

    score = score + 1

else

    output "That is not correct."


output "Mac Gargan is the alter ego of what Spider-Man villain? "

input answer

if answer == "Scorpion" then

    call correct()

    score = score + 1

else

    output "That is not correct."
```

Q By using the `correct()` function, how much coding is eliminated from the original Trivia program?

A For each question, the following two lines are reduced to simply `call correct()`.

```
    output "Correct!"

    output "You earn 1 point."
```

9.3 FUNCTIONS WITH PARAMETERS

Function Parameters (9.3.1, 9.3.2)

What if you want to create a function that outputs "Correct!" when the answer is correct, but "Not correct" when the answer is wrong? To output the appropriate message, the function needs to know if the answer was right or wrong. You can send data to a function. For example, you can send True to the function if the answer is correct but send False if the answer is wrong.

A function can use the data it receives to perform calculations, manipulate strings, control loops, output messages, and make decisions. A function with *parameters* uses data sent to the function as *arguments*. Let's explore the relationship between parameters and arguments.

Function parameters specify a template for data that a function can accept. Those parameters are listed as variables inside the parentheses at the end of the function name. When you specify the data type of a parameter, it is said to be a typed parameter. **Figure 9-4** shows how to create a function with one parameter that is used to determine whether to output "Correct!" or "Not correct."

The parameter for the `correct()` function is a Boolean variable named `answer_is_correct`. Be sure to include the data type for each parameter. For example, if you have multiple Boolean parameters, such as x and y, use a format such as `my_function(bool x, bool y)`.

Because `answer_is_correct` is a Boolean variable, it can have the value `true` or `false`. Trace the program so you understand how the if-then block uses the value of `answer_is_correct` to output the correct message.

```
void correct(bool answer_is_correct)          ──── Function parameter
{
  if (answer_is_correct)
  {
    cout << "Correct!" << endl;
    cout << "You earn 1 point." << endl;
  }
  else
    cout << "Not correct." << endl;
}
```

Figure 9-4 Function parameters

Function Arguments (9.3.3, 9.3.4)

How does a function get the value for a parameter? It receives the value from a function argument in the function call. A function argument is data that is *passed* to a function. For example, you could pass a Boolean value to the `correct()` function. Look for the function call and its argument in **Figure 9-5**.

```
void correct(bool answer_is_correct)
{
  if (answer_is_correct)
  {
    cout << "Correct!" << endl;
    cout << "Each correct answer is worth 1 point." << endl;
  }
  else
    cout << "Not correct." << endl;
}
int main()
{
  correct(false);
}
```

The function declaration contains a Boolean parameter called **answer_is_correct** that will receive false from the function call.

The function call contains an argument in parentheses. In C++ Boolean arguments must be lowercase.

Figure 9-5   Function arguments

Q What is the output of the program in Figure 9-5?

A The output is **"Not correct."**

The argument in the function call to **correct()** contains a Boolean value, which is passed to the variable **answer_is_correct. Figure 9-6** can help you visualize this handoff.

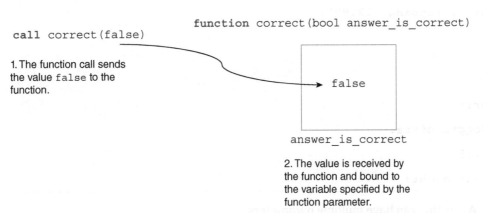

call correct(false)

function correct(bool answer_is_correct)

1. The function call sends the value false to the function.

false

answer_is_correct

2. The value is received by the function and bound to the variable specified by the function parameter.

Figure 9-6   The handoff copies the argument from the function call to the variable specified in the function declaration

The Handoff (9.3.5, 9.3.6)

The handoff between arguments and parameters is a powerful programming tool. Check out the function in **Figure 9-7** with its collection of parameters. Note that the function call can pass a variable, such as `topping`, as well as literals, such as 12 and 12.99.

When specifying the parameters for a function, make sure to include the data type for each one.

```cpp
#include <iostream>
using namespace std;


void receipt(int x, string y, float z)
{
  cout << "Your order:" << endl;
  cout << x << "-inch " << y << " pizza." << endl;
  cout << "Total $" << z << endl;
  cout << "Enjoy Trivia night!" << endl;
}


int main()
{
  string topping = "Veggie";
  receipt(12, topping, 12.99);
}


OUTPUT:
Your order:
12-inch Veggie pizza.
Total $12.99
Enjoy Trivia night!
```

Figure 9-7   A function can have multiple parameters

Q In the program shown in Figure 9-7, which function argument is passed to the **y** function parameter?

A The argument **topping** is passed. Because the variable **topping** contains the string "Veggie," that string is passed to the **y** function parameter and is printed on the receipt.

9.4 RETURN VALUES

Return Values (9.4.1, 9.4.2, 9.4.3)

In addition to passing data to a function, you can also return data from a function using a **return** statement at the end of a function. This data, called a return value, can be used for calculations or other operations in the main program.

Let's enhance the Trivia program so that the function assesses the user's answer to determine if it is correct. The function outputs "Correct!" and sends a 1 value back to the main program if the answer is correct. If the answer is not correct, the program outputs "That is not correct." and sends a 0 value back to the main program. The main program uses the return value to track the player's total score.

Trace through the following pseudocode to make sure you understand the algorithm.

```
function check_answer(guess, correct)

  if guess is correct then

      output "Correct!"

      return 1

  else

      output "That is not correct."

      return 0


output "Lake Chapala is the largest"

output "freshwater lake in which country? "

input answer

points = call check_answer(answer, "Mexico")

score = score + points
```

A lot is going on with this algorithm. Let's take it step by step.

1. Suppose that the user incorrectly answers "Brazil" to the first Trivia question. "Brazil" is stored in the variable **answer**.

2. The statement **points = call check_answer(answer, "Mexico")** calls the **check_answer()** function.

3. The function call passes two arguments to the function: the contents of **answer**—"Brazil"—and the literal, "Mexico."

4. The function has two parameters: **guess** and **correct**. "Brazil" is passed to **guess**. "Mexico" is passed to **correct**.

5. "Brazil" does not equal "Mexico" so the function returns 0 to the main program.

6. The 0 is stored in **points**. Why? The statement **points = call check_answer(answer, "Mexico")** puts the return value from the function into the variable called **points**.

7. In the main program, 0 is added to the score.

The concept embodied in the statement `points = call check_answer(answer, "Mexico")` gets to the core advantage of functions. You can create a variable and use it to store the result of the operations encapsulated in a function. **Figure 9-8** details the code for two Trivia questions.

```cpp
#include <iostream>
#include <string>
using namespace std;

int check_answer(string guess, string correct)
{
  if (guess == correct)
  {
    cout << "Correct!" << endl;
    return 1;
  }
  else
  {
    cout << "That is not correct." << endl << endl;
    return 0;
  }
}
int main() {
  string answer;
  int points = 0;
  int score = 0;
  cout << "Lake Chapala is the largest" << endl;
  cout << "freshwater lake in which country? ";
  cin >> answer;
  points = check_answer(answer, "Mexico");
  score = score + points;
  cout << endl;
```

Figure 9-8 Trivia code (*Continued*)

```
    cout << "Mac Gargan is the alter ego of" << endl;

    cout << "what Spider-Man villain? ";

    cin >> answer;

    points = check_answer (answer, "Scorpion");

    score = score + points;


    cout << "Your score: " << score << endl;
}
```

OUTPUT:

```
Lake Chapala is the largest
freshwater lake in which country? Mexico [Enter]
Correct!


Mac Gargan is the alter ego of
what Spider-Man villain? Joker [Enter]
That is not correct.


Your score: 1
```

Figure 9-8   Trivia code

Q To add another question to the Trivia program, you can copy and paste the four lines of code for one of the current questions. What would you have to change in the pasted text?

A You would just have to change the text of the question and the correct answer.

Return Type (9.4.4)

The Trivia program returns integer data to the main program. You might also create functions that return character, string, floating-point, or Boolean data. The **return type** corresponds to the data type that a function returns to the main program. **Figure 9-9** provides information about return types.

Syntax:

```
return_type function_name(parameter_type parameter)
```

Examples:

```
int check_answer(int guess, int correct)


float receipt(int pizza_size, bool trivia_winner)


bool check_id(int age)


string message(int score)
```

Rules and best practices:

- The return type does not have to match the parameter data types.
- The return type must match the data type for the data you plan to send back to the main program.
- Every non-void function should end with a **return** statement.
- The **return** statement for the **main()** function is optional. If you do not include one, the C++ compiler assumes return 0.

Figure 9-9   Specifying the function return type

The **return** statement at the end of a function passes data back to the main program. The data can be a literal, such as "Mushrooms" or 12.99, or it can be represented by a variable, such as **topping**. **Figure 9-10** illustrates how a function can pass a string using a variable.

```
#include <iostream>
#include<string>
using namespace std;                    The pizza() function
                                        has a string return type.
string pizza()
{
  string x = "Mushrooms";               The string "Mushrooms"
  return x;                             is assigned to a variable
}                                       called x.

                                        The string in x is returned
int main()                             to the main program.
{
  string topping = pizza();             The return value is
  cout << topping << endl;             assigned to a variable
}                                       called topping.

OUTPUT:

Mushrooms
```

Rules and best practices:
- You can return only one item from a function.
- Make sure the return type in the function declaration matches the type for the returned data.
- You can return literals such as "Cheese" or 1.
- You can also return the values stored in variables, such as **x**.

Figure 9-10 Return statements

Function Signature (9.4.5)

The return type is part of the **function signature** that uniquely defines a function for the compiler or interpreter. The components of a function signature may include the following:

- The function name
- The function parameters
- The function return type

In some programming languages, it is possible to have two functions with the same name, as long as they have different parameters. For example, you could have one function with a signature such as **check_answer(guess, correct)** and another function with a signature **check_answer(validate)**.

Although it is possible to have two functions with the same name, in practice you'll find it less confusing to use unique names for your functions.

9.5 SCOPE

Scope Basics (9.5.1, 9.5.2, 9.5.3, 9.5.4)

Here's a puzzler. Suppose you have a variable called **my_number** used as the argument in a call such as **experiment(my_number)**. The function declaration **experiment(my_number)** also uses **my_number** as a parameter. If the function is designed to add 1 to **my_number**, does the value in the original variable change?

Q Trace through the following pseudocode. What do you think is the output?

```
function experiment(my_number)

    output "Value passed to function : " + my_number

    my_number = my_number + 1

    output "Value after adding 1: " + my_number

    return my_number


my_number = 5

call experiment(my_number)

output "Value after returning to main program: " + my_number
```

A The output is:

```
Value passed to function: 5

Value after adding 1: 6

Value after returning to main program: 5
```

Are you surprised that the variable **my_number** in the main program was not changed to 6? This fascinating outcome is related to scope.

In the context of programming, **scope** refers to the visibility of program components, such as variables, to other parts of the program. In the **experiment()** function, the scope of the variable **my_number** was visible only within the function and was not accessible to other parts of the program.

In general, variables and other components that are limited to a specific part of a program are referred to as having a local scope. The variable called **my_number** in the **experiment()** function is a **local variable**.

In contrast, a **global variable** is accessible to an entire program. How do you know which variables are local and which are global? **Figure 9-11** answers this question.

The following program contains a global variable **g_earth**, a local variable called **village** in the function, and a local variable called **town** in the **main()** program. Both **g_earth** and **town** can be accessed by the **main()** program. The local variable **village** that is defined in the function cannot be accessed by the **main()** program and produces an error.

```
#include <iostream>

using namespace std;


int g_earth = 100;


void location()
```

Figure 9-11   Global and local variables (*Continued*)

```
{
  int village = 2;
  cout << village << endl;
  cout << g_earth << endl;
}


int main()
{
  int town = 50;
  cout << g_earth << endl;
  cout << village << endl;
  cout << town << endl;
}
```

OUTPUT:

```
main.cpp:16:11: error: use of undeclared identifier
      'village'
  cout << village << endl;
          ^
1 error generated.
compiler exit status 1
```

Rules and best practices:

- Global variables are defined at the beginning of a program, before functions and before the **main()** program code.
- Be sure to specify the data type for the global variable.
- Some programmers prefix global variables with g or g_ to annotate that they are global.
- Variables declared within a function are automatically classified as local. No additional coding is necessary.
- C++ best practices avoid the use of global variables because they disrupt modularization, making programs more difficult to modify and debug.

Figure 9-11   Global and local variables

It is possible to have two variables with the same name as long as they have different scopes. One variable could be global, but the other one is local. Or the two variables could be declared in different functions. With two variables of the same name, how do you sort out which variable has precedence? Let's find out.

Pass by Value (9.5.5)

Okay, so you use **my_number** in the main program and in a function. Because these variables have a different scope, they are stored in different memory locations. That is why in the following pseudocode, adding 1 to **my_number** in the **experiment()** function has no effect on the variable **my_number** in the main program.

```
function experiment(my_number)

    output "Value passed to function : " + my_number

    my_number = my_number + 1

    output "Value after adding 1: " + my_number

    return my_number


my_number = 5

call experiment(my_number)

output "Value after returning to main program: " + my_number
```

OUTPUT:

Value passed to function: 5

Value after adding 1: 6

Value after returning to main program: 5

The arguments passed to a function are copies of the data. The term **pass by value** refers to a function call that passes a copy of an argument to a function. The original variable retains its data. The variable in a function gets a copy of the data. Even if the main program variable and the function variable have the same name, any changes to the copy of the data only affect the variable in the function.

Figure 9-12 reinforces the idea that changing the contents of a local variable in a function does not change the contents of a variable of the same name, but with a different scope.

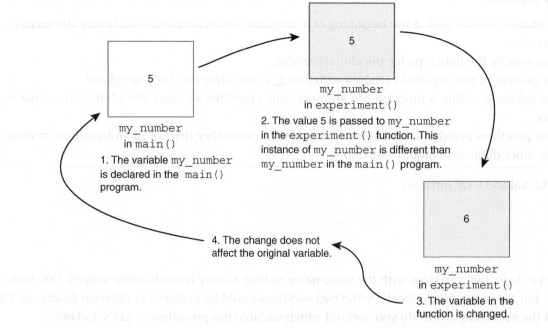

Figure 9-12   Pass by value sends a copy of data to a function

If you want to change the value of **my_number** in the main program, change the calling statement to include an assignment:

```
my_number = experiment(my_number)
```

The assignment statement explicitly changes the value of the variable **my_number** in the main program. To avoid confusion about the variables in the main program and the variables in a function, it is best to avoid using the same identifiers for arguments and parameters.

Pass by Reference (9.5.6)

In some programming languages, it is possible to create functions that directly modify a variable that is not local. These languages use a reference variable as an alias for the actual variable and its location in memory. The term pass by reference refers to a function call that uses a reference variable as a function parameter. **Figure 9-13** provides notes on passing by reference.

Reference variables begin with an ampersand symbol (&). In the following source code, look for the **&my_number** parameter in the function signature. Then notice that the last output value is 6, which means that changing **my_number** in the function changed the value in the memory location used for **my_number** in the main program.

```
#include <iostream>
using namespace std;


void experiment(int &my_number)
{
  cout << "Value passed to function: " << my_number << endl;
  my_number = my_number + 1;
  cout << "Value after adding 1: " << my_number << endl;
}


int main()
{
  int my_number = 5;
  experiment(my_number);
  cout << "Value after returning to main: " << my_number << endl;
}


OUTPUT:
Value passed to function: 5
Value after adding 1: 6
Value after returning to main: 6
```

Figure 9-13   Pass by reference

Pass by reference saves memory space because a copy of the variable is not needed. Some computational time is also saved. In modern computers loaded with memory and equipped with fast processors, those savings are small compared to the potential for accidentally changing the value of a variable by calling a function. Pass by reference should be reserved for special situations in programs with clearly constrained algorithms.

Namespaces (9.5.7)

Namespaces provide a way to manage the scope of variables. A **namespace** is essentially a named container that holds identifiers, such as variables, to avoid collisions with other identifiers that have the same name.

A simple way to explain namespaces is with shoe sizes. A size 9 is not the same for men's shoes as for women's shoes. To distinguish between the two, shoe manufacturers specify "Men's 9" or "Women's 9." In a similar way, namespaces serve to distinguish variables that might otherwise appear to be the same.

Namespaces can be implicit or explicit.

- **Implicit namespaces.** An implicit namespace is handled by your programming language. For example, a function defines a namespace for the variables it contains. The namespace for the main program might contain a variable called **my_number**, and the namespace for the **experiment()** function might contain a different variable also called **my_number**.
- **Explicit namespaces.** Programmers create explicit namespaces by declaring them. Once a namespace is declared, variables can be assigned to it. The combination of the namespace and the variable name provide the variable with a unique identifier, as shown in **Figure 9-14**.

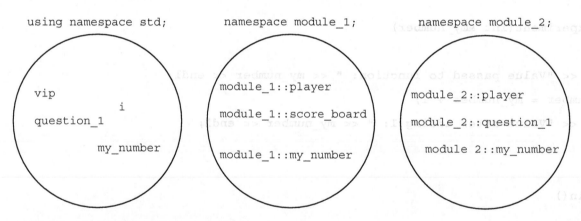

Rules and best practices:
- To declare a namespace, begin with the keyword `namespace`.
- End the `namespace` statement with a semicolon.
- Preface a namespace variable with the namespace and two colons as in `module_1::player`.
- To use the standard namespace, include `using namespace std;` at the beginning of the program.
- When using the standard namespace, variables do not need a namespace prefix.

Figure 9-14   Namespaces

Namespaces become especially important for large programs and for code that is produced by programming teams. On these large projects, namespaces help to ensure that variables and other identifiers operate within their intended scope and are not muddled with identifiers of the same name used in other parts of a program.

SUMMARY

- A function is a named block of program code that performs a specific task.
- Built-in functions are always available, without the need to import modules, libraries, packages, or other components.
- Imported functions are packaged in libraries and modules. They are typically distributed with a programming environment but need to be explicitly added to a program using a statement, such as `include` or `import`.
- Programmer-defined functions are created by you, the programmer, to perform customized operations within a program.
- Functions help programmers modularize code by grouping statements that perform a specific task.
- Functions reduce coding overhead by creating blocks of code that can be reused multiple times in a program.
- Functions help programmers debug efficiently because code is encapsulated in discrete groups.
- A function declaration can include the function name, return type, parameters, and parameter types.
- The body of a function contains the statements that define what the function does and may also include a `return` statement.
- Functions can be triggered by a function call from multiple locations in a program. A function call may include function arguments that are passed to the parameters of a function.
- Functions can send data back to the calling module by means of a `return` statement.
- Variables in a function have a different scope from the variables in the main program module or other functions. The scope of variables declared in a function have a local scope, making them visible only within the function. Variables with a global scope are visible throughout the entire program.
- In the context of functions, pass by value refers to a function call that passes a copy of an argument to a function.
- Pass by reference refers to a function call that passes a pointer to the variable that holds the argument.
- A namespace is a named container that holds the names of identifiers to prevent collisions with identifiers with the same name.

Key Terms

function argument	function signature	reference variable
function body	global variable	return type
function call	local variable	return value
function declaration	namespace	scope
function name	pass by reference	typed parameter
Function parameters	pass by value	void function

RECURSION

LEARNING OBJECTIVES:

10.1 KEY COMPONENTS OF RECURSION

10.1.1 Define recursion as a problem-solving approach.

10.1.2 Describe the purpose of recursion.

10.1.3 Explain the components of a recursive function.

10.1.4 List advantages and disadvantages of recursion.

10.2 USING RECURSION TO SOLVE COMPLEX PROBLEMS

10.2.1 Explain the application of recursion.

10.2.2 Differentiate recursive algorithms from algorithms that use repetition control structures.

10.2.3 Define the "divide and conquer" approach to problem solving.

10.2.4 Analyze how to use a base case and a recursive case to implement recursion into an iterative programming solution.

10.2.5 Construct a procedural program using recursion (pseudocode).

10.3 MANAGING MEMORY DURING RECURSION

10.3.1 Explain memory management and its importance with recursion.

10.3.2 Explain the use of a stack during recursion.

10.3.3 Explain tail-recursive functions.

10.1 KEY COMPONENTS OF RECURSION

The Recursive Mindset (10.1.1, 10.1.2)

Computer science, in general, is telling computers to solve problems. Similar to when you solve a problem, the computer can guess an answer randomly or it can try to be smarter about it. Suppose you are playing a guessing game where your friend is thinking of a number between 1 and 100, as in **Figure 10-1**. You say "27" as your first guess, and your friend responds, "No, my number is higher than that." You now know that the number must be between 27 and 100. How does your approach change? You use the response from your friend as a way to eliminate possibilities and arrive at the correct answer more quickly than randomly guessing.

The most efficient way to play this game is to start at 50. Guessing a number halfway between the smallest and largest numbers means that if you do not guess the correct answer, you still eliminate half of the options. If your friend responds "higher" to 50, you know the smallest possible value is 50. Your next guess

Dean Drobot/Shutterstock.com; majcot/Shutterstock.com

Figure 10-1   Numbers guessing game

is halfway between 50 and 100: 75. If your friend responds "lower," you have a new upper bound to the range of possible answers. You now know the number is between 50 and 75. Each time you guess, you update the range of possible numbers and perform the same task as when 1 and 100 were the boundaries. Your strategy is as follows:

1. Guess a number halfway between the smallest and largest number.
2. If told "higher," update the smallest number to this guess.
3. If told "lower," update the largest number to this guess.
4. Repeat steps 1–3 until you are correct.

When you use this strategy in the number guessing game, you are breaking down a large problem into smaller similar problems. Each piece can then be broken down until the problem is so small it is easily solved. Eventually, the number guessing game eliminates all except one number to guess. **Figure 10-2** shows an example of the game, starting with 1 and 10 as the smallest and largest numbers.

Recursion is the problem-solving approach that divides large problems into smaller, identical problems. The same steps are applied to each smaller version of the problem, although with different restrictions, such as the upper and lower boundaries for the number game.

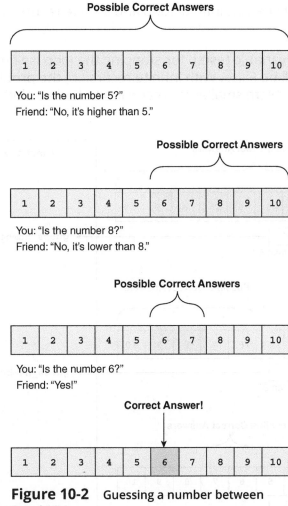

Figure 10-2 Guessing a number between 1 and 10

Recursion Basics (10.1.3)

The recursive mindset uses functions to solve problems. Following are brief reminders about function facts:

- Functions are named blocks of code that perform a specific task.
- Functions can have information passed to them as parameters.
- Functions can return information as return values, which can be used for calculations and other operations.
- Functions can be "called" to execute the lines of code inside the function.
- Functions can call other functions.

Take a moment to review that last point. Functions are like any other block of code. Anything you can do in one block of code, you can do in another. Therefore, functions can call other functions. This is one of the keys to elegant code design. A function can call any function in the scope of the code, including itself.

A **recursive function** calls itself at least once. At each function call, recursive functions use modified parameters to shrink the size of the problem. For the guessing game, the modified parameters are the lower and upper boundaries of the number range. If you don't modify the parameters for the recursive function, the recursive function does not stop; this is called **infinite recursion**.

Q What is the difference between an infinite loop and infinite recursion?

A With an infinite loop, the variable tested for stopping the loop isn't modified so that the conditional statement will be False. With infinite recursion, the problem size is never reduced. You need to make the problem smaller for recursion to find a solution.

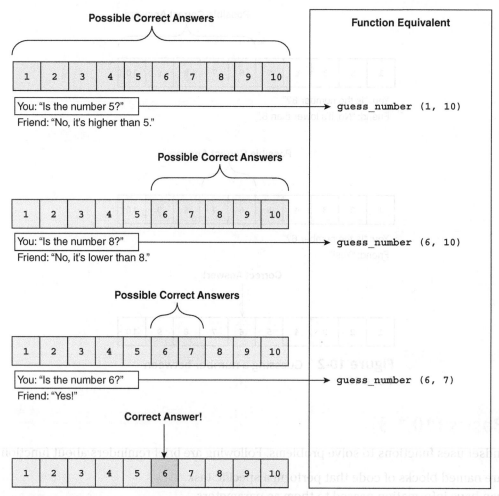

Figure 10-3   Guessing game using function calls

Figure 10-3 shows how Figure 10-2 looks using function calls.

In the number game, you stop guessing when you correctly guess the number. This is an example of a **base case**, a condition where you should stop trying to solve the problem. One type of base case signals an early exit from the function. If you guess the right number in the guessing game, you can stop without updating the number range.

A base case can also represent a problem small enough to solve quickly. For example, if you run out of numbers to guess, you know that your friend made a mistake in her answers, and that you need to tell her so. Recursive functions can have more than one base case, such as one to exit the function early and another to solve the program when it is small enough.

As with normal functions, a recursive function can return a value. If the recursive function does not need to return information, then recursion is easy. A simple program to print the numbers from 1 to 10 using recursion could be designed as follows:

```
function display_numbers(n)
    if n > 10
        return
    else
        display n
        call function display_numbers(n + 1)
```

Look over this program line by line to see how it works. The **function** statement in the first line indicates you are creating a function with the name **display_numbers**. Including the n in parentheses shows this function accepts one parameter. The if-else block sets the condition that if the parameter **n** is greater than 10, the function returns without doing anything. Otherwise, the function displays the value stored in **n** and calls itself, this time with the value increased by 1.

If the recursive function needs to return a value, it passes information in a chain. Think of a game of telephone, where people stand in a line and can only talk to two people: the person to their right and the person to their left. If the last person on the right has information to return to the first person, they have to tell the person to their left, who has to tell the person to *their* left, and so on until the information reaches the first person at the start of the line. (The good news is that computers don't mix up the information along the way, as usually happens when playing telephone.) For example, calculating the sum of numbers from 10 to 1 could be designed as follows:

```
function add_numbers(n)
    if n < 1
        return 0
    else
        initialize sum = n + call function add_numbers(n - 1)
        return sum
```

This function still has only one parameter, but now expects a returned value.

Q What is the returned value if **n** is 0?

A If **n** is 0, the base case of **n** < 1 is met, so 0 is returned.

Q What is the returned value if **n** is 1?

A If **n** is 1, the function makes one recursive call, then adds 1 to the result. This recursive call passes 0 to **add_numbers**, which returns 0. The returned value is 1.

The returned value is all values between 1 and **n** added together. Here, each function asks a recursive call for its result, and then adds the current value of **n** to the returned value and stores it in **sum**.

Recursion can represent a single line of problem solving, as in the example of the number guessing game. This type of recursive function calls itself once and is called **linear recursion**. Linear recursion is the easiest to program; most of the examples in this module are of linear recursion. Other versions of recursion known as **branching recursion** do not limit themselves to one recursive call. **Figures 10-4** and **10-5** show how these two flows of recursion work.

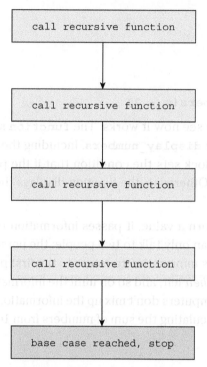

Figure 10-4   Linear recursive function calls

With the linear recursion shown in Figure 10-4, each time the code visits a function, the function calls itself at most once or stops when it reaches a base case.

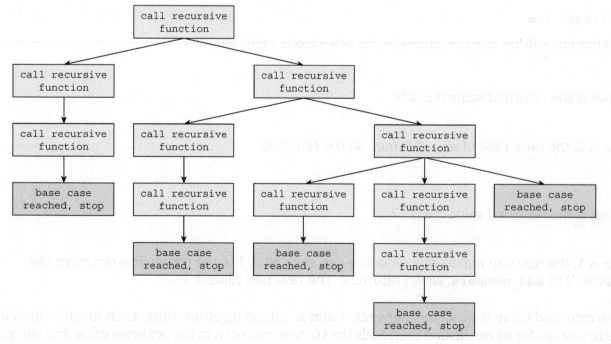

Figure 10-5   Branching recursive function calls

With the branching recursion shown in Figure 10-5, each time the code visits a function, the function calls itself one or more times, or stops when it reaches a base case.

When to Use Recursion (10.1.4)

Ask yourself the following key questions when deciding whether to use recursion to solve a problem:

- Can this problem be broken down into smaller problems?
- Are the smaller problems identical to the larger problems?
- Is there a way to divide the problem into smaller subproblems that are easy to solve?

While linear recursion and loops can be similar, keep a mental note of when it is easier to design a program with one or the other. The two are like a hammer and a saw. Technically, you could use a hammer to cut a piece of wood in half, but it would be easier if you used the appropriate tool.

Q When should you use loops? When should you use recursion?

A Use loops when you need to do the same thing without changing the situation. Use recursion when you need to reduce the problem to solve it.

Think of recursion as similar to delegating tasks. How can you delegate smaller problems to other people? How can you put the pieces back together after receiving the results? What should the smallest task be, at which point you cannot delegate anymore?

10.2 USING RECURSION TO SOLVE COMPLEX PROBLEMS

Designing Recursive Structures (10.2.1, 10.2.2, 10.2.3)

Use the following checklist when writing a recursive function:

1. Check for the base case.
2. Modify the parameters.
3. Invoke the function recursively.
4. Return the result to the calling function if appropriate.

Checking for a base case is the same as asking yourself "when should I stop?" To modify the parameters, ask "how is the problem changing through the recursive calls?" Finally, if a value is returned, you can do something with it. This could be as simple as returning the information unchanged to the calling function or calculating a new value to return.

The number guessing game uses linear recursion. **Figure 10-6** shows a working program for the game.

```cpp
#include <iostream>
using namespace std;


int guess_number(int low, int high)
{
    // Double slashes mean the line is a comment and not code!
    // Base case to detect cheating
    if (low > high)

        return -1;


    int middle = (low + high) / 2;

    char hint;


    cout << "Is your number " << middle << "?" << endl;

    cin >> hint;


    // Base case for correctly guessing the number
    if (hint == 'c')

        return middle;

    // Recursively try higher
    else if (hint == 'h')

        return guess_number(middle + 1, high);

    // Recursively try lower
    else

        return guess_number(low, middle - 1);


}

int main()
{
    cout << "Enter 'h' for higher, 'l' for lower, and 'c' for correct." << endl;
```

Figure 10-6   Program to play the guessing game (*Continued*)

```
cout << "Think of a number between 1 and 10!" << endl;

int number = guess_number(1, 10);

if (number != -1)

    cout << "Your number is " << number << "!" << endl;

else

    cout << "You cheated :(" << endl;


return 0;
}
```

Figure 10-6 Program to play the guessing game

Q Is the base case checked in Figure 10-6? If so, how?

A The code in Figure 10-6 has two base cases: cheating and correct answers. Cheating is when the lower boundary is higher than the upper boundary. Correct is when your friend tells you you're right.

Q Are the parameters modified in Figure 10-6? If so, how?

A If your friend replies "higher," then the lower boundary is increased to the guessed number. If your friend replies "lower," then the upper boundary is decreased to the guessed number.

Q Is the function invoked recursively in Figure 10-6? If so, how?

A Based on your friend's answers, "higher" invokes the function with a new lower boundary, and "lower" invokes the function with a new upper boundary.

Q Is anything returned in Figure 10-6? If so, what?

A The correctly guessed number is returned. Otherwise, −1 is returned if cheating was involved.

Anything done in a loop (an algorithm that uses a repetition control) can be done with recursion. **Figure 10-7** compares the earlier `display_numbers` pseudocode using an iterative structure and its recursive equivalent. (Because a loop uses iteration, its structure is called iterative.) The goal of both approaches is to display all numbers from 1 to 10. With a loop executing based on the variable `current_number`, it starts with `current_number` set to 1 and ends when `current_number` is greater than 10. The base case is when the variable `current_number` goes beyond 10.

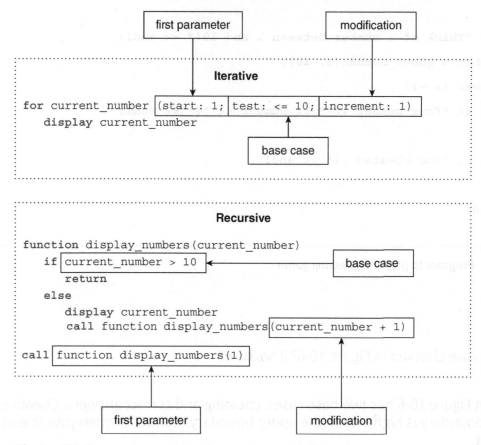

Figure 10-7 Loop and recursion to perform the same task

Some recursion modifies its parameters incrementally, like adding 1 in **display_numbers**. Another way to design recursive code is called "divide and conquer." As the name suggests, you divide the problem in order to conquer it. You took this approach in the number guessing game. Each time you guess, you divide the range of possible correct answers in half. Eventually, you conquer the problem by guessing the right number.

Linear Recursion (10.2.4, 10.2.5)

Identifying linear recursion problems is similar to knowing when you should use a loop. Can you solve a set of smaller problems in sequence? If so, use a loop or linear recursion. One example of an iterative problem is to add the numbers 1 to 10. The following for-loop takes an iterative approach:

```
initialize count = 0

for number (start: 1; test: <= 10; increment: 1)

    compute count = count + number

display count
```

Q How would you translate this pseudocode to recursion?

A Use the checklist. Start with the base case, which is the test case in the for-loop. In the recursive code, you reverse the test case to check if the current number is greater than 10 (instead of less than or equal to 10), because that is when you stop the sequence. The increment is how you modify the parameters, and the start is how you invoke the first recursive call.

The following pseudocode uses linear recursion to add the numbers 1 to 10:

```
function add_numbers(count, current_number)
    if current_number > 10
        return count
    else
        initialize next_count = count + current_number
        initialize next_number = current_number + 1
        return call function add_numbers(next_count, next_number)
```

Q Can you apply the recursive checklist to the linear recursion pseudocode?

A The base case is the line with `if current_number > 10`. The two `initialize` statements modify the parameters. The recursive call and returning value are in the last line.

To display the result, display the value returned by `add_numbers`, starting with 0 and 1 for the `count` and `current_number` parameters:

```
display call function add_numbers(0, 1)
```

The output is **55**, or the result of adding the numbers from 1 to 10.

Branching Recursion (10.2.5)

Some problems are more complicated than an iterative design can handle. Think of a computer folder containing files and other folders. Suppose you want to count the .txt files in the main folder. Assume the following functions are already programmed:

- **get_files**: Given a folder name, this function returns an array of all files in the folder. The variable that stores the result needs two square brackets [ ] next to its name to show that it is an array.
- **total_files**: Given a folder name, this function returns the total number of files in the folder.
- **ends_with**: Given a file name and an extension, this function returns True or False if the file name ends with the extension.

Can you solve this problem iteratively? You can use a for-loop to test each file and increase the count by 1 for each file with the extension .txt:

```
input folder
get files[] = call function get_files(folder)
get size = call function total_files(folder)
initialize count = 0
for index (start: 0; test: < size; increment: 1)
    if call function ends_with(files[index], ".txt")
        compute count = count + 1
```

The input is the name of the folder. The code collects the names of the files within that folder and then determines how many files it contains. A for-loop sets up the variable `count` to keep track of how many .txt files it identifies. Each file in the folder is examined for the .txt extension, and 1 is added to `count` if the file is a .txt file.

What happens if **folder** contains another folder, which also contains .txt files? In that case, you need to count the files in the nested folder. You could try to fix this by adding another for-loop:

```
input folder

get files[] = call function get_files("folderName")

get size = call function total_files("folderName")

initialize count = 0

for index (start: 0; test: < size; increment: 1)

    if call function ends_with(files[index], ".txt")

        compute count = count + 1

    else if files[index] is folder

        initialize folder2 = files[index]

        get files2 = call function get_files(folder2)

        get size2 = call function total_files(folder2)

        for index2 (start: 0; test: < size2; increment: 1)

            if call function ends_with(files2[index2], ".txt")

                compute count = count + 1
```

Now the pseudocode has an else-if condition to detect a nested folder. In the else-if block, the code is nearly identical to the code in the main program. It counts each file in **folder2** that has a .txt extension. However, that still doesn't solve the problem. What if **folder2** also contains a folder? What if that new folder also contains a folder? You need an infinite number of nested ifs and loops to solve this problem with an iterative algorithm.

You can't solve this problem iteratively. Each new folder you find means you have to go into the folder to count its files. This is a perfect time to use a recursive algorithm. For each new folder, you perform the same action on a smaller problem.

The following pseudocode shows how to solve the file-counting problem using recursion. Your base case is whether an item in a folder is a .txt file. If it is, increase the count of files by 1. If the item is a folder, then you count the .txt files it contains. You need to increase the total of .txt files by the result of counting the files in that folder. Each folder has its own count of .txt files, which must be summed to find the total count.

```
function count_txt_files(folder)

    get files[] = call function get_files(folder)

    get size = call function total_files(folder)

    initialize count = 0

    for index (start: 0; test: < size; increment: 1)

        if call function ends_with(files[index], ".txt")

            compute count = count + 1

        else if files[index] is folder

            initialize subcount = call function count_txt_files(files[index])

            compute count = count + subcount

    return count
```

This is an example of branching recursion, which includes more than one call to the recursive function, `count_txt_files`. It begins with a for-loop as in a standard iterative structure. Each time the code finds a folder instead of a file, it branches to the `count_txt_files` function to count the files in the folder. Although the code starts with a for-loop, it takes a recursive approach to perform a repetitive task and avoid impossible infinite code.

Another example of branching recursion is the computed list known as the Fibonacci sequence. The Fibonacci sequence is a weird series of numbers defined recursively, as follows:

- The first number is 1.
- The second number is 1.
- The third number is the second plus the first number.
- The fourth number is the third plus the second number.
- The nth number is the sum of $(n-1) + (n-2)$.

The sequence starts with the following 10 numbers:

1, 1, 2, 3, 5, 8, 13, 21, 34, 55

To find the next number in the Fibonacci sequence, you use recursion. The following code defines a function named `fibonacci` with a parameter called `number`, which refers to the position in the sequence. You have two base cases: if the value passed in `number` to `fibonacci` is 1 or 2, they both return 1, as shown in the `if` block. If `number` is something other than 1 or 2, you can call the function recursively by subtracting 1 and then 2 from `number`. The result of `number - 1` is stored in the variable `n1`, and the result from `number - 2` is stored in `n2`. The program then returns the sum of the two recursive calls.

```
function fibonacci(number)

    if number = 1 or number = 2

        return 1

    else

        initialize n1 = call function fibonacci(number - 1)

        initialize n2 = call function fibonacci(number - 2)

        return n1 + n2
```

Q If a program writes `fibonacci(2)`, how many times is the `fibonacci` function called recursively?

A None, because `fibonacci(2)` is one of the base cases.

Q If a program writes `fibonacci(4)`, how many times is the `fibonacci` function called recursively?

A The number 4 is not 1 or 2, so `fibonacci(3)` and `fibonacci(2)` are called recursively. Calling `fibonacci(3)` calls `fibonacci(2)` and `fibonacci(1)`. Both 1 and 2 are base cases, so there are no more recursive calls. The total number of recursive calls is 4.

Recall that the Fibonacci sequence starts with 10 numbers: 1, 1, 2, 3, 5, 8, 13, 21, 34, 55. How does the code calculate the eleventh Fibonacci number? The `fibonacci` function takes **11** as its argument. That number is not 1 or 2, so the `fibonacci` function is called recursively with arguments of **10** (**11 − 1**) and **9** (**11 − 2**). The first `fibonacci` function returns **55**, and the second returns **34**. Add the returned values to find the next number in the Fibonacci sequence, which is 89.

To program the Fibonacci sequence, see **Figure 10-8**.

```cpp
#include <iostream>

using namespace std;


int fibonacci(int n)
{

    // Base case

    if (n == 1 || n == 2)
        return 1;


    // Find the fibonacci number for n - 1

    int n1 = fibonacci(n - 1);


    // Find the fibonacci number for n - 2

    int n2 = fibonacci(n - 2);


    // Add together and return the result

    return n1 + n2;


}


int main()
{

    int n;

    cout << "Enter a number: ";
```

Figure 10-8   C++ code to program the Fibonacci sequence (*Continued*)

```
    cin >> n;


    int fibonacci_n = fibonacci(n);


    cout << "The Fibonacci number is " << fibonacci_n << endl;


    return 0;
}


OUTPUT:
Enter a number: 6
The Fibonacci number is 8
```

Figure 10-8   C++ code to program the Fibonacci sequence

10.3 MANAGING MEMORY DURING RECURSION

Memory Management (10.3.1, 10.3.2)

A function that calls itself many times can require a lot of memory when the program runs. A computer reserves a block of memory to keep track of the current state of the program. This block contains the names of all the variables in your program along with the values stored in each variable.

The following code sums the numbers from 1 to 10.

```
function sum(current_number)
    if current_number = 0
        return 0
    else
        initialize sum_total = call function sum(current_number - 1)
        return current_number + sum_total
call function sum(10)
```

Q How many variables does the above code need to remember?

A The line **return current_number + sum_total** follows the recursive call to the **sum** function. That means the program must remember **current_number** after the recursive call comes back. Each time a function is called, another memory block is set aside for that function's lifetime, and then marked as no longer needed once the function returns. Calling **sum(10)** means the code needs to remember 11 variables.

Figure 10-9 outlines the memory the code needs to hold variables when it calls **sum(10)**.

```
function sum(current_number)

   if current_number = 0

      return 0

   else

      initialize sum_total = call function sum(current_number - 1)

      return current_number + sum_total


call function sum(10)
```

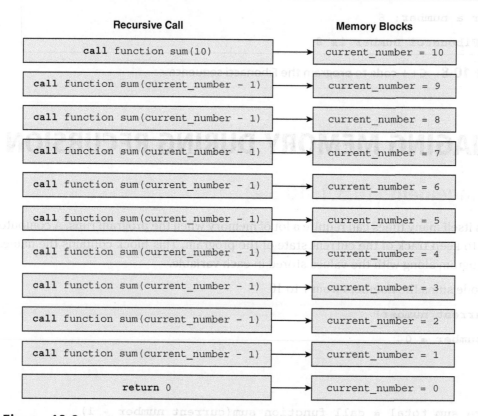

Figure 10-9   Calling sum(10) needs 11 memory blocks

Each time a recursive function finishes, it needs to return to the memory state directly before it. Computers use data structures called **stacks** to store the memory blocks for recursive function calls. As with a stack of pancakes, you can only place new pancakes on top and can only remove pancakes from the top. Each time a recursive function is called, a new memory block is placed on top of the stack as in **Figure 10-10**.

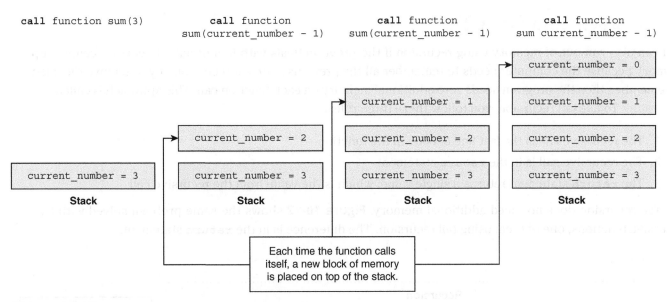

Figure 10-10   Memory stack for recursive function calls

Each time a function finishes, the top of the stack is removed, as in **Figure 10-11**.

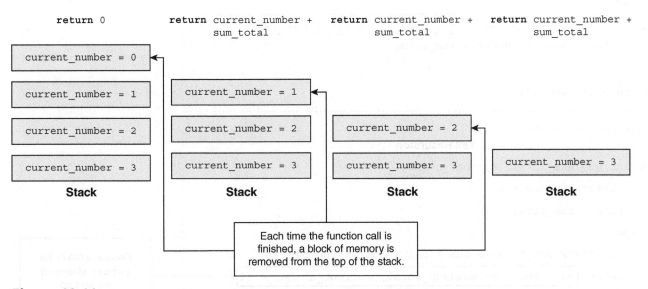

Figure 10-11   Memory stack when recursive function calls are finished

The longer a recursive chain of calls, the more memory is needed to keep track of what happened in the previous calls. In fact, the computer can run out of memory if the recursion goes on for too long. This is only a problem if you are working with exceptionally large datasets, such a list of everyone who has ever lived on Earth. For a recursive algorithm to deal with loads of data, it needs to get smart about its memory management.

Stable Recursion (10.3.3)

You can also run out of memory using recursion if the program deals with lots of data. Recursion can use up memory because the computer needs to remember all the previous states of recursion. If you remove the need to remember, then the program needs zero additional memory on each function call. This approach is called **tail recursion**. To use tail recursion, you follow these three rules:

1. The recursive call is the last line of code in the function.
2. The recursive call is in the **return** statement.
3. The **return** statement returns a single value, which is the value from the recursive call.

Tail recursion does not need additional memory. **Figure 10-12** shows the same problem solved with two recursive functions, one of them using tail recursion. The difference is in the **return** statement.

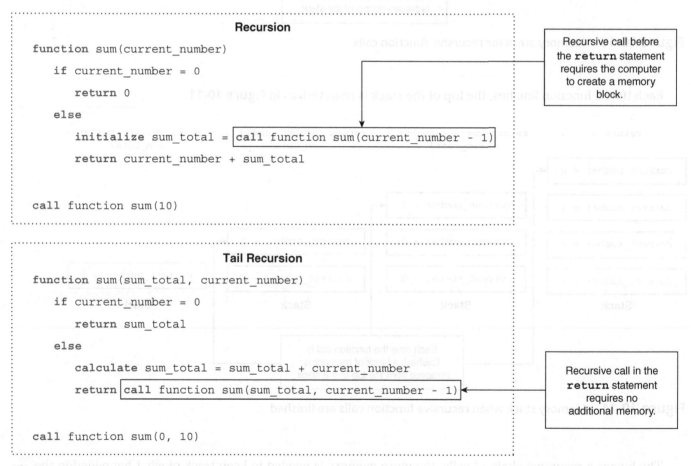

Figure 10-12   Using tail recursion

Both sets of code sum the numbers from 10 to 1. The tail recursive code passes the **sum_total** variable to the recursive function call instead of using a local variable. With this approach, the computer does not need to remember anything, so it does not use additional memory.

SUMMARY

- Recursion is a strategy for approaching large problems in computer science by breaking the problem down into smaller identical problems. The same steps are applied to each smaller version of the problem, although with different restrictions.
- A recursive function calls itself at least once. With each function call, a recursive function uses modified parameters to reduce the size of the problem.
- If the parameters of a recursive function are not modified, the recursive function does not stop, creating an infinite recursion.
- A base case is a condition that stops the recursion, such as guessing the correct number in a number guessing game. A base case can also represent a problem small enough that it can be solved quickly.
- A recursive function should check for the base case as its first step. Make sure the code also modifies the parameters, invokes the function recursively one or more times, and does something with any returned value.
- Linear recursion is a recursive function that calls itself once at most or stops when it reaches a base case.
- Branching recursion is a recursive function that calls itself more than once.
- Loops are similar to linear recursion, although you use each approach in different situations. Use loops when you need to do the same task without changing the conditions. Use recursion when you need to reduce the problem to solve it.
- Each recursive function call requires another block of memory from the computer unless the function is designed to use tail recursion.

Key Terms

base case

branching recursion

infinite recursion

linear recursion

Recursion

recursive function

stacks

tail recursion

EXCEPTIONS

LEARNING OBJECTIVES:

11.1 DEFINING EXCEPTIONS

11.1.1 Explain the use of exceptions being thrown in situations where the computer cannot continue.

11.1.2 Define an exception as a triggered event.

11.1.3 Describe the difference between a logic error (can be found by reading the code) and a runtime error.

11.1.4 Define exception objects as packages of information about what happened.

11.1.5 Contrast default exceptions with specific exception types.

11.1.6 Explain that different types of exceptions represent different general errors.

11.1.7 Explain that certain languages have defined exception types.

11.2 DEALING WITH EXCEPTIONS

11.2.1 Explain trying and error handling as logical flow controls.

11.2.2 Explain how code can try to achieve something.

11.2.3 Explain what happens when the code within a try block fails.

11.2.4 Explain how to use catching for error handling.

11.2.5 Describe the difference between a catch-all and catch exception specific.

11.2.6 Explain good design for including statements in the try block.

11.3 USING EXCEPTIONS

11.3.1 Discuss the advantages and disadvantages of exception handling versus robust code.

11.3.2 Explain statements that cause exceptions (raise/throw).

11.3.3 Describe the best practices for adding exceptions to a program.

11.3.4 Trace the flow of execution through variations of try-block statements.

11.1 DEFINING EXCEPTIONS

Errors in Code (11.1.1, 11.1.2, 11.1.3)

A fact of life for you as a programmer is that you must debug code to find and fix errors. In fact, you have to debug a lot of code. When you do, look for logic errors and runtime errors. **Logic errors** are probably the most familiar to you: Part of the code is incorrect, but it still runs and produces output. For example, you might be checking for numbers greater than zero when you mean to check for numbers less than zero. You typically find logic errors by carefully reading the code.

Logic errors are different from semantic errors, which are errors caught by the compiler. As you know, a runtime error is a flaw in a program that causes it to fail during execution.

Another type of problem can interrupt a program as it is running. Suppose you are coding part of a video game that includes a character named Iceabella. She can make ice cream for you and other users, as long as you bring her enough ice and cream (**Figure 11-1**). If you ask the character for ice cream before giving her any cream, what should she do? Should she create ice cream anyway? Should she close down her ice cream machine? Or, should she tell you what's wrong so you can fix it?

home_sweet_home/Shutterstock.com
Volhah/Shutterstock.com

Figure 11-1   Ice cream making video game

Ideally, when a program can't perform a task as instructed, it should gracefully inform the user. If Iceabella can create ice cream only if she is given cream first, then the program must make sure those conditions are met before Iceabella attempts to make ice cream. For example, the program can display a message reminding you that Iceabella needs cream and will then wait for you to supply it.

Code also has preconditions, or assumptions that need to be true for the code to work. If the preconditions aren't met, the code should fail gracefully instead of crashing, even in unusual situations.

In programming, an unusual situation is called an **exception**, an unexpected event that occurs as the program runs and prevents the program from completing execution. The unusual situation is said to trigger the exception and interrupt normal program flow.

Whereas an error is a design flaw that debugging should fix, an exception prevents part of a program from solving a problem on its own. The exception provides a way for one part of a program to ask for help from another part of the program. **Figure 11-2** shows the workflow communication between two program parts.

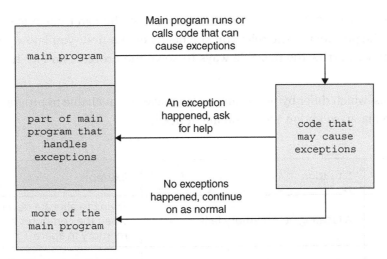

Figure 11-2   Communication between normal code and code with exceptions

When the main program encounters code that may cause an exception, the program flow can continue in two ways. If no exceptions occur, the flow can return a result to the main program, if one was requested. If an exception occurs, the code calls for help and is diverted to the part of the main program that handles exceptions. That part of the program resolves the exception and the program continues running.

A robust, well-written program checks for exceptions in situations where it might not otherwise continue, and then responds to the exceptions appropriately. That means you as a programmer must check for possible exceptions and write code to handle them. The program can then detect unexpected errors and manage them without letting an unwanted situation bring the program to a halt.

Exception Types (11.1.4, 11.1.5, 11.1.6, 11.1.7)

Programmers talk about exceptions as events, but an exception can also be a package of information indicating what went wrong. This information can be as simple as a numerical code or string description, or more complicated bundles of information including the state of the program when the exception occurred and the exception type.

Programming languages provide general exceptions, which can be used for all problems, but don't provide context that would help solve the problems. These non-specific exceptions are called **default exceptions**. Using default exceptions makes it easier to catch a problem but harder to know how to fix it. "Something bad happened" doesn't help you as much as "I have no cream for the ice cream." However, default exceptions can be useful to catch situations you may not realize will happen, such as operating system errors. When you receive an error message such as "Unknown error occurred," the program is using a default exception. The program detected the exception but did not correct it other than letting the user know it happened.

Specific exception types represent specific kinds of errors. They tell programmers the type of problem that happened, allowing them to find solutions faster. For example, if you receive an error message such as "Invalid parameter type," the problem obviously has something to do with a parameter being the wrong type. To fix this problem, you need to examine parameters.

For example, in the ice cream video game, Iceabella stating that she can't make ice cream doesn't help you understand how to fix the problem. If she tells you she needs cream first, you know you need to give her cream. Specific exception types narrow the possible ways to solve the problem and let the program return to its normal flow.

Many specific exceptions, which differ by programming language, are available to programmers. **Figure 11-3** shows some of the most common exception types you might need.

Type	Situation	Example
`bad_alloc`	Allocating new memory fails	Trying to allocate new memory when the computer has no memory to spare
`bad_function_call`	Invoking a function fails	Calling a function without defining it
`invalid_argument`	An argument is passed to a function or method that requires specific formats	Passing "0123" to a binary analysis calculator
`domain_error`	A mathematical function is given a number outside of the defined range	Passing –5 to a square root function
`out_of_range`	A location is accessed in a linear data structure that is larger than the maximum index	Accessing index 10 when the data structure has five items
`system_error`	The error originates from the system or outside the program	Operating system errors
`bad_array_new_length`	Creation of a new array cannot be completed due to the size provided	Creating an array with a size less than zero
`bad_exception`	Dynamic exception specifiers cause an error	A function that is supposed to cause a `bad_alloc` exception instead causes an overflow error

Figure 11-3   Common exceptions

Programming languages provide references, usually online, that define their exception types. It is the responsibility of a programmer to know, or know how to look up, the types of exceptions available in the language they use. Most programming languages also allow you to create your own exception types for special situations. For example, with Iceabella, you might make a specific `no_cream_error` exception.

Q Should you use a default exception to handle everything?

A No. Handling everything the same way would be similar to displaying only very generic computer messages. "Something went wrong" isn't as helpful as "You couldn't print your document because the printer needs ink."

11.2 DEALING WITH EXCEPTIONS

Handling Others' Exceptions (11.2.1, 11.2.2)

When code causes an exception, programmers say the code "throws" an exception. Programmers make their code **throw** exceptions when certain conditions are true. Handling the exception is more important than investigating why it was thrown in the first place. If Iceabella has no cream, it doesn't matter if someone took the cream, or that Iceabella used all the cream earlier. The problem is that Iceabella needs more cream before she can make ice cream. To handle thrown exceptions, all you need to know is what is wrong so you can fix the problem.

Suppose you are trying to program an image editor, which needs to be able to open image files. You find a library of functions that will load and display images for you. The normal flow of a program assumes everything works correctly: The program loads an image to the screen, and then lets users modify the image and save it on a storage device.

What should your program do if it can't load the image for some reason? For example, the program might not be able to find the image file or the file might not be in the correct format. You could take a few approaches to deal with the problem, depending on the tools available in the library of functions you are using, such as displaying an error message or a default image. Instead of dictating your approach, the programmer of the image library lets you control your program by throwing an exception. You can write code to detect the exception and handle it as you decide is best.

The code to detect an exception uses a similar logical control structure to an if-else block. The logical flow of the program changes depending on whether an exception occurs. Generally, to work with exceptions, programs **try** to do something and **catch** any exceptions that were thrown in the code.

Try and Catch Blocks (11.2.3, 11.2.4, 11.2.5, 11.2.6)

You can use a program flow control for trying and catching exceptions. The program flow control is called a **try-catch block**. (Some languages, including Python, refer to this program flow control as a try-except block). A try-catch block has two parts: the **try** block and the **catch** block. The **try** code attempts to proceed as if conditions are normal and nothing disrupts the program flow. If an exception is thrown in the **try** block, the program flow moves to the **catch** block. **Figure 11-4** shows a diagram of the flow for a try-catch block.

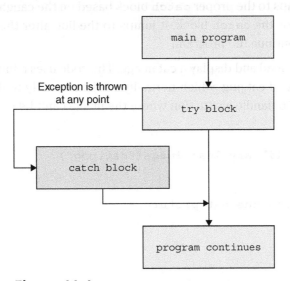

Figure 11-4   Try-catch block logic flow

If no exception is thrown, then the program executes normally through the **try** block. If an exception is thrown in the **try** block, however, the program stops executing code in the **try** block and jumps to the start of the **catch** block.

Unlike an if-else statement, a **try** block stops executing code when it detects an exception. The **catch** block can fix the problem or stop the program entirely. Fixing the problem can take many forms, including using default values to fill in the missing information, displaying an error message, or logging the error in a file.

Figure 11-5 shows the pseudocode for a simple example of calling two functions. Each function might throw an exception. The arrows show what direction the program takes at each point.

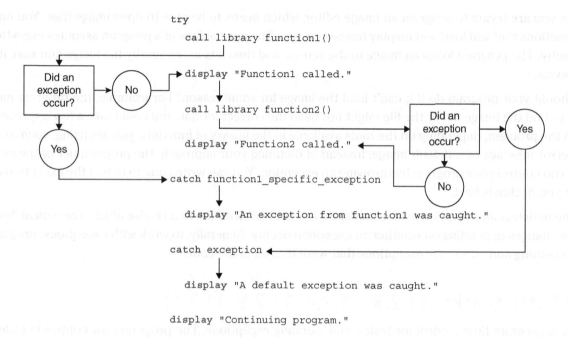

Figure 11-5   Pseudocode flow example

In the Figure 11-5, **function1** and **function2** can each throw an exception. The first function can throw a specific exception, while **function2** is handled by a default exception catch. If either function call triggers an exception event, then the logic jumps to the proper **catch** block based on the caught exception. When the code reaches the end of the **try** block or the **catch** block, it jumps to the line after the try-catch block (**display "Continuing program."**) to continue the program.

The following code attempts to load and display a cat image. The code uses a built-in function named **load_image** to display an image file named cat.png, which normally works correctly to display the image. However, the code is structured incorrectly to handle a situation where the image can't be displayed.

```
try
    initialize image = call library load_image("cat.png")
catch exception
    display "Could not display the cat picture."
display image
```

Q Consider the above example. What's wrong with the order of the statements?

A The last line (`display image`) is placed outside of the try-catch block. Displaying an image only works if the image loads successfully. The program could still crash at the last line if it tries to display an image that did not load correctly.

In the previous code, the `load_image` function can throw an exception if it can't display the cat.png file. However, because `display image` works correctly only if `load_image` can find and retrieve the image file, the `display image` statement belongs in the `try` block. You should include in the `try` block all the code that relies on the function that might throw an exception. The following pseudocode corrects this problem by including `display image` in the `try` block.

```
try

    initialize image = call library load_image("cat.png")

    display image

catch exception

    display "Could not display the cat picture."
```

When a statement in a `try` block fails and throws an exception, it signals the program to stop progressing through the block. If initializing the image fails (the program cannot find the file), or displaying the image fails (no display screen is connected), the code skips the `display image` statement and jumps to the `catch` block. If the `try` block completes without an exception being thrown, it skips over the `catch` block. If nothing was thrown, there's nothing to catch.

Catching a general exception with a statement such as `catch exception` makes any exception in the `try` block jump to the `catch` block. The generic message "Could not display the cat picture." fits a general exception, but a more specific message would be more helpful to users trying to solve the problem. Alternatively, you can program your code to only detect specific exceptions, as in the following code:

```
try

    initialize image = call library load_image("cat.png")

    display image

catch file_not_found_exception

    display "Could not find the cat picture."
```

Using a specific built-in exception such as `file_not_found_exception`, you can display a more helpful message suited to the exception, such as "Could not find the cat picture." The user can solve that problem by storing the file where the program can find it.

Additionally, you can include multiple `catch` statements, one for each exception you expect the program to throw.

```
try

    initialize image = call library load_image("cat.png")

    display image

catch file_not_found_exception
```

```
display "Could not find the cat picture."
catch file_format_not_supported_exception

display "The cat picture is in the wrong format."
```

The second `catch` statement addresses a second exception—the program finds the specified file, but it is in the wrong format.

Now think about how you might program your interactions with Iceabella. Assume that the interactions are a series of functions you can call: `make_ice_cream`, `add_cream`, and `add_ice`. A first start to the program would look like **Figure 11-6**.

```cpp
#include <iostream>

using namespace std;


int main()

{

    int choice = -1;
    int amount;



    cout << "Welcome to the Fantasy Ice Cream Shop!";

    cout << " What do you want to do?" << endl;

    while (choice != 0)
    {

        cout << "   1: Make ice cream" << endl;

        cout << "   2: Add cream" << endl;

        cout << "   3: Add ice" << endl;

        cout << "   0: Quit" << endl;


        cout << "> ";


        cin >> choice;


        if (choice == 1)
        {

            make_ice_cream();
        }

        else if (choice == 2)
        {
```

Figure 11-6   Program to interact with Iceabella (*continued*)

```
            cout << "How much?> ";

            cin >> amount;

            add_cream(amount);


        }
        else if (choice == 3)
        {
            cout << "How much?> ";

            cin >> amount;

            add_ice(amount);


        }


        cout << endl;


    }


    return 0;

}
```

Figure 11-6 Program to interact with Iceabella

The code in Figure 11-6 contains a loop that runs until the user inputs 0, indicating they are done interacting with Iceabella. The variable `choice` is set to -1 to indicate no choice has been made initially, and then is used as the flag for a `while` loop. The `choice` variable is set to the number the user enters via the command line. One of the three functions for interacting with Iceabella are called based on the number the user enters. Where could program this go wrong?

For simplicity's sake, assume that the only exceptions that could happen are:

1. Adding a negative amount of cream
2. Adding a negative amount of ice
3. Trying to make ice cream when there's no cream
4. Trying to make ice cream when there's no ice

Figure 11-7 shows one approach to handling these exceptions, though the approach is not ideal. All the code that relies on the function calls to Iceabella is within a `try` block, so that avoids the problem shown earlier in the pseudocode. However, the entire functionality, including parts that don't rely on Iceabella, are now within the `try` block.

```cpp
#include <iostream>
#include <exception>
#include <stdexcept>
using namespace std;


int main()
{

   try {

      int choice = -1;
      int amount = 0;


      cout << "Welcome to the Fantasy Ice Cream Shop!";
      cout << " What do you want to do?" << endl;
      while (choice != 0)
      {

         cout << "   1: Make ice cream" << endl;

         cout << "   2: Add cream" << endl;

         cout << "   3: Add ice" << endl;

         cout << "   0: Quit" << endl;


         cout << "> ";

         cin >> choice;


         if (choice == 1)

         {

            make_ice_cream();

         }
         else if (choice == 2)

         {

            cout << "How much?> ";
            cin >> amount;
            add_cream(amount);


         }
```

Figure 11-7   Program with try-catch block encompassing all code (*continued*)

```
            else if (choice == 3)
            {
                cout << "How much?> ";
                cin >> amount;
                add_ice(amount);

            }

            cout << endl;

        }

    }
    catch (runtime_error e)
    {
        cout << "Error happened " << e.what() << endl;
    }
    return 0;
}
```

Figure 11-7 Program with try-catch block encompassing all code

Q What would happen in the code shown in Figure 11-7 if there was no cream and you ask for ice cream to be made?

A The entire interaction with Iceabella will stop working if anything goes wrong. An exception would stop all code in the **try** block and exit to the **catch** block. In this case, that means the program stops entirely. You still want Iceabella to keep interacting with you, even if you make an impossible request.

Consider the alternative approach in **Figure 11-8**. This time, only the function call section of the code is surrounded by the **try** block, and the **catch** block displays what went wrong.

```
#include <iostream>
#include <exception>
#include <stdexcept>
#include <string.h>
using namespace std;
int main()
```

Figure 11-8 Program with the try-catch block encompassing the exception-throwing code (*continued*)

```
{
    int choice = -1;
    int amount = 0;

    cout << "Welcome to the Fantasy Ice Cream Shop!";
    cout << " What do you want to do?" << endl;
    while (choice != 0)
    {
        cout << "    1: Make ice cream" << endl;
        cout << "    2: Add cream" << endl;
        cout << "    3: Add ice" << endl;
        cout << "    0: Quit" << endl;

        cout << "> ";

        cin >> choice;

        try
        {
            if (choice == 1)
            {
                make_ice_cream();
            }
            else if (choice == 2)
            {
                cout << "How much?> ";
                cin >> amount;
                add_cream(amount);
            }
            else if (choice == 3)
            {
                cout << "How much?> ";
                cin >> amount;
                add_ice(amount);
```

try block includes only the function-calling code

Figure 11-8   Program with the try-catch block encompassing the exception-throwing code (*continued*)

```
            }
        }
        catch (runtime_error e) ←————————  catch block explains
        {                                           what went wrong

            const char*  type = e.what();

            if (strcmp(type, "cream") == 0)
            {
                cout << "I don't have enough cream." << endl;
            }
            else if (strcmp(type, "ice") == 0)
            {
                cout << "I don't have enough ice." << endl;
            }
            else if (strcmp(type, "amount") == 0)
            {
                cout << "You can't add a negative amount." << endl;
            }
        }

        cout << endl;

    }

    return 0;
}
```

Figure 11-8   Program with the try-catch block encompassing the exception-throwing code

Q How does the change in the code shown in Figure 11-8 change what happens if there's no cream?

A Iceabella will tell you something went wrong but will still wait for you to interact with her.

Professional program design tries to keep only the lines of code that rely on exception-throwing functions in the **try** block.

Figure 11-9 shows a general syntax for try-catch blocks. As in if-else blocks, the order of the **catch** statements matter. The first statement that matches the error condition will be selected, even if later **catch** statements also match.

```
Syntax:

try {

   // ... code that might have

   //     exceptions thrown

   ...

}

catch (int param) {

   cout << "int exception";

}

catch (char param) {

   cout << "char exception";

}

catch (invalid_argument_e) {

   cout << "invalid argument exception";

}

catch (...) {

   cout << "default exception";

}
```

C++ lets you throw or catch anything, including primitive types

The ellipsis `catch` statement catches any exceptions that haven't already been caught

Figure 11-9   General syntax for try-catch blocks

Q What would happen if you placed the general **catch** statement before specific **catch** statements?

A Because the general **catch** statement works for all exceptions, then none of the other **catch** statements would be triggered.

11.3 USING EXCEPTIONS

Throwing Exceptions (11.3.2, 11.3.4)

Like other programmers, you can throw your own exceptions. These **throw** statements act like a bail out: The program immediately stops your code and returns to where it was invoked with the exception information.

Recall that Iceabella has three functions you could call to interact with her. **Figure 11-10** shows what **make_ ice_cream**, **add_cream**, and **add_ice** look like without exceptions.

```cpp
#include <iostream>
using namespace std;


int cream_amount = 0;
int ice_amount = 0;


void make_ice_cream()
{
    cream_amount -= 1;
    ice_amount -= 1;
    cout << "Ice cream was made!" << endl;
}


void add_cream(int amount)
{
    cream_amount += amount;
    cout << "Thanks for the " << amount << " cups of cream!" <<
endl;

}


void add_ice(int amount)
{
    ice_amount += amount;
    cout << "Thanks for the " << amount << " cups of ice!" <<
endl;

}
```

Figure 11-10 Program to simulate Iceabella's interactions

Two global variables, `cream_amount` and `ice_amount`, are initialized to zero, indicating that Iceabella starts out with no supplies. If either the `add_cream` or `add_ice` functions are called, the `cream_amount` or `ice_amount` variables are each increased by the `amount` parameter. Calling `make_ice_cream` decreases the `ice_amount` and `cream_amount` variables and signals that ice cream was made.

One of the exceptions you might expect Iceabella to throw is if you try to add a negative amount to either the `cream_amount` or `ice_amount` variables. **Figure 11-11** shows one way to modify the code from Figure 11-10 to handle these situations.

```cpp
#include <iostream>
#include <exception>
#include <stdexcept>
#include <string.h>

int cream_amount = 0;
int ice_amount = 0;

void make_ice_cream()
{
    cream_amount -= 1;
    ice_amount -= 1;
    cout << "Ice cream was made!" << endl;
}


void add_cream(int amount)
{
    if (amount < 0)                          Check for positive
    {                                        values for cream
        throw runtime_error("amount");
    }
    cream_amount += amount;
    cout << "Thanks for the " << amount << " cups of cream!" <<
endl;

}

void add_ice(int amount)
{
    if (amount < 0)                          Check for positive
    {                                        values for ice
        throw runtime_error("amount");
    }
    ice_amount += amount;
    cout << "Thanks for the " << amount << " cups of ice!" <<
endl;
}
```

Figure 11-11   Program that checks for positive amounts

MODULE 11 EXCEPTIONS 201

Note the two **if** statements in the **add** functions. These statements test for the condition that the parameter **amount** is a value less than zero, and if true, throw an exception. You can have your code throw as many or as few exceptions as you see fit. Suppose the only requirements for starting to create ice cream is that both ice and cream are available to Iceabella in some amount greater than zero. **Figure 11-12** shows how you might program this exception to be thrown in **make_ice_cream**.

```cpp
#include <iostream>
#include <exception>
#include <stdexcept>
#include <string.h>
using namespace std;


int cream_amount = 0;
int ice_amount = 0;


void make_ice_cream()
{
    if (cream_amount <= 0)
    {
        throw runtime_error("cream");
    }
    else if (ice_amount <= 0)
    {
        throw runtime_error("ice");
    }

    cream_amount -= 1;
    ice_amount -= 1;
    cout << "Ice cream was made!" << endl;
}

void add_cream(int amount)
{
    if (amount < 0)
    {
        throw runtime_error("amount");
    }
    cream_amount += amount;
```

Figure 11-12 Program with exception thrown in a function (*continued*)

```
        cout << "Thanks for the " << amount << " cups of cream!" <<
    endl;
    }


    void add_ice(int amount)
    {
        if (amount < 0)
        {
            throw runtime_error("amount");
        }
        ice_amount += amount;
        cout << "Thanks for the " << amount << " cups of ice!" <<
    endl;


    }
```

Figure 11-12   Program with exception thrown in a function

The `make_ice_cream` function now has an `if` and an `else if` statement at the start. These conditions test for the ice and cream amounts before allowing Iceabella to state she has made ice cream. You do not need to wrap the remaining lines of the function code in an `else` block, because once an exception is thrown, the rest of the function will stop. In fact, in other situations, the thrown exception may be anywhere in a function call chain. Any thrown exception will be caught by the nearest try-catch block.

When to Bail (11.3.1, 11.3.3)

Being able to hand off problems to someone else adds another decision layer to designing your program. Exceptions allow you to "bail out" of a piece of code that reaches a situation it can't complete. Bailing out is like an emergency break to stop and find someone else who knows more to fix the problem. When should you try to handle the problem yourself, and when should you bail out? This decision is a balancing act between strong code that handles all possible situations and exceptions to your code where it can't continue. If your program would have to make up a solution, let someone else handle it instead. If Iceabella were to try to handle the lack of cream herself, she would need to somehow find the cream on her own, defeating the purpose of the interactions with her within the context of the game. Instead, she allows you to obtain the cream for her.

A general guideline is to think about what a function is requesting, such as "make ice cream." If the input provided makes that request impossible, throw an exception. Making ice cream assumes the ingredients are available to do so. A function should throw an exception instead of completing when those assumptions are broken. However, if your functions are often throwing exceptions, you may need to rethink your program design and change the assumptions.

Exceptions allow future users of your code libraries the control over how their program behaves. By throwing exceptions only in cases where your code cannot continue, you keep your code focused on its own goals (making ice cream) while leaving other goals to other parts of the program (getting the cream). However, if you throw exceptions at any inconvenience, your library becomes tedious to use. It puts more responsibility on other programmers, which might reduce the usefulness of your library.

When to use an exception is generally up to the programmer. Is the problem something you can fix on your own? How much trouble does it cause if someone asks you to make ice cream but doesn't give you cream? The answers to those questions help you decide whether an exception is useful.

Q If you ask Iceabella to clean her shop when her shop is already clean, should she throw an exception?

A No, this is not a state in which Iceabella cannot continue. She should just reclean the shop, or realize the shop is clean and do nothing.

Q If someone fills Iceabella's ice bucket with an angry ice-dragon instead of ice, should she throw an exception?

A Yes, Iceabella needs outside help to remove the angry ice-dragon from the ice bucket.

SUMMARY

- In programming, an unusual situation is called an exception, an unexpected event that occurs as the program runs and prevents the program from completing execution. The unusual situation is said to trigger the exception and interrupt normal program flow because the program could not otherwise continue.
- A robust, well-written program checks for exceptions in situations where it might not otherwise continue, and then responds to the exceptions appropriately.
- Programming languages provide general exceptions, which can be used for all problems, but don't provide context that would help solve the problems. These non-specific exceptions are called default exceptions.
- Specific exception types represent specific kinds of errors. They tell programmers the type of problem that happened, allowing them to find solutions faster. Many specific exceptions, which differ by programming language, are available to programmers.
- When code causes an exception, programmers say the code "throws" an exception. The code to detect an exception uses a similar logical control structure to an if-else block. The logical flow of the program changes depending on whether an exception occurs. Generally, to work with exceptions, programs try to do something and catch any exceptions that were thrown in the code.
- You can use a program flow control called a try-catch (or try-except) block for trying and catching exceptions. The `try` code attempts to proceed as if conditions are normal and nothing disrupts the program flow. If an exception is thrown in the `try` block, the program flow moves to the `catch` block.
- A `try` block stops executing code when it detects an exception. The `catch` block can fix the problem or stop the program entirely. Fixing the problem can take many forms, including using default values to fill in the missing information, displaying an error message, or logging the error in a file.
- Limit the amount of code inside a try-catch block to only the code which relies on the part that might fail.

Key Terms

catch	logic errors	try-catch block
default exceptions	throw	
exception	try	

MODULE 12

FILE OPERATIONS

LEARNING OBJECTIVES:

12.1 FILE INPUT AND OUTPUT

12.1.1 Describe directory structures.

12.1.2 Explain how to use the escape character in file paths.

12.1.3 Define absolute file path.

12.1.4 Define relative file path.

12.1.5 Identify the components of a file.

12.1.6 Recognize how a text file is represented in memory.

12.1.7 Define the term: file I/O.

12.1.8 List the operations available for file handling.

12.1.9 Describe the difference between handling a text file and a binary file.

12.1.10 List the file information that a programmer might request upon opening a file.

12.2 PROCESSING A FILE

12.2.1 Define linear access as it applies to files.

12.2.2 Define random access as it applies to files.

12.2.3 Define buffered streams.

12.2.4 Explain how stream readers and writers work.

12.3 READING FROM A FILE

12.3.1 Identify the generic syntax and permissions to open a file for reading.

12.3.2 Identify the default mode for opening a file for reading.

12.3.3 Explain how to verify that a file has been opened.

12.3.4 Identify an algorithm for reading an entire text file.

12.3.5 Explain how to derive numerical values from a text file.

12.3.6 Explain how to read records from a table in OOP.

12.3.7 Identify common exceptions that occur when reading files.

12.4 CLOSING A FILE

12.4.1 Explain why it is good practice to close a file after using it.

12.4.2 Identify the generic syntax for a close file statement that includes a try block.

12.5 CREATING AND WRITING NEW FILES

12.5.1 Identify the generic syntax for a statement to create a file.

12.5.2 Identify the generic syntax and permissions to open a file for writing.

12.5.3 Identify the default mode for opening a file for writing.

12.5.4 Explain the difference between append and write operations.

12.5.5 Describe the significance of including a newline argument in a write statement.

12.5.6 Identify an algorithm that writes multiple lines to a text file.

12.5.7 Identify common exceptions that occur while writing to a file.

12.1 FILE INPUT AND OUTPUT

The Purpose of Files (12.1.1, 12.1.2, 12.1.3, 12.1.4)

Programs can request input from users and display output on the screen. Using input and output this way makes the most sense when manipulating small amounts of data, such as a single character, word, or sentence. To work with larger amounts of data, your programs can use files.

A **file** is a digital container that stores data such as text, settings, or program commands. A file can be a document, picture, video, or other type of information. You can also use files to supply data to your programs. For example, you can use a file to store a list of your favorite songs and their ratings, as shown in **Figure 12-1**.

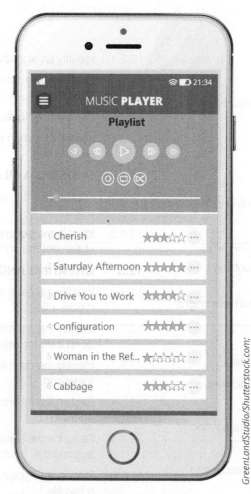

Figure 12-1   **Personal song list**

If you need to enter thousands of values and are not using files, you must type the values by hand and try to avoid making errors. Using a file to enter data is more efficient and less error prone.

Typically, when a program ends, its output data is lost. You can use files to permanently store data your code produces, no matter how much.

File handling is a way to read large amounts of data into your programs (more data than you'd reasonably expect a user to type) and to store data that your programs create.

You use a folder, also called a directory, as a storage space for organizing files into groups, similar to how you organize papers into physical folders as shown in **Figure 12-2**. A folder can hold zero or more files. In fact, a folder can hold other folders.

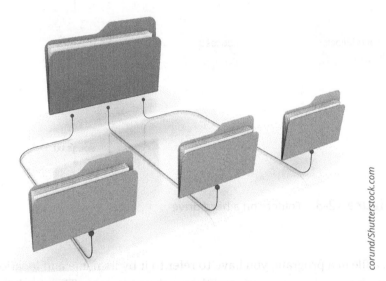

corund/Shutterstock.com

Figure 12-2   Physical folders organizing files

Every operating system (OS) uses files to store and access data and programs. The OS stores the files in a hierarchy of folders called a folder structure or directory structure, an arrangement that reflects how the OS organizes files and folders. A typical directory structure resembles a tree. All files have a specific location on your computer. For example, in **Figure 12-3**, the file songs.txt is in the Playlists folder, two levels below the hard drive, along with other Music files.

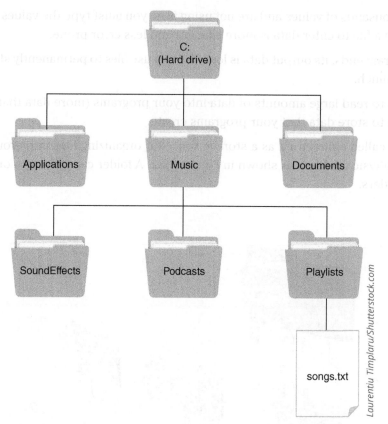

Figure 12-3   Folders on a hard drive

When you want to use a file in a program, you have to refer to it by its name and location. You can describe a file's location in two ways: the **absolute file path** and the **relative file path**. The absolute path tells the exact location of a file on the computer starting from the hard drive, or your computer's main storage. The drive is usually represented as a letter (such as C in Windows) or a slash (/ in macOS and Unix systems) to indicate the topmost level of the directory structure. Depending on the OS, you use a forward slash (/) or a backslash (\) to separate the folder and file names at each level. The relative path provides the location of a file starting from another location in the file system. The differences are shown in **Figure 12-4**.

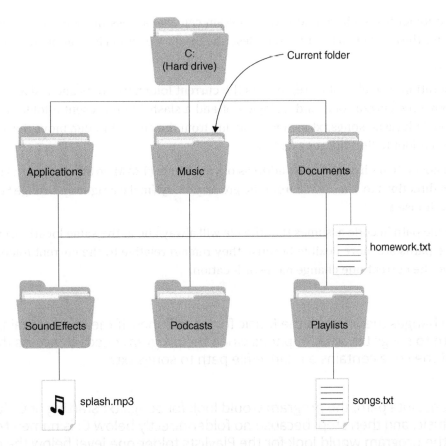

Figure 12-4 Relative and absolute paths to files and folders on a hard drive

Relative Paths	Absolute Paths
..\	C:\
..\Applications	C:\Applications
.	C:\Music
.\SoundEffects	C:\Music\SoundEffects
.\SoundEffects\splash.mp3	C:\Music\SoundEffects\splash.mp3
.\Podcasts	C:\Music\Podcasts
.\Playlists	C:\Music\Playlists
.\Playlists\songs.txt	C:\Music\Playlists\songs.txt
..\Documents	C:\Documents
..\Documents\homework.txt	C:\Documents\homework.txt

Laurentiu Timplaru/Shutterstock.com

Suppose that you exported your playlist to a text file and stored it locally in the Music folder. You also created a playlist analysis program that needs to access data in the songs.txt file, which is stored in the Playlists folder. The absolute path to the songs.txt file looks like this:

C:\Music\Playlists\songs.txt

Because the current folder is the Music folder, the program can also access the songs.txt file by following a relative path. To do so, use the notation in Figure 12-4 to describe the file's position in relation to the current folder:

.\Playlists\songs.txt

In a relative path notation, a single dot (.) represents the current folder, two dots and a slash (..\) represent the folder one level above the current one, and a single dot and a slash (.\) represent a folder below the current folder. The notation .\Playlists\songs.txt means, "starting from the current folder, move down in the folder structure to the Playlists folder to find the songs.txt file."

You can think of an absolute path as the exact address of your home (123 Main Street; Sunny, Florida, 32323) and the relative path as directions to your home from the grocery story (make a right on Orange Street, a left on Main Street, and stop at house #123).

Using the absolute file path in code assumes that the file will always be in the same location, even on different computers. Relative paths are more flexible because they remain relative to the current folder and are not affected if folders above the current one change name or location.

Q Suppose a user changes the name of the Music folder to Tunes. If the code contains an absolute file path to songs.txt, what happens when the program needs to access that file? What happens if the code contains a relative file path to songs.txt?

A When using an absolute path, the program would look for songs.txt starting at C:, look for a folder named Music, and then stop, because no folder directly below C: is named Music. With a relative path, the program would look for the Playlists folder one level below the current folder and then find the songs.txt file.

When specifying the name of a file, it may be necessary to use escape characters, which act as alternate interpretations of characters that have another meaning. Because these characters have special meanings to the system, you may need to escape single quotations, double quotations, backslashes, and question marks when working with the file system, as shown in **Figure 12-5**.

Character	Name	Escape Character
'	Single Quotation Mark	\'
"	Double Quotation Mark	\"
\	Backslash	\\
?	Question Mark	\?

Figure 12-5   Escape characters

Anatomy of a File (12.1.5, 12.1.6)

In a computer, a file is treated as a named collection of uninterrupted data stored in memory, as shown in **Figure 12-6**. Each piece of information in the file is stored as a sequence of bytes in memory.

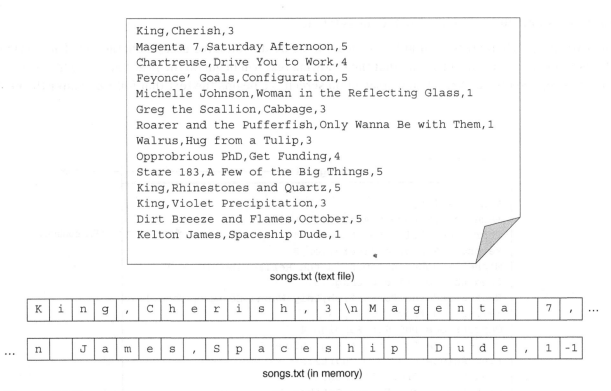

Figure 12-6   songs.txt represented in a text file and memory

A plain text file is the most basic type of data file used for input and output in programming. It arranges data in rows of text, which includes numbers and symbols. On a storage device, each character in a plain text file needs 1 byte of memory. For example, song.txt has 449 characters and takes up 449 bytes of memory. As you know, a computer stores characters in memory using binary code, so A is stored as 01000001. The main advantage of text files is that they are simple to create and read and they don't require much storage space, even when they contain a lot of data.

When you create a file, the OS reserves a named location on a storage device for the file contents. Next, you add data to the file, which a program does by writing to the file. The file is stored on disk until it is explicitly erased by the operating system.

In general, a file can have the following components:

File name. The file name is the complete name of the file, including the extension, such as songs.txt. The file name extension identifies the type of file. For example, .txt indicates a plain text file, and .mp3 is an extension for music files in a compressed format.

Contents. The contents include the text or other data in the file.

Delimiter. A delimiter is a tab character or punctuation mark such as a comma used to separate information, such as an artist's name from a song title.

End of file. The end of file (EOF) is a special character or code that represents the last element in a file. The EOF follows the last character of a file and is often represented as the number −1.

Newline. A newline is a special character (\n) indicating the end of a line.

Access point. An access point keeps track of your current position in a file, similar to a cursor or insertion point.

Figure 12-7 shows the components of the songs.txt file.

Similar to escape characters used in file names, file contents can have escape characters. The newline character is represented as **\n** and shows that the following text will begin on the next line in the file. The tab escape code is represented as **\t**. When displayed on screen, **\t** begins the text that follows it after the next tab stop.

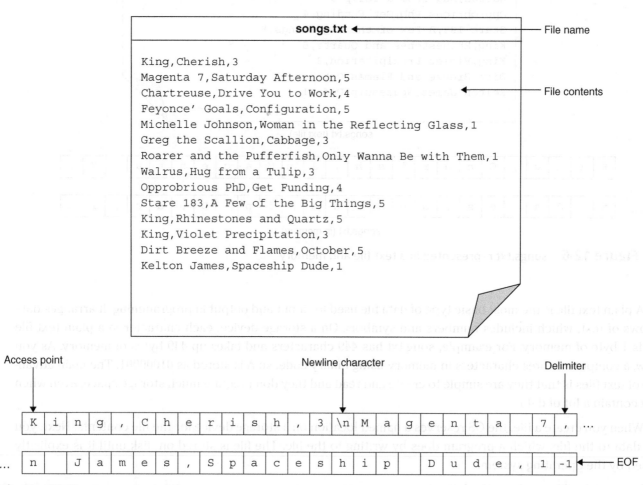

Figure 12-7 Elements of a file

File Usage (12.1.7, 12.1.8, 12.1.9, 12.1.10)

When code reads information from a file, it is called **file input**. When your code writes information to a file, it is called **file output**. Together they are called file input and output, or **file I/O**. Some common file handling operations include opening a file, reading the contents, writing information into the file, and closing it.

Two types of data files include text files and binary files. A **text file** stores its contents as individual 8-bit (1 byte) ASCII characters, such as text and numbers that people can easily read. If you open the songs.txt text file in a text editor, for example, you can read the list of artist names, song titles, and ratings. Text files usually have a .txt extension and are created using a plain text editor. Text files that store programs or markup code have the extensions .cpp, .java, .py, .csv, and .html.

Storing a text file using ASCII characters ensures that any type of operating system can handle the file. However, storing text as a series of 8-bit characters is a less efficient method that tends to consume memory.

In contrast, a **binary file** stores its contents in binary format, which you cannot easily read. The contents of binary files are not limited to ASCII text, but may contain byte patterns that do not print. For example, executable programs, music files, and images are binary files. If you open a binary file in a text editor, you will see symbols and other characters that do not form words except accidentally. Binary files can have a wide range of extensions such as .bin, .exe, .mp3, .pdf, and .doc.

The main advantage of binary files is that their encoding takes up less space than storing individual 8-bit ASCII characters, and computers can read them quickly. For example, a binary file can use a numeric format (such as IEEE 754) rather than text characters to store a value using less memory than ASCII.

Figure 12-8 compares text and binary files.

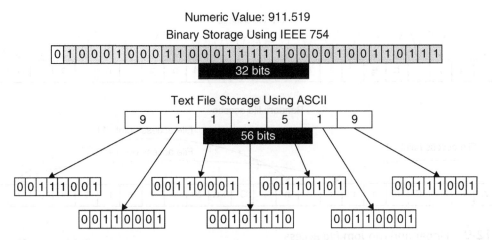

Figure 12-8 Binary vs text storage of the number 911.519

As you will see, your program needs to know whether it is using a text file or binary file to process it correctly. Binary files are encoded in a way that is specific to the type of file being read, so your program must read the code according to the encoding. Because text files simply store each character as its 8-bit ASCII representation, a program must only convert each character to its 8-bit set of binary codes.

Most programming languages have a **file handler**, a special built-in feature that allows you to interact with a file. You can use the file handler to request information about a file such as its size, type, location within the directory structure, the time it was created, and time it was last modified. The file handler also provides features to enable file I/O, opening files, and closing files.

12.2 PROCESSING A FILE

Accessing Files (12.2.1, 12.2.2)

Because files are stored in memory, consecutively, byte by byte, access is usually linear. A **file access point** is like a cursor—it indicates the current position in a file. You start at the first byte of the file and continue moving the file access point until the end of the file. Just as you are intended to read from a book, the computer reads each character or code in sequence, one by one, for the contents to have meaning. Reading a file this way is called **linear access** or sequential access.

In contrast, a program can also read a file using **random access**, which reads each character directly without first reading the character before it. Random file access is facilitated by changing the position of the file access point, a special variable that acts like a cursor indicating your position in a file. As a programmer, you can specify how many bytes to move the file access point from the current position. Positive values move the point towards the end of the file and negative values move the point towards the beginning of the file. As you work with files, you must keep track of the file access point position to avoid attempting to move outside of the memory limits of the file. **Figure 12-9** compares linear and random file access.

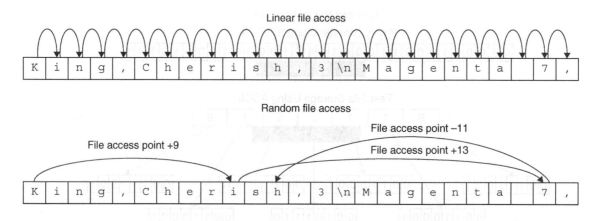

Figure 12-9   Linear and random file access

Q After the program has read some of the file, how do I go back to the beginning of a file?

A Each time you open a file, it places the file access point at the beginning of the file, allowing you to close and reopen the file. Alternatively, programming languages provide statements that reset the file access point to the beginning.

Streaming and Buffering (12.2.3, 12.2.4)

When your program uses file I/O, you are streaming information. The same way that you stream your favorite shows to binge watch on your computer, you stream to read information at a fixed rate into your program. Essentially, a **stream** is a channel that allows you to interact with files stored on your computer or another drive. See **Figure 12-10**.

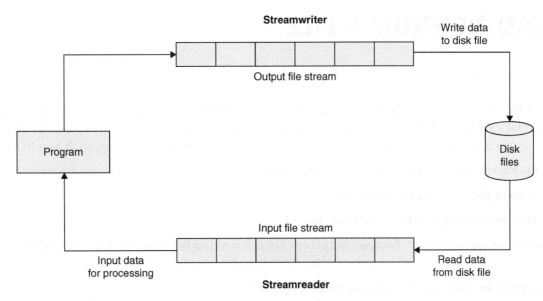

Figure 12-10 Streaming input and output streams using files

Some programming languages use a **streamwriter** to create a stream for writing text data to a file. The data from the text file is transferred to the stream and then written to the file. Similarly, a **streamreader** creates a stream for reading text from a file. The streamreader transfers the data from the file, into the stream, and then into your program.

Imagine that you are streaming a three-hour movie on your laptop. Previously, the laptop would need time to transfer the entire movie to your computer, and your computer would need a lot of space to hold the entire movie. Instead, your computer uses **buffering** to move data, bit by bit, into and out of a reserved part of memory (called a **buffer**) that your code can access.

Using a **buffered stream** can also improve performance when your program needs to read and write large amounts of data. Operating systems are constantly juggling many tasks. When reading a file, the OS does not read one byte at a time but reads a block of data and then switches to another task. While switching from one task to another, the OS needs to store the data somewhere, which is in a buffer. The advantages of buffering are shown in **Figure 12-11**.

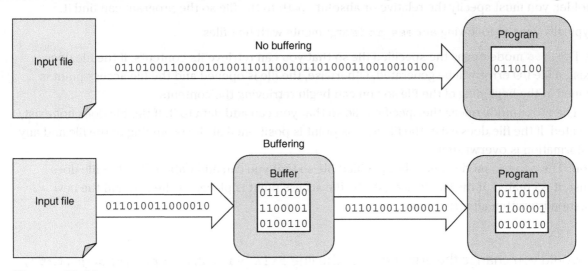

Figure 12-11 Buffering data from a file and into a program

The top part of Figure 12-11 shows reading from an input file without using buffering. The program has to wait for the entire input file to be read before it can use the data. For large input files, this can involve significant delays. With buffering, shown in the bottom part of Figure 12-11, the buffer stores some data from the input file and sends it to the program, which can use the data immediately without waiting for the entire file to be read.

12.3 READING FROM A FILE

Opening a File for Reading (12.3.1, 12.3.2, 12.3.3)

The songs.txt file lists the artist's last name, the song title, and a rating of each song on a 1–5 scale. You can write code to perform tasks such as calculating the average song rating or counting the songs by the artist named King. Before your program can do that, it must open the file by accessing it on a storage device, such as a hard drive.

Opening a file for reading has the following generic syntax:

```
declare file_variable as file_handler

file_variable.open("songs.txt", access_mode)
```

In most programming languages, escape characters are not needed because the file name is enclosed in double quotes.

The following breaks down the pseudocode piece by piece:

- The pseudocode includes the variable **file_variable**, which is assigned the type **file_handler**, a special type that enables you to interact with files. As a **file_handler**, the **file_variable** can open, close, and perform other tasks with files.
- To indicate that **file_variable** should open a file, use the dot operator followed by the word **open**, as in **file_variable.open**. You use the dot operator to specify which action to perform with a variable.
- Next, similar to passing arguments to a function, you specify the name of the file to open within parentheses. Enclose the file name in quotation marks, as in **"songs.txt"**.
- You can also include an **access_mode** argument that specifies how to access the file. The **access_mode** argument is optional and defines the purpose of opening the specified file. Common access modes are **read**, **write**, and **append**. If you do not specify an **access_mode**, the program uses the default mode, **r**, to open a file stream for reading from a text file.

The pseudocode assumes that songs.txt is in the same folder as the program code. If the file is stored in a different folder, you must specify the relative or absolute path to the file so the program can find it.

You typically use the following **access_mode** arguments with text files.

Read. The read mode opens the specified file so that you can retrieve its contents. If the file does not exist, a file I/O error will be generated. Otherwise, the file is opened and the file access point is positioned at the beginning of the file so you can begin retrieving the contents.

Write. The write mode opens the specified file so that you can add data to it. If the file does not exist, it is created. If the file does exist, the file access point is positioned at the beginning of the file and any new information is overwritten.

Append. The append mode opens the specified file so that you can add data to it. If the file does not exist, it is created. If the file does exist, the file access point is placed at the end and the new information is written after that point.

Q How would you change the arguments of the line **file_variable.open("songs.txt", access_mode)** to open songs.txt for reading?

A You would write **file_variable.open("songs.txt", "read")**.

Most of the time, the code shown earlier opens songs.txt so your program can perform other tasks with it. What if another program accesses songs.txt at the same time (perhaps to add new songs) or the name of the file is changed to my_songs.txt? An error will occur, so you want to include code to check that the file has actually been opened. You can use a **try** block to catch exceptions that occur, as shown in **Figure 12-12**.

```cpp
#include <iostream>

#include <fstream>

#include <stdexcept>

#include <string>


using namespace std;


int main ()

{

   ifstream input_file;

   try

   {

      input_file.open("songs.txt", ios::in);


      if(!input_file.is_open())

      {

         throw runtime_error("Could not open the file.");

      }

   }

   catch (runtime_error error)

   {

      cout << error.what() << endl;

      return 0;

   }


   return 0;

}
```

Figure 12-12   Using exception handling to open a file for reading

The code in Figure 12-12 opens the songs.txt file and handles an exception, should one occur. As in the pseudocode, first a file variable is declared. Next, the code that opens the file is enclosed within a **try** block. If an exception occurs, it is caught in the **catch** block. The message "Could not open the file" is displayed and the program exits because it cannot read from a file that does not exist.

Reading from a File (12.3.4, 12.3.5, 12.3.6, 12.3.7)

Now that your program opened songs.txt, it can read from it. Reading a file means that the OS starts at the beginning of the file (or wherever your file access point is currently placed) and delivers a copy of that information to your program. You use variables such as integers, characters, and strings to store the information given to your file. As the program reads each piece of data, the file access point updates and moves to the next item in the file.

Typically, programs read files character by character, in order, using a loop. The amount of data in a file is often unknown, so the loop stops when it reaches the EOF character.

A file is allocated a certain amount of space in memory. The EOF character keeps programs from accessing memory locations beyond the location of the file. A program cannot read past the EOF character because it violates file integrity and will crash the program.

When the file variable no longer has more information to read, the value of EOF becomes true, indicating that the program has reached the end of the file. Following is an example of checking for EOF:

```
declare c as character

while file_variable.eof != true

   c = file_variable.nextCharacter
```

The songs.txt file is formatted so that the data for each song is on its own line, with the artist, song title, and rating each separated by a comma, as shown in **Figure 12-13**.

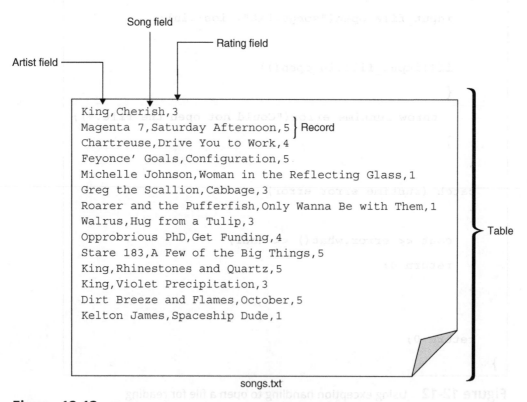

Figure 12-13   Fields and records in a comma-delimited file

Q How could you use the information about songs.txt to read the file more efficiently than character-by-character?

A Because you know that each line of the file has the same artist-song-rating format, you can read each line of the file, saving the information from the file in that order.

As Figure 12-13 shows, songs.txt is a comma-delimited text file, resembling records in a table in which each chunk of data is separated by a comma. Programs can read the comma-delimited text files more efficiently than character by character. Each chunk of data up to a comma is a field. One line containing an artist, song, and rating is a record. Because the data is arranged in fields and records, it is structured as a table.

In the program reading songs.txt, you can format `file_variable` to read up to each comma, assign that text to a variable, and then continue reading the rest of the line, as in **Figure 12-14**.

```cpp
#include <iostream>
#include <fstream>
#include <stdexcept>
#include <string>
#include <sstream>
using namespace std;

int main ()
{
    ifstream input_file;
    input_file.open("songs.txt", ios::in);
    string line_of_text;
    string artist;
    string song;
    string rating;
```

Figure 12-14 Reading a comma-delimited text file
(*continued*)

```
          while(!input_file.eof())
          {
              getline(input_file, line_of_text);
              stringstream s(line_of_text);

              getline(s, artist, ',');
              getline(s, song, ',');
              getline(s, rating, ',');
          }

          return 0;
}
```

Figure 12-14   Reading a comma-delimited text file

The program works as follows:

- Start the program by declaring variables to hold each field: artist, song, and rating.
- Also set the file variable to recognize that a comma is the delimiter used to separate each field in the record.
- Use a while loop to read through the file until it reaches the end.
- Each line reads the artist, song, and rating.
- Continue reading each line of the file until there is no more information to read.

Although rating is a number, it is declared as a **string**, so your code reads it as a **string**. If you plan to do math with the rating data, such as compute the average song rating, you need to convert the **string** to an integer. You could declare a new integer variable named **rating_num** and then add a statement to the end of the while loop:

rating_num = stringToInt(rating)

You can derive the numerical value by using a built-in string-to-integer converter. The command differs in each programming language, though the logic remains the same. As a **string**, the rating is the ASCII character representation of the number. You need to convert it to an integer before using it for mathematical operations. After this line of code runs, the numeric value is stored in **rating_num**.

The code in **Figure 12-15** reads the entire songs.txt file line by line (or song by song) and counts the number of songs in the file.

```
#include <iostream>
#include <fstream>
#include <string>
using namespace std;
```

Figure 12-15   Reading the songs.txt file (*continued*)

```
int main ()
{

    ifstream input_file;
    input_file.open("songs.txt", ios::in);
    string line_of_text;
    int song_count = 0;

    while(input_file.eof() == false)
    {
    getline(input_file, line_of_text);
        song_count++;
    }

    cout << "There are " << song_count << " songs in the file." << endl;

    return 0;
}

OUTPUT:
There are 14 songs in the file.
```

Figure 12-15   Reading the songs.txt file

Following are common exceptions that can occur when reading files:

The input stream is not open. There was an error creating the file handler, so the stream never gets created.

The file is empty. In this case, the file opens, but its only content is the EOF character.

Reading the wrong data type. You try to read a `string` variable as a numeric variable.

The file does not exist. The file you specified to open is not in the current location.

The file is actually a folder. The file that you requested to open is not a readable file, but actually a folder.

The file is already open by another program. Multiple file handlers can open the same file for reading with no problem, but once a program begins writing to the program, a lock is placed on the file and no one can open it until the writing has finished and the lock has been released.

In each case, it's a good programming practice to try and catch any generated exceptions and use the file handler to check for unintended states, such as an empty file or a locked file.

12.4 CLOSING A FILE

Closing Files after Use (12.4.1)

After you have read a file and are finished using it, the program should close it. For example, suppose that when you finish reading the songs.txt file to calculate your average song rating, your program unexpectedly stops due to some unforeseen error. This can lead to file corruption and loss of data. In larger programs, having too many files open at once can detract from performance. Closing a file restores resources (such as buffers) to the system. For these reasons, it is a good practice to close files as soon as you no longer need them.

After a file is closed, the input stream can be used to open another file, and the previous file becomes available to be opened by other code. To close the songs.txt file, include the following statement at the end of the program or as soon as the file is no longer needed by your program:

```
file_variable.close()
```

Be sure to close a file only when you are sure that your code no longer needs to access it. Trying to read from an already closed file may cause an error while your code is running.

Trying to Close a File (12.4.2)

Suppose your code tries to close a file that has already been closed somewhere else in your code. This leads to an exception that you need to address. Use **try** and **catch** blocks to handle the error. For example, the following code attempts to close a file that has already been closed. The **try** block attempts to close the already closed file. The **catch** block throws an I/O exception, and then displays an error message.

```
file_variable.close()

try

    file_variable.close()

catch IOexception

    display "File has already been closed elsewhere."
```

12.5 CREATING AND WRITING NEW FILES

Creating a File (12.5.1)

The same way that you use code to read information from a file, you can also create a new file. Suppose that you want to make another text file containing all of your favorite songs, ones you rated 4 or higher. In some programming languages, opening a file for writing with a unique name creates the file in the same folder as your program code. The new file is empty and contains only the EOF character, so you need to write data into the file before a program can use it. **Figure 12-16** shows a part of a program for creating and opening a file.

```
#include <iostream>
#include <fstream>
using namespace std;
int main()
{
    ofstream output_file;
    output_file.open("favorite_songs.txt", ios::out);
    return 0;
}
```

Figure 12-16   Creating a new file

To create a new file, you declare a variable as a file handler. By using the file handler to open a file for writing that does not exist, your program will create a new empty file named favorite_songs.txt in the same directory as your code.

Some programming languages, such as Java, provide a specific way to make blank files. In this case, you create a new file using the following code:

```
declare file_variable as file_handler
file_variable.create_new_file("favorite_songs.txt")
```

After declaring a file handler variable named **file_variable**, you can use the dot notation to execute the **file_variable.create_new_file** statement. The statement creates and opens a file named favorite_songs.txt.

Opening a File for Writing (12.5.2, 12.5.3, 12.5.4)

You open a file for writing after creating a new file or when you want to add data to an existing file. For example, you created favorite_songs.txt to hold your top songs, those rated 4 or 5, and now want to add the top-rated songs from songs.txt to favorite_songs.txt. Also, suppose that you bought some music and you want to add more songs to your list in songs.txt. In either case, you can use file I/O to write text into a file. The following pseudocode shows the generic syntax for opening a file for writing, in this case, the new favorite_songs.txt:

```
declare file_variable as file_handler
file_variable.open("favorite_songs.txt", access_mode)
```

You declare a variable with the type **file_handler** and use the dot operator to open the file and specify the access mode, as you did before. You'd use the same generic syntax to write to a new file or add to an existing file. The **access_mode** argument controls how the file will be written.

As with reading a file, **access_mode** is an optional argument for writing to a file. The values are usually **write** or **append**. The **write** mode begins writing text at the beginning of the file. If the file already exists, by default, using **write** mode writes over the entire file and erases any previous contents. The **append** mode starts writing at the end of the file, so it does not overwrite information. If you are uncertain whether a file already contains information, use **append** mode to avoid writing over information unintentionally.

Q Would you use the **write** or **append** access mode to add new songs to songs.txt?

A **Append** is the most appropriate in this case because you want to preserve the previous songs and add to the list.

Writing to and Appending a File (12.5.5, 12.5.6)

Suppose that your friends ask you to write code to help manage their music playlists as well. You can't give them your songs.txt file because they have different songs on their computer. You can, however, use a program to write files. The program asks your friends to enter their songs. It then creates a new text file named their_songs.txt. The program is shown in **Figure 12-17**.

```cpp
#include <iostream>

#include <fstream>

#include <string>
using namespace std;


int main ()
{
    ofstream output_file;

    output_file.open("their_songs.txt", ios::out);

    int num_songs;

    string artist;

    string song;

    int rating;

    cout << "Hello friend. How many songs would you like to enter? ";

    cin >> num_songs;

    cin.ignore();


    for(int i=0; i < num_songs;  i++)
    {
        cout << "Please enter the artist name. ";

        getline(cin, artist);

        cout << "Please enter the song name. ";
```

Figure 12-17 Writing a new file for a new song list (*continued*)

```
        getline(cin, song);
        cout << "Please enter the rating (1-5).";
        cin >> rating;
        cin.ignore();
        output_file << artist << "," << song << "," << rating << endl;
    }

    cout << "Thanks! Your file has been written." << endl;
    output_file.close();
    return 0;
}
```

OUTPUT:

Hello friend. How many songs would you like to enter? **1 [Enter]**

Please enter the artist name. **Rizzo [Enter]**

Please enter the song name. **Lies Hurt [Enter]**

Please enter the rating (1-5). **4 [Enter]**

Thanks! Your file has been written.

Figure 12-17   Writing a new file for a new song list

The program works as follows:

- Declare a file handler variable called **output_file**.
- Create the file called their_songs.txt by opening the output file for writing.
- Declare variables to hold the number of songs that your friend wants to enter, the artist name, song name, and rating.
- Prompt your friend to enter the number of songs to enter in the file and store the response in the variable **num_songs**.
- In a for-loop, iterate from 0 to the number of songs that your friend entered. Also prompt your friend to provide the artist name, song title, and rating for a song.
- Write the responses to the specified file. Because the file has to be formatted in a specific way, after the artist name is written, you write a comma, then the song name, a comma, and then the rating.
- After the rating, you write the newline character to the file, indicating that the next piece of information (that is, the next song) should start on the next line.
- Finally, you display a message stating that the file has been written and you close the output file.

If you want to go through your songs in songs.txt and write all of the favorites to a new file named favorite_songs.txt, you need to read and write at the same time. While you read each song from songs.txt, you check the rating score. If the rating is 4 or higher, then write the song data to favorite_songs.txt.

To write one song per line, you also need to include a newline character, which works like pressing the Enter key so that the following text appears on the next line. You specify a newline character using \n as the newline argument in a write statement, as in **Figure 12-18**.

```cpp
#include <iostream>
#include <fstream>
#include <string>
#include <sstream>
using namespace std;


int main ()
{
    ifstream input_file;
    ofstream output_file;
    input_file.open("songs.txt", ios::in);
    output_file.open("favorite_songs.txt", ios::out);
    string artist;
    string song;
    string rating;
    int rating_num;


    string line_of_text;

    while(!input_file.eof())
    {
        getline(input_file, line_of_text);
        stringstream s(line_of_text);
        getline(s, artist, ',');
        getline(s, song, ',');
        getline(s, rating, ',');
        rating_num = stoi(rating);
```

Figure 12-18   Saving the favorite songs to a new file (*continued*)

```
        if(rating_num >= 4)
        {
            output_file << artist;
            output_file << ",";
            output_file << song;
            output_file << ",";
            output_file<< rating << endl;
        }
    }

    return 0;
}
```

Figure 12-18   Saving the favorite songs to a new file

Figure 12-19 shows the songs.txt and favorite_songs.txt files after running the program shown in Figure 12-18.

songs.txt

```
King,Cherish,3
Magenta 7,Saturday Afternoon,5
Chartreuse,Drive You to Work,4
Feyonce' Goals,Configuration,5
Michelle Johnson,Woman in the Reflecting Glass,1
Greg the Scallion,Cabbage,3
Roarer and the Pufferfish,Only Wanna Be with Them,1
Walrus,Hug from a Tulip,3
Opprobrious PhD,Get Funding,4
Stare 183,A Few of the Big Things,5
King,Rhinestones and Quartz,5
King,Violet Precipitation,3
Dirt Breeze and Flames,October,5
Kelton James,Spaceship Dude,1
```

favorite_songs.txt

```
Magenta 7,Saturday Afternoon,5
Chartreuse,Drive You to Work,4
Feyonce' Goals,Configuration,5
Opprobrious PhD,Get Funding,4
Stare 183,A Few of the Big Things,5
King,Rhinestones and Quartz,5
Dirt Breeze and Flames,October,5
```

Figure 12-19   Contents of songs.txt and favorite_songs.txt

Nice! Now you have a list of your favorite songs. When it's time to add more favorite songs, you can update the favorite_songs.txt file. However, if you open favorite_songs.txt for writing, the file access will start at the beginning of the file, and you'll write over the current contents of the file. Instead, use the **append access_mode** argument, which keeps the current songs in the file and writes the new records at the end of the file. The code for appending resembles Figure 12-18, except you would change the line to open the output file from access mode **write** to **append**, as in the following pseudocode:

```
output_file.open("favorite_songs.txt", "append")
```

Q Can I code a program to read and write to the same file at the same time?

A It depends. Some operating systems let you write to a file while other programs (including your own) are reading from it. Others place a lock on the file, restricting access until someone closes the file. In general, reading and writing to the same file at the same time is a bad practice and should be avoided. If a file is being read while another program is writing to it, the read information may be out of date.

Anticipating Exceptions (12.5.7)

Suppose that a file was improperly formatted on one line, such as missing an artist title and rating for the last song. The code attempts to read the integer for the rating and reads past the end of the file instead. This causes your program to crash. For this reason, place any code that reads from a file in a **try** block.

A file operation could fail in other ways, such as not locating the file, having trouble transferring data from the buffer, or trying to read data into variables from a blank file. It makes sense to wrap the entire block of code dealing with files into one **try** block, instead of many separate **try** and **catch** blocks, as in the following pseudocode.

```
declare input_file as file_handler
declare output_file as file_handler


try

    input_file.open("new_songs.txt", "read")
    output_file.open("favorite_songs.txt", "append")


    declare artist as string
    declare song as string
    declare rating as string
    declare rating_num as integer
    input_file.setDelimiter(",")
```

```
    while input_file.peek() != EOF
        artist = input_file.nextString()
        song = input_file.nextString()
        rating = input_file.nextString()
        rating_num = stringToNum(rating)

        if rating_num >= 4
            output_file.write(artist)
            output_file.write(",")
            output_file.write(song)
            output_file.write("\n")

    input_file.close()
    output_file.close()


catch FileNotFoundException
    display "The specified file was not found."
catch EndOfFileException
    display "End of File reached. Exiting."
    return
catch CloseFileException
    display "Closing an already closed file. Exiting."
    return
```

SUMMARY

- A file is a named container of data stored in memory, such as a document, picture, or song. Use files as a way to read large amounts of data into your program or write large amounts of data from your program, also called file input/output (I/O).
- Folders contain and organize files into groups. An operating system stores files in an arrangement of folders called a folder structure or directory structure.
- The location of a file on your computer can be described by a relative path or an absolute path. The absolute path indicates the exact location of a file on the computer starting from the main storage device or drive. The relative path provides the location of a file starting from another location in the folder structure. Relative paths are more flexible than absolute paths because they are not affected if folders above the current one change name or location.
- Programs typically read two types of files: text files and binary files. Files can be read sequentially until the end-of-file character is reached, which is called linear access or sequential access.

- Buffering helps to stream large amounts of data into your program by moving data, bit by bit, into and out of a reserved part of memory called a buffer. Buffering can improve performance when your program needs to read or write a lot of data.
- Before a program can use a file, it must open the file by locating it on a storage device and then associating it with a file variable. To access the data in a file, a program reads from the file. The program can read unstructured data in a file character by character. In a structured file, such as a comma-delimited text file, the program can read the data field by field.
- In a delimited text file, you can use a loop to read a file efficiently. After reading a file, the program can process the file data to do operations such as performing calculations. You might need to convert string data to an integer or other numeric data type to use it for processing.
- A program writes to a file when it creates a file and then adds data to it, or when it appends new data to the end of an existing file. The file I/O mode depends on the data type and the desired operation, whether reading, writing, or appending a file.
- Programs should close files as soon as the files are no longer needed to avoid system performance problems.
- File operations can throw exceptions, so it's best to wrap file operations in a **try** block to catch the exceptions. Common exceptions include not finding the specified file, trying to close a file that has already been closed, and encountering improper formatting in a comma-delimited text file.

Key Terms

absolute file path	end of file (EOF)	linear access
access point	escape characters	newline
append	field	random access
binary file	file	read
buffer	file access point	record
buffered stream	file handler	relative file path
buffering	File handling	stream
comma-delimited text file	file I/O	streamreader
contents	file input	streamwriter
delimiter	file name	table
directory structure	file output	text file
dot operator	folder	write

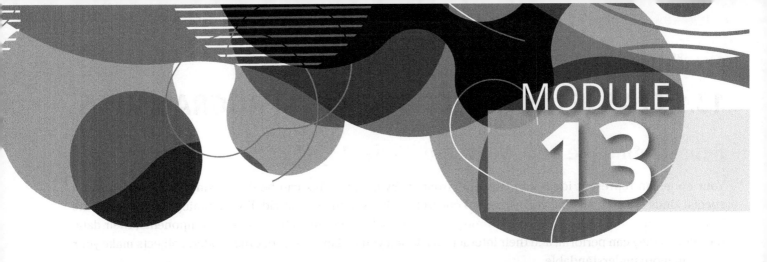

CLASSES AND OBJECTS

LEARNING OBJECTIVES:

13.1 CLASSES IN OBJECT-ORIENTED PROGRAMMING

13.1.1 Explain the difference between object-oriented programming (OOP) and procedural programming.

13.1.2 Define a class in OOP.

13.1.3 Explain how a class is similar to an architectural blueprint.

13.1.4 List the components that comprise a class.

13.1.5 Explain the function of the "class" keyword in creating a class.

13.2 USING OBJECTS

13.2.1 Describe objects and OOP.

13.2.2 Explain instances and objects.

13.2.3 Compare an object as an instance of the blueprint.

13.2.4 Define complex data types.

13.2.5 Identify the similarities of implementing primitive data types to implementing objects from classes.

13.2.6 Explain how encapsulation can enhance coding structures.

13.2.7 Explain the concept of information hiding.

13.3 USING STATIC ELEMENTS IN A CLASS

13.3.1 Explain how static variables are shared among instances of a class.

13.3.2 Explain the purpose of having static members of a class.

13.3.3 Define static methods.

13.3.4 Define static classes.

13.4 CHARACTERISTICS OF OBJECTS IN OBJECT-ORIENTED PROGRAMS

13.4.1 Define identity as it applies to OOP objects.

13.4.2 Define state as it applies to OOP objects.

13.4.3 Define behavior as it applies to OOP objects.

13.1 CLASSES IN OBJECT-ORIENTED PROGRAMMING

Representing the Real World with Code (13.1.1)

Your code can represent ideas and concepts from everyday life. This can be done using objects, which are special kinds of variables that correspond to concrete objects in the real world. Programming that uses objects is aptly called object-oriented programming (OOP). In OOP, you think in terms of key components, their data, the actions they can perform, and their interactions. When you collaborate with other coders, objects make your program more understandable.

In procedural programming, code is written step by step to create a set of instructions similar to a recipe for the computer to follow. When your program runs, it performs the exact steps in the same order as you wrote them. Procedural programming is useful for simple programs in which the algorithm has a finite number of steps, such as calculating the square root of a number. Object-oriented programming is more appropriate when your program needs to model a complex, real-world system with many components, actions, and relationships, such as a banking application.

Procedural programming is usually the first programming paradigm that new coders learn, but it has limitations. For example, imagine that you are writing a procedural program to manage hundreds of cars at a dealership. The information you need to store in variables about each car includes the make, model, color, year, mileage, and many other details, as shown in **Figure 13-1**.

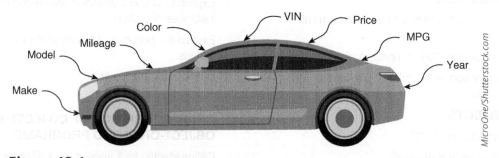

Figure 13-1   A car and its features

The amount of information for you and the program to keep track of would soon become overwhelming. If you need to change information, such as to add the vehicle identification number (VIN) to each car, you have to tediously modify every line of code corresponding to that change. As the number of changes increased, so would the difficulty of changing your code. OOP offers an alternative that allows you to easily modify the code in this scenario.

Using Classes (13.1.2, 13.1.3)

Classes make object-oriented programming possible. A class is a blueprint for creating an object. The same way that an architectural blueprint describes a building, a class describes an object. You use a class to create objects that share common characteristics, or properties, and build programs that use the objects. An architectural blueprint can be used to create many houses at different addresses, and a class can create many objects that share the same structure. The **Car** class is like a general model that can create objects such as a 2020 blue Honda Accord and a classic yellow Volkswagen Beetle.

A benefit of using classes is that it promotes code reuse. A programmer can reuse class code when making objects that have the same features. For example, if you want to store information about 500 cars in your dealership app, you could use one class file to describe all 500 cars.

Q How is the concept of a recipe (such as a cookie recipe) similar to a class?

A A recipe defines the characteristics of a cookie and you use it to create many cookies, which all have the same attributes, such as shape and crispiness, though the values of those attributes can vary.

Class Components (13.1.4, 13.1.5)

In many programming languages, the keyword **class** is a reserved word that you use only to define a class. A class is generally made up of the following components:

- **Class name**. A class name identifies the class by a specific name. The class name is usually a noun, such as **Car**.
- **Member variables**. The member variables, also called attributes or properties, make up the data stored in a class.
- **Methods**. The methods describe the actions an object can perform. Methods are like functions that belong to the class. A method is usually a verb phrase, such as **test_drive()**.
- **Accessors and mutators**. The accessors and mutators, commonly called getters and setters, are methods used only to control access to the member variables.
- **Access modifiers**. The access modifiers are keywords that describe what can access and change the member variables. Access modifiers can be set as **public**, **private**, or **protected**. This module covers **public** and **private** access. The **protected** keyword is discussed with inheritance and polymorphism.

A **Car** class (shown in **Figure 13-2**) has member variables to store a car's make, model, color, VIN, current price, miles per gallon (MPG), model year, and current mileage. The class also includes methods to describe the actions that can be performed on a **Car** object. For example, the **give_discount()** method sets a discount of a specific percentage on a car, **increase_mileage()** allows a dealer to increase the car's stated mileage after a test drive to accurately reflect the car's current mileage, and **sell_car()** sets the sold variable as True, stores the final **price**, and sets **on_lot** to False. The **test_drive()** method stores the driver's **license_number** of the person who took the car for a test drive and sets the value of **on_lot** to False.

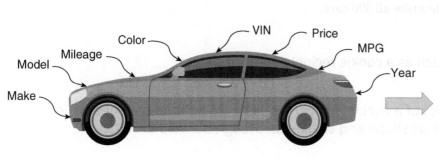

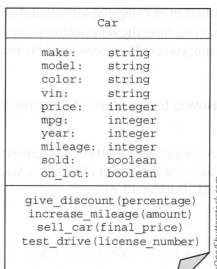

Car	
make:	string
model:	string
color:	string
vin:	string
price:	integer
mpg:	integer
year:	integer
mileage:	integer
sold:	boolean
on_lot:	boolean

give_discount(percentage)
increase_mileage(amount)
sell_car(final_price)
test_drive(license_number)

MicroOne/Shutterstock.com

Figure 13-2   Features of a car represented as a class

Figure 13-3 shows the code to create the **Car** class:

```
class Car
{
    public:
        void give_discount(percentage);

        void increase_mileage(amount);

        void sell_car(final_price);

        void test_drive(license_number);

        string get_make();

        void set_make(make);

        string get_model();

        void set_model(model);

        string get_color();

        void set_color(color);

        string get_vin();

        void set_vin(vin);

        int get_price();

        void set_price(price);

        int get_mpg();
```

Figure 13-3   Representation of the **Car** class (*continued*)

```
            void set_mpg(mpg);

            int get_year();

            void set_year(year);

            int get_mileage();

            void set_mileage(mileage);

            bool get_sold();

            void set_sold(sold);

            bool get_on_lot();

            void set_on_lot(on_lot);

    private:
            string make;

            string model;

            string color;

            string vin;

            int price;

            int mpg;

            int year;

            int mileage;

            bool sold;

            bool on_lot;
};
```

Figure 13-3   Representation of the `Car` class

- The code begins by using the **class** keyword to create a class named **Car**. Class names are capitalized by convention and are usually a noun (person, place, or thing). A class can have any name, except a reserved keyword. A class name follows similar rules as a variable name. It cannot begin with a number, but can consist of letters, numbers, and the underscore character.

- The access modifier **public** means that any methods or member variables listed in this section can be viewed or modified from anywhere outside of the class by anyone or any other part of the program. It is a common practice to make accessors and mutators **public**. The **public** parts of a class can be directly accessed by using the dot operator (.) to specify the name of the object, followed by the method or member variable.

- A method such as **give_discount(percentage)** consists of the method name, which is a single word beginning with a verb and containing no spaces. Method names are always followed by parentheses. The parentheses contain data to send to the method, such as a percentage value, that is required for the method to complete its action. Use empty parentheses for methods that do not require any data (as with accessors).

- The methods section of the code includes an accessor and mutator for each member variable. A method such as **get_make()** is an accessor (or getter), and a method such as **set_make(make)** is the corresponding mutator (or setter). When an object's getter is called (for example **get_make()**), the code making the method call must set the result of the call to a **string** variable. By convention, getters return the value of a specific member variable. Setters allow you to control how member variables are stored in an object and limit their accessibility. It is a good programming practice to include code in the setter to ensure the validity of the operation being performed. For example, the **set_price()** method checks if the price is a positive number.

- The access modifier **private** means that the methods and member variables in this section can be viewed or modified only by the class itself. In contrast to the **public** section, anything listed after **private** cannot be accessed by using the dot operator (.). It is customary to make all member variables **private** so that no outside code can directly change the features of the object in the class. Data and methods should be **private** if sharing them would cause problems. For example, suppose the **price** attribute were **public**. Code outside the **Car** class could change the price of a car, causing havoc at the dealership. By making the attributes **private**, only the methods of the **Car** class are allowed to change the car's attributes.

- An attribute such as **make** is a characteristic of a **Car**. As a member variable, its data type needs to be specified. Car makes are the brands, such as Honda, Ford, and Volvo, so **make** is declared as a **string**. The attributes can consist of any variable, including other objects.

Q Should every piece of data in an attribute have a getter and setter?

A Not necessarily. Although it's common practice to control access to data using getters and setters, you are not required to make getters and setters for every attribute.

13.2 USING OBJECTS

Creating Objects (13.2.1, 13.2.2, 13.2.3)

An object-oriented program manipulates objects, and you make objects from classes. Each object is an *instance* of its class, a realized physical entity, while a class is a logical entity. If a class is the blueprint, each house created from the blueprint is an object.

In a program, a class is defined once, but an object can be created from that class many times. In the same way a blueprint is not an actual building, a class is not the actual object. As shown in **Figure 13-4**, the **Car** class reflects the general concept of a car, while an object in the class refers to an actual car in the dealership.

Assume you have a 2020 Toyota Celica. In many programming languages, you use the keyword **new** to create an object of a specific class. The following pseudocode creates an object named **my_celica** in the **Car** class:

```
instantiate my_celica = new Car
```

Class   **Objects**

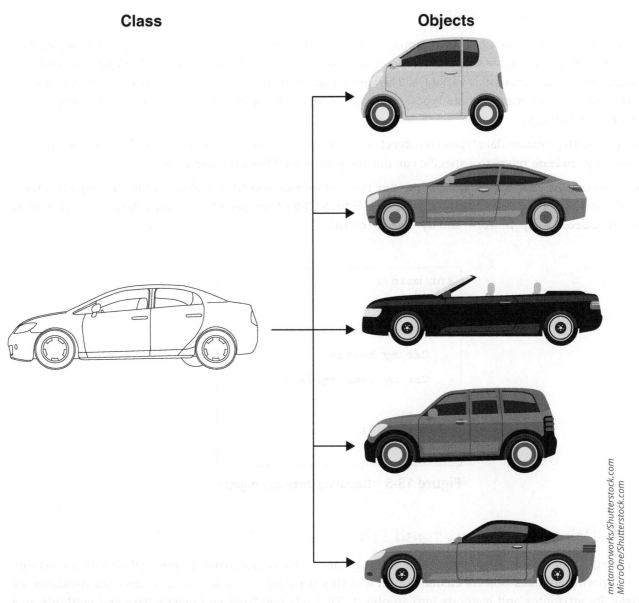

metamorworks/Shutterstock.com
MicroOne/Shutterstock.com

Figure 13-4 Class and objects

The code instantiates, or creates, a new object that is made from the class **Car**. The object is named **my_celica**. Code that refers to this specific car will reference the object by its name. The **new** keyword indicates that the computer should set aside memory to store the newly created **Car** object named **my_celica**.

Q Fill in the blanks with the correct words: A class includes _____ to describe the actions an object can perform, and it includes _____, also called attributes, that define the data the class can store. An instance of a class is an _____.

A methods; member variables; object

Objects as Variables (13.2.4, 13.2.5)

When you begin programming, you use simple variables, referred to as primitive data types or built-in data types, that hold a single value such as an integer, decimal, character, or Boolean value. In object-oriented programming, objects are treated as variables. They are considered complex data types because they can store more than one type of primitive data types. For example, **my_celica** has attributes that are of string, integer, and Boolean data types.

In code, both primitive data types and objects are referred to by their variable names. For example, the variable name **my_celica** refers to a specific car, the one you created from the **Car** class.

You can use the **public** mutators in the **Car** class to set the member variables of the **Car** objects. Create as many instances of the **Car** variable as you need. **Figure 13-5** shows code that creates three new **Car** objects named **my_corolla**, **my_beetle**, and **my_lamborghini**.

```
int main()
{
    Car my_corolla;

    Car my_beetle;

    Car my_lamborghini;


    return 0;
}
```

Figure 13-5   Declaring three Car objects

Object-Oriented Features and Principles (13.2.6, 13.2.7)

One of the goals of object-oriented programming is to make code easier to use. Bundling data with the actions they can perform makes objects easier to use, and this is called encapsulation. A class encapsulates, or encloses, its attributes and methods into an object. That lets you treat an object's data and methods as a single entity.

Encapsulation enhances coding structures by emphasizing your code's member variables and their available actions. In other words, a **Car** object contains all of its attributes and abilities, just as a real-life car does. It also gives you more control over how each object should function. For example, the **Car** class is a self-contained entity that bundles all of the data and actions that a **Car** object needs.

Encapsulation also aids with information hiding, which is concealing an object's data and methods from outside sources. An object can access its own data and methods, but other entities cannot. Also, users and other program components remain unaware of how an object's methods are carried out.

For example, the **Car** class includes the **increase_mileage()** method to change the mileage each time the car comes back from a test drive. Initially, your program allows a sales associate to update the mileage when the car is returned from a test drive. The dealership eventually installs a GPS tracker on each car to update the mileage as it is driven. The **Car** class includes a **public** accessor called **get_mileage()** that retrieves mileage information no matter the source, so your code does not need to change. The dealer can switch from updating mileage manually to an automatic GPS system without knowing about the inner workings of how the mileage is calculated. The same is true for other parts of the program that might report mileage. Information hiding gives the maker of the **Car** class the freedom to change how the class works "under the hood" without users or other program components needing to know the details.

13.3 USING STATIC ELEMENTS IN A CLASS

Static Member Variables (13.3.1, 13.3.2)

Suppose the owner of the dealership asks you to add a feature to your program. The dealer wants to keep a count of the cars in the dealership at any given time. To fulfill the request, you can add another attribute called **car_count** to the **Car** class. Each time the dealer receives a new car, **car_count** is incremented by one. Each time the dealer sells a car, **car_count** is decremented by one.

How should you modify the code to add the car-counting feature? Storing the same value in each **Car** object such as **my_celica**, **my_beetle**, and **my_lamborghini** takes up unnecessary space, especially as the number of **Car** objects increases. When a car is delivered to the dealership or sold, you'd also need to change the value of every **Car** object so that it has the correct value. It requires too many resources to store copies of the same thing when it needs constant updating. Instead, you can use a static variable to save resources and simplify the code.

A static variable is a member variable of a class and contains the same value in all instances of the class. Essentially, all objects of the same class share the same static member variable, as shown in **Figure 13-6**. In the **Car** class, **my_celica**, **my_beetle**, and **my_lamborghini** can share the value of the **car_count** static variable. Only one copy of the variable is stored in memory.

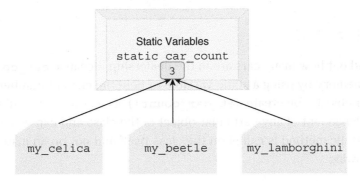

Figure 13-6   Each **Car** object shares the same static member variables

To create a static member of a class, include the keyword **static** as the member is declared. In the **Car** class, add get and set methods for **car_count**, such as **get_car_count()** and **set_car_count()** so you can use the methods to access and store the **car_count** values, which are **private**. Then add the following declaration in the **private** section of the class definition:

```
attribute: car_count as static integer
```

Figure 13-7 modifies the **private** member variables in the **Car** class to include a static member.

```
private:
    string make;
    string model;
    string color;
    string vin;
    int price;
    int mpg;
    int year;
    int mileage;
    bool sold;
    bool on_lot;
    static int car_count;    ← New static
                               member variable
```

Figure 13-7   Updated **private** member variables

In the **Car** class, the value of **car_count** needs to be updated only once. It then applies to every object in the **Car** class. Clearly, using a static member variable saves memory in your code. In general, consider using a static member variable in the following cases:

- The value of the variable is independent of the objects
- A value needs to be shared across all objects

Static Methods (13.3.3)

Suppose you now want to find out how many cars are in the dealership. Because **car_count** does not refer to a specific car, you can save memory by using a static variable to hold the current number of cars. In this case, you do not need to create an object. You create **get_car_count()** as a *static method* within the **Car** class. The static method is also independent of any particular object of the class and can be called without creating an instance of the object. A static method is called on the class itself and not on an instance of the class. The code would look like the following:

```
declare current_count as integer

current_count = Car.get_car_count()
```

The code first declares a new variable called **current_count** to hold the result of the following code. On the second line, the **Car** class is used with the dot operator (**Car.get_car_count()**) to access the static method **get_car_count()** and to return the value of the static member variable **car_count**. At the end of this code, **current_count** holds a copy of the value in **Car.car_count**.

Q When do I use static methods?

A Because static methods are not called on a specific object, you use them only to access static variables within a class and other static methods.

Static Classes (13.3.4)

Some languages include **static classes**. Similar to static methods, static classes can apply only to static member variables and static methods. They cannot be used to create instances of objects. A static class often organizes methods that operate only on input values and do not need to store information.

Suppose you want to create code so that the sales associates can do car-related computations for customers such as calculating the monthly payment for a car, the total sales tax, and estimates of the monthly gas expenses and the property tax. You could create a static class called **CarCalculations** to accomplish this. Provide the information to the static methods that return the desired result. The class would be defined as follows:

```
create class CarCalculations

    public

        static method: compute_monthly_payment(car_price, interest_rate, loan_length)

        static method: compute_sales_tax(car_price, tax_rate)

        static method: estimate_monthly_gas(mileage_per_month, car_mpg, current_gas_price)

        static method: estimate_property_tax(car_price, tax_rate)
```

This code creates the **CarCalculations** class. Each method of the car calculations class is declared as a static method:

- **compute_monthly_payment()** takes in the price of a car, the interest rate, and the length of the loan and then computes how much the person would pay each month.
- **compute_sales_tax()** takes in the car price and the tax rate for that state and returns the sales tax for the car.
- **estimate_monthly_gas()** takes in a driver's estimated driving mileage each month, the car's MPG, and the current price of gas to determine how much they would spend on gas each month.
- **estimate_property_tax()** takes in the price of the car and the current tax rate for that state to compute the property tax.

Each calculation is independent of any particular car, which is why the calculations can be static. To compute the sales tax for **my_celica** in a state with 5 percent sales tax, you'd write the following statement:

```
CarCalculations.compute_sales_tax(my_celica.get_price(), 0.05)
```

13.4 CHARACTERISTICS OF OBJECTS IN OBJECT-ORIENTED PROGRAMS

Object Identity (13.4.1)

In OOP, although you can create many objects that use the same underlying class, they all have a unique **identity**, which is how you distinguish objects created using the same class. You provide unique identities by giving the object instances different variable names. For example, the identity of any **Car** object is the object's variable name, as shown in **Figure 13-8**.

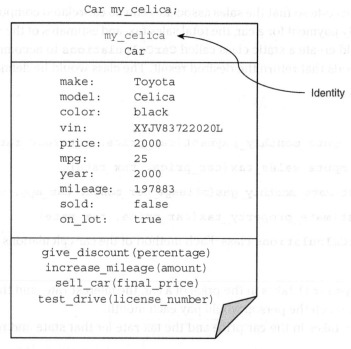

Figure 13-8   Identity of the `my_celica` object

In the **instantiate my_celica = new Car** statement, **my_celica** is the identity of the object. Any code that needs to reference this object will do so by using its variable name.

Q If two objects have the same values in all of their member variables, are they identical?

A Two objects can contain the same data, but it does not affect the object identity. They are separate instantiations of the same class, with different variable names, representing different objects stored in separate areas of memory within the program.

Object State (13.4.2)

An object's **state** represents the data held in an object's member variables at any time. During the execution of your code, the state of an object can change frequently. In general, when the value of an attribute changes, so does the state of the object.

Methods are typically used to change the state of an object. For example, when a car is sold, the **price** is updated, the status of **on_lot** is changed to False, and **car_count** is decremented. An example of an object's state is shown in **Figure 13-9**.

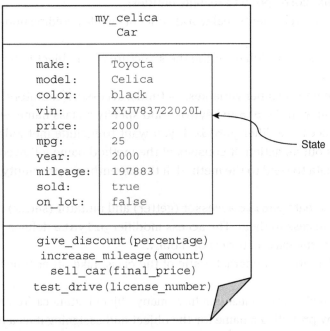

Figure 13-9   State of the **my_celica** object

Object Behavior (13.4.3)

Similar to people, an object's **behavior** describes what an object can do. Typically, behavior is thought of in terms of the methods or actions that an object can perform. The **Car** class can discount the price, increase the listed mileage after the car is taken out for test drives, set the car status to sold, and check it out for a test drive. These behaviors are shown in **Figure 13-10**.

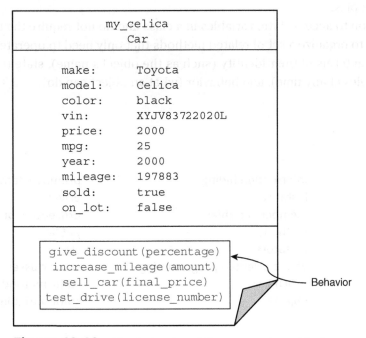

Figure 13-10   The behavior of the **my_celica** object

SUMMARY

- Object-oriented programming (OOP) allows you to represent ideas and concepts from everyday life in your code using objects that correspond to real-life entities.
- OOP promotes code reuse and represents real-world concepts while avoiding unnecessary, complicated variable declarations.
- Objects are created from classes, which describe the structure of an object in terms of its features and capabilities, like blueprints.
- A class consists of a class name, member variables, methods, accessors, mutators, and access modifiers.
- To create a class, you begin with the `class` keyword and specify a class name, which is capitalized by convention. Include the access modifier `public` if you want to include methods that any other class can use. A method carries out an action. It consists of the method name followed by parentheses. The parentheses can contain data to send to the method. If the parentheses are empty, the method does not require any data.
- It is a common practice to create `public` accessor (getter) and mutator (setter) methods for `private` member variables to limit access to them. The access modifier `private` defines methods and member variables as those that only the class can view or modify.
- A member variable, or attribute, is a characteristic of the class. Like other types of variables, its data type needs to be declared.
- An object is an instance of a class. One class can have many object instances. To create an instance of an object, you instantiate it by providing a name for the object and assigning it as a new object in a class.
- In OOP, objects are treated as variables and are considered complex data types because they can store more than one type of primitive data. For example, an object can have string, integer, and Boolean attributes.
- OOP makes code easier to use and understand through encapsulation and information hiding. A class encapsulates, or encloses, its attributes and methods into an object, which lets you treat the object's data and methods as a single entity. Information hiding refers to how OOP conceals an object's data and methods from outside sources.
- Static variables within a class allow you to share a variable among all members of the same class, without the need for multiple copies.
- Static methods allow you to access static variables in a class and do not require the use of an object.
- Static classes are used to organize a set of related methods that only need to operate on input values.
- Objects are described in terms of their identity (such as the object's name), state (the data held in an object's member variables at any time), and behavior (what an object can do).

Key Terms

access modifiers	information hiding	primitive data types
accessors	instance	private
behavior	member variables	procedural programming
class	methods	public
class name	mutators	state
complex data types	object-oriented programming	static classes
encapsulation	(OOP)	static method
identity	objects	static variable

MODULE

14

METHODS

LEARNING OBJECTIVES:

14.1 USING METHODS

14.1.1 Explain the purpose of modifying the behavior of an object.

14.1.2 Identify the components of a method.

14.1.3 Explain how to create and invoke a method.

14.2 CHANGING THE DEFAULT BEHAVIOR OF AN OBJECT

14.2.1 Explain operator overloading.

14.2.2 Identify when it is necessary to overload an operator.

14.2.3 Demonstrate overloading an equality operator.

14.2.4 Identify when it is necessary to overload a method.

14.2.5 Demonstrate overloading an assignment operator.

14.3 METHOD CASCADING AND METHOD CHAINING

14.3.1 Explain the purpose of method cascading.

14.3.2 Explain the utility of fluent interfaces.

14.4 USING CONSTRUCTORS

14.4.1 Explain how constructors are used in OOP.

14.4.2 Define memberwise initialization.

14.4.3 Explain how copy constructors are used in OOP.

14.4.4 Outline the syntax for using a copy constructor.

14.1 USING METHODS

Why Use Methods? (14.1.1)

In object-oriented programming (OOP), classes have special programmer-defined functions called methods. A method consists of a block of code that performs some action related to its object. A method is like a function that belongs to an object and performs a specific task, routine, operation, or process. Methods help us organize repetitive tasks related to an object.

You use methods to modify the behavior of objects because they make objects work. Without methods, objects would just be a collection of related data.

Suppose you are writing code to manage the cars in a car dealership called Zoe's Cars (**Figure 14-1**).

Figure 14-1   A dealership contains many kinds of cars

MicroOne/Shutterstock.com

As you may remember with functions, after the code in a function is run, it may or may not return a value to the line of code that called it. The same is true for methods. If the method returns a value, you will set the value to be equal to the method call. Otherwise, you only need to call the method. An object can have an infinite number of defined methods that determine how it behaves. The more methods that an object has, the more things it can do.

In a dealership, a `Car` object, for example, might have methods for discounting the price, increasing the mileage after a test drive, being sold, and registering a test drive. See **Figure 14-2**.

You can use a `Dealership` class to hold the member variables and methods that are relevant to running a dealership. The methods in the `Dealership` class (see **Figure 14-3**) include actions a car dealer performs, such as selling cars, adding new cars into inventory, initiating a test drive, and checking in a car for service.

In code, the `Dealership` class would resemble **Figure 14-4**. The member variables in the `Dealership` object include the following along with other dealership details:

- `owner` for the name of the owner
- `inventory` for the cars in the dealership's inventory
- `address` for the street address
- `capacity` for the number of cars the dealership can hold
- `num_cars` for the number of cars currently in the dealership

The `inventory` variable is an array of objects, each an instance of the `Car` class.

```cpp
#include <string>
using std::string;
class Car
{
   public:
      void give_discount(double percentage);
      void increase_mileage(int miles);
      void sell_car(double final_price);
      void test_drive(string license_number);
      string get_make();
      string get_model();
      string set_color();
      string get_vin();
      int get_price();
      int get_mpg();
      int get_year();
      int get mileage();
      bool get_sold();
      bool get_on_lot();
      void set_make(string m);
      void set_model(string m);
      void set_color(string c);
      void set_vin(string v);
      void set_price(int p);
      void set_mpg(int m);
      void set_year(int y);
      void set_mileage(int m);
      void set_sold(bool s);
      void set_on_lot(bool o);
   private:
      string make;
      string model;
      string color;
      string vin;
      int price;
      int mpg;
      int year;
      int mileage;
      bool sold;
      bool on_lot;
};
```

Accessors (Getters)

Mutators (Setters)

Methods

Figure 14-2   Car class definition in C++

The dealership is expecting some new cars this week. Zoe asks you to write some code to add cars into the inventory. You write a method called **add_car()** to help enter the new cars. The method has many of the components shown in **Figure 14-5**.

In the first line of the pseudocode in Figure 14-5, the add car method has **public** visibility. The keyword **void** specifies that the method does not return a value. The name of the class that the method belongs to is **Dealership** and the name of the method is **add_car()**. The method accepts one parameter, a **Car** object that it will add to the **inventory**, which is an array of **Cars**. First, the method checks to make sure that by adding this car, the dealership won't exceed its capacity. If it has space for the car, then the car is added to the inventory. If not, the method throws an exception and returns. Last, it updates the number of cars in the lot. The equivalent code is shown in **Figure 14-6**.

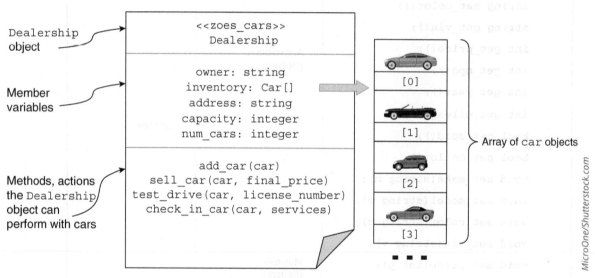

Figure 14-3   **Dealership** object containing **Cars** in inventory

```
#include <string>


class Dealership
{
    public:
        Dealership();
        void add_car(Car c);
        string get_owner();
        Car& get_inventory();
        string get_address();
        int get_capacity();
        int get_num_cars();
        void set_owner(string _owner);
        void set_inventory(Car *inventory);
        void set_address(string _address);
        void set_capacity(int capacity);
        void set_num_cars(int _num_cars);


    private:
        string owner;
        Car *inventory;
        string address;
        int capacity;
        int num_cars;
};
```

Figure 14-4   Dealership class definition in C++

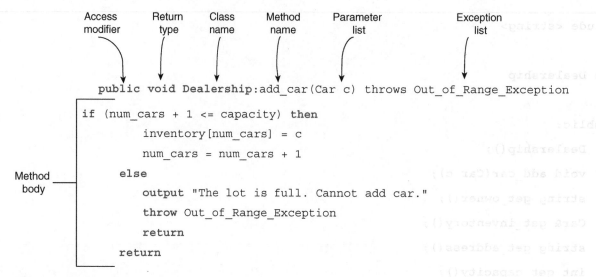

```
          Access      Return    Class     Method           Parameter                  Exception
          modifier    type      name      name             list                       list

          public void Dealership:add_car(Car c) throws Out_of_Range_Exception

          if (num_cars + 1 <= capacity) then
                  inventory[num_cars] = c
                  num_cars = num_cars + 1
              else
  Method
  body            output "The lot is full. Cannot add car."
                  throw Out_of_Range_Exception
                  return
              return
```

Figure 14-5   Method conventions

```
              #include <iostream>
              #include "Dealership.h"        The header files for the class
                                             and any other objects that the
              #include "Car.h"         ←──── class uses (Car in this case) are
                                             also included at the top of the
              using namespace std;           implementation file.

                                Scope resolution
           Return type   Class name  operator  Method name   Parameter list

              void Dealership::add_car(Car c)
              {
                  if(num_cars + 1 <= capacity)
                  {
                      inventory[num_cars] = c;
                      num_cars++;
                  }
                  else
  Method body
                  {
                      throw runtime_error("lot_full");
                  }
                  return;
              }
```

Rules and best practices:

- The name of the file is always the class name, followed by .cpp
- In C++, the access modifiers are not required in the method definition
- In C++ **the scope resolution operator** (::) is used to define a method outside of a class

Figure 14-6   Method to add a `Car` to the inventory in C++

Anatomy of a Method (14.1.2)

A method includes the following components:

- **Access modifier.** As with a class, the access modifier specifies whether a method is **public**, **private**, or **protected**.
  C++ methods may also have a **const** modifier to keep the method from modifying the state of the object. While not required, using **const** is considered by many a good practice to help avoid accidental code errors.
- **Method name.** The method name is the identifier to use when referring to the method in the code. The name is usually a verb followed by a noun, such as **add_car()**.
- **Class name.** Some programming languages include the name of the class to which the method belongs. In the **add_car()** method, the class name is **Dealership** because the **add_car()** method is a behavior that only the **Dealership** can perform.
- **Parameter list.** The parameter list specifies the input given to the method so it can perform its task. A parameter list can be empty. For example, the parameter list for the **add_car()** method has only one parameter, the **Car** being added to the inventory.
- **Method body.** The method body is the list of statements or other code that the method executes to perform its actions.
- **Return type.** The return type specifies the type of information, called the return value, that the method returns when it finishes executing. For example, the **add_car()** method has a **void** return type, indicating that it does not return a result. The return type can be any variable type, including complex data types.
- **Exception list.** In some programming languages, methods include an exception list, which names the exceptions that the method can possibly throw. The **add_car()** method can potentially throw an **Out_of_Range_Exception** if you attempt to add a car to an already full dealership.

A method must be defined before it can be used. Programmers define methods and can change them as necessary. For example, you may find a simpler way to perform the method's task. You can modify the behavior as appropriate for your context.

Using Methods (14.1.3)

When you want a method to perform an action, it can be triggered by a method call. Similar to functions, the flow of execution jumps to the method, performs the statements it contains, and then returns to the previous execution path. To make a method call, use the following syntax if the method returns a value:

```
return_value = call object.method(argument_1, argument_2, ...)
```

If the method does not return a value, use the following syntax:

```
call object.method(argument_1, argument_2, ...)
```

Let's break down the syntax examples piece by piece:

- **object.method()**: Identify an object's member variable followed by the name of the method you want to call. Separate the variable and method names with a period. For example, **add_car()** is a method in the **Dealership** class. Using **inventory.add_car()** indicates that you are trying to call the method to add a car to the inventory.
- **argument_1, argument_2**: You can pass zero, one, or more arguments to the object, which becomes the method's parameter list. For example, **add_car()** has one argument, an object of type **Car**.
- **return_value**: If the method has a result, it is returned to the variable specified in **return_value**. Similar to functions, if the method does not return a value, you can omit **return_value** from the method call. For example, **add_car()** does not return a value, so you do not have to set a return value.

Similar to a function, when a method is called, it starts executing the first statement in the method body and continues in order until the end of the method body. If a statement in the method causes an exception, then the exception is thrown back to the part of code that called the method. **Figure 14-7** shows the actual code for adding a `Car` into a `Dealership`.

```cpp
#include <iostream>
#include <string>
#include "Car.h"
#include "Dealership.h"
using namespace std;
int main()
{

    Dealership zoesZippyCars;        ← Declare a new Dealership object

    string owner;
    string address;                   Initialize variables to hold
                                      information about the
    int capacity;                     dealership
    int num_new_cars;

    cout << "What is your name?: ";
    getline(cin, owner);

    cout << "What is your address?: ";
    getline(cin, address);

    cout << "What is your lot's capacity?: ";    Get dealership
    cin >> capacity;                             information from the
                                                 user
    cin.ignore();

    cout << "How many cars would you like to enter?: ";
    cin >> num_new_cars;
    cin.ignore();


    zoesZippyCars.set_owner(owner);          Use mutators to set
    zoesZippyCars.set_address(address);      Dealership
    zoesZippyCars.set_capacity(capacity);    member variables


    Car new_car;
    string make;
    string model;
    string color;               Initialize variables to hold
    string vin;                 information about the
                                new car to add
    int price;
    int mpg;
    int year;
    int mileage;

    for(int i=0; i < num_new_cars; i++)     ← Use a for loop to prompt
    {                                          the user for the correct
                                               number of cars
```

Figure 14-7   Using the `add_car()` method to add a `Car` to a `Dealership` (*Continued*)

```
cout << "Please enter the car's make: ";
getline(cin, make);
getline(cin, make);
cout << "Please enter the car's model: ";
getline(cin, model);
cout << "Please enter the car's color: ";
getline(cin, color);
cout << "Please enter the car's vin: ";
getline(cin, vin);
cout << "Please enter the car's price: ";
cin >> price;
cin.ignore();
cout << "Please enter the car's mpg: ";
cin >> mpg;
cin.ignore();
cout << "Please enter the car's year: ";
cin >> year;
cin.ignore();
cout << "Please enter the car's mileage: ";
cin >> mileage;
cin.ignore();
```

Get car information from the user

```
new_car.set_make(make);
new_car.set_model(model);
new_car.set_color(color);
new_car.set_vin(vin);
new_car.set_price(price);
new_car.set_mpg(mpg);
new_car.set_year(year);
new_car.set_mpg(mileage);
```

Use mutators to set **Car** member variables

```
try
{
zoesZippyCars.add_car(new_car);
}
```

Call the **add_car()** method to add the **car** to the **inventory**

```
catch (runtime_error e)
{
  const char*  type = e.what();
  if(strcmp(type, "lot_full") == 0)
  {
  cout << "There is no more space in the lot." << endl;
  cout << "Sell more cars. Quitting Program." << endl;
  return 0;
  }
 }
}
}
 return 0;
}
```

Catch an exception if there isn't enough space in the lot

Figure 14-7   Using the `add_car()` method to add a `Car` to a `Dealership` (*Continued*)

Dealership.cpp

```cpp
#include <iostream>

using namespace std;

void Dealership::add_car(Car c)
{
    if(num_cars + 1 <= capacity)
    {
        inventory[num_cars] = c;
        num_cars++;
        cout << "Added a car to the inventory." << endl;
        cout << "There are now " << num_cars << " cars on the lot ";
        cout << "with a capacity of " << capacity <<  "." << endl;
    }
    else
    {
        throw runtime_error("lot_full");
    }
    return;
}
```

OUTPUT:

```
What is your name?: Zoe Zinger
What is your address?: 123 Main Street
What is your lot's capacity?: 50
How many cars would you like to enter?: 1
Please enter the car's make: Toyota
Please enter the car's model: Camry
Please enter the car's color: Silver
Please enter the car's vin: XYT7373932
Please enter the car's price: 16000
Please enter the car's mpg: 33
Please enter the car's year: 2004
Please enter the car's mileage: 23456
Added a car to the inventory.
There are now 1 cars on the lot with a capacity of 50.
```

Figure 14-7   Using the `add_car()` method to add a `Car` to a `Dealership`

Q How do I decide if I should use a function or a method?

A It depends on the organization of your code. If you need to perform an action that is performed on an object, then you should make it a method that belongs to the class. Otherwise, if the action does not need to be performed on the object, it should be a function.

14.2 CHANGING THE DEFAULT BEHAVIOR OF AN OBJECT

Using Objects as Regular Variables (14.2.1, 14.2.2, 14.2.3)

Programming languages provide many default or predefined operators that allow you to operate on primitive data types. These include add, subtract, divide, and multiply.

Suppose that in your car dealership program, you need a way to compare two cars to determine if they are the same car. For example, suppose that the dealership has a specific blue Celica listed on its website. A potential customer wants to test drive that car, but the dealership has five blue Celicas. How can you compare the Celica listed on the website to the Celicas on the lot so that the customer can drive the exact car they want? If `Car` objects were primitive data types, you would use the equality operator (`==`) to make this comparison. This would look like the following:

```
car_comparison = car_1 == car_2
```

The variable `car_comparison` holds a Boolean (`true` or `false`) value, depending on whether `car_1` is equal to `car_2`. However, with anything but primitive types, the statement creates a problem. With objects (not primitives), this statement actually compares the memory locations storing the `car_1` and `car_2` variables, not the contents of the `car_1` and `car_2` objects, which is what you want to do. This subtle difference is shown in **Figure 14-8**.

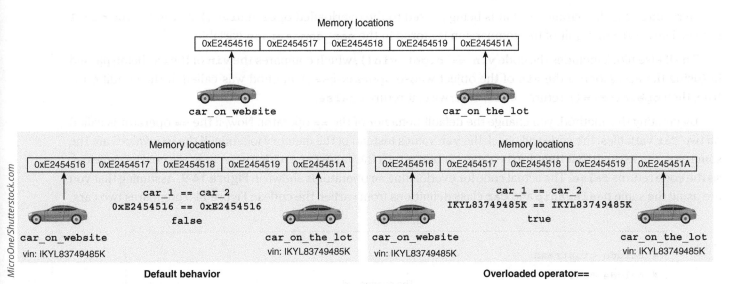

Figure 14-8   Using the default assignment operator on two `Car` objects

The statement `car_1 == car_2` compares the memory locations 0xE2454516 and 0xE2454519, finds they are different, and returns `false`. You need another approach to determine whether the `Car` objects, including their attributes and methods, are the same. Because `Car` objects are uniquely identified by a vehicle identification number (VIN), and `vin` is an attribute of the `Car` class, you can use the `vin` to test for equality. The statement `car_1.vin == car_2.vin` treats `car_1` and `car_2` as regular variables and compares the `vin` attributes for `car_1` and `car_2`, finds they are different, and returns `false`.

This is where you can use operator overloading, a programming technique that allows you to customize a built-in operator for objects of a particular class. Programmers overload operators to provide a concise, simple, and natural way to perform common operations on objects. Operators are overloaded the same way that methods are defined. Instead of specifying a method name, you specify the name of the operator that you are overloading. The overloaded operator should have the same return type and parameter list as the actual operator so that they can be used in a familiar way. You define the method in the method body, as you would a normal method. The completed overloaded operator definition goes in the same file as the other method definitions.

While the syntax varies among languages that support operator overloading, in pseudocode an overloaded operator definition resembles the following (using the equality comparison operator as an example):

```
public boolean Car::operator == (Car c)

    if (vin == c.get_vin()) then

        return true

    else

        return false
```

In the pseudocode, the first line `public boolean Car::operator == (Car c)` states that you are about to define a new **public** method in the **Car** class (that happens to be an overloaded operator). The keyword **boolean** states that the method is going to return a Boolean (**true** or **false**) value. **Car c** is the parameter that is passed to the method. This parameter is the **Car** object to compare to the **Car** whose method was called. Consider the following the statement:

```
car_comparison = car_1 == car_2
```

Here, **car_2** is the parameter that is being passed to the overloaded **operator==()** method of the **car_1** object. The **boolean** result of the comparison is stored in the **car_comparison** variable.

The if-else block includes the code **vin == c.get_vin()**, which compares the **vin** of the car being passed in (using the accessor) to the **vin** of the object whose **operator==()** method was called. If the condition is true, then **operator==()** returns **true**; otherwise, it returns **false**.

By creating this method, you change the default behavior of the **==** operator. Now, if the **==** operator is called on two **Car** variables, the code will check the **vin** values instead of the memory location. If the **vin** values are the same, you can assume that they are the same car and return the value **true**. Otherwise, they are not the same car, so the code returns **false**. The actual code for overloading an operator is shown in **Figure 14-9**. Assuming that you are using the same **Dealership** and **Car** class definitions from earlier, the code in Figure 14-9 compares two cars.

In Car.cpp

```
#include <iostream>

#include "Car.h"

using namespace std;

// other methods

bool Car::operator==(Car c)
{
    if (vin == c.get_vin())
        return true;
    else
        return false;
}
```

The overloaded operator==() method takes in a Car variable as a parameter and returns true if the VIN is the same as the VIN of the current object and false otherwise

Figure 14-9   Overloading the equality operator to compare two `Car` variables (*Continued*)

```
#include <iostream>
#include <string>
using namespace std;


int main()
{
    Car car_1;
    Car car_2;          } Declare two Car variables


    car_1.set_make("Toyota");
    car_1.set_model("Camry");
    car_1.set_color("gray");
    car_1.set_vin("XYZ2022690752");
    car_1.set_price(15639);
    car_1.set_mpg(30);
    car_1.set_year(2014);
    car_1.set_mileage(18123);
                                    Set the values
                                    of the attributes
                                    of two Car variables
    car_2.set_make("Volkswagen");   (car_1 and car_2)
    car_2.set_model("Beetle");
    car_2.set_color("red");
    car_2.set_vin("SMLGTR3483920");
    car_2.set_price(15000);
    car_2.set_mpg(25);
    car_2.set_year(2015);
    car_2.set_mileage(18123);
```

Figure 14-9   Overloading the equality operator to compare two Car variables (*Continued*)

```
    bool car_comparison = car_1 == car_2;

    if (car_comparison == true)
    {
        cout << "The two cars are the same." <<endl;
    }
    else
    {
        cout << "The two cars are different." <<endl;
    }
    return 0;

}

OUTPUT:
The two cars are the same.
```

Call the **operator==()** method to determine if they are the same. If they are, the message "The two cars are the same." will print to the screen. Otherwise, the message "The two cars are different." will print to the screen.

Figure 14-9   Overloading the equality operator to compare two `Car` variables

Because **vin** uniquely identifies the **Car** object, you do not need to check any other attributes to determine whether the objects are the same. In general, you do not have to test every member variable when one or a set of member variables uniquely identifies an object.

You can overload many types of operators besides the equality operator, including arithmetic, assignment, relational, and logical operators. It is not necessary to overload all available operators. Overloading operators is left to your discretion as a programmer in order to simplify commonly used operations for your specific program. As a rule of thumb, overloading an operator should help make your code easier to write and easier to understand to others.

Overloading Methods (14.2.4)

Car dealers often reduce prices during sale season. The dealership program should be flexible enough to discount car prices in different ways. For example, as a persuasive sales strategy, sales associates can take two cars made in the same year and discount the one with the higher price to match the price of a car with a lower price. Each car manufacturer can discount its cars as a percentage (between 0.01 and 0.99) of the sticker price. The dealership manager can also reduce a car's price by a specific dollar amount. One way to handle the three types of discounts is to create a different method for each one:

```
public void Car::discount_by_car_price(Car c)

public void Car::discount_by_percentage(float discount)

public void Car::discount_by_dollar_amount(integer discount)
```

The first method lets the sales associate obtain the price of the **Car** variable passed in, which is named c. If the price of **Car c** is lower than the price of the current **Car** variable on which the **discount_by_car_price(Car c)** method is being called, the price of the current object is now the price of c. Otherwise, the price stays the same.

The second method lets the car manufacturer specify a percentage (represented by a decimal value between 0 and 1) by which to discount the current **Car** variable on which the **discount_by_percentage(float discount)** method is being called.

The third method lets the dealership manager specify a dollar amount (represented by an integer) by which to discount the current **Car** variable on which the **discount_by_dollar_amount**(integer discount) method is being called.

However, defining a new name for each method is cumbersome and remembering which one to use is tedious. Anyone who codes a discount would need to remember the exact name of each method. Instead, you can apply method overloading, which means that you can write more than one method with the same name but different parameter lists. In general, you should overload a method when you have multiple methods that perform the same action but use different parameters. Java and C++ support method overloading, while Python does not.

The code determines the method to execute according to the arguments specified in the method call. So, you could change the pseudocode above to the following:

```
void discount_price(Car c)

void discount_price(float discount)

void discount_price(integer discount)
```

All of the methods listed in the pseudocode perform the same action. The only difference is that they have the same method name. Method overloading has two benefits. A single method such as **discount_price**() is short and easy to interpret and remember. The method is also reusable. You can use it for any type of discount, even if the discount calculations change. You create the method once but reuse it many times. The code for method overloading is shown in **Figure 14-10**.

```cpp
#include <iostream>
#include "Car.h"
using namespace std;
// other methods
void Car::discount_price(Car c)
{
    int other_car_price = c.get_price();
    if (other_car_price < price)
    {
        set_price(other_car_price);
    }
}
void Car::discount_price(float discount)
{
    float new_price = price - (discount * price);
    set_price(new_price);
}
void Car::discount_price(int discount)
{
    int new_price = price - discount;
    set_price(new_price);
}
```

Implementation of three overloaded methods for discounting the price of a car

Figure 14-10   Overloading a method to apply a discount to a car (*Continued*)

```
int main()
{

   Car car_1;
   Car car_2;        Declare three Car variables
   Car car_3;

   car_1.set_make("Toyota");
   car_1.set_model("Camry");
   car_1.set_color("gray");
   car_1.set_vin("XYZ2022690752");
   car_1.set_price(15639);
   car_1.set_mpg(30);
   car_1.set_year(2014);
   car_1.set_mileage(18123);

   car_2.set_make("Volkswagen");
   car_2.set_model("Beetle");
   car_2.set_color("red");
   car_2.set_vin("SMLGTR3483920");       Full variables with data
   car_2.set_price(15000);
   car_2.set_mpg(25);
   car_2.set_year(2015);
   car_2.set_mileage(18123);
   car_3.set_make("Nissan");
   car_3.set_model("Versa");
   car_3.set_color("blue");
   car_3.set_vin("ADKMY39203947");
   car_3.set_price(17000);
   car_3.set_mpg(22);
   car_3.set_year(2014);
   car_3.set_mileage(28447);
```

Figure 14-10   Overloading a method to apply a discount to a car (*Continued*)

```
    cout << "The price of car_1 is: " << car_1.get_price() << endl;

    cout << "The price of car_2 is: " << car_2.get_price() << endl;

    cout << "The price of car_3 is: " << car_3.get_price() << endl;


    float discount_1 = .1;
    car_1.discount_price(car_2);                    Call discount_price()
    car_2.discount_price(discount_1);                    using a Car
    car_3.discount_price(1500);                  variable, float, and integer


    cout << "After discounts, the price of car_1 is: " << car_1.get_price() << endl;

    cout << "After discounts, the price of car_2 is: " << car_2.get_price() << endl;

    cout << "After discounts, the price of car_3 is: " << car_3.get_price() << endl;
}


OUTPUT:
The price of car_1 is: 15639
The price of car_2 is: 15000
The price of car_3 is: 17000
After discounts, the price of car_1 is: 15000
After discounts, the price of car_2 is: 13500
After discounts, the price of car_3 is: 15500
```

Figure 14-10   Overloading a method to apply a discount to a car

Other members of your programming team benefit as well. Any programmer who uses your code can call the discount_price() method and pass in any type of discounts to apply the correct discount to the price of a car. The programmer does not have the additional overhead of remembering which method is correct to use for each type of discount.

Q Can I overload a method by creating a new method with the same parameter list, but different return types?

A No. The compiler tells methods apart by method name and parameter list. If you create two methods with the same parameter list but different return types, such as **int** and **void**, the compiler interprets this as declaring the same method twice and displays an error. Using the return type in a method invocation is optional. Consequently, if the return type is omitted in the call, nothing distinguishes the methods with otherwise identical signatures.

Setting One Object to Equal Another (14.2.5)

Suppose a car manufacturer is sending Zoe's Car dealership some cars to sell from another dealership named Cars Plus. The Cars Plus dealership will transfer cars to Zoe's Car dealership, where they will be added to the inventory.

To handle this situation in the dealership program, you might think you can pass the **Car (c)** to **add_car()** and then add it to the inventory as follows:

```
public void Dealership:add_car(Car c) throws Out_of_Range_Exception

    if (num_cars + 1 <= capacity) then

        inventory[num_cars] = c

        num_cars = num_cars + 1

    else

        throw Out_of_Range_Exception

    return
```

For the **add_car()** method, the assignment operator (=) is used to set the inventory **Car** variable at the next location equal to the new car passed in. Focus for a moment on the assignment operator and how it is working. In memory, what actually happens is shown in **Figure 14-11**.

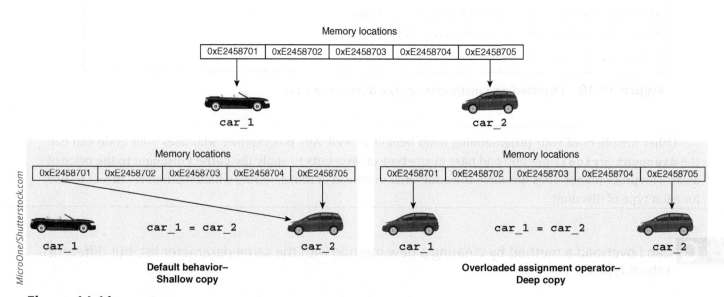

Figure 14-11   Shallow vs deep copy of an object using `operator =`

Usually, you use the assignment operator (=) to set one variable equal to the value of another. Assume you have **car_1** and **car_2** in memory as in the top of Figure 14-11. You want to make **car_1** equal to **car_2**. If you write **car_1 = car_2**, the default behavior happens. (See the left side of Figure 14-11.) Because **car_1** and **car_2** are complex data types, the variable name is regarded as the object's address in memory. The statement **car_1 = car_2** stores the memory location of **car_2** in **car_1**, so now **car_1** is also referring to the same object as **car_2**. To make things worse, the object that **car_1** was previously pointing to is now lost in memory because nothing is referring to it.

The **car_1** object is a shallow copy of **car_2**, meaning that the copy is superficial and does not refer to a unique object that no other variable refers to. This should be avoided. On the surface, the program appears to work as expected to add a transferred car to inventory. However if `car_2` is deleted or modified in memory (perhaps by the code that created it), then `car_1` is also deleted or modified.

To avoid this problem, you can overload the assignment operator as in the following pseudocode:

```
Car operator=(Car car_2)
    make = other_car.make

    model = other_car.model

    color = other_car.color

    vin = other_car.vin

    price = other_car.price

    mpg = other_car.mpg

    year = other_car.year

    mileage = other_car.mileage

    sold = false

    on_lot = true
```

This code overloads the assignment operator. Assume that the `operator=()` method has been called again as `car_1 = car_2`. The `operator=()` method of the `car_1` object is called, and `car_2` is passed in as a parameter. Every member variable of `car_2` is copied into `car_1`'s member variables. Now `car_1` and `car_2` have the exact same state and are the same car. When you call the `operator=()` method to set a `Car` in the `inventory` array equal to the transferred car, the code will make two duplicate objects, creating a deep copy, as shown on the right side of Figure 14-11.

14.3 METHOD CASCADING AND METHOD CHAINING

Calling Multiple Methods on the Same Object (14.3.1, 14.3.2)

The dealership managers at Zoe's Cars are so impressed with your work that they give you a month off. During that month, you decide to optimize your code to make it more efficient. In some parts of the code, you are calling multiple methods on the same object. For example, when entering a car into inventory, your code resembles the following:

```
instantiate new_car = new Car()

new_car.set_make(make)

new_car.set_model(model)

new_car.set_color(color)

new_car.set_vin(vin)

new_car.set_price(price)

new_car.set_mileage(mileage)

new_car.set_mpg(mpg)

new_car.set_year(year)

inventory.add_car(new_car)
```

In the code, you create a new **Car** variable and individually set the values of each of the member variables using the mutators. So, for each **new_car** object, the code calls eight different methods: **set_make()**, **set_model()**, **set_color()**, **set_vin()**, **set_price()**, **set_mileage()**, **set_mpg()**, and **set_year()**. How can you revise this code to be more efficient?

You can use **method cascading** (sometimes called method chaining), which calls many methods on a single object. Method cascading is a programming syntax preference that eliminates the need to list an object repeatedly. Your code can be rewritten as:

```
instantiate new_car = new Car()

new_car.set_make(make).set_model(model).set_color(color).set_vin(vin).set_
price(price).set_mileage(mileage).set_mpg(mpg).set_year(year)

inventory.add_car(new_car)
```

In this pseudocode, instead of calling eight methods on eight lines, you can join all of the methods together and execute them in the order in which they are written, going from left to right. **Fluent interfaces** are an object-oriented design methodology in which a programming language's syntax relies on method cascading to make code easier to read.

Q How would you change the pseudocode above to set the **on_lot** attribute to sold?

A Add

```
new_car.set_make(make).set_model(model).set_color(color).set_vin(vin).set_
price(price).set_mileage(mileage).add(newCar).set_on_lot(true)
```

Figure 14-12 shows how the method definition would be changed to allow for method cascading in code.

```
void Car::set_make(string m)
{
    make = m;
}
void Car::set_model(string m)
{
    model = m;
}
void Car::set_color(string c)
{
    color = c;
}
void Car::set_vin(string v)
{
    vin = v;
}
void Car::set_price(int p)
{
    price = p;
}
void Car::set_mpg(int m)
{
    mpg = m;
}
void Car::set_year(int y)
{
    year = y;
}
void Car::set_mileage(int m)
{
    mileage = m;
}
void Car::set_sold(bool s)
{
    sold = s;
}
void Car::set_on_lot(bool o)
{
    on_lot = o;
}
```

```
Car& Car::set_make(string m)
{
    make = m;
    return *this;
}
Car& Car::set_model(string m)
{
    model = m;
    return *this;
}
Car& Car::set_color(string c)
{
    color = c;
    return *this;
}
Car&  Car::set_vin(string v)
{
    vin = v;
    return *this;
}
Car& Car::set_price(int p)
{
    price = p;
    return *this;
}
Car& Car::set_mpg(int m)
{
    mpg = m;
    return *this;
}
Car& Car::set_year(int y)
{
    year = y;
    return *this;
}
...
```

In C++, method cascading requires the object to return access to itself in order to be used by the method call in the next cascading method. This is represented by return *this in every method definition.

Since we are returning access to an object, the mutators' return type changes from void to Car& which is the variable type for a reference to a Car.

Figure 14-12   Method definition to enable method cascading

14.4 USING CONSTRUCTORS

Specifying How to Construct an Object (14.4.1, 14.4.2)

So far, you've created a new **Car** object by typing code in the following format:

```
instantiate new_car = new Car()
```

Behind the scenes, your program calls a constructor, which is a special method that creates an object called **new_car** and allocates enough memory to hold all of the information associated with a **Car**. A constructor has no definable return type and uses the same method name as the class. Generally, programs call constructors when a new object is created to initialize objects of their class type. You may write and customize your own constructor, or the compiler will write one for you. The pseudocode for a simple constructor is as follows:

```
Car()

    mileage = 0

    on_lot = true

    sold = false
```

The constructor's method name is always the same name as the class. You use a constructor to initialize values for an object's member variables. For example, suppose that when adding new cars to the inventory, the **mileage** is always 0, **on_lot** is always **true**, and **sold** is always **false**. It would make sense to create cars that have those initial values already set as the default. This type of constructor is called the default constructor because it does not take in any parameters to use to set the values of the member variables. You would still create a new **Car** object in the same way as before; however, the default constructor sets the initial values for the three attributes as shown in the pseudocode.

The default constructor is called whenever your code creates a new **Car** object. When you write the equivalent of **instantiate new_car = new Car()**, in your code, the program creates a **Car** object named **new_car**, and the constructor sets the specified initial values for **mileage**, **on_lot**, and **sold**. The program can keep or change the default values as necessary for each new **Car** object.

If you do not define a constructor, the compiler creates an implicit default constructor for you. This constructor creates an object without any predefined values for the member variables. It defaults to whatever the language or operating system initializes new variables (if anything at all). Relying on the implicit default constructor can be risky. For example, the member variables may not get set with a value during the course of the program's execution and may contain garbage values, which are leftover, unwanted, and unusable values held in memory prior to a variable being initialized. If you try to access member variables and perform tasks with garbage data, an error will occur and may crash your program.

Q Is having no return type the same as a **void** return type?

A No. Technically, **void** is a return type. Constructors are defined without any type specified for return. A constructor actually returns the memory location of the object that was created.

Q Where are constructors defined?

A All constructors are defined in the same file as all of the other method definitions for the same class. Constructors are declared in the class definition alongside all of the other methods, with public access.

It is a good programming practice to use the default constructor to explicitly set the member variables, called memberwise initialization, even if the values are unknown. The default constructor can be rewritten as follows:

```
Car()
    make = ""
    model = ""
    color = ""
    vin = ""
    price = 0
    mileage = 0
    mpg = 0
    on_lot = true
    sold = false
```

The preceding pseudocode creates a full constructor, which initializes all member variables of the object when the object is created. When you write a full constructor, you no longer have to worry about accidentally crashing your program by performing operations using garbage values. You do not need to be concerned about the user trying to work with uninitialized data.

Like other methods, a constructor can also have a parameter list. This is called a parameterized constructor. The parameter list specifies the exact values to use to initialize the object's member variables when the object is created. A parameterized constructor is called as follows:

```
instantiate new_car = new Car(make, model, color, vin, price, mileage)
```

It is defined as follows:

```
Car(string _make, string _model, string _color, string _vin, integer _price, integer _mileage)
    make = _make
    model = _model
    color = _color
    vin = _vin
    price = _price
    mileage = _mileage
```

You call the parameterized constructor the same way as calling the default constructor, with the addition of parameters passed in that will be used to set the values of the member variables. In the constructor's definition, each of the parameters passed in is used to set the value of the corresponding member variable.

Constructing an Object from Another Object (14.4.3, 14.4.4)

From time to time, the cars in the dealership need to get serviced at the dealership to rotate the tires, change the oil, and ensure things are running smoothly. The service department wants to write code soon to handle checking cars in and out. Rather than copying every data member from all of your **Car** objects into theirs, you can create a *copy constructor*. It allows another object to be created that is an exact copy (or a deep copy) of the first object. Programmers may choose to create a copy constructor instead of overloading the assignment operator, depending on their context.

Previously, you overloaded the assignment operator to set one object equal to another. You will write similar code to make a copy constructor. It has the same format as the default constructor but takes in one argument, the object to copy. When the object to be copied is passed in, all of its member variables are copied to the new object. These two objects have the same member variables but exist in different locations in memory. It is not always necessary to have a copy constructor. For example, in a **Dealership** object, you'd never have two of the exact same **Dealership** at the same address.

A copy constructor for a **Car** object would look as follows:

```
Car(Car c)
    make = c.make
    model = c.model
    color = c.color
    vin = c.vin
    price = c.price
    mileage = c.mileage
    on_lot = c.on_lot
    sold = c.sold
```

Q What is the difference between a copy constructor and a deep copy?

A In memory they achieve the same outcome, but one is considered a method that can be called anytime and the other is a constructor that is called when an object is first created.

Q Can you define more than one constructor in an object?

A Yes. You can specify one default constructor, one copy constructor, and as many parameterized constructors as you need for the program design. This is called constructor overloading and it follows the same rules as operator overloading. The constructors may have the same name but must have different parameter lists.

SUMMARY

- In object-oriented programming, methods are special programmer-defined functions that belong to a class and perform some action related to objects made from the class.
- Methods are similar to functions and consist of an access modifier, method name, parameter list, method body, return type, and exception list.
- Methods must be invoked (or called) in order to perform an action. When a method is called, it starts executing the first statement in the method body and continues in order until the end of the method body.
- You can use methods to customize the default behavior of an object. Operator overloading allows you to specify how built-in operators should behave when operating on your objects. The default behavior often uses garbage data that can lead to errors in your program.
- You can make your code more usable with method overloading, which allows you to call the same method with different parameter lists. Overloading methods makes your code easier to interpret and reuse.
- When using the assignment operator (=) to make an object equal to another object, the default functionality creates a shallow copy, a new object that refers to the same memory location as another object. It is a good practice to overload the assignment operator to ensure that you create a deep copy of an object.
- Method cascading is a programming paradigm that allows you to call multiple methods on the same object in sequence, reducing the amount of code and improving efficiency. Programming languages that use method cascading are called fluent interfaces.
- Programs call constructors whenever a new object is instantiated. You can specify how a constructor sets the values of the member variables as an object is created. It is a good programming practice to use constructors to avoid performing operations with garbage values.
- Programs call the default constructor whenever an object is made. If you do not define the behavior of a default constructor, the compiler will do so for you.
- You can create a parameterized constructor to pass in any number of parameters to set the values of the member variables when creating an object.
- A copy constructor allows you to create a new object that is the exact copy of another object.

Key Terms

access modifier	garbage values	methods
constructor	implicit default constructor	operator overloading
copy constructor	memberwise initialization	parameter list
deep copy	method body	parameterized constructor
default constructor	method call	predefined operators
exception list	method cascading	return type
Fluent interfaces	method name	shallow copy
full constructor	method overloading	

MODULE 15

ENCAPSULATION

LEARNING OBJECTIVES:

15.1 COMPONENTS OF CLASS STRUCTURE

15.1.1 Explain how encapsulation can enhance coding structures.

15.1.2 Explain the concept of information hiding.

15.1.3 Explain the purpose of instance fields in classes.

15.1.4 Explain the purpose of methods in classes.

15.1.5 Explain the purpose of properties in classes.

15.1.6 Explain how to use a keyword to reference the current instance in OOP ("this").

15.1.7 Contrast implicit versus explicit self-reference.

15.2 ACCESSOR AND MUTATOR CONTEXT

15.2.1 Explain the purpose of an accessor.

15.2.2 Explain the purpose of a mutator.

15.3 USING CONSTRUCTORS

15.3.1 Explain the function of parameters in OOP.

15.3.2 Explain the function of arguments in OOP.

15.3.3 Define constructor overloading as it applies to OOP.

15.3.4 Define a default parameter as it applies to OOP.

15.4 ENCAPSULATION ENFORCEMENT WITH ACCESS MODIFIERS

15.4.1 Explain the purpose of access modifiers.

15.4.2 Explain public variables.

15.4.3 Explain private variables.

15.4.4 Explain how to test private data of an object.

15.5 INTERFACES AND HEADERS

15.5.1 Explain the purpose of interfaces.

15.5.2 Explain header files as they relate to interfaces.

15.5.3 Explain the function of method signatures in OOP.

15.5.4 Explain the purpose of header guards.

15.1 COMPONENTS OF CLASS STRUCTURE

Data Hiding (15.1.1, 15.1.2)

When driving a car, as in **Figure 15-1**, you understand that operating the car changes its behavior. Pressing the accelerator makes the car speed up, and pressing the brake slows it down. If you don't know anything else about how cars work, you could still use a car comfortably. It doesn't matter if pressing the accelerator adds gasoline to the combustion engine or increases the electrical signal to your electric car's engine; pressing the accelerator makes the car go forward.

guteksk7/Shutterstock.com

Figure 15-1   Driving a car does not require understanding of how the car works

You use a computer in the same way. You don't need to know how a computer was programmed in order to use it. You only need to know what it expects from you to provide output. When you move the mouse on your desk, you expect the output will be the computer updating the mouse pointer on the screen. In fact, hiding how the computer or car works makes it easy to use.

The details of how a car or a computer works depends on many properties and abilities bundled into one package. When you hear the word "car," you probably imagine an entire car. However, a car is made up of many independent parts, such as an engine, windows, wheels, doors, and seats, as shown in **Figure 15-2**. Each part has expectations and output. If you were to simulate a car for a simulation game, you should design each of these interworking parts according to its properties and abilities.

Digital Genetics/Shutterstock.com

Figure 15-2   A car has many parts

The bundling and hiding of information in computer science is called encapsulation. You use encapsulation to prevent trouble when designing and implementing classes and objects to organize their components. Writing programs is similar to making a meal. Encapsulation is being tidy in your workspace. Being tidy does not achieve the goal of making dinner, but it is still a good habit to build because tidiness makes it easier for someone else to use your workspace, less likely to use salt instead of sugar, or easier to move to other projects. In a similar way, using encapsulation properly creates code that is sturdier and easier to use.

Although the term "encapsulation" may be new to you, you've already used encapsulated features in your programs. For example, output to the screen is built into any programming language. You do not need to understand how a program produces output to display text. **Figure 15-3** shows code that prints text to the command line. If the compiler changes how it processes the statement to print text, your program would continue to work as you wrote it.

```
int main() {
    cout << "Printing to the command line!" << endl;
}
```

Figure 15-3   Printing a string to the command line

Designing Objects (15.1.3, 15.1.4, 15.1.5)

Classes are a fundamental part of object-oriented programming (OOP), which treats programs as objects, similar to real-world objects. A rubber ball is an object with specific attributes you can use to describe it. For example, the ball has a radius, color, and bounciness factor. These attributes are called the properties of an object. The possible properties of an object are stored in the class definition as member variables (also known as instance variables). Using the term "member variable" is a way to describe variables that are part of an object, rather than independent variables.

When designing an object in OOP, you start by identifying its properties. What are the defining features of this object that you, or another programmer, need to know about? Suppose you are a programmer at a company, and your boss asks you to program a basic **Car** class. Your boss also tells you that someone else will be using this class in their project without your help. The **Car** class needs to have a paint color, a year of manufacture, mileage, oil level, and current speed. (A real-life car would have many more properties.)

You use these properties to start to program a **Car** as a class, as shown in **Figure 15-4**. The code starts by defining the name of the class to be **Car**. It then sets up the property variables of **paint_color**, **year**, **mileage**, **oil_level**, and **current_speed**.

```
class Car
{
    string paint_color;
    int year;
    double mileage;
    double oil_level;
    double current_speed;
}
```

Figure 15-4   Properties of a car

Q **Figure 15-5** shows multisided gaming dice. These dice can have any number of sides, with the smallest number of sides being four. On each side is a number. When a die is rolled, one of the sides is considered "up." What do you think the properties of this object should be?

Mine Eyes Design/Shutterstock.com

Figure 15-5   Multisided gaming dice

A The number of sides should be a property (such as **num_sides**) so that you need only one class to represent all die types. The side facing up should also be a property (**face_up**) as it represents the state of the die.

Some properties of an object are important to the object itself, but do not need to be known by others. These properties are called instance fields. An **instance field** of an object is an internal variable not meant to be seen from the outside. The object itself may modify it, or leave it alone, but any outside code cannot access it. An example of an instance field for a **Car** object would be the oil level. A dashboard does not typically display the amount of oil in the car; it displays a "change oil" indicator light when the oil level is low. **Figure 15-6** shows the code for using an **oil_level** member variable.

```
class Car
{
    // ... other implemented parts of the car are omitted ... //

    bool should_change_oil()          oil_level instance
    {                                 field—other code
                                      cannot access it
        return this->oil_level < 0.5;
    }
}
```

Figure 15-6   Oil level is an instance field of a car

The code in Figure 15-6 shows a method that interacts with an instance field. Other implemented parts of the car are omitted for brevity. A method named **should_change_oil()** will return a **boolean true** or **false** value indicating whether the oil needs changing. It returns **true** if the **oil_level** of the car is less than 0.5, or **false** otherwise.

Q Consider the dice in Figure 15-5 again. What would be an instance field for a **Die** object?

A Recall that instance fields are properties of objects that cannot be seen from the outside but are used internally. One possible instance field for a **Die** object could be whether it is a weighted die that allows the user to cheat. If you are cheating, you do not want others to know you are being sneaky. So, if your dice need a cheating property to always land as "6" on a six-sided die, this property should be completely hidden from the outside.

Properties and instance fields describe the object's state. For example, the **current_speed** and **oil_level** properties describe a **Car** object's state. Actions are behaviors objects can use to change their state. A car can increase its speed or turn on its headlights. These actions are represented in code as methods. For example, a **Car** object can have an **accelerate()** method.

Another way to think about methods is as functions that are so useful to an object, they should always be included with an instance of that object. For example, all running cars can change speed, so all **Car** objects should have an **accelerate()** method. Each time you add a parameter to a function, you increase the requirements placed on others to use the function. If a function must always pass a **Car** object as an argument, then another programmer must always pass a car. Making the behavior a method instead removes the possibility of the other programmer forgetting to include the **Car** argument.

Q Return to Figure 15-5 again. What action should a **Die** object have?

A When interacting with dice, you can roll them to change which value faces up. The die in the upper-left corner of Figure 15-5 has four sides. A method such as **roll()** should randomly change the **face_up** value to any number from 1 to 4 for this instance of the **Die** object.

While **Figure 15-7** shows how to code a function to accelerate a car, **Figure 15-8** shows how to code a method to accelerate a car. Note that the **accelerate()** method requires less information to pass because it has fewer parameters.

```
void accelerate(Car car, double amount)
{
    double current_speed = car.get_current_speed();
    car.set_current_speed(amount + current_speed);
}
```

Car object must be passed to the **accelerate()** function.

Function gets the current speed with the getter method, then increases it with the setter method.

Figure 15-7   Code for an **accelerate()** function

```
class Car
{
    // ... other car code here ... //

    void accelerate(double amount)
    {
        this->current_speed += amount;
    }
}
```

Method is attached to a `Car` object, so it does not need to be passed a `Car` object as a parameter.

Method can directly access any property of the current object, so it can directly increase the speed.

Figure 15-8   Code for an `accelerate()` method

Self-Reference Scope (15.1.6, 15.1.7)

When talking about objects, context matters. "A car is red" doesn't mean much if you have five cars. However, "this car is red" tells you something about a specific car. To refer to the current object's properties and fields, use the **self-reference keyword**.

```
calculate this.year = 2002
```

In pseudocode, the keyword is `this`, but programming languages may use different words to indicate self-reference. **Figure 15-9** shows the keywords in several common programming languages, as well as the syntax for use.

Language	Self-Reference Keyword	Syntax for Use
C++	`this`	`this->identifier`
Java	`this`	`this.identifier`
Python	`self`	`self.identifier`

Figure 15-9   Common self-reference keywords

Some languages allow you to omit the self-reference keyword when using variable identifiers; this is called **implicit self-referencing**. An implicit self-reference requires the computer to figure out what variable you mean to use. Due to scope, the computer looks for a variable in a certain order. It references the first variable identifier that matches the one you've written, even if another variable has the same identifier in a different scope. The computer looks for a variable in the following order:

1. Local
2. Class
3. Global

Local scope includes the identifiers in the parameter list of the method signature. However, using **explicit self-referencing** forces the computer to look only at the class-level scope. **Figure 15-10** shows a code snippet that first references a local variable and then references a class variable with the same identifier. In this sample code, an object has the property `current_speed`, and a local variable is also declared with the identifier `current_speed`. When a local variable "overlaps" a class or global variable with the same identifier, it is often referred to as "shadowing."

```
class Car
{
    // ... omitted car code ... //

    void example()
    {
        int current_speed = 0;
        this->current_speed = 5;
    }
}
```

Local variable `current_speed`

Class variable `current_speed`

Self-reference keyword makes this declaration an explicit self-reference.

Figure 15-10   Local and instance variables with the same identifier

The code in Figure 15-10 has two variables with the same identifier: `current_speed`. The program can use a local and class variable with the same name because the class variable `current_speed` is defined with a self-reference keyword, making it an explicit self-reference.

Note that some languages, such as Python, cannot use implicit self-reference. For simplicity, the remaining examples in this module use explicit self-reference. Always using explicit referencing can make your code easier to read, as well as easier to match parameter identifiers, as shown in **Figure 15-11**. The code in Figure 15-11 sets a member variable to the value passed in as a parameter. To make it clear what the parameter matches, the parameter and the class property have the same identifier: `year`.

```
class Car
{
    // ... other implemented features omitted ... //

    void set_year(int year)
    {
        this->year = year;
    }
}
```

The parameter and member variable have the same name to indicate they match.

Figure 15-11   Matching parameters to the instance identifier

Q In Figure 15-11, what would happen if you left off the self-reference keyword and used `year = year`?

A The left side of the assignment statement would recognize the identifier `year` as the parameter name, instead of the member variable with the same identifier.

15.2 ACCESSOR AND MUTATOR CONTEXT

Viewing Data from an Object (15.2.1)

Limiting how someone interacts with an object reduces the chance for an error. Imagine a calculator with the standard set of numbers plus buttons labeled A, B, and so on. What if pressing a lettered button caused an error? You would wonder why the calculator had letter buttons in the first place. By allowing only access or changes to an object in certain situations, you make the code less prone to error. Instead of relying on direct manipulation of the state of the object, you use accessors and mutators to guide the interactions.

Recall that an **accessor** is a method used to access the state of an object. An accessor does not allow changes, or mutations, to an object. You should create an accessor for any property that should be visible from outside. For the `Car` class, this is `year`, `paint_color`, or `mileage`. Being "visible" means that other code can view or modify the property. Accessors are also known as **getters** because they get values from member variables outside of the class. **Figure 15-12** shows a possible accessor for the `Car` object.

```cpp
class Car
{
    // ... omitted code ... //

    string get_paint_color()
    {
        return this->paint_color;
    }
}

int main()
{
    Car my_car = Car(2002, "red");

    cout << "Car color: " << my_car.get_paint_color() << endl;

    return 0;

}
OUTPUT:
Car color: red
```

Single line of code to access the properties of an object.

Figure 15-12   An accessor (getter) for a `Car` object

Accessors usually do not require more than a single line of code in the method. At the bottom of Figure 15-12, the print statement uses the getter method instead of accessing the `paint_color` property directly. Because direct variable access allows many mistakes, such as setting the `paint_color` to "lizard," you don't want someone else to access `paint_color`, even to print its value.

Changing Data in an Object (15.2.2)

A **mutator** is a method used to change data. With encapsulation, you use mutators to control changes to your object by other users. By having other programmers use a mutator method instead of directly changing the property, you can limit how the property is changed. Mutators are also known as **setters** because they set the value for member variables. Imagine you are creating a method that sets the year a car was made. The earliest mass-manufactured car was the Ford Model T in 1908. The mutator shouldn't let anyone set the year to a value earlier than 1908. The paint color should also be limited, to prevent colors such as "lizard." **Figure 15-13** shows mutators for the **Car** object.

```
void set_paint_color(string paint_color)
{
    // Check against all valid paint colors.
    for (int i = 0; i < total_colors; i++)
    {
        if (available_colors[i] == paint_color)
        {
            this->paint_color = paint_color;
            return;
        }
    }

    // Set to a default color if the parameter does not
    //   contain a valid color.
    this->paint_color = available_colors[0];
}

void set_year(int year)
{
    // If the year is a valid year then set it.
    if (year >= 1908)
    {
        this->year = year;
    }

    // Otherwise, set the year to a default year.
    else
    {
        this->year = 1908;
    }
}
```

Annotations in figure:
- Setter for the paint color restricts the value to an approved list of colors.
- If the parameter does not contain a valid color, set the paint color to the default, the first color in the approved list.
- Setter enforces a minimum value for the year.
- If the year is incorrect, set it to a default value, the earliest possible year.

Figure 15-13   Setters for a car

The two mutators shown in Figure 15-13 check for invalid values in their parameters. First, **set_paint_color()** uses a loop to iterate over all possible colors, which are listed in the **available_colors** variable. If the parameter contains a color in **available_colors**, then it sets the member variable and returns. If the method reaches the end of the loop and has not quit, that means the value provided is not a valid color, so the method sets the value to the first valid color. Next, **set_year()** checks if the value given for a year is later than 1908. If the year is valid, the member variable is set; otherwise, it uses the default year of 1908.

Using getter and setter methods instead of directly modifying the object properties ensures that your code can make assumptions about the object's state. For example, you can be sure the **Car** object can't have a year earlier than 1908, and the paint is a valid color.

15.3 USING CONSTRUCTORS

Parameters and Arguments (15.3.1, 15.3.2)

Recall that a constructor is a special method that creates an object and allocates enough memory to hold the information associated with the object. Programs usually call constructors when a new object is created to initialize objects of their class type. You can use constructors for data hiding with encapsulation. When you create an object, you are the expert on the object and know the best way to set it up. The constructor is like a setup wizard for a new program. The constructor handles the complicated parts of an object and asks you only for the parts that might change. A car may have different paint colors, but the paint is still applied in the same way regardless of the color. **Figure 15-14** shows a possible **Car** constructor.

```
Car(int year, string paint_color) {        Constructor lets only
    // Using setters to enforce behavior    the color and year to
    this->set_paint_color(paint_color);     be set with two
    this->set_year(year);           Setters parameters.
    this->mileage = 0.0;
    this->oil_level = 1.0;                   Properties that do not need
    this->current_speed = 0.0;              setters because they have
                                             simple default values.
}
```

Figure 15-14   A constructor for a **Car** object

The constructor has two parameters, **year** and **paint_color**, which are passed to the two setter methods **set_paint_color()** and **set_year()**. Using setters ensures that the limitations created within the setters still are enforced in the constructor. The remaining lines of code set all properties of the **Car** object to starting values, such as the **mileage** starting at **0**.

Designing your object requires you to decide which parameters are important. What aspects of the object would someone want to change when setting up an instance of the object? What parts can be left alone? Address the aspects to change as parameters to the constructor. Each aspect is one parameter in the constructor, which in turn can be passed an argument to set that aspect to a value.

Q If someone is making a new **Car** object, what parts should they be allowed to set? Which parts should be off limits?

A They should be able to set the paint color and year because those properties are aspects of the car that you can change when building the car. The mileage shouldn't be changed because the car determines the mileage. A newly created car can be red, blue, or green, but it always has zero miles.

The parameters are the variables provided in the method signature. The **arguments** are the values provided to those parameters. The number of parameters you define for an object corresponds to the number of arguments to supply.

In Figure 15-14, the **Car** class has a constructor with two parameters of **year** and **paint_color**. A **Car** object can be created later with two unique arguments such as **2020** and **blue**.

Default Parameters and Constructor Overloading (15.3.3, 15.3.4)

As objects become more complicated, you might not want or need to supply all arguments to an object's constructor. You can specify default parameters to use if the constructor omits parameters for the object.

For example, because every new **Car** object needs to have a paint color, **paint_color** could be a default parameter with a color of **black**. List the default parameters after the parameter identifier in the parameter list.

Figure 15-15 shows how you could design the **Car** constructor so the user does not need to provide the color argument. Using black as the default color is arbitrary. You can assume that the other programmer will select the colors for each car. However, if the color does not matter to the final program, being able to write less code when creating cars is helpful.

```
                                                 Default parameter for
                                                 color is black.
Car(int year, string paint_color="black") {
    // Using setters to enforce behavior
    this->set_paint_color(paint_color);
    this->set_year(year);                        Setters
    this->mileage = 0.0;
    this->oil_level = 1.0;
    this->current_speed = 0.0;

}
```

Figure 15-15   A constructor with a default parameter

The code in Figure 15-15 shows a constructor with two parameters, **year** and **paint_color**. The use of the assignment syntax in the parameter list shows how to specify a default value. Assigning **paint_color** to **"black"** means that if only one parameter is provided to the constructor, then the computer fills in the missing argument for **paint_color** with **"black"**.

You can also use constructor overloading to handle this situation. Constructor overloading is similar to method overloading; you code multiple constructors with different parameter lists, and the computer selects the constructor that best matches the construction call. For example, the **Car** class could contain a constructor with no parameters, setting **year** and **paint_color** to default values, and a constructor with two parameters, one each for **year** and **paint_color**.

As with methods and functions, the constructor signatures must be distinct enough for the computer to know which one to select. (Recall that a signature is the name and parameters that uniquely define the function, method, or constructor.) Consider the following pseudocode for a constructor of a **Die** class, which includes two constructors.

```
Die (int sides, int face_up)
    this.sides = sides
    this.face_up = face_up


Die (int face_up, int sides)
    this.sides = sides
    this.face_up = face_up
```

Q If you were to create a new `Die` object by calling `Die(18, 4)` with two integer arguments, which constructor has the matching signature?

A Both defined constructors for `Die` have two integer parameters, so it is impossible for the computer to know which one was intended.

By providing multiple ways to call a constructor, your code can be used in many ways, as shown in **Figure 15-16**. The code constructs three cars, one without any arguments, one using a constructor that expects only the paint color as an argument, and one with a constructor expecting both the paint color and year.

```
int main()
{
    // Use the default constructor
    Car default_car = Car();          ← Constructor call without
                                        arguments matches the default
                                        constructor through constructor
                                        overloading.

    // Use the default parameter for color
    Car classic_black_car = Car(1980);  ← Constructor provides one
                                          argument for year and uses
                                          the default paint color.

    // Define all parameters with arguments
    Car red_2019_car = Car(2019, "red");  ← Constructor provides
                                            explicit arguments for
                                            both values.

    cout << "Default car color:";
    cout << default_car.get_paint_color() << endl;

    cout << "Classic Black color:";
    cout << classic_black_car.get_paint_color() << endl;

    cout << "Red 2019 color:";
    cout << red_2019_car.get_paint_color() << endl;

}

OUTPUT:

Default car color: black
Classic Black color: black
Red 2019 color: red
```

Figure 15-16   Multiple constructors used to create different cars

Some languages, such as Python, do not allow constructor overloading, though Python does allow default parameters. In contrast, Java does not allow default parameters, but does allow constructor overloading.

15.4 ENCAPSULATION ENFORCEMENT WITH ACCESS MODIFIERS

Access Modifiers (15.4.1)

Limiting access to the properties of an object is part of encapsulation and data hiding. The visibility of an object is how accessible it is to other locations in the code. Without visibility enforcement, someone could directly access the properties of an object and use them in an unintended way, even if the code contains getters and setters. For example, the mileage on a car should not be decreased, but someone could try to invoke `car.mileage -= 1` unless you can restrict access to the `mileage` member variable.

Remember that an access modifier is a keyword such as `public` or `private` that modifies the access level (or visibility) of the code. These keywords typically come before a variable, function, class, or method identifier, and usually are the first keyword on the line, as in the following pseudocode.

```
public int Car::get_speed()

    return current_speed


private void Car::increase_mileage(float amount)

    calculate mileage = mileage + amount
```

If you do not include an access modifier, the compiler uses the default visibility, which differs by language. **Figure 15-17** shows the default visibilities of common programming languages. Note that some programming languages, such as Python, do not have access modifiers. Typically, modifier-free languages have a naming convention to suggest visibility.

Language	Default Visibility
C++	Private
Java	Package
Python	Public (No visibility Modifiers)

Figure 15-17 Default visibility of common programming languages

Public Variables and Methods (15.4.2)

It is easiest to use public variables. Any other code or programmer can access a `public` variable from anywhere. Use `public` visibility when an aspect of an object does not need oversight. While `public` variables are the easiest to use when designing an object, you should resist making everything `public`. If you allow direct access to all the properties in an object, then a property such as `mileage` can be set incorrectly.

Recall that methods can also be **public**. In fact, most methods are **public**. **Figure 15-18** shows how to change the visibility of the **get_paint_color()** method for a **Car** object to **public**.

```
class Car
{
    // ... omitted code ... //

    // Anything following the colon after a visibility modifier
    // has that visibility.
                                    Keyword public
                                    followed by a colon.
    public:
        string get_paint_color()        get_paint_color()
        {                               method and its data type.
            return this->paint_color;
        }

        // Any following definitions are also public.

}
```

Figure 15-18   Making a `public` variable or method of an object

A good rule to follow is to assign **public** access to all accessors, mutators, and other behaviors the object can express.

Private Variables and Methods (15.4.3, 15.4.4)

Use the private access modifier to restrict how others interact with the object and to control how they can change the object. For example, you can make the **mileage** property **private** and allow only mileage increases. Defining a variable as **private** means that other code must use accessors and mutators to access the variable.

Recall that methods can also be **private**. A **private** method is useful when you have similar code used throughout the object, but outside code does not need to reference it. Some languages, such as Python, make all variables **public** and suggest the level of privacy with naming conventions. For example, a variable name starting with an underscore indicates that you should treat the variable as **private**.

For good object-oriented programming design, you should make most, if not all, your variables **private** so that your data can be changed only by the methods you allow and only in ways that you can control.

Q   Recall that instance fields are internal variables not intended to be seen from the outside. The earlier instance field example for the **Car** class was the **oil_level** variable. Should the **oil_level** of the **Car** be **public** or **private**?

A   All instance fields, because they should not be used outside of the object at all, should be made **private**.

Instance fields should not have any getters or setters, but rather be used by other methods in the object. The `oil_level` for a `Car` is `private`, and the only interaction with the property is through the `check_oil()` method.

Figure 15-19 shows how to change the visibility of a `Car` object's variables to `private`.

```
class Car
{

    private:
    // Private variables to enforce encapsulation
        string paint_color;
        int year;
        double mileage;
        double oil_level;
        double current_speed;


    public:
        // Anything following is now public
        // ... Methods, constructors go here ... //
        string get_paint_color()
        {
            return this->paint_color;
        }
        // ... etc ... //


}
```

Figure 15-19   Making a `private` variable or method of an object

As with any code you design, you must test it thoroughly to be confident that it is ready for someone else to use. Making parts of an object private makes it more complicated to test, but you don't want to have to change the visibility in order to run tests. **Figure 15-20** shows how you could design a test for private aspects of an object.

```
class Car {
    // ... all other car code ... //
    public:
        friend void print_speed(Car car);
};

void print_speed(Car car) {

    cout << "Car speed: " << car.current_speed << endl;

}

int main() {
    Car test_car = Car();
    test_car.accelerate(60);
    print_speed(test_car);

}

OUTPUT:
Car speed: 60
```

Keyword **friend** allows a function access to private properties of a class.

Main runs the test by creating a car, increasing the speed to 60, then calling **print_speed()**.

Because **print_speed()** is a friend of Car, it can access everything regardless of visibility.

Figure 15-20   Testing private property of an object

15.5 INTERFACES AND HEADERS

Interfaces (15.5.1)

When using code created by someone else, programmers only need to know the expected input and result. You can provide a shorthand guide to the expected input and output with **interfaces**, which are the minimum amount of information needed to interact with code. If an interface stays the same, but the implementation changes, the outside programmer can still use the code.

Consider the following function, which calculates the minimum of three numbers.

```
function min(x, y, z)

    if x <= y and x <= z

        return x

    else if y <= x and y <= z

        return y

    else

        return z
```

This function starts by comparing x to y and z, and if x is less than both, it returns x. Then it compares y to x and z, returning y if y is less than both. Finally, it returns z if it reaches the **else** part of the conditional block, because by this point z has to be the minimum. If you ran the **min()** function with the values 5, 10, and 2, the function would return 2. The function interface expects three numbers as parameters, called by the identifier `min()`, and returns the minimum of the three values passed to it. Pseudocode to use this function could look like the following:

```
input x

input y

input z

display "The smallest number is:"

display call function min(x, y, z)
```

Now consider the following alternative implementation for `min()`:

```
function min(x, y, z)

    initialize min_guess = x

    if y < min_guess

        compute min_guess = y

    if z < min_guess

        compute min_guess = z


    return min_guess
```

This version of `min()` starts by creating a variable called `min_guess`, which it initializes to the value in `x`. Next, it checks to see if `y` is less than the current value in `min_guess`. If `y` is less than `min_guess`, it updates `min_guess` to contain the value from `y`. It repeats this check with `z`. If you ran the `min()` function with the values 5, 10, and 2 in this implementation, the function would return 2 as before.

Q Does the code to use the `min()` function have to change when the implementation changes?

A Although the implementation changed, the input, expected behavior, and output did not. Externally, it's as if the function hadn't changed at all. If all you knew about `min()` was that it expects three numbers and will return the minimum of those three, you do not need to know how it is implemented in order to use it. Both implementations, given 5, 10 and 2 as arguments, return 2.

Programming an Interface (15.5.2, 15.5.3, 15.5.4)

You use interfaces to quickly show how to interact with a piece of code. As you saw earlier, you only need to know certain things to use code. Knowing how it is implemented is optional. If you are creating code for someone else, as your boss requested, creating an interface is a way to provide your coworker with all they need to succeed. To be useful, interfaces need to identify the following elements:

- How to invoke the function or method
- What the function or method will do
- What the function or method will return

Some interfaces are meant for humans only. This means that it conveys knowledge to people but doesn't provide any enforceable code. For example, a ReadMe text file is a human-only interface. It counts on a person to remember everything about the interface. In contrast, some programming languages provide a way to enforce the interface in the code.

Enforcing an interface using code lets you create a program that does not compile if the interface is used incorrectly. It can also remove human error when the code is used and reduces how much the programmer must memorize. Similar to how a compiler does not allow you to use the incorrect syntax in a for-loop, neither does a programming language let you use an interface incorrectly. Both will point to the exact place where the error occurred.

How to create code-enforced interfaces differs by programming language. C++ has **header files** (which end in .h instead of .cpp), while Java has an **interface** keyword. Python can simulate interfaces but not enforce interfaces, similar to how it simulates **private** variables.

Figure 15-21 shows how you could program the interface for the **Car** class. Only the method signatures are required in the interface in Java. The header file in C++ has method signatures and class variables, if necessary. Method signatures contain the three items listed earlier for indicating a useful interface: how to invoke the method, what it will do, and what it will return.

```
class Car
{
    private:
        // Private variables to enforce encapsulation
        string paint_color;
        int year;
        double mileage;
        double oil_level;
        double current_speed;

        // Static and constant variables
        const static string available_colors[];
        const static int total_colors;

    public:
        // Constructors
        Car();
        Car(string paint_color, int year=1908);

        // Getters
        string get_paint_color();
        int get_year();
        double get_mileage();
        double get_speed();

        // Setters
        void set_paint_color(string paint_color);
        void set_year(int year);

        // Other Methods
        void increase_miles(double amount);
        void change_oil();
        void accelerate(double amount);
        void travel(double time_in_seconds);
        void display();
        bool should_change_oil();
};
```

Interfaces in C++ have all the member variables and static variables.

How to call is the identifier name.

What information it needs is the parameter list.

Interfaces only list the methods available.

What to expect back is the return type.

Figure 15-21 Interface for the **Car** class

Note the difference between the interface and the implementation. The interface is only the method signature, while the implementation is the code within the method. An interface does not provide code you can run or show you how to achieve the end result. Interfaces are limited to method signatures that tell you how to interact with the code and what to expect back. An interface is usually stored in a separate file and defines the behavior only. C++ requires the interface definitions in a header file with a .h extension.

The implementation is the part of the code that actually does something. Implementations include for-loops, if-statements, and input commands, for example, that tell the computer what to do. You've primarily been working with implementations when you think of code. Implementations are stored in a file separate from the interface.

When the implementation is stored in another file, Java and C++ need to signal to which class these behaviors belong. In Java, the class signals its implementation with the keyword **implements**. In C++, the syntax changes to use **ClassName::** before each method name.

Figure 15-22 shows how the **Car** class implementation changes by including the interface from Figure 15-21.

```cpp
#include "car.h"                    Car:: indicates that
                                    this is part of a Car
Car::Car()                          class.
{
    this->paint_color = "black";
    this->year = 1908;
    this->mileage = 0.0;
    this->oil_level = 1.0;
    this->current_speed = 0.0;

}                                           Nothing else changes
                                            in how you program
                                            the features of a
                                            class.
Car::Car(string paint_color, int year) {
    // Using setters to enforce behavior
    this->set_paint_color(paint_color);
    this->set_year(year);
    this->mileage = 0.0;
    this->oil_level = 1.0;
    this->current_speed = 0.0;

}

// Getters
string Car::get_paint_color()
{
    return this->paint_color;
}
// ... etc ... //
```

Figure 15-22   Implementation of the **Car** interface

While most interfaces have no implementations, C++ allows you to place short implementations in the header file, such as a single line of code, similar to the getter method in Figure 15-12. Anything longer should not be in the header file.

C++ also has header guards, which are lines of code that prevent definition conflict, or two pieces of code having the same identifier but conflicting definitions. Header guards prevent conflicting definitions of the same function, class, or variable. To use header guards, you include three statements. Include `#ifdef` and `#define` at the beginning of the file. Include `#endif` at the end of the file.

SUMMARY

- Encapsulation is the practice of bundling and hiding information in one object. Using encapsulation allows you to design code for other programmers to use while still controlling your program design.
- When you design an object, you identify its properties and actions. The properties become variables within a class, while the behaviors and actions become as methods. Instance fields are variables the class might use but are never accessed from outside the class.
- To reference the current object instance, you use a self-reference keyword. The keyword is often `this`, depending on the programming language. Using explicit referencing forces the computer to look only at the class-level scope. If a programming language allows implicit referencing, the computer will look locally first, then at the class, then globally.
- Encapsulation is enforced by programming accessors and mutators, or getters and setters. These methods restrict how outside code can interact with your code by allowing access or mutation within certain parameters, such as never allowing a decrease in car mileage.
- Constructors set up an object to be used by other code. The parameters of a constructor indicate how much control outside code has over objects you've designed. Default parameters and constructor overloading give other programmers a shorthand way to program objects instead of detailing all the properties and methods in the construction.
- You use access modifiers to enforce encapsulation. The visibility of an object indicates where and whether a variable can be accessed directly in the code. `Private` variables can only be accessed from within the class it belongs to, while `public` variables are accessible by everyone everywhere.
- Interfaces are the minimal set of instructions a programmer needs to know about a piece of code to interact with it. The interface provides the input, output, and expected behavior to other programmers. Header files are files specific to C++ that are similar to interfaces and have the ability to use header guards to prevent multiple definitions of the same class.

Key Terms

access modifier	getters	private
accessor	header files	properties
arguments	header guards	public
constructor overloading	implicit self-referencing	self-reference keyword
default parameters	instance field	setters
default visibility	instance variables	visibility
encapsulation	interfaces	
explicit self-referencing	mutator	

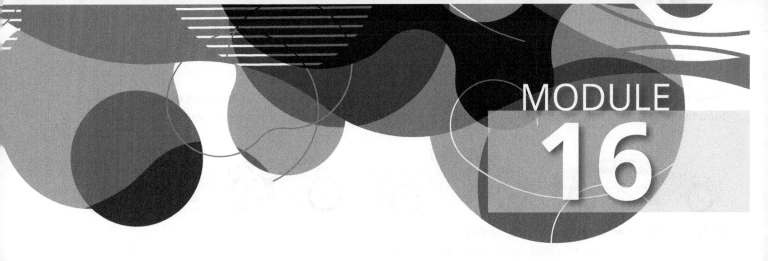

MODULE
16

INHERITANCE

LEARNING OBJECTIVES:

16.1   USING INHERITANCE

16.1.1   Explain the role of inheritance in building a class hierarchy.

16.1.2   Explain how inheritance is incorporated into building a class hierarchy.

16.1.3   Explain the terms parent, child, and ancestor in relation to OOP.

16.1.4   Explain the level of access between members of a hierarchy.

16.1.5   Explain protected variables.

16.2   NECESSARY COMPONENTS FOR INHERITANCE

16.2.1   Define a parent class.

16.2.2   Define a child class.

16.3   CREATING A CHILD CLASS THAT INHERITS FROM A PARENT CLASS

16.3.1   Outline the syntax used for creating an inherited class.

16.3.2   Write a statement that defines a child class that inherits at least one property from a parent class.

16.3.3   Write a statement defining a child class that inherits at least one method from a parent class.

16.3.4   Write a method that overrides the default behavior of the parent.

16.1 USING INHERITANCE

Creating Classes from Other Classes (16.1.1, 16.1.2)

Zoe's Car dealership has enjoyed success since you began writing code to manage the cars. The owner now has room to expand the dealership's capacity. With this new expansion, the inventory will include the sale of cars (gas, hybrid, and electric), motorcycles, trucks, and vans. Now is a good time to identify ways to better structure your code. Code reuse is a programming fundamental that you should strive to maintain in all of your programs.

The concept of inheritance will help you to write code for the dealership's expansion. In programming, inheritance is a way of creating a new class from an existing class. In the same way that children inherit genetic features from their biological parents (eyes, hair, and height, for example), classes can inherit the methods (including constructors) and member variables of other classes. Inheritance allows you to use the common properties of one class to define other classes, creating a hierarchy. Generally, a class created through inheritance is a more specialized or specific version of the original class.

As a rule of thumb, if you have logically related classes with common features, inheritance will likely make your code simpler. Inheritance is a useful tool when the same code uses related classes and needs to treat them similarly.

Using inheritance also helps you to avoid duplicating code. For example, the code for checking out a motor vehicle for a test run is the same, regardless of whether it is a car, truck, motorcycle, or van. See **Figure 16-1**.

Figure 16-1   Car, truck, motorcycle, and van

MicroOne/Shutterstock.com, Ivengo/Shutterstock.com, iman fanani/Shutterstock.com

The new version of the dealership code needs to manage cars, motorcycles, trucks, and vans. They are all logically related because they are all motor vehicles and sold in the dealership. You can create a new class called **MotorVehicle** to cover all of the inventory sold in the dealership (see **Figure 16-2**). If the owner decides to sell another type of motor vehicle in the future (such as a golf cart), you can add that object to the program with a minimal amount of code because it can inherit from **MotorVehicle**.

```
                    MotorVehicle

                  make : string
                  model : string
                  color : string
                  vin : string
                  price : integer
                  mpg : integer
                  year : integer
                  mileage : integer
                  fuel_level : double
                  tank_capacity : double
                  sold : boolean
                  on_lot : boolean

                  give_discount(percentage)
                  increase_mileage(amount)
                  sell_vehicle(final_price)
                  test_drive(license_number)
                  refuel(amount)
```

Figure 16-2   MotorVehicle class description

As shown in Figure 16-2, inheritance allows you to create a more general class with all of the common features found in the objects of that type. For example, all motor vehicles have a make, model, color, VIN, price, MPG, year, mileage, fuel level, and fuel tank capacity. In the dealership, motor vehicles also have a status to indicate if they are sold or on the lot. In addition, all motor vehicles in the dealership have similar actions that need to be performed, including discounting the price, increasing the mileage after a test drive, selling the vehicle, checking the vehicle out for a test drive, and refueling the vehicle.

Family Trees in OOP (16.1.3)

In a family tree linking family members, children inherit from parents and grandparents. The same terminology is used in inheritance for OOP. The diagram of the inheritance relationship between classes is called an **inheritance hierarchy**, or class hierarchy. Building an inheritance hierarchy starts when a class inherits from another class. See **Figure 16-3**.

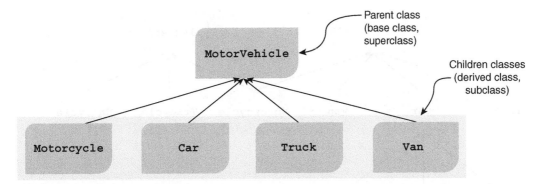

Figure 16-3   Inheritance class hierarchy for `MotorVehicles` sold in a dealership

The top class in the hierarchy is the **parent class**, also called the base class or superclass. It refers to the class from which all the other classes are created. For example, **MotorVehicle** is the parent class of the **Car** class. The types of motor vehicles, such as cars, motorcycles, trucks, and vans, are created (or derived) from the parent class. A **Car** is called a **child class**, or derived class, because it inherits the behavior and data members from the parent class.

The same way that each human parent is someone's child, a child class can also be a parent class. This feature is useful in the case of the **Car** class hierarchy. Three kinds of cars are sold at the dealership: gas-powered, electric-powered, and hybrid. Logically, each is a specialized version of a **Car**. You can create those classes so that they inherit from the **Car** class, making the hierarchy shown in **Figure 16-4**.

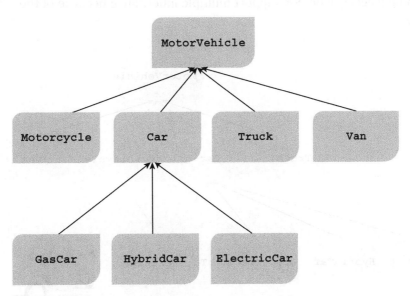

Figure 16-4   Classes inheriting from the `Car` class

Inheritance creates a hierarchy of classes, where the top class is the class from which all of the other classes are created. For example, **Motorcycle**, **Car**, **Truck**, and **Van** are types of motor vehicles, so they inherit directly from the **MotorVehicle** class. **GasCar**, **HybridCar**, and **ElectricCar** are specific kinds of cars, so they can inherit the properties of the **Car** class, which also inherits the properties of the **MotorVehicle** class.

GasCar, **HybridCar**, and **ElectricCar** have methods from **Car**, which also has the methods from **MotorVehicle**. **Car** and **MotorVehicle** are the **ancestors** of **GasCar**, **ElectricCar**, and **HybridCar**. In the hierarchy, any class that has one or more classes derived from it is an ancestor. Any class that is derived from a parent class is called a **descendant**.

In C++ and Python, a child class can be derived from more than one parent class. This concept is called **multiple inheritance**. If a child class inherits from more than one parent, it receives all the accessible methods and member variables of the parent. An example of multiple inheritance is shown in **Figure 16-5**.

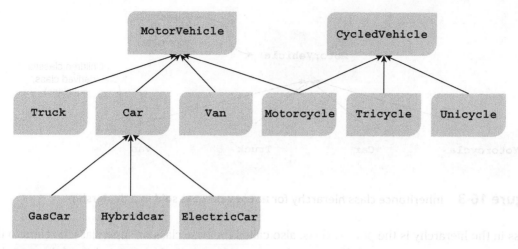

Figure 16-5   Multiple inheritance for the `Motorcycle` class

As shown in Figure 16-5, **Motorcycle** inherits from both **MotorVehicle** and **CycledVehicle**. **Motorcycle** inherits all of the features of **MotorVehicle** as well as features that are specific to **CycledVehicle**, such as handlebar length and kickstand. Multiple inheritance provides an easy way to create rich, complex objects by combining the features of preexisting related objects.

Although multiple inheritance saves time when creating complex objects that are a combination of other objects, some programming languages do not support multiple inheritance because of the **diamond problem**, illustrated in **Figure 16-6**.

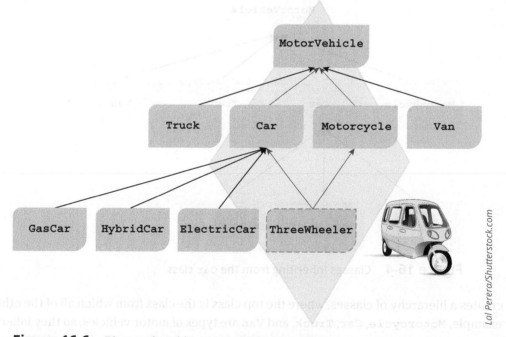

Figure 16-6   Diamond problem in multiple inheritance

Suppose that the dealership begins selling three-wheelers, which are a combination of a car and a motorcycle. It seems natural to create a new class called **ThreeWheeler** that has **Car** and **Motorcycle** as parents to inherit from. However, **Car** and **Motorcycle** share a common ancestor, **MotorVehicle**. Because **Car** and **Motorcycle** each have a copy of the methods and member variables in **MotorVehicle**, now **ThreeWheeler** has two copies of each member variable and method from **MotorVehicle**. Calling a method in **ThreeWheeler** causes ambiguity in the program because the computer does not know which method to use. It is for this reason that many programming languages do not allow or support multiple inheritance.

Q What should you do if multiple inheritance is unavoidable in your code?

A You must manually ensure that the diamond problem does not occur. If a child has multiple parents, you must trace the ancestry within the hierarchy to ensure that none of the parents share a common ancestor.

Levels of Access (16.1.4, 16.1.5)

In an inheritance hierarchy, when a child is derived from a parent, the parent can specify which methods and member variables are also inherited. As you may remember, the three access modifiers are **public**, **private**, and **protected**. You use these modifiers to specify which methods and member variables children can inherit. They function in the following way, also shown in **Figure 16-7**:

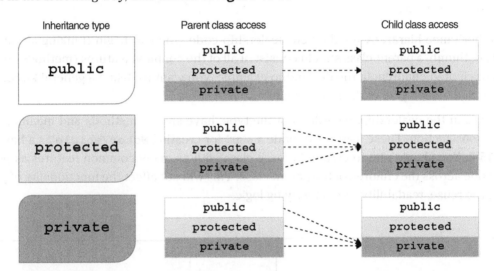

Figure 16-7   Inheritance according to inheritance type and access modifiers

public. Inherited by all derived classes
private. Not inherited by any derived classes
protected. Only inherited by the immediately derived class

When the child class is created, the inheritance type can be declared as **public**, **private**, or **protected**. The methods and attributes available in the child class depend on the access modifier specified in the class declaration.

The most common type of inheritance is **public** inheritance. If the inheritance type is **public**, the **public** methods and member variables of the parent become **public** members of the child class, and the **protected** members of the parent class become **protected** members of the child class. Members of the parent class that are **private** remain **private** to the parent class. As a rule of thumb, you should use **public** inheritance unless you have a specific reason not to use it.

The least common type of inheritance is **protected** inheritance. If the inheritance type is **protected**, the **public** and **protected** methods and member variables of the parent class become **protected** members of the child class.

If the inheritance type is **private**, the **public** and **protected** methods and member variables of the parent class become **private** members of the child class. Inheriting privately prevents further classes from inheriting these methods and member variables from the child class.

On the surface, **private** inheritance appears to contradict the goals of inheritance; however, you use **private** inheritance when you are interested in taking advantage of features available in the parent class, even if they are not logically or conceptually related. For example, suppose you want to create a **Bicycle** class. Logically, a bicycle is not a motor vehicle, but the **Bicycle** class can benefit from using the underlying structure of the **MotorVehicle** class.

In the past, you structured definitions so that the member variables are **private** and the methods are **public**. To change your code so that inheritance is possible, the **private** data members should be moved to the **public** section so that they can be inherited by children.

Inheritance is not mandatory. If you create a class that you do not want any other classes to inherit from, then you can include the keyword **final** in the class declaration, stating that this is the only definition of this entity. This creates a final class, which is a class that cannot have any other classes derived from it. If any class attempts to inherit from a **final** class, a compiling error occurs.

16.2 NECESSARY COMPONENTS FOR INHERITANCE

Defining a Parent Class (16.2.1)

After setting the inheritance hierarchy for the new dealership code, you can begin thinking about the inner structure. As a rule of thumb, a parent class should consist of all of the common features (methods and member variables) of the anticipated children. In the dealership example, you want to define a general **MotorVehicle** parent class, so you must identify all of the shared features.

All motor vehicles in the dealership, regardless of the type, have similar methods and member variables, as listed in the previous section. These features provide a start for creating **MotorVehicle** as a base class, as shown in **Figure 16-8**. You should aim to create the base class with as many common features as possible to avoid duplicating code across the children of the parent class. This will not affect the functionality of your code, but it will enhance the reuse, readability, and underlying logic.

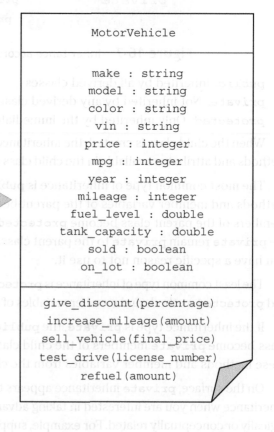

```
create class MotorVehicle
    public
        attribute: make as string
        attribute: model as string
        attribute: color as string
        attribute: vin as string
        attribute: price as integer
        attribute: mpg as integer
        attribute: year as integer
        attribute: mileage as integer
        attribute: fuel_level as double
        attribute: tank_capacity as double
        attribute: sold as boolean
        attribute: on_lot as boolean
        method: give_discount(percentage)
        method: increase_mileage(amount)
        method: sell_vehicle(final_price)
        method: test_drive(license_number)
        method: refuel(amount)
```

Figure 16-8 Defining a parent class

Because any class can become a parent class, the syntax for defining a parent class does not differ from the normal syntax for creating a class. For brevity purposes, all accessors, mutators, constructors, and overloaded operators are omitted from the examples in this module, but you should include them in your classes.

Defining a Child Class (16.2.2)

As previously described, a child class inherits the features of one or more of its parents. You can think of a child class as a customized version of the parent class. Not only does it contain the methods and member variables of the parent class, as specified by the inheritance settings, the child class can also include its own methods and member variables that are specific to the object. The following pseudocode shows the general syntax of defining such a class.

```
create class Child_Class_name : access_modifier: parent_class_1, parent_class_2 ...
  public
      method: additional_method_1(parameter_list)
      method: additional_method_2(parameter_list)
      attribute: additional_attribute_1 as type
      attribute: additional_attribute_2 as type
  protected
      method: additional_method_3(parameter_list)
      method: additional_method_4(parameter_list)
      attribute: additional_attribute_3 as type
      attribute: additional_attribute_4 as type
  private
      method: additional_method_5(parameter_list)
      method: additional_method_6(parameter_list)
      attribute: additional_attribute_5 as type
      attribute: additional_attribute_6 as type
```

As displayed, the pseudocode for defining a child class does not differ much from the pseudocode for defining a normal class. The two additions are the **access_modifier**, stating the inheritance type, and a list of the parent classes from which the child class should inherit.

Q Do I have to add methods and attributes when creating a child class from a parent class?

A No, but it is common to add class-specific variables to further customize the class. It's perfectly fine to create a child class that is identical to the parent class, though this practice is not useful because it does not take advantage of the opportunities inheritance provides for customizing.

For example, to create the **Truck** class that inherits from the **MotorVehicle** class, you would include attributes specific to the **Truck** class, which differentiate it from a general **MotorVehicle**, such as the width and length of the flatbed in the back of the truck. The pseudocode for customizing the class would resemble the following;

```
create class Truck : public MotorVehicle
  public
      attribute: flatbed_width as float
      attribute: flatbed_length as float
```

The compiler treats the **Truck** as though it has the following definition:

```
create class Truck

  public

    method: give_discount(percentage)

    method: increase_mileage(amount)

    method: sell_vehicle(final_price)

    method: test_drive(license_number)

    method: refuel(amount)

    attribute: make as string

    attribute: model as string

    attribute: color as string

    attribute: vin as string

    attribute: price as integer

    attribute: mpg as integer

    attribute: year as integer

    attribute: mileage as integer

    attribute: fuel_level as double

    attribute: tank_capacity as double

    attribute: sold as boolean

    attribute: on_lot as boolean

    attribute: flatbed_width as float

    attribute: flatbed_length as float
```

This pseudocode shows the methods and attributes inherited from **MotorVehicle** along with the additional attributes that are specific to a **Truck**. As the example shows, a child class can have additional methods and variables that are not included in the parent class. This is how the child class becomes a more specific, customized version of the parent.

16.3 CREATING A CHILD CLASS THAT INHERITS FROM A PARENT CLASS

Inheritance Syntax (16.3.1, 16.3.2, 16.3.3)

Now that you are familiar with the concept of inheritance and its components, you can create an inherited class. The syntax for writing code for a child class that inherits from a parent class differs from language to language. For example, **Figure 16-9** shows the code you would write for creating a **Truck** class that inherits from the **MotorVehicle** class.

Figure 16-9 shows the definition of the **MotorVehicle** class. After the **MotorVehicle** class is created, the **Truck** class can inherit from it. It inherits all of the properties and methods of **MotorVehicle**, and adds its own

MotorVehicle.cpp

```cpp
#include <iostream>
#include <string>
using namespace std;

class MotorVehicle
{
    public:
        void give_discount(double percentage);
        void increase_mileage(int miles);
        void sell_car(double final_price);
        void test_drive(string license_number);
        void refuel(int amount);
        string make;
        string model;
        string color;
        string vin;
        int price;
        int mpg;
        int year;
        int mileage;
        double fuel_level;
        double tank_capacity;
        bool sold;
        bool on_lot;
};

class Truck : public MotorVehicle
{
    public:
        double flatbed_length;
        double flatbed_width;
};

int main()
{
```

Define a parent class

Define a child class that inherits the public methods and properties of the parent class

Figure 16-9   C++ syntax for inheritance (*Continued*)

```
        Truck truck_1;  ◄──────────────────── Declare a Truck object


        truck_1.make = "Nissan";

        truck_1.model = "Frontier";

        truck_1.color = "blue";

        truck_1.vin = "TGR8374033974";

        truck_1.price = 19290;                    Initialize the data
                                                  members of the Truck
        truck_1.mpg = 25;                         object, including those
        truck_1.year = 2020;                      inherited from
                                                  MotorVehicle
        truck_1.mileage = 1000;

        truck_1.fuel_level = 20;

        truck_1.tank_capacity = 21.1;

        truck_1.sold = false;

        truck_1.on_lot = true;

        truck_1.flatbed_length = 8.1;

        truck_1.flatbed_width = 5.25;


        cout << "Made a truck with the following features: " << endl;

        cout << "Make: \t\t" << truck_1.make << endl;

        cout << "Model: \t\t" << truck_1.model << endl;

        cout << "Color: \t\t" << truck_1.color << endl;

        cout << "VIN: \t\t" << truck_1.vin << endl;

        cout << "Price: \t\t" << truck_1.price << endl;

        cout << "MPG: \t\t" << truck_1.mpg << endl;                    Write the
                                                                      contents
        cout << "Year: \t\t" << truck_1.year << endl;                 of the
                                                                      Truck
        cout << "Mileage: \t" << truck_1.mileage << endl;             object to
                                                                      the screen
        cout << "Fuel Level: \t" << truck_1.fuel_level << endl;

        cout << "Tank Capacity: \t" << truck_1.tank_capacity << endl;

        cout << "Sold Yet?: \t" << truck_1.sold << endl;

        cout << "On the lot?: \t" << truck_1.on_lot << endl;

        cout << "Flatbed length: \t" << truck_1.flatbed_length << endl;

        cout << "Flatbed width: \t" << truck_1.flatbed_width << endl;


        return 0;

    }
```

Figure 16-9 C++ syntax for inheritance (*Continued*)

```
Made a truck with the following features:
Make:           Nissan
Model:          Frontier
Color:          blue
VIN:            TGR8374033974
Price:          19290
MPG:            25
Year:           2020
Mileage:        1000
Fuel Level:     20
Tank Capacity:  21.1
Sold Yet?:      0
On the lot?:    1
Bed length:     8.1
Bed width:      5.25
```

Figure 16-9   C++ syntax for inheritance (*Continued*)

properties that define the length and the width of the flatbed. In the main section of the program, a **Truck** object is declared. All of the member variables of the **Truck** object, including those inherited from **MotorVehicle**, are initialized. Lastly, the contents of the member variables are written to the screen, with tabs inserted for readability.

Customizing Behavior (16.3.4)

As written, the **MotorVehicle** class includes a method to refuel the vehicle. The **refuel()** method is inherited from **MotorVehicle** by the **Car** class. The **GasCar**, **HybridCar**, and **ElectricCar** class each has a copy of the **refuel()** method. In the **MotorVehicle** class, the **refuel()** method specifies the number of gallons of gas to add to the tank. An electric car does not have a gas tank, so this version of the **refuel()** method inherited from **Car** does not apply.

Method overriding allows a child class to provide its own implementation of a method that is already inherited by one of its ancestors. Method overriding is useful when the way that the parent class has implemented a method doesn't apply to the child class and needs to change. Any method can be overridden to provide customized behavior. You can customize the **refuel()** method to fit the **ElectricCar** class. An example is shown in the following pseudocode.

```
create class MotorVehicle
  public
      method: give_discount(percentage)
      method: increase_mileage(amount)
      method: sell_vehicle(final_price)
      method: test_drive(license_number)
      method: refuel(amount)
      attribute: make as string
```

```
    attribute: model as string

    attribute: color as string

    attribute: vin as string

    attribute: price as integer

    attribute: mpg as integer

    attribute: year as integer

    attribute: mileage as integer

    attribute: fuel_level as double

    attribute: tank_capacity as double

    attribute: sold as boolean

    attribute: on_lot as boolean
create class Car : public MotorVehicle

  public

    attribute: fuel_type as string

create class ElectricCar : public Car

  public

    method: refuel(amount)

    attribute: battery_percentage as integer
```

The pseudocode shows the definition of the **MotorVehicle** class, followed by the definition of the **Car** class, which adds an attribute called **fuel_type**. Next is the definition of the **ElectricCar** class, which is a customized version of the **Car** class with a redefined **refuel()** method and an additional attribute to store the battery percentage. Now, whenever the **refuel()** method is called, the **ElectricCar** version of the method is used, instead of the definition inherited from **MotorVehicle**. Code demonstrating this concept is shown in **Figure 16-10**.

Figure 16-10 demonstrates method overriding. After the parent **MotorVehicle** class is defined, the **Car** class inherits from it, adding a member variable for the fuel type. Next, **ElectricCar** and **GasCar** are created as children of the **Car** class. The default behavior of the **MotorVehicle** class's **refuel()** method is to add the amount of gas (in gallons) specified in the parameter list to the **Car's** current amount of gas, as long as it does not overfill the tank.

The **refuel()** method behavior is fine for the **GasCar**; however, the **ElectricCar** requires electricity to recharge. The **ElectricCar** class overrides the **refuel()** method provided in the **MotorVehicle** class to redefine the method so that it adds a certain amount of charge to the battery (not to exceed 100 percent). Executing the overridden behavior is demonstrated in the main section of the program, which declares the **GasCar corolla** and the **ElectricCar tesla**. The **refuel()** method adds 3 gallons of gas to the **corolla** and 10 percent of charge to the **tesla**. The result of the methods is printed to the screen.

Q If I create a method in the child class that has the same name as a method in the base class but a different return type or different parameters, is this still method overriding?

A No, the method must have the same signature (name, parameters, and return type) to be considered overriding. If the method in the child class has the same name and return type, but different parameters, this is considered method overloading.

MotorVehicle.cpp

```cpp
#include <iostream>
#include <string>
using namespace std;

class MotorVehicle
{
    public:
        void give_discount(double percentage);
        void increase_mileage(int miles);
        void sell_car(double final_price);
        void test_drive(string license_number);
        void refuel(int amount);
        string make;
        string model;
        string color;
        string vin;
        int price;
        int mpg;
        int year;
        int mileage;
        double fuel_level;
        double tank_capacity;
        bool sold;
        bool on_lot;
};
```

Define the parent class, `MotorVehicle`

```cpp
class Car : public MotorVehicle
{
    public:
        string fuel_type;
};
```

Define the `Car` class that inherits the public members of `MotorVehicle`

```cpp
class ElectricCar : public Car
{
    public:
        void refuel(int amount);
        int battery_percentage;
};
```

Declare an `ElectricCar` object from the `Car` object

Figure 16-10   Overriding methods in a parent class (*Continued*)

```
class GasCar : public Car
{
  public:
     void refuel(int amount);
};
```

Declare a GasCar object from the Car object

```
void MotorVehicle::refuel(int amount)
{
   if(fuel_level + amount <= tank_capacity)
   {
      cout << "Current fuel level is: " << fuel_level << " gallons." << endl;
      cout << "Adding " << amount << " gallons of gas to the tank." << endl;
      fuel_level = fuel_level + amount;
      cout << "Current gas level is : " << fuel_level << " out of " <<
      tank_capacity << " gallons." << endl;
   }
   else
   {
      cout << "Cannot add gas. Will overfill." << endl;
   }
   return;
}
```

Definition of refuel() in MotorVehicle class

```
void GasCar::refuel(int amount)
{
   if(fuel_level + amount <= tank_capacity)
   {
      cout << "Current fuel level is: " << fuel_level << " gallons." << endl;
      cout << "Adding " << amount << " gallons of gas to the tank" << endl;
      fuel_level = fuel_level + amount;
      cout << "Current gas level is : " << fuel_level << " out of " <<
      tank_capacity << " gallons." << endl;
      cout << "You  can drive another " << fuel_level * mpg << " miles
      before refueling." << endl;
   }
   else
   {
      cout << "Cannot add gas. Will overfill." << endl;
   }

   return;
}
```

Figure 16-10　Overriding methods in a parent class (*Continued*)

```
void ElectricCar::refuel(int amount)

{

   if(battery_percentage + amount <= 100)

   {

      cout << "Current battery level is: " << battery_percentage << " percent." <<
endl;

      cout << "Charging the car to raise " << amount << " percentage points." <<
endl;

      battery_percentage = battery_percentage + amount;

      cout << "Current percentage amount is now: " << battery_percentage << " 
percent." << endl;

   }

   else

   {

      cout << "Cannot charge now. Will over charge the car." << endl;

   }

   return;

}

int main()

{

  GasCar corolla;
  ElectricCar tesla;

// some code to create a car
  corolla.fuel_level = 10.2;
  corolla.tank_capacity = 16;
  corolla.mpg = 32;
  tesla.battery_percentage = 42;

  corolla.refuel(3);
  tesla.refuel(10);

  return 0;

}
```

Redefinition of `refuel()` in `MotorVehicle` class

Test out `refuel()` in a `GasCar` and `ElectricCar` object

OUTPUT:

Current fuel level is: 10.2 gallons.

Adding 3 gallons of gas to the tank.

Current gas level is: 13.2 out of 16 gallons.

You can drive another 422.4 miles before refueling.

Current battery level is: 42 percent.

Charging the car to raise 10 percentage points.

Current percentage amount is now: 52 percent.

Figure 16-10   Overriding methods in a parent class (*Continued*)

Suppose that you want to create a base class that does not allow its children to modify the behavior of particular methods. For example, the `test_drive()` method requires an argument for a valid driver's license number of the person driving the car. This behavior should not change because it is required by law to have a valid driver's license to operate a motor vehicle. You do not want any of the children of this class to override the method and possibly change this requirement. You can use the keyword **final** in the method definition to create a final method that cannot be overridden by any of the children, as shown in **Figure 16-11**.

Figure 16-11 shows how a **final** method would be declared within a class. When the keyword **final** is added to the `test_drive()` method, the compiler prohibits any derived classes from redefining the method. If a derived class tries to provide its own definition of the `test_drive()` method, an error will occur and the code will not compile.

```cpp
#include <iostream>
#include <string>
using namespace std;

class MotorVehicle
{
    public:                                                    Keyword final
        void give_discount(double percentage);
        void increase_mileage(int miles);
        void sell_car(double final_price);
        virtual void test_drive(string license_number) final
        {
        cout << license_number;
        }
        void refuel(int amount);
        string make;
        string model;
        string color;
        string vin;
        int price;
        int mpg;
        int year;
        int mileage;
        double fuel_level;
        double tank_capacity;
        bool sold;
        bool on_lot;
};
```

Figure 16-11   Overriding methods in a parent class

SUMMARY

- In programming, inheritance is a way of creating a new class from another existing class. Inheritance builds a class hierarchy resembling a family tree, displaying which class has inherited from another class.
- A parent is the class that is being inherited from, a child is the class that is inheriting, and an ancestor is any parent or parent of a parent in a class hierarchy.
- A child can inherit from more than one parent, but you must make sure that the parents do not share an ancestor; otherwise the diamond problem will occur.
- The diamond problem happens when a child inherits duplicate copies of similar features from parents with a common ancestor.
- When a child inherits from a parent, the parent can specify which methods and member variables are also inherited using access modifier keyword, `public`, `private`, and `protected`.
- If you create a class that you do not want any other classes to inherit from, you can include the keyword `final` in the class declaration to prevent it from being inherited.
- Because any class can become a parent class, the syntax for defining a parent class does not differ from the normal syntax for creating a class.
- Defining a child class does not differ much from the pseudocode for defining a normal class. The two additions are the `access_modifier`, stating the inheritance type, and a list of the parent classes from which the child class should inherit.
- Method overriding is useful when the way that the parent class has implemented a method doesn't apply to the child class and needs to change. Any method can be overridden to provide customized behavior.
- If you do not want a child class to override a specific method, you can use the keyword `final` in the method definition to create a `final` method.

Key Terms

ancestors	final class	Method overriding
child class	final method	multiple inheritance
descendant	inheritance	parent class
diamond problem	inheritance hierarchy	

MODULE
17

POLYMORPHISM

LEARNING OBJECTIVES

17.1 THE PURPOSE OF POLYMORPHISM

17.1.1 Explain how polymorphism is used in OOP.

17.1.2 Define dynamic binding as it applies to OOP.

17.1.3 Explain the advantages of dynamic binding.

17.1.4 Describe how the compiler uses the overridden items of a parent class.

17.2 POLYMORPHISM BASICS

17.2.1 Explain the is-a relationship between a parent and child class.

17.2.2 Explain the has-a relationship between classes.

17.2.3 Write a statement that uses type casting.

17.3 VIRTUAL FUNCTIONS

17.3.1 Define pure virtual method.

17.3.2 Distinguish when to use a pure virtual method.

17.3.3 Write a statement that declares a pure virtual method.

17.3.4 Define an abstract class.

17.3.5 Identify when to use an abstract class.

17.1 THE PURPOSE OF POLYMORPHISM

Flexibility While Coding (17.1.1)

As a programmer, in addition to striving to write code that can handle any possible user input, you should also aim to create code that can handle any change in requirements. To provide this flexibility, many programming languages adopt the concept of **polymorphism**, a word combining the prefix *poly*, which means many, and *morph*, which means shape or form. In other words, polymorphism refers to an object that can take on many forms.

Simply put, polymorphism means that an object of a parent class can be used to refer to any of its descendants. If you are programming for a car dealership, for example, you are coding a system to help the owner sell many kinds of motorized vehicles, as shown in the class hierarchy in **Figure 17-1**.

All objects in the dealership inherit from the **MotorVehicle** class. Because of polymorphism, if you define a method that takes a **MotorVehicle** variable as a parameter, then that method can receive any object as a parameter, as long as it has been derived from **MotorVehicle**. **Motorcycle**, **Car**, **Truck**, **Van**, **GasCar**, **HybridCar**, and **ElectricCar** can be used in any method that specifies a **MotorVehicle** variable as a parameter.

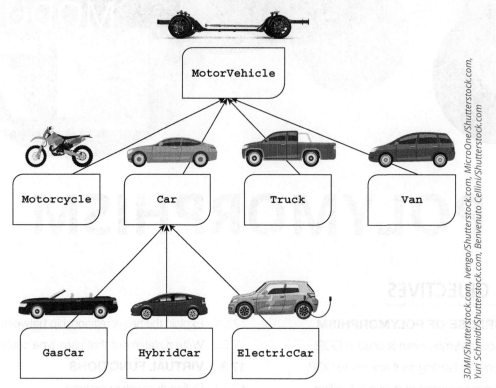

Figure 17-1 MotorVehicle inheritance hierarchy

The **add_vehicle()** method in the following code adds a vehicle to the car dealer's inventory. If the **add_vehicle()** method takes a **MotorVehicle** as input, the code works no matter which child of **MotorVehicle** is added.

```
public void Dealership:add_vehicle(MotorVehicle motor_vehicle) throws
Out_of_Range_Exception

    if (num_vehicles + 1 <= capacity) then

        inventory[num_vehicles] = motor_vehicle

        num_vehicles = num_vehicles + 1

    else

        throw Out_of_Range_Exception
return
```

This code takes as a parameter any **MotorVehicle** (or child of **MotorVehicle**) into the **add_vehicle()** method. If there is space in the inventory, the **MotorVehicle** is added. If there is no space, then an **Out_of_ Range_Exception** is thrown. By creating the **add_vehicle()** method like this, any other part of the code can add a **MotorVehicle** (or any child of **MotorVehicle**) to the inventory.

The following code declares three vehicles as objects in classes that are children of **MotorVehicle**: **HybridCar**, **Truck**, and **Motorcycle**. It also uses the **add_vehicle()** method to add the three vehicles to the inventory.

```
dealership zoes_zippy_cars

declare prius as HybridCar

declare tundra as Truck

declare harley as Motorcycle
```

```
zoes_zippy_cars.add_vehicle(prius)
```

```
zoes_zippy_cars.add_vehicle(tundra)
```

```
zoes_zippy_cars.add_vehicle(harley)
```

Any object that has been created from a class that inherits from the **MotorVehicle** class can be used with the **add_vehicle()** method to add vehicles to the inventory. In this case, you add **prius**, **tundra**, and **harley** to the inventory.

Suppose the dealership owner decides to sell scooters. You can create a **Scooter** class that inherits from the **MotorVehicle** class. A benefit of polymorphism is that if you need to add any other motor vehicles to the dealership and the class you are adding inherits from the parent class, you don't have to change much code. You would write code resembling the following to create a new object of type **Scooter** and add it to the inventory:

```
declare wolf as Scooter
```

```
zoes_zippy_cars.add_vehicle(wolf)
```

Q Can I make an object from the class type **MotorVehicle**?

A Yes, in theory you could. However, it would not make much sense in this context. It is impossible to go to a car dealership and purchase a generic motor vehicle. You would need to specify which kind.

Q Can I use **GasCar**, **HybridCar**, and **ElectricCar** in any place that specifies a **Car** variable?

A Yes, you can because **GasCar**, **HybridCar**, and **ElectricCar** are all children of **Car**. However, **Van**, **Motorcycle**, and **Truck** cannot be used in any place that specifies a **Car** variable.

The **Dealership** class represents the **inventory** object as an array of **Cars**. All of the methods use **Car** variables as parameters. When the **Dealership** expands to include other types of motor vehicles, you can use inheritance and polymorphism to change the **Dealership** object to hold an array of **MotorVehicles** (see **Figure 17-2**).

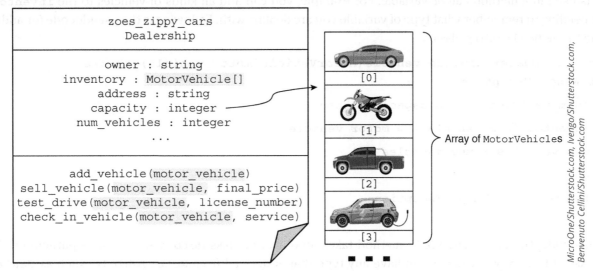

Figure 17-2 Defining the **Dealership** class using polymorphism

If you didn't use inheritance and polymorphism, related objects would have a lot of duplicate code. For example, the **inventory** would have six arrays (one for each type of motor vehicle). You would also have six of each method that the **Dealership** performs. This extra code adds overhead and is unnecessary. The code for defining the new **Dealership** class is shown in **Figure 17-3**. For brevity, constructors, overloaded operators, accessors, and mutators have been omitted from the code.

```cpp
#include <iostream>
#include <string>
using namespace std;
class Dealership
{
  public:
    Dealership();
    void add_vehicle(MotorVehicle motor_vehicle);
    void sell_vehicle(MotorVehicle motor_vehicle, double final_price);
    void test_drive(MotorVehicle motor_vehicle, string license_number);
    void check_in_vehicle(MotorVehicle motor_vehicle, string service);
  private:
    string owner;
    MotorVehicle inventory[50];
    string address;
    int capacity;
    int num_vehicles;
};
```

Figure 17-3   Defining a **Dealership** class

Now you can invoke any method in the **Dealership** class without being concerned about what type of motor vehicle is used in a method call or variable. For example, you can add all kinds of vehicles to the **inventory** without needing to remember what type of variable you are dealing with. Following is the pseudocode for adding a vehicle to the **Dealership** class:

```
public void Dealership:add_vehicle(MotorVehicle motor_vehicle) throws
Out_of_Range_Exception
    if (num_vehicles + 1 <= capacity) then
        inventory[num_vehicles] = motor_vehicle
        num_vehicles = num_vehicles + 1
    else
        throw Out_of_Range_Exception
    return
```

In this code, the **add_vehicle()** method takes an object of class **MotorVehicle** as a parameter. The object passed to **add_vehicle()** can have any type that is derived from **MotorVehicle**, such as **GasCar**, **Motorcycle**, or **Truck**. Regardless of the type, the code checks to determine if the **inventory** has enough space for the **MotorVehicle**, and then adds it to the **Dealership**.

Polymorphism allows you to perform one action in many ways. For example, you can perform the `add_vehicle()` behavior in six ways by adding six kinds of objects to the `inventory`. The code for adding a new motor vehicle to the `inventory` is shown in **Figure 17-4**.

in MotorVehicle.cpp

```cpp
void Dealership::add_vehicle(MotorVehicle motor_vehicle)
{
    if(num_vehicles + 1 <= capacity)          ← Check if there is space to
    {                                             add the vehicle
        inventory[num_vehicles] = motor_vehicle;  ← If so, add the vehicle and increase the number of
        num_vehicles++;                              vehicles in dealership
        cout << "Successfully added a new vehicle to the inventory." << endl;  ⎫
        cout << "There are now " << num_vehicles << " cars on the lot ";       ⎬ Print
        cout << "with " << capacity - num_vehicles <<  " spaces left." << endl; ⎭ current
    }                                                                             lot status
    else                                                                          to screen
    {
        throw runtime_error("lot_full");      ← Throw a runtime error
    }                                            if the lot is full
    return;
}
```

```cpp
#include <iostream>
#include <string>
using namespace std;

int main()                              ⎯ Create a Dealership variable
{
    Dealership zoesZippyCars;
    // some code to initialize data members of zoesZippyCars

    GasCar corolla;
    Motorcycle yamaha;          ⎯ Create different kinds of vehicles that
    Truck gmc;                    inherit from MotorVehicle
    ElectricCar tesla;

    // some code to initialize data members of the cars
    zoesZippyCars.add_vehicle(corolla);
    zoesZippyCars.add_vehicle(yamaha);
    zoesZippyCars.add_vehicle(gmc);
    zoesZippyCars.add_vehicle(tesla);     ⎯ Call add_vehicle() method (above)
                                            to add each vehicle to the Dealership's
    return 0;                               inventory
}
```

OUTPUT:

```
Successfully added a new vehicle to the inventory.
There are now 1 cars on the lot with 49 spaces left.
Successfully added a new vehicle to the inventory.
There are now 2 cars on the lot with 48 spaces left.
Successfully added a new vehicle to the inventory.
There are now 3 cars on the lot with 47 spaces left.
Successfully added a new vehicle to the inventory.
There are now 4 cars on the lot with 46 spaces left.
```

Figure 17-4 Method for adding a vehicle

By creating a method called **add_vehicle()** that can add anything derived from **MotorVehicle** (including **MotorVehicle**) to the **inventory**, you are using polymorphism. The **main()** portion of the code creates a **Dealership** variable and then creates vehicles that inherit from **MotorVehicle**. After initializing the member variables of each object, you can use the **add_vehicle()** method to add the object to the **inventory** of **zoes_zippy_cars**. The output shows that the behavior was successfully executed.

Dynamic Binding Under the Hood (17.1.2, 17.1.3, 17.1.4)

How does the computer know enough to execute such flexible code? How does the compiler know which variable or method to use in polymorphism? The answer is dynamic binding, also called late binding, which hides the differences between related classes in an inheritance hierarchy so they can be used interchangeably.

Recall that method overriding allows a child class to provide its own implementation of a method that is already inherited by one of its ancestors. Connecting a method call to the method's body is called binding. Because the connection is made while the program is running, polymorphism has dynamic binding.

Polymorphism in this instance means that a variable's method call executes a different method, depending on the type of the variable that called the method. In dynamic binding, the exact class that an object belongs to is decided when the code is running. The benefit is that the computer can decide the appropriate method implementation to execute as late as possible without being bound to a specific object type, thus enhancing code flexibility.

17.2 POLYMORPHISM BASICS

Classes Within Classes (17.2.1, 17.2.2)

Classes can have different kinds of relationships with each other to solve a problem. Inheritance makes the is-a relationship possible. The is-a relationship occurs between a parent and a child class where one class is a subclass of another class. In the **Dealership**, there is an "is-a" relationship between the **MotorVehicle** class (parent) and the **Motorcycle**, **Car**, **GasCar**, **HybridCar**, **ElectricCar**, **Truck**, and **Van** (children) classes. In an is-a relationship, you can treat a child class as though it is an instance of the parent class.

The second kind of relationship is called a has-a relationship, where a class is a member variable in another class. Composition makes the has-a relationship possible. Just because a class contains another class, it does not inherit the capabilities of the class it contains. For example, the **Dealership** class contains an array of **Motor-Vehicles**. This is a has-a relationship because a **Dealership** has **MotorVehicles**. The **Dealership** is not a **MotorVehicle**, nor does it inherit the capabilities of the **MotorVehicle** class. An example of the difference between the is-a and has-a relationship is shown in **Figure 17-5**.

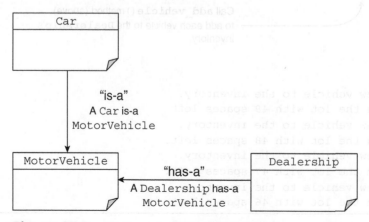

Figure 17-5 The has-a and is-a relationships

Objects as Other Objects (17.2.3)

Sometimes you need an object to act like an object of another type. For example, you can pass an object of type **Truck** to any method that takes a **MotorVehicle** object as a parameter. Inheritance also allows you to convert one object into another object, which is called type casting. Two kinds of type casting are implicit conversion and explicit conversion. Following is an example of implicit conversion. Assume that **Truck** and **MotorVehicle** have already been defined where **Truck** inherits from **MotorVehicle**. Implicit conversion allows the following code:

```
declare mv as MotorVehicle

declare t as Truck

t = mv
```

This pseudocode declares a **MotorVehicle** object and a **Truck** object. Implicit conversion occurs when an object of one type is set equal to an object of another type, which is what happens when the **Truck** object is set equal to the **MotorVehicle** object in the **t = mv** statement. Any code that uses **mv** will now treat it as an object of type **Truck**, and any code that explicitly uses a **Truck** object can use **mv** as input.

Implicit conversion requires you to either implement a copy constructor for the child class or overload the **operator=** method for the child class. In this pseudocode, the **operator=** method has been overloaded.

In strongly typed programming languages, such as C++, Java, and Python, every variable must be declared with a data type. Variables are bound to their data types. If the variable does not match the expected type in an expression or parameter list, an error will occur. For example, if a piece of code expects to use a **Truck** object, but is passed a **MotorVehicle** object, an error will occur because a **Truck** is a **MotorVehicle**, but a **MotorVehicle** is not a **Truck**. Because these languages are strongly typed, converting from one type to another requires an explicit conversion, as in the following code.

```
declare mv as MotorVehicle

declare t as Truck

mv = (MotorVehicle) t
```

This example again declares a **MotorVehicle** object and a **Truck** object. The **Truck** variable is explicitly cast as an object of the base class's type—**Truck** is a type of **MotorVehicle** object. The casting is explicit because the statement **mv = (MotorVehicle) t** specifically names the class (**MotorVehicle**) to which the variable **t** is cast. This type of casting is called upcasting because you are casting to an object that is higher in the class hierarchy, such as **Truck** being upcast to **MotorVehicle**.

You can also reverse the casting and replace the third line to read as follows:

```
t = (Truck) mv
```

This is an example of downcasting because you are converting an object to another object lower in the class hierarchy—a **MotorVehicle** is downcast to a **Truck**.

Q What is a possible concern with using downcasting?

A Suppose the **MotorVehicle** class does not have all the same member variables as **Truck**. For example, **Truck** might have two additional member variables to specify the length and width of the flatbed. In this case, downcasting produces an error, which is why it is considered dangerous.

17.3 VIRTUAL FUNCTIONS

Anticipating Customization (17.3.1, 17.3.2, 17.3.3)

If you review the code for the dealership, you might realize that there is no such thing as a generic **Car**. A **Car** should not implement some methods because its behavior varies depending on what type of **Car** is being used. For example, suppose the **Car** class implements a method called **calculate_fuel_cost()** that returns an estimated dollar amount for the car to travel a given number of miles.

This price calculation depends on whether the **Car** is a **GasCar**, **HybridCar**, or **ElectricCar**. A **GasCar** calculates the price based on the car's average MPG, the **HybridCar** calculates the price using the car's MPG and estimated battery usage, and the **ElectricCar** bases the price on the cost of the electricity to travel the distance. See **Figure 17-6**.

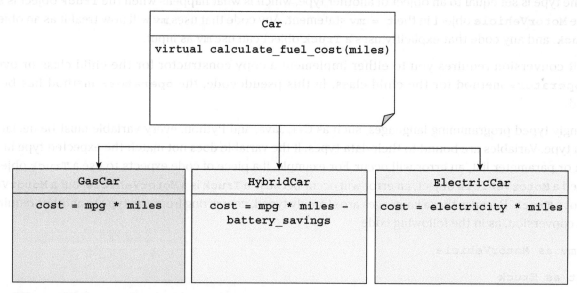

Figure 17-6   Differing method implementations

Because a **Car** is not a specific type of vehicle, it makes sense to require each kind of **Car** to indicate how it will implement the **calculate_fuel_cost()** method. You can use a pure virtual method to specify that the derived class will define the method inherited from the child class.

Pure virtual methods are not defined in the base class because any class derived from it should define its own version of the method. For example, **Car** does not define the behavior of **calculate_fuel_cost()**. Instead, any object derived from **Car** (**GasCar**, **HybridCar**, or **ElectricCar**) will create its own implementation of the method.

You use the keyword **virtual** in the method definition to indicate that a derived class will create its implementation of this method. The pseudocode for the method declaration in the base class definition resembles the following:

```
public virtual void Car: calculate_fuel_cost ()= 0
```

You define and implement a pure virtual method the same way you do for any method. A pure virtual method does not have an implementation, so it cannot be explicitly called in the base class. Instead, a pure virtual method must be defined within any class that inherits from it. Use the syntax = 0 at the end of the method declaration to indicate that the method is not defined in the base class. If a child class does not implement the method, the code will not compile. Code for defining and using a pure virtual method is shown in **Figure 17-7**.

The **Car** class inherits from the **MotorVehicle** class

The **= 0** syntax means the method is not defined here in the **Car** class, which is the base class for the **GasCar**, **HybridCar**, and **ElectricCar** classes

```
class Car : public MotorVehicle
{
   public:
      virtual double calculate_fuel_cost(int miles) = 0;
      string fuel_type;
};
```

```
class GasCar : public Car
{
   public:
      double calculate_fuel_cost(int miles);
      int fuel_level;
};
```

```
class HybridCar : public Car
{
   public:
      double calculate_fuel_cost(int miles);
      int fuel_level;
      int battery_percentage;
};
```

Each child of **Car** creates its own implementation of the **calculate_fuel_cost()** method

```
class ElectricCar : public Car
{
   public:
      double calculate_fuel_cost(int miles);
      int battery_percentage;
};
```

Figure 17-7   Pure virtual methods

Abstract Classes (17.3.4, 17.3.5)

When you create a pure virtual method, you are also creating an abstract class, which is any class that has one or more pure virtual methods. If a class has pure virtual methods, it cannot be instantiated, so you cannot create a variable of type **Car**. A car represented in the dealership must be a **GasCar**, **HybridCar**, or **ElectricCar**. An abstract class is generally used to represent a generic concept in a class hierarchy, such as a **Car**, rather than a specific object, such as a **HybridCar**.

As a rule of thumb, you should use an abstract class if you have closely related classes that need to implement multiple versions of the same method, as with the types of cars. Abstract classes are a good programming choice if you want to use inheritance but do not want to create an object with the same type as the base class. An abstract class often represents such an abstract idea that its instantiation does not make sense in the context of the program. For example, **Car** is an abstract idea that must be defined as a **GasCar**, **HybridCar**, or **ElectricCar** to have meaning within the program. A generic **Car** is not meaningful in this context.

Q Would the `MotorVehicle` class be a good candidate for an abstract class?

A On the surface, `MotorVehicle` is a generic concept from which you don't anticipate declaring objects. However, the `Dealership` has an array of `MotorVehicles`, which counts as an instantiation of the `MotorVehicle` class. Making `MotorVehicle` an abstract class would break this part of the code. In addition, you pass a `MotorVehicle` object to many methods, and the `MotorVehicle` object as a parameter would throw an error.

SUMMARY

- Polymorphism is a concept in object-oriented programming in which an object can have many types. Inheritance is the main driver of polymorphism, because a class derived from another class can be treated as the base class.

- Polymorphism means that an object of a parent class can be used to refer to any of its descendants. Inheritance and polymorphism help to avoid duplicate code within related objects.

- The compiler uses dynamic binding to determine which object's method to call as the program is running. A compiler cannot check for dynamic binding errors.

- The is-a relationship enables objects of a child class to be treated as an object of the parent or ancestor class. Inheritance fuels this relationship in OOP.

- The has-a relationship describes when a class has an object of another class as a member variable. In this type of relationship, the class does not inherit the capabilities of the class it contains.

- OOP languages allow the conversion of one object into another object, which is called type casting. Upcasting is type casting an object to a type that is above it in the inheritance hierarchy. Downcasting is type casting an object to a type that is below it in the inheritance hierarchy. Downcasting should be performed with caution, as it can lead to errors if the classes do not have similar member variables.

- In some programming scenarios, it makes sense to require the children of a base class to provide their own implementation of a method, especially if the functionality significantly varies between classes. This is called a pure virtual method.

- Any class with one or more pure virtual methods is called an abstract class. An abstract class cannot be instantiated and is generally used to represent a generic concept in a class hierarchy, rather than a specific object.

Key Terms

abstract class	explicit conversion	polymorphism
binding	has-a relationship	pure virtual method
downcasting	implicit conversion	type casting
dynamic binding	is-a relationship	upcasting

MODULE
18

TEMPLATES

LEARNING OBJECTIVES:

18.1 TEMPLATE BASICS

18.1.1 Define function templates.

18.1.2 Define class templates.

18.1.3 Explain how data and functions can be extended by using templates in OOP.

18.1.4 Explain the syntax for writing function templates.

18.1.5 Identify proper usage of the T parameter when using templates.

18.1.6 Explain the syntax for using templated functions or objects.

18.1.7 Explain how to use templates with classes in OOP.

18.1.8 Compare OOP template types.

18.2 TRICKY TEMPLATING

18.2.1 Explain how to mix template parameters.

18.2.2 Explain how to use multiple type parameters in a template.

18.2.3 Explain how to pass template classes to functions.

18.3 TEMPLATES AS A PROBLEM-SOLVING APPROACH

18.3.1 Explain how to create a template based on a given specification.

18.3.2 Discuss the advantages and disadvantages of using function templates.

18.1 TEMPLATE BASICS

Data Abstraction (18.1.1, 18.1.2, 18.1.3, 18.1.4)

You are probably familiar with the three types of grinding tools shown in **Figure 18-1**: a fruit or vegetable blender, a spice grinder, and a woodchipper. Incorporating three different objects like these in a program usually requires handling them separately. In this module, you learn how to save time by treating things generically rather than specifically.

Consider a minimum function named **my_min()**. When given two numbers, **my_min()** returns the minimum of the pair. What kinds of numbers should **my_min()** work on? Ideally, it would accept any numeric data type, including integers, doubles, and floats. However, you would need a copy of **my_min()** for each numeric type to perform the full range of calculations. Remember that you have to specify the kind of data you are using in code, including parameters. The requirement to specify the data type causes a problem when you want to reuse code, as shown in **Figure 18-2**.

Fruit and vegetable blender *Nerthuz/Shutterstock.com*   Spice grinder *Vectorpocket/Shutterstock.com*   Woodchipper *Yuliya Shatylo/Shutterstock.com*

Figure 18-1   Grinding tools for fruit, spices, and wood

Q What is the code in Figure 18-2 doing? Are the data types treated differently?

A The **my_min()** function is defined for the data types **int**, **double**, and **float**. The same conditional code follows the function signature for each data type. If the first number is smaller than the second, **my_min()** returns the first number. Otherwise, **my_min()** returns the second number. The code at the end tests each function with sample data, performs computations, and displays the output.

Figure 18-2 contains repetitious code you shouldn't have to write. Instead, you can use a **template** to substitute the three data types for a single placeholder. Templates, also known as generics in some languages, are a way to tell the compiler that although a data type does belong in a particular place, the data type isn't decided yet. Until the type is decided, use a generic stand-in identifier instead.

A function template is a function that uses a generic data type in its parameter list, its return type, or both. **Figure 18-3** shows a function template for tripling the value of passed in data.

After establishing a template with a generic data type **T**, the code defines the **triple** function using **T** as the data type instead of **int** or **double**. Inside the function, the code multiplies the **input** parameter by 3 and stores the result in the variable **result**, which is also of type **T**. The result is then returned.

A class template is a class that uses a generic type for one of its properties. Objects created from a class template are also known as templated objects. **Figure 18-4** shows a class template that can store any type of data as a member variable for a new class named **Storage**.

A more complicated example involves programming simulated grinders as in Figure 18-1. The grinders should work with things such as fruits (creating juice), spices (creating spice powder), or even wood (creating sawdust). The next section shows how to create a class template to simplify the code.

Because a template allows you to specify a parameter or property as a generic data type, you can reuse code by adapting it to more than one data type instead of repeating the code as in Figure 18-2.

```
#include <iostream>
using namespace std;

int my_min(int x, int y)
{
    if (x < y)
        return x;
    return y;
}

double my_min(double x, double y)
{
    if (x < y)
        return x;
    return y;
}

float my_min(float x, float y)
{
    if (x < y)
        return x;
    return y;
}

int main()
{
    int ix = 5;
    int iy = 12;
    double dx = 5.0;
    double dy = 12.0;
    float fx = 5.0f;
    float fy = 12.0f;

    cout << "int min: " << my_min(ix, iy) << endl;
    cout << "double min: " << my_min(dx, dy) << endl;
    cout << "float min: " << my_min(fx, fy) << endl;

    return 0;
}
OUTPUT:
int min: 5
double min: 5
float min: 5
```

For the three types of numbers, you need three identical functions with different signatures.

Function overloading detects the data type and then selects the appropriate function.

Figure 18-2   Creating a function for multiple data types

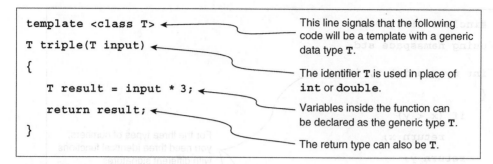

```
template <class T>                  This line signals that the following
                                    code will be a template with a generic
T triple(T input)                   data type T.
{
                                    The identifier T is used in place of
    T result = input * 3;           int or double.
    return result;                  Variables inside the function can
                                    be declared as the generic type T.
}
                                    The return type can also be T.
```

Figure 18-3   Function template syntax

```
template <class T>
                                    This line signals that the following code will
class Storage                       be a template with a generic type T.
{
    public:
        T stored_value;
}
                                    The identifier T is used in place of int or
                                    double to define the stored_value property
                                    of the Storage class.
```

Figure 18-4   Class template syntax

Template Structure and Use (18.1.5, 18.1.6, 18.1.7, 18.1.8)

The code in **Figure 18-5** shows how to set up a generic type **T**. This data type can use any identifier, but traditional naming conventions recommend using **T** for templates. The code that follows can use the generic identifier where you would use a variable type, such as **int** or **string**.

```
                                                Use the keyword template
                                                with <class T> to signal a
                                                template.
template <class T>
// ... code for one variable, function, or class ... //
template <class T>
// ... code for another variable, function, or class ... //



                    Each template applies to one variable, function, or class.
                    Other templated classes need to repeat the template
                    keyword.
```

Figure 18-5   Starting a template

Figure 18-6 shows a templated version of **my_min()** from Figure 18-2. The code starts by defining a template type **T**. The **my_min()** function signature then uses the identifier **T** instead of **int**, **float**, or **double** as the data

```
#include <iostream>
using namespace std;

template <class T>
T my_min(T x, T y)
{
    if (x < y)
        return x;
    return y;
}

int main()
{
    int ix = 5;
    int iy = 12;
    double dx = 5.0;
    double dy = 12.0;
    float fx = 5.0f;
    float fy = 12.0f;

    cout << "int min: " << my_min<int>(ix, iy) << endl;
    cout << "double min: " << my_min<double>(dx, dy) << endl;
    cout << "float min: " << my_min<float>(fx, fy) << endl;

    return 0;
}
OUTPUT:
int min: 5
double min: 5
float min: 5
```

Instead of assigning three data types, use the single generic data type **T**.

Only one function definition is necessary with templates.

When using the function, such as in a computation, you must supply the specific data type.

Figure 18-6　Creating a templated function

type. The remainder of the function is identical to the code shown in Figure 18-2, including an if-statement, test data, computations, and output. The test code at the bottom uses the templated function `my_min()` to find the minimum of two values. At this point, you assign specific data types to the `my_min()` function. When you use a templated function, class, or other templated piece of code, you must provide the data type.

When you create a template, you delay assigning data types until you use them, as in a computation. By using a template for `my_min()`, you reduce the amount of identical code (such as the if-statements in Figure 18-2).

Figure 18-7 contains simplified `Fruit`, `Spice`, and `Wood` classes. These are nonstandard defined classes, but you can still use them in templating. The generic type does not have to be a primitive type, such as `int`, but can be any type within the code's scope. (The code shown in other figures requires the code from Figure 18-7 to work.)

```
class Fruit
{
    public:
        string name;

        Fruit(string name="apple")
        {
            this->name = name;
        }

        void grind()
        {
            cout << this->name << " juice was made!" << endl;
        }

        void chunk()
        {
            cout << "lumpy " << this->name << " juice was made!" << endl;
        }
};


class Spice
{
    public:
        string name;

        Spice(string name="coriander")
        {
            this->name = name;
        }

        void grind()
        {
            cout << this->name << "powder was made!" << endl;
        }
}
```

Figure 18-7   Basic classes for the grinder example (*Continued*)

```
        void chunk()

        {

            cout << "coarse ground " << this->name << " was made!" << endl;

        }

};


class Wood

{

    public:

        string name;


        Wood(string name="oak")

        {

            this->name = name;

        }


        void grind()

        {

            cout << this->name << " sawdust was made!" << endl;

        }


        void chunk()

        {

            cout << this->name << " chips were made!" << endl;

        }

};
```

Figure 18-7   Basic classes for the grinder example (*Continued*)

This code defines three classes and a **name** property for each class. Each class also has the methods **grind()** and **chunk()**.

Figure 18-8 shows a **grind()** method that is templated to work for the **Fruit**, **Spice**, or **Wood** substance. The parameter list allows a substance to be passed in and then invokes **grind()** on the substance, but the type of the substance is not identified until the method is invoked.

This code runs only when it follows the code defining the classes shown in Figure 18-7. The classes are omitted here for brevity.

```cpp
// Code for Fruit, Spice, and Wood classes

template <class T>
void grind (T substance)
{
    substance.grind();
}

int main()
{
    // Create some substances to test
    Fruit apple = Fruit("apple");
    Fruit orange = Fruit("orange");
    Spice coriander = Spice("coriander");
    Wood oak = Wood("oak");

    // Test the templated function
    grind<Fruit>(apple);
    grind<Fruit>(orange);
    grind<Spice>(coriander);
    grind<Wood>(oak);

    return 0;
}
```

The **substance** parameter is assigned to the generic **T** data type.

The **substance** parameter is called in the **grind()** method.

The type of substance in angled brackets (**<>**) is passed to the **grind()** method.

OUTPUT:
```
apple juice was made!
orange juice was made!
ground coriander was made!
oak sawdust was made!
```

Figure 18-8   Grinder that can use any substance

Creating a templated class follows a similar syntax: define a generic type **T** and use it in place of a variable type. **Figure 18-9** shows a templated **Grinder** class for processing **Spice**, **Fruit**, or **Wood**. The **Grinder** class stores some substance in the variable **substance**, which is of type **T**, though again the type of substance is not identified. The member variable **level** indicates whether to invoke **grind()** or **chunk()** when the **Grinder** is told to process the substance using the **process()** method.

This code runs only when it follows the code defining the classes shown in Figure 18-7. The classes are omitted here for brevity.

```
// Code for Fruit, Spice, and Wood classes
// A templated grinder class
template <class T>
class Grinder
{
    public:
        T substance;
        int level;

        Grinder(T substance)
        {
            this->substance = substance;
            this->level = 0;
        }

        void setLevel(int level)
        {
            this->level = level;
        }

        void fill(T substance)
        {
            this->substance = substance;
        }

        void process()
        {
            if (this->level == 0)
            {
                this->substance.grind();
            }
            else if (this->level == 1)
            {
                this->substance.chunk();
            }
        }
};
```

Signals that the next class has a generic type **T**.

substance is of type **T**, so the constructor also has a parameter of type **T**.

substance is of type **T**, so any method to change the **substance** has a parameter of type **T**.

Figure 18-9   Grinder class that stores a substance (*Continued*)

```
int main()
{
    // Create some substances to test
    Fruit apple = Fruit("apple");
    Spice coriander = Spice("coriander");
    Wood oak = Wood("oak");

    // Create some templated grinders
    Grinder<Fruit> juicer = Grinder<Fruit>(apple);
    Grinder<Spice> spiceGrinder = Grinder<Spice>(coriander);
    Grinder<Wood> woodChipper = Grinder<Wood>(oak);

    // Test the templated classes
    juicer.setLevel(1);
    juicer.process();
    spiceGrinder.process();
    woodChipper.process();
    return 0;
}
```

The type of grinder is passed inside of angled brackets (`<>`) to the **Grinder** constructor call.

OUTPUT:

lumpy apple juice was made!

ground coriander was made!

oak sawdust was made!

Figure 18-9   Grinder class that stores a substance (*Continued*)

18.2 TRICKY TEMPLATING

Advanced Templating (18.2.1, 18.2.2)

You can use templates to assign a generic data type to more than one parameter or property in a single function or object. The syntax for using multiple types in a single template is shown in **Figure 18-10**.

```
template <class TFirst, class TSecond >
// ... code can use TFirst and TSecond as generic types ... //
```

Figure 18-10   Creating multiple generic types

If a function or object has more than one parameter or property of the same data type, they can share the same generic type. For example, three **int** parameters can each be assigned to the **T** type. However, if a function or object has more than one parameter or property of different data types, you need to use more than the single letter **T** for the template name. The best practice is to begin each type identifier with **T** followed by one or more words, as in **TFirst**. For example, a class with properties assigned to **int** and **string** data types could use **TFirst** for the **int** properties and **TSecond** for the **string** properties.

Using a template with multiple generic types requires you to provide a specific data type for each parameter or property. For example, if you created a **dual_grinder()** method that takes two different substances, you would have two parameters **substance_one** and **substance_two**. These two substances might not be the same type (**substance_one** is **Spice** and **substance_two** is **Wood**), so you would use the generic type identifiers **TSubstanceOne** and **TSubstanceTwo**. Two examples of a function template that takes two generic parameters and uses them is shown in **Figure 18-11**, one symbolic and the other the code for **dual_grinder()**.

This code runs only when it follows the code defining the **Spice** and **Wood** classes shown in Figure 18-7. The classes are omitted here for brevity.

```cpp
#include <iostream>
using namespace std;
// Code for Spice and Wood classes
template <class TFirst, class TSecond>          // Two types are made generic
                                                // with this template statement.
void two_templates(TFirst first, TSecond second)
{
    cout << "First param is " << first << endl;
    cout << "Second param is " << second << endl;
}

template <class TSubstanceOne, class TSubstanceTwo>
void dual_grinder(TSubstanceOne substance_one, TSubstanceTwo substance_two)
{
    substance_one.grind();
    substance_two.grind();
}

int main()
{
    // Some substances to grind with dual_grinder()
    Spice coriander = Spice("coriander");
    Wood oak = Wood("oak");
    two_templates<int, double>(5, 10.0);        // Two specific types are
                                                // needed when invoked.
    two_templates<string, float>("a string", 3.0f);
    dual_grinder<Spice, Wood>(coriander, oak);

    return 0;
}
```

OUTPUT:

```
First param is 5
Second param is 10
First param is a string
Second param is 3
coriander powder was made!
oak sawdust was made!
```

Figure 18-11   Multiple-typed function template

Templated Objects as Arguments (18.2.3)

Passing an object to a function or method requires the function or method to know the type, but templated objects might be of any type. To write a function that is not templated itself but can accept a templated parameter, you can take one of two approaches. One approach is to limit the templated generic type in the parameter list to a specific type. **Figure 18-12** shows how to force a function to accept only `Grinder` objects that have `Fruit` type substances.

```
This code runs only when it follows the code defining the classes shown in Figure 18-7.
The classes are omitted here for brevity.

// Code for Fruit, Spice, and Wood classes


void fruit_grinders(Grinder<Fruit> a)
{

    cout << "Only fruit grinders can be passed to this function." << endl;

}
```

Figure 18-12   Restricting a function to fruit-type grinders

The other way to handle templated parameters is to make the function templated as well. **Figure 18-13** shows how this is achieved by using the templating syntax for a function template.

```
This code runs only when it follows the code defining the classes shown in
Figure 18-7. The classes are omitted here for brevity.

// Code for Fruit, Spice, and Wood classes


template <class T>
void any_grinder(Grinder<T> a)
{

    cout << "Any grinder can be passed to this function." << endl;

}
```

Figure 18-13   A function which allows any `Grinder` as a parameter

When you would want to use one approach over the other depends on what your function is trying to achieve. Is it performing a task specific to fruit-only grinders, or does it work for any grinder? Also consider the intent of your code. Are you enhancing the template or using the template to solve a problem? Suppose you work for a smoothie stand business and they want to add a `add_protein_powder` function to work with the grinder templates. This function would use the grinder to solve a problem, though adding the function to the template wouldn't make the template better for others to use. Adding protein powder to wood doesn't improve wood chips. On the other hand, a **clean_blades** function would improve the template for all possible grinders. All grinders, regardless of the substance they use, can benefit from being cleaned.

18.3 TEMPLATES AS A PROBLEM-SOLVING APPROACH

Designing a Template (18.3.1)

Templates only work for data types that share an interface. Recall that an interface is the way you can interact with an object or data. For example, all numbers share an interface with mathematical operators such as + or *. If you create a template with objects in mind, then all objects used in the template should implement the same interface. For example, Figure 18-7 showed simplified class definitions for substances to use in a templated grinder.

Q Do the **Fruit**, **Spice**, and **Wood** classes have the same interface?

A Yes, they all have the same method signatures, so the way you interact with any of them is the same. However, while the classes implement the same methods, the way the methods work and their results are different. Implementing the same interface does not mean they behave the same.

When to Use Templates (18.3.2)

Normally, behavior you can achieve with templates can also be achieved with polymorphism. Remember that polymorphism is the use of object-oriented inheritance to create interchangeable objects with the same interface. **Fruit**, **Spice**, and **Wood** classes can all call the **grind()** or **chunk()** methods. The advantage of using templates is that the type determination occurs at compile time instead of runtime. That is, templates let the compiler figure out what data type to use when the code is compiled into machine code. Polymorphism figures out the data types during runtime, and therefore can be slightly slower than templating. The general guideline to follow is that if the code you are considering for templates or polymorphism is small or needs to run quickly, then you should use templates.

SUMMARY

- Because languages assign specific data types to information a program processes, you would need to duplicate code to perform the same task or achieve the same result on different data types. Templates allow you to assign a placeholder generic data type to objects, so you can reuse code with any data type.

- Templates require the intended replacement data types to have the same interface. Each data type that replaces the generic data type must have the same interactions so they are interchangeable. The data types do not have to behave the same way, but they do have to interact the same way.
- There are two solutions to pass a templated object as a parameter. You can force a specific data type instead of a generic type in the function definition, or you can template the function. When to use either depends on whether you have only specific data types or want to take a more generic approach.
- Templates and polymorphism have similar results. Templates are generally faster than polymorphism but harder to read and maintain. You should use templates when the code is small or needs to run quickly.

Key Terms

class template

function template

generic type

generics

template

MODULE
19

LINKED LIST DATA STRUCTURES

LEARNING OBJECTIVES:

19.1 LINKED LIST STRUCTURES

19.1.1 Explain the purpose of data structures, such as linked lists.

19.1.2 List commonly used data structures.

19.1.3 Classify data structures as linear or nonlinear.

19.1.4 List the operations associated with data structures.

19.1.5 Classify data structures as built-in, imported, or programmer defined.

19.1.6 Identify the components of a linked list.

19.1.7 Illustrate the physical layout of a linked list in memory.

19.2 TYPES OF LINKED LISTS

19.2.1 Draw a conceptual diagram of a singly linked list.

19.2.2 Characterize and identify use cases for a singly linked list.

19.2.3 Draw a conceptual diagram of a doubly linked list.

19.2.4 Characterize and identify use cases for a doubly linked list.

19.2.5 Draw a conceptual diagram of a circular linked list.

19.2.6 Characterize and identify use cases for a circular linked list.

19.2.7 Compare and contrast the characteristics of linked lists with arrays.

19.3 CODE A LINKED LIST

19.3.1 Express the high-level algorithm for creating a linked list based on a Node class and a LinkedList class.

19.3.2 State the purpose of the Node class.

19.3.3 Identify pointer declarations.

19.3.4 Identify elements of the LinkedList class.

19.3.5 Express the algorithm for appending a node to a linked list.

19.3.6 Express the algorithm for traversing a linked list.

19.3.7 Explain the use of a temporary pointer for traversing a linked list.

19.3.8 Identify code that finds a specific element in a linked list.

19.3.9 Diagram the way pointers shuffle when inserting an element in a linked list.

19.1 LINKED LIST STRUCTURES

Data Structure Selection (19.1.1, 19.1.2, 19.1.3, 19.1.4)

A musical composition is a series of notes. In the classical music of India, the notes of a basic scale are Sa Re Ga Ma Pa Dha and Ni, as shown in **Figure 19-1**. These notes can be arranged in many ways to form songs.

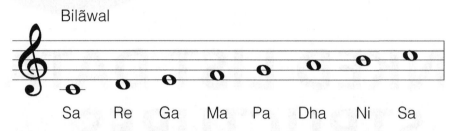

Figure 19-1   A basic scale for classical music of India

When composing a song, songwriters add, change, and delete notes. If you are coding a songwriting app, how would you organize the song data in memory so that it is easy to access and modify during runtime?

Computer scientists have devised many methods for organizing data in memory. These methods are referred to as data structures. More specifically, a **data structure** is a specific layout of data values in memory and a set of operations that can be applied to those values.

Figure 19-2 illustrates six data structures commonly used by programmers.

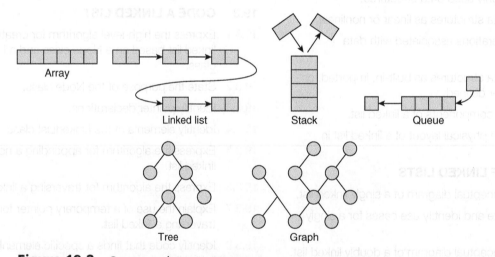

Figure 19-2   Common data structures

Arrays, linked lists, stacks, and queues are examples of linear data structures. A **linear data structure** arranges data elements in a sequential chain. A **nonlinear data structure** arranges data as hierarchies or webs in which there can be multiple links between data elements.

Q Which data structures in Figure 19-2 are nonlinear?

A Trees and graphs are nonlinear data structures because they connect a hierarchy or network of data elements rather than a linear sequence of elements.

The data structure you select for a set of data depends on how that data will be used. For example, for a music composition app, users create compositions that contain a varying number of notes. Notes need to be added, deleted, and changed. The final composition, though, is played sequentially.

You could use an array to work with the notes of a musical composition. Is that the best data structure you could select? An array holds data in consecutive memory locations. Each element has a corresponding index, such as [0], [1], or [2]. See **Figure 19-3**.

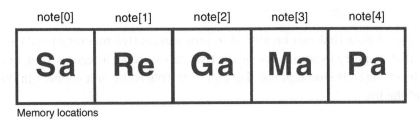

note[0]   note[1]   note[2]   note[3]   note[4]

| Sa | Re | Ga | Ma | Pa |

Memory locations

Figure 19-3   An array holds data in consecutive memory locations

The data in an array is easy to access using a statement such as **first_note = note[0]**. You can also change a note easily with a statement such as **note[4] = "Pa"**. Efficiently traversing an array can be accomplished using a loop.

When selecting a data structure, you should consider the efficiency of the following operations:

Accessing an individual element.
Appending a new element to the end of the structure.
Inserting an element within the structure.
Deleting an element.
Modifying an element.
Traversing the structure to display or manipulate each element.
Sorting the elements.

Q Arrays are a fixed size. What effect does that have on the efficiency of operations that manipulate array data?

A Because an array is a fixed size, it is not very efficient to append elements that would increase the size of an array, to insert elements within the array, or to delete elements.

Considering the limitations, an array might not be the best data structure for a musical composition app. Let's look at an alternative data structure called a linked list to see if it would be better suited for the data in your musical composition app.

Data Structure Implementation (19.1.5)

Your programming language could offer several ways to implement a linked list and other data structures. It might provide a built-in structure along with functions or methods to manipulate the structure's data. Data structures might also be available as modules that you can import or include from a library.

You can create programmer-defined data structures by coding relationships among primitive data types, such as integers, characters, and Booleans. You may also be able to take advantage of built-in functions for manipulating these primitives.

There can be several algorithms for coding a data structure. For example, you might code a linked list using a function or a class. Coding a linked list as a class is a common implementation, but first let's explore some basic information on how linked lists work.

Linked List Basics (19.1.6, 19.1.7)

A linked list is a collection of data that can be stored in nonconsecutive memory locations. In a simplified memory layout, assume that memory locations are boxes that can store an integer, string, or any other chunk of data. In **Figure 19-4**, the string Sa is stored in Box 6 of memory. This is the first element in the list, sometimes referred to as the head of the list.

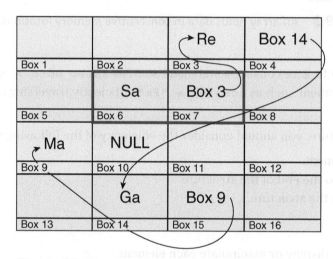

Figure 19-4   Linked list memory layout

Q Where is the second item of the list?

A The second element in the list, Re, is not stored in Box 7 or Box 8, which are the next consecutive memory locations. In a linked list, Re can be stored just about anywhere in memory. In this example, it is stored in Box 3.

To connect the elements in a linked list, each data element is associated with a link to the next address. These links connect the data elements into a linear structure in which each element links to one previous element and one subsequent element.

The link between two data elements is generally referred to as a pointer, though some programming languages refer to it as a reference. Technically, a pointer is a variable that holds the memory address of another variable. A reference accomplishes a similar goal by referring to the memory location of a variable or other object.

A pointer is stored in a memory location.

Q Look back at Figure 19-4. What is in Box 7?

A Box 7 contains "Box 3," which is a pointer that points to Re in Box 3.

Sa and the pointer to Re are two parts of a **node**. The first node in the linked list carries a pointer to Box 3, which is the location of Re, the second element in the list. The last element in a linked list typically points to NULL, null, or None, depending on your programming language.

19.2 TYPES OF LINKED LISTS

Singly Linked Lists (19.2.1, 19.2.2)

Conceptually, a linked list is often diagrammed as a sequence of nodes connected with arrows. A pointer called **head** references the first node in the linked list.

Each node has two parts. One part is for the data, and one part is for the pointer to the next data element. When each element in a linked list has a single pointer linking to the next element, the structure is called a **singly linked list**. **Figure 19-5** illustrates a conceptual diagram of a singly linked list.

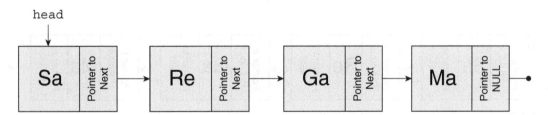

Figure 19-5   Conceptualization of a linked list

A singly linked list is useful for algorithms in which data links proceed in one direction. It is an efficient data structure for the notes in a song because the notes are always played from beginning to end.

Q What other activities can be represented by a singly linked list?

A Here are a few:
- Storing the frames for a video file that is played from beginning to end.
- Processing the people in a telephone queue as the person at the head of the list leaves and newcomers are added to the end.
- A navigation system that stores a list of directions that are followed in sequence from beginning to end.
- Storing a game character's path through a dungeon.

Doubly Linked Lists (19.2.3, 19.2.4)

But what if you're coding an app for a playlist of songs? Users might want to scroll forward or backward through the list of songs using controls such as those shown in **Figure 19-6**.

Figure 19-6 Playlist controls for cueing up the next or previous song

A **doubly linked list** has two pointers for each element. One pointer links to the next element, and the other pointer links to the previous element, as shown in **Figure 19-7**.

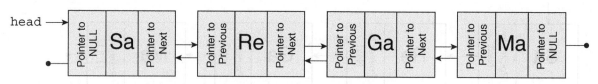

Figure 19-7 Conceptualization of a doubly linked list

A doubly linked list shines for algorithms that require traversing a list from beginning to end or from the end to the beginning.

Q In addition to a playlist app, can you think of other use cases for doubly linked lists?

A You might have thought of the following use cases:
- Using the Back and Next buttons in a browser to traverse a list of webpages.
- Using the up and down buttons in a file manager to traverse levels of folders.
- Storing the coordinates of a GPS tracker so that you can retrace your steps and find your way home.
- Tracking key presses for the Undo and Redo operations in a text editor.

Circular Linked Lists (19.2.5, 19.2.6)

For some algorithms, the list of data has no clear beginning or end. In a circular linked list, the last node points back to the first node as shown in **Figure 19-8**.

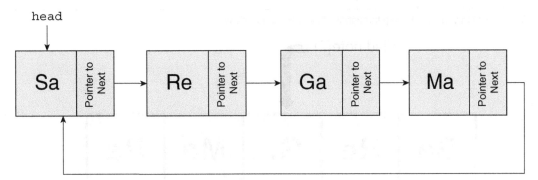

Figure 19-8   Conceptualization of a circular linked list

A circular list can be singly or doubly linked. You can use a circular linked list for algorithms in which data is cycled through repeatedly. You could use a circular linked list to store a list of players in a multiplayer game and use that list to rotate through each player's turns. Systems programmers might use a circular linked list to store a series of processes that the computer executes partially on a first pass, then continues to execute on subsequent passes.

Linked List Characteristics (19.2.7)

Singly, doubly, and circular linked lists have the following characteristics:

- *Extensible*. Elements can be easily appended to the end of the list.
- *Modifiable*. Elements can be efficiently inserted and deleted because to move a node, only the pointers to the data have to change.
- *Require extra memory space*. Memory space is required for the links as well as the data.
- *Sequential searching*. Traversing a linked list begins at the head and requires stepping through each element.

When planning the data structures for a program, a linked list might be a better choice than an array. Understanding the differences can help you choose the most efficient structure for your programs. Let's compare linked lists to arrays.

Access. Linked lists support sequential access, whereas arrays support random access. To access an element in a linked list, it is necessary to always begin at the head of the list and follow the links one by one until you reach the target element. In contrast, an array element can be reached simply by specifying its index number. See **Figure 19-9**.

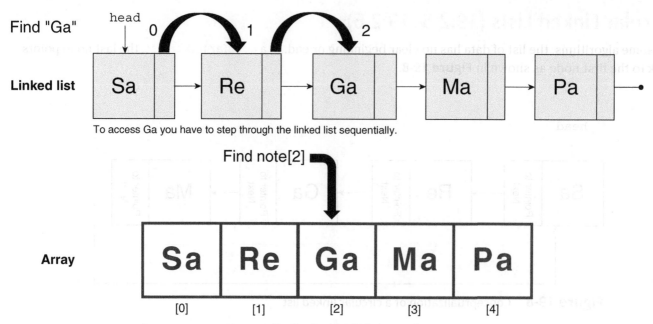

Find "Ga"

To access Ga you have to step through the linked list sequentially.

Find note[2]

In an array, you can access Ga directly using its index number.

Figure 19-9 Accessing elements in a linked list and an array

Extensibility. Linked lists are extensible simply by changing NULL at the end of the list to a pointer to the new element. In contrast, the size of an array is fixed when it is declared. If an array is full, adding an element requires you to copy the contents of the original array into a second, larger array before adding a new element. See **Figure 19-10**.

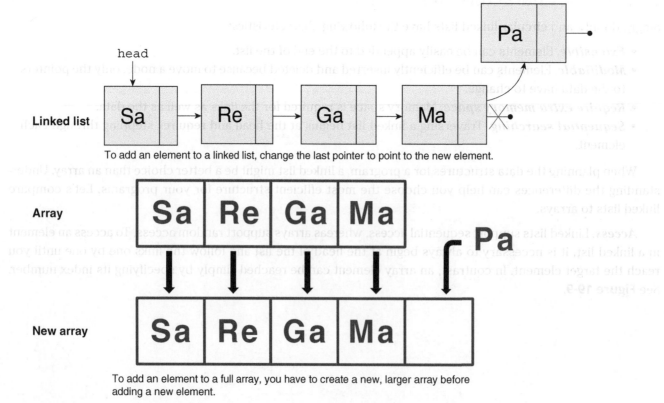

To add an element to a linked list, change the last pointer to point to the new element.

To add an element to a full array, you have to create a new, larger array before adding a new element.

Figure 19-10 Appending elements to a linked list and an array

Insertion. A new element can be inserted anywhere in a linked list by changing two pointers. Items in the original list remain in their current memory locations. In contrast, to insert an element into an array, multiple elements may need to shift to other memory locations to make space for the new element. See **Figure 19-11**.

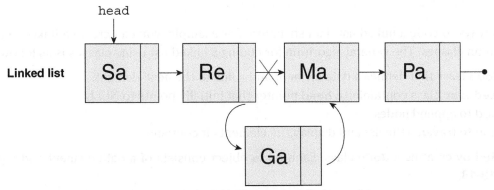

To insert an element into a linked list, you can adjust two pointers.

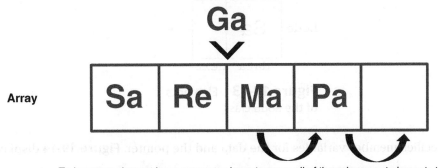

To insert an element in an array, you have to move all of the subsequent elements to create a space for the new element.

Figure 19-11   Inserting elements into a linked list and an array

Deletion. An element can easily be deleted from a linked list by changing pointers. As with insertions, elements remain in their original memory locations. Arrays are much less efficient for deletions because elements have to shift in memory to fill in the space produced by the deleted element. In **Figure 19-12** there are two Ga elements, and one is to be deleted.

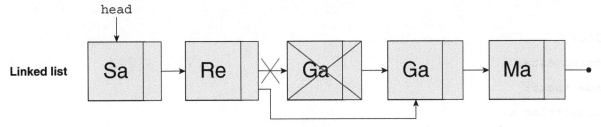

To delete an element from a linked list, simply change the pointer to the subsequent next element.

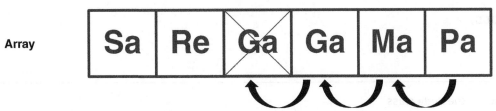

To delete an array element, move all the subsequent elements to fill in the gap.

Figure 19-12   Deleting elements in a linked list and an array

19.3 CODE A LINKED LIST

The Node Class (19.3.1, 19.3.2, 19.3.3)

There are several ways to code a linked list data structure. For example, you can create a linked list based on functions or based on classes. The general algorithm for coding a linked list using classes is as follows:

Construct a **Node** class that defines a data element and a link to the next element.

Create a **LinkedList** class containing a **head** pointer that initially points to NULL.

Create a method to append nodes.

Create a method to traverse the list and display the elements it contains.

Let's get started by creating a **Node** class. Each **Node** object consists of a data element and a pointer, as shown in **Figure 19-13**.

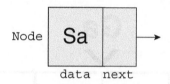

Node   Sa

data   next

Figure 19-13   Elements of the Node class

The **Node** class specifies member variables for the data and the pointer. **Figure 19-14** displays the code for the **Node** class.

The **Node** class has two member variables: a string called **data** and ***next**, which is a pointer to the next node of the list. The variable called **data** is declared as a string so it can hold a value such as Sa. The statement **Node *next** indicates that **next** is a pointer to an instance of a **Node** object.

Node(string d) is a constructor that initializes a **Node** object with data and sets the **next** pointer to **NULL**.

```cpp
class Node
{
  public:
    string data;
    Node *next;
    Node(string d)
    {
      data = d;
      next = NULL;
    }
};
```

Figure 19-14   Code for the Node class

The `LinkedList` Class (19.3.4)

The `LinkedList` class creates a pointer to the head of the list and initially sets it to NULL, None, or empty. The `LinkedList` class will also include methods that manipulate the linked list. **Figure 19-15** displays the code that creates the `LinkedList` class.

In the `LinkedList` class the statement `Node *head` creates a pointer to the head of the list. The `head` pointer is initially set to `NULL` because the list is empty.

```
class LinkedList
{
  public:
  Node *head;
  LinkedList()
  {
    head = NULL;
  }
}
```

Figure 19-15   Code for the `LinkedList` class

The `Append` Method (19.3.5)

A linked list is populated by appending elements, such as Sa, Re, and Ga, to the end of the data structure. When the list is empty, the element being appended becomes the head of the list. Otherwise, a loop traverses the list to the last element where you can append the new node.

The algorithm for the **append_node()** method goes like this:

Instantiate a node containing data and a **new_node** pointer that points to the node's location in memory.

If the **head** pointer for the linked list points to NULL then:

> set the **head** pointer so it references the same node as the **new_node** pointer, making the new node the head of the list.

Otherwise:

> Create a **temp** pointer that initially references the same node as the **head** pointer.
> While **temp** does not point to NULL at the end of the list,
>> set **temp** to reference the same node as **temp next** and move to the next node.

At the end of the list, set the last pointer (**temp next**) to reference the same node as the **new_node** pointer so that the new node is linked to the list.

Q How can you tell if a list is empty?

A The **head** points to NULL.

Figure 19-16 details the code for appending a new element to the end of the linked list.

The `append_node()` method begins with `Node *new_node = new Node(d)`, which creates a new node containing a data value and an associated pointer called `new_node`.

If `head == NULL`, the list is empty, and the `head` pointer takes on the value of `new_node` to make the new node the head of the list. Otherwise `Node *temp = head` creates a pointer called `temp` that references the same node as the `head` pointer where the traversal begins.

A while-loop handles the traversal. If `temp->next` is not `NULL`, it is not the end of the list, so the next pointer is loaded into `temp` using the statement `temp = temp->next`. When `temp` contains `NULL`, it is the end of the list and the new node can be added using the statement `temp->next = new_node`.

```
void append_node(string d)
{
  Node *new_node = new Node(d);
  if (head == NULL)
    head = new_node;
  else
  {
    Node *temp = head;
    while (temp->next != NULL)
      temp = temp->next;

    temp->next = new_node;
  }
}
```

Figure 19-16   Code for the `append()` method

The driver code that creates an instance of a linked list and calls the `append_node()` method is simple. The code in **Figure 19-17** creates a linked list called `my_list` and appends three nodes for strings Sa, Re, and Ga.

```
#include <iostream>
#include <string>
using namespace std;

int main()
{
  LinkedList my_list;
  my_list.append_node("Sa");
  my_list.append_node("Re");
  my_list.append_node("Ga");
}
```

Figure 19-17   Driver code to append elements to the linked list program

Linked List Traversal (19.3.6, 19.3.7)

You'll want to see the results of the append operation by displaying the list. For that you can create a method called **display()**. This method begins at the head of the list and uses a while-loop to traverse the list by following the pointers from one element to the next until it reaches the NULL pointer at the end of the list. Here is the algorithm:

If **head** points to NULL then
>   display "The list is empty."

Otherwise,
>   Create a **temp** pointer that initially references the same node as the **head** pointer.
>   While **temp** does not point to NULL at the end of the list,
>>   Display the data pointed to by **temp**.
>>   Set **temp** to reference the same node as **temp next** and continue to loop.

Trace through the code in **Figure 19-18** and look for the statement that moves the temporary pointer along.

The **display()** method begins by checking if the list is empty. If there are elements in the list, **Node *temp = head** creates a pointer called **temp** that references the same node as the **head** pointer.

The reference **temp->data** holds the data for the first node and the **cout** statement displays it. Then **temp = temp->next** loads **temp** with the pointer to the next node.

```
void display()
{
  if (head == NULL)
    cout << "List is empty!" << endl;
  else
  {
    Node *temp = head;
    while (temp != NULL)
    {
      cout << temp->data << endl ;
      temp = temp->next;
    }
    cout << endl;
  }
}
```

Figure 19-18   Code for traversing the list to output of all the elements

---

Q If the list contains Sa Re Ga Ma, what is the output when the driver program calls **display()**?

A The output is:
```
Sa
Re
Ga
Ma
```

The Find Method (19.3.8)

You can use the general algorithm for traversing a linked list to look at each element and determine if it matches a specified target value. The algorithm goes like this:

> Load the value you want to find into a variable called **target**.
> If **head** points to NULL then:
>> display "The list is empty."
> Otherwise:
>> Create a **temp** pointer that initially references the same node as the **head** pointer.
>> While **temp** does not point to NULL at the end of the list:
>>> Compare the data pointed to by **temp** to the data in **target**.
>>> If **temp** and **target** match, display a message that the target data is in the list.
>>> Otherwise, set **temp** to reference the same node as **temp next** and continue to loop.

Figure 19-19 illustrates the code for the **find_it()** method.

The **find_it()** method accepts one argument for the target value. If the list is empty, the target is not in the list.

Node *temp = head sets a temporary pointer to the first item in the list. If **temp->data** is the target value, the "Found" message is displayed. Otherwise, **temp** is set to the **temp->next** pointer and the loop iterates to the next list element.

```cpp
void find_it(string target)
{
  if (head == NULL)

    cout << "List is empty!" << endl;

  else
  {

    Node *temp = head;

    while (temp != NULL)
    {

      if (temp->data == target)

          cout << "Found " << target << " in the list. " << endl;

      temp = temp->next;

    }

  }
}
```

Figure 19-19 Code for finding an element in a linked list

Q If the linked list contains Sa Re Ga Ma and the driver program calls `find_it("Ga")`, what is the output?

A The output is `Found Ga in the list`.

The Insert Method (19.3.9)

Inserting an element into a linked list requires you to shuffle pointers. Pay attention to the pointers in **Figure 19-20**.

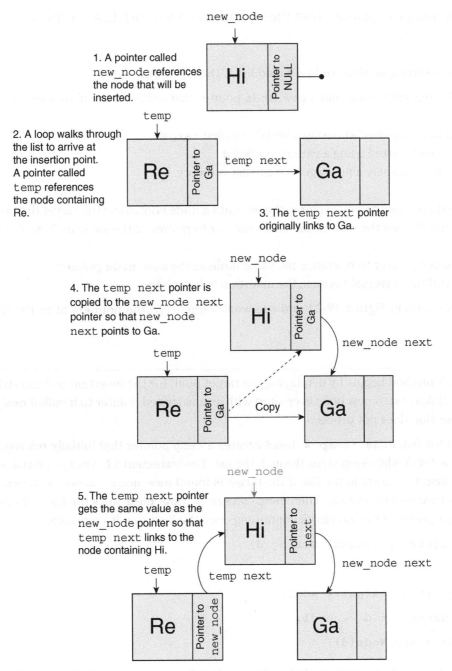

Figure 19-20   Pointer shuffling for inserting a new node between Re and Ga in a linked list

Q Where does `temp next` point before the insertion? Where does it point after the insertion?

A Before the insertion, `temp next` points to Ga. After the insertion, it points to the node containing Hi.

Q Where does the pointer from the Hi node point before the insertion? Where does it point after the insertion?

A Before the insertion, the pointer from the Hi node points to NULL. After the insertion, it points to Ga.

The algorithm for inserting an element in a linked list is the following:

Instantiate a node containing data, and a `new_node` pointer that points to the node's location in memory.
Display the location of the insertion using a variable called `target`.
Display the data to be inserted using a variable called `d`.
If `head` points to NULL, display a message that the list is empty.
Otherwise:
    Assign each node to `temp` as you traverse the list until a node containing the target data is reached.
    At the insertion point, set the `new_node next` pointer to reference the same node as the `temp next` pointer.
    Set the `temp next` pointer to reference the same node as the `new_node` pointer.
    Use `break` to end the traversal because the insertion is complete.

Trace through the code in **Figure 19-21** and see what happens to the pointers after the "Found target!" statement.

The `insert_node()` method begins by displaying the target point for the insertion and the string that is to be inserted into the linked list. A new node is created with an associated pointer to it called `new_node`. If the list is empty, the insertion does not proceed.

If there are nodes in the list, `Node *temp = head` creates a `temp` pointer that initially references the same node as the `head` pointer. A while-loop steps through the list. The statement `if (temp->data == target)` looks for the target insertion point in the list. If the target is found `new_node->next = temp->next` links the new node to the next node in the list. Then `temp->next = new_node` links the target to the new node. The `break` statement prevents the loop from continuing once the insertion is complete.

```
void insert_node(string target, string d)

{

  cout << "Target:" << target<< endl;

  cout << "New data:" << d << endl;

  Node *new_node = new Node(d);
```

Figure 19-21   Code for inserting a node in a linked list (*continued*)

```
if (head == NULL)

  cout << "List is empty!" << endl;

else

{

  Node *temp = head;

  while (temp != NULL)

  {

    if (temp->data == target)

    {

      new_node->next = temp->next;

      temp->next = new_node;

      break;

    }

    temp = temp->next;

  }

}

}
```

Figure 19-21   Code for inserting a node in a linked list (*continued*)

After you've defined the **Node** class, the **LinkedList** class, and methods for appending, traversing, finding, and inserting elements, you can use a driver program such as the one in **Figure 19-22** to experiment with linked lists.

```
#include <iostream>

#include <string>

using namespace std;


int main()

{

  LinkedList my_list;

  my_list.append_node("Sa");

  my_list.append_node("Re");

  my_list.append_node("Ga");
```

Figure 19-22   Linked list driver code to append, traverse, find, and insert (*continued*)

```
        cout<< "The original list:" << endl;
        my_list.display();


        my_list.find_it("Sa");
        cout << endl;


        my_list.insert_node("Re", "Hi");
        cout << "The list after the insertion: " << endl;
        my_list.display();
}
```

OUTPUT:

```
The original list:
Sa
Re
Ga


Found Sa in the list.


Target:Re
New data:Hi
The list after the insertion:
Sa
Re
Hi
Ga
```

Figure 19-22   Linked list driver code to append, traverse, find, and insert
(*continued*)

SUMMARY

- A linked list is a linear data structure. A data structure is a specific layout of data values in memory and a set of operations that can be applied to those values. Other data structures include arrays, stacks, queues, trees, and graphs. Data structures are used to hold data in memory during program execution.
- A linked list is a collection of data that can be stored in nonconsecutive memory locations. Each element in a linked list is called a node. Each node consists of data and a pointer to the next node. The first node in a linked list is referred to as the head.

- When each element in a linked list has a single pointer linking to the next element, the structure is called a singly linked list. A doubly linked list has two pointers for each element. One pointer links to the next element; the other pointer links to the previous element. In a circular linked list, the last node points back to the first node.
- Linked lists are easy to extend and modify. However, they require extra memory for the pointers and must be accessed sequentially beginning at the head of the list.
- There are a variety of algorithms for coding linked lists. One popular way is to create a `Node` class for each data element and a `LinkedList` class with methods for appending elements, traversing the list, inserting elements, finding elements, displaying elements, and other operations.
- Many programming languages provide a linked list structure and methods either as a built-in or as a module that you can import or include. Coding a linked list is one of the challenges you might experience in a technical interview when seeking a programming job, so you'll want to keep linked lists in your programming skill set.

Key Terms

circular linked list	linear data structure	pointer
data structure	linked list	reference
doubly linked list	node	singly linked list
head	nonlinear data structure	

STACKS AND QUEUES

LEARNING OBJECTIVES:

20.1 STACKS

20.1.1 Explain why stacks are considered limited access, linear data structures.

20.1.2 Explain the meaning of LIFO in the context of stacks.

20.1.3 Use the terms "push" and "pop" in the context of stacks.

20.1.4 State the efficiency of push, pop, and search operations performed on a stack.

20.1.5 Provide examples illustrating the use of stacks in computer programs.

20.1.6 Identify built-in stack functions.

20.1.7 Identify the classes that are used when implementing a stack based on a linked list.

20.1.8 Diagram the processes for pushing and popping elements from a linked list stack.

20.2 QUEUES

20.2.1 Classify a queue as a linear, limited access data structure that is accessed as FIFO.

20.2.2 Contrast the FIFO operation of a queue with the LIFO operation of a stack.

20.2.3 Apply the terms "enqueue" and "dequeue" in the context of queues.

20.2.4 Label the elements of a queue.

20.2.5 State the efficiency of queuing operations, such as enqueue and dequeue.

20.2.6 Provide examples illustrating the use of queues in computer programs.

20.2.7 Describe the classes that are used when coding a queue based on a linked list.

20.2.8 Recall the algorithms for enqueuing and dequeuing elements from a linked list queue.

20.1 STACKS

Stack Basics (20.1.1, 20.1.2, 20.1.3, 20.1.4)

Cafeteria food. It's not always great, but after queuing up in a line, you can quickly grab a tray off the stack, slide it down the rails, and pile it up with food. See **Figure 20-1**. That experience provides a foundation for understanding two important data structures: stacks and queues. Let's start with stacks.

Claudio Divizia/Shutterstock.com

Figure 20-1 A cafeteria has stacks and queues

In programming, a **stack** is a limited access, linear data structure in which the last data element added is the first element removed. As an analogy, visualize a busy cafeteria. The trays are stacked one on top of another. The top tray on the stack—the last one added—is the first one that can be removed. To reach the tray at the bottom of the stack, all the other trays have to be removed first.

The data in a stack is controlled by a last-in-first-out algorithm referred to as **LIFO** (pronounced LIE foh). Adding a data element to the top of the stack is accomplished with a **push** operation. Deleting an element from the top of a stack is accomplished with a **pop** operation.

Stacks may also support a **peek** operation that retrieves the value of the top element without removing it from the stack. **Figure 20-2** shows a conceptual diagram of a stack, along with its push and pop operations.

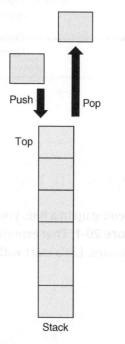

Figure 20-2 The stack data structure

The characteristics of a stack data structure include the following:

Linear. Elements in a stack are related linearly, not hierarchically. Each element is chained to one previous element and one next element.

Homogeneous. The elements in a stack are all the same data type.

Efficient addition and removal. No matter how many elements a stack contains, adding or removing an element from the stack can be accomplished in a single operation. Push and pop can only be applied to the top element of the stack, so theoretically the number of additional elements in the stack has no effect on the efficiency of the push and pop operations.

Extensible. Stacks allocate memory dynamically as elements are added. Unlike arrays, the length of a stack does not need to be declared.

Limited access. Only the top element in a stack can be accessed. The elements further down the stack cannot be accessed directly. There is no easy way to iterate through all the elements in a stack. To search for an element in a stack, you have to remove elements one by one until the target element is found. If you want to keep the original stack, you have to store all of the elements that you pop off, then push them back to the stack when you are done.

Q Which is easier: accessing an element in the middle of an array or in the middle of a stack?

A Array elements can be directly accessed using the element's index number, whereas to access an element in a stack, you have to pop elements off until you reach the target element.

Stack Use Cases (20.1.5)

Stacks are a handy tool for your programming toolkit. Consider using a stack when you are working with data that requires operations such as the following:

Reversing order. Stacks work well for algorithms that reverse words or other objects. **Figure 20-3** can help you visualize how to use a stack to reverse the letters in a word. You push each letter onto the stack. The first letter ends up at the bottom. The last letter ends up at the top. As you pop off each letter, the word is spelled backwards.

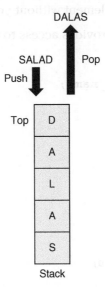

Figure 20-3 Reversing a word using a stack

Q If you push BURRITO onto a stack, in what sequence will the letters pop off?

A The letters will pop off in reverse order: OTIRRUB.

Undo and redo. Stacks are also useful for undo and redo operations. For example, a word processing program can use a stack to collect each keystroke and command the user makes. Suppose the user deletes a word. That operation is pushed to the top of the stack. The user decides that the word should not have been deleted and selects Undo. The word processing program pops the Undo operation off the stack, then pops the deleted word off the stack. Presto! The word is undeleted.

Retracing steps. A stack might also be used to keep a list of websites visited by a browser. Every new page pushes a link onto the stack. The Prev button pops a link off the stack and goes back to the previous page that the browser displayed. This aspect of stacks is also handy for solving maze problems in which choosing the wrong path requires you to reverse to an intersection to try a different path.

Testing symmetry. Stacks are useful for testing symmetry. Here's an example. Word processing programs use the " symbol for opening a quotation, but the " symbol for closing a quotation. How does it know which to use? When the quotation symbols are stored on a stack, popping the top element indicates if the last one was an opening or closing quotation mark.

Built-in Stacks (20.1.6)

Most programming languages have a built-in stack function, method, or class. **Figure 20-4** provides an example that does the following:

> Pushes 1 onto the stack.
> Pushes 2 onto the stack.
> Outputs the top number of the stack. (It is 2 at this point in the program.)
> Pops the top number off the stack.
> Outputs the top number of the stack. (It is 1 after popping off 2.)

The C++ Standard Template Library (STL) includes a stack container with **push()**, **pop()**, and **top()** functions. The **top()** function peeks at the top element without popping it off the stack.

The statement **#include <bits/stdc++.h>** provides access to the stack container and its functions.

Syntax:

Declare the stack: `stack <data_type> stack_name;`

Push: `stack_name.push(data);`

Pop: `stack_name.pop();`

Peek: `stack_name.top();`

`#include <bits/stdc++.h>`

`using namespace std;`

Figure 20-4 A built-in `stack()` function (*continued*)

```
int main ()

{

  stack <int> the_stack;

  the_stack.push(1);

  the_stack.push(2);

  cout << "The top of the stack is: " << the_stack.top() << endl;


  the_stack.pop();

  cout << "The top of the stack is: " << the_stack.top()<< endl;

}
OUTPUT:

The top of the stack is: 2

The top of the stack is: 1
```

Figure 20-4   A built-in `stack()` function (*continued*)

Code a Stack (20.1.7, 20.1.8)

You can also implement a stack based on a linked list. A linked list stack is essentially a "from scratch" solution that gives you total control over the behavior of the stack and its operations.

As a quick review, recall that a linked list is a chain of nodes, each with a pointer to the next node. The diagram in **Figure 20-5** illustrates a linked list in a vertical orientation that resembles a stack.

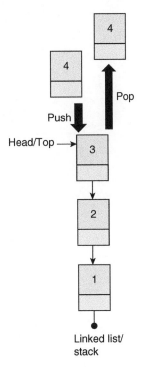

Figure 20-5   A linked list can be used to implement a stack

Q What part of a linked list is equivalent to the top of a stack?

A The head of a linked list is equivalent to the top of a stack. When you picture the head of a linked list as the top of a stack, then you can see how the two structures are related.

It is easy to implement a stack as a linked list with methods to push and pop data elements. The code for a linked list stack begins by defining a **Node** class and a **Stack** class, as shown in **Figure 20-6**. The **Node** class defines a node as having data and a link to the next node. The **Stack** class creates a pointer called **top** that initially points to NULL, null, or None, depending on your programming language.

The following segment of code declares a **Node** class and a **Stack** class. The **Node** class has two attributes: an integer called **data**, and a pointer called ***next** that references the next node. **Node(int d)** is a constructor for a **Node** object containing data set to **d** and a **next** pointer to NULL.

In the **Stack** class, the statement **Node *top** creates a pointer called **top** and **top = NULL** initially sets the **top** pointer to NULL because the stack has no nodes when it is first created.

```cpp
#include <iostream>
using namespace std;


class Node
{
  public:
  int data;
  Node *next;
  Node(int d)
  {
    data = d;
    next = NULL;
  }
};
class Stack
{
  public:
  Node *top;
  Stack()
  {
    top = NULL;
  }
```

Figure 20-6   Code for the **Node** and **Stack** classes

Q Why does **top** initially point to NULL, null, or None?

A The stack does not yet include a node that **top** can point to.

Push(). The **Stack** class includes a **push()** method that places an element at the top of the stack, which is the head of the linked list. The algorithm for the **push()** method goes like this:

Create a new node with an associated pointer to it called **temp**.

Load data into the node referenced by **temp**.

Change the **temp next** pointer to reference the same node as the **top** pointer.

Set the **top** pointer to reference the same node as **temp** so that **top** points to the top node in the stack.

The diagram in **Figure 20-7** illustrates what happens when an element is pushed to the top of the linked list stack.

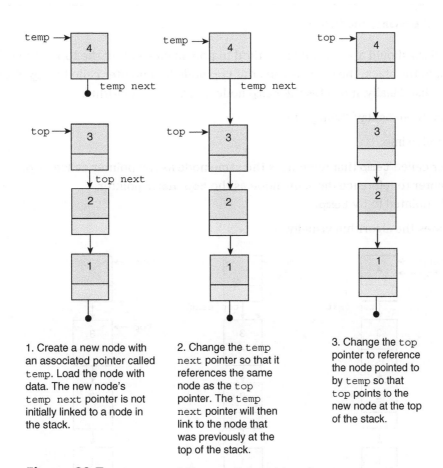

1. Create a new node with an associated pointer called temp. Load the node with data. The new node's temp next pointer is not initially linked to a node in the stack.

2. Change the temp next pointer so that it references the same node as the top pointer. The temp next pointer will then link to the node that was previously at the top of the stack.

3. Change the top pointer to reference the node pointed to by temp so that top points to the new node at the top of the stack.

Figure 20-7   Conceptual diagram for pushing elements onto the linked list stack

Q To which node does **temp next** link during the **push()** method?

A The **temp next** pointer initially points to NULL, but then links to the **top** node.

The code for pushing an element to the top of the stack is detailed in **Figure 20-8**.

The statement `Node *temp = new Node(d)` creates a new node referenced by a pointer called `temp` and populates the node with data `d`. Then `temp->next = top` links the new node's next pointer to the current top of the stack. The statement `top = temp` changes the `top` pointer so it references the new node that is now the top of the stack.

```
void push(int d)

  {

    Node *temp = new Node(d);

    temp->next = top;

    top = temp;

    cout << top->data << " is pushed onto the stack." << endl;


  }
```

Figure 20-8 Code for the `push()` method

Pop(). The `Stack` class should also include a method to pop an element off the top of the linked list stack. As long as there is data in the stack, the code assigns the `top` node to a pointer called `temp`. It then makes the next node the top of the list. Finally, it deletes the `temp` node. Here is the algorithm:

If the stack is empty, then display "Empty stack."

Otherwise, do the following:

> Create a pointer called `temp` that references the same node as the pointer called `top`.
> Set the `top` pointer to reference the same node as the `top next` pointer.
> Delete the node pointed to by `temp`.

Figure 20-9 illustrates the algorithm visually.

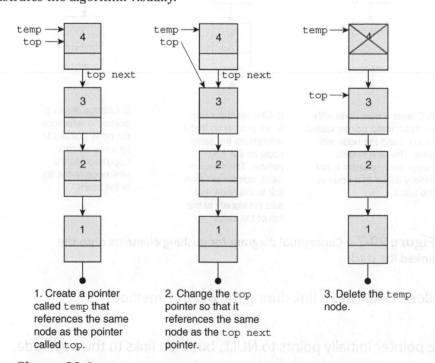

1. Create a pointer called `temp` that references the same node as the pointer called `top`.

2. Change the `top` pointer so that it references the same node as the `top next` pointer.

3. Delete the `temp` node.

Figure 20-9 Conceptual diagram for popping elements off the linked list stack

Q Why do you have to create a `temp` pointer instead of just deleting the `top` node?

A If you do not create a `temp` pointer, the pointer to the next element would be lost and it would be impossible to relocate the top of the stack.

In the linked list implementation, you'll first check whether the stack is empty and display "Empty stack" if that is the case. If there are elements on the stack, the `pop()` method proceeds according to the algorithm. The code for popping the top element from a stack is detailed in **Figure 20-10**.

The if-clause checks if the stack is empty. Otherwise, the stack contains nodes and `Node *temp = top` creates a pointer called `temp` that references the node at the top of the stack. The statement `top = top->next` points top to the second (next) node in the stack. Finally, `delete(temp)` deletes the node referenced by `temp`.

```
void pop()
{
    if(top == NULL)

        cout << "Empty stack." << endl;

    else

    {
        Node *temp = top;

        cout << top->data << " is popped off the stack." << endl;

        top = top->next;

        delete(temp);

    }
}
```

Figure 20-10   Code for the `pop()` method

After you have defined the `push()` and `pop()` methods, you can use them in programs. Remember to create the `Stack` object in your driver code. In **Figure 20-11**, the driver code creates a `Stack` object called `my_stack`. It pushes 1, then 2 onto the stack. After that, the code attempts to pop off three items. Because the stack contains only two items, the last `pop()` method produces the "Empty stack" message.

```
int main()
{
    Stack my_stack;

    my_stack.push(1);

    my_stack.push(2);

    my_stack.pop();
```

Figure 20-11   Driver code for the linked list stack (*continued*)

```
    my_stack.pop();

    my_stack.pop();

}
OUTPUT:

1 is pushed onto the stack.

2 is pushed onto the stack.

2 is popped off the stack.

1 is popped off the stack.

Empty stack.
```

Figure 20-11   Driver code for the linked list stack (*continued*)

20.2 QUEUES

Queue Basics (20.2.1, 20.2.2, 20.2.3, 20.2.4, 20.2.5)

A **queue** is a limited access, linear data structure in which elements are removed from the front and added to the rear. The people in line at a cafeteria form a queue. The first person in line is the first person to be served and leave the line. New arrivals are added to the end of the line.

Like a line of people, the data in a queue is controlled by a first-in-first-out algorithm referred to as **FIFO** (pronounced FI foh). Adding a data element to the rear of a queue is accomplished with an **enqueue** operation. Deleting an element from the front of the queue is accomplished with a **dequeue** operation.

Queues may also support a peek operation that retrieves the value of the front element without removing it from the queue.

Figure 20-12 illustrates a conceptual diagram of a queue, along with its enqueue and dequeue operations.

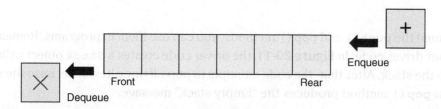

Figure 20-12   The queue data structure

Data in a queue can be efficiently enqueued and dequeued, but as with stacks, traversal is less efficient. Additional characteristics of queue data structures are similar to those of a stack.

- Homogeneous
- Linear
- Efficient addition and removal
- Extensible
- Limited access

Queue Use Cases (20.2.6)

The basic characteristic of a queue is that it can hold data and eventually release it in sequential order. Queues shine for algorithms that represent a sequence of tasks that must be processed in the order in which they occur. Here are some examples:

Scheduling. Operating systems track and schedule the processes from multiple programs that all require CPU processing time.

Asynchronous data transfer. Data that cannot always flow freely may be held in a buffer and then released. Keyboards include buffers that store keypresses until they can be handled by a software application. Print spoolers hold character data until a printer is ready to receive it.

Flood fill algorithms. Games such as Go and Minesweeper use queues to determine which squares are cleared. In Paint software, a queue controls the bucket tool that fills connected, similarly colored areas with a specified new color. See **Figure 20-13**.

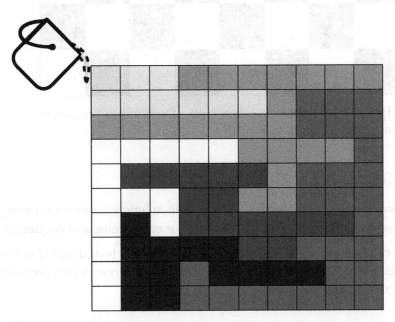

Figure 20-13   Flood fill algorithms are based on queues

First come, first served. Applications that control commercial phone systems place callers on hold and connect them to agents on a first come, first served basis. Print queues hold a series of documents and print them out in the order that they were received.

Traversal algorithms. Queues are used to follow a path through a hierarchical structure called a tree.

Shortest path. A queue is a key part of the solution to mapping problems such as the classic Chess Knight Problem to find the minimum number of steps taken by the Knight to move from point A to point B on a chessboard. See **Figure 20-14**.

Figure 20-14   The algorithm for the Chess Knight Problem is based on a queue data structure

Code a Queue (20.2.7, 20.2.8)

Although most programming languages provide a variety of built-in functionality for queues, you have the most control if you create a linked list and provide it with methods for enqueueing and dequeuing.

Conceptually, a queue can be a linked list in which the head of the list is designated as the front of the queue where data elements are removed. The tail of the linked list becomes the rear of the queue where data elements are added, as shown in **Figure 20-15**.

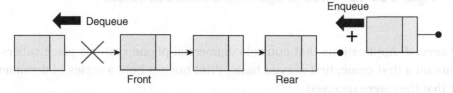

Figure 20-15   A linked list can be used to implement a queue

Q Is the head of a linked list equivalent to the front or rear of a queue?

A The head of a linked list is equivalent to the front of a queue.

The code for a linked list queue begins by creating a **Node** class and a **Queue** class, as shown in **Figure 20-16**.

The **Node** class includes a variable for the data and a pointer to the next node. **Node(int d)** is a constructor for a **Node** object containing data set to **d** and a **next** pointer to NULL.

The **Queue** class tracks both the front and rear of the queue with those pointers initially set to NULL in the **Queue** constructor.

```cpp
#include<iostream>
using namespace std;


class Node
{
  public:
    int data;
    Node *next;
    Node(int d)
    {
      data = d;
      next = NULL;
    }
};


class Queue
{
  public:
  Node *front, *rear;
  Queue()
  {
    front = rear = NULL;
  }
}
```

Figure 20-16   Code for the **Node** and **Queue** classes

Q In a queue, which pointers are initially set to NULL, null, or None?

A The front and rear nodes are initially empty, so the front and rear pointers are set to NULL, null, or None.

Enqueue(). The **enqueue()** method is designed to add a data element to the rear of the linked list queue, as shown in **Figure 20-17**.

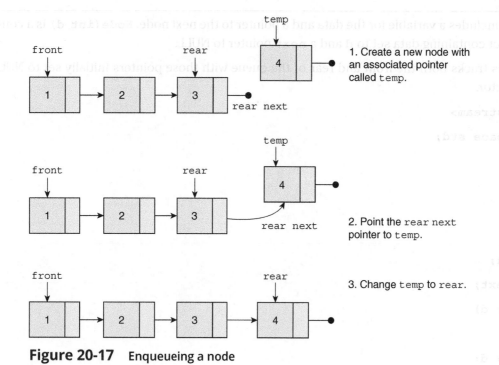

Figure 20-17   Enqueueing a node

Q Initially, what is the value of the **rear next** pointer?

A The **rear next** pointer is initially NULL, null, or None.

The enqueue algorithm goes like this:

Create a new node with a pointer to it called **temp**.
Load data into the node referenced by **temp**.
If the queue is empty, the new node becomes the front and the rear of the queue.
Otherwise, point the **rear next** pointer to the node referenced by **temp** and then change **temp** to **rear**.

The code for the **enqueue()** method is detailed in **Figure 20-18**.

The statement **Node *temp = new Node(d)** creates a new node containing data **d** with an associated pointer called **temp**. The if-clause makes the new node the front and rear of the queue if the queue is empty. If the queue contains nodes, **rear->next = temp** points the last node in the queue to the new node. The statement **rear = temp** moves the **rear** pointer to the newly enqueued node.

```
void enqueue(int d)

{

    Node *temp = new Node(d);


    if (rear == NULL)
```

Figure 20-18   Code for the **enqueue()** method (*continued*)

```
  {

    front = rear = temp;

    cout << front->data;

    cout << " is the front and rear of the queue." << endl;

  }

  else

  {

    rear->next = temp;

    rear = temp;

    cout << rear->data << " is the rear of the queue." << endl;

  }

}
```

Figure 20-18   Code for the `enqueue()` method (*continued*)

Dequeue(). The `dequeue()` method removes a data element from the front of the linked list queue. This method is similar to the `pop()` method in a stack and uses a similar algorithm. Here's the algorithm:

If the queue is empty, then display "Empty queue."
Otherwise, do the following:
> Create a pointer called `temp` that references the same node as the pointer called `front`.
> Set the `front` pointer to reference the same node as the `temp next` pointer.
> Delete the node referenced by `temp`.

The code for the `dequeue()` method is in **Figure 20-19**.

The if-clause checks if the queue is empty. If the queue is not empty, `Node *temp = front` creates a pointer called `temp` that refers to the same node as the `front` pointer. The statement `front = temp->next` points `front` to the second node in the queue, making that node the front of the queue. Then `delete(temp)` deletes the node referenced by `temp`.

```
void dequeue()

  {

    if (front == NULL)

      cout << "Empty queue."<< endl;

    else

    {

      Node *temp = front;

      front = temp->next;

      cout << temp->data << " is dequeued." << endl;

      delete(temp);

    }

  }
```

Figure 20-19   Code for the `dequeue()` method

Q Which pointers reference the same node when the dequeue operation begins?

A The `front` and `temp` pointers both reference the front node when the dequeue operation begins.

Your driver code can create an instance of the `Queue` class such as `my_queue` and use the `enqueue()` and `dequeue()` methods to add or remove elements from the queue. The driver code in **Figure 20-20** enqueues two elements, then dequeues them.

```
int main()
{

    Queue my_queue;

    my_queue.enqueue(1);

    my_queue.enqueue(2);

    my_queue.dequeue();

    my_queue.dequeue();

}

OUTPUT:

1 is the front and rear of the queue.

2 is the rear of the queue.

1 is dequeued.

2 is dequeued.
```

Figure 20-20   Driver code for the linked list queue

Q Review the code for the `dequeue()` method. What would be the output if the driver code had a third `dequeue()` statement?

A The if-statement in the `dequeue()` method would produce the "Empty queue" message, so the output would be:

```
1 is the front and rear of the queue.
2 is the rear of the queue.
1 is dequeued.
2 is dequeued.
Empty queue.
```

SUMMARY

- A stack is a limited access, linear data structure in which the last data element added is the first element removed. The data in a stack is controlled by a last-in-first-out algorithm referred to as LIFO.
- Adding a data element to the top of the stack is accomplished with a push operation. Deleting an element from the end of a stack is accomplished with a pop operation. Stacks may also support a peek operation that retrieves the value of the top element without removing it from the stack.
- Stacks are linear, homogeneous, and extensible. Adding and removing elements from the top of a stack is very efficient. Stacks are limited access, however, so traversing the data is less efficient because it requires popping elements off the stack one by one.
- Stacks are a handy tool for algorithms that rely on reversing, retracing, undoing, or testing symmetry.
- Most programming languages have built-in stack support. An alternative is to implement a stack based on a linked list. The code for a linked list stack typically includes a **Node** class, a **Stack** class, a **push()** method, and a **pop()** method.
- A queue is a limited access, linear data structure in which elements are removed from the front and added to the rear. The data in a queue is controlled by a first-in-first-out algorithm referred to as FIFO.
- Adding a data element to the rear of a queue is accomplished with an enqueue operation. Deleting an element from the front of the queue is accomplished with a dequeue operation. Queues may also support a peek operation that retrieves the value of the front element without removing it from the queue.
- Queues have characteristics similar to those of a stack. They are homogeneous, linear, and extensible. Enqueuing and dequeuing are efficient, but limited access makes traversal activities less efficient.
- Queues are useful tools for algorithms that represent a sequence of tasks that must be processed in the order in which they occur.
- As with stacks, queues can be implemented based on linked lists. A linked list queue includes a **Node** class, a **Queue** class, an **enqueue()** method, and a **dequeue()** method.

Key Terms

dequeue	LIFO	push
enqueue	peek	queue
FIFO	pop	stack

MODULE 21

TREES AND GRAPHS

LEARNING OBJECTIVES:

21.1 NONLINEAR DATA STRUCTURES

21.1.1 Describe the difference between linear and nonlinear data structures.

21.1.2 Explain the design of nonlinear data structures.

21.1.3 Define "nodes" and "edges" in nonlinear data structures.

21.2 TREE STRUCTURES

21.2.1 Classify trees as nonlinear abstract data structures.

21.2.2 Identify the key elements of a tree data structure.

21.2.3 Associate the term "hierarchical" with tree data structures.

21.2.4 Identify the height and depth of a tree data structure.

21.2.5 Explain why a tree structure can be described as recursive.

21.3 SOLVING PROBLEMS USING TREES

21.3.1 Provide examples that use trees to represent hierarchical data.

21.3.2 State the key characteristic of a binary tree.

21.3.3 Differentiate between a binary tree and a binary search tree.

21.3.4 Define the term "traversal" as it relates to tree data structures.

21.3.5 Trace the path of a depth first traversal.

21.3.6 Trace the path of a breadth first traversal.

21.4 GRAPH STRUCTURES

21.4.1 Classify a graph as a nonlinear abstract data structure.

21.4.2 Compare diagrams of graphs to diagrams of trees.

21.4.3 State four characteristics that differentiate graphs from trees.

21.4.4 Explain the difference between directed and undirected graphs.

21.5 SOLVING PROBLEMS WITH GRAPHS

21.5.1 Provide examples of using graph data structures to represent data.

21.5.2 Associate the term "network model" with graph data structures.

21.5.3 Define the term "shortest path" as it relates to graphs.

21.5.4 Provide examples of using shortest paths in the real world.

21.5.5 Trace Floyd's Algorithm.

21.1 NONLINEAR DATA STRUCTURES

Linear versus Nonlinear Structures (21.1.1, 21.1.2)

The easiest information for a computer to manage is a linear data structure where data elements are arranged sequentially and each element is connected to the previous and next one, such as the guest list for a party or the high scores on a video game.

Not all data is linear, however, but is arranged as a hierarchy or a web with one or more links between data elements. Examples of nonlinear data include an organizational chart, family tree, and a website map that shows how each webpage connects to the home page.

Imagine you are in a hedge maze, shown in **Figure 21-1**. Consider a path through the maze as a series of choices. At each intersection, you choose a direction to continue through the maze or exit.

Figure 21-1   Hedge maze

Figure 21-2 shows a simpler maze with each decision point labeled with a letter from A through G. The entrance is shown with a blue arrow pointing into the maze, and the exit is shown with a blue arrow pointing out of the maze.

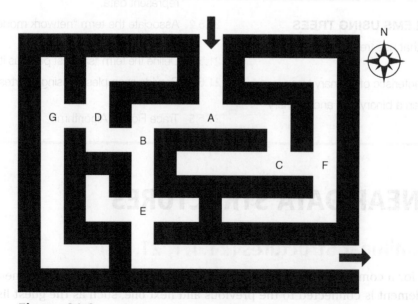

Figure 21-2   Computer-friendly maze

Suppose you want to display all possible routes through the maze, including paths that result in a dead end. You could represent each route as a list of instructions, which is a linear data structure. For example, how would you describe traveling to the D intersection? Take the path south to intersection A, then west to intersection B, then west again to reach intersection D. How would you describe the path to intersection E? Go south, west, and south to reach E. The first two instructions to intersections D and E create overlapping paths—first go south, then go west—because the paths to D and E each pass through intersection B. Listing all possible routes creates many redundant instructions.

Mazes are web-like structures that are best represented nonlinearly. A linear description of the maze is possible, but is tedious and repetitive.

Nonlinear Building Blocks (21.1.3)

Recall that in a linear data structure, a node stores a piece of information and a pointer to another node somewhere else in the computer's memory. Nonlinear structures use the same idea of nodes, except the number of connections is not limited to a single link. Instead, each node can have one or more connections. **Figure 21-3** compares a linear structure and a nonlinear structure.

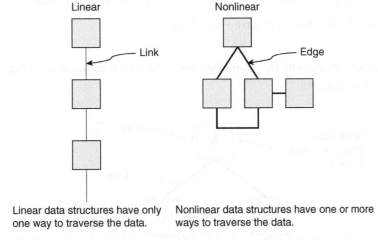

Linear data structures have only one way to traverse the data.

Nonlinear data structures have one or more ways to traverse the data.

Figure 21-3   Linear versus nonlinear data structures

In a nonlinear data structure, the connections between nodes are called edges. An edge can be directed, which means it is like a one-way street. A directed edge can go from A to B, but not in reverse. An edge can also be undirected, which means it can be taken in either direction: A to B or B to A. How edges are restricted affects the design of each data structure.

21.2 TREE STRUCTURES

Tree Basics (21.2.1, 21.2.2, 21.2.3)

A tree is a hierarchical nonlinear data structure. As with a linked list, a tree has a starting point and a connection from one data element to the next. Unlike linked lists, each node in a tree can have more than one connection to other data elements.

Imagine a tree with branches that split into leaves. Now imagine a piece of information at each point where the tree splits. The splitting points are nodes. Although trees grow and branch out upwards, traditionally coding trees are drawn upside down so the starting point appears at the top of the diagram. **Figure 21-4** shows the nodes in a tree data structure. The image on the right shows how trees are traditionally diagrammed in computer science.

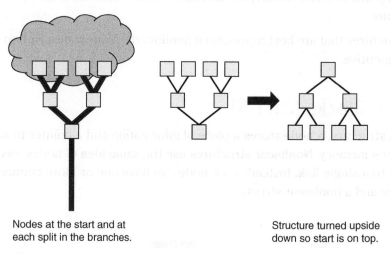

Nodes at the start and at
each split in the branches.

Structure turned upside
down so start is on top.

Figure 21-4   Nodes in a tree structure

The edges in a tree structure represent the branches and connect one node to other nodes. **Figure 21-5** shows nodes and edges in a tree diagram.

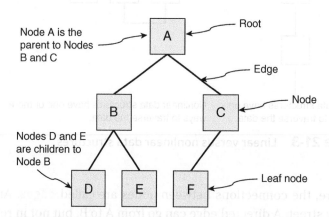

Node A is the
parent to Nodes
B and C

Root

Edge

Node

Nodes D and E
are children to
Node B

Leaf node

Figure 21-5   Nodes and edges in a basic tree

Two nodes are related if they are connected by an edge, such as Node A and Node C in Figure 21-5. Each node can have only one edge connecting it to another node. That means the number of edges in a tree equals the number of nodes minus one. The tree in Figure 21-5 has six nodes and five edges.

One node can be a **parent** or **child** of another node. In Figure 21-5, Node A is the parent of Node B and Node C. The children of Node B are Nodes D and E. A tree is hierarchical because of these parent–child relationships, with nodes above or below one another.

The nodes at the top and bottom of a tree have special names. The **root** node is at the top of the tree and has no parent node. The nodes at the bottom, which have no children, are called **leaf nodes**. In Figure 21-5, the root is Node A, and the leaf nodes are Nodes D, E, and F. A tree can have only one parent node. A node may have zero or more children, but only one parent. The only exception to this rule is the root node, which does not have a parent.

In the maze example, you could represent the choices at each intersection as a tree. Each intersection is a node, and the paths are edges. See **Figure 21-6**. From intersection A, you have two choices: west takes you to intersection B, and east takes you to intersection C.

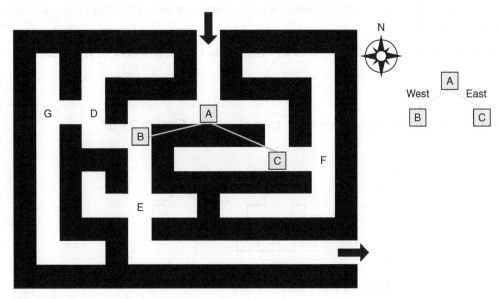

Figure 21-6   Tree structure in a maze

Q In Figure 21-6, which node is the root of the tree for the maze paths?

A The starting point of the maze, intersection A, is the root because it has no parent node. There is no decision to make before intersection A.

Figure 21-7 shows the full decision tree for the maze paths. Nodes with no letters represent dead ends.

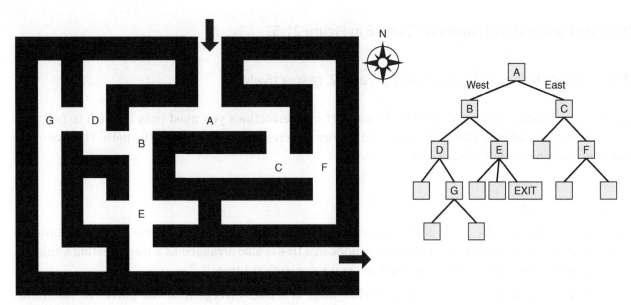

Figure 21-7   Full tree structure for the complete maze

Tree Properties (21.2.4)

A tree's shape can be described by its size, height, and width.

Size. The size refers to the number of nodes in the tree.

Height. The height is determined by the number of node rows in a tree, including the root node. A tree's height cannot be greater than its size.

Width. The width is determined by the number of children in the largest row of the tree. This row is not always the bottom of the tree.

Q What are the size, height, and width of each tree shown in **Figure 21-8**?

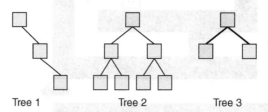

Tree 1   Tree 2   Tree 3

Figure 21-8   Several trees

A Tree 1 has a size of 3, a height of 3, and a width of 1; tree 2 has a size of 7, a height of 3, and a width of 4; and tree 3 has a size of 3, a height of 2, and a width of 2.

You describe the location of a node by its depth into the tree. To calculate a node's depth, start at the root, which has a depth of 0. Add 1 to the depth each time you follow an edge to a child node. Note the difference between height and depth: a tree has a height, and a node has a depth. The smallest tree has a height of 1, which means it has only one row of nodes and a single node in that row. The shallowest node has a depth of 0, which means it is the root node.

Q What are the depths of Nodes A, C, and E in Figure 21-5?

A The depths of Nodes A, C, and E are 0, 1, and 2, respectively.

In a maze, the height of a tree represents the number of intersections you must pass through to find your way out or to reach a dead end. The taller the tree, the more directions you select along the path. The size of the tree represents how many paths the maze contains.

Trees as Recursive Structures (21.2.5)

Remember that recursion is the act of dividing a problem into smaller copies of the same problem in order to solve it. Trees are recursive structures in that every node in a tree is also arranged as a tree, creating a subtree. To solve the problem posed by a tree data structure, you solve each subtree.

Although each tree has only one root, any other node is a tree, disregarding the parent of that node. In **Figure 21-9**, Node B is a subtree attached to Node A. The other nodes are also tree structures.

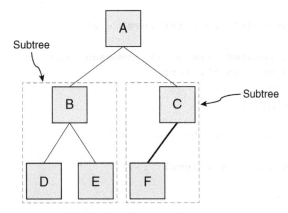

Figure 21-9   Nodes as subtrees

Each node, even nodes without children, are subtrees. This means that a tree has a recursive definition. A tree or subtree is one of the following:

- A single node, or a tree of height 1
- A node with children subtrees of smaller heights

Properties of a tree can also be defined recursively. The size of Node A in Figure 21-9 is the size of subtrees B and C added together, plus 1, which equals 6. The height of Node A is the height of the tallest subtree plus 1, which is 3.

Figure 21-10 shows how you can code a tree structure using a `Node` class for a nonlinear data structure. The code is for a specific type of nonlinear `Node`, a tree with only two children, labeled `left` and `right`.

```
#include <iostream>
#include <string>

using namespace std;

class Node
{
    public:
        int data;

        Node* left;     left and right are the paths to take for
        Node* right;    a binary tree.

        Node(int data, Node* left = NULL, Node* right = NULL)
        {
            this->data = data;
            this->left = left;
            this->right = right;
        }

};
```

Figure 21-10   Modifying the `Node` class and printing a tree (*continued*)

```cpp
void print_tree(Node* tree, int level = 0)
{
    // Prints a rotated tree to the command line
    // with the root on the left.
    string s = "";
    if (tree != NULL)
    {
        print_tree(tree->right, level + 1);

        for (int i = 0; i < level; i++)
        {
            s += "| ";
        }
        s += to_string(tree->data);
        cout << s << endl;

        print_tree(tree->left, level + 1);
    }
}


int main()
{
    // Build a tree
    Node* tree = new Node(5);

    // depth 1
    tree->left = new Node(2);
    tree->right = new Node(8);

    // depth 2
    tree->left->left = new Node(1);
    tree->left->right = new Node(3);
    tree->right->left = new Node(7);
    tree->right->right = new Node(10);

    print_tree(tree);

    return 0;

}

OUTPUT:
| | 10
| 8
| | 7
5
| | 3
| 2
| | 1
```

Figure 21-10   Modifying the Node class and printing a tree (*continued*)

21.3 SOLVING PROBLEMS USING TREES

Tree Applications (21.3.1, 21.3.2)

You can use trees to solve many hierarchical problems beyond mazes. A video game often has moments in the story when the player can make choices. Each choice leads the story down one of many possible paths. A tree is a perfect way to organize these choices, as shown in **Figure 21-11**.

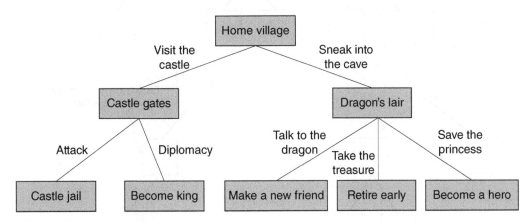

Figure 21-11   Tree for a story-driven game

Translating Morse code is also a good time to use a tree. Morse code is a communication method that uses short and long sounds to represent letters. For example, "dot dot dash dot" means the letter "F." The tree in **Figure 21-12** shows how to translate Morse code into letters. Each node has a left edge for dot (.) and a right edge for dash (-). You follow the left path for each dot in the code, and you follow the right path for each dash to arrive at the node containing the translated letter. To translate "dot dot dash dot," you go left, left, right, and left through the tree to end up at the leaf node containing "F."

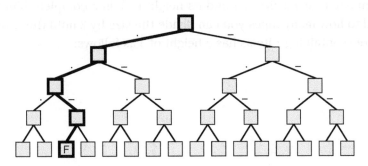

Figure 21-12   Morse code tree with "F" highlighted

Most often, trees are used in a binary format, where each node has up to two options, similar to the Morse code tree in Figure 21-12. **Binary trees** have no more than two children per node. In other words, a node in a binary tree can have zero, one, or two children, as shown in **Figure 21-13**.

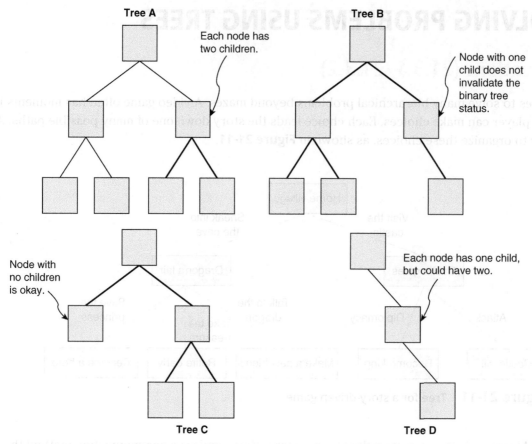

Figure 21-13   Binary trees

Each new row in a binary tree has room for twice as many children as the previous row, because each node can have two children. In a complete (or full) binary tree, each node except a leaf node has two children. In Figure 21-13, Tree A is a complete tree. Its size is 7 and its height is 3. In a complete binary tree, the height is log2(n) rounded up, or equal to how many times you can divide the size by 2 until the result is less than 1. You can calculate that a binary tree containing 7 items has a height of 3 as follows:

7 / 2 = 3.5
3.5 / 2 = 1.75
1.75 / 2 = 0.875

Data Storage in Trees (21.3.3, 21.3.4, 21.3.5, 21.3.6)

Each node in a tree can contain data or information. In Morse code, the letter "U" translates to "dot dot dash." This translation follows the same path as "F" in a Morse code tree, but stops one node above "F," where the letter "U" is stored. See **Figure 21-14**.

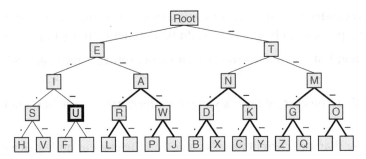

Figure 21-14   Morse code tree with "U" highlighted

A commonly used tree is a binary search tree (BST), a binary tree used to search for a specific value. Each node in a BST contains one piece of searchable information. **Figure 21-15** shows a possible BST with a number in each node.

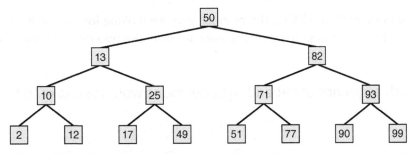

Figure 21-15   Binary search tree (BST)

To search a BST, you start at the root and look at the data contained within each node. As in a maze, each edge from a node represents a decision. Each node in a BST has two edges, one representing "left" and the other representing "right." The left path takes you to a number less than the current number, and the right path takes you to a number greater than the current number. In **Figure 21-16**, the root node contains the value 50. The nodes to the left contain values less than 50, and the nodes to the right contain values greater than 50. Such an organization simplifies a search.

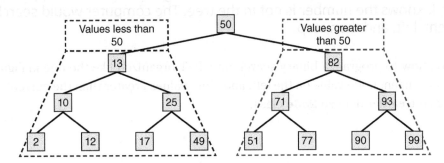

Figure 21-16   BST highlighting left and right choices

Remember that trees are recursive in design. This means that you can apply a recursive design to most algorithms that use a tree. For example, a search on a BST could be defined with the following algorithm:

Check the current node, and if it is equal to the search value, return a message indicating that you have found the search value.

If the search value is less than the current node's value and the current node has a left child, search the left child, and return the result.

If the search value is greater than the current node's value and the current node has a right child, search the right child, and return the result.

Otherwise, return a message indicating that you cannot find the search value.

You can use this algorithm to find a number in a tree. Suppose you want to find the number 17 in the BST shown in Figure 21-15. First look at the data stored in the root node, which contains 50. That number is not 17, so you need to keep looking. Because 17 is less than 50, follow the edge on the left to the node containing 13. Because 17 is greater than 13, follow the edge on the right to the node containing 25. Because 17 is less than 25, follow the node on the left to the node containing 17, the number you want to find.

Although 17 is in a leaf node in Figure 21-15, the number you are looking for can be in any node, including a leaf node. If you reach a leaf node without locating the search value, the tree does not include that number.

Q In Figure 21-15, which sequence of left and right decisions would you take to find the number 51?

A The path to find 51 starts at the root. The root does not contain 51, so the search continues. Taking paths right, left, and left leads to the node containing 51.

Q In Figure 21-15, which sequence of left and right decisions would you take to find the number 18?

A While you can tell at a glance that 18 is not in the tree, a computer would search for the value until it reaches a leaf node and cannot continue left or right. When the computer runs out of edges to follow, it knows the number is not in the tree. The computer would search the BST by going left, right, left, and then stop.

Figure 21-17 shows how to program a binary search on a BST organized like the one in Figure 21-15, with child values less than the current node value on the left, and child values greater than the current node value on the right. The code uses the earlier defined **Node** class.

```cpp
#include <iostream>
#include <string>

using namespace std;

void binary_search(Node* tree, int data)
{
    if (tree == NULL)
    {
        cout << "The item " << data << " IS NOT in the tree!" << endl;
    }
    else
    {
        if (tree->data == data)
        {
            cout << "The item " << data << " IS in the tree!" << endl;
        }
        else if (tree->data > data)
        {
            binary_search(tree->left, data);
        }
        else
        {
            binary_search(tree->right, data);
        }
    }
}

int main()
{
    // Build a tree
    Node* tree = new Node(5);

    // depth 1
    tree->left = new Node(2);
    tree->right = new Node(8);

    // depth 2
    tree->left->left = new Node(1);
    tree->left->right = new Node(3);
    tree->right->left = new Node(7);
    tree->right->right = new Node(10);

    binary_search(tree, 7);
    binary_search(tree, 3);
    binary_search(tree, 12);

    return 0;
}

OUTPUT:
The item 7 IS in the tree!
The item 3 IS in the tree!
The item 12 IS NOT in the tree!
```

Annotations:
- Refers to the Node class from Figure 21-10.
- If the current node to search doesn't exist, end the search.
- If the current node has data equal to what you are searching for, then you found the number.
- Otherwise, go left if the search data is less than the data in the current node, or go right.

Figure 21-17   Programming a binary search on a BST

The path to find the number 16 in the BST shown in Figure 21-16 and the path from the start to the exit in the maze are both instances of a single path in a tree. In contrast, a traversal must visit every node, not take a single path through the branches. A traversal requires some backtracking as each node includes multiple choices that need to be explored to make a complete traversal. All traversals start at the root node.

There are two common ways to traverse a tree. The first traversal is called a depth first (DF) traversal, which begins at the root and charges ahead with its decisions along a branch, backtracking only if it has nowhere else to go.

Figure 21-18 shows a simple binary tree where each node has a color and two edges, left and right.

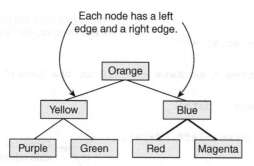

Figure 21-18   Binary tree with color values

A DF traversal explores the binary tree as follows:

1. The first node is the orange node. At this point you select a preference for decisions, such as continuing left before right.
2. The next node on the left contains yellow.
3. The next node on the left contains purple.
4. The traversal has nowhere to go, so it backs up to the previous node, which contains yellow.
5. One decision at the yellow node has not been traversed yet, so the traversal continues to the right node, which contains green.
6. The traversal has nowhere to go, so it backs up to yellow.
7. The yellow node offers no more choices, so the traversal backs up to orange.
8. The remaining decision is to continue to the right, so the traversal follows the path to blue.
9. The pattern continues to visit the red node, and then the magenta node. The final DF traversal order of colors is orange, yellow, purple, green, blue, red, and magenta.

In contrast to a DF traversal is a breadth first (BF) traversal. Instead of committing to a decision path and backtracking when all options are exhausted, a BF traversal visits each node at a level within the tree before moving on.

To use a BF traversal with the color tree in Figure 21-18, you again start at orange, and then visit yellow. Although a DF traversal visits the purple node next, a BF traversal visits the blue node next because the blue node is on the same level (or row) as the yellow node. The current level does not contain other nodes, so the BF traversal continues to the next row and visits purple, green, red, and then magenta. The final BF traversal is orange, yellow, blue, purple, green, red, and magenta.

Figure 21-19 uses the earlier defined `Node` class to demonstrate both depth first and breadth first traversals. To program these two traversals, you need to use two linear data structures: a queue and a stack.

```cpp
#include <iostream>
#include <string>
#include <bits/stdc++.h>

using namespace std;

void depth_first_traversal(Node* tree)
{
    stack<Node*> node_stack;
    Node* item;

    node_stack.push(tree);

    while (!node_stack.empty())
    {
        item = node_stack.top();
        node_stack.pop();

        cout << item->data << " ";

        if (item->right != NULL)
        {
            node_stack.push(item->right);
        }
        if (item->left != NULL)
        {
            node_stack.push(item->left);
        }
    }

    cout << endl;
}

void breadth_first_traversal(Node* tree)
{
    queue<Node*> node_stack;
    Node* item;

    node_stack.push(tree);
```

Refers to the **Node** class from Figure 21-10.

Figure 21-19   Programming depth and breadth first traversals (*continued*)

```cpp
    while (!node_stack.empty())
    {
        item = node_stack.front();
        node_stack.pop();

        cout << item->data << " ";

        if (item->left != NULL)
        {
            node_stack.push(item->left);
        }
        if (item->right != NULL)
        {
            node_stack.push(item->right);
        }
    }

    cout << endl;
}


int main()
{
    // Build a tree
    Node* tree = new Node(5);

    // depth 1
    tree->left = new Node(2);
    tree->right = new Node(8);

    // depth 2
    tree->left->left = new Node(1);
    tree->left->right = new Node(3);
    tree->right->left = new Node(7);
    tree->right->right = new Node(10);

    depth_first_traversal(tree);
    breadth_first_traversal(tree);

    return 0;
}

OUTPUT:
5 2 1 3 8 7 10
5 2 8 1 3 7 10
```

Figure 21-19   Programming depth and breadth first traversals (*continued*)

Note how similar the code is for the two traversals. The logic for the traversals is mostly handled by the queue and stack data structures. The only difference between the two traversals is the node to visit next, which the queue and stack keep track of for you.

21.4 GRAPH STRUCTURES

Graph Basics (21.4.1, 21.4.2, 21.4.3)

Graphs are another variant of nonlinear abstract data structure. The difference between graphs and trees is that graphs have no enforced hierarchy. The nodes in a graph are connected to other nodes, but no one node is the start of the structure. Think of a map of your town, with blocks of buildings and the streets connecting them. When trying to figure out directions from one place to another, the starting and ending points are relative to your current location.

Figure 21-20 shows three graphs. Note that trees and graphs can look quite similar. Unlike trees, however, graphs have no root nodes, no limit on edges between nodes, no parent-child relationships, and possibly more than one path between nodes.

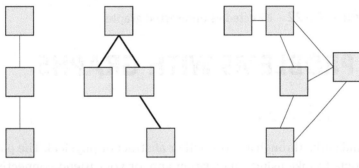

Figure 21-20   Basic graphs

Types of graphs include the following:

Sparse graph. A **sparse graph** does not contain many edges between the nodes.
Complete graph. In a **complete graph**, every node has an edge to every other node.
Connected graph. In a **connected graph**, all nodes are connected by at least one edge to a group of nodes.
Unconnected graph. An **unconnected graph** has islands of nodes not connected to the main group.

Figure 21-21 shows examples of each type of graph.

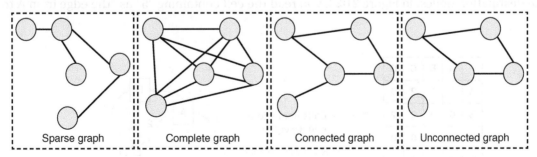

Figure 21-21   Types of graphs

Directed and Undirected Graphs (21.4.4)

Sometimes roads are one-way only, so that they must be traveled in only one direction. A **directed graph** has edges like one-way roads. A directed edge can link from Node A to Node B, but not from Node B to Node A. An **undirected graph** does not restrict the direction of any edge. **Figure 21-22** shows directed and undirected graphs, with arrows indicating a directed edge.

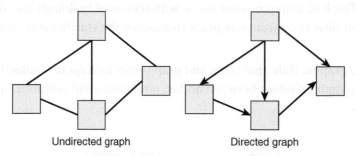

Undirected graph   Directed graph

Figure 21-22   Directed vs undirected graphs

21.5 SOLVING PROBLEMS WITH GRAPHS

Graph Applications (21.5.1, 21.5.2)

Graphs are typically used to find paths through an area, either abstract or physical. The paths could be the way to find the exit to a maze, a route to take using a navigation app, or your friend connective network on social media. This connective network used by most social media sites can also be called a network model.

In graphs, edges can include weights. These **edge weights** can represent many things, but typically are related to the "cost" to take that edge. In a driving map, for example, the edge weights are the physical distances in miles.

Representing graphs in code is tricky, as graph nodes have an unknown number of edges. Instead of representing the graph as a series of edges attached to nodes, you can use an **adjacency matrix**. This matrix is a two-dimensional grid, with a row and column for each node. The value at the intersection of two nodes represents the edge weight.

Figure 21-23 shows an adjacency matrix. If a node has no edge, then it has an edge weight of 0. Otherwise, the matrix contains a positive number. The labels in the left column are the starting nodes, and the labels in the top row are the destination nodes. In Figure 21-23, you read the cell containing "5" as "the edge from A to B has a weight of 5."

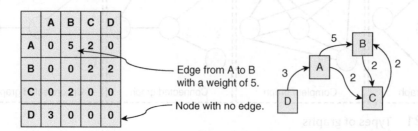

Figure 21-23   Adjacency matrix and graph it represents

Q Does the adjacency matrix in Figure 21-23 describe a directed graph or an undirected graph? How can you tell?

A The matrix includes an edge from A to B, but not from B to A, creating a one-way path. Therefore, the matrix describes a directed graph. An undirected graph would not have any one-way paths.

Computing Paths (21.5.3, 21.5.4, 21.5.5)

When driving somewhere or exploring a maze, you typically want the shortest path to the destination. In a graph, you find the shortest path by adding the edge weights of the nodes. The minimum sum of edges is the shortest path.

Figure 21-24 shows a maze and its graph. You can find the exit easily by looking at the graph, but a computer can't. A computer has to compare nodes and paths one by one.

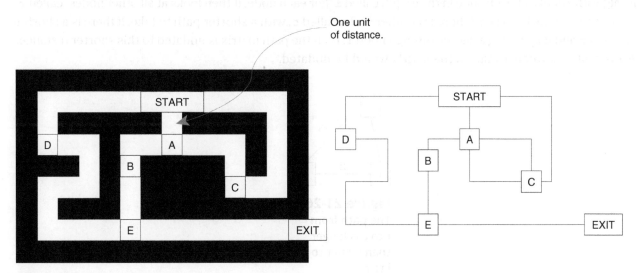

Figure 21-24   Maze and its graph

To have a computer solve the maze and find the exit, you need to convert the maze into an adjacency matrix. The size of the square containing a letter represents 1 unit of distance. For example, the distance between START and A is 2, as it takes two squares to arrive at A. **Figure 21-25** shows the adjacency matrix for the maze in Figure 21-24.

	START	A	B	C	D	E	EXIT
START	0	2	0	11	7	0	0
A	2	0	3	5	0	0	0
B	0	3	0	0	0	3	0
C	11	5	0	0	0	0	0
D	7	0	0	0	0	12	0
E	0	0	3	0	12	0	8
EXIT	0	0	0	0	0	8	0

Figure 21-25   Adjacency matrix for the maze

Q Does the adjacency matrix in Figure 21-25 describe a directed graph or an undirected graph?

A The matrix does not indicate any one-way paths, so it describes an undirected graph.

To calculate the shortest path from a starting point to a destination, you can use an algorithm called **Floyd's Algorithm**. It calculates the shortest distance between two nodes and the shortest distance between all nodes in the graph. Given an adjacency matrix like the one in Figure 21-25, Floyd's Algorithm creates a new matrix where the values are the shortest distance between two nodes, not just edges. The outline for Floyd's Algorithm is as follows:

```
for each node index i
    for each node index r
        for each node index c
            A[r][c] = min(A[r][c], A[r][i] + A[i][c])
```

The algorithm looks at each node in the graph, called i. For each node, it then looks at all other nodes, called r. For each node r, it checks to see if there is another node, called c, with a shorter path to take. If there is a shorter path between r and c by taking a detour through node i, then the path matrix is updated to this shorter distance. **Figure 21-26** shows when a value in the matrix would be updated.

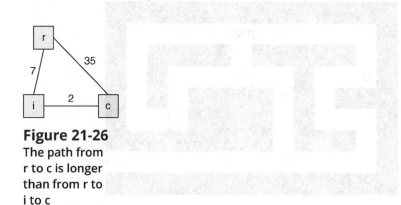

Figure 21-26
The path from
r to c is longer
than from r to
i to c

Figure 21-27 shows a program for applying Floyd's Algorithm. To interpret the results, consider that each entry in the matrix now has the shortest possible path between the two nodes. For example, the output in Figure 21-27 shows first the adjacency matrix and then Floyd's results. If you look at the row labeled **START** and read across to the column labeled **EXIT**, the shortest path out of the maze takes 16 steps.

```
#include <iostream>

#include <iomanip> // Allows you to specify the width of cout with setw

using namespace std;



void print_matrix(int matrix[7][7], string nodes[7])
```

Figure 21-27   Program to apply Floyd's Algorithm (*continued*)

```
{
    // Uses setw to specify the number of characters to pad out the printed values
    //  setw(10) means "make sure this is 10 characters long, use spaces before it
to ensure"
    cout << setw(10) << " |";
    for (int r = 0; r < 7; r++)
    {
        cout << setw(6) << nodes[r] << " |";
    }

    cout << endl;

    for (int r = 0; r < 70; r++)
    {
        cout << "-";
    }

    cout << endl;

    for (int r = 0; r < 7; r++)
    {
        cout << setw(8) << nodes[r] << " |";
        for (int c = 0; c < 7; c++)
        {
            cout << setw(6) << matrix[r][c] << " |";
        }

        cout << endl;
    }
}

void floyds(int matrix[7][7])
```

Figure 21-27 Program to apply Floyd's Algorithm (*continued*)

```cpp
{
    for (int i = 0; i < 7; i++)
    {
        for (int r = 0; r < 7; r++)
        {
            for (int c = 0; c < 7; c++)
            {
                // Check to see if there is an edge between ri, ic, and we are not
                // comparing a node to itself
                if (r != c and matrix[r][i] != 0 and matrix[i][c] != 0)
                {
                    // If the value is zero then we can update it regardless
                    if (matrix[r][c] == 0)
                    {
                        matrix[r][c] = matrix[r][i] + matrix[i][c];

                    }
                    // Else update to the minimum
                    else
                    {
                        matrix[r][c] = min(matrix[r][c], matrix[r][i] + matrix[i][c]);
                    }
                }
            }
        }
    }

}

int main()
{

    string nodes[] = {"START", "A", "B", "C", "D", "E", "EXIT"};
```

Figure 21-27   Program to apply Floyd's Algorithm (*continued*)

```
int matrix[7][7] = {{0,2,0,11,7,0,0},
                    {2,0,3,5,0,0,0},
                    {0,3,0,0,0,3,0},
                    {11,5,0,0,0,0,0},
                    {7,0,0,0,0,12,0},
                    {0,0,3,0,12,0,8},
                    {0,0,0,0,0,8,0}};


    print_matrix(matrix, nodes);

    floyds(matrix);


    cout << endl << endl<<"Floyd's:" << endl << endl;


    print_matrix(matrix, nodes);

}
```

OUTPUT:

	START	A	B	C	D	E	EXIT
START	0	2	0	11	7	0	0
A	2	0	3	5	0	0	0
B	0	3	0	0	0	3	0
C	11	5	0	0	0	0	0
D	7	0	0	0	0	12	0
E	0	0	3	0	12	0	8
EXIT	0	0	0	0	0	8	0

Floyd's:

	START	A	B	C	D	E	EXIT
START	0	2	5	7	7	8	16
A	2	0	3	5	9	6	14
B	5	3	0	8	12	3	11
C	7	5	8	0	14	11	19
D	7	9	12	14	0	12	20
E	8	6	3	11	12	0	8
EXIT	16	14	11	19	20	8	0

Figure 21-27   Program to apply Floyd's Algorithm (*continued*)

SUMMARY

- Use a nonlinear data structure for data arranged as a hierarchy or web with one or more connections between data elements.
- In a nonlinear data structure, each node can have one or more connections, called edges.
- A tree is a hierarchical nonlinear data structure with a starting point and nodes where each node is connected by an edge to another node. A tree is hierarchical because it establishes parent–child relationships between nodes. The root node at the top of the tree has no parent node, and the leaf nodes at the bottom of the tree have no children.
- A tree's shape is described by the size, height, and width of the tree. You describe the location of a node by its depth into the tree.
- Trees are recursive structures because every node in a tree is also arranged as a tree, creating a subtree.
- A binary tree has no more than two children per node. A tree that translates Morse code is a binary tree. You use a binary search tree (BST) to search for a specific value. Each node in a BST contains one piece of searchable information.
- The route from the start to the exit in a maze is a single path in a tree. A traversal, on the other hand, visits every node in the tree, starting from the root node. A depth first (DF) traversal begins searching at the root and continues along a branch, backtracking after it reaches a leaf node. A breadth first (BF) traversal visits each node at a level (or row) within the tree before continuing to the next level.
- Graphs are nonlinear data structures similar to trees, but do not arrange nodes in a hierarchy. In addition, graphs have no root nodes and allow more than one path between nodes.
- Graphs can be directed or undirected. A directed graph has edges like one-way roads, where an edge links Node A to Node B, but does not link Node B to Node A. An undirected graph does not restrict the direction of its edges.
- Graphs are typically used to find paths through an abstract or physical area, such as a city or maze. Edges in a graph can include weights that might indicate the cost to take that edge. In a driving map, for example, the edge weights are the distances between locations.
- An adjacency matrix represents a graph as a grid instead of a series of edges attached to nodes. The matrix includes a row and column for each node, and the value at the intersection of two nodes indicates the edge weight.
- To calculate the shortest path from a starting point to a destination, you can use Floyd's Algorithm.

Key Terms

adjacency matrix	directed graph	shortest path
binary search tree (BST)	edge weights	sparse graph
Binary trees	edges	traversal
breadth first (BF) traversal	Floyd's Algorithm	tree
child	Graphs	unconnected graph
complete graph	leaf nodes	undirected graph
connected graph	parent	
depth first (DF) traversal	root	

ALGORITHM COMPLEXITY AND BIG-O NOTATION

LEARNING OBJECTIVES

22.1 BIG-O NOTATION

22.1.1 Explain why programmers are interested in algorithm performance.

22.1.2 Name two factors that affect algorithm efficiency.

22.1.3 Differentiate runtime from time complexity.

22.1.4 Identify asymptotic analysis as a way to evaluate the performance of an algorithm as the size of its input grows.

22.1.5 Identify the three asymptotic notations that apply to algorithm performance.

22.2 TIME COMPLEXITY

22.2.1 State the purpose of Big-O notation.

22.2.2 State that Big-O is expressed based on the size of the input "n."

22.2.3 Identify the general format for Big-O notation.

22.2.4 Identify the Big-O notation and graph for constant time and provide an example of an algorithm that has linear time complexity.

22.2.5 Identify the Big-O notation and graph for linear time and provide an example of an algorithm that runs in quadratic time.

22.2.6 Identify the Big-O notation and graph for quadratic time and provide an example of an algorithm that runs in logarithmic time.

22.2.7 Identify the Big-O notation and graph for logarithmic time.

22.2.8 Correctly identify that the order of efficiency is $O(C)$, $O(\log n)$, $O(n)$, $O(n^2)$.

22.3 SPACE COMPLEXITY

22.3.1 State that space complexity is the amount of memory space required by an algorithm to execute an algorithm.

22.3.2 Differentiate instruction space, data space, and auxiliary space.

22.3.3 State that the calculation for space complexity can be based on data space, auxiliary space, or both.

22.3.4 Identify algorithms that have constant space complexity.

22.3.5 Identify algorithms that have $O(n)$ space complexity.

22.3.6 Associate appending elements to an array as an algorithm that requires linear space complexity.

22.3.7 Identify an example of a loop that does not have $O(n)$ space complexity, but has $O(n)$ time complexity.

22.4 COMPLEXITY CALCULATIONS

22.4.1 Determine the Big-O time complexity for each line of a program.

22.4.2 Determine the time complexity of loops.

22.4.3 Combine Big-O terms.

22.4.4 Simplify Big-O terms.

22.4.5 Determine the overall Big-O for the code representing an algorithm.

22.1 BIG-O NOTATION

Algorithm Complexity (22.1.1, 22.1.2, 22.1.3)

A Big Mac (**Figure 22-1**) is a double-decker hamburger, the flagship product of a popular fast food restaurant chain. But what's a Big-O? It is not something to eat, but it does relate to computer programming.

apertursound/Shutterstock.com

Figure 22-1   Big Mac or Big-O?

Many programming problems can be solved with more than one algorithm. How do you know which algorithm is best?

For many programming problems, the best solution is the most efficient one. Programmers and computer scientists are interested in ways to make programs most efficient so that applications run quickly and use a minimal amount of system resources. But exactly what makes one algorithm more efficient than another? Let's find out.

Algorithm efficiency can be measured by time and by space.

- **Time complexity** refers to the amount of time required to run an algorithm as its data set grows. In general, algorithms that execute most quickly are most time efficient. Algorithms that require more time as the data set grows have more time complexity.
- **Space complexity** refers to the amount of memory required by an algorithm as its data set grows. Algorithms that require the least memory space are likely to be the most space efficient. Algorithms that require more space as the data set grows have more space complexity.

In computing, the concept of time is slippery. Time could refer to runtime—the number of microseconds required for an algorithm to complete execution. But runtime on what hardware platform and with what data set? Exactly what is included in runtime? File access time? Transmission time? Build time?

Q Why might runtime not be a good metric of program efficiency?

A Runtime is hardware dependent. It is not a good metric for efficiency because an algorithm might require more time to run on a cloud-based hardware platform than on a local hardware platform.

Asymptotic Analysis (22.1.4)

A set of metrics can be used as objective measures of an algorithm's time efficiency or space efficiency. **Asymptotic analysis** provides programmers with a way to evaluate the performance of an algorithm as the size of its data set grows.

Q Suppose you have two different algorithms for sorting data. One algorithm sorts 10 items in 10 ms, but takes 100 ms to sort 100 items. The other algorithm sorts the 10 items in 20 ms, but takes 40 ms to sort 100 items. Which algorithm is more efficient for large data sets?

A You can hypothesize that the second algorithm is much more efficient for large data sets. Although the first algorithm sorts a small amount of data quickly, processing time increases linearly as the data set grows. The second algorithm takes longer to sort 10 items, but less time to sort a larger data set.

Figure 22-2 shows graphs of these two algorithms. You can see that the time complexity of the first algorithm continues to increase as the data set grows. In contrast, the time complexity of the second algorithm levels off for larger data sets.

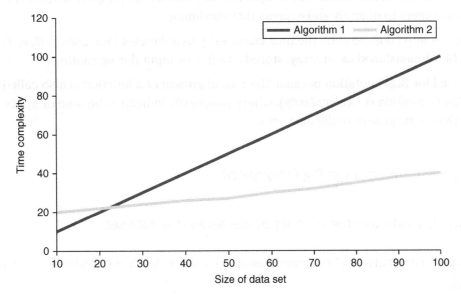

Figure 22-2 Time complexity varies for different algorithms and data set size

Asymptotic analysis reveals the efficiency of algorithms. You can use it to compare various algorithms before selecting the one to use.

Asymptotic Notation (22.1.5)

The performance of an algorithm can be expressed in **asymptotic notation**. Three of these notations are commonly applied to programming:

Big-O notation is used to express the worst-case time complexity or space complexity of an algorithm. Worst-case is sometimes referred to as upper bounds because it measures the maximum complexity of an algorithm.

Big-Omega notation (Big-Ω) is used to express the best-case time complexity or space complexity. Because an algorithm will never perform faster or take less space than its Big Omega, this metric delineates the lower bound.

Big-Theta notation (Big-θ) encompasses both the upper and lower bounds of an algorithm, a situation sometimes referred to as a tight bound.

Of these three notations, Big-O is most frequently used to measure the efficiency of algorithms. Familiarity with Big-O notation is not only useful for evaluating algorithms for your programs, it is also an important concept to have in hand for job interviews.

22.2 TIME COMPLEXITY

Big-O Metrics (22.2.1, 22.2.2, 22.2.3)

Programmers are primarily concerned with the worst-case scenarios for time and space complexity because it is important to know the maximum amount of time or space an algorithm might require when it is executed. Big-O notation allows programmers to quantify and express that maximum.

Big-O notation takes into consideration the time complexity as a data set increases in size. That data might be accessed from a file, dimensioned as an array, stored as a list, or input during runtime.

The letter O is used for Big-O notation because the rate of growth of a function is also called its *order*. The general format for Big-O notation is O(*complexity*), where *complexity* indicates the time or space requirements of an algorithm relative to the growth of the data set *n*.

Q What do you think *n* stands for in Big-O notation?

A In Big-O notation, *n* indicates the number of elements in a data set.

The following Big-O metrics are most commonly used to measure the time complexity of algorithms.

O(C) Constant time
O(*n*) Linear time
O(*n*²) Quadratic time
O(log *n*) Logarithmic time

Let's take a quick look at each of these metrics and the kinds of algorithms to which they apply.

Constant Time (22.2.4)

Suppose you have a list of fast food restaurants sorted in order by the date they were first established. The first element in the list is White Castle because it was established in 1921. You write a program to find the first element in this list.

Finding the first element in a list requires one line of code that specifies one operation: get the item at index [0].

```
first_item = fast_food_list[0]
```

It does not matter how many fast food restaurants are in the data set. There could be five or five million. The algorithm to find the first one will operate in the same amount of time. In Big-O notation, this type of algorithm executes in **constant time** because it does not change as the data set becomes larger.

A line plot with the number of data elements on the x-axis and the number of operations on the y-axis is a flat line for constant time, as shown in **Figure 22-3**.

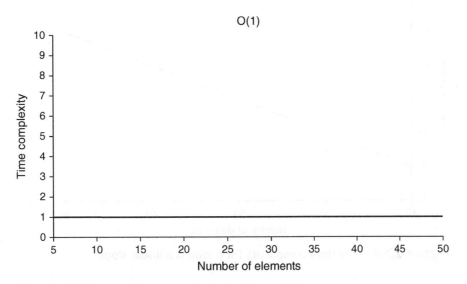

Figure 22-3   The graph of constant time is a flat line

The Big-O notation for constant time is O(C), where C is the number of operations required to complete the algorithm.

Q Finding the first element in a list requires only one operation in constant time. What is the Big-O notation for this operation?

A For finding the first element in a list, the time complexity is a single operation, so the Big-O notation would be O(1).

Linear Time (22.2.5)

What about an algorithm to find any specific fast food restaurant that is in the list? Is Jollibee in the list of fast food restaurants? To search the list, you need to loop through the list to examine each item.

```
assign i = 0
while not end of list
```

```
if fast_food_list[i] = "Jollibee" then

output "Found it!"

break

    else

        i = i + 1
```

The worst case for this search would be when Jollibee is the last item in the list. If it is the last item in a list of 10 fast food restaurants, the algorithm requires 10 loops. If the list contains 50 fast food restaurants, the algorithm requires 50 loops. As the data set of items in the list grows, the time complexity increases at a linear rate shown in **Figure 22-4**.

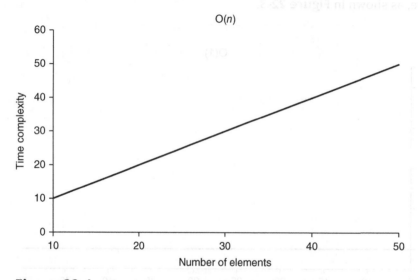

Figure 22-4   The time complexity for a loop is a linear slope

This type of time complexity is referred to as **linear time**. It relates directly to the number of items in a data set. If the number of items is n, then the time complexity is expressed in Big-O notation as $O(n)$.

Q Which is more efficient, constant time or linear time?

A Algorithms of linear complexity are less efficient than algorithms that run in constant time. $O(n)$ algorithms require more and more processing time as the size of the data set increases.

Algorithms based on iterative structures, such as finding an item in an unsorted list, typically have linear time complexity. Inserting, deleting, and searching array elements, searching a stack or linked list, and hash table operations are also typical examples of algorithms with linear complexity.

Quadratic Time (22.2.6)

White Castle is the first item in the list of fast food restaurants because it was the first one established. To sort the list in alphabetical order, you can use an insertion sort based on nested loops.

In the worst-case scenario, both loops execute for all of the items in the list. If the list contains five items, the outer loop executes five times and each of those iterations executes five times. That's 5^2, or 25, iterations. If the list contains 50 fast food restaurants, the time complexity is 50^2, or 2500 iterations. Wow! Increasing the number of items in the list significantly increases the time complexity of the insertion sort, as shown in **Figure 22-5**.

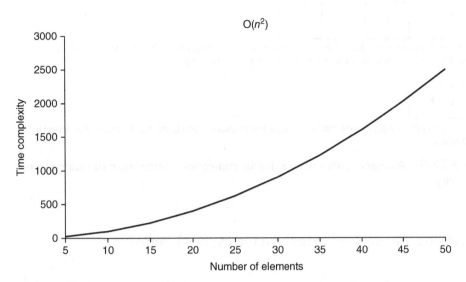

Figure 22-5   The time complexity for a nested loop increases more sharply as the data set grows

This type of time complexity is referred to as quadratic time. It increases more sharply than linear time complexity as the data set grows. Because the number of iterations is n^2, quadratic complexity in Big-O notation is expressed as $O(n^2)$.

Simple sorting algorithms, such as quick sort, bubble sort, selection sort, and insertion sort, have quadratic time complexity. They are best avoided when working with large data sets. You can use alternative, more efficient, sorting algorithms in your programs.

Q Suppose you have a program that searches through a data set one element at time and another program that uses an insertion sort to put the elements in alphabetical order. Which program has the better time efficiency?

A The search has $O(n)$ complexity. The sort has $O(n^2)$ efficiency. That means the search is more efficient.

Logarithmic Time (22.2.7, 22.2.8)

Computer scientists and programmers are always looking for clever algorithms that divide and conquer. Using a binary search to find items in a sorted list is an example of this divide-and-conquer strategy.

Suppose you have a list of 11 fast food restaurants sorted alphabetically. We'll simplify this list as [A, B, C, D, E, F, G, H, I, J, K]. A binary search locates the middle item in the list and checks to see if it is the target. If not, half of the list is discarded based on whether the target is greater than or less than the middle item. This process of discarding half the list continues until the target is found. See **Figure 22-6**.

A	B	C	D	E	F	G	H	I	J	K

1. To check if J is in the list, look at the midpoint. If the midpoint is not what you're looking for and it is less than the target value, throw out half the list that is less than or equal to the midpoint.

G	H	I	J	K

2. Check the midpoint in the sublist. If that midpoint is not the target and it is less than the target value, discard half of the sublist that is less than or equal to the target.

J	K

3. With only two elements left, use the first one as the midpoint. That is the target value. You found it in three steps.

Figure 22-6   A binary search uses a divide-and-conquer algorithm to reduce time complexity

 How many iterations are required to find J in the list of 11 items?

A Three iterations are required. The first uses F as the midpoint in the whole list. The second uses I as the midpoint in the sublist. The third uses J as the midpoint of the last half of the sublist. J is found in the third iteration.

In a binary search, the iterations do not grow dramatically with the size of the list because with each iteration, half of the list is eliminated. **Figure 22-7** illustrates this growth pattern that decreases in slope as the data set grows.

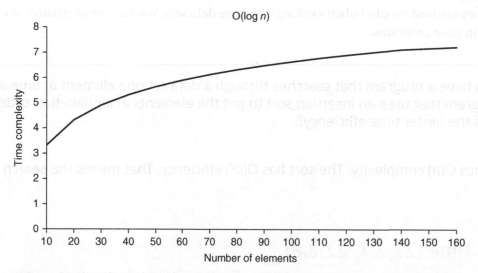

Figure 22-7   The graph of logarithmic time decreases in slope as the number of data elements increases

At most, four iterations are required for a binary search to find an item in a 10-item list. A maximum of five iterations are required for a 20-item list; seven iterations for a 100-item list. This trend is characteristic of logarithms.

A logarithm is the opposite of exponentiation. Whereas an exponent multiplies, a logarithm divides. Binary searches and operations on binary trees run in logarithmic time characterized by the ratio of operations decreasing as the size of the data set grows.

Because the number of iterations is log n, logarithmic time in Big-O notation is expressed as $O(\log n)$. Logarithmic time is considered to be more efficient than either linear or quadratic time. Algorithms that run in logarithmic time are your buddies.

22.3 SPACE COMPLEXITY

Memory Space (22.3.1, 22.3.2, 22.3.3)

As a programmer, you should be aware of the memory requirements for the programs that you code. Today's computers have lots of memory, but may be called upon to process huge data sets. Using asymptotic analysis to get a handle on the space complexity of your algorithms can help you understand memory requirements as your programs scale up to large data sets.

Computer programs require three types of memory space to hold instructions and data.

Instruction space is the memory used to store the code for a program. When a program runs, memory space is used to store the compiled version of a program, its bitcode, or the source code that will be processed by an interpreter. Writing efficient code can reduce the amount of instruction space required to execute an algorithm.

Instruction space is not affected by the size of the data set. For example, the set of instructions to sort a list doesn't change if the list contains 10 items or 10,000 items. Because time complexity metrics are tied to the size of the data set, the size of the instruction set does not play a role in determining space complexity.

Data space is the memory required to hold data that is accessed by a program, input to a program, or generated by the program. As that data grows, more memory is required. Suppose you write a program to generate random numbers and store them in an array. When that program generates 50 random numbers, it requires more data space than when it generates 10 random numbers.

Data space is a significant factor in space complexity because memory usage corresponds to the size of the data sets you expect a program to process.

Auxiliary space is the memory required to temporarily hold variables and data as a program runs. This space may be allocated to hold temporary variables or arrays.

Space complexity can be measured in terms of the data space, the auxiliary space, or a combination of both. For sorting algorithms, for example, it is customary to measure only the auxiliary space because it is assumed that the data being sorted will consume n amount of space where n is the number of items to be sorted.

Q Why isn't the instruction space for a sort included in the complexity calculation?

A Because the set of program instructions does not change as the size of the data set changes.

Programs typically exhibit two types of space complexity:

$O(1)$ Constant space
$O(n)$ Linear space

Constant Space Complexity (22.3.4)

Algorithms with **constant space complexity** require the same amount of memory regardless of the size of the data space. A bubble sort is an example of an algorithm that uses constant space.

To code a bubble sort, begin by comparing the first two elements. If the first element is larger than the second element, put the first element in a temporary variable, move the second element into the first position, and then move the value in the temporary variable to the second position, as shown in **Figure 22-8**.

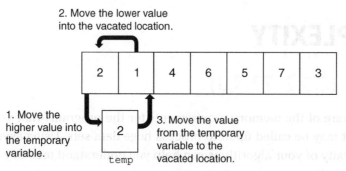

2. Move the lower value into the vacated location.

| 2 | 1 | 4 | 6 | 5 | 7 | 3 |

1. Move the higher value into the temporary variable.

2
temp

3. Move the value from the temporary variable to the vacated location.

If a pair of numbers is out of order, switch them by rotating through a temporary variable.

Figure 22-8   A bubble sort uses one temporary memory location regardless of the number of elements in a data set, so the space complexity is constant O(1)

The bubble sort continues to compare pairs of elements and swap them as necessary. After several passes, the elements are sorted. This algorithm requires only one temporary variable for the sort, regardless of how many elements are to be sorted. Because the auxiliary space requirements do not change as the data set grows, the algorithm runs in constant space, O(1).

Bubble sorts, heap sorts, insertion sorts, selection sorts, and shell sorts all operate in constant space. These algorithms are sometimes referred to as *in-place sorts* because they essentially overwrite the data in the original array, rather than creating a new array to hold the sorted data.

Linear Space Complexity (22.3.5, 22.3.6, 22.3.7)

Algorithms with **linear space complexity** require more space as the size of the data set grows. A brute force sorting algorithm is an example of linear space complexity. It uses two arrays: the original unsorted array and a new array to hold sorted elements.

To carry out the sort, your program looks through the unsorted array to find the smallest element and puts it in the first position of the new array. The program then looks through the unsorted list to find the next smallest element and puts it in the second position of the new array. This process repeats for every item in the unsorted array. See **Figure 22-9**.

Original array

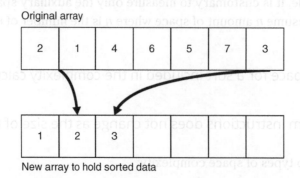

| 2 | 1 | 4 | 6 | 5 | 7 | 3 |

| 1 | 2 | 3 | | | | |

New array to hold sorted data

Figure 22-9   A brute force sort uses two arrays, so the space complexity O(*n*) increases as the data set grows

Because this code generates a second array of the same size as the unsorted list, the algorithm's space complexity is $O(n)$. The complexity increases as the size of the data set increases.

Merge sorts and tree sorts operate in linear space. They are less space efficient than in-place sorts, so they may not be suitable for large data sets.

Algorithms do not have to operate in the same time and space complexity. For example, a bubble sort has $O(1)$ space complexity, but $O(n)$ time complexity.

Q What are the space and time complexities for searching an array?

A The space complexity of searching an array is $O(1)$ because the search requires no additional memory space. The time complexity of the search is $O(n)$ because it depends on the number of elements in the array.

22.4 COMPLEXITY CALCULATIONS

Line-by-Line Time Complexity (22.4.1, 22.4.2)

Suppose that you have a list of numbers, such as 1, 2, 3, 4, 5 or 5, 4, 3, 2, 6, 3, 2, 9, 2. The list could be any length. You've devised the following algorithm that looks through the list to count the number of 3s it contains:

```
initialize total = 0

    for element in the_list:

        if element = 3 then

            total = total + 1

    next
```

Q What do you think is the time complexity of this algorithm?

A It is linear time, $O(n)$. Let's find out why.

The first line of the program is an assignment statement. Within the processor, this statement requires a single step that takes place in constant time. So far, the algorithm has a time complexity of $O(1)$.

```
initialize total = 0      O(1)
```

The for-next loop requires the processor to look at each element in the list to check if it is a 3:

```
for element in the_list:

        if element = 3 then
```

The process of checking one list element to determine if it is 3 is a constant time operation, but this operation takes place for every element in the list. You don't know the size of the list because this general algorithm could be used for any list of numbers. You can use n to represent the number of items in the list.

The time complexity of stepping through the list to check each number is O(n)—one step for each item in the list. Including the O(1) time complexity for the initialization step of the algorithm, your time complexity so far is O(1 + n).

```
initialize total = 0                        O(1)

    for element in the_list:

        if element = 3 then                 O(n)

                                   Total: O(1 + n)
```

Incrementing the total with **total = total + 1** also takes place within the loop. Potentially, every element in the list could be 3. Therefore, this operation also depends on the number of items in the list. You can add this to the list of time complexities as another n.

```
initialize total = 0                        O(1)

    for element in the_list:

        if element = 3 then                 O(n)

            total = total + 1               O(n)

next

                                 Total: O(1 + n + n)
```

So far, the complexity is 1 + n + n, based on the initial assignment statement and the two statements within the loop. Mathematically, this is the same as 1 + 2n.

Q How would you express this in Big-O notation?

A: It is O(1 + 2n).

Combine and Simplify (22.4.3, 22.4.4)

Now things get interesting. Although you have calculated the number of steps for the algorithm, Big-O time complexity is only focused on the upper bounds of a program's runtime. You can simplify O(1 + 2n).

The limiting factor is not the constant operation, so you can simply eliminate the 1. You can also eliminate the 2 from the 2n notation. Why? Because 2n and n are both linear functions. They indicate the same *type* of growth, even if the *rate* of growth is different. As the number of elements in the list increases, the rate of growth is the same for n as for 2n. **Figure 22-10** illustrates this somewhat nonintuitive concept.

For the purposes of Big-O notation, O(2n) is the same as O(n). As a result, the algorithm for counting the number of 3s in a list is bounded by linear time complexity, which you can express in Big-O notation as O(n).

To summarize, when you want to determine the time complexity of an algorithm, do the following:

1. List the complexity for each line of code.
2. Mathematically combine terms.
3. Select the most time complex term, as O(C), O(log n), O(n), or O(n²).

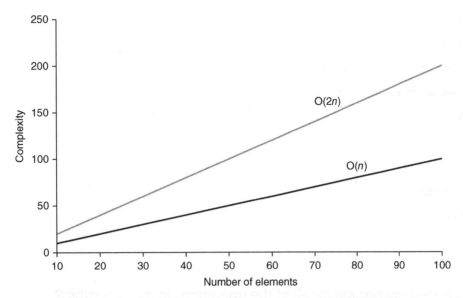

Figure 22-10   Algorithms with O(*n*) and O(*2n*) time complexities both increase linearly

A Mystery Algorithm (22.4.5)

Let's take a look at one more example to make sure that you've got the hang of these Big-O calculations.

Suppose that once again, you have a list called **the_list**, which could be any length. Here is a mystery algorithm designed to process the list. The algorithm is a mystery, because its purpose doesn't matter. You're only concerned with its time complexity.

```
initialize a = 5
initialize total = 0
    for i in the_list:
        for j in the_list:
            print(i)
            print(j)
        next
    for k in the_list:
        total = total + 1
    next
```

Q Take a moment to jot down the time complexity for each operation of the mystery function. What is the extended expression for all of the operations in this algorithm?

A Your initial list of operations should look something like the following.

```
initialize a = 5                    1
initialize total = 0                1
    for i in the_list:              n
        for j in the_list:          2n
            print(i)
            print(j)
        next
    for k in the_list:              n
        total = total + 1
next
```

Q What is the expanded expression for all of the operations in this algorithm?

A It is $2 + n * 2n + n$.
The 2 is derived from the first two assignment statements.
n is derived from the "i" loop.
$2n$ is derived from the "j" loop's two print statements.
The final n is derived from the addition operation within the "k" loop.

You might wonder where the multiplication comes from. Notice the nested for-next loops. The outside for-next loop begins with the first number in the list, but then the inner for-next loop steps through each element in the list. If the list contains four elements, the two loops will not execute $4 + 4$ times. They will execute 4×4 times. Aha! That is the source of the multiplication.

Now, simplify the expression. $2 + n * 2n + n$ simplifies to $2 + 2n^2 + n$.

Q What is the result when you eliminate the constants?

A It is $n^2 + n$.

Now, all you have to do is choose the term that represents the fastest growing time complexity and convert it into Big-O notation. Of n^2 and n, n^2 is the fastest growing time complexity. In Big-O notation, the time complexity for the mystery algorithm is $O(n^2)$.

To recap, you can figure the time complexity of a function by listing the operations required for each line of code. You can mathematically combine the terms and eliminate any coefficients. Finally, select the most time complex term as the boundary to use in the Big-O expression.

SUMMARY

- Time complexity refers to the amount of time required to execute an algorithm as its data set grows. In general, algorithms that execute most quickly are most time efficient. Algorithms that require more time as the data set grows have more time complexity.

- Space complexity refers to the amount of memory required by an algorithm as its data set grows. Algorithms that require the least memory space are likely to be the most space efficient. Algorithms that require more space as the data set grows have more space complexity.

- A set of metrics can be used as objective measures of an algorithm's time efficiency or space efficiency. Asymptotic analysis provides programmers with a way to evaluate the performance of an algorithm as the size of its data set grows.

- Asymptotic notations include Big-O, Big-Omega, and Big-Theta. Of these three notations, Big-O is most frequently used to measure the efficiency of algorithms.

- Big-O notation is used to express the worst-case time complexity or space complexity of an algorithm. Worst-case is sometimes referred to as upper bounds because it measures the maximum complexity of an algorithm.

- The efficiency of algorithms that execute in constant time do not change as the data set becomes larger. The Big-O notation for constant time is $O(C)$.

- Algorithms that increase linearly as the data set becomes larger execute in linear time, expressed as $O(n)$. Algorithms of linear complexity, such as those containing a loop, are less efficient than algorithms that run in constant time.

- Algorithms, such as those containing nested loops, that require multiple passes through a data set execute in quadratic time, expressed as $O(n^2)$.

- Divide-and-conquer algorithms, such as a binary search, execute in logarithmic time, expressed as $O(\log n)$.

- Space complexity may measure data space, auxiliary space, or both and is typically either $O(C)$ or $O(n)$. Computer scientists typically use space complexity when evaluating the efficiency of sorting algorithms.

- To determine the complexity of an algorithm, you can perform a line-by-line asymptotic analysis by listing the complexity for each line of code, mathematically combining terms, and selecting the most complex term.

Key Terms

Asymptotic analysis	constant time	$O(\log n)$
asymptotic notation	Data space	$O(n)$
Auxiliary space	Instruction space	$O(n^2)$
Big-O notation	linear space complexity	quadratic time
Big-Omega notation	linear time	Space complexity
Big-Theta notation	logarithmic time	Time complexity
constant space complexity	$O(C)$	

SEARCH ALGORITHMS

LEARNING OBJECTIVES:

23.1 USING SEARCH ALGORITHMS

23.1.1 State the purpose of a search algorithm.

23.1.2 Define the term "search space."

23.2 PERFORMING A LINEAR SEARCH

23.2.1 Identify the algorithm for a linear search.

23.2.2 Identify data structures that can be searched linearly.

23.2.3 State the time complexities of a linear search.

23.2.4 Explain why linear search is rarely used.

23.3 PERFORMING A BINARY SEARCH

23.3.1 Categorize binary search with the computational thinking concept of divide and conquer.

23.3.2 Identify the characteristics of data structures that support a binary search.

23.3.3 List examples of databases that have the characteristics required for a binary search.

23.3.4 Distinguish between the iterative and recursive algorithms for the binary search of an array.

23.3.5 Identify the following in a binary search algorithm: min index, max index, middle index.

23.3.6 Analyze what happens if the search space contains more than one target value.

23.3.7 State the time and space complexities for a binary search.

23.4 USING REGULAR EXPRESSIONS IN SEARCH ALGORITHMS

23.4.1 Define a regular expression as a sequence of characters that define a search pattern.

23.4.2 Associate "regex," "re," and "regexp" with the term regular expression.

23.4.3 Identify algorithms that use regular expressions.

23.4.4 Match regex metacharacters to their operations.

23.4.5 Analyze regular expressions that use [], *, ?, |, !, and +.

23.1 USING SEARCH ALGORITHMS

Search Basics (23.1.1, 23.1.2)

Computers can store large amounts of information represented as text, images, spreadsheets, music, and many other formats. All of this information exists as a collection of ones and zeros in your system's memory, which can hold terabytes of data. To make this information useful to you, the computer must be able to search for and retrieve the information you need. Special algorithms called search algorithms find a specific piece of information within a large set of data as efficiently as possible. Search algorithms are typically evaluated based on how fast they return the desired result.

You can think of searching for information on a computer as similar to searching for a contact in a phone book. The contact information is sorted alphabetically to help you to find a phone number faster. For example, imagine that your cell phone lists contacts in random order, as in **Figure 23-1**.

Figure 23-1   Contacts in a cell phone

To find a specific contact name such as Sandra Taylor in a random list, you would need to look through the list of contact names. If you have a short list of contacts in your phone, then looking for Sandra Taylor is easy. However, as you add more contacts to the list, the task gets more difficult because the search space, or the amount of data you are searching, gets larger.

23.2 PERFORMING A LINEAR SEARCH

Looking for a Needle in a Haystack (23.2.1, 23.2.2)

Sometimes, searching for data seems like you are looking for a needle in a haystack. The search space contains a huge amount of information and you need to find the one value that you need. Consider the unordered list of contacts shown in **Figure 23-2**.

| Riah Justice | George Castile | Amauhd McClain | Sandra Taylor | Floyd Garner | Elijah Arbery | Pamela Sterling | Breonna Bland |

Sapann Design/ Shutterstock.com

Figure 23-2   Unordered contact list

Suppose you need to call Sandra Taylor but you have no idea where her name is located within your unordered list of contacts. Your first instinct might be to scroll through the entire list, looking at each name one at a time to find Sandra Taylor. This type of search algorithm is called linear search, where you look at each item in a list one by one to find what you are looking for. Linear search is the simplest search algorithm when the information you are searching is in a random order.

You typically use a linear search algorithm when your data is stored in an array or a list. Generally, linear search can be used for any contiguous data structure. When coding a linear search algorithm, a loop is often used. Following is the algorithm for linear search:

Specify a cursor variable to start searching at the beginning of the search space.
Inspect the current element at the cursor and determine if it is the value you are looking for.
If the current element is the item that you are looking for, return the index of the item, the item itself, or the value **true** and end the search.

Otherwise, do the following:

Iterate to the next element and begin the inspection process again.
If you have reached the end of the search space, end the search.
Return a sentinel value to indicate that the search has terminated without finding the element.

In coding, a sentinel value (or flag value) is a special value used to indicate that a search should end. The sentinel should not be a valid value that you'd expect to find within the search space. For example, -1 is an appropriate sentinel value to put at the end of a list of positive integers to show that the end of the list has been reached. Within objects, you can create sentinel values by manipulating the values of the data members.

Figure 23-3 illustrates the code for the **linear_search()** method.

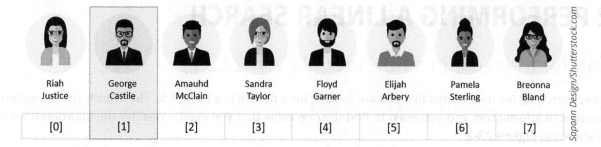

Riah Justice	George Castile	Amauhd McClain	Sandra Taylor	Floyd Garner	Elijah Arbery	Pamela Sterling	Breonna Bland
[0]	[1]	[2]	[3]	[4]	[5]	[6]	[7]

in ContactList.cpp

```cpp
class Contact
{
  public:
    Contact();
    Contact(string _first_name, string _last_name, string _mobile_number);
    string get_first_name();
    string get_last_name();
    string get_mobile_number();
  private:
    string first_name;
    string last_name;
    string mobile_number;
    string home_number;
    string work_number;
    string company;
    string address;
    string email;
};

#include <iostream>
#include <string>
using namespace std;

int main()
{
    Contact person_1("Riah", "Justice", "202-345-8643");
    Contact person_2("George", "Castile", "301-753-4543");
    Contact person_3("Amauhd", "McClain", "240-243-6532");
    Contact person_4("Sandra", "Taylor", "443-567-9544");
    Contact person_5("Floyd", "Garner", "734-546-6950");
    Contact person_6("Elijah", "Arbery", "313-809-6352");
    Contact person_7("Pamela", "Sterling", "864-754-3227");
    Contact person_8("Breonna", "Bland", "352-429-4372");
```

Initialize some Contacts with data.

Figure 23-3 Code for linear search within an array of Contacts (*Continued*)

```
Contact contact_list[8];                    Declare an array of Contacts, representing the
                                            contact_list.

contact_list[0] = person_1;
contact_list[1] = person_2;
contact_list[2] = person_3;
contact_list[3] = person_4;
contact_list[4] = person_5;                 Put the Contacts, into the      Determine the length of
contact_list[5] = person_6;                 contact_list.                   the contact_list.
contact_list[6] = person_7;
contact_list[7] = person_8;

int length = sizeof(contact_list)/sizeof(contact_list[0]);

int found = linear_search(contact_list, length, "George", "Castile");

                                                            Call the linear_search()
                                                            method to find a specific contact.

if(found != -1)
{
   cout << "The value was located at index: " << found << endl;
}
else                                                        If the contact was
{                                                           found, print the index,
   cout << "The value was not found in the list" << endl;   otherwise print that it
}                                                           was not located.

return 0;
}

int linear_search(Contact list[], int length, string _first, string _last)
{
   for (int i = 0; i < length; i++)                 Loop through the list of Contacts.
   {
      if (list[i].get_first_name() == _first && list[i].get_last_name() == _last)
      {
         return i;
      }                                             If the first name and the last name match the
   }                                                first and last name passed in, return the index
   return -1;            Return -1 if you've reached of where the value was found.
}                        the end of the list and the
                         value was not found.


OUTPUT:
The value was located at index: 1
```

Figure 23-3   Code for linear search within an array of `Contacts`

Q How do I know if my search algorithms should return the index of the data I am searching for, the data itself, or `true`?

A The value that should be returned depends on the context and purpose of the search. If you need to know only the location of the information, return the index. If you need to manipulate the data, return the data item itself. If you just need to verify that the desired value is in the search space, it is appropriate to return the value `true`.

Evaluating Search Time (23.2.3, 23.2.4)

The linear search found the Sandra Taylor contact quickly because the name was near the beginning of the list. Suppose the contact you were looking for happened to be at the end of the list. A linear search would take longer because it examines everything within the search space before it can find the solution. If the item you're looking for is not in the search space, a linear search also examines every item before determining that the item cannot be found. As you may imagine, linear search is considered the slowest search method.

In the worst-case scenario, a linear search looks through an entire list before it can find the desired object. As the size of the list grows, search performance can decrease significantly because it takes longer to find the target data. For this reason, linear search is rarely used. You can use other strategies to reduce the time necessary to search for an item in a list.

23.3 PERFORMING A BINARY SEARCH

Shrinking the Search Space (23.3.1, 23.3.2, 23.3.3)

As the size of the search space increases, the amount of time that it takes to find a solution also increases. For example, an unordered list of contacts would take a long time to search one by one. Now, imagine that the list is sorted. Each contact is listed alphabetically by first name, as shown in **Figure 23-4**.

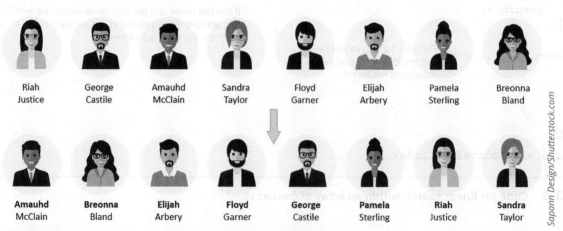

Figure 23-4   List of contacts in alphabetic order by first name

Sapann Design/Shutterstock.com

Suppose you want to find contact information for Breonna Bland. In an unordered search, you'd need to look through every contact until you reached Breonna's contact information at the end of the list. The search takes a long time because as the amount of information increases, you lose time examining many contacts until you find the one you want.

If your data is ordered, the search becomes easier. You can take advantage of the inherent ordering system for letters (A to Z) and for numbers (0 to 9). Suppose you are looking up the word "dog" in the dictionary. If you open the dictionary to a page with words that begin with the letter "m," then you know that the definition of dog is listed before this page. You do not need to look at any words that come after the letter "m" because you know the first letter in "dog" comes before "m." In essence, you have reduced the search space by 50 percent.

Search becomes easier when you can eliminate part of the search space. To take advantage of the ordering of data, you can use a binary search algorithm, which divides the search space in half until the target value is located. This approach is typically referred to as a divide-and-conquer technique because each step divides the search space and eliminates part of it on the path to a solution.

Any data structure that uses binary search must have the data in the search space in sorted order. Binary search algorithms do not work on unsorted data or data with duplicate values. An ordered collection of data, such as a dictionary, has the characteristics necessary for binary search. In general, any collection of data that consists of unique values that can be ordered is required for binary search. (For example, the dictionary does not list the same word twice.)

When coding a binary search algorithm, you use recursion or iteration. The algorithm for binary search is the following:

1. Specify a cursor variable called `min` to point to the first element in the search space.
2. Specify a cursor variable called `max` to point to the last element in the search space.
3. Specify a cursor variable called `current` to begin at the middle of the search space, the size of the array/2.
4. If the current element is the item that you are looking for, return the index of the item, the item itself, or the value `true` and end the search.
5. Otherwise, do the following:

   Determine if the target you are looking for comes before or after the current element.
   If the target comes before the current element:
   - Move `max` to the item before `current`.
   - Move `current` to the middle of the new array formed between `min` and `max`.
   - Start again at step 4 (recursively).

   If the target comes after the current element:
   - Move `min` to the item after `current`.
   - Move `current` to the middle of the new array formed between `min` and `max`.
   - Start again at step 4 (recursively).
6. If the `min` and `max` indexes cross each other (i.e., `min` is on the right, and `max` is on the left), then return −1 and end the search.

Implementing Binary Search (23.3.4, 23.3.5, 23.3.6, 23.3.7)

At the beginning of the binary search algorithm for finding Breonna Bland's contact information in a sorted list, `min` is set at index [0], `max` is index [7], and `current` is index [3], as shown in **Figure 23-5**.

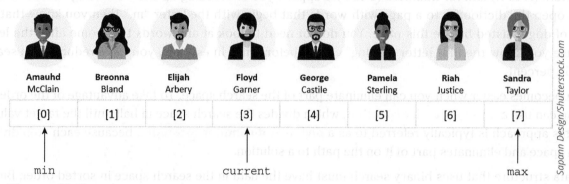

Figure 23-5   Binary search, stage 1

The `current` index is not pointing to Breonna Bland, so you update `max` to point to the index to the left of `current` (index [2]), and update `current` to point to the index between `min` and `max` (index [1]). Now `current` is pointing to index [1], which is the location of the target. See **Figure 23-6**.

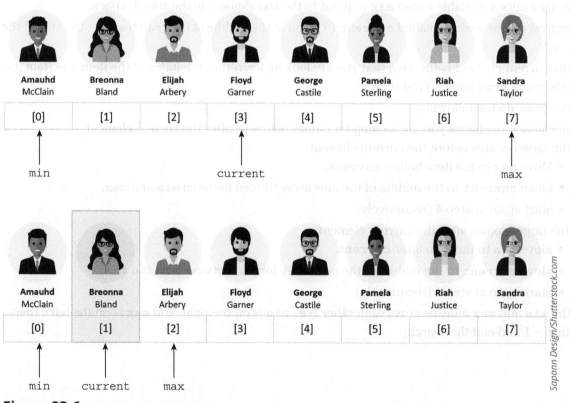

Figure 23-6   Binary search, stage 2

As you may have noticed, the binary search algorithm requires each value in the search space to be unique. What would happen if the search space contained duplicate values? Suppose index [2] held a contact identical to index [1] so that both contacts had the name Breonna Bland. The algorithm would still work the same and return index [1] as the result. Index [2] would be ignored as a possible solution. Depending on the context of your problem and the solution requirements, this behavior may be undesirable. For example, suppose you need to count the number of times a certain value appears within your ordered search space. Ignoring duplicates would be a problem in this case.

A binary search algorithm can be correctly implemented using recursion or iteration. Generally speaking, the recursive algorithm is simpler to code, but the iterative solution takes up less computer memory to use. This is because recursion adds multiple function calls to the call stack as it copies subsections of the data in each recursive call. Regardless, both algorithms can successfully return a solution. The code for implementing a binary search recursively is shown in **Figure 23-7**.

Sections of code from ContactList.cpp showing how to implement a binary search recursively.

```cpp
bool Contact::operator==(Contact c)
{
  if (first_name == c.get_first_name() && last_name == c.get_last_name())
  {
    return true;
  }
  return false;
}
```

```cpp
bool Contact::operator>(Contact c)
{
  if (first_name > c.get_first_name())
  {
    if(last_name > c.get_last_name())
    {
      return true;
    }
  }
  return false;
}
```

Figure 23-7   Recursive code for binary search (*Continued*)

```cpp
#include <iostream>
#include <string>
using namespace std;

int main()
{
    Contact person_1("Amauhd", "McClain", "240-243-6532");
    Contact person_2("Breonna", "Bland", "352-429-4372");
    Contact person_3("Elijah", "Arbery", "313-809-6352");
    Contact person_4("Floyd", "Garner", "734-546-6950");
    Contact person_5("George", "Castile", "301-753-4543");
    Contact person_6("Pamela", "Sterling", "864-754-3227");
    Contact person_7("Riah", "Justice", "202-345-8643");
    Contact person_8("Sandra", "Taylor", "443-567-9544");

    Contact contact_list[8];

    contact_list[0] = person_1;
    contact_list[1] = person_2;
    contact_list[2] = person_3;
    contact_list[3] = person_4;
    contact_list[4] = person_5;
    contact_list[5] = person_6;
    contact_list[6] = person_7;
    contact_list[7] = person_8;

    int length = sizeof(contact_list)/sizeof(contact_list[0]);

    int found = binary_search(contact_list, 0, length-1, person_2);

    if(found != -1)
    {
        cout << "The value was located at index: " << found << endl;
    }
    else
    {
        cout << "The value was not found in the list" << endl;
    }
    return 0;
}
```

Initialize some **Contacts** with data in alphabetical order by first name.

Declare an array of **Contacts**, representing the **contact_list**.

Put the **Contacts** into the **contact_list**.

Call **binary_search()** to find **person_2**.

If the contact was found, print the index; otherwise print that it was not located.

Figure 23-7   Recursive code for binary search (*Continued*)

```
int binary_search(Contact list[], int min, int max, Contact target)
{
    if (max >= min)                    ←————————— Continue only if max comes after or is the same as min.
    {
        int current = min + (max - min) / 2;  ←——— Calculate the middle index between min and max.

        cout << "Min is: " << min << endl;
        cout << "Max is: " << max << endl;        ←——— Output the index values.
        cout << "Current is: " << current << endl;

        if (list[current] == target)
        {                                   If the target is the element that current points to,
            return current;                 return the index.
        }

        else if (list[current] > target)          If the target is smaller
        {                                         than the current
            return binary_search(list, min, current - 1, target);  value, redo the binary
        }                                         search on the left half
                                                  of the contact list
        else                                      array.
        {                                         Else, if the target is
            return binary_search(list, current + 1, max, target);  larger than the
        }                                         current value, redo
    }                                             the binary search on
                                                  the right half of the
    return -1;     ←————————                      contact list array.
}                    Return −1 if you've
                     reached the end of
                     the list and the value
                     was not found.
```

```
OUTPUT:

Min is: 0
Max is: 7
Current is: 3
Min is: 0
Max is: 2
Current is: 1
The value was located at index: 1
```

Figure 23-7   Recursive code for binary search

The code for implementing a binary search iteratively is shown in **Figure 23-8**.

Section of code from ContactList.cpp showing how to implement a binary search iteratively.

```
int binary_search(Contact list[], int min, int max, Contact target)
{
    while (min <= max)  ←————— Continue only if max comes after or is the same as min.
    {
        int current = min + (max - min) / 2;  ←————— Calculate the middle index
                                                      between min and max.
        cout << "Min is: " << min << endl;
        cout << "Max is: " << max << endl;     }— Output the index values.
        cout << "Current is: " << current << endl;

        if (list[current] == target)
        {                                }— If the target is the element that current
            return current;                  points to, return the index.
        }

        if (list[current] < target)
        {                                }— If the target is smaller than the current value,
            min = current + 1;               then update the min pointer to refer to the
        }                                    right half of the list.

        else
        {                                }— Else, if the target is larger than the current
            max = current -1;                value, then update the max pointer to refer to
        }                                    the left half of the list.
    }

    return -1;  ←————— Return –1 if you've reached the end of the list and the value was not found.
}
```

```
OUTPUT:
Min is: 0
Max is: 7
Current is: 3
Min is: 0
Max is: 2
Current is: 1
```

Figure 23-8 Iterative code for binary search

A binary search reduces the search space by half on each iteration. This behavior reduces the number of evaluations needed to find your target. For this reason, if the search space contains n items, binary search takes $\log_2(n)$ comparisons at most to determine the answer. For example, the contact list has eight contacts. A linear search needs up to eight evaluations to find a match. However, using a binary search, you only need to perform two comparisons (index[3] and index[1]) to find the target. The expression $\log_2(8)$ results in 3, so the binary search performed less than the maximum of eight evaluations with a linear search.

23.4 USING REGULAR EXPRESSIONS IN SEARCH ALGORITHMS

Specifying a Search Pattern (23.4.1, 23.4.2, 23.4.3)

In a search scenario (such as a search engine), after you optimize the underlying search algorithm, you need a way to locate the information you want. Suppose you have a database full of contact information. The database grows as you add contacts over time. You recall the exact name of only some contacts. For other contacts, you remember partial names. In these cases, you can use a regular expression to search for a desired contact. A regular expression is a string of characters that describe the pattern of the text you are searching for. "Regular expression" is sometimes abbreviated as "regex," "re," or "regexp."

Regular expression algorithms are used in text editors (such as in the find operation), search engines, and lexical analysis, as seen in **Figure 23-9**.

Figure 23-9   Examples of regular expressions in a search engine and text editor

Regular Expression Search Operators (23.4.4, 23.4.5)

To create a regular expression, you use a string of characters that describes the pattern of the information for which you are searching. The characters that describe the patterns used in regular expressions are called metacharacters. Metacharacters can be used alone or in combination with other metacharacters to describe patterns, such as those shown in **Figure 23-10**. Keep in mind that metacharacters in regular expressions can vary from one programming language to another. However, the available features usually remain the same.

Metacharacters	Description	Usage
\d	Any single digit number from 0–9	\d\d\d matches any three-digit number such as 202
\w	Any single letter (a–z), (A–Z) or number (0–9)	\w\w\w = 313
\W	Any single symbol	\W\W = @@ \W\W = @$
[a–z]	A set of characters where exactly one must match	Ta[iy]lor = Tailor or Taylor
[0–9]	A set of numbers where exactly one must match	1[028] = 10 1[028] = 12 1[028] = 18
(abc)	A set of characters that must be matched in this exact order	Tay(lor) = Taylor
(123)	A set of numbers that must be matched in this exact order	Tay(123) = Tay123
|	Logical OR; allows alternate patterns to be matched	Ta(i|y)lor = Tailor or Taylor
?	The character immediately before the question mark occurs 0 or 1 time only	Breon?a = Breona or Breoa
*	The character immediately before the asterisk occurs 0 or more times	fre* matches fr fre free freee freeee
+	The character immediately before the + occurs 1 or more times	fre+ matches fre free freee freeee
.	The period matches any single letter, number, or symbol	fre. matches free fred fre# fre!

Figure 23-10   Regular expression metacharacters, meanings, and examples (*Continued*)

Metacharacters	Description	Usage
{n}	A quantifier that matches when the specified character or group of characters occurs exactly n times	\d**{4}** matches 2945 1738 0525 1229 fr[et]**{2}** matches free fret frte frtt
{n,m}	A quantifier that matches when the specified character or group of characters occurs at least n times, but no more than m times	\d**{2,4}** matches 68 678 6789 12 123 1234

Figure 23-10   Regular expression metacharacters, meanings, and examples

Q How would you search for any 10-digit phone number (no dashes)?

A [0–9]{10}

Q How would you search for any year in this millennium (2000–2999)?

A 20/d/d

Q Which contact's first name would match the regular expression Br(e|i)(o|a)nna?

A Breonna Bland

SUMMARY

- To make the large amounts of information that computers store useful to you, a computer needs to efficiently search for desired information. Search algorithms are special algorithms that describe how to find a specific or target piece of information.
- The search space defines the amount of data that needs to be examined to find the target. Generally, as the search space increases, the time needed to find the target also increases.
- Linear search is the simplest search algorithm. Each element in the search space is examined until the target is located.
- Linear search can be performed on any contiguous data structure such as an array or linked list.
- In the worst-case scenario, linear search requires you to look at every item in the search space before you find the solution, which is why linear search is rarely used.
- A binary search algorithm consecutively divides the search space in half until the target value is located. This approach is typically referred to as a divide-and-conquer technique because each step divides the search space on the path to a solution.
- Binary search reduces the search space by half on each iteration. This behavior reduces the number of times you have to evaluate an item to determine if it is equal to your target. If the search space contains n items, binary search takes at most $\log_2(n)$ comparisons to determine the answer.
- In a search scenario (such as a search engine), when you have optimized the underlying search algorithm, you need a way to specify the information you are seeking. When searching, you can use a regular expression to search for an item, such as a desired contact. A regular expression is a string of characters that describe the pattern of the text for which you are searching.
- The characters that describe the patterns used in regular expressions are called metacharacters. You can use metacharacters alone or in combination with other metacharacters to describe patterns.

Key Terms

binary search algorithm	metacharacters	search space
divide-and-conquer technique	regular expression	sentinel value
linear search	search algorithms	

MODULE 24

SORTING ALGORITHMS

LEARNING OBJECTIVES

24.1 QUALITIES OF SORTING ALGORITHMS

24.1.1 Explain why sorting algorithms are an important programming tool.

24.1.2 Explain why programmers should know the best-case, average-case, and worst-case time complexities of a sorting algorithm.

24.1.3 Explain the meaning of an in-place sort.

24.1.4 Explain the meaning of a stable sort.

24.2 BUBBLE SORT

24.2.1 Trace the path of a bubble sort on a set of sample data.

24.2.2 Identify the bubble sort algorithm.

24.2.3 Explain why a bubble sort is an example of a stable sorting algorithm.

24.2.4 Classify bubble sort as an in-place sorting algorithm.

24.2.5 State the best-, average-, and worst-case time complexities of a bubble sort.

24.2.6 Recognize that if a data set is already sorted, a bubble sort has a best-case time complexity of O(n).

24.2.7 Recognize data sets for which a bubble sort might be practical.

24.3 QUICKSORT

24.3.1 Trace the path of a quicksort on a set of sample data.

24.3.2 Identify the quicksort algorithm.

24.3.3 Classify quicksort as a divide-and-conquer algorithm and as an in-place sorting algorithm.

24.3.4 Explain why the quicksort algorithm is an example of recursion.

24.3.5 Recognize that quicksort is not a stable sorting algorithm.

24.3.6 State that the worst-case time complexity of a quicksort is O(n^2), but explain why that is rarely required.

24.3.7 State that the best and average time complexities of a quicksort are $n \log n$.

24.3.8 Explain why quicksort is regarded as the best general-purpose sorting algorithm.

24.4 MERGE SORT

24.4.1 Trace the path of a merge sort on a set of sample data.

24.4.2 Identify the merge sort algorithm.

24.4.3 Classify merge sort as a divide-and-conquer algorithm.

24.4.4 Classify merge sort as a stable sorting algorithm.

24.4.5 Recognize that merge sort is not an in-place algorithm.

24.4.6 State that the performance of a merge sort is always O($n \log n$).

24.4.7 State that merge sort is efficient for sorting linked lists.

24.1 QUALITIES OF SORTING ALGORITHMS

Ordering Items (24.1.1)

Imagine you have a contacts book like the one in **Figure 24-1**, with one contact per page. Typically the contact pages are organized alphabetically, but what if the pages fell out of the book when the binder rings were open? Finding someone's contact information would be tedious, as you would have to look at each page in a random order until you found the right one. If the contact pages were in alphabetical order, however, you could find information more easily. Instead of bundling all the pages together in random order, you would sort the pages before returning them to the contacts book.

Figure 24-1   Contacts book, organized by name

Sorting is an important topic in computer science as it makes data easier to find. Because computers commonly deal with large sets of data, you should know how to sort data (to find things more easily) and understand how the computer sorts. You can approach the task in a few ways using sorting algorithms.

To sort data items, a computer needs to know how the items relate to each other, such as whether one item is the same, less than, or greater than another item. Computers are set up to make numerical and alphabetical sorting easy, so that when you compare two numbers or letters, the computer knows how to order them. The character "a" is less than the character "b," and so on. The ability to use comparison operators, such as less than (<), is built into most programming languages.

Time Complexity in Sorting Algorithms (24.1.2)

How would you put the pages of your contact book back in order? You could use many strategies to sort the contact pages. You could spread out the contact pages and look for patterns, or you could put a few pages in alphabetic order and then insert each other page in its correct place. The strategy a computer takes is determined by the sorting algorithm it uses. Each algorithm has advantages and disadvantages.

Picking up a contact page is considered one unit of work. Comparing one page to another page is also one unit of work. The total amount of work you must do to sort the contact pages depends on how many pages you have and the strategy you're using. The total amount of work a computer does to complete a task is known as the runtime of an algorithm. Runtimes are described in terms of the variable n, where n represents the number of items to sort. (In this case, "variable" refers to a letter or symbol that represents a value.)

Assume your sorting approach requires you to compare each contact page to every other contact page, as shown in **Figure 24-2**. If you have one stack of 10 items to sort and another stack of 100 items to sort, the overall time is greater for sorting the 100 items. The same is true for the runtime of an algorithm—it is the same proportionally compared to its input.

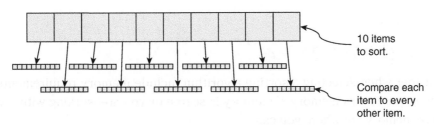

10 items to sort.

Compare each item to every other item.

Figure 24-2 Ten items with 10 work units per item

Q What is the runtime of the strategy that requires you to look at every page as you sort each page?

A If you have n contact pages, and each page requires n comparisons, the runtime is $n * n$, or n^2. Sorting 10 contact pages results in $10 * 10 = 100$ comparisons, while sorting 100 contact pages results in $100 * 100 = 10,000$ comparisons.

Recall that describing an algorithm's runtime in terms of a mathematical variable is known as **Big-O** runtime. The n^2 runtime is $O(n^2)$ in Big-O syntax. Big-O time complexity is focused only on the upper bounds of a program's runtime. If a full polynomial expression such as $n^3 + 2n^2 + n + 10$ describes a runtime, you would write the runtime as $O(n^3)$ instead of the full polynomial. **Figure 24-3** shows how, as n increases, the other parts of the polynomial equation matter less. In other words, n^2 and $n^2 + n$ are close in value as n increases.

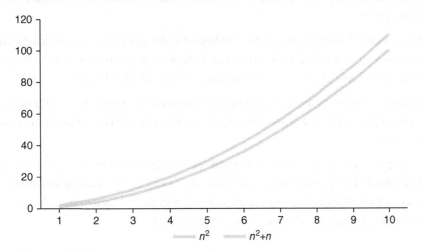

Figure 24-3 Comparing n^2 and $n^2 + n$

The runtime of an algorithm can be described in three ways: the best case, the worst case, and the average case. The best-case runtime is the fastest an algorithm can possibly run. Suppose you pick up all your contact pages, look through them once, and realize they're already in sorted order. This is the best-case scenario because no more work is needed. The worst-case runtime is the longest an algorithm can possibly run. Provided a sorting algorithm doesn't rely on luck to sort the items, eventually the algorithm stops; the worst-case runtime is how long that takes. The average-case runtime is how long the algorithm takes on average, given the unsorted items are shuffled an average amount.

Typically, the average case is the most useful information about a sorting algorithm. However, also knowing the worst-case and best-case runtimes and how those cases occur helps you select an algorithm. If you know that the worst case is likely to happen often when you use an algorithm, then you can select a different algorithm.

Sorting Properties (24.1.3, 24.1.4)

Other properties to consider when selecting a sorting algorithm include memory requirements and stability. Some sorting algorithms require extra memory. If memory is scarce or you are working with a very large data set, you need to conserve memory anywhere you can.

One way to conserve memory is to use an in-place algorithm. An in-place algorithm uses zero extra memory. If you have 10 items to sort, an in-place algorithm uses only the memory already available and no more. An example of an in-place algorithm is a bubble sort, which you'll examine shortly.

Another property of an algorithm is whether it is stable. A stable algorithm means that the items to sort are not rearranged during the sorting process. For example, suppose you are sorting contacts and two contacts are named Sarah B. A stable algorithm sorts the two contacts after the "A" contacts and before the "C" contacts, but keeps the two Sarah B. contacts in their original order. If Sarah B. with the birthday in June is listed before Sarah B. with the birthday in August in your book, then after the sorting is complete, Sarah B. with the June birthday still comes first.

A common algorithmic tactic for computers is to use a divide-and-conquer technique. This means the algorithm splits the problem, usually in half, to solve it. If you're looking for a contact whose last name starts with "J," for example, you start in the middle of the contact book. If the middle page contains names starting with "M," you know your contact is on a page in the previous part of the book. The divide-and-conquer approach has a runtime equivalent to how many times you can divide the total search space in half. If you have 16 contacts and check the middle, then you eliminate eight contacts you don't have to check. If you check the middle of the remaining contacts, you eliminate four, then two, and then one. Using a divide-and-conquer approach results in less work for you or the computer.

The "divide by 2 until you can't" approach can be mathematically expressed as a logarithm. The log base 2 of a number is how many times you can divide that number in half. In Big-O terms, it is $O(\log_2 n)$, or sometimes simplified to $O(\log n)$ because you are almost always dividing in half, so the 2 can be implied.

Of the many sorting algorithms you can use, this module introduces those that help you understand how runtimes come into play when you are using a program to sort data. The sorting algorithms covered are bubble sort, quicksort, and merge sort.

To test and visualize these sorting algorithms, **Figure 24-4** shows two helping procedures: **shuffle()** and **print_items()**. The **shuffle()** code rearranges the numbers in the **items** parameter randomly, and **print_items()** displays each number in the **items** parameter, separated by a space. Any code examples that reference **shuffle()** or **print_items()** use the code in Figure 24-4.

```
void shuffle(int items[], int length)
{

   // A quick shuffling function to mix up the numbers in items randomly


   for (int i = 0; i < length; i++)
   {
      int index = rand() % (length - i) + i;
      int temp = items[index];
      items[index] = items[i];
      items[i] = temp;

   }
}


void print_items(int items[], int length)
{
   // To display each number in items
   for (int i = 0; i < length; i++)
   {
      cout << items[i] << " ";
   }

   cout << endl;

}
```

Figure 24-4   Code for `shuffle()` and `print_items()`

24.2 BUBBLE SORT

Defining the Bubble Sort Algorithm (24.2.1, 24.2.2)

Bubble sort is an easy-to-program but inefficient sorting algorithm. The bubble sort algorithm has two parts: a pass and a swap. A pass is a loop that traverses over all the items to sort. For each item, it checks to see if a swap needs to be made. A swap is made when the two neighboring items are out of order. The pseudocode for a swap is as follows:

```
if numbers[index] > numbers[index + 1]

    temp_variable = numbers[index]

    numbers[index] = numbers[index + 1]

    numbers[index + 1] = temp_variable
```

If the number at the current index is greater than the number one spot to the right, then the numbers are out of order. The value in the current index is stored in a temporary variable, the number to the right is placed in the current index, and then the value originally in the current index is placed in the index one to the right.

The pseudocode for one pass in a bubble sort algorithm is as follows:

```
for index (start: 0; test: < len(numbers) - 1)

    if numbers[index] > numbers[index + 1]

        temp_variable = numbers[index]

        numbers[index] = numbers[index + 1]

        numbers[index + 1] = temp_variable
```

The first pass starts the **index** at 0. The index test for the for-loop stops at one position less than the end position. This is different from a normal for-loop because a swap checks the current index and the index one to the right. Inside the loop body is the code for a swap.

Q Why does the for-loop need to stop one index position earlier than normal for-loops?

A All indexes need to be valid when used to access items in an array. In the loop's code, **index + 1** is used as an index. If the index continued to the normal stopping point, then **index + 1** would be an invalid index.

One pass of a bubble sort visits each item in the array once and tries to swap it so they are in ascending order (A–Z or 0–9). **Figure 24-5** shows one pass through an unsorted list.

Each bar in Figure 24-5 represents a number, with the height of the bar corresponding to the number. The first pass of this bubble sort of 10 items takes nine steps:

1. Step 1 shows the entire list of numbers as unsorted (in gray).
2. Step 2 compares the two numbers highlighted in red. The two numbers are not out of order, so they are not swapped.
3. The numbers in step 3 are also not out of order, so they are not swapped.
4. Step 4 compares two numbers that are out of order.
5. Step 5 swaps the numbers.
6. Step 6 does not swap numbers because they are already in order.
7. Step 7 compares two numbers that are out of order.
8. Step 8 swaps the numbers.
9. Step 9 shows the final array after one pass, with the rightmost number highlighted in green.

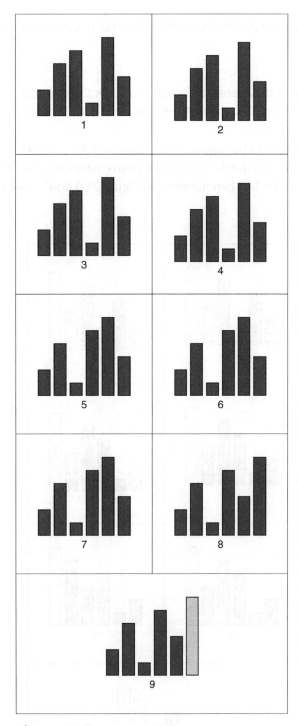

Figure 24-5   One pass of bubble sort

Q What can you claim about the numbers in the last step of Figure 24-5? What has one pass achieved? What is true about the green highlighted number?

A One pass has sorted ("bubbled") one item to the last index. The item that is sorted to the end is the largest value in the entire array of numbers, and therefore must be placed at the last index. One pass of bubble sort puts exactly one number in its sorted location.

Q If one pass of bubble sort sorts one number, how many passes are needed to sort all *n* numbers?

A Bubble sort needs at most *n* passes to sort all numbers. Because each pass puts one number in the correct place, *n* passes puts *n* numbers in the correct place.

Figure 24-6 shows a second pass to bubble sort the numbers. After the second pass, two numbers are sorted correctly. Because each pass sorts one number, each successive pass can ignore the sorted locations instead of checking all positions for swaps. The last two numbers in Figure 24-6 don't need to be compared.

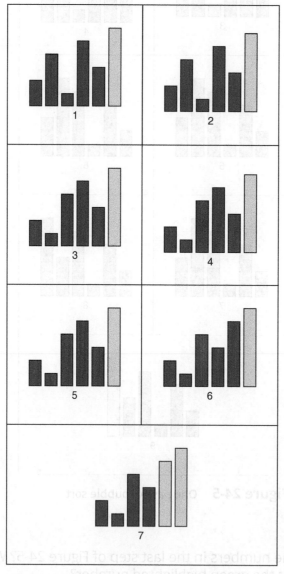

Figure 24-6   Second pass of bubble sort

Figure 24-7 shows the array after the remaining passes are completed.

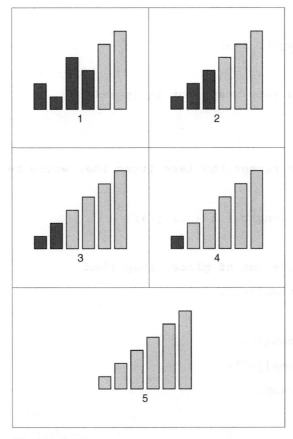

Figure 24-7   All passes of bubble sort

Although the items are sorted in step 4, the bubble sort continues to do a final comparison in step 5. You can program a bubble sort and stop as soon as the items are sorted. If no swaps are made during a pass, then the numbers are in sorted order and no more passes need to be made. **Figure 24-8** shows how to code a bubble sort.

The following code uses the functions shown in Figure 24-4 to run.

```
#include <iostream>
#include <stdlib.h>
#include <time.h>


using namespace std;
```

Figure 24-8   Bubble sort code (*Continued*)

```
void bubble_sort(int items[], int length)
{
    // Do n passes
    for (int i = 0; i < length; i++)
    {
        // Keep track of how many swaps for early exit
        int swaps = 0;


        // Look at each item except the last items that would be sorted
        // (i items)
        for (int j = 0; j < length - 1 - i; j++)
        {
            // If two items are out of place, swap them
            if (items[j] > items[j+1])
            {
                int temp = items[j];
                items[j] = items[j+1];
                items[j+1] = temp;


                swaps += 1;


            }
        }

        // If no swaps happened during a pass, you can stop early
        if (swaps == 0)
        {
            break;
        }
    }

}
```

Figure 24-8   Bubble sort code (*Continued*)

```
int main()
{
    // Seed the random module for shuffle to work
    srand (time(NULL));


    // Create 10 items
    int items[] = {1, 2, 3, 4, 5, 6, 7, 8, 9, 10};


    // Test bubble sort
    cout << "Bubble Sort" << endl;
    shuffle(items, 10);
    print_items(items, 10);
    bubble_sort(items, 10);
    print_items(items, 10);
    cout << endl;


    return 0;
}
```

OUTPUT (your output may differ because of rand()):

```
Bubble Sort
6 3 2 7 8 5 9 10 4 1
1 2 3 4 5 6 7 8 9 10
```

Figure 24-8   Bubble sort code

Bubble Sort Properties (24.2.3, 24.2.4, 24.2.5, 24.2.6, 24.2.7)

If you program bubble sort to stop if it makes no swaps during a pass, then its best-case scenario is starting with an already sorted list. The program checks each item once on a pass, makes no swaps, and then stops. The best-case runtime of bubble sort of n items is $O(n)$.

The worst-case scenario is that the program needs to make all n passes to sort n items. If bubble sort does not stop early, then it has to make n passes, with each pass taking n comparisons. The worst-case runtime is $O(n^2)$. The worst-case scenario is triggered when the items are in reverse order, which is the opposite of the best case.

The average case is more difficult to figure out. Consider the "stopping early" part of bubble sort. To calculate an average of six numbers, for example, you add all the numbers and then divide by six. Bubble sort could stop early after one, two, or three passes, each equally likely assuming a random shuffle of the numbers. To find an average runtime, you can add the runtimes of all possible stopping-early situations, and then divide by n, as in the following:

$$\frac{1\ pass + 2\ passes + 3\ passes + \dots + n\ passes}{n}$$

The summation pattern of $1 + 2 + 3$ up to some n is the following known summation:

$$1 + 2 + 3 + \dots + n = \frac{n(n + 1)}{2}$$

Apply this formula into the original summation and simplify the fractional on the right as follows:

$$\frac{\frac{n(n + 1)}{2}}{n} = \frac{n + 1}{2}\ passes$$

Each pass takes n work, so you rewrite the equation as follows:

$$n\left(\frac{n + 1}{2}\right) = \frac{n^2 + n}{2}\ work$$

Remember that in Big-O notation, you can retain only the largest part of the polynomial and drop constant multipliers or divisors. As a result, even on average, bubble sort is still $O(n^2)$ work.

Bubble sort swaps items many times to order them, so it does not need additional memory to store items. Therefore, bubble sort is an in-place sort. Bubble sort swaps items only when they are strictly out of order. Because it does not swap identical items, bubble sort is also a stable algorithm.

Bubble sort is not the best option for most data sets. Instead, it is a simple and easy-to-program approach to sorting and provides a good introduction to how computers can sort items. If the data set is small enough that the runtime does not matter, then you could use bubble sort, though it is not the best sorting algorithm. If your data set is already mostly sorted, bubble sort has the best-case runtime of $O(n)$ because it can stop early. Otherwise, use a different sort.

24.3 QUICKSORT

Defining the Quicksort Algorithm (24.3.1, 24.3.2, 24.3.4)

Quicksort approximates an efficient sort. It relies on probabilities to ensure it generally performs well, despite having an undesirable worst-case scenario. Quicksort uses a divide-and-conquer approach. Like bubble sort, quicksort has two parts: a partitioning step and a recursive step.

In effect, the partitioning step picks a random item as a pivot, then figures out where that one item belongs in the sorted order. Imagine that to sort your unordered contacts pages, you pick the page for your friend Megan Lee. You put Megan's page aside and create two piles: one for contact pages that should come before Megan's page, and another pile for contact pages that should come after Megan's page. After you have two piles, then you know that Megan's page goes between the two piles, as in **Figure 24-9**.

Figure 24-9   Divide and conquer to place a contact page

A quicksort algorithm selects the middle item as the pivot, and then moves the pivot out of the way, as in **Figure 24-10**.

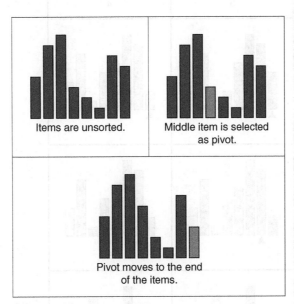

Figure 24-10   Quicksort pivot selection and movement

Next, to partition the values into two piles, the quicksort algorithm keeps track of a boundary index. The boundary index indicates that everything to the left is less than the pivot, and everything to the right is greater than the pivot. The boundary index starts at the leftmost index, and then iterates over all values other than the pivot (which is conveniently out of the way). If a value at an index is less than the pivot, it is moved to the boundary index, and the boundary index is increased by one. If the value at an index is greater than the pivot, then both that value and the boundary index are left alone.

Figure 24-11 shows how the quicksort algorithm works with a boundary index. The boundary index is indicated by a black arrow below the number bars.

The quicksort algorithm works as follows:

- In steps 1 through 4, the examined values in red are greater than the pivot in blue, so nothing is changed.
- In step 5, the examined value in red is less than the pivot, so it is swapped in step 6 with the value at the boundary index.
- In step 7, the boundary index is moved to the right by one.
- The process continues until all values other than the pivot have been examined.
- In the last step, the pivot is swapped with the value at the boundary index.

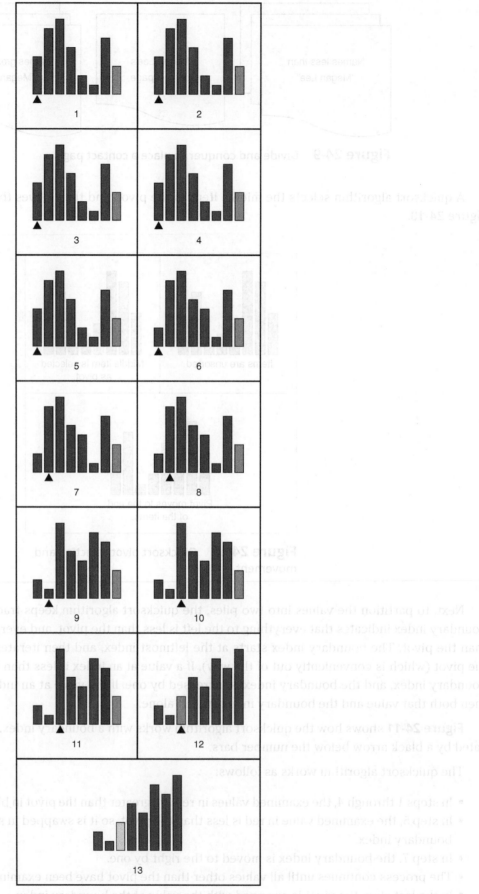

Figure 24-11   Partitioning for quicksort

As with bubble sort, after one partition in a quicksort, one item is sorted. In addition, the left and right sections have different characteristics.

Q What can you say about the numbers to the left of the green bar after step 13 in Figure 24-11? What about the numbers to the right of the green bar?

A The numbers to the left of the green bar are less than the pivot. The numbers to the right of the green bar are greater than the pivot.

Given an array of numerical values stored in the variable `items`, and given `left` and `right` index variables, the pseudocode for partitioning is:

```
middle = (left + right) // 2
boundary = left


pivot = items[middle]
items[middle] = items[right]
items[right] = pivot


for index (start: left; test: < right; increment: 1)
    if items[index] < pivot
        temp = items[index]
        items[index] = items[boundary]
        items[boundary] = temp
        boundary = boundary + 1


temp = items[right]
items[right] = items[boundary]
items[boundary] = temp
```

After using a quicksort to partition items, you have two sections of unsorted numbers. The numbers to the left of the pivot should never end up on the right, nor should the numbers on the right end up to the left of the pivot. You can sort the left and right sections independently and maintain the order. You've created two smaller subproblems, which is exactly what recursion needs.

Quicksort recursively tries to partition the items to the left and right of the pivot until only one item remains to sort. If only one item remains, it is guaranteed to be in sorted order. **Figure 24-12** shows how quicksort works recursively on the left by picking a pivot, moving it away, and so on, as in Figure 24-11. Only two items remain to the left of the pivot, so the left section is sorted quickly.

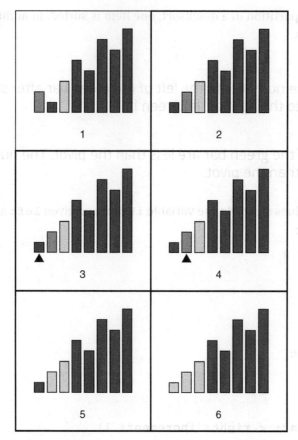

Figure 24-12   Recursive partitions in the left section

Figure 24-13 shows the progress continued with the numbers to the right of the pivot.

Quicksort continues this way until all items are sorted. The pseudocode outline for the recursive step in quicksort is:

```
function recurse(items[], left, right)
    if left = right
        return
    elseif left < right
        pivot_position = partition(items, left, right)
        recurse(items, left, pivot_position - 1)
        recurse(items, pivot_position + 1, right)
```

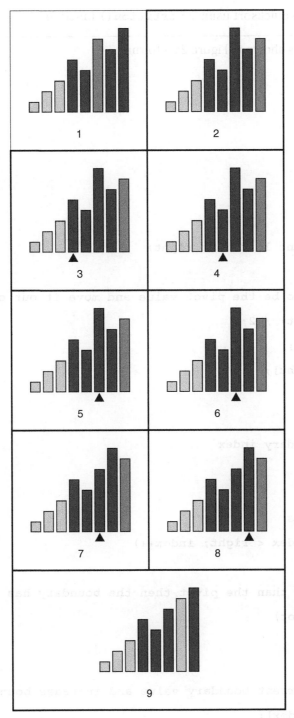

Figure 24-13 Recursive partitions in the right section

Figure 24-14 shows the code for a quicksort using a `partition()` function.

The following code uses the functions shown in Figure 24-4 to run.

```cpp
#include <iostream>
#include <stdlib.h>
#include <time.h>

using namespace std;

int partition(int items[], int left, int right)
{
    // Pick the middle item to be the pivot value and move it out of the way
    int middle = (left + right) / 2;
    int pivot = items[middle];
    items[middle] = items[right];
    items[right] = pivot;


    // Keep track of the boundary index
    int boundary = left;


    // Look at all other items
    for (int index = left; index < right; index++)
    {
        // If the item is less than the pivot then the boundary has to move
        if (items[index] < pivot)
        {

            // Swap with the current boundary value and increase boundary by 1
            int temp = items[index];
            items[index] = items[boundary];
            items[boundary] = temp;

            boundary += 1;
        }
    }
```

Figure 24-14   Quicksort code (*Continued*)

```
    // Move pivot to between the two groups of numbers as indicated by
    // the boundary index
    int temp = items[right];
    items[right] = items[boundary];
    items[boundary] = temp;


    // Return the boundary to inform quicksort how to recurse
    return boundary;

}


void quick_recurse(int items[], int left, int right)
{
    // Check for base case
    // Did the left and right boundaries pass each other? Then stop.
    if (left >= right)
    {
        return;
    }


    // Find the pivot's position after partitioning
    int pivot_position = partition(items, left, right);


    // Recurse left and right of pivot
    quick_recurse(items, left, pivot_position - 1);
    quick_recurse(items, pivot_position + 1, right);

}


void quick_sort(int items[], int length)
{
    // Start the recursion to include all valid indexes
    // (length - 1 instead of length)
    quick_recurse(items, 0, length -1);

}
```

Figure 24-14 Quicksort code (*Continued*)

```
int main()
{
    // Seed the random module for shuffle to work
    srand (time(NULL));


    // Create 10 items
    int items[] = {1, 2, 3, 4, 5, 6, 7, 8, 9, 10};


    // Test quick sort
    cout << "Quick Sort" << endl;
    shuffle(items, 10);
    print_items(items, 10);
    quick_sort(items, 10);
    print_items(items, 10);
    cout << endl;


    return 0;
}
```

OUTPUT (your output may differ because of rand()):

```
Quick Sort

6 3 2 7 8 5 9 10 4 1

1 2 3 4 5 6 7 8 9 10
```

Figure 24-14   Quicksort code

Quicksort Properties (24.3.3, 24.3.5, 24.3.6, 24.3.7, 24.3.8)

The runtime of a quicksort algorithm depends on how partitioning works out. Each partition requires O(n) work, where n is the total number of values to compare to the pivot. Even during recursive steps, considering all partitions at the same recursive depth requires O(n) work. See **Figure 24-15**.

Quicksort's runtime is n multiplied by the number of times **partition()** is called. The best runtime is when quicksort evenly divides a list of numbers into two equal piles, similar to starting in the middle of a dictionary to find a word. In this case, each section of the list is about half the size of the starting list. Each section repeats the partition, which in the best case divides each section in half again.

Assuming that each partition is divided exactly in half, how many times can **partition()** be called? The mathematical function log represents the concept of "how many times can something be divided in half." Log base 2, also written as $\log_2$, or simplified to log in Big-O notation, returns the "how many times you can divide in half" value for a number, stopping when it reaches a value of 1 or lower. Log(2) is 1, log(4) is 2, log(8) is 3, and so on. Therefore, the best-case runtime for a quicksort algorithm is O(n log(n)).

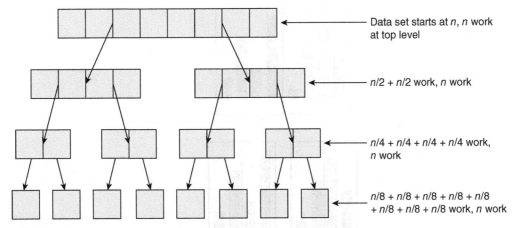

Figure 24-15   Dividing in half results in *n* work at each level

Quicksort has problems when it does not divide unsorted values equally. Consider the pivot picking: what happens if the largest value is selected as the pivot? What about when it recursively calls **partition()** and selects the second largest value as the pivot?

Q If quicksort picks each value in descending order from largest to smallest for its pivots, how many times is **partition()** called?

A Each partition would sort one value in the correct location, but leave most items unsorted to the left. This could happen *n* times.

If quicksort uses each value in descending order for its pivots, the runtime is $O(n^2)$. Despite this worst-case scenario requiring too much runtime (more than $O(n \log(n))$), quicksort is considered the best general-purpose sorting algorithm. This is because the worst case is unlikely. The probability that the worst pivot is picked at each **partition()** call is 1 in *n*, meaning that the worst-case scenario has about a $1/n^n$ chance, which is very unlikely, especially if *n* is large. On average, quicksort has a runtime of $O(n \log(n))$.

Quicksort is an in-place algorithm because it uses no additional memory. However, quicksort is not stable, as moving pivots and partitioning values can swap the positions of identical values. In general, quicksort is a fast and memory-efficient sorting algorithm to use in any situation. You might consider a different algorithm if you need to guarantee the $O(n \log(n))$ runtime.

24.4 MERGE SORT

Defining the Merge Sort Algorithm (24.4.1, 24.4.2, 24.4.4)

Merge sort is another divide-and-conquer algorithm. The two parts of merge sort are partitioning and merging. Partitioning is easy: the algorithm splits a list of numbers in half and calls a sorting function such as **merge()** recursively on each half. See **Figure 24-16**.

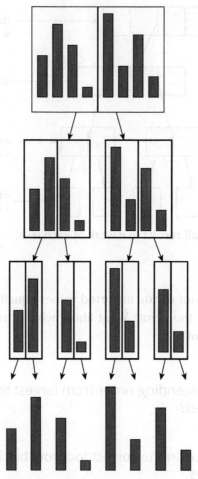

Figure 24-16   Merge sort
always divides in half

The base case for the recursive call is when the list contains only one item, meaning it is already sorted. The interesting part is when the recursive calls return two lists that are sorted. The recursive merge sort pseudocode logic is as follows:

```
function recurse(items[], left, right)

    if left >= right
        return


middle = (left + right) / 2


recurse(items, left, middle)
recurse(items, middle + 1, right)


merge(items, left, middle, right)
```

Assuming it works correctly, the function **recurse()** stores the two halves in the indexes indicated from **left** to **middle**, and from **middle + 1** to **right**. Next, you must use **merge()** to merge the two halves. Consider the lists in **Figure 24-17**.

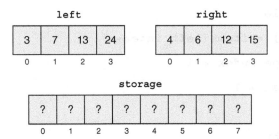

Figure 24-17   `left` and `right` can be merged into `storage`

Q Which number from the sorted `left` and `right` lists should be the first item in the `storage` result? How do you find it?

A You know the two lists of numbers are already sorted, so the smallest number (the number that must come first in the merged result) is either the first number in `left` or the first number in `right`. You can move the smallest number in the two lists to the first index of `storage`. In Figure 24-17, the smallest number is 3.

The second number for the merged result again has to be one of two numbers from `left` and `right`. The number for index 1 of `storage` is 4. Merge 6, 7, 12, 13, 15, and then 24 from the sorted lists to `storage`. This process can repeat until one of the lists runs out of numbers, but each time you only need to look at two values.

The logic for merge sort is as follows:

```
function merge(items, left, middle, right)

    initialize storage[right - left]


    left_index = left
    right_index = middle + 1
    storage_index = 0


    while left_index <= middle and right_index <= right
        if items[left_index] <= items[right_index]
            storage[storage_index] = items[left_index]
            storage_index = storage_index + 1
            left_index = left_index + 1
        else
            storage[storage_index] = items[right_index]
            storage_index = storage_index + 1
            right_index = right_index + 1
```

```
while left_index <= middle

    storage[storage_index] = items[left_index++]

    storage_index = storage_index + 1

    left_index = left_index + 1


while right_index <= right

    storage[storage_index] = items[right_index]

    storage_index = storage_index + 1

    right_index = right_index + 1


for i (start: left; test: <= right; increment: 1)

    items[i] = storage[i - left]
```

Figure 24-18 shows the code for a merge sort.

The following code uses the functions shown in Figure 24-4 to run.

```
#include <iostream>

#include <stdlib.h>

#include <time.h>


using namespace std;


void merge(int items[], int left, int middle, int right)

{

  // Create enough storage to merge the two sections of the items array
  int storage[right - left];


  // Three indexes to keep track of the place in the left section,
  // right section, and merged storage.
  int left_index = left;

  int right_index = middle + 1;

  int storage_index = 0;


  // While there is something in both the left and right sections

  while (left_index <= middle and right_index <= right)
```

Figure 24-18   Merge sort code (*Continued*)

```
{
    // If the left section has a number smaller than the right section
    // copy it over to the storage
    if (items[left_index] <= items[right_index])
    {
        storage[storage_index++] = items[left_index++];
    }

    // Otherwise copy the number from the right section to storage
    else
    {
        storage[storage_index++] = items[right_index++];
    }
}


// Check to see if there are any numbers in the left section and
// copy them over
// Numbers would only be in the left section if the right section ran out
while (left_index <= middle)
{

    storage[storage_index++] = items[left_index++];
}


// Check to see if there are any numbers in the right section
// and copy them over
// Numbers would only be in the right section if the left section ran out
while (right_index <= right)
{
    storage[storage_index++] = items[right_index++];
}


// Copy the merged numbers back into the correct place in the items array.
for (int i = left; i <= right; i++)
```

Figure 24-18   Merge sort code (*Continued*)

```cpp
    {
        items[i] = storage[i - left];
    }
}

void merge_recurse(int items[], int left, int right)
{
    // If the left and right indexes pass each other it is the base case
    if (left >= right)
    {
        return;
    }

    // Find the middle
    int middle = (left + right) / 2;

    // Recurse left and right
    merge_recurse(items, left, middle);
    merge_recurse(items, middle + 1, right);

    // Merge the sorted left and right sections
    merge(items, left, middle, right);
}

void merge_sort(int items[], int length)
{
    // Start the recursion with all valid indexes
    // (length - 1 instead of length)
    merge_recurse(items, 0, length-1);
}

int main()
{
    // Seed the random module for shuffle to work
    srand (time(NULL));
```

Figure 24-18   Merge sort code (*Continued*)

```
    // Create 10 items
    int items[] = {1, 2, 3, 4, 5, 6, 7, 8, 9, 10};


    // Test merge sort
    cout << "Merge Sort" << endl;
    shuffle(items, 10);
    print_items(items, 10);
    merge_sort(items, 10);
    print_items(items, 10);
    cout << endl;


    return 0;
}


OUTPUT (your output may differ because of rand()):
Merge Sort
6 3 2 7 8 5 9 10 4 1
1 2 3 4 5 6 7 8 9 10
```

Figure 24-18   Merge sort code

Merge Sort Properties (24.4.3, 24.4.5, 24.4.6, 24.4.7)

Unlike bubble sort, merge sort cannot stop early. The best, worst, and average runtimes for merge sort are the same because it always takes the same amount of work to complete the sort. Merging takes *n* work for the same reason partitioning did in Figure 24-15. Splitting a list of values in half takes $O(\log(n))$ work, as it does for quicksort. Merge sort always takes $O(n \log(n))$ work.

Merge sort needs extra memory for the recursive steps. Whenever you make a temporary copy of information in a computer, it requires more memory. Therefore, merge sort is not an in-place sorting algorithm. However, merge sort is stable because it favors the left side in ties in the merge code.

Merge sort guarantees the fast runtime of $O(n \log(n))$, which is important to consider when selecting a sorting algorithm. Merge sort, with a bit of modification, is also good for sorting linked lists. Recall that linked lists have poor random access, so sorts like quicksort are inefficient.

SUMMARY

- Sorting algorithms try to efficiently organize items in a sorted order.
- You express the runtime of a sorting algorithm in terms of n, where n is the number of items to be sorted. Computer scientists use Big-O analysis, which includes only the largest part of a polynomial expression of n as the overall runtime. Algorithms can have best, worst, and average runtime cases.
- In-place algorithms do not need additional memory to run. Stable algorithms do not change the order of identical items, such as two contacts with the same name.
- A common tactic for computers is to divide and conquer, which tries to reduce the problem into two equal halves to make the runtime logarithmic.
- The bubble sort algorithm is easy to program but slow to run. Bubble sort uses passes to swap adjacent items if they are out of order, setting one item as sorted after one pass. After n passes, bubble sort is complete. Bubble sort can stop early if it makes a pass and no swaps occur. Bubble sort's runtimes are $O(n^2)$ for worst and average cases and $O(n)$ for the best case.
- The quicksort algorithm relies on probability to perform well. Quicksort uses partitioning and recursion to divide and conquer an unsorted list. Partitioning picks the middle item as a pivot and moves it out of the way. Quicksort then places all items less than the pivot on the left and all items greater than the pivot on the right before moving the pivot between these two groups. Quicksort next performs two smaller quicksorts on the left and right groups. Quicksort's runtimes are $O(n^2)$ in the worst case, which happens infrequently, and $O(n \log(n))$ for its average and best cases.
- The merge sort algorithm uses extra memory to guarantee a fast runtime. Merge sort splits an unsorted list in half to sort two smaller lists, and then merges the two sorted results together. Merge sort has the same runtime for the best, worst, and average cases: $O(n \log(n))$.

Key Terms

average-case runtime	in-place algorithm	sorting algorithms
best-case runtime	Merge sort	stable algorithm
Big-O	Quicksort	worst-case runtime
Bubble sort	runtime	
divide-and-conquer technique	Sorting	

MODULE
25

PROCESSOR ARCHITECTURE

LEARNING OBJECTIVES:

25.1 PROCESSOR ORGANIZATION

25.1.1 List the key components of an integrated circuit.

25.1.2 Identify transistors as one of the most important components of an integrated circuit.

25.1.3 State Moore's law.

25.1.4 Analyze the current relevance of Moore's law.

25.1.5 Diagram the foundational computer components now referred to as von Neumann architecture.

25.1.6 Illustrate how von Neumann architecture maps to the components of a CPU.

25.1.7 Explain the function of a CPU.

25.1.8 Associate CPUs with microprocessors.

25.1.9 Classify a microprocessor as a type of integrated circuit.

25.2 LOW-LEVEL INSTRUCTION SETS

25.2.1 List the most common operations in a microprocessor instruction set.

25.2.2 Differentiate between CISC and RISC architectures.

25.2.3 Associate machine language with the instruction set of a CPU.

25.2.4 Differentiate between an op code and an operand.

25.2.5 Classify machine language as a low-level programming language.

25.2.6 List the characteristics of machine language.

25.2.7 Define assembly language as a low-level programming language with instructions that have a strong correspondence to machine language instructions.

25.2.8 Differentiate a machine language instruction from an assembly language instruction.

25.2.9 State advantages and disadvantages of low-level languages for creating software.

25.3 MICROPROCESSOR OPERATIONS

25.3.1 Identify the roles that registers, the instruction pointer, the ALU, and the control unit play in processing an instruction.

25.3.2 Identify the three phases of the instruction cycle: fetch, decode, execute.

25.3.3 Trace the execution of a short assembly language program that loads data into registers.

25.4 HIGH-LEVEL PROGRAMMING LANGUAGES

25.4.1 Define the term "high-level programming language."

25.4.2 Provide examples of early high-level programming languages.

25.4.3 Provide examples of high-level programming languages that are currently in widespread use.

25.4.4 List the key characteristics of high-level programming languages.

25.4.5 List the advantages of high-level programming languages.

25.4.6 List the disadvantages of high-level programming languages.

25.1 PROCESSOR ORGANIZATION

Integrated Circuits (25.1.1, 25.1.2)

The computing devices that you use come in all shapes and sizes. They include tiny smart sensors, digital watches and smartphones, portable tablets and laptops, desk-sized workstations, and room-sized server farms.

Regardless of the shape, size, function, or cost of these devices, they all contain integrated circuits. An integrated circuit, similar to those in **Figure 25-1**, contains microscopic electronic circuitry and components, such as transistors, capacitors, and resistors, etched onto a flat slice of silicon.

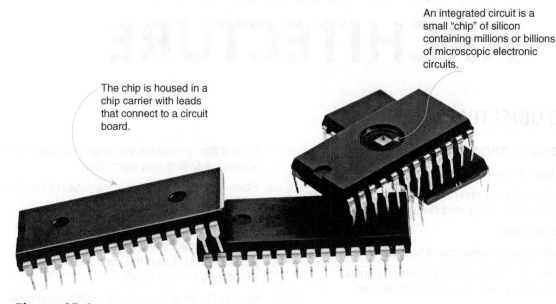

An integrated circuit is a small "chip" of silicon containing millions or billions of microscopic electronic circuits.

The chip is housed in a chip carrier with leads that connect to a circuit board.

Figure 25-1   Integrated circuits

Integrated circuits are sometimes referred to as "computer chips" or just "chips." Some integrated circuits are designed to carry out processing activities, while other chips are designed to handle memory, storage, input, or output.

A transistor is an electronic circuit that controls the flow of current. Transistors are one of the most important components in an integrated circuit because they perform two essential tasks:

Amplify signals. Transistors can make a signal stronger so that it has enough "juice" to travel through a circuit.

Act as switches. Transistors act as switches to control the flow of electronic signals. **Figure 25-2** shows how a transistor controls the flow of current from a Collector to an Emitter.

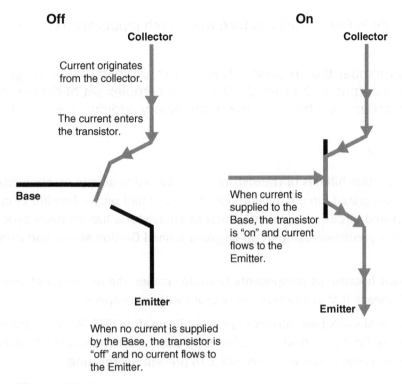

Figure 25-2   Transistors

Transistors link to other components, such as capacitors and resistors, to form logic gates. A logic gate manipulates electrical signals to perform logical and arithmetic operations. For example, the XOR logic gate in **Figure 25-3** can be used to add two bits.

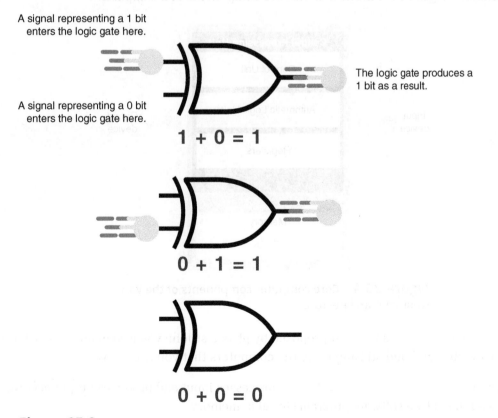

Figure 25-3   XOR logic gates

Q What will the logic gate in Figure 25-3 produce when both inputs are 1?

A It will produce 0. Remember that in binary, there is no "2." When this circuit gets 1 + 1 as the input, it has only one output, so it produces 0. A more complex set of circuits is needed for the operation that carries the 1 bit to complete the binary addition 1 + 1 = 10.

Moore's Law (25.1.3, 25.1.4)

Today, integrated circuits contain billions of transistors and other microscopic components, but that wasn't always the case. The first integrated circuits invented in the 1950s had only a handful of components. Since then, the number of integrated circuit components, such as transistors, has doubled every two years. This phenomenon was based on a prediction made by an engineer named Gordon Moore and came to be known as Moore's Law.

Moore's law is important because as components become smaller, the distance between them decreases. Signals travel faster, which means that computers can operate with more speed.

Experts question whether Moore's Law will continue to hold true after 2025. With current silicon technology, miniaturization can only go so far. As electrons move faster through smaller and smaller circuits, they generate more and more heat. At some point, it may not be possible to prevent overheating.

CPUs (25.1.5, 25.1.6, 25.1.7, 25.1.8, 25.1.9)

A computer can be defined as a multipurpose device that accepts input, processes that input based on a stored set of instructions, and produces output. Abstracting away the details of circuit boards, silicon, integrated circuits, and transistors, **Figure 25-4** illustrates the core components of a computer.

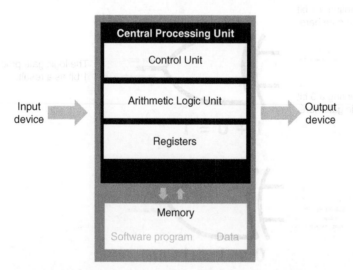

Figure 25-4   Core computer components of the von Neumann architecture

This abstract view of computers was first proposed by physicist John von Neumann in 1945. It is referred to as "von Neumann architecture" and still applies to the computers that you use today.

- Your computer's **central processing unit (CPU)** processes input and produces output according to the instructions supplied by a software program stored in memory.
- The CPU contains a control unit, an arithmetic logic unit, and registers.

- The control unit manages processing activities by collecting instructions and data, then sending them to the ALU.
- The arithmetic logic unit (ALU) performs arithmetic and logical operations.
- Registers are temporary areas for holding data.
- Computer programs and data are stored in memory where they can be accessed by the CPU.

The CPU for each of your digital devices is housed in a single integrated circuit called a microprocessor. A microprocessor is a complex integrated circuit containing billions of components designed to process data. On the circuit board of any digital device, you can easily identify the microprocessor because it is typically the largest integrated circuit. See **Figure 25-5**.

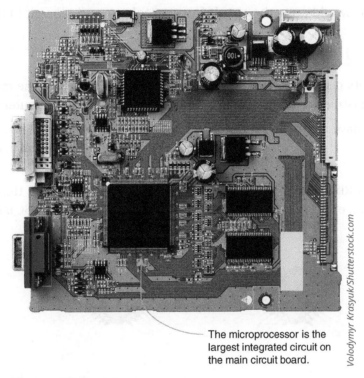

The microprocessor is the largest integrated circuit on the main circuit board.

Volodymyr Krasyuk/Shutterstock.com

Figure 25-5 Microprocessor

25.2 LOW-LEVEL INSTRUCTION SETS

Microprocessor Instruction Sets (25.2.1)

Computers perform billions of operations each second to accomplish relatively simple tasks, such as calculating your daily fitness activity or inserting an address in an email message. The reason for all this processing activity is that microprocessors are hard-wired to perform a limited set of operations for processing data.

A collection of preprogrammed microprocessor operations is called an instruction set. Each operation corresponds to a seemingly insignificant task, such as comparing two numbers to see if they are the same or moving a number from memory into the arithmetic logic unit. Here is a set of very basic microprocessor operations:

LOAD: Place a value in a CPU register.

MOVE: Copy a value from memory into a CPU register.

ADD: Add the values in two CPU registers.

SUBTRACT: Subtract the value in one CPU register from the value in another register.

MULTIPLY: Multiply the values in two CPU registers.

DIVIDE: Divide the value in one CPU register by the value in another register.

STORE: Copy a value from a CPU register into memory.

COMPARE: Check if the values in two registers are the same.

JUMP: Go to a different instruction.

END: Stop executing instructions.

Q Suppose the processor completed an ADD operation. Which operation would copy the result to a location in memory?

A The STORE operation would copy the result from a register and place it in memory.

RISC and CISC (25.2.2)

Although all microprocessors perform similar operations, the instruction set for the microprocessor in your phone is different from the instruction set for the microprocessor in a desktop computer optimized for gaming.

Some microprocessors have instruction sets consisting of hundreds of operations. These processors are classified as complex instruction set computers (CISC). Microprocessors with small instruction sets are classified as reduced instruction set computers (RISC).

As you might imagine, a RISC processor has to perform many more operations than a CISC processor to accomplish the same task, but each RISC instruction executes more quickly than a CISC instruction. **Figure 25-6** compares CISC and RISC.

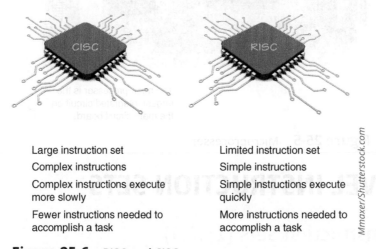

Large instruction set	Limited instruction set
Complex instructions	Simple instructions
Complex instructions execute more slowly	Simple instructions execute quickly
Fewer instructions needed to accomplish a task	More instructions needed to accomplish a task

Mmaxer/Shutterstock.com

Figure 25-6   RISC and CISC

In their simplicity, RISC processors use less power and require less cooling, which makes them ideal for mobile devices and high-performance servers. The ARM processor in your mobile phone is an example of a RISC processor.

The IBM PC that your grandmother used back in 1985 contained an x86 CISC processor, and the descendants of these microprocessors are still preferred for general-purpose computing devices such as desktop computers.

Machine Language (25.2.3, 25.2.4, 25.2.5, 25.2.6)

Each operation that a microprocessor performs has a corresponding instruction in machine language that is coded as a string of 0s and 1s. A machine language instruction has an op code that specifies an operation, such as load, add, move, or compare.

A machine language instruction can also have one or more operands that specify the data to process, its location in memory, or its destination in a register. The long strings of 0s and 1s in **Figure 25-7** contain an op code and operands that instruct the processor to load 5 into Register 1.

Op code   Operands

10000101   00000101   00000001
LOAD   5   Register 1

Figure 25-7   Op codes and operands in machine language instructions

Machine language is classified as a low-level programming language because it provides very little abstraction from the binary operation of computer circuits. If you were programming in machine language, you would have to understand many details about microprocessor operations and remember the op codes corresponding to long sequences of 0s and 1s.

Assembly Language (25.2.7, 25.2.8, 25.2.9)

To avoid dealing with perplexing strings of 0s and 1s, programmers turned to assembly language, which uses text abbreviations for op codes that directly correspond to the op codes of machine language. Where a machine language op code might be 0000 0000, the assembly language equivalent might be ADD.

Q Can you guess the meaning of assembly language op codes such as MOV, LDI, and CMP? Hint: Look back at the list of microprocessor operations.

A MOV is the op code that moves a value from memory into a CPU register. LDI is the "load immediate" op code that puts a specific value, such as 5, into a register. CMP is the op code for comparing the values in two registers.

An assembly language op code is usually two or three characters long. Data and addresses used as operands are specified as hexadecimal numbers.

By comparing the machine language instruction to an assembly language instruction in **Figure 25-8**, you can see how the op codes and operands correspond.

Figure 25-8   Compare a machine language instruction to its assembly language equivalent

If your interests lean toward programming controllers, device drivers, and operating systems, then you'll need assembly language skills. With assembly language, you can work directly with registers and memory addresses to optimize code so that it runs swiftly and efficiently. Hackers use assembly language to create and modify viruses. To thwart hackers, assembly language is also an important tool for security professionals.

25.3 MICROPROCESSOR OPERATIONS

Processing an Instruction (25.3.1)

In von Neumann's CPU architecture, a control unit and ALU work together to process instructions. The control unit has an **instruction register** that holds the instruction being processed.

The ALU has registers that hold the data being processed and the data that is produced. **Figure 25-9** shows how the CPU sets up an instruction to add the contents of two registers.

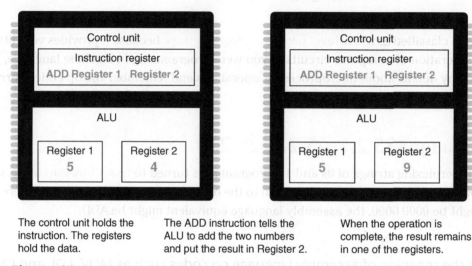

The control unit holds the instruction. The registers hold the data.

The ADD instruction tells the ALU to add the two numbers and put the result in Register 2.

When the operation is complete, the result remains in one of the registers.

Figure 25-9   Adding the contents of two registers in the ALU

The Instruction Cycle (25.3.2, 25.3.3)

Computers are like swans in the sense that on the surface everything seems to float effortlessly, but under the surface there is lots of activity, as those swan feet cycle through the water. A machine language or assembly language instruction seems very detailed, but even more detailed activity is going on in the microprocessor.

The execution of a machine language or assembly language instruction happens in three phases referred to as an **instruction cycle**, shown in **Figure 25-10**.

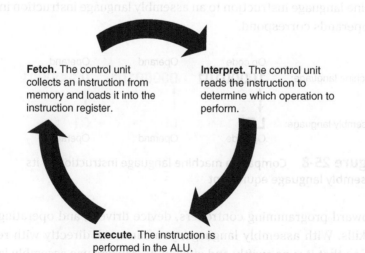

Fetch. The control unit collects an instruction from memory and loads it into the instruction register.

Interpret. The control unit reads the instruction to determine which operation to perform.

Execute. The instruction is performed in the ALU.

Figure 25-10   The instruction cycle

The machine language instructions for a program are held in a sequence of memory locations. To keep track of the instruction being executed, the control unit uses an instruction pointer. When the program begins, the instruction pointer holds the memory address of the first instruction. At the end of the instruction cycle, the instruction pointer is updated to point to the memory location that holds the next instruction.

Suppose a program begins with an instruction to load the value 5 into Register 1 of the ALU. **Figure 25-11** illustrates what happens as that instruction is executed.

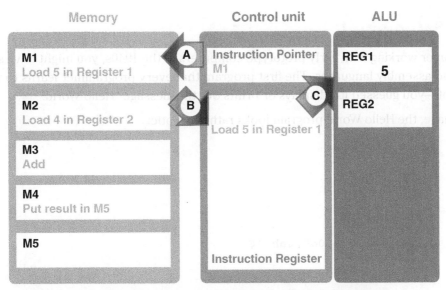

(A) The instruction pointer indicates M1 as the memory location of the first instruction.
(B) The control unit fetches the instruction and copies it to the instruction register.
(C) The instruction is interpreted and then executed by placing 5 in Register 1 of the ALU.
    Then the instruction pointer advances to M2 to fetch the next instruction.

Figure 25-11   Adding the contents of two registers in the CPU

Q Now that you know the basics of the instruction cycle, trace through the short assembly language program in **Figure 25-12**. What is the result of execution? Where does that result end up? What is in the instruction pointer? What is in the instruction register?

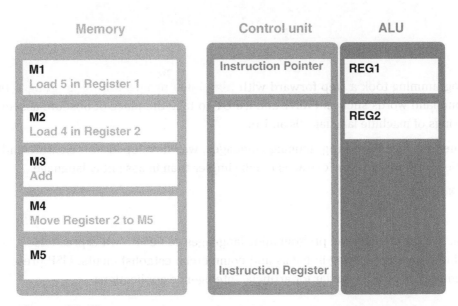

Figure 25-12   What is the result of executing the instructions in memory?

A The value 9 is in Register 2 and at memory location M5. The instruction pointer holds M5. The instruction register contains the last instruction: "Move Register 2 to M5."

25.4 HIGH-LEVEL PROGRAMMING LANGUAGES

Evolution (25.4.1, 25.4.2)

If you were a programmer working with early prototype computers in the 1940s, you might have struggled with machine languages and assembly languages. The first program that every programmer learns to write is "Hello World," a program that—you guessed it—displays or prints out the message "Hello World!"

In assembly language, the Hello World program looks rather cryptic:

```
Dosseg
.model small
.stack 100h
.data
hello_message db 'Hello World!',0dh,0ah,'$'
.code
main proc
mov ax,@data
mov ds,ax
mov ah,9
mov dx,offset hello_message
int 21h
mov ax,4C00h
int 21h
main endp
end main
```

By the 1950s, programming took a step forward with high-level programming languages that provided easy-to-remember command words such as PRINT and INPUT to take the place of obscure assembly language op codes and long strings of machine language 0s and 1s.

Fortran, one of the first high-level programming languages, was developed for scientific and engineering applications. The Hello World program in Fortran is much simpler than in assembly language.

```
PRINT *, "Hello World!"
END
```

In the Fortran era, two other high-level programming languages came into widespread use. COBOL became the language for business data processing in banks and commercial establishments. LISP presented a unique approach to programming and is still popular for artificial intelligence applications.

Teaching Languages (25.4.2)

If you wanted to become a self-taught programmer in the 1980s, a programming language called BASIC was included with every personal computer. In BASIC, each instruction is numbered, usually beginning with line 100. The Hello World program in BASIC looks like this:

```
100 PRINT "Hello World!"
```

At universities, the prevailing teaching language was Pascal. In elementary schools, students used Logo to program an on-screen turtle robot to create geometric patterns, as shown in **Figure 25-13**.

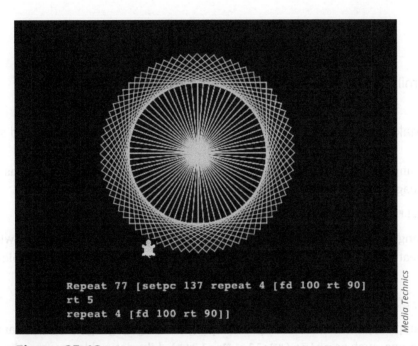

```
Repeat 77 [setpc 137 repeat 4 [fd 100 rt 90]
rt 5
repeat 4 [fd 100 rt 90]]
```

Figure 25-13 Logo program

The C Family (25.4.2, 25.4.3)

In the 1970s, the C programming language was an important development in high-level languages. Originally designed for creating utilities and operating systems, C became the parent for several of today's popular languages, such as C++, C#, and Objective-C.

C and its derivatives use extensive punctuation, such as parentheses, curly brackets, and semicolons, to ensure that each instruction is clear and unambiguous.

```
#include <iostream>

using namespace std;


int main( )
{
cout << "Hello World!" << endl;
return 0;
}
```

Web Programming Languages (25.4.3)

With the popularity of the web in the 1990s came languages such as JavaScript, Java, Python, Ruby, and PHP. If you are interested in creating online apps, these programming languages are in demand.

In Java, the Hello World program looks like this:

```
public class Hello {

    public static void main(String []args) {

        System.out.println("Hello World!");

    }

}
```

Q What are some similarities that you recognize between C and Java?

A Both C and Java make extensive use of punctuation, such as curly brackets and semicolons.

Python is a programming language created by a team of programmers whose philosophy was "simple is better than complex." The language has the simplicity of BASIC with minimal punctuation:

```
print ("Hello World!")
```

New programming languages are still being developed. In 2014, Apple introduced the Swift programming language designed for creating applications that run on iPhones, iPads, iMacs, and other Apple devices.

Characteristics (25.4.4)

From the Hello World examples, you can see that high-level programming languages use familiar words to formulate sentence-like instructions, such as `print("Hello World!")`. Like natural languages, these programming languages also have basic grammar rules for structure and punctuation.

For computer scientists, the key characteristic of a high-level language is the level of abstraction that differentiates it from machine language. Few elements of a high-level language have a one-to-one correspondence to machine language instructions. Instead, a single high-level language command such as `print` takes the place of a whole list of detailed assembly or machine language op codes. See **Figure 25-14**.

```
                              Dosseg
                              .model small
                              .stack 100h
                              .data
                              hello_message db 'Hello
                              World!',0dh,0ah,'$'
                              .code
                              main proc
print("Hello World!")         mov ax,@data
                              mov ds,ax
                              mov ah,9
                              mov dx,offset hello_message
                              int 21h
                              mov ax,4C00h
                              int 21h
                              main endp
                              end main
```

Figure 25-14   A single instruction in a high-level programming language requires multiple instructions in a low-level language

The abstraction of high-level languages decouples programmers from the digital and binary aspects of physical devices. Using a high-level language, you rarely have to deal directly with registers within the microprocessor or addresses within RAM chips. When coding a print command, you don't need to know which display device or printer will be used. Your programming language manages the details of arranging pixels on a screen display or controlling the printer ink dispenser.

Advantages and Disadvantages (25.4.5, 25.4.6)

As you might expect, high-level languages have many advantages over low-level languages, but they have a few disadvantages, too. Here are the significant pros and cons.

- **+ Easy to understand.** Imagine having to memorize strings of 0s and 1s that correspond to op codes. Commands such as `print`, `continue`, `return`, and `try` are easy to learn and remember. The sentence-like structure of high-level code makes it easy to understand and share with other programmers on your team.
- **+ Error detection.** In 1947 a programmer named Grace Hopper was troubleshooting a computer error and discovered a moth in one of the relay mechanisms. Removing the "bug" got the computer running properly. Since then, coding errors have been referred to as "bugs," and correcting those errors is called debugging. Programs written in high-level programming languages are relatively easy to debug because they use command words and punctuation similar to natural languages.
- **+ Machine independent.** The programs that you code using a high-level programming language are portable. You can write a program on one computer and distribute it for use on other computers.
- **– Require translation.** Programs written in high-level languages cannot be directly executed by a microprocessor. The program code has to be converted into machine language. The conversion requires an extra step when coding or when the program runs.
- **– Abstraction penalty.** Because high-level programming languages are separated from machine code by levels of abstraction, they may not be able to optimize processing tasks by taking advantage of low-level, machine-specific shortcuts. Programs coded in high-level languages typically run somewhat slower and require more memory than their machine-language or assembly-language counterparts.

SUMMARY

- A computer can be defined as a multipurpose device that accepts input, processes that input based on a stored set of instructions, and produces output.
- The key components of today's computers are integrated circuits, which contain millions or billions of microscopic transistors, resistors, capacitors, and circuitry. Transistors are important because they amplify signals, act as switches, and form logic gates.
- Moore's Law states that the number of components manufactured in integrated circuits doubles every two years, producing faster computing devices.
- Modern computers are based on von Neumann architecture with a central processing unit that contains a control unit, an arithmetic logic unit, and registers. These elements are integrated into microprocessors that perform the operations contained in an instruction set.
- Microprocessors can be programmed using low-level machine language and assembly language, or a high-level programming language.

- Low-level programming language statements consist of an op code and an operand that correspond directly to the microprocessor's instruction set.
- High-level programming languages, such as BASIC, C++, Java, and Python, use natural language commands and offer a level of abstraction that distances programmers from the detailed instruction set.

Key Terms

arithmetic logic unit (ALU)	instruction cycle	microprocessor
assembly language	instruction pointer	Moore's Law
central processing unit (CPU)	instruction register	op code
complex instruction set computers (CISC)	instruction set	operands
	integrated circuit	reduced instruction set computers (RISC)
computer	logic gate	
control unit	low-level programming language	Registers
high-level programming languages	machine language	transistor

DATA REPRESENTATION

LEARNING OBJECTIVES:

26.1 BITS AND BYTES

26.1.1 Define the term "digital data" and contrast it with the term "analog data."

26.1.2 Provide examples that differentiate digital data from analog data.

26.1.3 State that the term "bit" stands for "binary digit."

26.1.4 Confirm that a bit can have one of two states, conceptually represented by 0 or 1.

26.1.5 Define the term "bit" as the smallest unit of data representation.

26.1.6 Identify "b" as the symbol for bit.

26.1.7 List some of the ways that bits can be physically represented.

26.1.8 Associate bits with powers of 2.

26.1.9 Calculate the number of states that can be represented by one bit of data.

26.1.10 Define the terms "byte" and "octet" as a series of eight bits.

26.1.11 Identify "B" as the symbol for a byte.

26.1.12 Calculate the number of states that can be represented by 8 bits of data.

26.1.13 Define kilo, mega, giga, tera, peta, and exa in terms of powers of 2.

26.1.14 List examples of technologies that are measured in bits.

26.1.15 List examples of technologies that are measured in bytes.

26.2 BINARY

26.2.1 Associate the term "binary number" with the base-2 number system that uses only two symbols: 0 and 1.

26.2.2 Associate binary numbers with digital data representation.

26.2.3 Convert decimal numbers to binary.

26.2.4 Convert binary numbers to decimal.

26.2.5 Add binary numbers.

26.2.6 Calculate the one's complement of a binary number.

26.2.7 Calculate the two's complement of a binary number.

26.2.8 List three ways computers represent negative numbers.

26.3 HEXADECIMAL

26.3.1 Provide examples of technology applications that use hexadecimal.

26.3.2 Explain the RGB color system.

26.3.3 Associate the term "hexadecimal number" with the base-16 number system that uses symbols 0, 1, 2, 3, 4, 5, 6, 7, 8, 9, A, B, C, D, E, and F.

26.3.4 Identify 0xFF and other common notations for hexadecimal numbers.

26.3.5 Calculate that two hexadecimal digits can be represented in one byte of data.

26.3.6 Convert hexadecimal numbers to binary.

26.3.7 Convert binary numbers to hexadecimal.

26.3.8 Convert hexadecimal numbers to decimal.

26.3.9 Define the term "information density" as the amount of information that can be represented using a set number of bits.

26.3.10 Compare the information density of hexadecimal to binary.

26.3.11 Identify which notation has better readability: binary or hexadecimal.

26.4   ASCII AND UNICODE

26.4.1   Define the term "ASCII" as a standard method of representing non-numeric data using seven bits.

26.4.2   Understand why 7-bit ASCII can represent 128 characters.

26.4.3   Use an ASCII table to find the binary or decimal representation of a letter or symbol.

26.4.4   Define "control characters" as non-printable data such as line feeds or backspaces.

26.4.5   Identify Extended ASCII as a notation for representing 256 characters.

26.4.6   Define the term "Unicode" as the use of multiple bytes to represent characters included in most modern languages.

26.4.7   Associate UTF-8 with Unicode.

26.5   MEMORY ALLOCATION

26.5.1   Explain the difference between memory and storage.

26.5.2   Differentiate between online and offline storage.

26.5.3   Explain the term "volatile" in the context of computer memory.

26.5.4   Explain the difference between read-only and read-write.

26.5.5   Classify memory and storage devices according to their technology: solid state, magnetic, or optical.

26.5.6   Differentiate bits, bytes, and words.

26.5.7   Identify RAM as the type of memory used to temporarily hold the operating system, programs that are being executed, and the data needed by those programs.

26.5.8   Explain that memory consists of multiple storage locations that typically each hold one byte of data.

26.5.9   Define a "memory address" as a unique identifier for a memory location, usually represented by a hexadecimal number such as 0x9FFF.

26.1 BITS AND BYTES

Digital Data (26.1.1, 26.1.2)

Q Here's a puzzler. What do each of the diagrams in **Figure 26-1** have in common?

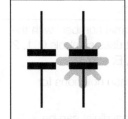 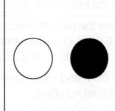 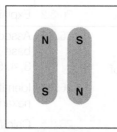 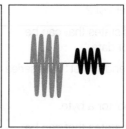 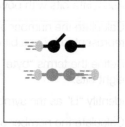

Figure 26-1   What do these diagrams have in common?

A Each diagram is a digital, binary pair that represents two unique states. For example, an uncharged circuit is one state. A charged circuit is the other state.

Surprisingly, any of the digital, binary pairs in Figure 26-1 can be used to represent all kinds of data, such as letters, symbols, numbers, and even colors.

Digital data is discrete and chunky. The data shown by a digital clock can be 10:52 or 10:53, but the clock can't show the split seconds in between. In contrast, **analog data** is continuous. For example, the second hand on an analog clock sweeps through a continuous range of time.

Computers store and manipulate many types of digital data, such as words, numbers, symbols, colors, sounds, images, and video. That data is processed within electronic circuits, sent as wired and wireless signals all over the world, stored as microscopic dots on CDs, saved as magnetic particles on hard drives, and held in electronic gates within flash drives.

Data representation refers to the way data is abstracted or modeled. When data is abstracted into a series of units that can have one of two states, the data representation is binary. The exact mechanism for data representation may vary from one device to another, but as shown in **Figure 26-2**, the data retains two important characteristics: it is digital, and it is binary.

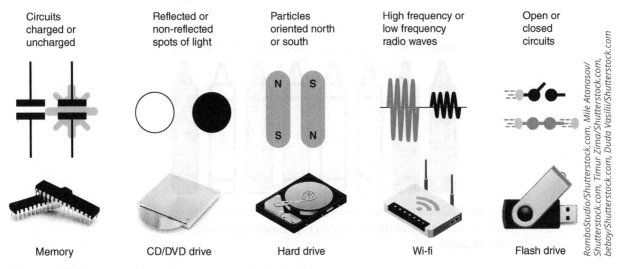

Circuits charged or uncharged	Reflected or non-reflected spots of light	Particles oriented north or south	High frequency or low frequency radio waves	Open or closed circuits
Memory	CD/DVD drive	Hard drive	Wi-fi	Flash drive

RomboStudio/Shutterstock.com, Mile Atanasov/Shutterstock.com, Timur Zima/Shutterstock.com, beboy/Shutterstock.com, Duda Vasilii/Shutterstock.com

Figure 26-2 Computer data is digital and it is binary

Bits (26.1.3, 26.1.4, 26.1.5, 26.1.6, 26.1.7, 26.1.8, 26.1.9)

Although computers might use on/off signals, frequencies, colored dots, or magnetized particles to physically represent data, you can envision those two states as the binary digits 0 and 1.

A binary digit is commonly referred to as a bit, abbreviated as a lowercase "b." A bit is the smallest unit of data manipulated by a digital device.

A single bit can be either a 0 or 1—that's two possibilities. A single bit could represent true or it could represent false. Or, a single bit could represent yes or no. As shown in **Figure 26-3**, one bit can be used to represent either of two units of information.

Bits: *0*   1

Sunny   Rainy

Figure 26-3 One bit can represent two units of information

To represent any one of four pieces of information, you need two bits. To represent any one of eight pieces of information, you need three bits. **Figure 26-4** provides examples.

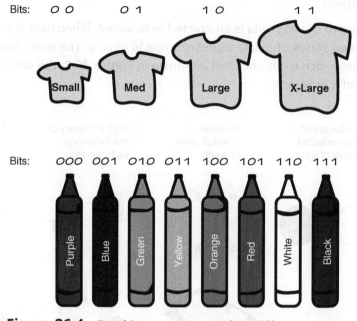

Figure 26-4   Two bits can represent four different units of information, and three bits can represent eight units of information

One bit: 2 possible units of information. Two bits: 4 possible units of information. Three bits: 8 possible units of information. You might be noticing a pattern. Each additional bit doubles the amount of information that can be represented.

Bits are based on the binary number system and correspond to powers of 2. To figure out how many units of information can be represented by any number of bits, simply plug in the number as the power of 2. One bit represents 2^1 units of information. For two bits, it is 2^2, for three bits it is 2^3.

Q How many different units of information can be represented using 5 bits?

A Five bits can be used to represent 32 different units of information. You can use a scientific or programmer calculator to find the value of 2^5 or multiply 2 five times: 2 x 2 x 2 x 2 x 2.

Bytes (26.1.10, 26.1.11, 26.1.12, 26.1.13, 26.1.14, 26.1.15)

Computers work with groups of eight bits called a **byte**. Here are the must-know basics about bytes:

- Byte is abbreviated as an uppercase "B."
- Bytes are sometimes called "octets."
- 00001010 is a byte of data.
- Each byte can represent one of 2^8, or 256, different units of data.
- A byte of data is commonly used to store text: a letter, symbol, or punctuation mark.

Bits and bytes are used to measure transmission speed and storage capacity of digital devices. Bits for speed. Bytes for capacity. These measurements can get quite large. For example, the speed of an Internet connection might be clocked at more than 50 million bits per second. A flash drive might store several billion bytes of data.

Such large numbers are often expressed using terms such as megabits and gigabytes.

The tricky thing about these numbers is that they commonly use binary measurements based on powers of 2, not powers of 10.

For example, in the world of computers, a kilo is 2^{10}, which is 1,024. But in everyday life, a kilo is just 1,000 because it is derived from the decimal value 10^3. You can see the difference in **Figure 26-5**.

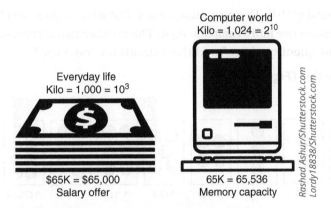

Figure 26-5   Measurements that relate to computers are based on powers of 2

Q Suppose your Visa chip card has 2K memory capacity. How many bytes of data can your card store?

A 2K is 1,024 × 2, which equals 2,048 bytes.

Figure 26-6 lists commonly used prefixes and abbreviations for binary measurements of bits and bytes.

Prefix	Abbreviation for bits	Abbreviation for bytes	Number of bits or bytes
Kilo	Kb	KB	$2^{10} = 1,024$
Mega	Mb	MB	$2^{20} = 1,048,576$
Giga	Gb	GB	$2^{30} = 1,073,741,824$
Tera	Tb	TB	$2^{40} = 1,099,511,627,776$
Peta	Pb	PB	$2^{50} = 1,125,899,906,842,624$
Exa	Eb	EB	$2^{60} = 1,152,921,504,606,846,976$
Zetta	Zb	ZB	$2^{70} = 1,180,591,620,717,411,303,424$
Yotta	Yb	YB	$2^{80} = 1,208,925,819,614,629,174,706,176$

Figure 26-6   Binary measurements for bits and bytes

26.2 BINARY

Binary Numbers (26.2.1, 26.2.2)

Computers were originally designed to process numerical data, and today's computers still carry out many tasks involving calculations. Because computers are electronic devices, they manipulate bits—1s and 0s. The **binary number system** also uses 1s and 0s to represent numbers, so this system is used to represent numbers in most digital devices.

In binary notation, numbers are represented using only the digits 0 and 1. This system is sometimes called **base-2** because it uses two digits.

When counting in binary, begin with 0. The next number is 1. But what comes next? There is no "2" digit. To make the next number, you'll need to use more than one digit. The number two is represented by 10, pronounced "one zero." The 1 stands for "one quantity of two" and the 0 stands for "no ones."

Counting in binary goes like this (**Figure 26-7**):

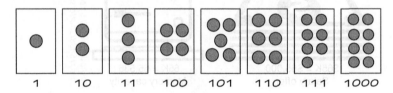

Figure 26-7   Counting in binary

Q After 1000, what's the next binary number?

A The next binary number is 1001.

In computer memory, binary numbers are stored in microscopic electronic circuits called **capacitors**. The symbol for a capacitor looks like the letter T and its upside-down reflection. A charged capacitor represents a 1 bit. An uncharged capacitor represents a 0 bit. **Figure 26-8** illustrates a series of capacitors that represent the binary number 00000101.

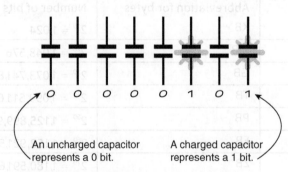

An uncharged capacitor represents a 0 bit.

A charged capacitor represents a 1 bit.

Figure 26-8   Computer memory uses capacitors to represent binary data

It is usually easy to identify a binary number because it is typically a long string of 1s and 0s. However, a number such as 101 could mean five in binary or one hundred and one in decimal. To differentiate, binary numbers can be written using any of the following notations:

- 101b
- 101_2
- %101
- 0b101
- 101_{binary}

An additional clue that a number is binary would be zeros in the left place values. Binary numbers are often written as bytes containing 8 bits. A binary number such as 101 could be written as 00000101. The leftmost zeros do not add any value to the number and may be omitted.

Binary to Decimal (26.2.3)

Programmers are expected to understand how binary can be used to represent prices, miles, wages, quantities, and other numbers that computers manipulate for everyday tasks. Suppose a computer stores 1010 for the number of penguins in a zoo. That number is more understandable when converted into our familiar decimal system.

In the binary number system, each place value is a power of 2. The rightmost place value is 2^0, which is 1 in decimal. The next place value is 2^1, which is two in decimal. In **Figure 26-9**, you can see how to convert the binary number 1010 into the decimal number 10.

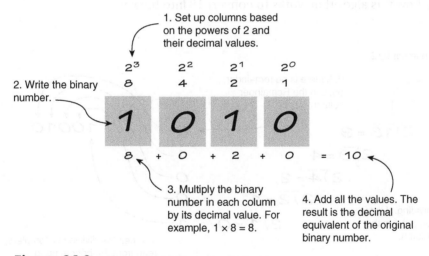

Figure 26-9   Converting binary to decimal

Q Let's see if you have the hang of binary to decimal conversion. What is the decimal equivalent of the binary number 11010?

A Here's the answer. As shown in **Figure 26-10**, there is one value of 16 plus one value of 8 and one value of 2 for a total of 26.

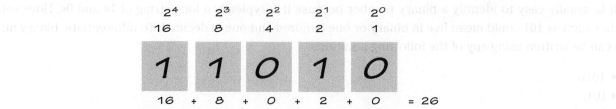

Figure 26-10   11010 is the binary representation of 26

Decimal to Binary (26.2.4)

A palindrome is a word or number that reads the same backward as forward. Kayak is a palindrome. Numbers can also be palindromes. The number 15351 is a palindrome with a secret. To discover that secret, you'll need to know how to convert decimal numbers to binary.

Converting decimal numbers to binary is easy if you use a division trick. The algorithm goes like this:

Write down the decimal number.
Divide the decimal number by 2.
If there is a remainder, write 1 in the remainder column.
If there is no remainder, write 0 in the remainder column.
Continue dividing until you reach 0.
Read up the remainder column for the binary number.

Figure 26-11 shows how this algorithm works to convert 18 into binary.

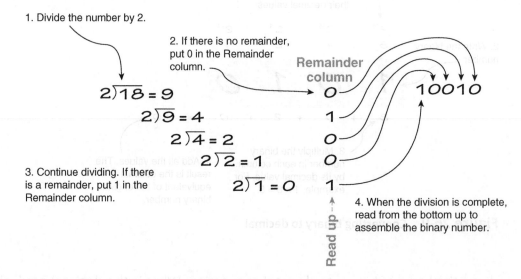

Figure 26-11   Converting a decimal number to binary requires repeated division by 2

Converting the palindrome 15351 into binary involves lots of division operations. You can use a programmer's calculator like the one in **Figure 26-12** to find the result.

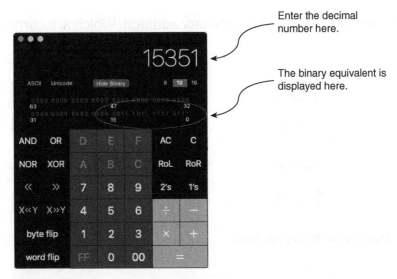

Enter the decimal
number here.

The binary equivalent is
displayed here.

Figure 26-12   Use a scientific or programmer calculator for decimal to binary conversions

The binary for 15351 is 11101111110111. Both the decimal and binary numbers are palindromes! That's the secret of 15351.

Binary Addition (26.2.5)

Computers perform arithmetic operations based on binary numbers. Understanding binary addition can give you insight into digital arithmetic and the way computers represent negative numbers.

When adding 1 + 1 in binary, there is no "2" digit. So, what happens? The addition algorithm for binary numbers is similar to adding 9 + 1 in base-10. You write a zero as a placeholder and carry the 1 to next place value as shown in **Figure 26-13**.

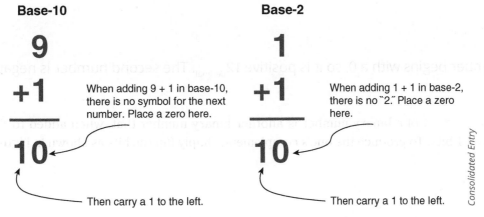

Base-10

9
+1
─────
10

When adding 9 + 1 in base-10, there is no symbol for the next number. Place a zero here.

Then carry a 1 to the left.

Base-2

1
+1
─────
10

When adding 1 + 1 in base-2, there is no "2." Place a zero here.

Then carry a 1 to the left.

Consolidated Entry

Figure 26-13   The algorithm for binary addition is similar to using a "carry" in base-10

Q Figure 26-14 shows a few more examples of binary addition. Which are correct and which are not?

$$\begin{array}{r} 1 \\ + 11 \\ \hline 100 \end{array} \qquad \begin{array}{r} 101 \\ + 10 \\ \hline 111 \end{array} \qquad \begin{array}{r} 1011 \\ + 10 \\ \hline 1001 \end{array} \qquad \begin{array}{r} 1111 \\ + 111 \\ \hline 10110 \end{array}$$

Figure 26-14   Examples of binary addition

A The third sum is not correct. 1011 + 10 = 10101.

Negative Numbers (26.2.6, 26.2.7, 26.2.8)

Computers have to deal with negative numbers, but there is no electronic negative symbol. Computers represent negative numbers in three ways:

- Signed magnitude
- One's complement
- Two's complement

Signed magnitude uses the leftmost bit to indicate whether a number is positive or negative. If that bit is 0, the number is positive. If that bit is 1, the number is negative.

Q Which of these numbers is negative?

00001100
10001100

A The first number begins with a 0, so it is positive $12_{decimal}$. The second number is negative: $-12_{decimal}$.

The **one's complement** of a binary number is another binary number that, when added to the original number, produces all 1 bits. To produce the one's complement, simply flip the bits as shown in **Figure 26-15**.

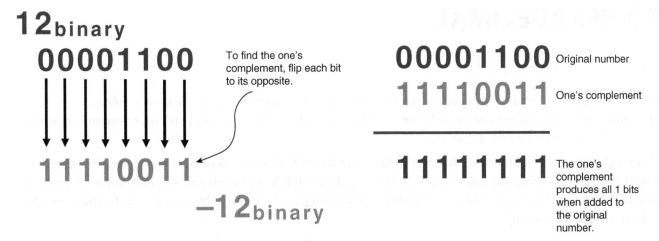

Figure 26-15   The one's complement of a binary number can represent its negative

The **two's complement** of a binary number is another binary number that, when added to the original number, produces all 0 bits. Producing the two's complement is a multistep algorithm as shown in **Figure 26-16**.

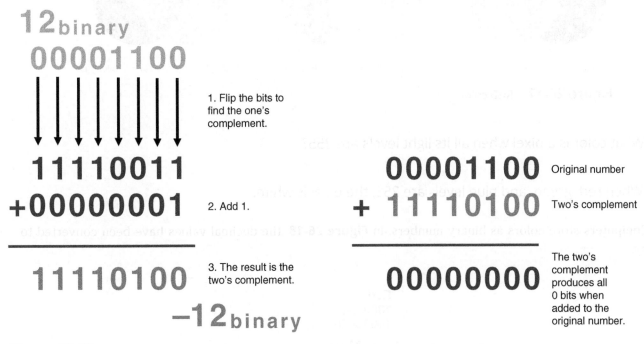

Figure 26-16   The two's complement of a binary number can represent its negative

With three ways of representing negative numbers, you might be thinking that 10001100, 11110011, and 11110100 all could represent −12. You would be correct, but most modern computers use the two's complement for negative numbers.

26.3 HEXADECIMAL

Colors (26.3.1, 26.3.2)

The color display on a computer or smartphone is divided into thousands of picture elements called pixels. Each pixel contains a group of three miniature lights: one red, one green, and one blue. This color system is referred to as RGB, which stands for red, green, blue.

Each light can have an illumination level ranging from 0 to 255. The light is off and black when its value is 0. The light is brightest when its value is 255. In the purple swatch in the center of the first color diagram in **Figure 26-17**, the red light is on at level 130, which is half strength. The green light is off at level 0. The blue light is on full strength at level 255.

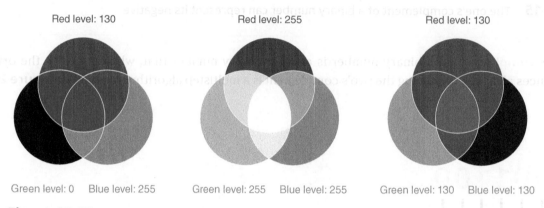

Figure 26-17   RGB color

Q What color is a pixel when all its light levels are 255?

A When red, green, and blue levels are 255, the pixel is white.

Computers store colors as binary numbers. In **Figure 26-18**, the decimal values have been converted to binary.

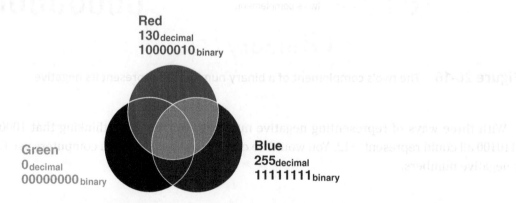

Figure 26-18   Binary values for red, green, and blue combine to display purple

The 24-bit binary number for the color purple is 100000100000000011111111. That's very long. Computers don't have any trouble with such a long number, but humans find it cumbersome. Programmers use hexadecimal notation to deal with colors because it requires only six digits instead of 24.

The hexadecimal notation for the purple swatch is #8200FF. That's much shorter than the 24-bit binary notation. Finding out why hexadecimal notation is so much shorter requires a quick introduction to the hexadecimal number system.

Hexadecimal Numbers (26.3.3, 26.3.4)

The hexadecimal number system, or base-16, has 16 digits: 0 1 2 3 4 5 6 7 8 9 A B C D E F. This number system is commonly used to specify the colors of icons, images, and text. Web designers are well-versed in hexadecimal for specifying the colors of text and links on webpages.

Programmers usually say "hex" instead of "hexadecimal." Counting in hex goes like this:

0 1 2 3 4 5 6 7 8 9 A B C D E F 10 11 12 13 14 15 16 17 18 19

To distinguish hex numbers from binary and decimal numbers, you might see any of these notations:

- 0x101
- #101
- 101h
- 0h101
- 101_{hex}
- 101_h
- 101_{16}
- &H101
- U+0101

Binary-Hex-Binary Conversions (26.3.5, 26.3.6, 26.3.7)

Q Here's something interesting. Take a look at the binary numbers in **Figure 26-19** and their hex equivalents. Do you notice a pattern?

Hex	0	1	2	3	4	5	6	7
Binary	0000	0001	0010	0011	0100	0101	0110	0111

Hex	8	9	A	B	C	D	E	F
Binary	1000	1001	1010	1011	1100	1101	1110	1111

Figure 26-19   Do you notice a pattern between hex and binary digits?

A For every four binary digits, there is a one-digit hex number. For example, the four binary digits 1011 and the single hexadecimal digit B both represent the decimal number 11.

This correspondence makes it easy to convert from binary to hex. The algorithm for converting binary numbers into hex is shown in **Figure 26-20**.

101011111001001	1. Begin with the original number.
10101111100 1001	2. Working from the right, separate a group of four digits.
101 0111 1100 1001	3. Continue separating into groups of four.
0101 0111 1100 1001	4. If the leftmost group has less than four bits, pad it with zeros.
5 7 C 9	5. For each group of four digits, write the corresponding hex value.
#57C9	6. The result is the hexadecimal value.

Figure 26-20   Convert binary to hex

To convert from hex to binary, just reverse the process. For each hex digit, write out the 4-bit binary number.

Q To be sure you can convert hex to binary, try converting A1 into binary.

A The binary for A is 1010. The binary for 1 is 0001. So A1 is 10100001 in binary.

Hex-Decimal Conversion (26.3.8)

The hexadecimal system has place values that are powers of 16. The algorithm for converting hex to decimal is shown in **Figure 26-21**.

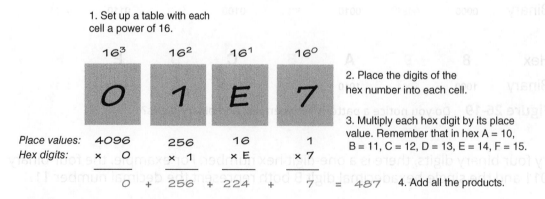

1. Set up a table with each cell a power of 16.

16^3	16^2	16^1	16^0
O	1	E	7

2. Place the digits of the hex number into each cell.

Place values: 4096   256   16   1
Hex digits: × O   × 1   × E   × 7

3. Multiply each hex digit by its place value. Remember that in hex A = 10, B = 11, C = 12, D = 13, E = 14, F = 15.

O + 256 + 224 + 7 = 487

4. Add all the products.

Figure 26-21   Convert hex to decimal

Information Density (26.3.9, 26.3.10, 26.3.11)

Information density is the amount of information that can be represented by a single symbol. You've worked with three number systems: decimal, binary, and hex. Which system do you think has the greatest information density?

Recall that $15_{decimal}$ is 1111_{binary} or F_{hex}. In decimal, the number requires two digits. In binary, four digits. In hex, only one digit. Hexadecimal provides higher information density than binary or decimal, so it is more efficient—at least for humans.

Because hex notation is efficient and relatively easy to read, it is used not only for designating colors, but also for memory readouts, raw file readouts, IPv6 Internet addresses, and storage addresses in computer memory.

Hollywood uses hex, too. You've seen all the garble that appears on hacker screens in movies. That Hollywood illusion is created by displaying the contents of a file with binary bits converted to hex. In **Figure 26-22**, each two-digit pair is a hex value.

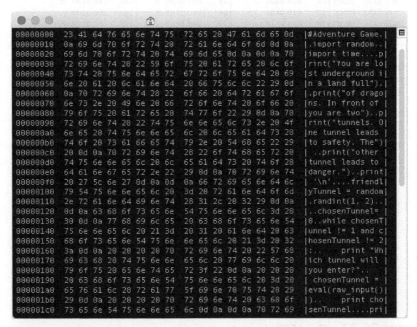

Figure 26-22   A raw file readout displays hex values for the binary data in a document or program

26-4 ASCII AND UNICODE

ASCII (26.4.1, 26.4.2, 26.4.3, 26.4.4)

Computers work with text as well as numbers, so there has to be an **encoding system** for representing text with 0 and 1 bits. **ASCII** is the American Standard Code for Information Interchange.

ASCII uses 7 bits to represent text. For example, the ASCII representation of an uppercase A is 1000001. When you type the letter "A" in a word processing document, the computer stores it as 1000001.

With 7 bits, ASCII can represent 128 different elements, including:

- Lowercase and uppercase letters of the alphabet
- Numerals from 0 to 9
- Punctuation symbols
- Arithmetic operators
- Symbols such as @ # $ % &
- Control characters, which include non-printable data such as a space and a line feed

The characters and their encoded equivalents are called a character set. The character set table in **Figure 26-23** illustrates the binary and decimal representations for each character.

Dec	Bin	Char	Dec	Bin	Char	Dec	Bin	Char	Dec	Bin	Char
0	000 0000	[NUL]	32	010 0000	space	64	100 0000	@	96	110 0000	`
1	000 0001	[SOH]	33	010 0001	!	65	100 0001	A	97	110 0001	a
2	000 0010	[STX]	34	010 0010	"	66	100 0010	B	98	110 0010	b
3	000 0011	[ETX]	35	010 0011	#	67	100 0011	C	99	110 0011	c
4	000 0100	[EOT]	36	010 0100	$	68	100 0100	D	100	110 0100	d
5	000 0101	[ENQ]	37	010 0101	%	69	100 0101	E	101	110 0101	e
6	000 0110	[ACK]	38	010 0110	&	70	100 0110	F	102	110 0110	f
7	000 0111	[BEL]	39	010 0111	'	71	100 0111	G	103	110 0111	g
8	000 1000	[BS]	40	010 1000	(	72	100 1000	H	104	110 1000	h
9	000 1001	[TAB]	41	010 1001	)	73	100 1001	I	105	110 1001	i
10	000 1010	[LF]	42	010 1010	*	74	100 1010	J	106	110 1010	j
11	000 1011	[VT]	43	010 1011	+	75	100 1011	K	107	110 1011	k
12	000 1100	[FF]	44	010 1100	,	76	100 1100	L	108	110 1100	l
13	000 1101	[CR]	45	010 1101	-	77	100 1101	M	109	110 1101	m
14	000 1110	[SO]	46	010 1110	.	78	100 1110	N	110	110 1110	n
15	000 1111	[SI]	47	010 1111	/	79	100 1111	o	111	110 1111	o
16	001 0000	[DLE]	48	011 0000	0	80	101 0000	P	112	111 0000	p
17	001 0001	[DC1]	49	011 0001	1	81	101 0001	Q	113	111 0001	q
18	001 0010	[DC2]	50	011 0010	2	82	101 0010	R	114	111 0010	r
19	001 0011	[DC3]	51	011 0011	3	83	101 0011	S	115	111 0011	s
20	001 0100	[DC4]	52	011 0100	4	84	101 0100	T	116	111 0100	t
21	001 0101	[NAK]	53	011 0101	5	85	101 0101	U	117	111 0101	u
22	001 0110	[SYN]	54	011 0110	6	86	101 0110	V	118	111 0110	v
23	001 0111	[ETB]	55	011 0111	7	87	101 0111	W	119	111 0111	w
24	001 1000	[CAN]	56	011 1000	8	88	101 1000	X	120	111 1000	x
25	001 1001	[EM]	57	011 1001	9	89	101 1001	Y	121	111 1001	y
26	001 1010	[SUB]	58	011 1010	:	90	101 1010	Z	122	111 1010	z
27	001 1011	[ESC]	59	011 1011	;	91	101 1011	[	123	111 1011	{
28	001 1100	[FS]	60	011 1100	<	92	101 1100	\	124	111 1100	|
29	001 1101	[GS]	61	011 1101	=	93	101 1101	]	125	111 1101	}
30	001 1110	[RS]	62	011 1110	>	94	101 1110	^	126	111 1110	~
31	001 1111	[US]	63	011 1111	?	95	101 1111	_	127	111 1111	[DEL]

Figure 26-23   The ASCII character set

Q What is the binary representation for an uppercase letter M and its decimal equivalent?

A An uppercase M is 100 1101 in binary. The decimal equivalent for 100 1101 is 77.

Extended ASCII (26.4.5)

Seven bits provides 128 possible elements for the ASCII character set. Recall that the number of units of information represented by binary digits corresponds to powers of 2.

$2^1 = 2$ units
$2^2 = 4$ units
$2^3 = 8$ units

$2^4 = 16$ units

$2^5 = 32$ units

$2^6 = 64$ units

$2^7 = 128$ units

Seven-bit ASCII was fine for English text, but it lacked symbols for international monetary units such as the ₤ (pound) and ¥ (yen). It also lacked letters of the alphabet with diacritic marks, such as ë and à, found in Spanish, French, and other languages.

ASCII was eventually extended to 8 bits, which allows representation of 256 (that's 2^8) different elements. Those elements include diacritic marks, international symbols, and a variety of small lines and shapes. **Figure 26-24** illustrates some symbols added to the Extended ASCII character set.

Figure 26-24 Symbols from the Extended ASCII character set

Unicode (26.4.6, 26.4.7)

As the popularity of computers spread throughout the world, it became important to support languages, such as Russian, Mandarin, Hindi, and Arabic, that use non-European character sets. Unicode is a variable-length standard that is at least 16 bits but may extend to 48 bits.

Unicode assigns each symbol a binary number called a codepoint. A codepoint is usually written as a hexadecimal number such as U+006F. The U+ means Unicode. Hexadecimal notation is used instead of binary because it is easier to read.

Q Here's a challenge. You know that 8-bit ASCII can be used to represent 256 characters. The decimal number 256 is 0100 in hex. Which of these symbols would not be in the ASCII character set, but would be in the Unicode character set?

€   U+20AC

@   U+0040

$ U+0024

A The euro symbol € is not in the 8-bit ASCII character set. Its hexadecimal assignment is 20AC, which is 8,364 in decimal—a number far higher than the 256-limit placed on the ASCII character set. The @ symbol is hex 0040, which is 64 in decimal. The $ symbol is hex 0024, which is 36 in decimal. Because 64 and 36 are within the 256 ASCII limit, the @ and $ symbols are in the ASCII character set.

There are several versions of Unicode. **UTF-8** is a popular standard today. It is the most common character set used on the web.

With encoding methods such as ASCII, Extended ASCII, Unicode, and UTF-8, programmers and web designers may have to specify which one to use. If you have received an email message sprinkled with weird symbols such as HÐ‾â¾€ or connected to a webpage that contained garbled text, you've seen the result of a mismatched encoding method. Your device might have been expecting UTF-8, but was sent data formatted for plain ASCII text.

Programming languages and web design tools make provisions for specifying encoding systems and character sets. Keep this fact in mind when working on a coding project that involves languages other than English.

26.5 MEMORY ALLOCATION

Memory and Storage (26.5.1)

The terms "memory" and "storage" are used inconsistently in the computer industry. **Storage** technically refers to devices that hold data *permanently*, in contrast to **memory** that holds data only *temporarily*. But devices such as flash drives are popularly called "memory sticks" even though they store data permanently. Disk drives are sometimes called "secondary memory" even though they essentially store data permanently. You can see why there is confusion.

To take a programmer's view, however, memory is different from storage. Memory has a direct line to the processor. Storage is a step removed from the processor. **Figure 26-25** is a useful abstraction showing a programmer's view of memory and storage.

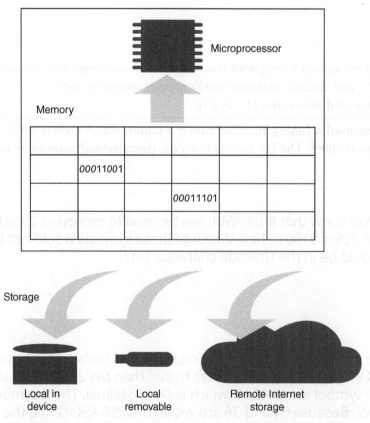

Figure 26-25   A programmer's view of memory and storage

Storage Devices (26.5.2, 26.5.3, 26.5.4, 26.5.5, 26.5.6)

The bits and bytes that represent data and computer programs can be stored in a variety of devices, such as hard drives, flash drives, solid state drives, SD cards, and CD/DVD drives.

Storage devices can be classified in several ways.

Locality. Online storage is provided by Internet-based cloud services, such as Amazon Web Services, Microsoft Azure, and Google Cloud Platform. Offline storage (local storage) includes devices such as hard drives that are typically connected directly to a digital device and removable devices such as flash drives.

Volatility. Volatile storage requires a power source to hold data. Nonvolatile storage holds data even when a device is turned off. Nonvolatile storage is sometimes referred to as "permanent storage," whereas volatile storage is sometimes referred to as "temporary storage."

Changeability. Most storage devices save data by a process called "writing," and they retrieve data by a process called "reading." Storage devices such as CD ROMs are read-only, which means that the data they contain cannot be changed. Other storage devices, such as hard drives and flash drives, have read-write capabilities that allow data to be stored, retrieved, and changed.

Technology. Magnetic storage technology arranges microscopic magnetic particles that represent 0s and 1s. Optical storage technology recognizes the presence or absence of reflected light. Solid state storage technology opens or shuts miniature logic gates to represent "on" or "off" bits (**Figure 26-26**).

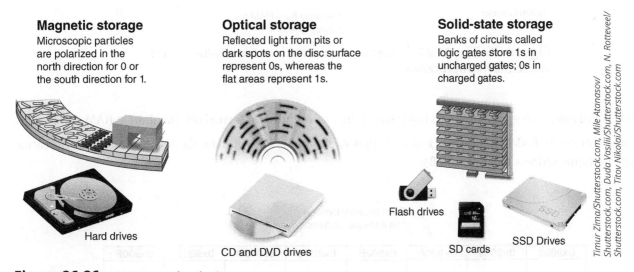

Magnetic storage
Microscopic particles are polarized in the north direction for 0 or the south direction for 1.

Hard drives

Optical storage
Reflected light from pits or dark spots on the disc surface represent 0s, whereas the flat areas represent 1s.

CD and DVD drives

Solid-state storage
Banks of circuits called logic gates store 1s in uncharged gates; 0s in charged gates.

Flash drives

SD cards

SSD Drives

Timur Zima/Shutterstock.com, Mile Atanasov/ Shutterstock.com, Duda Vasilii/Shutterstock.com, N. Rotteveel/ Shutterstock.com, Titov Nikolai/Shutterstock.com

Figure 26-26   Storage technologies

Computer storage is divided into locations for holding data. Those locations can be designated as blocks, pages, tracks, or sectors, each with a unique address. A byte consisting of 8 bits is usually the minimum amount of space allocated to store a single item of data. Several bytes can be combined to store longer data, such as Unicode characters, integers, or floating-point numbers.

Memory (26.5.7, 26.5.8, 26.5.9)

Programmers are interested in RAM (random access memory) because it provides local, temporary storage for data, programs, and the computer's operating system. When programmers use RAM effectively, programs run efficiently. For example, a list stored in successive memory locations can be accessed more quickly than if the list is scattered randomly in memory.

RAM is classified as memory because it is directly linked to the processor. RAM is housed within one or more integrated circuits that reside on the main circuit board of a digital device (**Figure 26-27**).

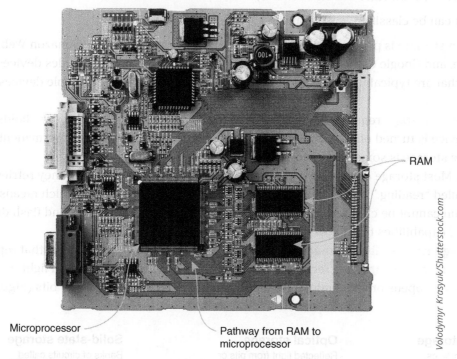

RAM

Microprocessor

Pathway from RAM to microprocessor

Volodymyr Krasyuk/Shutterstock.com

Figure 26-27   **RAM is located on the main circuit board with a direct link to the microprocessor**

RAM is volatile. It requires power to hold data. When a computer is turned off, the data in RAM disappears.

You can envision RAM as a gridwork of cells that each hold a byte of data. Each cell is a memory location that has a unique address (**Figure 26-28**).

Each memory location has a unique address.

0×9008	0×9009	0×900A	0×900B	0×900C	0×900D	0×900E	0×900F
			00100011	11001010			

0×9010	0×9011	0×9012	0×9013	0×9014	0×9015	0×9016	0×9018
	00100010			11100111	01010011		

Each memory location can hold one byte of data such as one ASCII character or one integer in the range 0 to 255.

Longer data such as Unicode characters can be stored in consecutive memory locations.

Figure 26-28   **RAM addresses and data**

A **memory address** such as 0x9FFF begins with 0x to indicate it is in hexadecimal. Familiarity with this notation is helpful for two reasons:

Manual memory management. Occasionally when coding, you might want to directly manipulate the contents of a memory location.

Tracking down coding errors. You might want to check the contents of memory variables to fix coding errors.

RAM capacity is typically measured in gigabytes, in contrast to storage options, which may hold terabytes of data. Today's computers and smartphones are usually shipped with somewhere between 1 and 8 GB of RAM.

SUMMARY

- Data representation refers to the way information is abstracted so that it can be manipulated, transmitted, and stored as data by today's computing devices.
- Whether data takes the form of radio signals, electric charges, magnetized particles, or reflected light, it retains two important characteristics: it is digital, and it is binary.
- One binary digit is called a bit. Eight bits are a byte.
- Digital devices use the binary number system to represent positive and negative numbers. Text data is represented using ASCII, Unicode, and UTF-8 encoding.
- Binary representations are typically long strings of 0s and 1s, which are difficult for humans to read. Hexadecimal notation is easier to read than binary and has higher information density, so it is often the preferred notation used by programmers. Hexadecimal is used to refer to memory addresses and for raw file readouts.
- Digital data is held temporarily in memory and more permanently in storage devices, such as hard drives and flash drives.
- Storage devices can be classified in several ways, including by technology. Magnetic storage technology arranges microscopic magnetic particles that represent 0s and 1s. Optical storage technology recognizes the presence or absence of reflected light. Solid state storage technology opens or shuts miniature logic gates to represent "on" or "off" bits.
- RAM is classified as memory because it is directly linked to the processor. RAM provides local, temporary storage for data, programs, and the computer's operating system. Each RAM location has a unique address and holds one byte of data.

Key Terms

analog data	Digital data	pixels
ASCII	encoding system	RAM (random access memory)
base-2	hexadecimal number system	read-only
binary	Information density	read-write
binary digits	Magnetic storage technology	RGB
binary measurements	memory	Signed magnitude
binary number system	memory address	Solid state storage technology
bit	Nonvolatile storage	Storage
byte	Offline storage	two's complement
capacitors	one's complement	Unicode
character set	Online storage	UTF-8
Data representation	Optical storage technology	Volatile storage

MODULE 27

PROGRAMMING PARADIGMS

LEARNING OBJECTIVES:

27.1 IMPERATIVE AND DECLARATIVE PARADIGMS

27.1.1 Define the term "programming paradigm."

27.1.2 Differentiate between imperative and declarative programming paradigms.

27.2 THE PROCEDURAL PARADIGM

27.2.1 Associate procedural programming with step-by-step algorithms that specify *how* a computer should perform a task.

27.2.2 Associate the procedural paradigm with imperative programming.

27.2.3 List the key characteristics of the procedural paradigm.

27.2.4 List advantages and disadvantages of the procedural paradigm.

27.2.5 Associate procedural programming with early high-level languages such as Fortran, BASIC, Pascal, and C.

27.3 THE OBJECT-ORIENTED PARADIGM

27.3.1 Associate the object-oriented paradigm with creating data models of a problem's entities, actions, and relationships.

27.3.2 Explain the significance of classes, objects, attributes, and methods in the object-oriented paradigm.

27.3.3 List the key characteristics of OOP.

27.3.4 List advantages and disadvantages of the object-oriented paradigm.

27.3.5 Identify problems that can best be solved using the object-oriented paradigm.

27.3.6 Identify programming languages that support the object-oriented paradigm.

27.3.7 State that a programming language can support multiple paradigms.

27.4 DECLARATIVE PARADIGMS

27.4.1 Identify the approach of declarative paradigms as expressing the logic of a problem rather than specifying a step-by-step algorithm.

27.4.2 List the key characteristics of declarative paradigms.

27.4.3 Identify problems that can best be solved using the declarative paradigm.

27.4.4 List logic programming, functional programming, and database query as examples of the declarative paradigm.

27.4.5 Associate various programming languages with each type of declarative paradigm.

27.4.6 List advantages and disadvantages of the declarative paradigm.

27.1 IMPERATIVE AND DECLARATIVE PARADIGMS

Think Outside the Box (27.1.1, 27.1.2)

Q Can you use pen and paper to duplicate the drawing in **Figure 27-1** without lifting the pen from the paper?

Figure 27-1
Can you draw this diagram without lifting your pen from the paper?

A The trick is to fold over a corner of the paper as shown in **Figure 27-2**.

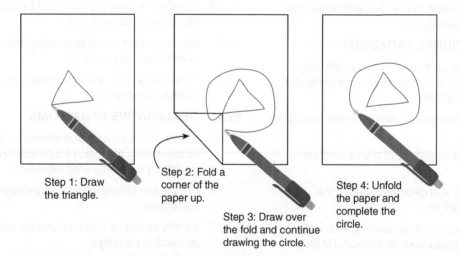

Step 1: Draw the triangle.

Step 2: Fold a corner of the paper up.

Step 3: Draw over the fold and continue drawing the circle.

Step 4: Unfold the paper and complete the circle.

Figure 27-2   One solution to the puzzler

The circle puzzler has another solution. Using a ballpoint pen, you can retract the point after drawing the triangle, move the pen, and then extend the point to draw the circle.

Solving the circle-drawing challenge requires creative thinking and illustrates that there can be more than one approach to a solution.

Programmers have several ways to approach a programming task:

- View the task as a problem that can be solved by specifying a series of steps for the computer to execute.
- Visualize the computer manipulating data for several objects, people, or places.
- Create a solution based on a series of rules.

The various approaches to programming are referred to as programming paradigms. To use an analogy, suppose you are planning a trip from New York City to Philadelphia. As in **Figure 27-3**, you have several "paradigms" for transportation: car, plane, train, or scooter!

By car, you need turn-by-turn directions.

Once you book a flight, you don't have to worry about the route details.

A scooter trip might be cheap, but won't get you there very fast.

Taking a train is not fast, but you can leave the driving to the engineer.

Figure 27-3   Transportation paradigms

Each transportation paradigm has advantages and disadvantages. You might even use more than one paradigm by driving to the airport and then taking a plane. Programming paradigms also have advantages and disadvantages. Here are the important takeaways:

- A programming paradigm affects the way you think about a program and the style in which you code it.
- Each programming paradigm has advantages and disadvantages.
- One paradigm might be a more suitable approach to a programming problem than another paradigm.
- Some programs might require you to use more than one paradigm.
- The features for implementing paradigms vary from one programming language to another.

Programming paradigms fall into one of two categories: imperative or declarative. Each category includes a subset of specialized paradigms.

- Imperative programming paradigms focus on *how* by specifying the steps required to carry out a task. This category includes procedural and object-oriented paradigms.
- Declarative programming paradigms focus on *what* by describing the problem or task. This category includes logic, functional, and database query paradigms.

Let's take a look at the most popular imperative and declarative programming paradigms to see how they can contribute to your programming skills.

27.2 THE PROCEDURAL PARADIGM

Procedural Basics (27.2.1, 27.2.2)

The traditional approach to programming uses the procedural paradigm, which helps you visualize a program as a step-by-step algorithm. Programs based on the procedural paradigm typically consist of instructions that indicate *how* a computer should perform a task or solve a problem.

Because the procedural paradigm focuses on step-by-step algorithms, it is classified as an imperative programming paradigm.

Let's use a road trip as an example and look at a program that calculates the total cost of gas for two trips. One trip is along the 2700-mile, once-glamorous Route 66. The other trip is along the scenic but rugged 2000-mile Alaska Highway. You would like the program to determine which trip would have the lowest total gas cost. A procedural algorithm for this calculation might look like the steps in **Figure 27-4**.

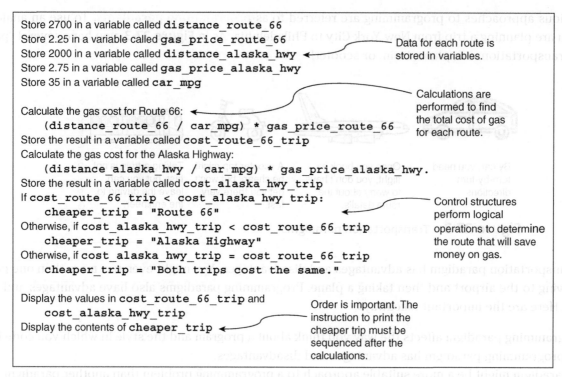

Store 2700 in a variable called `distance_route_66`
Store 2.25 in a variable called `gas_price_route_66`
Store 2000 in a variable called `distance_alaska_hwy` ← Data for each route is stored in variables.
Store 2.75 in a variable called `gas_price_alaska_hwy`
Store 35 in a variable called `car_mpg`

Calculate the gas cost for Route 66: ← Calculations are performed to find the total cost of gas for each route.
    `(distance_route_66 / car_mpg) * gas_price_route_66`
Store the result in a variable called `cost_route_66_trip`
Calculate the gas cost for the Alaska Highway:
    `(distance_alaska_hwy / car_mpg) * gas_price_alaska_hwy.`
Store the result in a variable called `cost_alaska_hwy_trip`
If `cost_route_66_trip < cost_alaska_hwy_trip`:
    `cheaper_trip = "Route 66"` ← Control structures perform logical operations to determine the route that will save money on gas.
Otherwise, if `cost_alaska_hwy_trip < cost_route_66_trip`
    `cheaper_trip = "Alaska Highway"`
Otherwise, if `cost_alaska_hwy_trip = cost_route_66_trip`
    `cheaper_trip = "Both trips cost the same."`

Display the values in `cost_route_66_trip` and
    `cost_alaska_hwy_trip`
Display the contents of `cheaper_trip` ← Order is important. The instruction to print the cheaper trip must be sequenced after the calculations.

Figure 27-4 A procedural algorithm specifies how the computer determines the trip with the lowest gas cost

In keeping with the step-by-step focus of the procedural paradigm, the code for this program would closely match the steps of the algorithm; one line of program code for each step in the algorithm.

Characteristics of Procedural Programs (27.2.3)

The three sections of the algorithm in Figure 27-4 are typical of programs based on the procedural paradigm. The program has an input section where data is loaded into variables, a processing section where calculations are performed, and an output section where data is displayed, printed, or transmitted. Here are some other characteristics of programs based on the procedural paradigm:

Order is important. A crucial element of procedural programming is specifying the correct order of the steps in an algorithm.

Use of variables. Procedural programs typically store data in variables and use those variables for computations, output, and other operations.

Use of selection control structures. Simple procedural programs execute the steps of an algorithm in sequence. But control structures can change that sequence. A selection control structure tells the computer what to do based on whether a condition is true or false. The following section of the road trip pseudocode tells the computer to put **"Route 66"** in the variable `cheaper_trip` if the cost of gas for traveling Route 66 is cheaper than the cost on the Alaska Highway.

```
if cost_route_66_trip < cost_alaska_hwy_trip then

    cheaper_trip = "Route 66"

    else if cost_alaska_hwy_trip < cost_route_66_trip then

    cheaper_trip = "Alaska Highway"

    else if cost_alaska_hwy_trip = cost_route_66_trip then

    cheaper_trip = "Both trips cost the same. "
```

Q How many possible branches does the above control structure include?

A It includes three possible branches:
1. Route 66 is cheaper.
2. The Alaskan Highway is cheaper.
3. The two routes cost the same.

Use of repetition control structures. A repetition control structure tells the computer to repeat one or more instructions until a certain condition is met. Here is an example of a procedural control structure that uses a repetition control to print "There's no place like home" three times.

```
for count = 1 to 3

    print "There's no place like home."

next
```

Top-down decomposition. Complex tasks can be divided into smaller tasks, a process called decomposition. These smaller tasks can be coded as separate, but linked programs, or they can be included in a comprehensive program but abstracted into segments of code called subroutines, procedures, or functions. These functions are sometimes given data to use for calculations and may return results back to the main program that called them. You can think of these code segments as branches from the main program, as shown in **Figure 27-5**.

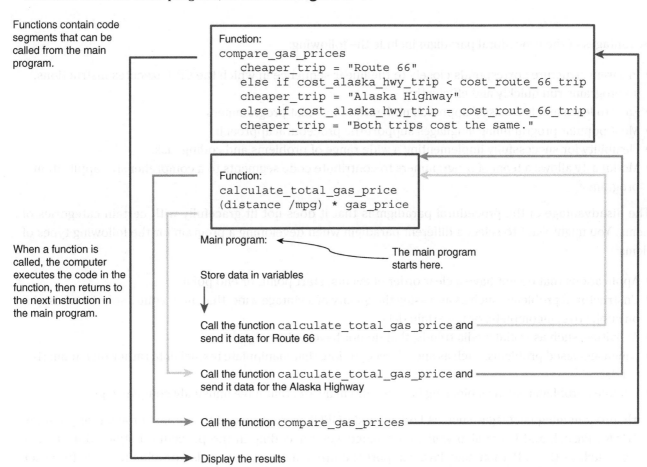

Figure 27-5 Procedural programs have a main execution path, but subroutines, procedures, and functions serve as side trips

Procedural Paradigm Applications (27.2.4, 27.2.5)

As a programmer, you can apply the procedural paradigm to any programming problems that can be approached as a series of steps. It is a particularly effective approach for problems and tasks such as those in **Figure 27-6**.

Repetitive tasks where the same set of steps can be applied to different data sets

Large applications that can be divided into modules

Systems that require optimized performance

Any problem where the solution naturally involves a series of sequential steps or calculations

Processing paychecks requires the same calculations every week, but for varying work hours

Online stores with modules for inventory management, shopping carts, payment processing, and delivery logistics

Launching spacecraft

Processing survey data

davooda/Shutterstock.com

Figure 27-6   The procedural paradigm works well for these types of applications

Advantages of the procedural paradigm include the following:

- Program structure corresponds closely to the linear sequence in which the CPU executes instructions, so programs run quickly and efficiently
- Easy to learn and is a classic approach understood by most programmers
- Most popular programming languages support the procedural approach
- Flexibility for successfully implementing a wide range of problems and coding tasks
- Modularity allows a team of programmers to contribute code segments to a comprehensive application program

The disadvantage of the procedural paradigm is that it does not fit gracefully with certain categories of problems. You might want to select a different paradigm when developing a program for the following types of problems:

- Applications that do not have a clear order of events, start point, or end point
- Unstructured problems, such as assessing the quality of a vintage wine, that may require solutions based on subjective, incomplete, or uncertain data
- Activities, such as social media trends, that do not have a clear algorithm
- Language-based problems, such as speech recognition, that manipulate textual data rather than numerical data
- Complex problems, such as blocking hackers and malware, that have unusually complex logic

Early programming languages such as Fortran and COBOL were designed to support procedural programming. BASIC, Pascal, and C are also well-known languages for coding in the procedural style. More recent languages, such as C++, Python, and Java, support the procedural style, but also provide features for other programming paradigms.

27.3 THE OBJECT-ORIENTED PARADIGM

Objects, Classes, and Methods (27.3.1, 27.3.2)

The object-oriented paradigm is based on the idea that programs can be designed by visualizing objects that interact with each other. The objects in an object-oriented program are abstractions of real-world entities, such as people, places, and things.

For a road trip, you might be considering whether to drive your Mustang or your friend's Camaro. You can create Mustang and Camaro objects as specific instances of a template called a class. **Figure 27-7** explains.

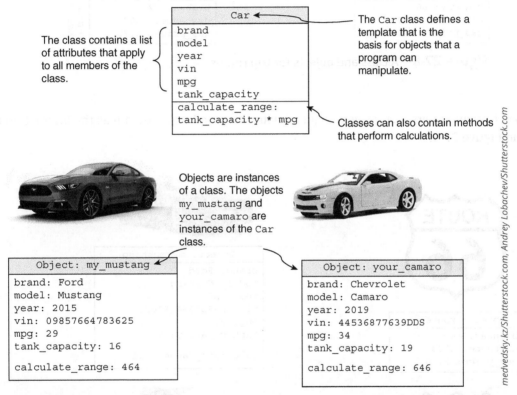

Figure 27-7 The object-oriented paradigm focuses on defining classes and creating objects

A class defines attributes, such as `mpg` and `tank_capacity`. Classes also define methods that perform tasks, such as collecting input, executing decisions, making calculations, or producing output.

Q In Figure 27-7, what is the method in the `Car` class?

A The `Car` class contains the `calculate_range` method, which computes the range of a car using the formula `tank_capacity * mpg`.

A `Car` class could be part of a program that determines the cost of a road trip. You need another class for the road trip program, one that generates objects for various trip routes such as those in **Figure 27-8**.

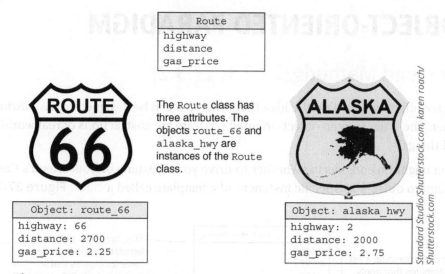

The Route class has three attributes. The objects route_66 and alaska_hwy are instances of the Route class.

Figure 27-8   A class and objects for trip routes

From an object-oriented perspective, you might visualize the road trip program as the interaction between objects shown in **Figure 27-9**.

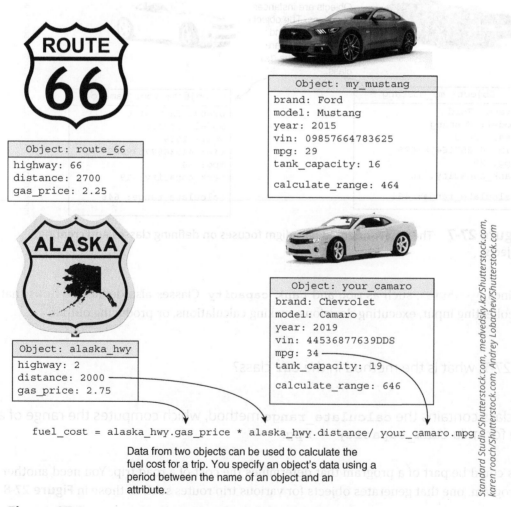

```
fuel_cost = alaska_hwy.gas_price * alaska_hwy.distance/ your_camaro.mpg
```

Data from two objects can be used to calculate the fuel cost for a trip. You specify an object's data using a period between the name of an object and an attribute.

Figure 27-9   In the object-oriented paradigm, objects interact

Based on the visualization in Figure 27-9, you can approach the coding process by doing the following:

Define the **Route** class.

Define the **Car** class.

Use the **Route** class to create objects for Route 66 and the Alaska highway.

Use the **Car** class to create objects for a Camaro and a Mustang.

Calculate the fuel cost for the Alaska trip using data from the Alaska Highway object and the Camaro object.

Characteristics of Object-Oriented Programs (27.3.3)

Object-oriented programming (OOP) incorporates classes, objects, and methods. The object-oriented paradigm is also characterized by the use of inheritance, polymorphism, and encapsulation.

Inheritance The classes in an object-oriented program can be reused, which leads to programming efficiencies. Suppose you're thinking of taking an electric car on your road trip. Gas mileage won't apply.

Instead of making a completely different class for electric cars, you can use the **Car** class for attributes that apply to all types of cars, but create one subclass for gas guzzlers and another subclass for electric cars.

Inheritance is a feature of object-oriented programming that allows subclasses to acquire common attributes from a parent class, as shown in **Figure 27-10**.

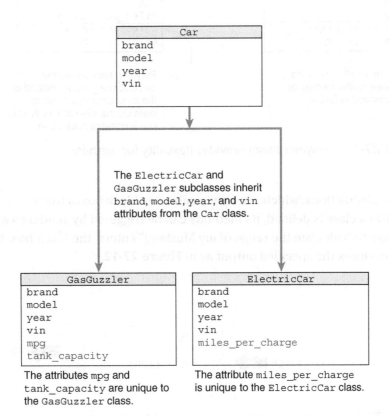

Figure 27-10   Inheritance creates subclasses

Polymorphism The `Car` class uses the `calculate_range` method to find the number of miles a car can drive on a tank of gas. That method doesn't apply to electric cars. For the `ElectricCar` subclass, you can modify the `calculate_range` method so that it simply uses the `miles_per_charge` data. Polymorphism gives your program the flexibility to have multiple methods named `calculate_range`, but the way those methods process objects depends on their class. See **Figure 27-11**.

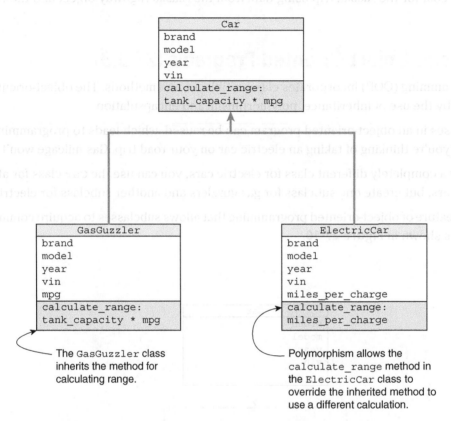

Figure 27-11   Polymorphism provides flexibility for methods

Encapsulation Classes are abstractions, which can be visualized as black boxes that encapsulate data attributes and methods. After a class is defined, its methods can be triggered by sending a message. In the road trip program, a message to "calculate the range of my Mustang" enters the black box, triggers the appropriate method, and produces the specified output as in **Figure 27-12**.

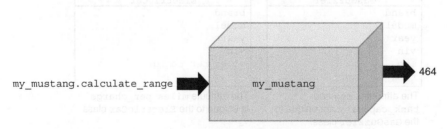

Figure 27-12   Encapsulation treats classes as black boxes

The object-oriented paradigm joins the procedural paradigm under the umbrella of imperative program-ming. With both paradigms, programmers specify the steps for *how* to accomplish a task or perform a method defined in a class.

Object-Oriented Applications (27.3.4, 27.3.5, 27.3.6, 27.3.7)

If you score a job on a programming team, you'll most likely work on a project that is based on an object-oriented approach. Familiarity with OOP is mandatory for today's IT and computer science careers.

The object-oriented approach is the top choice for a wide variety of software development projects, but it is particularly appropriate for the following types of applications:

- Simulation and modeling systems
- Office automation systems that communicate and share information
- Internet services
- Web apps
- Mobile apps

The object-oriented paradigm has several advantages:

- Classes reflect real-world objects, allowing program structure to mirror reality.
- Inheritance and polymorphism provide flexibility within programs.
- Encapsulated classes and methods can be reused in other programs for faster development.
- Programs are fairly easy to test, debug, and maintain because methods perform specific tasks.
- Today, it is widely used for most software development.

The object-oriented paradigm is not perfect. Its disadvantages include the following:

- Large programs. Defining classes, generating objects, and specifying methods tend to require more lines of code than procedural programs.
- Nonoptimal processing speed. Programs containing more lines of code require more processing time.
- Not appropriate for every application. Problems with complex rule sets or those that require natural language processing are among the tasks best tackled with other paradigms.

Simula, developed in the 1960s, and SmallTalk, developed in the 1970s, were two of the original programming languages for object-oriented programming. The paradigm was not popular, however, until the 1990s when languages such as Java, Python, Ruby, and C++ started to appear.

Many of today's popular programming languages support both procedural and object-oriented programming approaches. Such languages allow programmers to create classes, objects, and methods, but do not require them as the foundation for program code.

27.4 DECLARATIVE PARADIGMS

Declarative Basics (27.4.1)

Although the dominant programming paradigms are procedural and object-oriented, other programming paradigms are worth your attention. Declarative paradigms approach programming by describing *what* a program is supposed to accomplish. This approach is very different from imperative paradigms, which focus on the steps for *how* to accomplish a task.

Declarative paradigms are similar to booking a flight: you specify when you want to leave, where you want to go, and the fare class that you can afford. Your specifications tell the booking app *what* you want, not how to book the flight or pilot the plane to your destination.

To get a handle on the declarative approach, let's delve into the fascinating world of logic programming.

In logic programming, you use three types of statements: facts that form a database, rules that define the logic, and queries that trigger processing. A fact supplies basic information in the form of a predicate expression that specifies a relationship. **Figure 27-13** explains.

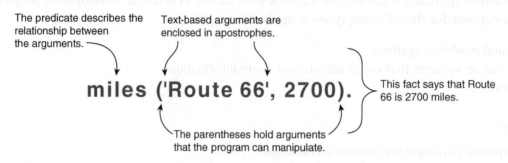

The predicate describes the relationship between the arguments.

Text-based arguments are enclosed in apostrophes.

This fact says that Route 66 is 2700 miles.

miles ('Route 66', 2700).

The parentheses hold arguments that the program can manipulate.

Figure 27-13   Logic programming uses predicate expressions

Using predicate expressions, you can create a program that contains facts about routes, gas prices, and cars. Without viewing the facts it contains, users who understand the way facts are structured can interact with the program to enter queries. In **Figure 27-14**, you'll see a set of facts and the results of a query that asks, "What is the price of gas on the Alaska Highway?"

```
miles('Route 66', 2700).
miles('Alaska Hwy', 2000).
gas_price('Route 66', 2.25).
gas_price('Alaska Hwy', 2.75).
mpg('Camaro', 34).
mpg('Mustang', 29).

?- gas_price('Alaska Hwy', What).


What = 2.75
```

Facts specify data about the routes and cars.

This query has two arguments: **'Alaska Hwy'** and **What**. Because **What** is capitalized and not set off by apostrophes, it is a variable. The query looks for a **gas_price** fact with an **'Alaska Hwy'** argument. When it finds one, it replaces **What** with the value of the second argument: 2.75.

The result of the query specifies the value of the variable **What**.

Figure 27-14   A query searches the database for matching facts

Q What do you think will be produced by the query ?- miles('Alaska Hwy', What).

A The query produces **What = 2000**, based on the fact miles('Alaska Hwy', 2000).

Adding a rule to the program specifies the logic for calculating the cost of any trip, as **Figure 27-15** explains.

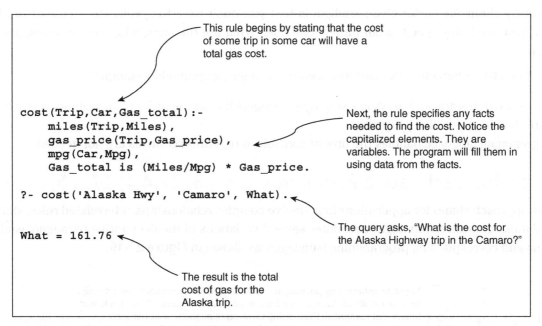

Figure 27-15 Rules provide the logic for processing the data provided by the program's facts

Q How would you change the query in Figure 27-15 to ask for the cost of a trip on Route 66 in the Mustang?

A The query would be `cost('Route 66', 'Mustang', What)`.

To automate the query, you can add a `show_costs` rule. Does it matter where you put that rule? No. One of the key characteristics of the declarative paradigm is that the sequence of instructions is not important. That contrasts with the imperative paradigm where instructions must be coded in sequence for the program to produce the correct result. Here is the rule:

```
show_costs:-
    cost(Trip, Car, Gas_total),
    write(Trip), write(' '),
    write(Car), write(' '),
    write(Gas_total).
```

With the `show_costs` rule in place, the query `? - show_costs.` produces this output:

```
Route 66 Camaro 178.67

Route 66 Mustang 209.48

Alaska Hwy Camaro 161.76

Alaska Hwy Mustang 189.65
```

Notice that the program repeated this query for both routes and both cars without a repetition control. Programming languages that support the declarative paradigm have internal mechanisms to handle the flow of control.

Characteristics of the Declarative Paradigm (27.4.2)

The main takeaway about the declarative paradigm is that you don't have to specify the steps for producing output. Instead you need only specify *what* rather than *how*: What are the facts, what are the rules, and what are the queries.

Let's recap two other characteristics that surfaced in the logic programming example:

- Declarative programs are not based on a step-by step algorithm, so the order of statements is much less important than in imperative programs.
- The programming language handles the flow of control, so repetition controls are not needed.

Applications for Declarative Paradigms (27.4.3, 27.4.4, 27.4.5, 27.4.6)

The declarative approach shines for applications that involve complex relationships, interrelated rules, statistical analysis, and database queries. You might encounter several variations of the declarative paradigm, each with its unique focus and corresponding programming languages, as shown in **Figure 27-16**.

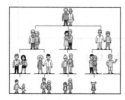

Logic programming paradigm. Genealogy involves complex relationships between mothers, fathers, children, siblings, and spouses. The data is text-based, not numerical. Processing involves relationships, rather than calculations. The **logic programming paradigm** is an effective approach for dealing with complex relationships, decisions, and rule sets that are expressed as text. Programming languages such as Prolog support this declarative approach.

Functional programming paradigm. Social networking services have policies against spam, malware, and other inappropriate activities. Identifying abuses involves statistical analysis and processing policy rules. The **functional programming paradigm** is an effective approach for applications that have interacting text-based or numerical rules. Programming languages such as Haskell, Scheme, OCaml, Scala, and Clojure support a declarative approach to programs that deal with mathematical functions.

Database query programming. Databases may contain hundreds or millions of records. Database query languages such as SQL include built-in declarative commands, such as **SELECT**. The following statement uses the **SELECT** command to find the price of gas along the Alaska Highway:

`SELECT gas_price FROM TripDatabase WHERE Trip = "Alaska Highway"`

This statement is another example of the declarative paradigm's focus on *what*, rather than how. It is in contrast to the imperative paradigm, which would require many lines of code specifying how to look at every entry in the database until finding the Alaska Highway trip and its corresponding gas price.

Figure 27-16   Variations of the declarative paradigm

In addition to applications for which they are well suited, declarative paradigms have some general advantages and disadvantages that are important to keep in mind:

Advantage: Because languages that support the declarative paradigm handle program flow, programmers do not have to code background control structures.

Advantage: Relatively simple program code is required for tasks that involve complex and interrelated rules or conditions.

Disadvantage: Program execution speed is not optimal because declarative programming languages handle program flow in the same way for every program.

Disadvantage: Programmers have to think outside of the imperative-paradigm box.

SUMMARY

- Programming paradigms provide various approaches to designing, developing, and implementing computer programs.
- Programming paradigms can be classified as imperative or declarative. Imperative programming paradigms focus on *how* by specifying the steps required to carry out a task. Declarative programming paradigms focus on *what* by describing the problem or task.
- The procedural paradigm is an imperative approach based on step-by-step algorithms. It is characterized by the use of variables, selection control structures, repetition control structures, and top-down decomposition. Programs based on the procedural paradigm typically run efficiently, but the approach is not optimal for all types of applications.
- The object-oriented paradigm is an imperative approach based on the concept of objects interacting with each other. Programmers define templates called classes, generate objects from these classes, and define methods that perform tasks related to the objects. Features such as inheritance, polymorphism, and encapsulation provide flexibility and reusability, but at a possible cost to execution speed.
- Declarative paradigms include logic programming, functional programming, and database query programming. These paradigms shine for applications that involve complex relationships, interrelated rules, statistical analysis, and data base queries.

Key Terms

attributes

class

Declarative programming
  paradigms

encapsulate

Imperative programming
  paradigms

Inheritance

methods

object-oriented paradigm

objects

Polymorphism

predicate expression

procedural paradigm

programming paradigms

repetition control structure

selection control structure

MODULE
28

USER INTERFACES

LEARNING OBJECTIVES:

28.1 USER INTERFACE BASICS

28.1.1 Define the term "user interface."

28.1.2 Explain the difference between a user interface and a user experience.

28.1.3 Describe the focus of the computer science discipline called Human-Computer Interaction.

28.1.4 Distinguish between physical and abstract interface components.

28.1.5 Describe how programmers select appropriate user interfaces.

28.1.6 Explain the purpose of APIs in the context of user interfaces.

28.2 COMMAND-LINE USER INTERFACES

28.2.1 List the characteristics of command-line user interfaces.

28.2.2 Identify use cases for command-line user interfaces.

28.2.3 Delineate the general algorithm for programs with command-line user interfaces.

28.2.4 Identify and apply conventions for formatting command-line input and output.

28.3 GRAPHICAL USER INTERFACES

28.3.1 List the characteristics of graphical user interfaces.

28.3.2 Explain how APIs relate to developing programs with graphical user interfaces.

28.3.3 Explain the relevance of event-driven programs to graphical user interfaces.

28.3.4 Recall the steps for the high-level algorithm on which an event-driven program is based.

28.4 VOICE USER INTERFACES

28.4.1 Identify use cases for voice user interfaces.

28.4.2 Outline the algorithm for speech recognition.

28.4.3 Describe the process of concatenative speech synthesis.

28.4.4 Compare and contrast voice user interfaces to other types of user interfaces.

28.5 VIRTUAL ENVIRONMENT INTERFACES

28.5.1 Differentiate between applications of virtual reality, augmented reality, and mixed reality.

28.5.2 List user interface components for virtual environment interfaces.

28.5.3 Explain the significance of vector graphics for virtual reality programs.

28.5.4 List three types of tools for building programs with virtual environments.

28.6 ACCESSIBILITY AND INCLUSION

28.6.1 Define "accessibility" as it relates to software design and use.

28.6.2 Match examples of common accessibility problems with best practices solutions.

28.6.3 Define "inclusion" as it relates to software design and use.

28.6.4 Match examples of common inclusion problems with best practices solutions.

28.6.5 Classify usability problems as accessibility or inclusion.

28.1 USER INTERFACE BASICS

UI and UX (28.1.1, 28.1.2, 28.1.3)

In *Star Trek IV: The Voyage Home*, the crew of the starship Enterprise travels back in time to 1986. Scotty, the ship's engineer, walks over to an Apple Macintosh computer like the one in **Figure 28-1**. When he says, "Hello, computer!" nothing happens, so he picks up the mouse and tries to use it as a microphone.

Is it a microphone?

iStock/RyanJLane

Figure 28-1   The way to interact with a digital device might not be obvious to everyone

Scotty is familiar with computers that respond to voice commands. The way he expects to interact with the Macintosh computer is not the way the computer is expecting to interact with him. Scotty has a user interface problem.

In the context of programming, a **user interface (UI)** is a collection of physical, graphical, and logical constructs that facilitate interaction between humans and digital devices. The purpose of a user interface is to simplify a complex system so it is easy to use.

A similar concept, **user experience (UX)** is broader in scope and goes beyond user interaction to include an entire realm of consumer involvement. Apple provides an example of a crafted user experience that includes physical stores, online stores, product packaging, branding, equipment design, product support, and a standard look and feel for devices' home screens and apps.

The takeaway is this: UX design is all about an overall product experience, while UI design is all about the way users interact with a digital device.

In computer science, **Human-Computer Interaction (HCI)** is an important and in-demand discipline. HCI encompasses UI and UX design. It is a key aspect of all software design, from creating fantastic game worlds to formulating mundane online tax forms.

UI Components (28.1.4)

User interfaces have both physical and abstract components. Physical components, such as those in **Figure 28-2**, include input and output devices.

Elena Blokhina/Shutterstock.com, JenWalters/
Shutterstock.com, wacpan/Shutterstock.com,
iceink/Shutterstock.com, Benoit Daoust/Shutterstock.com,
gd_project/Shutterstock.com, AG-PHOTOS/Shutterstock.com

Figure 28-2   User interfaces have physical components

Q What are the main physical components of a smartphone user interface?

A The touch screen and microphone are the primary physical UI components, but the phone's speaker is also a UI component. Some phones have a Home button that is a key UI component.

User interfaces also have abstract components. Modern programs contain abstract user interface components, such as the screen-based controls in **Figure 28-3** that represent actions and objects.

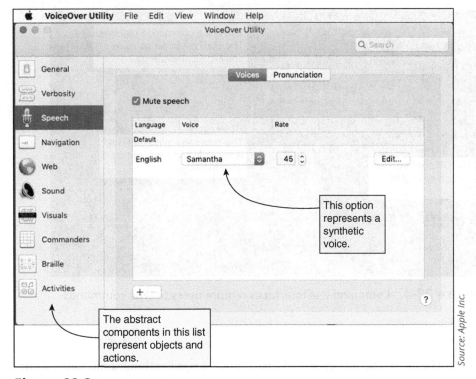

Source: Apple Inc.

Figure 28-3   User interfaces have abstract components

Selecting a UI (28.1.5, 28.1.6)

The user interface for a software product does not emerge from the vacuum of space. It has context defined by the platform conventions of operating systems, programming languages, design standards, and web protocols, including HTTP and HTML. Your selection of user interface elements for a program should reflect this context.

Operating systems, such as Microsoft Windows, Android, macOS, and iOS each feature a unique user interface defined by the look and feel of menus, icons, and other screen-based controls. When programming, you can access application program interfaces (APIs) that contain platform-specific interface elements, such as the Windows toolbar or a scrollable iPhone menu.

Physical and abstract interface components combine in various ways to produce four main classifications of user interfaces. Let's take a look at each one to discover the applications where they shine.

28.2 COMMAND-LINE USER INTERFACES

Command-Line Basics (28.2.1, 28.2.2)

Early generations of computers featured command-line user interfaces that required users to type commands. Some modern digital devices provide access to a command-line interface that you can use to expertly work with the operating system. On computers running the Windows operating system, the command-line is accessed using the Windows command prompt. On an Apple computer running macOS, access is provided by the Terminal app.

Although command-line interaction with the operating system is similar to carrying out a conversation with the computer, the conversation is based on a set of command words and punctuation rules that users have to memorize. Mistakes produce frustrating error messages such as the one in **Figure 28-4**.

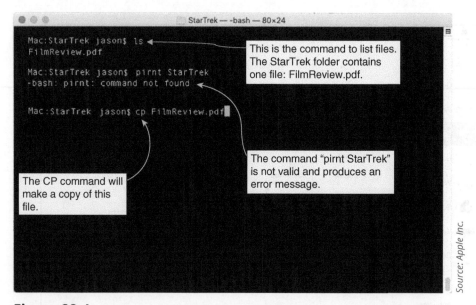

Figure 28-4   Command-line interfaces require users to type commands

Command-Line Program Design (28.2.2, 28.2.3, 28.2.4)

Command-line user interfaces can be incorporated into software applications. Judicious use of prompts and a sprinkling of artificial intelligence can alleviate the burden of memorizing commands.

A chatbot program called Eliza is an iconic example of a program based on a command-line user interface. Chatbots such as Eliza are designed to carry out a conversation. Originally, chatbots used bland generic replies, but more sophisticated chatbots use artificial intelligence algorithms to determine the meaning of user input. **Figure 28-5** shows a typical Eliza conversation.

```
I am the psychotherapist. Please describe your problems.
Each time you are finished talking, type RET twice.

>I seem to have trouble making decisions.
Can you elaborate on that?
>You know, trouble deciding what to do.
Why do you say that?
> I can't make up my mind.
Really?
>You're not being very helpful.
What makes you believe that I'm not being very helpful?
```

Figure 28-5   A conversation with the Eliza chatbot software

The overarching algorithm for a program with a command-line user interface is similar to a conversation in which the computer and user take turns asking questions and making responses.

Repeat until task is complete:

Computer prompts user to enter a query or other input data.
User enters data.
Computer responds to input data.

For simple entry-level practice programs, you may choose to use command-line user interfaces. You can incorporate some basic user interface principles to format input and output as shown in **Figure 28-6**.

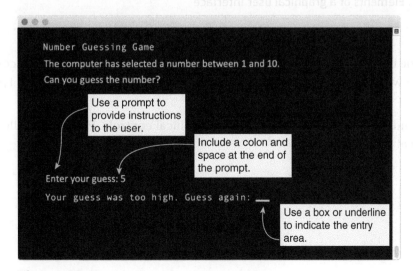

Figure 28-6   Command line best practices

28.3 GRAPHICAL USER INTERFACES

GUI Basics (28.3.1)

Most digital devices today are equipped with a graphical user interface (GUI), which displays screen-based objects and menus that can be manipulated using a mouse, keyboard, or touch gesture. The acronym for "graphical user interface" is GUI, sometimes pronounced "gooey."

A GUI is based on a desktop or home screen populated with graphical representations of objects and actions. GUIs are sometimes called "WIMP" user interfaces because they contain workspaces, icons, menus, and a pointer, as shown in **Figure 28-7**.

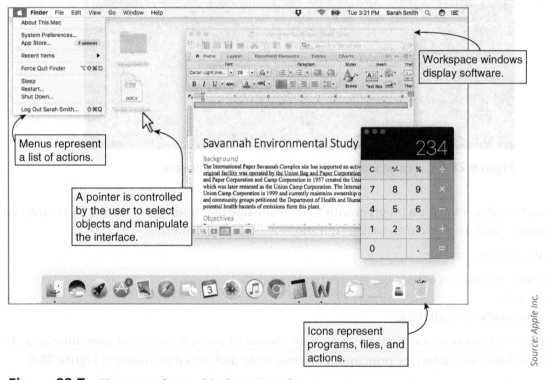

Figure 28-7   Elements of a graphical user interface

Menus, such as the one in Figure 28-7, address the memorization problem associated with command-line user interfaces. When working with a GUI, users can select commands from a menu rather than typing memorized commands.

In addition to icons and menus, GUIs offer a variety of graphical controls. **Figure 28-8** illustrates the most common types of graphical controls.

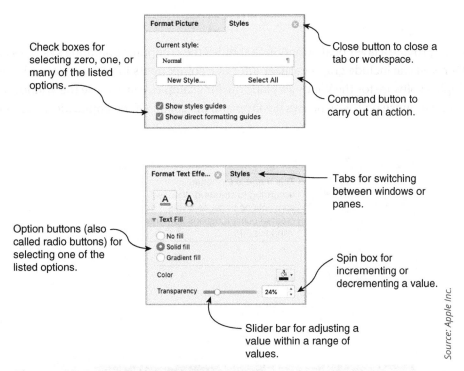

Check boxes for selecting zero, one, or many of the listed options.

Close button to close a tab or workspace.

Command button to carry out an action.

Tabs for switching between windows or panes.

Option buttons (also called radio buttons) for selecting one of the listed options.

Spin box for incrementing or decrementing a value.

Slider bar for adjusting a value within a range of values.

Source: Apple Inc.

Figure 28-8   Graphical controls

Q Can you identify the controls in **Figure 28-9**?

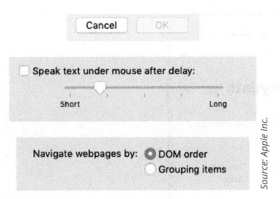

Source: Apple Inc.

Figure 28-9   Can you identify these GUI controls?

A From the top, these controls are command buttons, a slider bar, and option, or "radio," buttons.

GUI Program Design (28.3.2, 28.3.3, 28.3.4)

Graphical user interfaces provide a layer of abstraction that hides the computer operating system's command-line detail. As a programmer, you can include graphical user interface components in your programs by using libraries and APIs. When developing software for the Windows platform, for example, you can use the Windows API to design menus that look and act like those on the Windows desktop and Microsoft Office applications. See **Figure 28-10**.

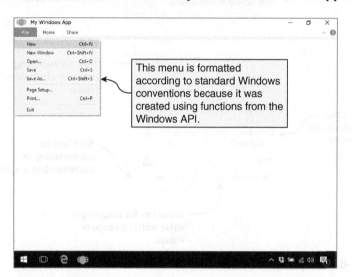

Figure 28-10   The Windows API provides tools for menus, command buttons, and other Windows UI elements

Programs with GUI interfaces have an open-ended **event-driven** flow, rather than a linear flow from beginning to end. The flow of the program is determined by user actions called "events," as shown in **Figure 28-11**.

Figure 28-11   UI events

Source: Apple Inc., GreenLandStudio/Shutterstock.com

For example, your smartphone's music app might have a menu with options for accessing albums, randomizing a playlist, and playing a specific song. You can select these options in any order. Your selection is an event that triggers an action such as playing the Star Trek soundtrack. Your code for handling an event is referred to as an **event handler**.

The high-level algorithm for developing an event-driven program goes something like this:

Create the icons, menus, and other interface elements that can trigger events.

Organize those interface elements inside a screen window.

Define and code an event-handler function for each interface element.

Initiate the program as an infinite event-loop that waits for users to trigger events.

28.4 VOICE USER INTERFACES

Voice Interface Basics (28.4.1)

Today, Scotty could pick up any smartphone and speak to a digital assistant using a voice user interface characterized by spoken communication. Just think of the ways that voice user interfaces shine:

- Hands-free communication while driving
- Text message dictation
- Digital assistants, such as Siri and Alexa
- Telephone interactive voice response systems
- Word processor dictation systems

Voice user interfaces are based on two technologies: speech recognition and speech synthesis. Speech recognition uses sophisticated algorithms to identify spoken words and convert them into text that can be processed for meaning. During speech synthesis, machines such as computers generate audio output that sounds like human speech.

Speech Recognition (28.4.2)

To get a handle on the complexity of speech recognition algorithms, suppose you use a voice command to call a phone number beginning with "six." A microphone collects samples from the sound wave, and from that wave attempts to identify a unit of speech, called a phoneme, that corresponds to each sample. Those phonemes then have to be interpreted to find the correct meaning. **Figure 28-12** highlights the difficulty of this process.

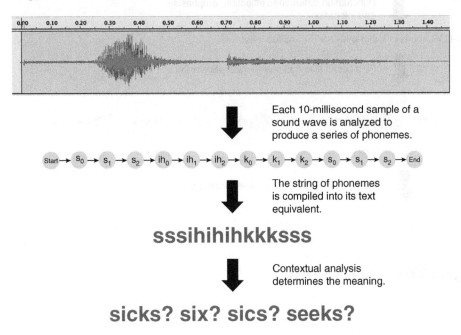

Each 10-millisecond sample of a sound wave is analyzed to produce a series of phonemes.

The string of phonemes is compiled into its text equivalent.

Contextual analysis determines the meaning.

Figure 28-12   Speech recognition

To efficiently convert speech to text, computer scientists apply sophisticated algorithms such as Connectionist Temporal Classification, Fourier transforms, and Hidden Markov Models. The process is computationally intensive, as you can imagine. A typical sentence contains thousands of 10-millisecond speech samples, and each one has to be compared to a huge universe of possible phonemes.

After converting speech to text, further processing is required to determine its context and meaning. Is it a number? Is it part of a phone number? Is it the area code? As speech input becomes more complex, deriving meaning requires algorithms based on a branch of artificial intelligence called natural language processing.

Speech Synthesis (28.4.3)

The first generation of speech synthesizers produced robotic voices that mangled the pronunciation of many words. Modern speech synthesis produces speech that sounds natural. The most common speech synthesis technology, **concatenative synthesis**, is based on a collection of prerecorded phonemes that can be assembled into words and sentences.

To derive the phonemes, live voice actors record words and sentences contained in a series of phoneme-rich scripts. Expert linguists slice the recordings into speech components, such as frequently used words and language-specific phonemes. The experts tag these speech segments and then load them into an extensive database. Speech segments are retrieved from this database during the speech synthesis process outlined in **Figure 28-13**.

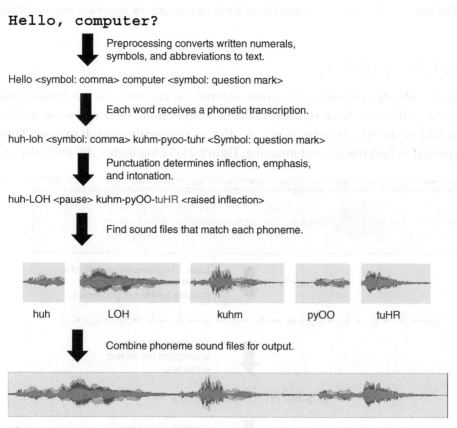

Figure 28-13   Speech synthesis

Designing Programs for Voice User Interfaces (28.4.4)

Programmers can add audio input and output features to existing software. For example, text messaging apps accept either typed or spoken input. Such applications can be classified a GUIs with speech input capabilities.

A purely voice-activated application, however, has no visual interface. Its design requires a programming mindset based on conversational communication rather than visual screen-based interactions.

To design a voice-activated application, your first step is to define the contextual domain. Are you creating a game? A digital assistant? By mapping out typical interactions, you can design a series of audio prompts and responses.

 Would you say that the logic underlying a program with a voice user interface resembles a program with a command-line interface or a GUI?

 The logic of a program with a voice user interface surprisingly has more similarities to command-line user interfaces than to GUIs. The conversation that takes place is linear rather than event driven.

Implementing voice user interfaces requires speech recognition and speech synthesis APIs. Programs can access comprehensive speech recognition from cloud-based services such as Google Cloud, but access requires an Internet connection. Speech recognition within local devices is more limited, but advancements in speech processing algorithms continue to provide better functionality for programs that operate independently of the Internet.

28.5 VIRTUAL ENVIRONMENT INTERFACES

Virtual Environments (28.5.1)

Virtual reality uses computer technology to create a simulated, three-dimensional world that users can manipulate through head, hand, and body movements. Doesn't that sound a lot like the futuristic holodeck on the starship Enterprise where the crew could "vacation" in exotic simulated locations?

While waiting for holodecks, you can work with virtual reality games, flight simulators, field trips, and architectural walkthroughs. Technologies similar to virtual reality include augmented reality and mixed reality. See **Figure 28-14**.

Virtual reality is a three-dimensional world containing objects that users can manipulate.

Augmented reality adds tags to images of real places.

Mixed reality adds three-dimensional objects to real-world images.

deymos/Shutterstock.com, Source: Yelp, Inc., Source: Pokemon Go

Figure 28-14   Virtual environments

Virtual Environment Interface Components (28.5.2, 28.5.3)

The primary input device for virtual reality software is a head-mounted display, which contains two display screens—one for each eye. As shown in **Figure 28-15**, the two images are slightly offset and produce the sense of three dimensions when viewed.

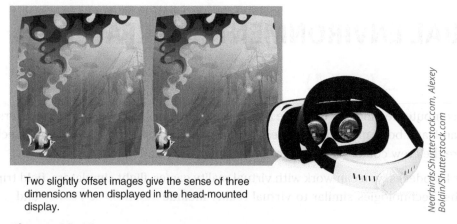

Two slightly offset images give the sense of three dimensions when displayed in the head-mounted display.

Nearbirds/Shutterstock.com, Alexey Boldin/Shutterstock.com

Figure 28-15   Virtual reality head mounted display

Haptic technologies play an increasingly important role as part of a virtual interface. Haptic devices simulate the sense of touch. For example, users wearing haptic gloves in a virtual environment would be able to "feel" the surface of a simulated object.

Virtual, augmented, or mixed reality user interfaces may also include one or more of the following devices:

Hand-held controllers, such as joysticks and digital wands, to select objects

Smartphone cameras to capture real-world images

Smartphone displays to provide the screen for a head-mounted display

Haptic gloves for tactile feedback from virtual objects

Microphones for speech recognition

Motion tracking body suits to sense a user's body movements

Programming virtual applications is all about collecting data from interface devices and using it to control variables that affect the virtual environment and the objects it contains.

Environments can be based on footage from 360-degree motion photography or three-dimensional vector animations. Vector graphics define shapes as a set of instructions for drawing lines and curves.

Vector graphic instructions can form three-dimensional objects. The structure for a vector graphic is called a wireframe, and that wireframe can be filled with color, shaded, highlighted, and endowed with various levels of transparency. See **Figure 28-16**.

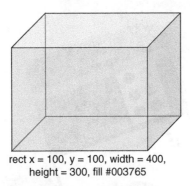

rect x = 100, y = 100, width = 400, height = 300, fill #003765

Figure 28-16 3D vector graphics are formed from instructions that specify shape, size, color, and lighting

Assembling a collection of vector graphics produces a virtual reality environment that users can navigate in three dimensions, viewing objects from all sides. Because each vector object is independent, users can also move them within the virtual world.

Programming the Virtual Interface (28.5.4)

Extending the user interface to a three-dimensional environment requires linkages from the user's equipment. For example, if haptic gloves are used to manipulate objects, each glove gesture is an interface input that you have to deal with in program code.

Development tools provide functions and libraries for assigning actions to the entire spectrum of inputs. Development tools for virtual environments include the following:

- Modeling languages such as VRML
- Application program interfaces such as WebVR
- Game engines such as Unity

28.6 ACCESSIBILITY AND INCLUSION

Accessibility Guidelines (28.6.1, 28.6.2)

Imagine using digital devices with your eyes closed. You can't see the screen. You can't look at the labels on your keyboard. Millions of people with disabilities use braille keyboards, screen narrators, and other adaptive technologies such as the eyes-free texting app in **Figure 28-17**.

Figure 28-17   Adaptive devices include this app for eyes-free texting

In the context of software development, accessibility means providing user interfaces that can be used by everyone, including people with disabilities. Most software development projects include detailed accessibility requirements based on in-house guidelines and standards developed by advocacy organizations.

Both Microsoft and Apple have detailed guidelines for developing accessible software and apps. The W3C organization promotes its Web Content Accessibility Guidelines (WCAG) and a variation of those guidelines for nonweb information and communications technologies. Many countries, including the United States, have enacted laws and regulations that apply to hardware and software accessibility.

Programming for accessibility may require you to provide alternative modes of interaction for people with visual, audio, motor, or cognitive limitations. Including individuals with special needs in software testing cycles can help you gauge the success of your accessibility efforts. Best practice guidelines for accessibility include the following.

Visual accessibility: Many people have impaired vision. Individuals without sight may use special adaptive equipment to interact with digital devices. Color blindness prevents people from differentiating some colors. People with low vision may have difficulty deciphering text that blends into the background.

To increase accessibility for individuals with impaired vision:

• Provide an audio alternative to visual cues. Alt text, for example, provides an audio description of a graphic, image, or diagram.

- Organize screen elements to make sense when interpreted by a screen reader.
- Avoid using color as the only cue for differentiating significant text and controls.
- Select a color palette that presents high contrast between foreground objects, text, and backgrounds.

Audio accessibility: Because audio interaction with digital devices has become popular, developers should take the following steps to assist individuals with acute hearing loss:

- Avoid using audio as the only cue signaling events and alerts.
- Provide an option to view a transcript of audio exchanges.
- Provide closed captions for video streams.

Motor and cognitive accessibility: Physical disabilities can make using a keyboard and mouse difficult. Because adaptive devices interact with the operating system, software is generally more accessible when it adheres to standard conventions of the host operating system. Also consider the following guidelines:

- Ensure that your software functions correctly when users have activated accessibility features provided by the operating system.
- Be mindful of response times, allowing for delayed responses from persons with motor disabilities.
- Avoid flashing screen objects that may cause seizures in some people.
- Provide alternatives to mouse operations, such as drag and drop, that may be difficult for individuals with impaired motor skills.
- Consider ways someone might use your software by issuing voice commands.

Inclusive Design (28.6.3, 28.6.4, 28.6.5, 28.6.6)

Inclusive design ensures that a software product is usable by people with diverse abilities, backgrounds, and equipment access. It includes accessibility principles but extends to encompass gender identity, ethnicity, nationality, technical skill level, and equipment availability.

Best practices for inclusive design require you as a developer to view projects from the perspective of people who may speak different languages, identify with different genders, have various skill sets, and who may not have access to state-of-the-art equipment.

Inclusive language: You may not be able to speak Hindi or read Devanagari script, but you can probably identify the Search link in **Figure 28-18** because the software developers included a magnifying glass icon.

Source: Google LLC

Figure 28-18   Icons and images can help to overcome language barriers

Tech products get worldwide use, so think globally when you design software.

- Use simple language and intuitive controls to increase usability for people with diverse language preferences.
- Enhance on-screen controls with icons to show their purpose.
- Use standard buttons and menus placed at standard locations, which may help users transfer skills from other similar software.

Inclusive identity: Cultural heritage and personal identity affect the way people use and interpret content. Wording and visual techniques can help to ensure a positive experience for every user. See **Figure 28-19**.

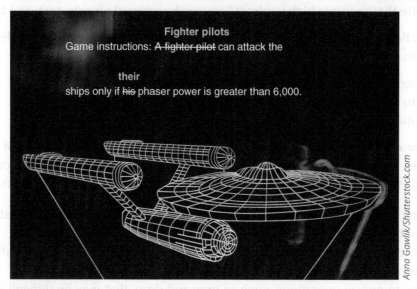

Figure 28-19   Inclusive language is gender neutral

Guidelines for identity inclusion include the following:

- Be mindful of pronouns. Using plurals, such as "their," helps to avoid use of "he," "she," and other gender-specific terms.
- Remain aware of cultural sensitivities, including the meanings attached to colors, symbols, and gestures.
- Avoid sarcasm and inside jokes that may be easily misinterpreted by users with diverse cultural backgrounds.

Inclusive skill sets: Novice users may need help to overcome the initial learning curve for your software, but expert users don't want to wade through multiple help screens before getting right to the task. In **Figure 28-20**, expert users can opt out of the introductory help.

Figure 28-20   Let users opt out of hints and instructions that they don't want

Following are guidelines for including users of varying skillsets:

- Assume your users could have skill levels ranging from novice to expert.
- Supply a full range of cues to help novice users, but do not let them interfere with the streamlined interaction demanded by power users.

Inclusive equipment: Consumers use many devices to access software, and not everyone has a high-speed Internet connection. Designing your software to include as many devices as practical might require different versions for computer and mobile platforms, as shown in **Figure 28-21**.

Source: Opentable, Mosika/Shutterstock.com, Source: Airbnb, Inc., GreenLandStudio/Shutterstock.com

Figure 28-21   Different platforms may require different versions of a software product

Here are some additional tips for extending your software to a larger user base:

- Test your software on legacy devices that might not have state-of-the-art processing power, cutting-edge graphics capability, or high-speed Internet access.
- Customize versions of your software for various screen sizes, orientations, and resolutions to accommodate users with smartphones, desktop computers, tablets, or laptops.
- Aim for cross-platform compatibility so that your software works on multiple operating systems and your online apps operate with multiple browsers.

Q In the scene from Star Trek when Scotty tries to use voice commands to interact with a 1986 Macintosh computer, how would you classify his interface problem? Is it an accessibility problem or an inclusive problem?

A Scotty does not have a hearing, visual, cognitive, or motor disability, so his problem must be with inclusive design. In theory, the Macintosh computer design did not take into account the experiences and expectations of a person from another cultural time period. In reality, this fanciful example also points out that developers can only implement available technologies but may have opportunities to add accessible and inclusive features in the future.

SUMMARY

- A user interface (UI) is a collection of physical, graphical, and logical constructs that facilitate interaction between humans and digital devices. A broader concept, user experience (UX) goes beyond user interaction to include an entire realm of consumer involvement.

- User interfaces have both physical and abstract components. Programmers have control over abstract user interface components, such as screen-based controls that represent actions and objects. Programmers can access application program interfaces (APIs) that contain platform-specific interface elements, such as the Windows toolbar or a scrollable iPhone menu.

- Command-line user interfaces requiring typed interaction can be used to manipulate the operating system and for simple entry-level practice programs.

- A graphical user interface (GUI) displays graphical objects and menus that can be manipulated using a mouse, keyboard, or touch gesture. GUIs are sometimes called "WIMP" user interfaces because they contain workspaces, icons, menus, and a pointer.

- Programs with GUI interfaces have an open-ended, event-driven flow, rather than a linear flow from beginning to end. The flow of the program is determined by user actions called "events."

- A voice user interface is characterized by spoken communication, based on underlying speech recognition and speech synthesis technologies. The logic of a program with a voice user interface has similarities to command-line user interfaces.

- Virtual reality uses computer technology to create a simulated, three-dimensional world that users can manipulate through head, hand, and body movements. Augmented reality tags real-world scenes with computer-generated data. Mixed reality layers three-dimensional interactive objects over real-world scenes.

- When developing the user interface for a program, be sure to consider accessibility and use inclusive design so that your work is available to the widest possible audience.

Key Terms

accessibility

application program interfaces
  (APIs)

augmented reality

Chatbots

command-line user interfaces

concatenative synthesis

event-driven

event handler

graphical user interface (GUI)

Haptic

Human-Computer Interaction (HCI)

Inclusive design

mixed reality

phoneme

Speech recognition

speech synthesis

user experience (UX)

user interface (UI)

Vector graphics

Virtual reality

voice user interface

MODULE
29

SOFTWARE DEVELOPMENT METHODOLOGIES

LEARNING OBJECTIVES:

29.1 SOFTWARE DEVELOPMENT

29.1.1 List the key tasks that take place during the software development process.

29.1.2 Describe the importance of efficiency, security, and quality throughout the software development process.

29.2 THE WATERFALL MODEL

29.2.1 Describe the general methodology of the waterfall development model.

29.2.2 Identify each phase of the waterfall model.

29.2.3 List advantages and disadvantages of the waterfall model.

29.2.4 Select software development projects that can be best approached using the waterfall model.

29.3 THE AGILE MODEL

29.3.1 Describe the general approach of incremental, iterative development methods.

29.3.2 Classify Scrum, Extreme Programming, Feature-Driven Development, and Rapid Application Development as agile development methodologies.

29.3.3 List advantages and disadvantages of agile development.

29.3.4 Select software projects that can be best approached using an agile development methodology.

29.4 CODING PRINCIPLES

29.4.1 Describe the DRY principle.

29.4.2 Describe the single responsibility principle.

29.4.3 Explain the purpose of clean coding.

29.4.4 Explain how statement blocks assist readability and constrain scope in a structured program.

29.4.5 Describe the importance of secure coding.

29.4.6 List principles for secure coding.

29.4.7 List success factors for creating top-notch software.

29.5 TESTING

29.5.1 Identify testing levels for software development.

29.5.2 Describe unit testing and the use of test cases.

29.5.3 State the purpose of integration testing.

29.5.4 Explain why system testing is classified as a "black box" methodology.

29.5.5 Explain the use of alpha and beta passes in the acceptance test phase.

29.5.6 Identify the purpose of regression testing.

29.1 SOFTWARE DEVELOPMENT

The Software Development Life Cycle (29.1.1)

Like plants and animals, software has a life cycle. This software development life cycle begins with conception and progresses through the phases in **Figure 29-1**.

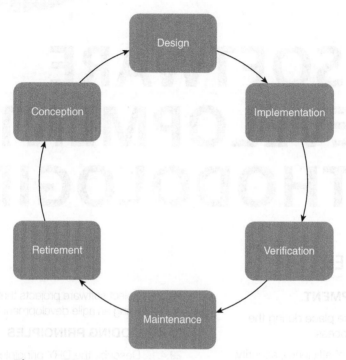

Figure 29-1 The software development lifecycle

As an individual or as part of a development team, you'll contribute to one or more phases of the software development life cycle.

Conception and Planning. The initial idea for an information system, software program, or app is based on business necessities, problems that need to be solved, niches that need to be filled, or markets that have profit potential. The software begins as a plan, which contains requirements for *what* the software is expected to do. Those requirements are created by various stakeholders, such as users, business owners, consultants, and programmers.

Design. In the design phase, developers formulate a model of the software using algorithms and data structures that specify *how* the software is supposed to accomplish the list of requirements.

Implementation. The software materializes as programmers generate lines of code and populate data structures to implement the design.

Verification. Testing is an integral phase in which software gains durability and stability as programmers correct errors and optimize performance.

Maintenance. After deployment, software can perform for months, years, or decades. Its lifetime may span generations of hardware and encompass innovations that affect its functionality. Software evolves in the maintenance phase as programmers supply incremental improvements to maintain peak performance.

Retirement. Eventually, the useful lifespan of a software program comes to an end because of factors such as changing user requirements and hardware innovations. As software nears the end of its useful life, maintenance activities wind down and user support is discontinued. If new, updated software is required, stakeholders restart the software development life cycle for a new state-of-the-art edition.

Q Can you identify three important takeaways from the software development life cycle that affect the way you should approach a programming project?

A The software development life cycle highlights the following important takeaways for you as a programmer:

- *Plan before you code.* Prior to coding, be sure to have a clear idea of what the software is supposed to do and how you plan to structure your code.
- *Testing is mandatory.* A program may appear to run correctly, but rigorous testing can eliminate coding errors that produce incorrect results with certain data sets.
- *Done is not finished.* Because software tends to have a long lifespan, be prepared to revise and improve your code.

Efficiency, Quality, and Security (29.1.2)

It might seem like the focus of software development is coding for functionality; in other words, making software that works. Functionality is important, but efficiency, security, and quality are also essential in all phases of the software life cycle.

Efficiency. Efficient programs have a smaller hardware footprint, but better response time.

Security. Secure software protects itself, its users, its underlying hardware, and its communication system from unauthorized activities.

Quality. Software rises to the top of the quality scale when it is correct, reliable, easy to use, flexible, testable, and maintainable.

The checklist in **Figure 29-2** provides examples of best practices that integrate efficiency, security, and quality during every phase of the software life cycle.

Conception

☑ Make sure the list of requirements is targeted to essential tasks.

☑ Include a list of security concerns in the requirements document.

☑ Gather factors that define usage expectations.

Design

☑ Decompose the software scope into modules, functions, and classes that perform specific tasks.

☑ Ensure that the design incudes all of the required tasks.

☑ Include directives for secure coding practices in the software specifications.

Implementation

☑ Follow secure coding practices.

☑ Write code that can be easily understood and modified.

☑ Walk through code to identify potential inefficiencies and security vulnerabilities.

Verification

☑ Follow a testing plan that verifies correct operation for all branches of the program.

☑ Include tests that attempt to gain unauthorized access to the software code or data.

Maintenance

☑ Provide ways to monitor the software's performance throughout its life.

☑ Provide monitoring routines to log attempted security breaches.

Retirement

☑ Have a plan for gracefully decommissioning the software.

Figure 29-2   Best practices for software efficiency, quality, and security in each phase of software development

29.2 THE WATERFALL MODEL

Structured Analysis and Design (29.2.1, 29.2.2)

Back in the days when computers were room-sized mainframes, going digital was all about converting manual business processes into computerized information systems. Teams of systems analysts were nearly overwhelmed by all the tasks associated with implementing new information systems. See **Figure 29-3**.

Figure 29-3   Developing new information systems involves many tasks

Out of the chaos emerged a systematic approach to software development based on a rigidly structured sequence of analysis and design phases. This approach, known as the waterfall model, divides software development into a series of cascading tasks that are performed one after the other. As shown in **Figure 29-4**, each phase produces a deliverable that is the input for the next phase.

Q Suppose you are a member of a development team producing an advanced driver assistance system (ADAS) that monitors blind spots, helps drivers stay in their lane, and autonomously avoids collisions. Your team is using the waterfall development method. What documentation would you be given as you begin coding the collision detection module?

A The software specifications documentation.

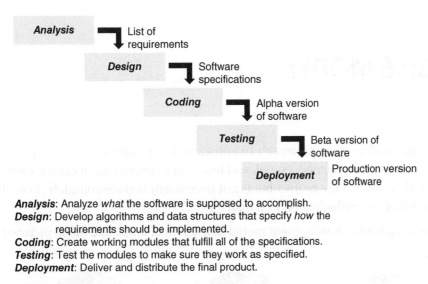

Analysis: Analyze *what* the software is supposed to accomplish.
Design: Develop algorithms and data structures that specify *how* the requirements should be implemented.
Coding: Create working modules that fulfill all of the specifications.
Testing: Test the modules to make sure they work as specified.
Deployment: Deliver and distribute the final product.

Figure 29-4   Phases of the waterfall development model

Waterfall Advantages and Disadvantages (29.2.3, 29.2.4)

The main advantage of the waterfall model is its emphasis on planning. During the analysis and design phases, developers lock down specifications for the software. These two phases may take up to 40 percent of the total development time, and once coding begins, few changes are made to the specifications. Additional advantages include:

- With specifications locked down, programmers have a clear mandate and don't need to be concerned with last-minute change orders that might have a domino effect throughout the code.
- The documentation created during the analysis and design phases needs only minor edits to become documentation for the final software product.

The major criticism of the waterfall model is its lack of flexibility. During the analysis and design phases, developers rarely can anticipate every way in which users will interact with the software. Business policies and regulations might change while development is ongoing. Because the software specifications are locked down at the beginning, developers have limited leeway to add or improve features during the coding phase.

Based on its advantages and disadvantages, the waterfall model is appropriate for development projects when:

- The scope and size of the project are well defined.
- The requirements are clear at the beginning of the project.
- The underlying system and use cases are stable.
- The project has a defined completion date during which requirements are not likely to change.

Q How suitable is the waterfall model for developing your collision avoidance module of the ADAS system?

A The waterfall method might not be suitable because as you develop the system, you could discover additional requirements based on scenarios that were not anticipated during the design phase.

29.3 THE AGILE MODEL

Incremental Development (29.3.1)

In response to the waterfall model's rigid approach to software development, an incremental development model emerged in which software is designed, coded, and tested in a succession of cycles. Each cycle produces a module that works and adds value to the project but is not necessarily feature complete. In each cycle, requirements can change as the software gradually takes its final form.

You can visualize the incremental development model as a series of loops like those pictured in **Figure 29-5**.

Plan: Determine the scope and focus of the iteration.
Design: Create specifications for coding an instance of a module.
Code: Write the code for the module.
Test: Test the module.
Release: Circulate the module to get user feedback.
Review: Analyze user feedback.
Iterate: Launch the next iteration to improve and extend the feature set and functionality.

Figure 29-5   The incremental iterative design approach

Agile Methodologies (29.3.2)

Incremental, iterative development is the basis for today's popular agile development methodologies. When you hear team leaders mention Scrum, Extreme Programming, Rapid Application Development, or Feature-Driven Development, they are referring to various agile methodologies.

The general agile approach was devised by a group of programmers who published the Agile Manifesto, shown in **Figure 29-6**.

The Agile Manifesto

We are uncovering better ways of developing software by doing it and helping others do it. Through this work we have come to value:

Individuals and interactions over processes and tools

Working software over comprehensive documentation

Customer collaboration over contract negotiation

Responding to change over following a plan

That is, while there is value in the items on the right, we value the items on the left more.

_____

© 2001-2019 Agile Manifesto Authors
This declaration may be freely copied in any form, but only in its entirety through this notice.

Source: Agile Alliance

Figure 29-6   The Agile Manifesto

Q From reading the Agile Manifesto, what are the four important principles of the Agile philosophy?

A The four important principles of the Agile philosphy are:

- Interacting with users and team members rather than following a set process
- Focusing on coding and testing rather than maintaining documentation
- Getting feedback from users throughout the development process
- Allowing the specifications to change as developers respond to feedback

Agile Advantages and Disadvantages (29.3.3, 29.3.4)

For many of today's innovative software projects, agile development methodologies have several advantages over the waterfall model:

- Agile methodologies are more flexible, allowing programmers to alter requirements going into each iteration.
- Functional software is released at the end of each iteration, unlike the waterfall model, which produces a functional product only at the end of the testing phase.
- Each release is thoroughly tested to ensure software quality.
- User interaction during multiple deployment and review phases provides developers with continuous feedback that can be incorporated into the final product.
- Because of feedback during each iteration, the final product tends to satisfy user needs.

Q In agile methodologies, how does user involvement differ from the waterfall method?

A In the waterfall method, users typically provide input once during the analysis phase and then again during the testing phase. With agile methodologies, users participate in each iteration.

The major criticisms of agile methodologies include:

- Measuring progress is difficult.
- The number of iterations that will be required for the final product is unknown.
- Developers can get sidetracked by requests to add features that are not essential to the software functionality.
- The lack of a comprehensive design plan tends to be reflected in haphazard documentation.

Q Which criticism of agile methodologies is most likely to affect the software delivery date?

A Because the number of iterations is unknown, the software delivery date may be difficult to estimate.

Based on advantages and disadvantages, an agile methodology is appropriate for development projects when:

- The requirements are not obvious when the project begins.
- It is acceptable for the design to emerge through prototyping.
- It is important to get users involved in the development process.

29.4 CODING PRINCIPLES

Efficient Coding (29.4.1)

DRY, WET, DIE, SRP, Clean, STRIDE, KISS. Programmers toss these terms around like baseballs at an MLB game warmup. These terms are acronyms for principles that can help you during the coding phase of the software development cycle.

> **Don't Repeat Yourself (DRY)** is a programming principle that promotes efficient code through efficient use and reuse of functions, classes, and methods. **Duplication is Evil (DIE)** is the same idea.
>
> **Write Every Time (WET)** is the opposite of DRY. WET code contains needless repetition. **Figure 29-7** shows the difference between WET and DRY code.

The takeaway from the DRY principle is to check your code for redundancies. If necessary, restructure your algorithms, classes, or methods to eliminate repetitive code.

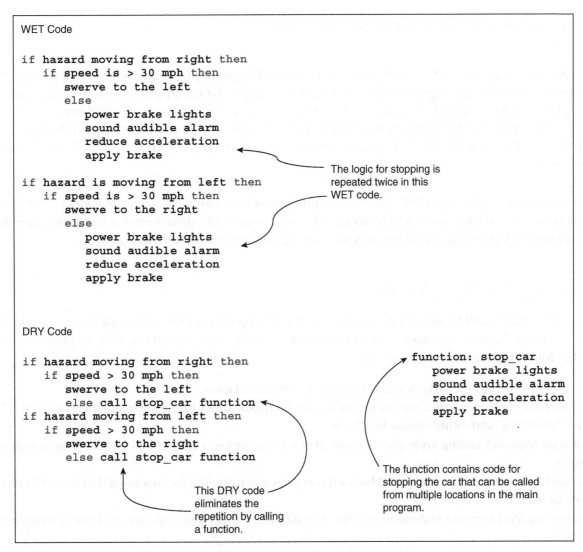

Figure 29-7   The difference between WET and DRY code

Modularized Code (29.4.2)

The **single responsibility principle (SRP)** suggests each function or class should have only one responsibility and one reason to change. When you have more than one reason to change a function or a class, it might have too much responsibility and is a candidate for restructuring.

Your collision avoidance module for the ADAS software needs to deal with various hazards. You might initially think that hazards should be defined in a class like the one in **Figure 29-8**.

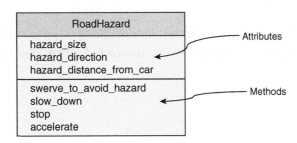

Figure 29-8   A class that violates SRP

Q Can you guess why the RoadHazard class violates SRP?

A The RoadHazard class has four methods, so it is handling many possible hazards. The code for the class or its methods might need to change for many reasons. In the future, sensors might be able to detect the speed of a hazard, which could require changes to several methods in the class. Another reason: it might become apparent that collision avoidance with the car ahead should be handled differently than avoiding random hazards that pop up from the side of the road.

To ensure that your code follows SRP, consider the purpose of each function, class, and method. Make sure these elements are fully decomposed and focus on one task. Look at the dependencies and make sure that changes won't have a domino effect that requires altering multiple class structures or methods.

Clean Coding (29.4.3, 29.4.4)

Clean code can be easily understood; not just by you, but by other programmers who might test your modules or modify them in the future. Clean code should be elegant, readable, simple, and testable. To produce clean code, keep the following best practices in mind:

- Use descriptive names for variables, functions, methods, and classes.
- Use consistent naming conventions for functions and methods. Don't prefix some functions with "get," but use "calculate" with other similar functions.
- Adopt a naming and coding style that is consistent with accepted conventions for the programming language.
- Keep functions and methods short and focused on doing one task. Aim for functions that have 15 lines of code or less.
- Use white space to create statement blocks that delineate functions, classes, and other program segments.
- Use comments sparingly. Your code should be self-explanatory. Be sure to update comments with each release.

Q How can you create a visual delineation for a block of code that represents a decision control structure?

A Insert an extra line to add white space before and after the decision block.

Secure Coding (29.4.5, 29.4.6)

When you find your STRIDE in programming, you're in the habit of taking steps to make sure your code is secure. STRIDE is a mnemonic for the six types of security threats shown in **Figure 29-9** that take advantage of code vulnerabilities.

Spoofing: Pretending to be someone else

Tampering: Unauthorized changing, adding, or deleting data

Repudiation: Hiding malicious activity to avoid detection

Information disclosure: Data breaches that access confidential information

Denial of service: Preventing access to legitimate users

Escalation of privileges: Modifying user rights to gain access to data

Mooi Design/Shutterstock.com

Figure 29-9   The STRIDE framework of security vulnerabilities

You might wonder what these threats have to do with your code. Let's look at an example: buffer overflows. A **buffer overflow** is a condition in which data in memory exceeds its boundaries and flows into memory areas intended for other data or program code. **Figure 29-10** illustrates a simplified example of a buffer overflow exploit.

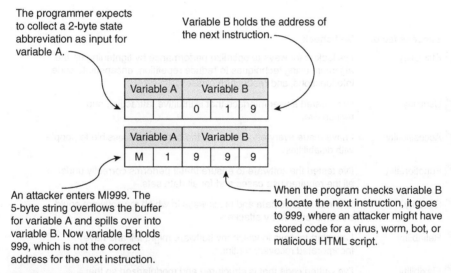

The programmer expects to collect a 2-byte state abbreviation as input for variable A.

Variable B holds the address of the next instruction.

Variable A	Variable B		
		0	1	9

Variable A		Variable B		
M	1	9	9	9

An attacker enters MI999. The 5-byte string overflows the buffer for variable A and spills over into variable B. Now variable B holds 999, which is not the correct address for the next instruction.

When the program checks variable B to locate the next instruction, it goes to 999, where an attacker might have stored code for a virus, worm, bot, or malicious HTML script.

Figure 29-10   How a buffer overflow exploit works

Cybercriminals can trigger buffer overflows with input specifically designed to execute malicious code, such as a computer virus. In the STRIDE model, buffer overflow exploits are an example of tampering that can lead to information disclosure.

You can protect your code from buffer overflows and other security exploits by implementing the following principles of **secure coding**:

Security from the start: Be mindful of ways in which your application might be exploited by cybercriminals.

Separation of privilege: Allow each user to access only those parts of a program that are required to perform their allocated tasks. By doing so, you minimize exposure if an account is compromised.

Economy of mechanism: Follow the KISS (Keep It Simple and Secure) doctrine that simpler code means less can go wrong.

Code defensively: Check user input for suspicious nonprintable control characters, and place strict boundaries on the values that can be stored in variables. Check the validity of input parameters in methods. Use containers that don't allow overruns instead of raw buffers that do.

Fail securely: Anticipate and handle exceptions that might cause your program to fail. Log all failures or suspicious activity. For example, if a user enters an incorrect password many times, it may be a break-in attempt.

Q If you allow open access to the ADAS system, it might be possible for remote users to control the braking system for a car. Which two principles of secure coding does this violate?

A It violates the security-from-the-start principle and the separation-of-privilege principle.

Success Factors (29.4.7)

When creating software, your initial concern might be "I hope it works!" But that is not the only criteria for successful coding. In a production environment, the quality of your code depends on several **success factors**. **Figure 29-11** offers a checklist of success factors that can increase the quality of the software you create.

Success factor	Self-check
✓ Efficiency	I've looked for ways to optimize performance by tightening up the algorithm using techniques to reduce repetition, encapsulate code into functions, and restructure classes.
✓ Usability	I've created a user interface that is intuitive, attractive, and responsive.
✓ Accessibility	I have made every effort to make the software accessible to people with disabilities.
✓ Functionality	I've tested the software to ensure that it performs correctly under all the required use cases and for all data sets.
✓ Security	I've tried to anticipate and block ways in which my software could be compromised by attackers.
✓ Reliability	I am alert to ways in which my software might fail and have incorporated recovery routines.
✓ Flexibility	I've written code that is structured and modularized so that necessary modifications can be implemented in narrowly targeted segments of code.
✓ Maintainability	I've written code that can be understood by other programmers who might be revising it.
✓ Testability	I've written and executed unit tests for my code which can be easily run again for regression testing after any future changes.

Figure 29-11   Coding success factors

29.5 TESTING

Levels of Testing (29.5.1)

Developing software to assist drivers is not trivial. Drivers' lives depend on the reliability of the code that you contribute. Testing is crucial.

Software development involves four levels of testing, shown in **Figure 29-12**.

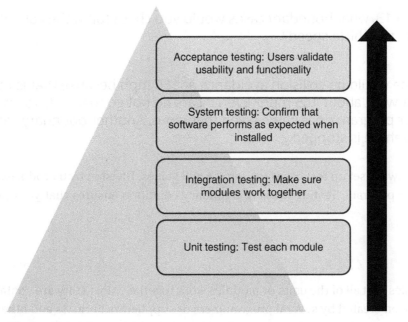

Figure 29-12   Software testing levels

Unit Testing (29.5.2)

Unit testing ensures that each module operates correctly for a comprehensive range of test cases. A **test case** is a set of preconditions, steps, and data that should produce a specific result called a "post condition." When a test case is executed, the actual results should correspond to the expected post condition.

If your module of the ADAS is supposed to stop the vehicle before an imminent collision, you must ensure that it correctly accounts for factors such as vehicle speed, stopping distance, and road conditions.

Unit testing can be carried out by manually entering test data, or testing can be automated using a companion program to feed in test cases. The goal of unit testing is to try all probable combinations of data, statements, decisions, branches, and conditions to ensure that they produce the expected output.

When setting up test cases, you should include boundary cases. A **boundary case** is a data point that is just at or beyond the maximum or minimum limits of expected data. See **Figure 29-13**.

Sergey85/Shutterstock.com

Figure 29-13   Boundary conditions for vehicle speed

Q Based on Figure 29-13, what boundary cases would you check for in the collision avoidance module that relate to vehicle speed?

A One boundary case would be collision avoidance at 160 mph because that is the maximum vehicle speed. But what about 165 mph? Even if cars do not go that fast, you would also want to know what your program does when given that input. Another boundary case would be at 0 mph when the vehicle is stopped.

Savvy programmers always set up test cases for zero or null values. Division by 0 produces errors and exceptions that can terminate a program. Testing the zero-boundary condition ensures that your program gracefully handles the result.

Integration Testing (29.5.3)

Integration testing verifies that all of the units or modules work together. Most software contains a collection of modules that may have been created by several programmers or supplied as libraries and other preprogrammed tools. When combined, these modules might not coordinate as expected.

Integration testing is based on test cases that focus on the flow of data between modules. For example, in the ADAS software, the module that detects objects has to send actionable data to the module that controls the vehicle's speed. When the detection module sends data such as "Moose ahead," the speed module should process that data to stop the vehicle (**Figure 29-14**).

⚠ **Large object detected. Stop vehicle.**

ArtMari/Shutterstock.com

Figure 29-14   Collision avoidance

System Testing (29.5.4)

System testing validates that the fully integrated software application performs as expected when installed on target hardware platforms. The software is tested under load to make sure it maintains good response time and stability.

System testing is classified as "black box testing" because it focuses on inputs and outputs, rather than the underlying code. In contrast, unit testing is classified as "white box testing" because all the details of the code are under scrutiny. See **Figure 29-15**.

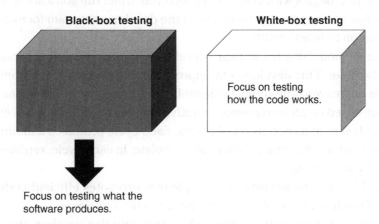

Figure 29-15   Black box and white box testing

Acceptance Testing (29.5.5)

Acceptance testing is typically performed with the help of users to ensure that the software meets usability requirements and the objectives for which it was created. Acceptance testing includes alpha and beta test passes.

Alpha testing is performed internally by professional testers. Your ADAS system would likely be tested on a closed course with professional drivers. **Beta testing** is performed by a select group of "real users" who are not members of the development team or professional testers. This phase of testing helps to identify problems that may occur in real-world environments on various hardware platforms and in a wide variety of unexpected scenarios.

Q Software for complex information systems requires a formal test plan prepared by developers. What level of testing is appropriate for casual programming projects and course assignments?

A For casual programming, unit testing can verify that your software functions correctly for a variety of data sets. You can also carry out simple acceptance testing by imagining that you are a typical user.

Regression Testing (29.5.6)

One additional type of testing is important in multiple phases of the software development cycle. **Regression testing** is performed to ensure that recent code modifications do not have adverse effects. This type of testing can be performed during unit, integration, system, or acceptance testing. It may also be required for changes made during the maintenance phase of the system life cycle.

Whenever code is modified, no matter how small the change, appropriate tests should be performed. Usually, you can use existing test cases; if not the entire test suite, then a subset that probes any likely side effects of the modified code.

SUMMARY

- Software has a life cycle that begins with conception and ends when the software is decommissioned.
- During the software development process, members of the development team focus on efficiency, security, and quality, in addition to functionality.
- The waterfall development model divides software development into a series of cascading tasks that are performed one after the other. This development approach is suitable when the application domain is well defined and stable but leaves little room for flexibility and changing requirements.
- Agile methodologies are based on an incremental, iterative approach to software development. Software is designed, coded, and tested in a succession of cycles. Each cycle produces a module that works and adds value to the project but is not necessarily feature complete. In each cycle, requirements can change as the software gradually takes its final form.
- Don't Repeat Yourself (DRY) is a programming principle that promotes efficient code. The opposite is Write Every Time (WET) code that contains repetitions and redundancies.
- The single responsibility principle (SRP) suggests that each function or class should have only one responsibility and one reason to change.
- Clean code can be easily understood; not just by you, but by other programmers who might test your modules or modify them in the future.
- Secure coding begins with an awareness of exploits that can compromise code and continues throughout the coding process in the form of simplifying code, establishing input checks, and handling exceptions.
- Software quality, security, functionality, and usability are evaluated during four testing phases: unit testing, integration testing, system testing, and acceptance testing.

Key Terms

Acceptance testing	Don't Repeat Yourself (DRY)	software development life cycle
agile development methodologies	Duplication is Evil (DIE)	success factors
Alpha testing	incremental development model	System testing
Beta testing	Integration testing	test case
boundary case	Regression testing	Unit testing
buffer overflow	secure coding	waterfall model
Clean code	single responsibility principle (SRP)	Write Every Time (WET)

MODULE 30

PSEUDOCODE, FLOWCHARTS, AND DECISION TABLES

LEARNING OBJECTIVES

30.1 PSEUDOCODE

30.1.1 Define the term "pseudocode" as a set of structured statements that programmers use to delineate the steps of an algorithm.

30.1.2 Explain the purpose of pseudocode.

30.1.3 Contrast pseudocode with code written in a programming language.

30.1.4 Recognize the relationship between algorithm steps and pseudocode statements.

30.1.5 Incorporate common style conventions to write pseudocode.

30.1.6 Apply an organized approach to writing pseudocode.

30.2 FLOWCHARTS

30.2.1 Define the term "flowchart" as a diagrammatic representation of an algorithm.

30.2.2 State that flowcharts can be used instead of, or in conjunction with, pseudocode.

30.2.3 Identify the shapes used in flowcharts and the purpose of each.

30.2.4 Trace a path through a flowchart.

30.2.5 List tools that can be used to create flowcharts.

30.3 DECISION TABLES

30.3.1 Define a decision table as a grid of rows and columns used to distill a set of complex decisions and actions into a set of rules that can become the statements in a computer program.

30.3.2 Identify the four quadrants of a decision table.

30.3.3 Calculate the maximum number of conditions.

30.3.4 Formulate the unique combinations of conditions.

30.3.5 Specify the action for each unique combination.

30.3.6 Interpret the rules produced by a decision table.

30.3.7 Optimize the rule set.

30.3.8 Check the decision table for completeness and accuracy.

30.1 PSEUDOCODE

From Algorithms to Pseudocode (30.1.1, 30.1.2, 30.1.4)

A company has gathered a team of programmers to create a fantastic new multiplayer adventure game. You're on the team and responsible for the module that walks players through creating a wizard or warrior for the game.

The adventure game begins by allowing each player to create a game character. **Figure 30-1** explains the initial parameters for wizards and for warriors.

(a)   (b)

Wizard
Energy points: 25
Spells: 3
Location: 0,0

Warrior
Energy points: 25
Weapon: 1
Weapon choice: bow
Location: 0,0

Algol/Shutterstock.com

tsuneomp/Shutterstock.com

Figure 30-1   Adventure game characters

Try to visualize the algorithm necessary to help a game player create a character. Here is one sequence of steps that could accomplish that task.

Ask player to enter a name for the game character.
Give player's character 25 energy points.
Give player the choice of being a wizard or a warrior.
If the character is a warrior, then allow the player to choose one weapon.
If the character is a wizard, then allow the player to choose three spells.
Set the character at the starting location.

Writing down the steps for an algorithm is a good start, but refining those steps into pseudocode can reduce the time you spend coding and help you produce a more efficient program.

Pseudocode is a set of structured statements for delineating the steps of an algorithm. This development tool goes beyond a simple list of steps because the wording is more precise.

Writing pseudocode can help you develop the detail and precision for expressing an algorithm in terms that can be easily transformed into statements coded in a programming language such as Python, Java, or C++.

In **Figure 30-2**, compare the pseudocode to the algorithm. You can't help but notice that the pseudocode is more detailed and more structured.

Pseudocode	Algorithm Steps

`begin`
`display What is your character's`
`    name?`
	Ask player to enter a name for the game character

`input character_name`	
`energy_points = 25`	Give player's character 25 energy points
`display Is your character a` `    wizard or warrior?`	Give player the choice of being a wizard or a warrior
`input character_type`	

`if character_type = warrior then`
`    display weapons list`
`    input selected_weapon`
	If the character is a warrior, then allow the player to choose one weapon

`if character_type = wizard then`
`    for count <= 3`
`        display spell list`
`        input selected spell`
`    next`
	If the character is a wizard, then allow the player to choose three spells

`location = 0,0` `end`	Set the character at the starting location

Figure 30-2 Pseudocode expresses an algorithm in structured detail

Q In Figure 30-2, which pseudocode statement is equivalent to "Give player's character 25 energy points" in the algorithm?

A The equivalent is `energy_points = 25`.

Q Two statements in the pseudocode correspond to "Give player the choice of being a wizard or a warrior." What are they?

A They are:

```
display Is your character a wizard or warrior?
input character_type
```

Pseudocode Basics (30.1.3)

Pseudocode includes commands and control structures. **Commands** indicate an action. **Control structures** indicate decisions or repetitions. Let's take a closer look at the adventure game pseudocode. In **Figure 30-3**, commands and control structures are highlighted in bold purple text to help you identify them.

```
begin
display What is your character's name?
input character_name
energy_points = 25
display Is your character a wizard or warrior?
input character_type


if character_type = warrior then
   display weapons list
   input selected_weapon


if character_type = wizard then
   for count <=3
      display spell list
      input selected spell
   next
location = 0,0
end
```

Figure 30-3   Pseudocode delineates commands and control structures

Q In Figure 30-3, would you classify `display` and `input` as commands or control structures?

A `Display` and `input` are commands, as are `begin` and `end`.

Q What are the two control structures in Figure 30-3?

A `If..then` is a control structure for a decision. `For..next` is a control structure for a repetition.

Pseudocode is fairly detailed and precise, but it is not program code. Typically, pseudocode has less punctuation than code in Java or C++. Also, the exact command words for a programming language may differ from those that you use in pseudocode.

Q In **Figure 30-4**, can you differentiate the pseudocode from the program code?

Sample 1	Sample 2
`{`	`display Please enter your name`
`string user_name;`	`input user_name`
`cout << "Please enter your name: " << endl;`	
`cin >> user_name;`	
`}`	

Figure 30-4   Differentiating between program code and pseudocode

A Sample 1 is program code in C++. Sample 2 is pseudocode. The C++ code required quite a bit more punctuation and parameters.

Pseudocode Guidelines (30.1.5)

There are no hard and fast rules for pseudocode syntax, punctuation, or phrasing, but some keywords and style conventions are derived from programming languages. **Figure 30-5** summarizes common naming conventions for pseudocode elements.

Pseudocode Element	Naming Conventions	Example

Variables
Function names
Method names
	Use a single letter, such as i, j, or k, for loop counters. For other variables, use a descriptive name. Be consistent in the use of case and underlines.	Three styles for variable names are common. Select one:
		`dragon_master`
		or
		`DragonMaster`
		or
		`dragonMaster`

Constants	Use all uppercase.	`MAX_SPEED`
Class names	Use camel case with each word capitalized.	`MyClass`

Command words	Be consistent with the style you use for command words. All lowercase is common, but lowercase bold and all uppercase are also common styles.	`display Hello!`
		or
		`DISPLAY Hello!`
		or
		`display Hello!`

Figure 30-5   Pseudocode naming conventions

Q How would you specify a constant, such as the number of seconds in a minute?

A Use uppercase for the constant as in SECONDS = 60.

In pseudocode you will want to work with variables and computations. Variables hold values that might change during program execution. Computations, functions, and methods often trigger those changes. The guidelines in **Figure 30-6** summarize best practices.

Pseudocode Element	Guideline	Example
`initialize`	Use to assign the initial value to a variable.	`initialize loop_counter = 1`
`declare`	Use to declare a variable before it is initialized. Include the variable name and its data type	`declare loop_counter as integer`

`create`	Use to describe a class, with the class name in CamelCase. Use the words "attribute" and "method" as necessary.	`create class Wizard`
		`    attribute: energy_points`
		`    attribute: spell`
		`    method: calculate_score`

`instantiate`	Use when instantiating an object. Use = new (equal sign "new") and the class name, followed by a list of attributes.	`instantiate gandalf = new`
		`Wizard with 100 energy points`
		`and lumous spell`

`compute`	Use the word `compute` followed by a mathematical expression with operators + − / * () % > < = <= >=.	`compute x = x + 1`

Figure 30-6   Pseudocode for variables and computations

Q What is the difference between initializing a variable and declaring a variable?

A When a variable is initialized, it receives a value, such as 0. When a variable is declared, it does not necessarily receive a value, but it is assigned a data type, such as integer or string.

Pseudocode commands specify actions. **Figure 30-7** outlines the use of common pseudocode commands.

Pseudocode Element	Guideline	Example
`display`	Use to prompt users for input or to display text or images on the screen.	`display Enter the name for` `your character:`
`input`	Use to collect external information from keyboard or touch interfaces and indicate the variable that will hold the input.	`input character_name`
`get` `read`	Use for collecting data from a source such as an array, file, or database.	`get array[5]` `read "myfile.txt"`

Figure 30-7   Pseudocode for commands

Finally, the guidelines in **Figure 30-8** can help you specify control structures in your pseudocode.

Pseudocode Element	Guideline	Example

`if..then`	Use for decision control structures. Use indents when the structure contains multiple lines.	```if score = 500 then```
		``` display Here is a bonus```
		``` score = score + 10```

`if..then..else`	Use for decisions with more than one possible outcome.	```if energy_points > 25 then```
		``` spell = success```
		``` else```
		``` spell = fail```

`for..next`	Use for loops that repeat a specific number of times.	```for count = 1 to 3```
		``` display spell list```
		``` input spell selection```
		```next```

`repeat..until`	Use for loops that continue until a specific condition is reached.	```repeat```
		``` strike door```
		``` yell "Open up!"```
		```until door = open```

`while..do`	Use for loops that continue only while a condition is true.	```while next_square NOT wall do``` ``` move to next_square```

`call`	Use to call a function, library, or method.	```call function get_score```
		```call method cast_spell```
		```call library random```

`return`	Use to specify a variable whose value will be sent from a function to the main program.	```return spell_result```

Figure 30-8 Pseudocode for control structures

Writing Pseudocode (30.1.6)

Writing pseudocode is not complex if you follow these easy steps:

1. Begin by jotting down the algorithm in your own words.
2. Identify variables in the algorithm and assign names to them.
3. Begin your pseudocode in a new column or document by writing statements that declare and initialize the variables.
4. Use a consistent style for command words and variable names.
5. Continue working through each step of the algorithm using corresponding pseudocode commands, computations, and control structures.
6. Identify computations and write them as mathematical expressions using variables as necessary.
7. Identify decision structures and write them in `if..then` format.
8. Identify repetition structures. Write the repetition pseudocode block using `for..next`, `repeat.. until`, or `while..do`, as appropriate.
9. Use indents for multiline decision and repetition structures.
10. Use blank lines as whitespace to set off decision and repetition structures.

30.2 FLOWCHARTS

Flowchart Basics (30.2.1, 30.2.2)

A **flowchart** is a diagram that represents the sequence and flow of steps in an algorithm. Programmers sometimes use flowcharts instead of pseudocode. Some development projects require the use of both flowcharts and pseudocode.

Flowcharts use a standard set of shapes that are connected by flowline arrows. The most commonly used flowchart shapes are described in **Figure 30-9**.

Shape	Name	Purpose
	Terminator	Represents the start or end of the algorithm
	Process	Indicates a mathematical or logical operation
	Decision	Represents a decision point that branches to different sets of steps
	Data	Represents data input or output
	Connector	Indicates a connection between two separate sections of a flowchart

Figure 30-9   Flowchart shapes

Drawing Flowcharts (30.2.3, 30.2.4)

Flowcharts begin and end with a **terminator shape**. The first shape contains the word Start. Additional shapes are stacked vertically to indicate sequential program flow, as shown in **Figure 30-10**.

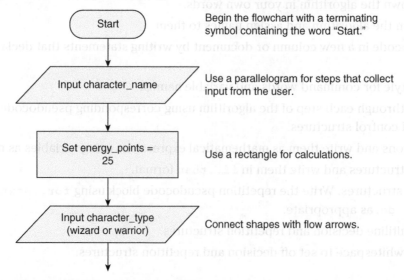

Begin the flowchart with a terminating symbol containing the word "Start."

Use a parallelogram for steps that collect input from the user.

Use a rectangle for calculations.

Connect shapes with flow arrows.

Figure 30-10   Sequential flow

Flowchart decision control structures correspond to `if..then` statements in pseudocode. Use a diamond shape and branching arrows for decisions in your flowchart, as in **Figure 30-11**.

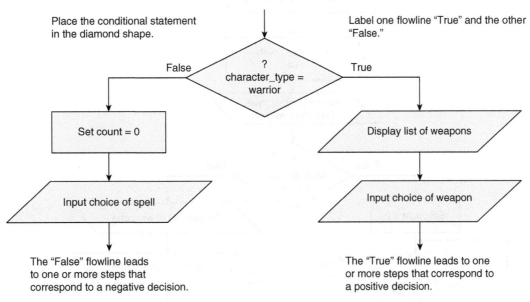

Figure 30-11   Decision structures

You can represent `for..next`, `repeat..until`, and `while..do` repetition control structures in your flowcharts using the shapes and flowlines in **Figure 30-12**.

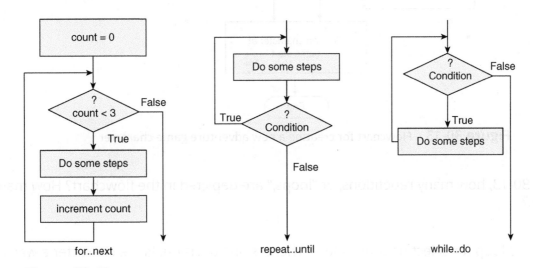

Figure 30-12   Repetition structures

Flowchart Tools (30.2.5)

To create a flowchart, you can use diagramming software or an online diagramming app. Trace the flow of steps in **Figure 30-13** to discover how the shapes fit together to diagram an algorithm that creates a character for an adventure game.

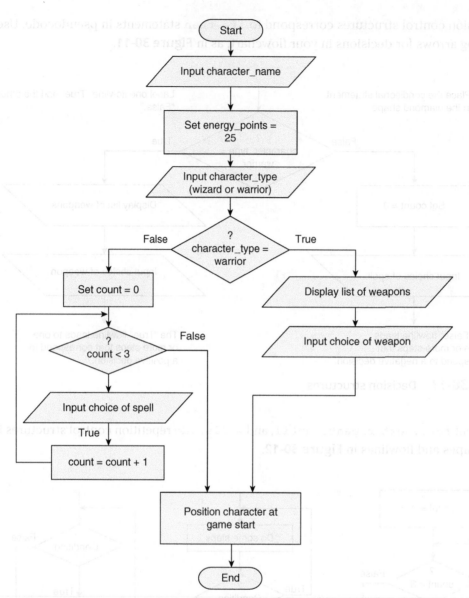

Figure 30-13   Flowchart for creating a new adventure game character

Q In Figure 30-13, how many repetitions, or "loops," are depicted in the flowchart? How many decisions?

A There is one loop for selecting three spells. There is one decision: Is the character a warrior?

When using a flowchart app, you can drag shapes into the work area to position them. Most flowchart apps include a feature that also allows you to drag connecting arrows between two shapes. After the shapes are connected, the arrows stretch, shrink, or bend as necessary when the shapes are moved.

Check your completed flowchart to make sure that every shape, excluding the Start and End terminators, has at least one input and one output. Also, check that all the flow arrows point in the correct direction to indicate the sequence of steps.

30.3 DECISION TABLES

Decision Table Basics (30.3.1)

Think about developing an adventure game that allows wizards and warriors to cast a simple flame spell under certain conditions, depending on the type of character, the character's energy points, and whether there is daylight. All the possibilities could become complex.

To make sure that your program includes all of the possible conditions when a spell can be successfully cast, you can construct a decision table. A **decision table** uses rows and columns to distill a set of complex decisions and actions into a set of rules that can become the statements in a computer program.

Figure 30-14 illustrates a decision table for the flame spell. Take a quick look, then we'll explore how to construct one.

Wizard	Y	Y	Y	Y	N	N	N	N
Daylight	Y	Y	N	N	Y	Y	N	N
Energy level > 50	Y	N	Y	N	Y	N	Y	N
Spell produces flame	✔	✔	✔					
Spell produces spark				✔	✔			
Spell fails						✔	✔	✔

Figure 30-14   A decision table for the flame spell

List the Conditions (30.3.2)

To create a decision table, you can use a spreadsheet, word processor, pencil and paper, or a decision table wizard. The table will have four quadrants, as shown in **Figure 30-15**.

Upper-left quadrant: **Conditions**	Upper-right quadrant: **Alternatives**
Lower-left quadrant: **Actions**	Lower-right quadrant: **Action entries**

Figure 30-15   Decision table quadrants

Begin by filling in the **Conditions quadrant** with factors that affect the decision. Three conditions affect flame spells. Those conditions go in the upper-left quadrant. See **Figure 30-16**.

Wizard								
Daylight								
Energy level > 50								

Figure 30-16   The Conditions quadrant

Q What do you notice about the way these conditions are formulated?

A They all have yes or no possibilities. For example, the condition Wizard would be "yes" for wizards, but "no" for warriors.

List All Possible Alternatives (30.3.3, 30.3.4)

For each condition, there are two alternatives: Y or N. A character can be a wizard (Y) or not (N). It can be daylight (Y) or not (N). The character's energy can be more than 50 (Y) or not (N).

To identify all the options for the **Alternatives quadrant**, first calculate the number of possible combinations. For the spell, there are two alternatives (Y and N) and three conditions (wizard, daylight, and energy level). The calculation is 2^3, or $2 \times 2 \times 2$, which is 8. You will have eight columns in the Alternatives quadrant. Fill in the alternatives as shown in **Figure 30-17**.

Wizard	Y	Y	Y	Y	N	N	N	N
Daylight	Y	Y	N	N	Y	Y	N	N
Energy level > 50	Y	N	Y	N	Y	N	Y	N

Figure 30-17   The Alternatives quadrant

Notice the pattern in each row. In the first row, one half is filled with Ys and the other half is filled with Ns, so four Ys are followed by four Ns. In the second row, the pattern is two Ys followed by two Ns. The last row alternates between Ys and Ns.

Reading from top to bottom, each column has a unique set of alternatives.

Q What is the first set of alternatives?

A The first set is Y Y Y indicating that the character is a wizard, it is daylight, and the character's energy level is above 50.

Specify Results and Rules (30.3.5)

Your next step is to specify possible actions in the **Action quadrant**. There are three possible actions: the spell will produce a steady flame, the spell will produce a small spark, or the spell will fail. See **Figure 30-18**.

Wizard	Y	Y	Y	Y	N	N	N	N
Daylight	Y	Y	N	N	Y	Y	N	N
Energy level > 50	Y	N	Y	N	Y	N	Y	N
Spell produces flame								
Spell produces spark								
Spell fails								

Figure 30-18   The Action quadrant

The fun part is filling in the **Action Entries quadrant**. For each series of Ys and Ns in a vertical column, place a checkmark in the lower-right quadrant to indicate the correct action. The set of alternatives and the action entries combine to form a rule. See **Figure 30-19**.

Wizard	Y	Y	Y	Y	N	N	N	N
Daylight	Y	Y	N	N	Y	Y	N	N
Energy level > 50	Y	N	Y	N	Y	N	Y	N
Spell produces flame	✔	✔	✔					
Spell produces spark				✔	✔			
Spell fails						✔	✔	✔

Figure 30-19   Decision table rules

For the first set of alternatives, Y Y Y, the character is a wizard, it is daylight, and the wizard has an energy level that is greater than 50. This character can cast the flame spell to produce a steady flame.

Q Take a close look at the other sets of alternatives. What happens when non-wizards cast the flame spell?

A A warrior can use a flame spell to produce a spark only when it is daylight and the warrior has more than 50 energy points.

Interpret Rules (30.3.6)

The information in a decision table can be converted into pseudocode and eventually into program code. For the first rule, the character is a wizard, it is daylight, and the character's energy level is above 50, so the spell produces a flame. The pseudocode for this rule might be:

```
if wizard = Y and daylight = Y and energy_level > 50 then
    flame_spell = flame
```

Can a wizard always cast the flame spell? Rule 4 says that if there is no daylight and the wizard has an energy level less than 50, the spell will only produce a spark. The pseudocode for this rule would be:

```
if wizard = Y and daylight = N and energy_level <= 50 then
    flame_spell = spark
```

Q Can you find the rule that allows a non-wizard to cast the flame spell? How would you express this rule in pseudocode?

A The rule is the fifth column of alternatives. The pseudocode would be:

```
if wizard = N and daylight = Y and energy_level > 50 then
    flame_spell = spark
```

This decision table has eight rules. Are all eight rules required, or can these rules be combined to produce pseudocode and program code that is more efficient? Is the table complete and is it accurate? Before depending on a decision table for the logic that is the basis for program code, three simple steps help to ensure optimization, completeness, and accuracy.

Optimize the Rules (30.3.7)

Some rules can be combined. Notice the pattern of Ys in the first and second rules of **Figure 30-20**. Those rules both produce a flame as long as the character is a wizard and it is daylight. The wizard's energy level doesn't matter.

Wizard	Y	Y	Y	Y	N	N	N	N
Daylight	Y	Y	N	N	Y	Y	N	N
Energy level > 50	Y	N	Y	N	Y	N	Y	N
Spell produces flame	✔	✔	✔					
Spell produces spark				✔	✔			
Spell fails						✔	✔	✔

Figure 30-20   Redundant rules

Rules 1 and 2 can be combined using a dash to eliminate the energy level. The resulting table looks like **Figure 30-21**.

Wizard	Y	Y	Y	N	N	N	N
Daylight	Y	N	N	Y	Y	N	N
Energy level > 50	–	Y	N	Y	N	Y	N
Spell produces flame	✔	✔					
Spell produces spark			✔	✔			
Spell fails					✔	✔	✔

Figure 30-21   A dash indicates combined rules

Q Can you combine the last two rules?

A Yes, the energy level has no effect on non-wizards who are in the dark. The revised decision table will look like **Figure 30-22**.

Wizard	Y	Y	Y	N	N	N
Daylight	Y	N	N	Y	Y	N
Energy level > 50	–	Y	N	Y	N	–
Spell produces flame	✔	✔				
Spell produces spark			✔	✔		
Spell fails					✔	✔

Figure 30-22   The last two rules combined

Check for Completeness and Accuracy (30.3.8)

The final step for creating a decision table is to make sure it is complete and accurate.

Check for completeness. The optimized decision table contains six rules. The table is complete if it contains all of the possible conditions and actions. Suppose that non-wizard users could cast flame spells if they carried a magic candle. That condition is not included in the upper-left quadrant, so the decision table would be incomplete. To complete the table, it would need to be revised for four conditions and sixteen rules.

Check for accuracy. Sometimes decision tables produce redundant rules or impossible situations. Redundant rules exist when two rules have the same conditions and produce the same result. Impossible rules contain conditions that contradict each other.

Q Here is a slightly different decision table. Can you find any redundant rules or impossible rules in **Figure 30-23**?

	1	2	3	4	5	6	7	8
Wizard	Y	Y	Y	Y	N	N	N	N
Energy level <= 50	Y	Y	N	N	Y	Y	N	N
Energy level > 50	Y	N	Y	N	Y	N	Y	N
Spell produces flame	✔	✔						
Spell produces spark			✔	✔				
Spell fails					✔	✔	✔	✔

Figure 30-23   Can you find any redundant or impossible rules in this decision table?

A Did you find these problems:

- Rules 1 and 5 are impossible. A character cannot have an energy level greater than 50 and less than 50 at the same time.
- Rule 4 is impossible. It refers to a character that does not have an energy level above, equal to, or below 50!
- Rules 5, 6, 7, and 8 are redundant. They can be combined.

Decision tables are fun to construct and can help you sort through complex logic. Make sure to keep this tool handy in your program development toolbox.

SUMMARY

- Pseudocode is a set of structured statements for delineating the steps of an algorithm, including control structures.
- There are no hard and fast rules for pseudocode syntax, punctuation, or phrasing, but some keywords and style conventions are similar to programming languages.
- When writing pseudocode, use a consistent style for command words and variable names.

- A flowchart is a diagram that represents the sequence and flow of steps in an algorithm. Flowcharts use a standard set of shapes that are connected by flowline arrows.
- Control structures are easy to visualize when depicted in a flowchart.
- When drawing flowcharts, make sure that every shape, excluding terminators, has at least one input and one output.
- A decision table uses rows and columns to distill a set of complex decisions and actions into a set of rules that can become the statements in a computer program.
- To create a decision table, fill in the four quadrants: Conditions, Alternatives, Actions, and Action Entries. Read down each vertical column of Ys, Ns, and checkmarks to formulate rules.
- Decision tables can be optimized by combining rules to eliminate rules that are redundant and those that are impossible.

Key Terms

Action Entries quadrant

Action quadrant

Alternatives quadrant

Commands

Conditions quadrant

Control structures

decision table

flowchart

Impossible rules

Pseudocode

Redundant rules

terminator shape

Variables

UNIFIED MODELING LANGUAGE

LEARNING OBJECTIVES:

31.1 PURPOSE OF UNIFIED MODELING LANGUAGE (UML)

31.1.1 Associate "UML" with "unified modeling language."

31.1.2 Define the purpose of UML as helping programmers visualize the design of a software system.

31.2 UML DIAGRAM PARTS

31.2.1 Define a class diagram.

31.2.2 Identify the parts of class notation.

31.2.3 Differentiate class notation from object notation.

31.2.4 Define a use case diagram.

31.2.5 Identify the parts of use cases.

31.2.6 Demonstrate a use case with UML.

31.2.7 Define a sequence diagram.

31.2.8 Identify the parts of a sequence diagram.

31.3 USING UML TO STRUCTURE PROGRAMS

31.3.1 Associate UML with the analysis and design of systems that will be implemented with object-oriented programming.

31.3.2 Construct a class diagram for a real-world object.

31.3.3 Contrast real-world examples for relationship diagrams.

31.3.4 Showcase UML associations and their notations for class diagrams.

31.3.5 Demonstrate the translation of UML to code.

31.1 PURPOSE OF UNIFIED MODELING LANGUAGE (UML)

Communicating Ideas to Other Programmers (31.1.1, 31.1.2)

The way you communicate with others relies on your mutual agreement about what terms mean. When you see or hear the word "teapot," you probably think of an item similar to the one shown in **Figure 31-1**. If "teapot" means something else to a friend or colleague, you might end up arguing about how to use the item. Communication requires agreement on the representation of ideas.

Danny Smythe/Shutterstock.com

Figure 31-1   Standard teapot

Computer scientists also need to agree on terms when communicating ideas. Instead of reading someone else's code, which can be time consuming and difficult, you can use the Unified Modeling Language (UML). UML helps programmers visualize the design of complicated programs and coordinate large projects where many people are working on parts of a whole. Each of those parts needs to work with the other parts. Using UML, programmers define the code relationships and behaviors for everyone to reference. UML can also be used for tasks other than programming, such as communicating or creating use cases for programs.

31.2 UML DIAGRAM PARTS

Class Diagram Basics (31.2.1, 31.2.2, 31.2.3)

UML is used to define the components of a system, or scenario, including consistent names. UML consists of many types of diagrams, including a class diagram, which represents the structure of a system, showing relationships between classes, objects, methods, functions, and member variables.

For example, suppose you need to create a `Teapot` class, which contains all of the methods and variables associated with a teapot. Instead of writing the code for the `Teapot` class, you can start by creating a class diagram in UML to describe the structure of the class, as shown in **Figure 31-2**.

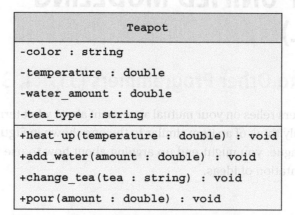

Figure 31-2   Class diagram of the `Teapot` class

In a class diagram, a class is represented by a rectangle divided into sections. A class diagram includes the following symbols and notations:

Class name. Write the class name in the top section of the rectangle. Format it as bold, centered, and with the first letter capitalized, as in `Teapot`.

Attributes. List the class attributes in the second section. Attributes are not bold, left aligned, and lowercase. Each attribute is listed in the format `identifier : variable_type`, as in `color : string`.

Methods. List the methods in the third section. Methods are not bold, left aligned, and lowercase. Each method is listed in the format `method_name( argument(s) ) : return_type`. Each argument appears in the format `argument_name : type`. For example, a complete method is `heat_up(temperature : double) : void`.

Visibility markers. A visibility marker specifies what can access the methods and attributes in a class. The public marker is a **+** sign, the protected marker is a **#** sign, and the private marker is a **–** sign. For example, `-color : string` indicates that `color` is a private attribute. Markers are optional.

Q Since an object is an instance of a class, can I represent an object in UML using the same notation as in a class diagram?

A For the most part, yes. The only difference in the notation is that you write the object name in the top section instead of the class name. In addition, the object name is underlined, as in `red_teapot`, to distinguish an object from a class.

Use Case Diagram Basics (31.2.4, 31.2.5, 31.2.6)

In UML, a use case diagram communicates how a user interacts with the system to achieve a goal. In general, a use case is a list of actions or steps showing the interactions between a person and a system in order to accomplish a task. The use case depicts who does what with the system and for what purpose.

Specifying use cases helps to organize the functional requirements of the system. In software engineering, functional requirements are the behaviors that a system must perform, usually specified by the customer. For example, for a teapot to be useful, it must have the functional requirements of allowing a person to add water, heat the water, change the tea, and pour out the contents.

Q What's the difference between a functional requirement and a use case?

A You can think of use cases as a way to identify and document the functional requirements of a system.

A scenario is a single use case, or a single action path through the system. Generally, a use case diagram communicates a high-level overview of the relationships between system components. A use case diagram of the Making Tea system is displayed in **Figure 31-3**.

A use case diagram consists of the following components:

System. Represent the system being described by a bounding box. Anything outside of the box is considered as outside of the system. In the example, Making Tea is the system.

Actors. The actors are the types of people using the system. An actor is represented by a stick figure. Other systems that interact with this system can also be represented as actors. In the example, a generic Person is the actor.

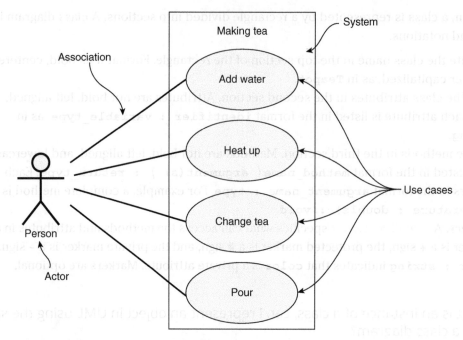

Figure 31-3 Use case diagram for the Making Tea system

Use cases. The use cases describe the actions a user can take in the system. The use cases are represented by horizontal ovals. In the example, the use cases are Add Water, Heat Up, Change Tea, and Pour.

Association. An **association** is a line drawn between an actor and a use case. In complex diagrams with many actors and use cases, the associations help to clarify which actors are associated with which use cases.

A more complex example involving a car dealership management system is shown in **Figure 31-4**.

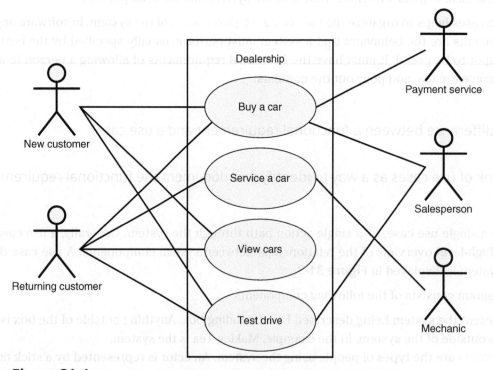

Figure 31-4 Use case diagram for a Dealership management system

The actors in the car dealership management system include new customers, returning customers, the payment service, a salesperson, and a mechanic. The use cases supported include buying a car, servicing a car, viewing the available cars, and test driving a car. The straight lines represent which actors are associated with which use cases.

Sequence Diagrams (31.2.7, 31.2.8)

In UML, a **sequence diagram** shows the relationship among parts of code and the exact sequence of events. When coding a system, developers use a sequence diagram to understand the order in which actions need to occur. Sequence diagrams can help to describe the logic of complex processes within a system without focusing on small details.

To create a sequence diagram, you first need to determine all of the entities necessary to make the code run. In the teapot example, a person, teapot, water source such as a sink, tea, and a heating device are necessary to make tea. Usually, one sequence diagram is drawn per use case. The sequence diagram in **Figure 31-5** shows how to use a teapot to make a cup of tea.

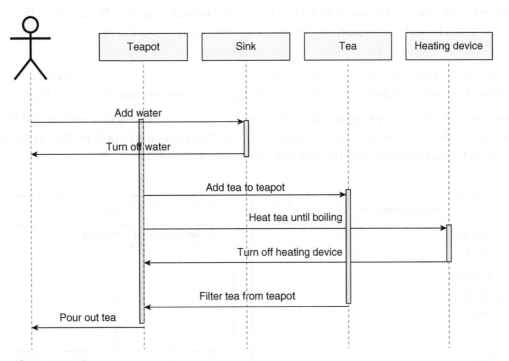

Figure 31-5   Sequence diagram for making tea

A sequence diagram consists of the following components:

Actors. The actors are represented as stick figures (similar to use case diagrams). Actors are always outside of the scope of the diagram.

Objects. The objects are represented as rectangles. The objects are not necessarily classes in the system, but they represent entities that interact in the system. They are usually placed in sequential order from left to right. In Figure 31-5, the objects are a teapot, sink, tea, and heating device.

Lifelines. A lifeline represents the existence of an actor or object over time. Lifelines appear as dashed vertical lines. As you move forward in time, the sequence moves down the lifeline.

Messages. A message shows the interaction between components as discrete steps. Methods are often used as the messages. In the diagram, messages appear as filled arrows and include text describing the interaction, as in "Add water." Generally, messages point from left to right; however a

return message (or reply message) points from right to left, usually indicating the result of an action, similar to a return value. If a message requests information, a return message indicates the result. The return message is denoted with a dashed line. The sequence diagram in Figure 31-5 does not use any return messages.

Activation boxes. An **activation box** shows when and how long an object performs an action or is otherwise active. An activation box is depicted as a long narrow rectangle on the lifeline, extending from the object's first message to its last message.

31.3 USING UML TO STRUCTURE PROGRAMS

UML Associations (31.3.1, 31.3.2, 31.3.3, 31.3.4)

Professional programming teams use UML to design and analyze systems that will be coded using object-oriented programming. The teams use the UML diagrams as a rule book, where everyone agrees on how parts of the program should work. If everyone agrees on the parts and how they fit together, they break the project into smaller tasks for others to work on. In this way, UML provides a cheat sheet for communication in big projects.

Class diagrams can be combined with other classes in a **relationship diagram**. The lines connecting the classes indicate how the classes relate to, and interact with, the other classes, also known as their associations.

Figure 31-6 shows the UML class diagram for a car using **inheritance**. The arrow with an unfilled triangle signifies that the class inherits from the class it points to. The **Car** class inherits from **MotorVehicle**, the **ElectricCar** class inherits from **Car**, and the **GasCar** class inherits from **Car**.

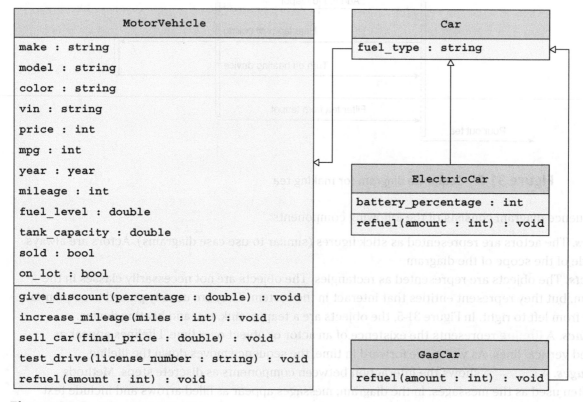

Figure 31-6 Inheritance in UML

Sometimes classes depend on the definition of another class even though they are not literally part of that class. For example, a washing machine can clean clothes, but it does not own them. To represent this dependency in UML, you use a dashed line with an open arrow. **Figure 31-7** shows a `WashingMachine` class that has a dependence on the `Clothing` class.

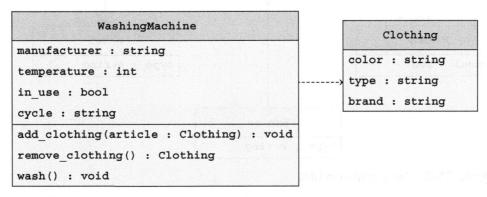

Figure 31-7   Dependency in UML

Aggregation describes a class that contains one or more members of another class, but the lifetimes of those members are not inherently connected to the containing class. For example, a business has multiple stores to manage, but if one store closes, the business still exists. A deck of cards contains many cards, but some cards can be removed without destroying the deck.

In a UML diagram, aggregation is shown as a solid line ending in an unfilled diamond. **Figure 31-8** shows a `Deck` class that aggregates multiple objects of a `Card` class. The numbers on the aggregation line indicate the numerical relationship between the two classes. Here, zero or more cards make up one deck, and each card can exist in only one deck.

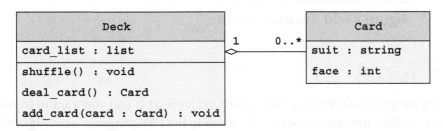

Figure 31-8   Aggregation in UML

Composition is similar to aggregation, where a class contains one or more member classes, except the classes directly rely on each other to exist. A `Vehicle` class can be made up of other member classes. For example, a vehicle contains wheels, but if the wheels are destroyed, the vehicle is, too, since it can no longer function.

In a UML diagram, composition is shown as a solid line ending in a filled diamond. **Figure 31-9** shows a `Vehicle` class composed of `Window`, `Engine`, and `Wheel` classes. Numerical values are used as in aggregation to indicate the relationships.

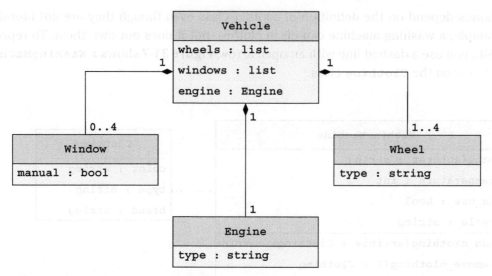

Figure 31-9   Composition in UML

The term **realization** is used in UML when an interface is fulfilled by a class. Realization is shown as a dashed line ending in an unfilled triangle. In **Figure 31-10**, the `VideoPlayer` and `AudioPlayer` realize the `MediaPlayer` interface.

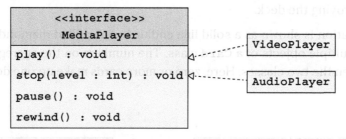

Figure 31-10   Realization in UML

Translating UML to Code (31.3.5)

Suppose you've created a `Teapot` class diagram like the one in Figure 31-2, and you want to translate it to code. The best way to start is to outline the code based on the items in the UML diagram, as in **Figure 31-11**.

```
class Teapot
{
  private:
      string color;
      double temperature;
      double water_amount;
      string tea_type;
```

Figure 31-11   Outline of code based on a UML diagram (*Continued*)

```
    public:

        void heat_up(double temperature)
        {

        }


        void add_water(double amount)
        {

        }


        void change_tea(string tea)
        {

        }


        void pour(double amount)
        {

        }
};
```

Figure 31-11   Outline of code based on a UML diagram

Depending on how the programming team determined that these methods should behave, you can fill in the rest of the code as in **Figure 31-12**.

```
#include <iostream>
using namespace std;


class Teapot
{
    private:
        string color;
        double temperature = 0;
        double water_amount = 0;
        string tea_type;
```

Figure 31-12   Implementing the `Teapot` class (*Continued*)

```
public:
    Teapot(string color)
    {
        this->color = color;
    }


void heat_up(double temperature)
{
    this->temperature = temperature;
}


void add_water(double amount)
{
    this->water_amount += amount;
}


void change_tea(string tea)
{
    this->tea_type = tea;
}


void pour(double amount)
{
    this->water_amount -= amount;
}


string get_color()
{
    return this->color;
}
int get_temperature()
{
    return this->temperature;
}
```

Figure 31-12 Implementing the Teapot class (*Continued*)

```cpp
    string get_tea_type()
    {
        return this->tea_type;
    }

    double get_water_amount()
    {
        return this->water_amount;
    }
};

int main()
{

    Teapot t = Teapot("blue");
    t.change_tea("oolong");
    t.add_water(25.5);
    t.heat_up(95);
    t.pour(2.75);

    cout << "Teapot status:" << endl;
    cout << "Color: " << t.get_color() << endl;
    cout << "Temperature: " << t.get_temperature() << endl;
    cout << "Tea Type: " << t.get_tea_type() << endl;
    cout << "Water Amount: " << t.get_water_amount() << endl;


    return 0;
}
```

OUTPUT:

```
Teapot status:
Color: blue
Temperature: 95
Tea Type: oolong
Water Amount: 22.75
```

Figure 31-12   Implementing the `Teapot` class

SUMMARY

- The Unified Modeling Language (UML) is a standardized way for computer scientists to communicate ideas to other programmers. Using a common means of communication helps to ensure that everyone on a project team has the same understanding of the program design and solution.
- A class diagram is a visual representation of a class to be used by a program. The diagram uses a rectangle to indicate each class, with sections inside the class rectangle to show the member variables and methods. Access modifiers are also included in the class diagram.
- A use case diagram conveys how a user will interact with the programmed system. The use case diagram is made up of use cases that organize the functional requirements of the system.
- The use case diagram consists of the system, actors, use cases, and associations.
- A scenario represents a single path of action through the system at a high level.
- A sequence diagram shows the relationships of entities within code and the exact sequence of events. This information helps developers understand the logic and process of the system. A sequence diagram also conveys how long each object is act ive within the system.
- A sequence diagram consists of actors, objects, lifelines, messages, return messages, and activation boxes.
- Classes that rely on other classes but don't own other classes as part of their design are called dependent. UML diagrams show dependency with a dotted line ending with an open arrow.
- A class can contain other classes and use them as part of its whole definition, as in a deck of cards, but the containing class and its member classes are not directly connected. This relationship is called aggregation. UML diagrams show aggregation with a solid line ending in an unfilled diamond.
- When one class is made up of another class and cannot exist without the second class, the relationship is called composition. UML diagrams show composition with a solid line ending with a filled diamond.
- Implementing an interface is called realization. UML diagrams show realization with a dashed line ending in an unfilled triangle.
- Based on UML diagrams, you can create skeleton outlines of a class to fill in with code later. This strategy can help in structuring your code while brainstorming a solution.

Key Terms

activation box	functional requirements	scenario
actors	inheritance	sequence diagram
Aggregation	lifeline	Unified Modeling Language (UML)
association	message	use case
class diagram	realization	use case diagram
Composition	relationship diagram	visibility marker
dependence	return message	

GLOSSARY

A

absolute file path   A notation that indicates the exact location of a file on the computer, from a point starting at the hard drive.

abstract class   Any class that has one or more pure virtual methods.

abstraction   The process of hiding details or substituting a generalization for something specific.

Acceptance testing   A user-focused testing process designed to ensure that the software meets usability requirements and the objectives for which it was created.

access modifiers   Keywords that describe who can see and change the member variables. They can be set as public, private, or protected.

access point   A point such as a cursor that keeps track of your current position in a file.

accessibility   The availability of a place, service, or software to people with disabilities.

accessors   A special method in a class that returns the value of a specific member variable in a class.

Action Entries quadrant   The lower-right quadrant of a decision table that contains actions corresponding to each set of alternatives.

Action quadrant   The lower-left quadrant of a decision table that contains a list of possible outcomes.

activation box   In a sequence diagram, a narrow rectangle that shows when and how long an object is performing an action or is active.

actors   The types of people using a system in a UML use case diagram.

adjacency matrix   A way to represent a graph in code with a two-dimensional matrix of edge weights.

Aggregation   When a class contains other independent classes as part of its structure.

agile development methodologies   A variety of incremental, iterative approaches based on the Agile Manifesto.

algorithm   A series of steps for solving a problem or task.

Alpha testing   A type of acceptance testing performed by internal testers.

Alternatives quadrant   The upper-right quadrant of a decision table that contains Ys and Ns denoting all possible combinations of conditions.

analog data   Data that has continuous values.

ancestors   Any classes that have one or more classes derived from them.

append   A mode to open a file for writing so that you can add data to it, without writing over any existing data.

application program interfaces (APIs)   A set of routines that can be included in programs to enhance functionality, such as constructing platform-specific user interfaces.

arguments   The term for the values provided to a method or function that are placed inside the parameters.

arithmetic logic unit (ALU)   The component of the CPU that performs arithmetic and logical operations.

arithmetic operators   Mathematical symbols such as $+$, $-$, $*$, $/$, and $\%$.

array   A data structure that stores a collection of elements that all have the same data type.

array index   The reference in [ ] square brackets that identifies an array element.

ASCII (American Standard Code for Information Interchange)   A method for encoding letters, symbols, and numerals using seven bits or eight bits.

assembly language   A low-level programming language that corresponds closely to the machine language instruction set for a CPU.

assignment statement   A statement that sets or changes the value that is stored in a variable.

association   A line drawn between items in a UML diagram.

Asymptotic analysis   A method for evaluating the performance of an algorithm in relation to the size of the data set.

asymptotic notation   The expression of asymptotic analysis, typically as Big-O, Big-Omega, or Big-Theta.

attributes   The characteristics that describe an object.

augmented reality   The use of computer technology to add digital tags to real-world images.

Auxiliary space   The memory required to temporarily hold variables and data as a program runs.

average-case runtime   The amount of time an algorithm needs to run to completion on average, given a random order of data.

B

base case   A situation in which a recursive function can stop trying to solve a problem.

base-2   Another name for the binary number system.

behavior   Describes what an object can do. Typically thought of in terms of the methods or actions that an object can perform.

best-case runtime   The smallest amount of time possible an algorithm needs to run to completion.

Beta testing   A type of acceptance testing performed by a select group of users in real-world environments.

Big-O   A generalization of a runtime. Only the largest growing factor of the polynomial matters in Big-O.

Big-O notation   Asymptotic notation for the worst-case time complexity or space complexity of an algorithm.

Big-Omega notation   Asymptotic notation for the best-case time complexity or space complexity.

Big-Theta notation   Asymptotic notation that encompasses both the upper and lower bounds of an algorithm, a situation sometimes referred to as a tight bound.

binary   A representation of data that can have one of two states.

binary digits   A binary digit is a 0 or 1 representing the smallest unit of information in a computer.

binary file   A file that stores the contents in binary format (ones and zeros) which is not human readable, but takes up less space.

binary measurements   Megabytes, gigabytes, and similar measures based on powers of 2.

binary number system   A system for counting that uses only numerals 0 and 1.

binary search algorithm   An algorithm that divides the search space in half until the target value is located.

binary search tree (BST)   A binary tree that enforces a meaning to the left and right children. Stored items are sorted by putting items "less than" the current node to the left, and items "greater than" to the right.

Binary trees   Trees limited to two children per node.

binding   Connecting a method call to the method's body.

bit   A binary digit; 0 or 1.

Boolean expressions   Expressions containing relational operators and operands, such as choice == 1, that evaluate to True or False.

Boolean literal   A literal that has a value of True or False.

boundary case   A data point that is just at or beyond the maximum or minimum limits of expected data.

branching recursion   A type of recursion that makes more than one recursive function call.

breadth first (BF) traversal   A traversal that visits the nodes in a tree by depth level.

breakpoint   A location with program code that triggers the debugging utility to halt while a programmer identifies an error.

Bubble sort   A simple algorithm which sorts items by swapping adjacent pairs if the two items are out of order.

buffer   The common piece of memory used to transfer pieces of information into and out of memory during file I/O.

buffer overflow   A condition in which data flows into unexpected memory locations.

buffered stream   An input or output stream that uses an intermediary buffer when reading from a file or writing to a file.

buffering   Moving data, bit by bit, into and out of a common piece of memory (called a buffer) which is accessed by your code and an external source (like memory).

build tools   Tools, such as a preprocessor, compiler, and linker, that convert source code into a program that a computer can execute.

byte   A group of eight bits; commonly used to store a number, letter, symbol, or punctuation mark.

bytecode   Code that is compiled into an intermediate file that a virtual machine compiles and executes.

C

Camel case   A text format that begins with a lowercase letter but uses an uppercase letter for subsequent words.

capacitors   Electronic circuits that store an electrical charge and are commonly used to store signals that represent data in computers.

case sensitivity   The differentiation that makes a lowercase letter different from its uppercase version.

catch   To remedy a problem that caused the exception to occur.

central processing unit (CPU)   The components of a computer that perform processing tasks.

character data type   The data type assigned to variables that hold one character of data.

character literal   A single character or symbol.

character set   Alphanumeric characters and their encoded equivalents.

Chatbots   Interactive programs that respond with seeming intelligence to user interaction.

child   In a tree data structure, a node that is below and connected to another node.

child class   A class created using methods and data members inherited from the parent class.

circular linked list   A linked list in which each node links sequentially to one other node, and there is no null pointer to the end.

class diagram   A diagram in UML which details the structure of classes.

class name   A noun that identifies the class by a specific name.

class template   A class that uses a generic type for one of its properties.

classes   The blueprint containing attributes and methods that describe a collection of objects.

classification patterns   The pattern of attributes and methods that apply to a collection of objects.

Clean code   The principle that code should be easily understood, elegant, simple, and testable.

code block   A group of program statements that perform a specific function, and that may be visually set off from other statements or blocks using blank lines.

code editor   A type of text editor that is specially designed for entering program code.

Coercion   The process by which a literal is automatically converted into a different data type.

comma-delimited text file   A text file in which chunks of data resemble records in a table separated by a comma.

command-line user interfaces   A form of interacting with a computer that requires typed commands.

Commands   Actions, such as display and input, that can be specified in pseudocode or a programming language.

comment   An explanatory notation within program code that is not executed by a computer.

compiler   Utility software that translates code written in one programming language into another language.

complete graph   A graph in which each node has an edge to every other node.

complex data types   Data types that store more than one kind of primitive data.

complex instruction set computers (CISC)   An instruction set that includes many operations, some of which require multiple CPU cycles.

Composite data types   Data types that are programmer defined, available as functions, or provided by methods.

Composition   When a class contains other dependent classes as part of its structure.

compound operators   Mathematical operators that offer shortcuts for basic assignment operations.

Computational thinking   A set of techniques, such as decomposition, pattern identification, and abstraction, designed to formulate problems and their solutions.

computer   A multipurpose device that accepts input, processes that input based on a stored set of instructions, and produces output.

computer program   A collection of statements written in a programming language, such as C++, Java, or Python, that performs a specific task when executed by a digital device.

concatenation   Combining data using the + concatenation operator.

concatenative synthesis   The process of combining a series of prerecorded phonemes to create synthesized speech.

conditional logical operator   Operators, such as AND and OR, that combine the outcomes of two or more Boolean expressions.

conditional statement   A statement, such as if choice == 1, that initiates a decision control structure.

condition-controlled loop   A repetition control structure that is governed by a logical expression either at the beginning or the end of the loop.

Conditions quadrant   The upper-left quadrant of a decision table that contains factors affecting a decision.

connected graph   A graph where all nodes are connected by at least one edge to the rest of the group of nodes.

constant   A named memory location that holds data, which is used but not changed by the statements in a program.

constant space complexity   The asymptotic, or Big-O, status for algorithms that do not require additional space as the data set increases.

constant time   The asymptotic, or Big-O, status for algorithms that are not affected by the size of the data set.

constructor   A special method that creates an object and allocates enough memory to hold the information associated with the object. The constructor has the same method name as the class.

constructor overloading   Creating multiple constructors for a class with differing parameter lists. The compiler will deduce which one to use based on the arguments provided (not available in all languages).

contents   The text or information contained in a file.

control statement   A statement that controls the conditions under which a loop continues to execute.

control structure   One or more statements that alter the sequential execution of a computer program.

control unit   The component of the CPU that interprets instructions and manages processing activity.

copy constructor   A constructor that creates a new object as a copy of the one passed in the parameter list and initializes the member variables.

count-controlled loop   A repetition control structure that repeats a specified number of times.

D

Data representation   The way data is presented and abstracted.

Data space   The memory required to hold data that is accessed by a program, input to a program, or generated by the program.

data structure   A specific layout of values in memory and a set of operations that can be applied to those values.

data type   A category of data such as integer, floating point, or character.

Debugging   The process of finding and correcting errors–bugs–in a computer program.

debugging utilities   Software that can be used to find and correct errors in program code.

decision control structure   One or more statements that alter the sequential flow based on a condition or decision.

decision table   A grid of rows and columns that distill a set of complex decisions and actions into a set of rules that can become the statements in a computer program.

Declarative programming paradigms   Any approach to software development and programming that focuses on "what" by describing the problem or task that is the scope of a computer program.

declare a variable   The process of specifying a name that is assigned, or bound, to a memory location.

decomposition   A technique for breaking a task into smaller parts.

deep copy   A copy of an object in which all member variables from the source object are copied into the destination object.

default constructor   A constructor that is called without specifying any parameters. You can define a default constructor, or the compiler will create one for you with default variables for each member variable.

default exceptions   A generic exception handling statement to catch any unhandled exception event.

default parameters   A default value to use for a parameter if no argument is provided (not available in all languages).

default visibility   If no specific access modifier is provided, each language sets the visibility to a default value.

delimiter   A punctuation mark or tab character that denotes the separation of information in a file.

dependence   When a class depends on another independent class's definition.

depth first (DF) traversal   A traversal that tries to go as deep as possible in a tree before backing up to find more nodes to visit.

dequeue   The operation that removes a data element from the front of a queue.

descendant   Any class that has been derived from a parent class.

diamond problem   A multiple inheritance scenario where two of the parents of a child share a common ancestor, thus giving the child duplicates of methods and data members.

Digital data   Data that has discrete, rather than continuous, values.

directed graph   A graph where edges are one-way paths.

directive   In the context of programming, a statement that tells the computer how to handle the program rather than how to perform an algorithm.

directory structure   A hierarchy of folders and files on a computer.

divide-and-conquer technique   An algorithmic technique in which each step divides the problem space and eliminates part of it on the path to a solution.

Don't Repeat Yourself (DRY)   A programming principle that encourages programmers to eliminate redundancies in their code.

dot operator   An operator that lets you specify which action to perform with a variable.

double precision   Floating-point numbers stored usually in 8 bytes of memory.

doubly linked list   A linked list in which each element has two pointers: one to the next element and one to the previous element.

downcasting   Type casting to an object that is lower in the class hierarchy.

Duplication is Evil (DIE)   An acronym for the concept that programmers should eliminate redundancies in their code.

dynamic binding   Connecting a method call to the method's body at run-time.

dynamically typed   A programming language feature that allows a variable to take on any type of data during program execution.

E

E notation   A way of expressing floating-point numbers as powers of 10.

edge weights   The cost to take an edge, sometimes used to represent a physical distance, but can be a value that represents other measurements.

edges   The connections between nodes in a nonlinear data structure.

else-if structure   A decision control structure that handles multiple conditions.

encapsulate   A feature of object-oriented programming in which classes become black box abstractions.

encapsulation   An object-oriented concept of constructing objects by bundling relevant data with the actions they can perform.

encoding system   A method for converting data, such as the letters of the alphabet, into a format such as binary.

end of file (EOF)   A special character to represent the last element in a file.

enqueue   The operation that adds a data element to the rear of a queue.

equal operator   The == symbol that compares one value to another and returns True if the values are equal.

escape characters   An alternate interpretation of a character that has another meaning.

escape sequence   Embedded characters beginning with a backslash (\ ) to insert special symbols into a string.

event handler   The code for handling a program event.

event-driven   A paradigm for a program controlled by user events, such as clicking an icon.

exception   An event triggered by a situation that cannot be resolved by the program. An exception is also a package of information about the situation.

exception list   Names the exceptions that the method can possibly throw during its execution.

executable file   A file that has been compiled into machine code and that can be directly executed by a computer.

explicit conversion   Type casting in strongly typed languages in which you specify the variable class to which to convert.

explicit self-referencing   Explicitly telling the compiler to use a member variable by using the self-reference keyword.

expression   A programming statement that has a value and usually includes arithmetic operators and operands.

F

Fall through   Program execution that continues to the next sequential statement.

field   Each piece of data separated by a delimiter (such as a comma) in a table

FIFO   The acronym for "first in, first out."

file   A digital container that stores data, information, settings, or program commands. In programming, a file can provide input to a program or store the results of a program's execution.

file access point   A special variable that acts like a cursor indicating your position in a file.

file handler   A special, built-in feature that allows you to interact with a file, in abstract terms.

file handling   Reading data into programs and storing data that your program produces.

file I/O   The common term for the combined acts of file input and output.

file input   Using code to read information from a file.

file name   The name of a file, including the extension.

file output   Using code to write information into a file.

final class   A class that cannot have any other classes derived from it.

final method   A method declared with the final keyword indicating that it cannot be overridden.

floating-point data types   Numbers that include decimal and fractional parts; expressed in decimal or E notation.

flowchart   A diagram that represents the sequence and flow of steps in an algorithm.

Floyd's Algorithm   A simple algorithm that calculates the value of the shortest paths between all nodes in a graph given an adjacency matrix.

Fluent interfaces   An object-oriented design methodology in which a programming language's syntax relies on method cascading to make code easier to read.

folder   A digital storage space for organizing files and other folders. Also called a directory.

for-loop   A count-controlled loop that is controlled by the conditions in a statement beginning with the keyword for.

formatting parameters   Elements that can alter the appearance of numeric and text output.

full constructor   A constructor that initializes all member variables of the object when the object is created.

function   A named procedure that performs a specific task.

function argument   The data that is passed in parentheses to a function by the function call.

function body   The block of code in a function that defines what the function does.

function call   A statement that transfers program flow to a function.

function declaration   The first line of a function that provides the function name and optionally parameters and return type.

function name   The name of a function, which ends with ( ) parentheses.

Function parameters   The variables enclosed in parentheses in the function declaration.

function signature   The function name and parameters that uniquely define a function.

function template   A function that uses a generic data type in its parameter list, its return type, or both.

Functional decomposition   A technique for dividing modules into smaller actions, processes, or steps.

functional requirements   The specific behaviors a system must perform.

G

garbage values   Leftover, unwanted, and unusable values held in memory prior to a variable being initialized.

generic type   A type defined by templating to signal that the data type is to be defined later.

generics   Another word for templates, or code that uses a placeholder identifier to stand for a generic data type, which is unknown until later in the code.

getters   Another term for "accessors": they "get" the data.

global variable   A variable that is visible throughout the entire program.

graphical user interface (GUI)   A type of user interface that displays graphical objects such as workspaces, icons, menus, and a pointer.

Graphs   A nonlinear data structure with no hierarchical structure. A graph has no starting point or ending point.

H

Haptic   A term used for devices that simulate the sense of touch.

has-a relationship   A class relationship where a class contains an object of another class as a data member.

head   The first element in a data structure.

header files   C++ specific interfaces.

header guards   C++ specific flags to prevent conflicting definitions of classes, methods, variables, or functions.

hexadecimal number system   A system for counting that uses 16 digits: 1 2 3 4 5 6 7 8 9 A B C D E F.

high-level programming languages   Systems for issuing instructions to a CPU that abstract away the detail of low-level machine language to provide programmers with natural language commands.

homogeneous   A characteristic of arrays in which all the elements are of the same data type.

Human–Computer Interaction (HCI)   A computer science discipline that focuses on improving ways that people interact with digital devices.

I

identity   A way to refer to unique objects in order to distinguish them from other objects created from the same class. Oftentimes the identity is synonymous with the variable's name.

if-then structure   A decision control structure with one branch based on a True Boolean expression.

if-then-else structure   A decision control structure that has two branches: one for True and one for False.

Imperative programming paradigms   Any approach to software development and programming that focuses on "how" by specifying the steps required for a computer to carry out a task.

implicit conversion   A type casting that requires you to either implement a copy constructor for the child class or overload the assignment operator for the child class.

implicit default constructor   A constructor that creates an object without any predefined values.

implicit self-referencing   Implying the use of a member variable without the use of the self-reference keyword (not available in all languages).

Impossible rules   Rules in a decision table that have contradictory actions.

Inclusive design   The concept of developing software and other consumer items so they are available and acceptable to the widest possible audience.

incremental development model   An approach to software development in which software is designed, coded, and tested in a succession of cycles.

index   The position of a character in a string, beginning with position [0].

index error   A coding fault in which the index value is not within the range of index values associated with an array.

infinite loop   A loop that never terminates.

infinite recursion   A recursive function that does not modify its parameters and therefore never stops.

Information density   The amount of information that can be represented by a single symbol.

information hiding   The object-oriented programming principle to only allow the object to have access to the underlying details of the object and hide the data and internal workings from entities outside of it.

inheritance   A feature of object-oriented programming in which subclasses acquire attributes of a parent class.

inheritance hierarchy   Graphical depiction of the inheritance relationship between classes.

initialize a variable   The process of specifying a name and value for a variable.

in-place algorithm   An algorithm which does not need additional memory beyond the input.

instance   An object created from a class.

instance field   A variable of an object which is never seen or accessed by anything outside of the object.

instance variables   Another term for "member variables."

instruction cycle   The activity that takes place in the CPU to complete a single instruction: fetch, interpret, execute.

instruction pointer   A component of the CPU's control unit that indicates the location of each instruction to be executed.

instruction register   A component of the CPU's control unit that holds the instruction that is currently being executed.

instruction set   The collection of operations that a computer's central processing unit can perform.

Instruction space   The memory used to store the code for a program.

integer data types   Whole numbers that can be signed or unsigned and expressed in decimal, binary, or hexadecimal notation.

integrated circuit   A thin slice of silicon that contains microscopic electronic circuitry.

integrated development environment (IDE)   Software that includes all of the tools needed to code, compile, link, and debug programs.

Integration testing   A testing process for verifying that all of the software units or modules work together.

interfaces   The instructions for how to interact with a piece of code. Includes: how to call it, what arguments it expects, and what to expect back from the code.

interpreter   In the context of computer software, it is utility software that preprocesses and executes program statements one by one.

is-a relationship   A class relationship between a parent and a child, in which a child inherits directly from a parent class or one of its descendants

iteration   One repetition of a loop.

Java Virtual Machine (JVM)   The virtual machine software that compiles and executes bytecode produced by the Java programming language.

K

keywords   Words in a programming language that have special meaning, such as a command to perform an action.

L

leaf nodes   In a tree data structure, nodes at the bottom, which have no children.

level of abstraction   The degree to which the details of an object or concept are hidden.

lifeline   In a sequence diagram, represents the existence of an actor or object over time.

LIFO   The acronym for "last in, first out."

linear access   Reading a file in memory, consecutively, byte by byte, in a sequence.

linear data structure   A data structure such as an array, linked list, stack, or queue that arranges data elements in a sequence.

linear recursion   A type of recursion that represents a single line of problem solving and therefore makes one recursive function call.

linear search   A type of search algorithm that examines each item in a list or array one by one to find a particular value.

linear space complexity   The asymptotic, or Big-O, status for algorithms that require additional space for each data element as the size of the data set increases.

linear time   The asymptotic, or Big-O, status for algorithms that require one step for each element in the data set and therefore increase linearly as the data set grows.

linked list   A data structure that organizes a collection of data elements in non-consecutive memory locations.

linker   Utility software that converts one or more object files into a binary executable file.

literal   An element of data used by a computer program.

local variable   A variable that is visible in a function or other defined area of a program.

logarithmic time   The asymptotic, or Big-O, status for algorithms with a time or space complexity that tends to level out as the size of the data set increases.

Logic errors   Errors that do not prevent the program from running but do result in incorrect output.

logic gate   A circuit that manipulates electrical signals to perform logical and arithmetic operations.

loop   A structure in a program that repeats.

loop counter   The variable that tracks the number of times a count-controlled loop executes.

low-level programming language   A system for issuing instructions using machine language or assembly language that correspond closely to the CPU instruction set.

M

machine code   A series of binary machine language instructions.

machine language   The set of binary instructions that a CPU can directly execute.

Magnetic storage technology   Devices that polarize magnetic particles as a means to store data.

member variables   Variables that comprise the data that is stored in a class.

memberwise initialization   Using a constructor to set the values of the data members of an object.

memory   A temporary data-holding area that is typically integrated into the main circuit board of a digital device.

memory address   A location in memory with a unique identifier, usually written as a hexadecimal number.

Merge sort   An algorithm which guarantees a fast runtime at the expense of additional memory. Uses divide-and-conquer.

message   In a sequence diagram, shows the interaction between components as discrete steps. Generally, a message is a method or function.

metacharacters   Characters that describe the patterns used in regular expressions.

method body   The list of statements that the method executes to perform its operations.

method call   The way in which a method in an object is invoked.

method cascading   A programming syntax preference that uses one statement to call many methods on a single object.

method name   The way in which a method is referred to in code when it is being used. Conventionally, the method name is a verb followed by a noun.

method overloading   To write more than one method with the same name but different parameter lists.

Method overriding   Functionality that allows a child class to provide its own implementation of a method that is already inherited by one of its ancestors.

methods   The actions that an object can perform.

microprocessor   A complex integrated circuit that contains the components for a computer's CPU.

mixed reality   The use of computer technology to add interactive, three-dimensional objects to a real or simulated experience.

modules   The cohesive, structural units of an algorithm.

Moore's Law   The prediction that manufacturers would be able to double the number of components in an integrated circuit every two years.

multiple inheritance   A child class that is derived from more than one parent class.

mutators   A special method in a class that changes the value of a specific member variable in a class.

N

namespace   A named container that holds identifiers such as variables, to prevent collisions for identifiers with the same name.

nested-if structures   Decision control structures that have a decision within a decision.

nested-loop   A loop within a loop.

newline   A special character (usually \n) indicating the end of a line.

node   A basic unit of a data structure, usually containing a data element and optionally a link to other nodes.

non-linear data structure   A data structure such as a tree or graph that arranges data elements in a hierarchy, web, or network.

Nonvolatile storage   Storage or memory devices that do not require power to hold data.

null variable   A variable that has no value.

numeric literal   A literal composed of one or more digits that represent integers or floating-point numbers.

O

O(C)   The Big-O notation for constant time or space.

O(log n)   The Big-O notation for logarithmic time or space complexity.

O(n)   The Big-O notation for linear time or space.

$O(n^2)$ The Big-O notation for quadratic time.

object code   The binary program code that is produced by a compiler.

object-oriented decomposition   A technique for dividing a problem or task into logical and physical objects that a computer program will manipulate.

object-oriented paradigm   A type of imperative programming based on the idea that programs can be designed by visualizing objects that interact with each other.

object-oriented programming (OOP)   Programming that heavily relies on the concept of objects.

objects   Specific instances of a class; for example, Rover is a specific object of the class Dog.

Offline storage   Local storage devices that are connected to a computer or can be conveniently removed.

one-dimensional array   A linear array stored in consecutive memory locations with elements referenced by an index.

one's complement   A binary number that when added to another binary number produces all 1 bits.

online IDE   An integrated development environment that runs in a browser and requires no installation. Also called a web IDE.

Online storage   Storage provided by Internet-based cloud services.

op code   An operation code that is the machine language or assembly language command for a processing instruction.

operands   The part of a machine language or assembly language instruction that specifies the data to be processed, its location in memory, or its destination register.

operator overloading   A technique that allows programmers to customize predefined operators for objects of a particular class.

Optical storage technology   Devices that use light to store and access data.

order of operations   The sequence in which addition, subtraction, and other mathematical operations are performed.

P

parameter list   Specifies the input that is given to the method so it can perform its task.

parameterized constructor   A constructor that includes a parameter list to initialize its member variables.

parent   In a tree data structure, a node that is above and connected to another node.

parent class   The class from which other classes are created during inheritance.

pass by reference   A function call that passes a pointer to the actual data.

pass by value   A function call that passes a copy of an argument to a function.

pattern identification   A technique for finding patterns in procedures and tasks.

peek   The operation that accesses the first item in a stack or queue without removing it.

phoneme   The smallest sound that is a part of speech.

pixels   The miniature picture elements of a display screen that emit red, green, and blue light.

pointer   A variable that holds the address of another variable.

polymorphism   A concept of object-oriented programming in which an object in a child class can be treated uniquely by redefining methods derived from an inherited class.

pop   The operation that removes the top element from a stack.

post-test loop   A condition-controlled loop in which the first pass is always executed because the test condition is at the end of the loop.

predefined operators   Operators that are already defined in a programming language. They often include operators for arithmetic, logic, relations, assignment, input, and output.

predicate expression   The basic format for statements in logic and functional programming.

preprocessor   Utility software that performs housekeeping tasks before source code is compiled.

preprocessor directives   Program statements that provide instructions to the preprocessor, but are not executed by the compiler.

pre-test loop   A condition-controlled loop that begins with a condition and loops only if that condition is true.

Primitive data types   Data types that are built into a programming language.

private   An access modifier keyword indicating that the member variable or method is only accessible by the class itself.

procedural paradigm   A type of imperative programming paradigm that specifies how a computer is supposed to carry out a task using variables, control structures, and ordered instructions.

procedural programming   Code that is written "step-by-step" like a set of instructions, like a recipe, for the computer to follow.

program animation   A feature of debugging utilities that steps through code one statement at a time.

program code   The set of statements written in a programming language.

programming algorithm   A set of steps that specify the underlying logic and structure for the statements in a computer program.

programming language   A formal language with semantics and syntax for instructing a computer to perform a specific task.

programming paradigms   Various approaches to software development and programming. Major paradigms are classified as imperative or declarative.

prompt   A message that specifies what a user should enter when a program is running.

properties   A way of describing the variables connected to an object as an aspect or feature.

Pseudocode   A set of structured statements for delineating the steps of an algorithm.

public   An access modifier keyword indicating that the member variable or method is accessible by anywhere outside of the class.

pure virtual method   A method that requires the derived classes to override the implementation of its functionality.

push   The operation that adds a data element to the top of a stack.

Q

quadratic time   The asymptotic, or Big-O, status for algorithms with a time or space complexity that increases more sharply than linear time as the data set grows.

queue   A limited access, linear data structure in which the first data element added is the first element removed.

Quicksort   An approximation of a fast algorithm which uses probability and divide-and-conquer to achieve a good runtime.

R

RAM (random access memory)   A volatile type of memory that provides a temporary holding area for data.

random access   Reading a file in memory by accessing each character directly without first reading the character before it.

read   A mode to open a file to examine its contents.

read-only   A device or file that can be accessed, but not altered.

read-write   A device or file that can be created, accessed, altered, or deleted.

realization   When a class implements an interface.

record   One line of fields in a table.

Recursion   A problem-solving approach that divides large problems into smaller, identical problems.

recursive function   A function that calls itself at least once.

reduced instruction set computers (RISC)   A streamlined instruction set with a roster of simple operations.

Redundant rules   Two or more rules in a decision table that have the same outcome when differences in alternatives are eliminated.

reference   A name, usually in the form of a variable, that refers to a specific location in memory of a value or other data object.

reference variable   A variable that points directly to a variable, rather than to a copy of the data it contains.

Registers   Temporary areas for holding data in the CPU.

Regression testing   Testing to ensure that modifications to code do not have unexpected side effects.

regular expression   A string of characters that describe the pattern of the text you are searching for.

relational operator   An operator such as ==, >, or < that specifies a comparison between two operands.

relationship diagram   A UML diagram showing how classes interact.

relative file path   Tells the location of a file, from another location in the file system.

repetition control structures   Blocks of code that are executed repeatedly based on a control condition.

reserved words   The words that a programming language reserves for its use to specify commands and other actions.

return message   A type of message, similar to a return value.

return type   The data type that the function passes back to the main program.

return value   The data that is passed from a function back to the main program.

RGB   A color system that uses a mixture of red, green, and blue light to produce the spectrum of colors.

root   In a tree data structure, the topmost node; it has no parents. Also considered the "starting point" of a tree.

runtime   How long an algorithm takes to complete in terms of the total number of items, "n."

runtime error   A flaw in a program that causes a program to fail during execution.

S

scenario   A single use case, or single action path through a system.

scope   The visibility of program components, such as variables.

search algorithms   Special algorithms that find a specific piece of information within a large set of data as efficiently as possible.

search space   The amount of data you are searching.

secure coding   Programming that includes routines to protect code from security exploits.

selection control structure   An executable statement that directs program flow based on a condition or decision.

self-reference keyword   The keyword used in object methods to reference itself.

semantic error   A flaw in the logic of one or more statements that causes a program to produce incorrect results.

Semantics   In the context of programming, the meaning and validity of program statements.

sentinel value   A special value in an algorithm that signals the end of a loop or recursion.

sequence diagram   A UML diagram used to show how parts of code are related and the exact sequence of events.

setters   Another term for "mutators": they "set" the data.

shallow copy   Pointing the reference variable for a new object to another, preexisting object.

shortest path   The path between two nodes that costs the least, as represented by the sum of the edges taken along the path.

signed integer   A whole number that is preceded by a + or − sign.

Signed magnitude   The use of the leftmost bit in a binary representation to indicate a negative number.

single precision   Floating-point numbers usually stored in 4 bytes of memory.

single responsibility principle (SRP)   The concept that each function or class should have only one responsibility and one reason to change.

singly linked list   A linked list in which a single pointer links one element to the next element.

Snake case   A text format that uses all lowercase and separates words with an underscore.

software development kit (SDK)   A set of tools for developing platform-specific software.

software development life cycle   The progression of a software application from conception to retirement.

Solid state storage technology   Devices that use non-volatile circuitry to store data.

Sorting   The act of placing items in a deterministic order, typically numerically or alphabetically.

sorting algorithms   Programming approach to sorting items stored in computer memory.

source code   A set of statements usually written in a high-level programming language.

Space complexity   The amount of memory required by an algorithm as a function of the size of the data set.

sparse graph   A graph with few edges between the nodes.

Speech recognition   The process by which spoken words are transformed into digital text.

speech synthesis   The process by which digital text is transformed into audible speech.

stable algorithm   An algorithm which does not mix up equivalent items' relative orders.

stacks   A limited access, linear data structure in which the last data element added is the first element removed.

state   Represents the data held in an object's member variables at any time.

statement   Each instruction written in a high-level programming language.

static classes   Classes with the restriction of only containing static member variables and static methods. Often used to organize a set of methods that only need to operate on input values, and do not need to store any information.

static method   A special method that is independent of any particular object of the class and can be called without making an instance of the object. This type of method is called on the class itself.

static variable   A member variable of a class that contains the same value in all instances of the class.

statically typed   A programming language feature that requires a variable to hold only the type of data that was specified when the variable was declared or initialized.

Storage   A term used to refer to devices that can hold data on a relatively permanent basis.

stream   A channel that allows you to interact with files stored on your computer or another drive.

streamreader   A programming language device that creates a stream for reading data from a file.

streamwriter   A programming language device that creates a stream for writing data to a file.

string   A sequence of characters.

string data type   The data type assigned to variables that hold a sequence of characters.

string literal   A literal that contains more than one character.

Structural decomposition   A process that identifies structural units of a task or problem.

success factors   Best practices that can improve the quality of a programmer's code.

switch-case structure   A decision control structure that contains a series of cases and executes with fall through by default.

syntax   In the context of programming languages, the grammar rules for word order and punctuation.

syntax error   A flaw in a program statement that results from incorrectly using punctuation or word sequencing.

System testing   A testing process for validating that the fully integrated software application performs as expected when installed on target hardware platforms.

T

table   A collection of records.

tail recursion   A way to structure recursive code so that the program requires no additional memory during function calls.

template   A piece of code that uses a placeholder identifier to stand for a generic data type, which is unknown until later in the code.

terminating condition   The condition that terminates a loop.

terminator shape   The rounded rectangle shape at the beginning or end of a flowchart.

test case   A set of preconditions, steps, and data that should produce a specific result called a "post condition."

test condition   A part of the control statement that contains the expression used to control loop execution.

text editor   Software that can be used to enter plain ASCII text.

text file   A file that stores its contents as ASCII characters.

throw   When a program stops executing code and moves to error-handling in a situation where it cannot continue.

Time complexity   The amount of time, measured in number of operations, required to run an algorithm as its data set grows.

transistor   A key component of integrated circuits because of its ability to amplify signals, act as a switch, and form logic gates.

traversal   A way to visit all nodes in a tree.

traversing an array   The process of accessing each element in an array, usually with a loop.

tree   A nonlinear data structure that enforces a hierarchical form, and looks like an upside-down tree.

truth table   A table that specifies the outcome of conditional logical operators such as AND and OR.

try   An attempt for code to complete as normal, unless an exception occurs; then the code stops trying and moves to handle the thrown exception.

try-catch block   A syntactic block of code where exceptions occur and are handled. The try part indicates code to try, and the catch part catches and handles exceptions from the try part.

two-dimensional array   An array consisting of rows and columns stored in consecutive memory locations with elements referenced by row and column indexes.

two's complement   A binary number that when added to another binary number produces all 0 bits.

type casting   Converting a variable of one type into another type.

type inference   A programming language feature that deduces the data type based on the presence or absence of a decimal point.

typed parameter   A parameter that has an explicitly stated data type.

U

unconnected graph   A graph with isolated groups of nodes not connected by edges.

undefined variable   A variable that has not been specified by the programmer.

undirected graph   A graph where edges are two-way paths.

Unicode   A variable-length encoding system that includes representation for the written glyphs used by most of the world's languages.

Unified Modeling Language (UML)   A standardized way of visualizing programs to enable better communication with others.

Unit testing   A process that tests each program module to ensure that it operates correctly.

unsigned integer   A positive whole number that has no + or − sign.

upcasting   Type casting to an object that is higher than the class hierarchy.

use case   A list of actions or steps showing the interactions between a person and a system in order to accomplish a task.

use case diagram   A UML diagram that communicates how a user interacts with a system.

user experience (UX)   A concept that encompasses aspects of user activities beyond interacting with the user interface.

user interface (UI)   A collection of physical, graphical, and logical constructs that facilitate interaction between humans and digital devices.

user-controlled loop   A loop that executes or terminates based on input collected from the user at runtime.

UTF-8   A popular version of Unicode, used extensively on the Web.

variable   A named memory location that temporarily holds text or a numeric value.

V

Vector graphics   A format for specifying digital images as instructions for lines, colors, and basic shapes.

virtual machine   Utility software that operates on a specific hardware platform to execute bytecode.

Virtual reality   The use of computer technology to create simulated three-dimensional worlds populated by objects that users can manipulate.

visibility   How visible a property or behavior of an object is to other locations in code.

visibility marker   UML symbols that indicate the access modifiers of variables or methods.

voice user interface   A type of user interface characterized by spoken communication between a user and a digital device.

void function   A function that does not return a value to the main program.

Volatile storage   Storage or memory that requires power to hold data.

W

waterfall model   An approach to software development in which the project is divided into a series of cascading tasks that are performed one after the other.

while-loop   A pre-test loop that begins with a while statement.

worst-case runtime   The largest amount of time possible an algorithm needs to run to completion.

write   A mode to open a file and insert content, writing over any existing content.

Write Every Time (WET)   The opposite of DRY; code that contains redundancies.

INDEX

A

abs( ) function, 51
Absolute path, 208
Abstract Class, 317
Abstraction
  basics, 9–10
  black boxes, 11–12
  classes and objects, 10–11
  defined, 10
  levels of, 12
Abstraction penalty, 467
Acceptance testing, 539
Accessibility guidelines, 520–521
Accessing files, 214
access_mode arguments, 216
Access modifier, 233, 251, 283
Accessors, 233, 277–278
Access point, 211
Accumulators, loops, 111–112
Action entries quadrant, 553
Action quadrant, 552
Activation box, 562
Actors, 559
add_car( ) method, 252–254
add_vehicle( ) method, 310–311
Adjacency matrix, 388
Aggregation, 563
Agile development methodologies, 530
Agile model
  advantages and disadvantages, 531–532
  incremental development, 530
  methodologies, 530–531
Algorithm complexity
  space, 396
  time, 396
Algorithms
  basics, 2
  "good," 3–4
  programming, 2–3
  selecting and creating, 4
Alpha testing, 539
Alternatives quadrant, 552
American Standard Code for Information
        Interchange (ASCII), 65–66
Analog data, 470
Ancestors, 293
AND operator, 100–101
Anticipating exceptions, 228–229
Appendite mode, 216
Append method, 343
append_node( ) method, 344
Application program interfaces (APIs), 510

Arguments, 280
Arithmetic logic unit (ALU), 459
Arithmetic operators, 54–55
Array
  characteristics, 127
  defined, 126
  index, 127
  input and output, 130–135
  magic rectangles, 126
  one-dimensional, 128–130
  operations, 135–137
  two-dimensional, 137–143
  use cases, 128
Array element
  change, 135
  find, 135–136
  sum, 137
ASCII (American Standard Code for
        Information Interchange), 65–66
  character set, 484
  defined, 483
  extended, 484–485
  unicode, 485–486
Assembly language, 461
Assigning variables, 43–44
Assignment operator (=), 269
Assignment statements
  assigning variables, 43–44
  declaring variables, 41–42
  initializing variables, 42–43
Association, 560
Asymptotic analysis, 397–398
Asymptotic notation, 398
Asynchronous data transfer, 363
Attributes, 7, 497
Audio accessibility, 521
Augmented reality, 517
Auxiliary space, 403
Average-case runtime, 430

B

Base-2, 474
Base case, 168
Best-case runtime, 430
Beta testing, 539
Big-Omega notation, 398
Big-O notation, 398
  algorithm complexity, 396–397
  asymptotic analysis, 397–398
  asymptotic notation, 398
Big-O runtime, 429
Big-Theta notation, 398

Binary

Binary
  addition, 477–478
  data representation, 471
  decimal, to, 475–477
  digits, 471
  measurements, 473
  negative numbers, 478–479
  number system, 474–475
Binary file, 213
Binary search algorithm, 417
Binary search performance
  implementation, 418–422
    iterative code, 422
    recursive code, 419–421
  search space, 416–417
Binary search tree (BST), 381
Binary trees, 379
Binding, 314
Bits, 471–472
Black box abstraction, 11–12
Black box testing, 539
Boolean expressions, 89
Boolean literal, 38
Boundary case, 537
Boundary index, 439
Branching recursion, 170, 175–179
Breadth first (BF) traversal, 384
Breakpoint, 30
Bubble sort
  algorithm, 431, 432
  code, 435–437
  properties, 437–438
  remaining passes, 435
  second pass, 434
  unsorted list, 433
Buffering, 215
Buffer overflow, 535
Build tools
  compilers, 23–24
  interpreters, 26–27
  preprocessors and linkers, 24–25
  toolset, 22–23
  virtual machines, 25–26
Built-in functions, 146
Built-in stacks, 356–357
Bytecode, 25
Bytes, 472–473

C

Capacitors, 474
Case sensitivity, 73
Casting types, 315

Catch exception, 191
Central processing unit (CPU), 458–459
Character
  manipulation, 68–69
  memory allocation, 65–66
  output format, 67
Character data types
  defined, 64
  digits, 66–67
  manipulation, 68–69
  memory allocation, 65–66
  output format, 67
Character literal, 37
Character set, 484
Chatbots, 511
Child class, 297–298
Child node, 374
Circular linked lists, 339
Class diagram, 558
Classes, 9, 232–233, 497
  and objects, 10–11
Class hierarchy, 310
Classification patterns, 9
Class inhierarchy
  ancestors, 293
  descendant, 293
  diagram, 293
  diamond problem, 294
  multiple inheritance, 294
Class structure
  data hiding, 271–273
  encapsulation, 273
  objects, 273–276
  self-reference scope, 276–277
Class template, 320
Clean code, 534
Closing file
  after use, 221
  try/catch blocks, 221
COBOL, 496
Code block, 22
Code editor, 21
Code linked list
  append method, 343–344
  find method, 346–347
  insert method, 347–350
  linkedlist class, 343
  node class, 342
  traversal, 345–346
Coding principles
  clean coding, 534
  efficient coding, 532–533
  secure coding, 534–536
  single responsibility principle, 533–534
  success factors, 536
Coding tools
  basic structure, 21–22
  program editors, 20–21
Coercion, 78
Cohesion, 7
Command-line user interfaces
  defined, 510
  program design, 510–511
Commands, 544
Comment, 21
Compiler, 23–24
Complete graph, 387

Completeness and accuracy,
  checking, 555
Complex data types, 238
Complex instruction set computers
  (CISC), 460
Composite data types, 51
Composition, 563
Compound operators, 56–57
Computational thinking, 4
Computer program, 2, 16
Concatenation
  defined, 76
  output, 76–77
  variables, 77–78
Concatenative synthesis, 516
Conditional logical operators
  AND operator, 100–101
  OR operator, 101
Conditional statement, 86
  Boolean variable, 90
Condition-controlled loop, 116
Conditions quadrant, 551
Connected graph, 387
Constants, 39
Constant space complexity, 404
Constant time, 399
Constructor overloading, 281
Constructors
  copy constructor, 268
  default parameters, 266, 281
  garbage values, 266
  implicit default constructor, 266
  memberwise initialization, 267
  object, 266
  overloading, 281
  parameterized constructor, 267
  parameters/arguments, 280
Contents, 211
Control statement, 105
Control structures, 84, 544
Control unit, 458
Conversion
  binary-hex-binary, 481–482
  binary to decimal, 475
  decimal to binary, 476–477
  hex-decimal, 482
Core elements, programming
  language, 19
Count-controlled loops
  basics, 104–105
  control statements, 105
  for-loop, 105–108
  traverse an array, 132–133
  user-controlled loops, 108–109
Counters, loops, 109–111
Creating files, 222–223

D

Data abstraction, 319–322
  class template, 320
  function creation, 321
  function template, 320
  template
    class, 322
    function, 322
Database query programming, 504

Data representation
  binary, 471
  defined, 471
Data space, 403
Data storage
  BF traversal, 384, 385–386
  BST, 381, 381
  DF traversal, 384, 385–386
  node class, 382–383
Data structure, 334
Data types
  and Boolean expressions, 89–90
  composite, 51
  defined, 50
  numeric (see Numeric data types)
  primitive, 50–51
Dealership class, 311–314
Debugging, 27
Debugging tools
  debugging utilities, 30–31
  programming errors, 27–28
  runtime errors, 29
  semantic errors, 29–30
  syntax errors, 28
Debugging utilities, 30–31
Decimal to binary, 476–477
Decision control structure, 84
Decision tables
  accuracy checking, 555
  action entries quadrant, 553
  action quadrant, 552
  alternatives quadrant, 552
  basics, 551
  completeness checking, 555
  conditions, 551–552
  interpret rules, 553–554
  rules, 554
Declarative paradigms, 492–493
  applications, 504
  basics, 501–503
  characteristics, 504
  variations, 504
Declarative programming paradigms, 493
Declaring variables, 41–42
Decomposition
  basics, 4–5
  defined, 4
  dependencies and cohesion, 7
  functional, 6
  object-oriented, 7
  structural, 5–6
Default assignment operator, 255
Default behavior
  default assignment operator, 255
  predefined operators, 255
  setting one object to equal another,
    262–263
Default constructor, 266
Default exceptions, 187
Default parameters, 281
Default visibility, 283
Deletion, 341
Delimiter, 211
Dependence, 7, 563
Depth first (DF) traversal, 384
Dequeue( ) method, 367–368
Dequeue operation, 362

Descendant, 293
Diamond problem, 294
Digital data, 470
Digits, 66–67
Dimensioning an array, 129
Directed graph, 388
Directives, 21
Directory structure, 207
display( ) method, 345
Divide-and-conquer approach, 439
Divide-and-conquer technique, 417, 430
Do-loops, 120–122
Don't repeat yourself (DRY), 532
Double precision, 54
Doubly linked lists, 338
Downcasting, 315
dual_grinder( ) method, 329
Duplication is Evil (DIE), 532
Dynamically typed programming
        language, 43
Dynamic Binding, 314

E

Edges, 373
Edge weights, 388
Efficiency, 527
Efficient coding, 532–533
Encapsulation, 238, 500
    access modifiers, 283
    private variables/methods, 284–286
    public variables/methods, 283–284
    visibility, 283
Encoding system, 483
End of file (EOF), 211
E notation, 53
enqueue( ) method, 365–367
Enqueue operation, 362
Equality operator (==), 255–267
Equal operator, 87–88
Error detection, 467
Errors
    exception, 186
    logic, 185, 186
    runtime, 185
    workflow communication, 187
Escape characters, 70–71, 210
Escape sequence, 70–71
Event-driven, 514
Event handler, 514
Exception list, 251
Exceptions
    anticipation, 228–229
    bailing out, 202–203
    default, 187
    definition, 186
    error in code, 185–186
    handling, 189
    logic errors, 185
    no_cream_error, 187
    throw, 189
    types, 187–188
    workflow communication, 187
Executable file, 23
Explicit conversion, 315
Explicit namespaces, 162
Explicit self-referencing, 276

Expression, 54
Extensibility, 340

F

Fall through, 98
File
    absolute *vs.* relative path, 208, 209
    access point, 211
    binary, 213
    closing, 222
    components, 211, 212
    contents, 211
    delimiter, 211
    digital container, 206
    directory, 207
    EOF, 211
    escape characters, 210
    folders, hard drive, 208
    input/output, 212
    name, 211
    newline, 211
    opening, 223–224
    reading, 216–221
    relative path, 208
    sequence of bytes, 210–211
    usage, 212–214
    writing/appending, 224–228
File handling, 207
file_not_found_exception, 191
Final class, 296
find_it( ) method., 346–347
Find method, 346
First-in-first-out algorithm (FIFO), 362
Flag value, 413
Floating-point data types, 53–54
Flowcharts
    basics, 548
    drawing, 548–549
    tools, 549–550
Flow of execution, 147
Floyd's Algorithm, 390
Fluent interfaces, 264, 269
For-loop
    defined, 105
    flowchart, 106
    repetitions of bench press guidance,
        107–108
    syntax and rules, 107
Formatted output, 60
Formatting parameters, 60–61
Fortran, 496
Function, 51
    advantages, 147–148
    classifications, 146
    components, 148
    flow of execution, 147
    parameters, 150–152
    programmer-defined, 146–147
    pseudocode, 149
    return values, 153–157
    scope, 157–162
Functional decomposition, 6
Functional programming paradigm, 504
Functional requirements, 559
Function argument, 150–151
Function body, 148

Function call, 147
Function declaration, 148
Function name, 148
Function signature, 157
Function template, 320

G

Garbage values, 266
Generics, 320
Generic type, 322
give_discount( ) method, 233
Global variable, 158–159
"Good" algorithms, 3–4
Graph applications
    adjacency matrix, 388
    edge weights, 388
Graphical user interface (GUI)
    defined, 512
    elements, 512
    graphical controls, 513
    program design, 514–515
Graphs, 387
Graph structures
    definition, 387
    directed, 388
    types, 387
    undirected, 388
Guessing game, 172–173

H

Hand-held controllers, 518
Handoff, 152
Haptic, 518
Head, 336
Hello World!, 16
Hexadecimal
    binary-hex-binary conversions,
        481–482
    colors, 480–481
    conversion, 482
    information density, 483
    number system, 481
High-level programming languages, 16
    advantages/disadvantages, 467
    C family, 465
    characteristics, 466–467
    evolution, 464
    teaching languages, 465
    web programming language, 466
Homogeneous, 127, 355
Human-Computer Interaction (HCI), 508

I

If-then
    control structures, 84–85
    decision logic, 85
    else structures, 91–93
    structures, 85–87
If-then-else structures
    defined, 91
    sample code, 92–93
    syntax and rules, 92
Imperative programming paradigms, 493
Implicit conversion, 315

Implicit default constructor, 266
Implicit namespaces, 162
Implicit self-referencing, 276
Imported functions, 146
Impossible rules, 555
Inclusive design, 521–523
Inclusive equipment, 523
Inclusive identity, 522
Inclusive language, 521
Inclusive skill sets, 522
Incremental development
    model, 530
Index, 71
Index errors, 131–132
Infinite loop, 117–118
Infinite recursion, 167
Information density, 483
Information hiding, 238
Inheritance, 499
    child class, 297–298
    creating classes, 291
    customizing behavior, 301–306
    level of access, 295–296
    OOP, hierarchy, 292–295
    parent class, 296–297
    syntax, 298–301
    UML, 562
Initializing variables, 42–43
Inner and outer loops, 113–115
In-place algorithm, 430
Input and output, 44–45
Input array elements, 133–135
Insertion, 341
Insert method, 347
insert_node( ) method, 348–349
Instruction pointer, 463
Instruction space, 403
Integer data types, 52–53
Integrated circuits, 456–457
Integrated development environments
    (IDEs), 32
Integration testing, 538
Interfaces
    Car class implementation, 289
    elements, 287
    header files, 288
Interpreter, 26–27

Linear search performance
    array of contacts, 414–415
    data search, 413
    evaluating time, 416
Linear space complexity, 404
Linear time, 399–400
Line-by-line time complexity,
    405–406
LinkedList class, 343
Linked lists, 336
    characteristics, 339–341
    circular, 339
    code
        append method, 343–344
        class, 343
        find method, 346–347
        insert method, 347–350
        node class, 342
        traversal, 345–346
    double, 338
    single, 337
    types, 337–341
Linked list structure
    data structure
        implementation, 335–336
        operators, 335
        selection, 334–335
        types, 334
    memory layout, 336
Linked List Traversal, 345
Linker, 24
Literals
    character and string, 37
    numeric, 36–37
    tricky, 38
Local variable, 158–159
Logarithmic time, 401–403
Logic errors, 185–186
Logic gate, 457
Logic programming paradigm, 504
Loop counter, 105
Loops
    accumulators, 111–112
    block of code, 104
    breaking out, 118–119
    counters, 109–111
    terminating condition, 123
Low-level instruction sets
    assembly language, 461
    CISC, 460
    machine language, 460–461
    microprocessor, 459–460
    operands, 461
    RISC, 460

Member variables, 233
Memberwise initialization, 267
Memory, 486
Memory address, 489
Memory allocation
    memory and storage, 486
    RAM, 487–489
    storage devices, 487
Memory connection, 41
Memory management, 179–181
Merge sort
    code, 450–453
    divide-and-conquer algorithm, 447
    logic, 449–450
    properties, 453
    recurse( ) function, 448
Message, 561
Metacharacters, 423
Method cascading, 263–265
Method implementation, 316
Method overloading, 259
Method overriding
    final method, 306
    parent class, 303–305
    refuel( ) method, 301
    test_drive( ) method, 306
Methods, 7, 233, 314, 497
    anatomy, 251
    Car class, 247
    conventions, 250
    dealership details, 246
    inventory variable, 246
    programmer-defined functions, 245
Microprocessor, 459
    instruction cycle, 462
    instruction pointer, 463
    instruction sets, 462
min( ) function, 286
Mixed reality, 517
Modules, 5
Moore's law, 458
Motor and cognitive accessibility, 521
MotorVehicle class, 309
Multiple conditions
    else if structures, 96–97
    fall through, 97–99
    if-then-else structures, 91–93
    nested-if structures, 93–95
Multiple inheritance, 293
Mutators, 278–279, 233
Mystery algorithm, 407–408

Java Virtual Machine (JVM), 25–26

Keywords, 17

Last-in-first-out algorithm (LIFO), 354
Late binding, 314
Leaf nodes, 374
Level of abstraction, 12
Lifeline, 561
Linear access, 214
Linear data structure, 334
Linear recursion, 170, 174–175
Linear search, 413
linear_search( ) method, 413–415

Machine code, 23
Machine independent, 467
Machine language, 460–461
Magic rectangles, 126
Magnetic storage technology, 487
main( ) function, 21
Manual memory management, 489
Mathematical expressions
    arithmetic operators, 54–55
    compound operators, 56–57
    order of operations, 56

Namespace, 162
Negative numbers, 478–479
Nested-if structures, 93–95
Nested loops
    flowchart, 113
    inner and outer loops, 113–115
    loops within loops, 112–113
no_cream_error exception, 188
Node, 337
Node class, 342
Nonlinear
    building blocks, 373
    data structures, 334, 371–373
    edges, 373

vs. linear, 371–373
    tree structure, node class, 377–378
Nonvolatile storage, 487
Null variable, 43
Numeric data type conversion
    convert integers, 58–59
    floating-point numbers, 58–59
    rounding quirks, 59–60
Numeric data types
    floating-point, 53–54
    integer, 52–53
Numeric literals, 36–37

O

Object code, 23
Object-oriented decomposition, 7
Object-oriented paradigm
    applications, 501
    characteristics, 499–500
    classes, 497
    methods, 497
    objects, 497, 498
Object-oriented programming (OOP), 499
    characteristics, 242–243
    class, 232–233
    components, 233–236
    procedural programming, 232
Objects, 7, 497
    accelerate( ) method, 275
    behavior, 243
    class Car, 237
    encapsulation, 238
    features/principles, 238–239
    identity, 242
    instance, 236
    instance field, 274
    member variables, 273
    state, 242–243
    variables, 238
Offline storage, 487
One-dimensional arrays
    declare and initialize, 129
    memory allocation, 127
    numeric arrays, initialize, 128–129
    string arrays, initialize, 130
One's complement, 478
Online IDE, 32
Online storage, 487
Op code, 460
Opening file, 223–224
operator= method, 315
Operator overloading, 256
Optical storage technology, 487
Ordering items, 428
Order of operations, 56
OR operator, 101
Overloading operators, 258–261

P

Parameterized constructor, 267
Parameter list, 251
Parameters, function, 150
Parent class, 296–297
Parent node, 374
Partition( ) function, 444–446
Pass by reference, 161–162

Pass by value, 160
Pattern identification
    basics, 8
    classification, 9
    defined, 8
    repetitive, 8–9
Peek operation, 354
Personal identification number (PIN), 2
Phoneme, 515
Pixels, 480
Pointer, 336
Polymorphism, 309, 500
    classes, 314
    dynamic binding, 314
    method, 314
    objects, 315
    purpose, 309–314
pop( ) method, 360–362
Pop operation, 354
Post-test loops
    do-loops, 120–122
    flowchart, 116
    test conditions and terminating
        conditions, 123
Predicate expression, 502
Preprocessor, 24
Preprocessor directives, 24
Pre-test loops
    breaking out of loops, 118–119
    infinite loop, 117–118
    while-loops, 116–117
Primitive data types, 50–51, 238
Private variables, 284–286
Problem solving
    using graphs
        computing paths, 389–393
        graph applications, 388–389
    using tree
        data storage, 380–386
        tree application, 379–380
Procedural paradigm
    applications, 496
    basics, 493–494
    characteristics, 494–495
Procedural programming, 232
Processing file
    accessing, 214
    streaming/buffering, 214–215
Processor organization
    CPU, 458–459
    integrated circuits, 456–457
    logic gate, 457
    Moore's law, 458
    transistor, 456
Program animation, 31
Program code, 16
Program design
    command-line user interfaces, 510–511
    graphical user interface (GUI), 514–515
    voice user interface, 517
Program editors, 20–21
Programmer-defined functions, 146–147
Programming algorithm, 2–3
Programming errors, 27–28
Programming languages
    basics, 16–17
    core elements, 19

Hello World!, 16
    syntax and semantics, 17–19
    toolbox, 19–20
Programming paradigms, 493
Protected inheritance, 295
Pseudocode
    algorithms, 542–543
    commands and control structures, 544
    defined, 542
    function, 149
    guidelines, 545–547
    writing, 547
Public inheritance, 295
Public variables, 283–284
Pure virtual method, 316–317
push( ) method, 359–360
Push operation, 354

Q

Quadratic time, 400–401
Quality, 527
Queue
    code, 364–368
    data structure, characteristics, 362
    definition, 362
    FIFO, 362
    use cases, 363–364
Quicksort
    algorithm, 438
    array, numerical values, 441
    boundary index, 439
    divide-and-conquer approach, 439
    partition( ) function, 444–446
    partitioning, 440
    properties, 446–447
    recursive partition, 442, 443

R

RAM (random access memory), 487–488
Random access, 214
rating_num variable, 220
Reading file
    comma-delimited text file, 219
    EOF character, 218
    exceptions, 221
    opening, 216–217
Read mode, 216
Read-only, 487
Read-write, 487
Realization, 564
Recurse( ) function, 448
Recursion
    basics, 167–171
    branching, 175–179
    designing recursive structures, 171–174
    linear, 174–175
    memory management, 179–181
    problem-solving approach, 166
    recursive mindset, 165–167
    stable recursion, 182
Recursive function, 167
Recursive structure, 376–378
Reduced instruction set computers (CISC),
    460
Redundant rules, 554, 555
Reference, 336

Reference variable, 161
Refuel( ) method, 301
Registers, 458
Regression testing, 539–540
Regular expressions, 423
   search operators, 423–425
   search pattern specification, 423
Relational operators
   Boolean expressions and data types,
      89–90
   equal operator, 87–88
   operands, 88
Relationship diagram, 562
Relative path, 208
Repetition control structures,
   104–105, 495
Repetitive patterns, 8–9
Reserved words, 17, 39
Return message, 562
Return type, 156–157, 251
Return values, 153–155
RGB color, 480
Root node, 374
Runtime errors, 29, 185

S

Scenario, 559
Scheduling, 363
Scope
   global and local variables, 158–159
   namespaces, 162
   pass by reference, 161–162
   pass by value, 160–161
Scope resolution operator (::), 250
Search algorithms, 412
Search space, 412
Secure coding, 534–536
Security, 527
Selection control structure, 494
Self-reference keyword
   explicit, 276
   implicit, 276
   local/instance variables, 277
Semantic error, 29–30
Semantics, 17
Sentinel value, 413
Sequence diagram, 561
set_price( ) method, 236
Setters, 278
Shortest path, 363, 389
Signed integer, 52
Signed magnitude, 478
Single precision, 54
Single responsibility principle
   (SRP), 533
Singly linked lists, 337
Software development
   efficiency, quality, and security, 527–528
   life cycle, 526–527
Software development kit (SDK), 32–33
Solid state storage technology, 487
Sorting algorithm
   ordering items, 428
   properties, 430–431
   time complexity, 428–430
Source code, 23

Space complexity, 396
   constant, 404
   linear, 404–405
   memory space, 403
Sparse graph, 387
Speech synthesis, 516
Stable algorithm, 430
Stable recursion, 182
Stack code, 357–362
Stacks, 180, 353–362
   built-in, 356–357
   code, 357–362
   data structure, 354–355
   definition, 354
   LIFO, 354
   use cases, 355–356
Stack use cases
   retracing steps, 356
   reversing order, 355
   testing symmetry, 356
   undo and redo, 356
Statements, 16, 22
Statically typed, 43
Static elements
   classes, 241
   member variables, 239–240
   methods, 240–241
Storage, 486
Streamreader, 215
Streamwriter, 215
String, 69
String arrays, 130
String data types
   escape characters, 70–71
   string indexes, 71–72
   working, 69–70
String functions
   change case, 73–74
   length, 72–73
   location of character, 74–75
   manipulation, 72
   retrieve substring, 75–76
String indexes, 71–72
String length, 72–73
String literal, 37
String manipulation, 72
Structural decomposition, 5–6
Structure and use
   basic classes, 324–325
   grinder class, 327–328
   process( ) method, 326
   templated function, 323
Structured analysis and design, 528–529
Substring, 75–76
Success factors, 536
Switch-case structure, 98–99
Syntax error, 28
Syntax, programming language, 18
System testing, 539

T

Tail recursion, 182
Template
   advance, 328–329
   arguments objects, 330–331
   data abstraction, 319–322

designing, 331
   problem-solving approach, 331
   structure and use, 322–328
   use, 331
Template designing, 331
Template use, 331
Terminating condition, 123
Terminator shape, 548
Test case, 537
Test condition, 105
test_drive( ) method, 233, 306
Testing
   acceptance, 539
   integration, 538
   levels of, 536–537
   regression, 539–540
   system, 539
   unit, 537–538
Testing symmetry, 356
Text editor, 21
Text file, 212
Throw exceptions, 189
Throwing exceptions
   add functions, 201–202
   checks for positive amounts, 200
   program to simulate Iceabella's
      interactions, 198
   statements, 198
Time complexity, 396
   average-case runtime, 430
   best-case runtime, 430
   Big-O metrics, 398
   Big-O runtime, 429
   constant time, 399
   linear time, 399–400
   logarithmic time, 401–403
   quadratic time, 400–401
   runtime, 429
   worst-case runtime, 430
Toolbox, programming language, 19–20
Tools, flowchart, 549–550
Toolset, 22–23
Top-down decomposition, 495
Tracking down coding errors, 489
Transitors, 456
Traversal, 384
Traversal algorithms, 363
Traversing an array, 132–133
Tree properties, 376
Tree structure
   application, 379–380
   data storage, 380–386
   definition, 373
   node, 374
   properties, 376
   recursive, 376–378
Tricky templating
   advance template, 328–329
   object as argument, 330–331
Truth table
   AND operator, 100–101
   OR operator, 101
Try and catch block
   exceptions, 193
   file_not_found_exception, 191
   function calls, 194–197
   if-else statement, 190

load_ image function, 190, 191
logic flow, 189
pseudocode flow, 190
syntax, 198
variable choice, 193
Two-dimensional arrays
basics, 137–138
declare and initialize, 138–139
output, 139–140
sum array columns and rows, 141–143
Two's complement, 479
Typecasting, 78–80, 315
Typed parameter, 150
Type inference, 43

U

Unconnected graph, 387
Undefined variable, 41
Undirected graph, 388
Unicode, 485–486
Unified modeling language (UML)
associations, 562–564
class diagram, 558–559
defined, 558
sequence diagrams, 561–562
translating to code, 564–567
use case diagram, 559–561
Unit testing, 537
Unsigned integer, 52
Upcasting, 315
Use case, 559

Use case diagram, 559
User-controlled loop, 108–109
User experience (UX), 508
User interface (UI)
components, 508–509
defined, 508
selection, 510
UTF-8, 486

V

Variables
assigning, 43–44
camel case, 39
choice, 193
concatenation, 77–78
declaring, 41–42
defined, 38
initializing, 42–43
input, 44–45
output, 45
pseudocode, 546
reserved word, 39
snake case, 39
Vector graphics, 519
Vehicle identification number (VIN), 232
Virtual environment interfaces
augmented reality and mixed reality, 517
components, 518–519
programming, 519
virtual reality, 517
Virtual functions, 316–318

Virtual machine, 25
Virtual reality, 517
Visibility, 283
Visibility marker, 559
Visual accessibility, 520
Visual platform, 20
Voice user interface
basics, 515
program design, 517
speech recognition, 515–516
speech synthesis, 516
Void functions
basics, 148
pseudocode, 149
Volatile storage, 487

W

Waterfall model
advantages and disadvantages,
529–530
structured analysis and design, 528–529
Web content accessibility guidelines
(WCAG), 520
While-loops, 116–117, 193
Word processor, 20
Worst-case runtime, 430
Write Every Time (WET), 532
Write mode, 216
Writing/appending file
newline character, 226
program, 225